School of American Research
Advanced Seminar Series

DOUGLAS W. SCHWARTZ, GENERAL EDITOR

The Archaeology of
Lower Central America

THE ARCHAEOLOGY OF LOWER CENTRAL AMERICA

Edited by
Frederick W. Lange
AND
Doris Z. Stone

A SCHOOL OF AMERICAN RESEARCH BOOK
University of New Mexico Press ● *Albuquerque*

Library of Congress Cataloging in Publication Data
Main entry under title:

The Archaeology of lower Central America.

(School of American Research advanced seminar series)
"A School of American Research book."
Papers presented at an advanced seminar held Apr. 8–14, 1980.
Bibliography: p.
Includes index.
1. Indians of Central America—Antiquities—Congresses. 2. Central America—
Antiquities—Congresses. I. Lange, Frederick W., 1944–   . II. Stone, Doris,
1909–   . III. School of American Research (Santa Fe, N.M.) IV. Series.

F1434.A84   1983   972.8′01   83-21747
ISBN 0-8263-0717-5

Dedicated to the memory of a pioneer
in Central American archaeology,
SAMUEL KIRKLAND LOTHROP

Preface

The advanced seminar on lower Central American archaeology was held April 8–14, 1980, in the seminar facilities at the School of American Research, Santa Fe, New Mexico. The central themes had evolved in conversations and correspondence among the organizers and some of the participants over the preceding two years. The need for the seminar was dictated by rapidly accumulating data from lower Central America, and by the desire among some of the people actively working there to meet to exchange detailed ideas, speculations, and hypotheses. Many of the recent data were regional in nature, and there had been only limited contact among researchers in Panama, Costa Rica, Canada, New York, and Germany; they realized that letters and brief discussions at national and international meetings did not really allow for the exchange of new information, ideas, and impressions, or for the elaboration of theoretical viewpoints or general syntheses.

Dr. Douglas Schwartz, president of the School of American Research, was convinced of the importance of a seminar and the appropriateness of the School of American Research advanced seminar format for data presentation, discussions, and summation of the results for the broader scientific community and interested public. The emphases of the seminar were to draw together available information, to reevaluate currently held conceptions about cultural and historical process in the area, to focus our attention on problem areas (either geographical or chronological) where significant data gaps existed, and to articulate our goals and objectives for future research.

Ten papers were originally solicited for the seminar and were distributed in advance to the participants as a basis for the discussions. Following the seminar, an additional paper was solicited from Warwick Bray, which he generously agreed to provide despite the handicap of not having attended the discussion sessions. The participants were: Richard Cooke (Smithsonian Tropical Research Institute, Panama); Wolfgang Haberland (Museum für Völkerkunde und Vorgeschichte, Hamburg); Paul Healy (Trent); Frederick Lange (Illinois State); Allison Paulsen (Hartwick); Robert Sharer (University Museum, Pennsylvania); Payson Sheets (Colorado); Michael Snarskis (National Museum of Costa Rica); Doris Stone (Harvard, Tulane); and Gordon Willey (Harvard).

The planning committee for the seminar consisted of Gordon Willey, Frederick Lange, and Doris Stone. Lange and Stone agreed to serve as coorganizers of the symposium, and Willey consented to chair the discussion sessions. Snarskis and Sharer assisted in compiling the summary chronological chart (fig. 1.2).

Some of the participants in the seminar were known to one another only through the published results of their investigations; some had worked together on field projects or had been closely associated institutionally. It was very useful to establish a common basis of knowledge among many people working in the area. In the discussions, and in the revised papers, the participants were all generous in sharing unpublished data. In his summary, Willey has occasionally drawn on discussion data that were not incorporated in any of the individual chapters. Some of the ideas we discussed might best be described as speculative or intuitive, but were integral to helping to form a better picture of pre-Columbian cultural development in the area. We all mutually recognize an intellectual debt to one another; the discussions in Santa Fe helped us all to improve, refine, and revise our papers for the final volume.

We would very much like to thank Doug Schwartz and members of his office staff, specifically Jeton Brown, without whose organizational aid the seminar never would have taken place. Jane Barberousse and her kitchen staff took care of the marvelous household and dining arrangements, which made the living aspects of the seminar as pleasant, effortless, and enjoyable as they possibly could have been. During the week of the seminar, participants also enjoyed the hospitality of Mrs. Marshall L. McCune, Dr. and Mrs. Douglas Schwartz, Dr. and Mrs. Andrew Hunter Whiteford, Mr. and Mrs. Frank Sandstrom, and David and Ruth Noble.

Winifred Creamer initiated the compilation of the master bibliography, Lynette Norr cross-checked and verified many of the entries, and Holley Lange assisted greatly in its completion. Many of the fine maps in the volume, including Figure 1.1, were drawn by Carol Cooperrider. Jane Kepp took over as director of publications at the School of American Research after the seminar. The volume has benefited greatly from her editorial efforts and insights.

This volume is dedicated to the memory and contributions of Samuel K. Lothrop. He was a pioneer of Central American archaeological research and anticipated many of the problems of cultural development, prehistoric cultural interactions, and other themes with which we are concerned today, and which the reader sees reflected in our efforts.

Contents

PART ONE

Introduction

1
Introduction

FREDERICK W. LANGE

Department of Anthropology
University of Colorado, Boulder

DORIS Z. STONE

Peabody Museum, Harvard University
Middle American Research Institute, Tulane University

Lower Central America, defined archaeologically, encompasses most of El Salvador and Honduras, and all of Nicaragua, Costa Rica, and Panama (fig. 1.1). A more general consideration of Central America would have included Guatemala and placed more emphasis on western Honduras to the north and west, but these were excluded here except in the consideration of Mesoamerican influence on lower Central America. In similar fashion, an examination of the more conceptually satisfying Intermediate Area would have stressed lower Central America's lowland tropical forest and riverine affinities to the south and to the east. Both the terms *Central America* and the *Intermediate Area* would have stretched the geographical coverage beyond that included here. Our main constraints in geographical coverage were limits on the size of the seminar group and the sheer bulk of new data from lower Central America.

In planning the seminar, we decided to confine discussion to the large volume of data from the area somewhat arbitrarily defined as lower Central America. We are fully aware that the data discussed in this volume have broader geographical and cultural implications.

The seminar papers focused on a part of the New World which was a cultural periphery, rather than a cultural core such as Mesoamerica or the Andes. Not only do these studies explore the relationship of Central America

3

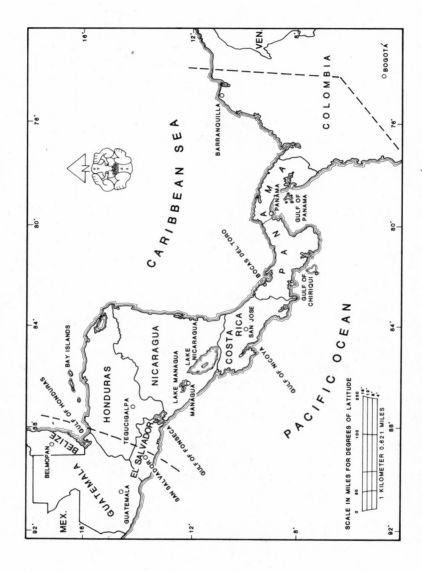

Figure 1.1. The boundaries of lower Central America as established for this volume.

to various core areas, they also look at cultural development in that region for its own value and integrity. The conclusions demonstrate that there were contacts and exchanges between various regions of lower Central America and the more evolved core areas to the north and south. However, development in lower Central America was not dependent on external influences for its cultural growth and diversity, nor was it dominated to any great degree by external forces—it evolved significant cultural patterns of its own. These papers also afford an important opportunity to look at cultural patterns that emerged away from the limelight that often shines on the high civilizations of the Nuclear American core areas. The size and splendor of these core areas have frequently obscured the examination of basic patterns and processes.

Great geographical and cultural variability within a very limited land surface area is a significant characteristic of lower Central America. For example, the generally dry Pacific side contrasts with the wetter Atlantic side, and major river systems are found mainly on the Atlantic and not on the Pacific. Despite the ecological differences, pre-Columbian social and economic interaction spheres linked the wetter Atlantic side and the dry Pacific side in some locations; in other parts of the area, these linking networks seem not to have been as well defined.

The geographical and cultural variability of lower Central America contributed to the emergence of a diversity of cultural patterns and levels of social evolution. With some notable exceptions, the basis for scientific research in lower Central America was established in the 1950s and 1960s and saw rapid expansion in the 1970s. The combined results of these decades of research fill the pages of the following chapters, highlighting both accomplishments to date and research needs for the future.

Within the whole of lower Central America, the chronological sequence stretches from the Paleo-Indian era to the Spanish contact period. Sites representative of any pre-fluted-point-manufacturing peoples are absent, but from approximately 10,000 B.P. on, there is a complete regional picture of human cultural adaptation and evolution.

Numerous systematic settlement pattern studies have been made in each of the five countries, with the exception of Nicaragua. These studies have demonstrated the differences between Pacific and Atlantic coast settlement practices and have emphasized the importance of quality soils, access to transportation routes, and proximity to raw materials and commodities as significant locational determinants. The importance of coastal settlement, at different times and places in different areas, is now clearly recognized.

Data relating the impact of natural events such as earthquakes and volcanic eruptions have also been accumulated from different locales within the region, and indications are that this will be an important avenue of research for the future. The geomorphology of tropical river systems, and their impact on preservation of the archaeological record, has also been detailed in some areas as a result of the systematic settlement pattern studies. We are no longer dependent on purely cultural explanations, or speculations, for the absence of sites of a particular size, function, or temporal affiliation in specific areas.

Subsistence data are available for many parts of lower Central America and demonstrate significant variability even between small contiguous areas. Preservation of vegetable matter is, of course, capricious, but we do see distinct patterns emerging from a combination of perishable and nonperishable data. The importance of marine resources is clearly defined: where such resources were abundant in estuary or near-shore environments, settlement near and exploitation of these resources were intensive; where they were low in density or lacking, intensive settlement did not occur.

We have become increasingly aware of the wide diversity of material culture. Although there are broad overall similarities in some ceramic styles, lower Central America demonstrates a plethora of ceramic types. Numerous regional ceramic typologies and sequences have been formulated and provide the chronological framework for the area. These sequences have been generalized into the chronological sequence shown in figure 1.2 and are presented in regional detail in the individual chapters. The data are most numerous for the period post–500 B.C. and much sketchier for earlier times.

A general sense of the distribution of such important commodities as gold, jade, and obsidian has emerged and contributes to a greatly improved, although still limited, consensus on trade routes and trade mechanisms. This improvement results partially from recovery of these "exotic" materials from secure excavation contexts, and is also a result of greatly improved methods of analysis of physical properties, source materials, and interregional comparisons.

The increase in archaeological excavations has produced a variety of data from controlled contexts and has hence improved our intrasite and subsistence information. Another important area of interpretation that has benefited has been that of personal status, social organization and stratification, and elite behavior. The fine ceramics—gold, jade, and stonework—that were for so long seen almost exclusively in museums or private collections are now being recovered from primary contexts. The contextual recovery of this information is not only permitting us to describe more accurately the social aspects of these societies, but is also shedding light on the manner in which elite persons from different locations may have interacted.

In spite of the great strides in research in the past two decades, we still lack information on some periods and areas, and we have not focused equally on all our data. The amount of information currently available on Paleo-Indian and Archaic occupations is limited, as are data for the late prehistoric/protohistoric period. These imbalances cause difficulties in assessing broad themes of cultural evolution. In the summary chronological chart (fig. 1.2),

PERIODS		YEARS
VI	Spanish Conquest and survivals	A.D. 1550
	more organized and developed chiefdoms; civil rather than shamanistic control becomes prevalent; echo of secularization in Mesoamerica	
V	Change and Upheaval	A.D. 1000
	shifting emphasis on trade routes and politics; first reaction to over-competition	
IV		A.D. 500
	A.D. rise of ranked societies	
	B.C. full-fledged Formative communities	
	widespread, small, sedentary agricultural communities	
III		1000 B.C.
	expansion and diversification	
	Introduction of Ceramics	
II		4000 B.C.
	Tropical Archaic	
I		ca. 8000 B.C.
	Paleo-Indian	

Figure 1.2.   Periods of cultural evolution in lower Central America.

the overall pattern of cultural development is portrayed in large spans of time; the chart is broadly evolutionary, but has been left as nonspecific as possible so that elasticity and flexibility exist for future refinements.

More research has been done on the Pacific coast than on the Atlantic. This has been for two main reasons. First, our research paradigm stressed the interrelationship of Pacific coastal Central America with Mesoamerica and was dedicated primarily to demonstrating formative and other cultural links. Until recently, no such conceptual umbrella existed to stimulate research on the Atlantic coast, but a paradigm focusing on expansion out of a South American tropical forest heartland has begun to emerge. A second reason for the focus on the Pacific is simply the logistics of doing archaeology in Central America. Transportation systems and overall field conditions have generally made research easier on the Pacific than on the Atlantic.

The research foci of scholars have also varied. Some have emphasized ceramic analysis and the development of cultural chronological schemes, while others have primarily emphasized environmental considerations. Preservation of cultural remains plays an important role in determining research emphasis. In some parts of the region, for example, relatively large skeletal populations (100 +) have been excavated, while in others none have been recovered. The frequency of radiocarbon specimens varies in similar fashion.

The long coastline is a dominant geographical feature on both the Atlantic and Pacific. However, we still have very little idea of the complexity of coastal systems or of how people on the coast interacted with those in the interior. We also know little of the extent to which there were social and trade networks between the coasts during the prehistoric period.

Such an uneven data base makes broad comparative efforts difficult, and there are still large areas of lower Central America where we honestly cannot say much at all about what happened. These gaps are particularly frustrating in attempts to deal with processes of cultural evolution and to learn why most of lower Central America never evolved beyond a low or intermediate chiefdom stage. Two of the purposes of the seminar, then, were to define fundamental research problems and to suggest objectives for future research.

Stone's paper provides a historical perspective on the development of research in lower Central America. She traces these efforts both chronologically and as reflections of major changes in archaeological and anthropological research emphasis. In so doing, she reviews the past and also sets some goals for the future.

Lange's first paper reviews the cultural geography of lower Central America. He examines and delineates those geographical features—such as rivers, fertile soils, and available raw materials—which might have been strong positive locational factors and those—such as poor soils, mountain ranges, and lack of apparent natural resources—which may have had a negative impact on locational decisions. The seminar also decided this area was better described as a buffer zone (Lange 1979a) than as a cultural frontier, and the limits and mechanics of this zone are described. This paper provides the ecological background from which geographically based cultural and archaeological problems—such as resource utilization, subsistence patterns, trade networks, and population growth—in specific areas of lower Central America can be examined.

The specific studies on different regions proceed from north to south, perhaps reflecting the bias that we know more about Mesoamerican than South American connections with lower Central America. Sharer's paper examines relationships between southern Mesoamerica and lower Central America. He sees the area in terms of the frontier/buffer model and views trade networks as the bridging mechanisms. He reviews the nature of trade and other relationships between the regions, with particular emphasis on the Maya period. Sheets's paper focuses on El Salvador and makes use of very important cultural data related to volcanic activity. He also emphasizes the importance of lithic analyses as indicators of cultural activity and the intersite and period comparisons of population concentration.

The following paper is Healy's, on Honduras, part of which was clearly in the Mesoamerican sphere of influence and the rest definitely outside it during the same period of cultural evolution. Healy draws clear contrasts between western and eastern Honduras and also notes traits characteristic of both. He thereby begins to delineate some of the cultural features that seem to be associated more with either northern or southern relationships. His Caribbean coastal data seem comparable to those from Atlantic Nicaragua, Costa Rica, and Panama.

Lange's discussion of Greater Nicoya (northwestern Pacific coastal Costa Rica and Pacific Nicaragua including the southern periphery of the Gulf of Fonseca) articulates geographically and culturally with the western Honduran area discussed by Healy. His paper also shares a common eastern boundary with Snarskis's paper on the Atlantic watershed of Costa Rica and Nicaragua. Greater Nicoya seems to be the heart of the buffer zone between northern- and southern-derived cultural phenomena.

Snarskis's paper deals with the Atlantic watersheds of Costa Rica, Nicaragua, and Panama. The bulk of his data derive from intermediate zones between the highlands and the coast, and not from the coast proper. In addition to the apparent connections with Healy's data mentioned earlier, Atlantic coastal Costa Rica also ties in with the rest of the eastern watershed of Central America and with northern South America, as discussed in Warwick Bray's paper.

Haberland's paper deals with a more limited geographical area, and his focus is on the Grand Chiriqui region of western Panama and its extension into Costa Rica. This area has been known archaeologically for decades, and in terms of patterns of socio-cultural development it was an important one in pre-Columbian Central America. He particularly emphasizes population movements and social evolution as seen in the archaeological record. Recent research by Robert Drolet in the Boruca area is reported as a note at the end of this chapter.

Richard Cooke's paper covers central and eastern Panama more extensively. After developing a basic culture history, he focuses on ecologically related themes by examining the utilization of particular animal species, domestic patterns, and evolution of a mortuary complex.

Warwick Bray's paper focuses on relationships between lower Central America and Colombia, particularly on data regarding settlement patterns, locational expansion, social evolution, and development of subsistence practices. All these data are related to data presented by Snarskis and, to a lesser extent, Healy for the Atlantic watershed of lower Central America.

Willey synthesizes the information from a region where he sparked some of the initial modern research interest more than two decades ago. The detailed bibliography and radiocarbon charts are designed to aid further research in the area.

Chronology

The development of a chronological framework for lower Central America has been a slow, ongoing process. Many parts of the area are still unrepresented in even the simplest fashion on time-space summaries. Nonetheless, in comparing Wauchope (1954) and Haberland (1978), it is clear that considerable progress has been made. Appendixes 1 through 10 contain over 190 dates reliable for dating purposes; none of these were available 25 years ago. Many of the problems which Wauchope (1954: 20) identified as "dangers of the possible contamination of specimens, incorrect archaeological dating of specimens, and drawing conclusions from small samples" are still with us. However, while Wauchope (1954: 19) complained that "C14 standard deviations are seldom under 200 years," the tables and chart presented with this paper have eliminated all dates with a standard deviation of 150 years or more with no loss of interpretive value.

This progress is related to improved archaeological techniques in the recovery of carbon specimens, to their care and conservation until they can be submitted to a laboratory, and to improved laboratory preparation and analytical techniques. The tables include samples processed during a span ranging from practically the dawn of radiocarbon calibration to the latest sophisticated technology. Because of changes in technology, the dates processed more recently have a higher level of confidence than do the older ones.

Some of the natural processes discussed in this paper pose particular hazards to accurate radiocarbon analysis, although we cannot define their magnitude. The upwelling effect along the Pacific coast of Central America causes substantial difficulty in dating shell specimens, with a tendency to increase the age. Some shell dates in the tables are reinforced by analyses of wood carbon, while others are without independent confirmation.

Concerns about the general effect of volcanic activity on radiocarbon samples exist as a result of general environmental contamination, but the specific effects are undemonstrated. Since upwelling and volcanic conditions jointly affect such a broad stretch of the Pacific coast, we do need to keep potential environmental anomalies firmly in mind. The Atlantic coast, though not affected nearly as much by volcanism or upwelling, has moist, humid conditions and molds and fungi which have deleterious impacts on analytical results.

No region in lower Central America or adjacent areas has a complete sequence of human occupation. In some cases this reflects lack of research or gaps in exploitation of the available record; in others, the lack of substantive data may reflect low population totals and densities, the impact of natural events on the archaeological record, and the shift of populations through time.

In appendixes 1 through 10, dates are usually identified by laboratory number, and the material treated (vegetal carbon or shell) is identified when known. In reporting the actual years calculated from results of the individual calibrations, dates are given in radiocarbon years with laboratory numbers and standard errors and also with MASCA corrections. In some cases it was impossible to ascertain whether one or two standard deviations were being presented; in the absence of contrary evidence one standard deviation was used.

Most dates with standard deviations of 150 years or more were omitted from the regional tables; all omitted dates are included in appendix 9. A very few dates with deviations of 150 years or more, which have particular importance or represent reasonable approximations of the beginnings of particular cultural sequences, have been retained. Associated phase and period data, with annotations of contextual or interpretive significance, have also been recorded; most of these assessments were provided by contributors to the volume.

The dates presented for El Salvador (appendix 1) are from Andrews V (1976) and Sheets (1979); the latter focused on relating volcanic episodes to human habitation, and the former dated various architectural components at Quelepa. In Honduras (appendix 2), dates are from Healy (1980: T2) and Baudez and Becquelin (1973); the former emphasizes settlement in a coastal environment, and the latter inland settings. Dates from the important Gulf of Fonseca area are completely lacking. There are few dates from the Isthmus of Rivas in Nicaragua (appendix 3), and more dates are available from the Atlantic coast of Nicaragua (appendix 4).

There are relatively more dates for northwestern Costa Rica (appendix 3), with some originally obtained in the late 1950s and early 1960s by Coe and Baudez; additional dates from Coe's excavations were presented by Sweeney (1975), and, finally, other analyses have resulted from recent efforts by Bay of Culebra and Guanacaste–San Carlos research teams. No radio-carbon dates have yet been reported from the important Gulf of Nicoya area, and, likewise, very few are known from Costa Rica's central highlands (appendix 5). Kennedy's (1976: 88) dates for the Atlantic watershed of Costa Rica had standard deviations too large for inclusion on the master chart; therefore, dates obtained by Snarskis (appendix 6) are the basis for the regional sequence. No dates are available for southern Costa Rica.

Haberland (1978) and Linares and Ranere (1980) have published a rel-atively large group of dates from western Panama (appendix 7). From east of Chiriqui, Willey and McGimsey (1954), Linares and Ranere (1980), and Cooke (1976c) have formed perhaps the best and most useful chronology from lower Central America (appendix 8). No radiocarbon results came from Drolet's work in eastern Panama, and that area still must be cross-correlated with other sequences. Relevant dates from Colombia are in ap-pendix 10 and are a solid comparative base.

General Considerations

We conducted this seminar within the framework of our own research efforts. In addition, we were sensitive to political, social, and educational processes in lower Central America and our concern for cultural resource management in the area. The seminar clearly expressed the need for sub-stantially greater participation by local professionals, the training and teach-ing of local professionals where they currently do not exist, and a greater attention to sharing the results of the research. With all of its lacunae, a nonetheless much more concise, cohesive, and united picture of prehistoric lower Central America, with its not-yet-defined-boundary, emerges in the following pages. Neither the seminar discussions nor the published papers allowed for coverage of as much detail and as many different aspects as any of us (or some readers) may have hoped. However, we have attempted to give a comprehensive picture to ensure that new avenues for future research are readily apparent.

2
A History of
Lower Central American
Archaeology

DORIS Z. STONE

Peabody Museum, Harvard University
Middle American Research Institute, Tulane University

The purpose of this chapter is to trace the main lines of archaeological investigation in lower Central America from the nineteenth century to the present day. Early archaeology in lower Central America was primarily a part of exploration; sites and surface finds were discovered and described by observant travelers, engineers, art historians, and only occasionally by excavators.

Later stages of archaeological work in this area involved careful excavation, taking into account each item no matter how minute, be it foodstuff or plant material, and, most important, noting the stratigraphic position of all objects as they were uncovered. This trend is visible in reports dating from the late 1920s and increases in regional excavations during the 1950s, coming into its own in the 1960s and 1970s. Attention to climate change, ecology, subsistence, and social patterns as well as reconstruction of social status systems also became more prevalent in the 1970s and continues to be emphasized in the 1980s.

Another important activity has been the classification of the associated ceramics and their placement in time. All these approaches are still useful, for we are just beginning to understand the complex systems that lie behind lower Central American cultures and their local variations.

In a wider sense my review was anticipated by Willey and Sabloff (1980) in their critical history of American archaeology, but their volume is far more theoretical and scientific than this paper, which is not only limited geographically but stresses individual achievements within set physical boundaries.

Early Central American Pioneers

In the nineteenth and early twentieth centuries, few explorers were interested in more than one Central American country, because of the great distances and difficulties of travel (figs. 2.1 and 2.2). Living conditions were primitive, food was barely adequate, and foot, mule, and dugout were the only means of transportation. These journeys or expeditions could take months; some took years, and little communication could be maintained with the outside world. Frequently the traveler was faced with a change in government, or with floods or earthquakes—all of which prolonged the undertaking. Nevertheless, these early pioneers were scholars, and some were also collectors of antiquities.

In the nineteenth century, E. G. Squier, United States chargé d'affaires to the republics of Central America and an educated traveler and engineer, reported on the stone monuments of Zapatera and other islands in Lake Nicaragua, which illustrate diverse pre-Columbian artifacts and pictographs (1850, 1852, 1853a). In his book *The States of Central America* (1858), Squier wrote about the five countries the isthmus then comprised and also included some archaeological observations. His chapter on Honduras describes ruins such as Tenampua, Maniami, and Calamulla in the Department of Comayagua. Others of his writings, "Some Account of the Lake of Yojoa or Taulabe in Honduras" (1860) and "Tongues from Tombs" (1869), were firsthand accounts of previously unknown sites and cultural artifacts.

Two Germans, S. Habel, a medical doctor (1878), and Karl Sapper, a geographer (1896, 1902), also contributed to Central American archaeological knowledge. But it was the scholar Walter Lehmann, in the early twentieth century, who really first concerned himself with the non-Maya prehistory of Central America including Panama. Trained as an art historian, he reported (1910) his journey through Central America and Mexico from 1907 to 1909, giving a picture of previously unknown pre-Columbian cultures. Undoubtedly influenced by the Americanists Eduard Seler and C. H. Berendt, Lehmann traced northern intrusions into most of this territory and also delimited archaeological centers in Costa Rica.

While gathering linguistic data, during a lengthy journey overland from El Salvador to Costa Rica, Lehmann made over a thousand drawings of stone and clay artifacts, including rock art and painted and incised motifs on pottery. These drawings are preserved in the Ibero-Amerikanischen Bib-

Figure 2.1.   On the trail in Guatemala, 1935.

Figure 2.2. On the trail in Honduras, 1935.

liothek in Berlin and stress Mexican influences in Central America as seen in design elements and their combinations. They also indicate Lehmann's concept of cultural trends from both the north and the south, a concept that has persisted to the present day.

It is hard to ascertain the influence of Lehmann on his North American contemporary, Herbert Joseph Spinden, an explorer, art historian, and cultural theorist. Spinden's explorations and fieldwork in Central America during the early years of the twentieth century led to the publication (1915) of a survey of Salvadorean archaeology in which he noted the importance of the little-known Lenca. He later wrote a general introduction (1917) to Mexican and Central American cultures. Both volumes emphasized the importance of artistic and technological traits that indicated a cultural unity throughout the greater part of Central America, much of which had been unknown to the scientific world (e.g., the Mosquito coast of Honduras and Nicaragua).

Spinden also recognized the southern roots of eastern Central American culture but considered them a recent intrusion. He broadened Lehmann's concept of the archaeological culture center to include three provinces of lower Central America: (a) northern Honduras east of La Ceiba and eastern Nicaragua north of Rivas and west of the forest zone; (b) southern Nicaragua; and (c) northern Costa Rica, subdivided into six sections. These provinces, he believed, were derived from a Mayanized Chorotegan culture based on an art style, a concept he termed the "Chorotegan Culture Area." Spinden furthermore (1925) conceived of the Chorotega as people who were southern in origin but who had pushed their way north at the time of the Spaniards' arrival. This was contrary to Lehmann's idea of a northern or Chiapanecan homeland for the Chorotega (1920:2: 864–65).

Samuel Kirkland Lothrop was one of the last scholars to extend his work to all of Central America. He shared Lehmann's regard for northern and southern elements in the Isthmian region and for pottery classification. In 1926 he produced his monumental two volumes *Pottery of Costa Rica and Nicaragua*, which were based principally on museum and private collections and which stressed design motifs and evaluated vessel forms. Lothrop (1927a) made a small but significant excavation with the Salvadorean geologist and scholar Jorge Larde in central El Salvador at Cerro Zapote and, as a result, was among the first to recognize cultural diversity in Central America through stratified ceramics.

In 1950 Lothrop produced a ceramic sequence from the Diquis River Delta, but it lacked radiocarbon verification. His chronological sequence was not published until 13 years later (1963: 109–11). The reports of his excavations at Cocle (1937–42), in Veraguas (1950), and at Playa Venado, Canal Zone (1954, 1960), were backed by painstaking fieldwork and scholarly use of historical documentation. Most of these publications are still standard references.

Lothrop made a valuable map of Tenampua (1927b; Stone 1957) and was also concerned with theoretical considerations. He evolved, in collaboration with George C. Vaillant, the concept of the "Q Complex," a theory based on a widespread variety of pottery traits primarily associated with non-Maya cultures but including Playa de los Muertos in the Sula Plain (Popenoe 1934; Vaillant 1933: 59, 1934). This hypothesis was the motivating idea behind Doris Stone's "The Basic Cultures of Central America" (1948) and may well have served as an impetus for James Ford's "Formative" concept (1969). Lothrop, as one of the first to deal with the question of the southern frontier of the Maya (1939), sparked later studies by Longyear (1947), Stone (1959), Thompson (1970), Sharer (1974), Andrews V (1977), and Henderson (1978). Lothrop also compiled a synthesis of lower Central American archaeology (1966).

An Englishman, Thomas Athol Joyce, trained in the classics at Oxford, became one of the great Americanist scholars of his time. Long a member of the staff of the British Museum, he served in his later years as deputy keeper of the Sub-Department of Ethnography. Joyce's only fieldwork was in British Honduras (Belize), an area outside lower Central America. He was one of the first, however, to write a synthesis of Isthmian archaeology. His book *Central America and West Indian Archaeology* (1916) is based on the archaeological and ethnological collections from major American and European museums as well as historical sources. This volume made a profound impact on the leading Americanists of the Old and New worlds (Carmichael 1973: 38–40) and still remains one of the prime contributions to our knowledge of Central American prehistory.

Regional Pioneers

Honduras

Regional pioneers were by necessity explorers, and data collecting was their objective. The Central American country that drew the earliest attention of dirt archaeologists was Honduras, unquestionably because of the superb Maya ruins at Copan. However, when political problems prevented further work at Copan, George Byron Gordon began excavations in 1896 at Playa de los Muertos, Santana, and other sites in the Ulua Valley. As a result of the unique and aesthetic quality of some of the ceramics he found, he made a classification and chronological alignment of the ceramic complex called Ulua Polychrome Ware. Gordon sorted ceramics by vessel form, decorative motif, color, and, to a certain degree, paste. In what we call Ulua Polychrome Ware, he recognized two principal groups: (a) painted motifs recalling figures from the Maya codices and (b) vessels with motifs derived from Maya symbolism but emphasizing animal features—heads, for example. He turned to Maya ceramics, as most researchers have done since, in an effort to affiliate this pottery, but he was unable to place it temporally (1898a: 27–41).

Ulua Polychrome pottery has consistently attracted the attention of archaeologists in Honduras and El Salvador and has been the source of controversial speculation about its ethnic origin. Even those who did not concentrate on its classification have expressed opinions regarding the early people responsible for it. Among those who attempted a classification from the laboratory were Vaillant (1927) and Harry Tschopik (1937), both of whom concluded that the designs had a late southern influence, although Tschopik also saw Maya affiliations. Willey believed that Ulua Polychrome ceramics were "truly Maya-made" (1969), while J. Eric S. Thompson observed that this pottery showed a combination of Maya and locally developed motifs (1970: 84–85).

William Duncan Strong worked with Alfred Kidder II and A. J. Drexel Paul, Jr., in the Ulua Valley and at Los Naranjos, Lake Yojoa. They recognized cultural strata in pottery and discovered two early ceramic types— Ulua Monochrome and Ulua Bichrome—but their attempt to classify Ulua Polychrome Ware was also unsatisfactory (1938; Strong 1948).

At Copan, John M. Longyear III defined an Archaic (Preclassic) period containing pottery decorated with the Usulutan technique. He was the first person to establish the temporal position of the Ulua Polychrome complex through his find of Full Classic tombs and graves at Copan that contained this ware. He indicated that it was "at least partially contemporaneous" with the last period of Copan but came to the conclusion that Ulua Polychrome was probably created by the Lenca and only influenced by the Maya (Longyear 1952).

Two later scholars, Joel S. Canby (1951) and Jeremiah Epstein (1959), became interested in this ware from a chronological point of view. Canby tried to correlate Ulua Polychrome Ware with the Maya calendar using his well-documented Formative culture sequence from Yarumela in the Comayagua Valley. The presence of Usulutan pottery in this sequence was of particular significance (1951: 83–84). Epstein developed a basic ceramic sequence for each of the two cultures of the Honduran north coast: the northeast and the northwest. By stylistically analyzing Ulua Polychrome sherds from different sites, he concluded that the ware showed Maya influence and belonged in the Late Classic period.

In 1957 Stone also made an unsatisfactory classification of this pottery using, as Longyear had, form and design. John B. Glass followed the same model (1966) and included in this division the Bold Geometric style, which does not belong in this complex. Stone (1967, 1969a) extended Glass's hypothesis of design analysis through the interpretation of religious motifs on certain Mayoid vessels of Ulua Polychrome Ware. She stressed a Nahuat influence (Stone 1972) in her attempts to pinpoint the external connections and cultural contacts.

During the 1960s reliable auto and air travel became available, making it possible to collect hundreds of potsherds at a single site instead of depending on what saddlebags, which had to accommodate food and clothing first, could hold. As a result, the trend in archaeology turned sharply from a reliance on historical documents for orientation at the most recent stratigraphic levels to utilization of sherd sequences based on innumerable examples according to stratum and site. This was not a new approach, but it was now applied to samples in quantity. Also in vogue was a trend to change the names of pottery types to allow for type-variety nomenclature.

Claude F. Baudez proposed a series of regional sequences founded on material he excavated from Choluteca (1966) and the Comayagua Valley (Baudez and Becquelin 1969) and which he compared with material from other regions, including Copan and the Ulua-Yojoa area. For classifying Ulua Polychrome Ware, he used a type-variety system based on pottery from the Maya zone as well as a breakdown of ceramic types and successive complexes in an attempt "to solve cultural evolution" (Baudez 1966: 334).

From 1967 to 1969 Baudez and Pierre Becquelin excavated at Los Naranjos on Lake Yojoa (1969, 1973) and concluded that the cultural ties were closer to the Olmec and the Maya in the north than to lower Central America, a premise that leads to further discussion and more investigation. Baudez and Becquelin distinguished a type which they termed Babilonia Polychrome belonging to their Yojoa phase but which resembled the Mayoid style associated with Ulua Polychrome Ware (1969: 225–26). In 1977, they recognized iconographic diversity in this group but were unable to break it down into stylistic varieties on the basis of their Los Naranjos samples.

A new program of salvage archaeology in the Ulua-Yojoa area has promoted fieldwork under the auspices of the Instituto Hondureño de Antropologia e Historia (IHAH). The tendency of these recent investigators (e.g., James J. Sheehy in 1978) has been to demonstrate the interrelationships of regional sites through ceramic wares. Irene Stearns Wallace analyzed Naco-style pottery and Ulua Polychrome Ware in an effort to determine typical motifs and their combinations. She coded sherd samples from different sites and used the computer to establish the significant design mixtures and other characteristics of the ware as a way to clarify geographical relationships (1978).

Eugenie Robinson has worked out a breakdown of Ulua Polychrome Ware (1978) and, along with Rene Viel (1977), stresses the "reading" of pottery decoration. Both see a "design vocabulary" based on painted motifs and vessel form of the Mayoid class as a means of identifying the ethnic group of the makers and their markets as well as showing "how social interactions are reflected in ceramic design." Viel argues that variability in design reflects a social and a functional sense and makes use of classes modeled on morphological categories which he sees as syntax rules. Above all, he sees pottery with high aesthetic value, like the Babilonia group, as being of great help in a socio-cultural reconstruction.

Regional reports on Honduras have been published by several investigators. Dorothy H. Popenoe discussed the ceremonial nature of Tenampua and its partial association with a southern culture (1928, 1936). Strong made studies of northeastern Honduras and the Bay Islands (1934a, 1934b, 1935) and wrote a synthesis of Central American archaeology (1948). Jens Yde, a Dane, published one of the first archaeological surveys of the northwest (1938). Stone reported Los Naranjos, Lake Yojoa (1934a), the site of Guaimoretta Lagoon (1934b), and surveyed northern Honduras. Her report on the north coast included a partial plan and photographs of the now destroyed site of Travesia and provides the only record of architectural remains in the Sula Plain (1941).

Stone also made a survey of southern and central Honduras (1957) and, along with Conchita Turnbull, excavated a pre-Columbian pottery kiln— direct archaeological evidence of ceramic production in the Sula Valley (Stone and Turnbull 1941). At that time she erroneously felt that the Ulua Polychrome sherds in the kiln indicated that this ware continued up to Conquest times, an idea stimulated by the presence of this type on the surface in the Comayagua Valley, particularly at the site of Lo de Vaca, which she first reported in 1957.

H. J. Boekelman worked in a shell midden at Guaimoretta (1935) which contained symbols of a South American phallic cult. Ripley Bullen and William Plowden, Jr., reported what may be evidence from mountain tops and terraces in the Sierra region (1963, 1964) of the route pursued by preceramic man through the highlands of Honduras. Vito Veliz, along with Healy and Willey, classified Roatan ceramics (Veliz, Healy, and Willey 1975); he also found human footprints in vitrified rhyolite near Guaimaca (1978a).

In the 1970s exploration and factual reportage took a new direction, giving archaeologists more than one interest to keep in mind. The first to take this course in Honduras was Paul F. Healy, one of the few professionals to explore the Cuyamel Caves, which he assigned to the Early/Middle Preclassic period on the basis of ceramics (1974a). Between 1973 and 1976 Healy investigated subsistence and settlement patterns in the vicinity of Trujillo and the Aguan Valley. He collected 10,000 potsherds, 200 lithic samples, and molluscan and faunal remains, which provided ample evidence for a study of the ecology and life pattern—a new approach. Radiocarbon dating confirmed Epstein's chronology of this region and extended it from A.D. 300 to the Spanish Conquest (Healy 1973, 1974a, 1975, 1976a, 1977, 1978a, 1978b, 1978c, 1978d).

A renewed study of the movements of pre-Columbian peoples is a trend initiated during the last decade by Epstein. He recently worked on the Bay Islands and postulated from his finds that non-Mesoamerican people did not reach those parts before A.D. 1000 (1978). On the contrary, Nedenia C. Kennedy (1978: 213–14) sees non-Mesoamericans on the mainland prior to Playa de los Muertos.

John S. Henderson has shown particular interest in trade networks and ports of call at the sites of Naco and La Sierra, higher up in the Chamelecon Valley. His aim was to find a cultural frontier marked by zones of maximum density of foreign enclaves (1976, 1978).

Among the new projects in Honduras is the site of Curruste (CR 32), partly encircled by hills on the highway to Ticamaya Lagoon. Here, mounds with stairways and platforms are arranged in a semicircle. A group of enthusiastic laymen, with Antonio Bogran in charge, made the excavation possible and gave the property to the University of San Pedro Sula along with the proposal to develop a field school for archaeologists and a park for tourists.

The preliminary report was made by George Hasemann, Vito Veliz, and Lori van Gerpen (1978). The project is now under the supervision of Ricardo Agurcia Fasquell and calls for the restoration of a Late Classic living site. The study encompasses social and political organization, including the way of life in the Sula Plain during this period. Agurcia Fasquell is also undertaking, along with Henderson, a regional survey of the Sula Valley and a study of settlement patterns. Veliz is heading the El Cajon project, where the Sulaco and Comayagua rivers meet. His co-workers are Kenneth Hirth and George Hasemann; the latter excavated on Utila Island (1977) and along the Sulaco River, where he found 18 Late Classic sites with Bold Geometric pottery but no Mayoid polychromes (manuscript report).

The trend toward a synthesis of regional prehistory seen in the discussion of Costa Rica later in this chapter is paralleled by Honduran investigators. Roberto Reyes Mazzoni (1976a, 1976b) published a one-volume summary accompanied by a second volume, consisting solely of bibliography, as part of his M.A. thesis in Mexico. Much of the text refers to the geology-geography of the country. Another M.A. thesis by Rudy Radillo (1978), California State University, Los Angeles, stressed Honduran cultural sequences and site classification as well as archaeological problems.

El Salvador

All the uncertainties as to what constitutes the area termed lower Central America culminate in the archaeology of El Salvador. The region has mixed, though ample, remains of Maya and Mexican (Pipil) cultures even east of the Lempa River, where historical documentation locates the Matagalpa and the Ulva, fundamentally Central American peoples.

Among the earliest reports on central and eastern El Salvador is an article by F. de Montessus de Ballore, a captain in the French artillery stationed in San Salvador. He noted that the ceramics from Tehuacan suggest affiliations with Mexico, Peru, and Bolivia but no connections with the intermediate region of Central America (1892: 527, 529). A more important contribution, however, is his atlas of pottery samples from private collections, published in 1891 and followed by a commentary in 1892 by Desire Pector. In reviewing this publication Pector noted that the ceramics from El Salvador brought to light two important ethnological problems: (a) the original extent of the non-Maya/non-Mexican peoples and (b) the date when the northerners first appeared, a question that still bothers investigators (Sharer 1974, 1978a).

In the 1920s, the introduction of the utilization of stratigraphy linked this early period to that of the pioneer excavators. This transition owed itself to Jorge Larde, who had a fundamentally geological approach to archaeology (1926a) and noted an archaic culture below the remains of a volcanic eruption near Lake Ilopango (1926b). He also recognized the reoccupation of sites after volcanic eruptions. A year later he and Lothrop excavated at Cerro Zapote, where Preclassic ceramics with Usulutan decoration first came into prominence (Lothrop 1927a). Following the trend established by Larde and Lothrop, Antonio E. Sol recognized three distinct cultures in a ravine at Quelepa in 1929 and presented descriptive accounts of Cihuatan and Tehuacan (1929a, 1929b, 1939).

In the 1940s, investigators began to give more attention to dirt archaeology than to exploration. Foremost among them in El Salvador was Stanley H. Boggs, who established archaeological zones within the country as a whole and initiated the search for Salvadorean culture areas that were free from northern influences (1944: 53). The work of Boggs at Tazumal and Campaña San Andres (1943a, 1943b), coupled with his interest in the relationships between sites, probably led Longyear into this same direction (1966).

Longyear worked at Los Llanitos in eastern El Salvador. His stratigraphic excavations concentrated on the cultural and temporal sequences of ceramics and strengthened his original hypothesis of the chronological position of Ulua Polychrome Ware in the Late Classic period. He also examined the distribution of cultural products, a new trend in Salvadorean archaeology (1944). Muriel N. Porter also belongs in the category of pioneer excavators. Her find of Preclassic material from San Salvador provided sound information on non-Maya/non-Mexican culture in the central part of the country (1955).

In attempting to clarify the labyrinth of culture complexes in El Salvador, Wolfgang Haberland established ceramic sequences in three regions: the western, linked with Guatemala and Mesoamerica; the eastern, essentially Central American; and the central area, which he found heavily influenced by the first two regions but in the main Mesoamerican (1958, 1960a, 1960b,

1961a). Haberland's sequences stressed the need for further investigation, particularly in the Late Preclassic and Early Classic periods (Andrews V 1976: 143). He also devoted himself to a search for early man in eastern El Salvador and, with W. H. Grebe, reported a Preclassic site with footprints in this area (1957).

During the 1970s the Lempa Dam required salvage archaeology in El Salvador, which brought an influx of investigators and new trends. Most of the work has been carried out in the central part of the country, particularly the project known as Cerron Grande and at Cihuatan, the Early Postclassic site associated with the Pipil. The approach of the participants was multi-disciplinary ecological research. New methods of gathering ecological data include flotation and pollen analysis, along with opal phytalith studies. The work of Payson D. Sheets on natural hazards such as volcanism, floods, and their effects has inspired many recent investigators (1976, 1979). Sheets also wrote (1975) an important summary of Salvadorean lithics.

Karen Olsen Bruhns shows a decided break with former traditions. Her interest lies in settlement patterns as seen from a socio-political viewpoint. She also gives renewed emphasis to trade routes in combination with trading communities or ports of call (1977, 1978, 1979, 1980).

Luis Casasola Garcia worked out a ceramic phase at Jayaque, a Preclassic site in central El Salvador. He thinks the site is related to the same time span at Kaminaljuyu and El Baul in Guatemala, Los Naranjos in Honduras, Chalchuapa, and Quelepa in El Salvador. He also searched for areas of cultural elements and traits (1977). This methodology promotes an effort to discover, using ecology and history, the causes of diverse ceramic types in a given country and their external as well as internal relationships to the site.

Intersite variability, coupled with ecology and the local environment, lies behind Jane Holden Kelley's work at Cihuatan (1980). The search for Post-classic sites and their part in cultural exchange has been prominent in recent archaeological activities (Andrews V 1976; Fowler and Solis Angula 1977).

E. Wyllys Andrews V made a thorough excavation and study of an eastern Salvadorean site (Quelepa) first described by Atilio Peccorini (1913, 1926). Andrews established a cultural sequence which began in 400 B.C. Lower Central American influence was strongest during the Early Classic, but Quelepa became Mesoamericanized by A.D. 650. This ended in A.D. 1150 with the beginning of the Late Classic. He also successfully formulated a sequence for Usulutan-type pottery. Contrary to former ideas, Andrews V suggested that this technique originated either in western El Salvador or in highland Guatemala. From there, it was spread to the east and north in El Salvador and Honduras by the Lenca peoples. Adhering to the concept of a cultural sphere (Willey, Culbert, and Adams 1967: 306), Andrews V sees a resemblance between Copan Archaic, Ulua Bichrome (Santa Rita), Ya-

rumela II, Lo de Vaca, and Eden I (Los Naranjos), with the Uapala complex
at Quelepa due to the Lenca. He believes that the Late Classic at Quelepa
indicated a relationship oriented more to Veracruz and the Gulf coast (in
other words, a lowland Mesoamerican pattern) than to lower Central America (1976: 179–86).

Nicaragua

Nicaragua is archaeologically the least known of the Central American
republics. Its prehistory has been overshadowed by historical documentation
since the Conquest, perhaps because it was from lower Central America
that the Spanish takeover of the whole Isthmus began.

The intrepid Englishman Frederick Boyle was an astute observer with
the makings of an equally good archaeologist. His journey on mule from
the Caribbean coast westward led him through the Department of Chontales, where he was the first person to refer to looters sacking graves in
mounds on the savannas. Boyle's mention of a sculptured alabaster vessel
hints at trade with Honduras; his account of funerary urns, piles of human
teeth, and burnt, headless bodies recalls Panamanian practices. He was also
the first to notice the difference between the monoliths of Chontales, Ni-
quiran, and others in Nicaragua (1868:1: 294) that were later studied by
Francis B. Richardson (1940). Boyle also illustrated Luna Ware, shoe vessels,
and stone faces from Ometepe and Zapatera islands, Mombacho, and Chontales (1868:1: facing 43, 96).

Thomas Belt, an English naturalist, made observations that seem to
foreshadow the thoughts of more recent investigators. He noted, for example,
that from Cape Gracias a Dios southward on the east coast, manioc was
favored over maize and that the petroglyphs along the Rio Mico resembled
many in South America and the Virgin Islands (1874: 53, 55).

Two North Americans and another European made contributions of particular interest during this period: a navy doctor, J. F. Bransford (1881); Earl
Flint, an investigator for the Smithsonian Institution (letters to George
Putnam in 1882, 1884–85, 1889); and a Swedish botanist, Carl Bovallius
(1886, 1887).

Bransford and Flint conducted some of the first careful excavations in
southern Pacific Nicaragua and the Nicoya Peninsula of Costa Rica and
obtained collections now in the Smithsonian Museum. It was through
Bransford's efforts that Luna Ware (1881: 20–44), a curious mixture of
northern and southern motifs, and Palmar Ware (1881: 69–70), one of the
oldest Central American bichromes, were named and recognized. He also
illustrated examples with the bold interpretations of the Mexican feathered
serpent (1881: 54, 58) of what we call Papagayo and Underslipped Incised
Ware. Flint identified a pottery style called Tola and presented the first

scientific report on the human footprints of Acahualinca. These footprints were later examined by Richardson, who published a diagram of the site (1954). Bovallius, like Squier, published drawings of statues, artifacts, and pictographs from Zapatera Island (1886, 1887), and also described Punta del Zapote, a site later ruined by looters.

Ceramic sequences in Nicaragua were first established by Albert H. Norweb (1961) for the Isthmus of Rivas, part of what Norweb referred to as the Greater Nicoya subarea (1964). Norweb's detailed sequences were based on ceramic modes from southwestern Nicaragua and related wherever possible to those from the Nicoya Peninsula. He came to the conclusion that the Zoned Bichrome and Early Polychrome periods were lower Central American in character but that the culture acquired Mesoamerican characteristics during the Middle Polychrome period. Michael D. Coe (1963) saw the Early Polychrome as "contributing" to Mesoamerica.

Haberland's ceramic sequence from Ometepe Island (1966b) broadened the knowledge of ceramic interrelationships between Nicaragua and northwestern Costa Rican sites from 300 B.C. to A.D. 800. It also suggested horizon markers for the Zoned Bichrome period and the first part of the Early Polychrome period (Haberland 1969: 234). Hno. Hildeberto Maria, F.S.C. (Matillo Vila 1968), made a study of rock art.

Lydia L. Wyckoff derived a ceramic sequence from a collection in the Heye Museum of the American Indian and from her excavation at San Francisco on the Rivas Peninsula (1974). She suggested that the extensive use of Papagayo Polychrome in the Middle Polychrome period and its discovery at Isla de Sacrificios, Mexico, imply migration, not trade. Papagayo is a Mesoamericanized polychrome ware characteristic of the Greater Nicoya area. It was traded north but has been misidentified at many sites. If what has been identified in Veracruz really is Papagayo, it most likely was brought by pilgrims.

Karen Olsen Bruhns reported (1974) on fieldwork at Punto de las Figuras and Punto Zapote on Zapatera Island. The object of the survey was to date the Zapatera statues, but efforts were hampered by looting. Neither a date nor connection between pottery and the alter-ego figures was established. Punto Zapote seems to have combined residential with ceremonial remains, and Bruhns noted that the reports of Squier and Bovallius are still necessary to understand the site.

Linda Anne Reynolds (n.d.) classified the sherds from Punto de las Figuras and divided them into two large groups according to paste, temper, surface color, and decorative treatment. Applying both ceramic and historical evidence, she placed the site in the Middle Polychrome period within the Chorotegan "tradition."

Healy analyzed 80,000 sherds from Willey and Norweb's earlier excavations on the Peninsula of Rivas and on Ometepe Island. He employed the type-variety method of analysis and produced a sequence covering 2,000 years that paralleled sequences already established for northwestern Costa Rica and showed the interrelationship of the two areas (1974b, 1976b, 1980).

Richard W. Magnus worked on the Atlantic coast with the aim of establishing a chronological sequence and the cultural relationships of the area from Pearl Lagoon to the southern limits of Bluefields Bay. He recognized a polychrome and a monochrome tradition, the latter with or without incised and punctated decoration (1975, 1976, 1978). Magnus also noted that villages were inland, and the coast was used for fishing, a situation we see applicable to the Linea Vieja and Talamanca, Costa Rica, as well.

Costa Rica

Geographically, Costa Rica has been one of the most difficult countries to penetrate, especially in the south, where excessive rainfall for at least nine months a year produces dense forest lands that cover the steep, high ranges as well as the low, swampy coast. The first archaeological work in Costa Rica was done by Bransford (1884) and Flint, who limited themselves to the upper part of the Nicoya Peninsula.

Anastacio Alfaro, a natural scientist, should be considered the father of Costa Rican archaeology (Stone 1956a). Alfaro was sent at age 22 by the Costa Rican government to the Smithsonian Institution to learn museum work. He later became the first director of the National Museum. Honest, scholarly, and dedicated, he was commissioned to enlarge the state collections destined for exhibition in 1892 at Madrid. He worked at El Guayabo de Turrialba and in different parts of the country (1893, 1896).

Carl Vilhem Hartman, a Swedish botanist, was the first to carry out a series of systematically recorded excavations in Costa Rica. He noted the structure and contents of graves (Rowe 1959: 272) and established two distinct cultural units in the highlands—Stone Cist and Curridabat Ware, the forerunner of Costa Rican culture sequences. He also worked at Las Mercedes (1901) and on the Pacific side at Las Huacas (1907). While in the area, he purchased a fluted point which eventually found its way to the Carnegie Museum in Pittsburgh (Swauger and Mayer-Oakes 1952). Pedro Perez Zeledon (1907–8) and Jorge A. Lines (1935, 1936a, 1936b, 1942) were other early investigators who supplied new archaeological information in published texts.

Stone was the first to report the lithic spheres in the Diquis Delta and to excavate there (1943). She found Black and Red Line Ware with iron tools, which strengthens Haberland's placement of this pottery in the Boruca phase (Haberland 1957a; Stone 1966a, fig. 7, b–d). This time span also applies to the unpainted appliqued tripod vessels with millefiore beads and iron articles reported by Stone (1966a: 47, fig. 1). She was one of the first to use ecology and plants in reconstructing the pre-Columbian environment of the country and to indicate the importance of the peach palm and tuber agriculture (1956b). She also named the three archaeological regions of Costa Rica (1958a). Her discovery of a Mesoamerican type of maize in a pre-Columbian Guanacaste burial supported her earlier hypothesis of Meso-american influence in Costa Rica (1977: 90, 95 note 2; Dunn 1978: 97).

Carlos Balser, another pioneer, has concentrated on the techniques in working jadeite and metal (1953, 1962; Stone and Balser 1958). Stone and Balser (1957) conducted a study on the function of the two types of grinding stones in lower Central America.

Carlos H. Aguilar excavated an unusual ceremonial cache containing stone and wooden objects at Retes (1953). Aguilar worked at El Guayabo (1972), a site which has seen greatly expanded research efforts by the Archaeology Laboratory of the University of Costa Rica (Fonseca Zamora 1979). Aguilar also conducted salvage archaeology at Pavas, where he found bottle or pit graves (1974) and at El Molino in Cartago (1975). He obtained a ceramic sequence at both places (1976).

Matthew W. Stirling was yet another pioneer excavator who worked at Las Mercedes and other sites on the Linea Vieja. He was the first (1969) to correlate in time the axe-god image and nasal snuffers with ceramic vessels of the Early Period on the Atlantic watershed, establishing a date, A.D. 144. The association of "chocolate pots" in this find is at least four centuries earlier than those in a subsequent sequence by Snarskis (1976b: 107).

Archaeological pioneers in the Diquis Region besides Stone (1943) include Haberland, who established a ceramic sequence for the upper area (1959) that, along with his ceramic typology, tied in this section with the adjoining Chiriqui Province in Panama and caused him to apply the term Gran Chiriqui to this border region (1961c, 1962, 1976); Laura Laurencich de Minelli and Luigi Minelli (1966, 1973), whose excavations have given us the most complete information on the earliest or Aguas Buenas phase; and Maria Eugenia Bozzoli de Willi, who is one of few to furnish reliable reports on the Middle to Late period Diquis and the Boruca phase in the western part of the General and Parrita valleys (1962, 1966).

Michael D. Coe (1962b) and Claude F. Baudez (1962, 1967) started investigations on the Nicoya Peninsula about the same time. These two archaeologists combined the results of their studies to produce a chrono-logical and ceramic type sequence not only for Guanacaste but also as a model for comparison with southwestern Nicaragua (Coe and Baudez 1961; Baudez and Coe 1962).

William J. Kennedy developed a sequence for the Reventazon Valley (1968, 1969, 1975, 1976) and used surface finish and color, paste color, texture, and temper to classify plain or monochrome wares. He relied on the technique of ornamentation to classify the decorated pottery. His sequence can be correlated with that from the Nicoya region. Characteristic of the Atlantic watershed, however, is the development of painted-line wares, the intrusion of negative-painted pottery from the south, and an almost total lack of a polychrome tradition, except for trade wares from Nicoya.

Frederick W. Lange's primary objective has been to integrate settlement patterns with subsistence patterns by examining a specific geographical area and testing the cultural deposits at selected sites, some of which were later excavated more extensively. He has established a ceramic sequence, which wisely follows previous nomenclature whenever possible, for northern coastal Guanacaste and the Sapoa River area (Lange 1971a, 1971b, 1972, 1976, 1978). Lange also finds in the pre-Columbian culture of the Nicoya region a circum-Caribbean pattern of ecological adaptation instead of a Mesoamerican one (1971c). He has also focused on the importance of climatic variations and foodstuffs as factors in population and economic changes. Along with Richard M. Accola, Lange has helped to prove the existence of metalworking in Costa Rica (1979). Among general problems to be resolved in the future, Lange lists as one of the most provocative the need to investigate the relationships and differences between sites of inland valleys and coastal bays (Lange 1976: 45–66; 1978).

Jeanne W. Sweeney (1975, 1976) worked toward Guanacaste and ceramic analysis. Her results are based on 20,000 sherds collected by M. Coe, whose sequence she used and amplified. Curiously, Sweeney sees the ceramics of the Nicoya Peninsula as predominantly non-northern and comments that "the inclusion of Nicoya in Mesoamerica is unwarranted" (1976: 39). This line of thought seems hard to justify in view of the number of late polychromes with motifs from the Central Mexican highlands (Stone 1982).

A pottery sequence based on individual modes was tentatively proposed by Michael J. Snarskis for the Atlantic watershed (1976a). His excavations were carried out in a multicomponent site which yielded possible Paleo-Indian remains and a ceramic complex termed El Bosque. This complex is composed of traits of the Formative and Zoned Bichrome periods but with small differences. Maize of the *Pollo* species, found in conjunction with the El Bosque complex, has been claimed as the most primitive form and native to Colombia (Snarskis 1975: 8–11), an opinion not shared by all botanists (Dunn 1978).

Skeletal remains from Barrahonda, Guanacaste, have been studied by Laurencich de Minelli (1979). The site appears to be Zoned Bichrome, but radiocarbon dates obtained thus far are inconclusive.

A synthesis of regional prehistory was first published by Stone (1972) and covered the geographical Central American Isthmus. The same pattern, but relating only to Costa Rica, was followed by Luis Ferrero (1977). Stone also presented a synthesis, with historical documentation, of Costa Rican archaeology emphasizing trade routes (1977) and which also included previously unpublished reports of sites.

Panama

The looting of Panamanian graves did not cease in 1519 when the conquistador Gaspar de Espinosa sacked a house containing three bodies of chieftains prepared for burial with all their golden finery (Espinosa 1873), but rather has continued. The most serious damage to archaeology, however, was the discovery of gold-filled graves at Bugabita, Chiriqui, in 1858 and the subsequent publication of this find in 1895 by F. M. Otis, a North American surgeon on board the steamer *Moses Taylor*. It is estimated that gold objects worth in those days more than $100,000 were pillaged from over 4,000 graves in the area, a feat that stimulated expeditions by foreign institutions and whetted local appetites. Earlier articles by Squier (1859), J. King Merritt (1860), J. T. Bateman (1861), William Bollaert (1861, 1863), and A. de Zeltner (1865) caused similar problems.

These activities were closely followed by the North American William H. Holmes. He based most of his studies on the large collections of artifacts at Yale University and the U.S. National Museum, the majority of which had been gathered by an explorer, J. A. McNeil (Holmes 1888). Holmes recognized two types of plain ware and nine painted ones based on the method of manufacture, clay, shape, finish, decoration, and evidence of use (1888: 84). Holmes's use of collections instead of fieldwork as a means of reconstructing Chiriquian prehistory started a trend among archaeologists to do the same.

George Grant MacCurdy (1911) also based his study on the Yale collection. Although he adhered to Holmes's classification, MacCurdy changed some of the terminology, a tack that is occasionally good but frequently confusing (1911: 47). Nevertheless, the volumes of Holmes and MacCurdy were outstanding for their precise and numerous illustrations and furnished a model for future archaeological studies. Cornelius Osgood classified the Yale vessels as well but included private collections in David, Panama, in his study. This additional material enabled him to reduce previous groupings to four types and to trace some wares beyond Panamanian boundaries (1935).

A. Hyatt Verrill wrote a tantalizing account (tantalizing because one wishes the author had included more details) of his investigations at Rio Caño (1927), which yielded lithic statues. These monoliths show a relationship to stone figures from varied sites on the west coast of lower Central America, particularly Honduras.

The report of Sigvald Linne, a Swede, on his explorations and excavations on the peninsula of Darien and the Pearl Islands in 1929 is still the best for this area. Linne was also the first to do scientific fieldwork in Chiriqui (1936).

Lothrop's excavations in Panama came soon after, and he was also responsible for a later summary of lower Isthmian archaeology (1966). J. Alden Mason worked at Cocle and decided that the graves were those of warriors buried with their chief and not sacrificial victims as suggested by Lothrop (Mason 1940, 1941, 1942). Olga F. Linares interprets the reports differently and sees only a ceremonial burial ground attributable to political alliances and mainly reserved for warriors and their leaders (1977a: 76–77).

In 1948 the discovery of human remains at Venado Beach led to the formation of what later became the Archaeological Society of Panama, whose members carried out constructive fieldwork. The results were published in a journal, *Panama Archaeologist* (1958–65), and covered a wide range of investigations—Venado Beach, a Madden Lake cave, fluted points, Villaba Island, shaft graves on Guacamayo Volcano, and the rising Panamanian coastlines.

Matthew Stirling was the first to excavate at the Late Preclassic ceremonial site of Barriles and to report on its petroglyphs and lithic statues (1950) as well as on ceramics from the vicinity (Stirling and Stirling 1964a). Alain Ichon is another archaeologist who has been interested in the problems of Barriles pottery (1968).

A search for sites related to preceramic peoples and early pottery makers characterized much of the 1950s, beginning with Willey and McGimsey's Monogrillo study (1954), which included finding the preceramic site of Cerro Mangote, dated around 4900 B.C. (McGimsey 1956), and establishing a ceramic sequence for later periods.

Haberland's work in Panama convinced him that a common cultural background united three basically Central American complexes—Aguas Buenas and La Concepcion of Panama with those of central Costa Rica—but with regional differences (1961c, 1973). Baudez compiled a regional chronology of Central America (1963) and also a survey that accepts Mesoamerican influences (1970). Reina Torres de Arauz has written a synthesis of Panamanian archaeology (1966).

In 1964 John Ladd published a ceramic sequence and study of Parita and Santa Maria. The pottery types were later shown by R. G. Cooke to be missing at Cocle (1976d), thus changing the terminal period of the site to an earlier date. Leo Biese has concerned himself with the archaeology of Panama Viejo (1964). Various reports of excavations and finds have also appeared in the *Boletin del Museo Chiricano*, particularly in 1966, nos. 1, 2, and 3. Linares has made the only survey of the Gulf of Chiriqui, where she established a pottery sequence (1968a, 1968b).

Archaeologists of the 1970s focused on hypothesis testing and have stressed pre-Columbian ecology. Beginning with a concentrated search for preceramic cultures in part inspired by Junius Bird's hunt for early projectile points (Bird and Cooke 1974, 1977), more such sites have appeared (Ranere 1975a, 1975b; Ranere and Hansell 1978).

Linares, along with Ranere and Cooke, made controlled comparisons between different areas of the Panamanian coast and subsequent developments. They indicate that the greater the natural resources, the more frequent are the changes in subsistence patterns and social systems (Linares and Ranere 1971, 1980; Linares and Cooke 1975; Cooke 1976a, 1976d; Linares 1977b). While Linares has directed her inquiry as to how and why the circum-Caribbean type of chiefdom developed in lower Central America, she has misinterpreted the basis for this social system. The clan with its moieties, reciprocal and nonreciprocal groups, and professions connected with them functioned as a social class and so gave rise to a rank society (Stone 1962a: 35–36; 1977).

The historical development of archaeology in lower Central America has been thoroughly influenced by the geographical, political, and cultural characteristics of the different regions. The intricacies, differences, and problems set forth in the following articles vary in scope and emphasis and reflect these historical patterns.

In the 1970s settlement patterns and ecological methodologies began to appear in archaeological studies. Analytical procedures reflecting increasing sophistication in modern instrumentation were also being used. These efforts became part of the research summarized in the other chapters and are discussed in that context.

3
Cultural Geography of Pre-Columbian Lower Central America

Frederick W. Lange

Department of Anthropology
University of Colorado, Boulder

Introduction

A geographically/ecologically based understanding of lower Central America is essential in order to comprehend the cultural development of the region. Particular aspects of the physical landscape affected settlement patterns, subsistence, and acquisition of natural resources, encouraged or impeded human movement, and established the limits for human cultural development in the region. The region's principal physical features are the thin and elongated lower Central American Isthmus, bulging to broader width only in northeastern Nicaragua and eastern Honduras; the almost continuous chain of volcanoes down the backbone of the Isthmus; the contrasting wet and dry Pacific coastal lowlands; and the wetter Atlantic coastal lowlands.[1]

Landforms

The basic landforms of the area are shown in figure 3.1. In general lower Central America is divided into central highlands and plateaus and Atlantic and Pacific coastal lowlands, but there are a number of cross-cutting features as well. These features are mostly structural depressions in old graben systems or valleys between volcanic peaks and should be considered natural conduits for human movement. Of particular interest are the depressions linking the Gulf of Fonseca, via the Nicaraguan lakes, with the Atlantic coastal lowland of Costa Rica.

In northern Honduras a number of narrow but fertile lowlands "similar to the lower Motagua in Guatemala, occupy the numerous northeast-southwest trending depressions that open onto the Caribbean coast" (West 1964a: 70). In western Honduras Sapper (1902) earlier noted a north-south "structural depression [that] forms a trans-isthmian passway from the Gulf of

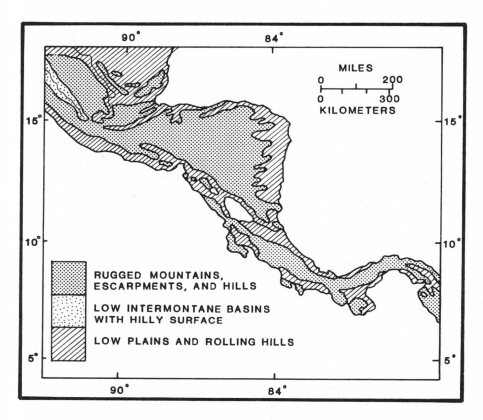

Figure 3.1. Basic landforms of lower Central America (West and Augelli 1976: 22).

Fonseca, up the Goascoran River Valley, through Comayagua Valley to the Ulua depression on the Caribbean coast" (West 1964a: 70).

On the very northern limits of lower Central America, but potentially very significant in terms of the jade and obsidian trade and other cultural contacts, is the "Valle de las Vacas, the locale of Guatemala City . . . a transverse, north-south graben structure [that] . . . affords an easy pass across the volcanic range from the Pacific coastal plains to the Motagua Valley" (West 1964a: 77). The cultural significance of the various depressions and other natural corridors that link subregions of lower Central America is little studied and poorly understood. Two of these depressions place the Gulf of Fonseca at an intersection of natural corridors crossing practically the whole lower Central American area. Limited work by Baudez (1966, 1976a) suggested extensive pre-Columbian occupation in the Gulf of Fonseca area. Purely geographical-locational criteria suggest it should be a prime target for future research.

Coastal Systems and Intercoastal Contacts

Prehistoric peoples in the interior were very seldom more than a few days' journey from either coast, reinforcing Voorhies's (1978) important point that coastal systems are never isolated, but always have broader systemic relationships with noncoastal areas. The relatively small distances between coasts in the Isthmus suggest the possibility that pre-Columbian social and trade networks linked the coasts, but only in western Panama (Linares 1977b; Linares and Ranere 1980) and in northern Costa Rica (Lange 1978; Norr 1978) have attempts been made to assess cultural similarities and differences along coast-to-coast corridors. Drolet reported little evidence of Pacific coastal cultural contacts from his work on the Atlantic coast of eastern Panama (1980). According to Cooke (Chap. 10, this volume), there is ethnohistoric evidence and a consensus that Atlantic coast Panamanian groups were deeply involved in Pacific coastal trade, although regional artifact assemblages remained distinct. The data suggest that the ecological differences between the Atlantic and Pacific coasts formed a boundary between pre-Columbian groups. Other than the obvious ecological differences, we have little idea of what the mechanisms of boundary maintenance were, although Drolet has some tantalizing insights (1980) that suggest differences in cosmological relationships for which the environment may have been partially responsible.

The Atlantic Caribbean Coast

While least known archaeologically, the Atlantic coastal lowlands cover the largest space in lower Central America. West (1964a: 81) divided the Caribbean coast from Guatemala to Panama into four subareas: (a) the Guatemala-Honduras coast; (b) the Mosquito (or Miskito) coast in northwestern Honduras and Nicaragua; (c) the eastern lowlands of the Nicaraguan depression and its Costa Rican appendage; and (d) the coast of southeastern Costa Rica and Panama (fig. 3.2).

Along the Guatemala-Honduras coast, data from the Bay Islands (Epstein 1957) suggest contacts with Pacific Costa Rica and other parts of Central America. More recently, reflecting the general shift in research emphases, Healy (1974a, 1975, 1977, 1978a, 1978b, 1978c, and this volume) has begun to produce detailed settlement, subsistence, and cultural data indicating that pre-Columbian peoples not only farmed the fertile river valleys, but also exploited the rich marine resources. Henderson et al. (1979) have also carried out extensive research in the Naco Valley of Honduras.

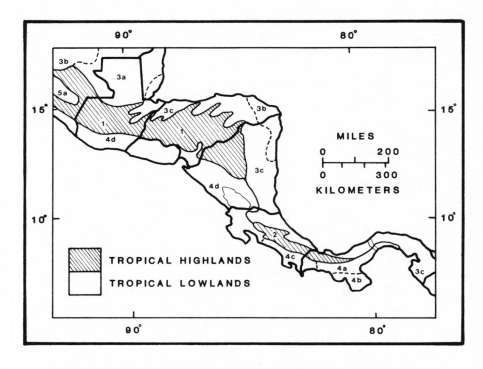

TROPICAL HIGHLANDS AND EXTRATROPICAL APPENDAGES
1   Highlands of northern Central America
2   Highlands of Costa Rica and western Panama

TROPICAL LOWLANDS
3   Caribbean-Gulf lowlands
  3a Peten-Yucatan rain-forest area
  3b Mosquito coast
  3c Caribbean rain-forest area of Central America
4   Pacific lowlands
  4a Savanna of Central Panama
  4b Azuero rain-forest area
  4c Rain forest of southwestern Costa Rica
  4d Volcanic lowlands of Central America
5   Dry interior tropical basins
  5a Valley of Chiapas

Figure 3.2.   Natural regions of lower Central America (West 1964b: 368).

The Mosquito coastal lowland is almost 1000 kilometers long and 150 kilometers wide in some places and is one of the more extensive coastal plains in lower Central America (West 1964a: 81). On the northern part of this lowland the Patuca and Coco rivers have produced large deltas. These delta formations have geomorphological implications for archaeological research. The coastal lagoon areas are rapidly filling, the coast is expanding, and prehistoric sites may have been either swept away or buried, or they may be as many as 20 kilometers inland. Immediately offshore is the Mosquito Bank, where cays and reefs stimulate the production of rich marine life, certainly a factor in settlement and subsistence practices. Archaeological research in the area has been limited to studies by Magnus (1976: 1978), who suggested that pre-Columbian peoples exploited both coastal marine and inland farming resources, a pattern mirrored by Nietschmann's (1973) contemporary studies.

Tamayo (1964: 98) has noted that "the lower courses of the . . . Honduran and Nicaraguan rivers . . . are wide, fairly deep and voluminous, and therefore navigable for small craft." In Honduras the combined Chamelecon-Ulua drainage basin is perhaps the largest in lower Central America and has an extensive floodplain with fertile soils that were the center of the pre-Columbian cacao trade with the Yucatec Maya. The Sula Plain was also Maya at the time of the conquest (Stone 1941). The Aguan River drains another fertile depression toward the Caribbean, and farther to the east numerous other large rivers drain the eastern highlands of Honduras (Tamayo 1964: 88). The complete hydrology of lower Central America is summarized in figure 3.3.

In northern Nicaragua the Patuca is the largest river system and its Rio Guayape tributary is well known for placer gold deposits. South of the Patuca is the extensive Coco River system which, although it rises in the northwestern highlands of Nicaragua a scant 75 kilometers from the Pacific coast, winds a 750-kilometer route to the Caribbean and is navigable along the lower 500 kilometers. In general, the entire Caribbean coast of Nicaragua is drained by rivers similar to, but shorter than, the Coco (Tamayo 1964: 97).

The eastern lowlands of the Nicaraguan depression straddle the Nicaraguan–Costa Rican Atlantic border. The San Juan River has formed a massive delta that is rapidly èxpanding; it also drains the inland lakes of Nicaragua and has numerous tributaries entering from north-central Costa Rica. Its largest tributary is the Rio San Carlos, but there are numerous others (Tamayo 1964: 97–98). Many of the San Juan's tributaries rise near valleys between volcanoes on the Atlantic slopes of the Costa Rican central volcanic range. These valleys offer paths of communication between Guanacaste and the San Carlos Plain.

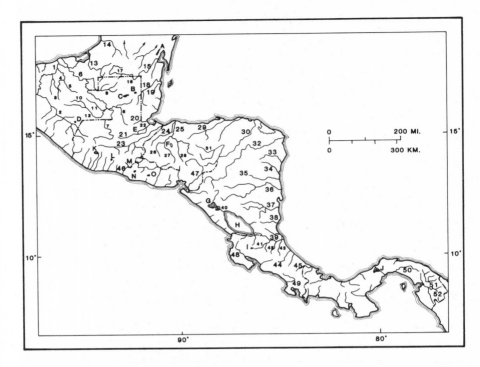

Figure 3.3. Hydrology of lower Central America (Tamayo 1964: 89).

RIVERS

ATLANTIC WATERSHED

1. Grijalva
2. Rio Grande de Chiapas
3. Tacotalpa
4. Macuspana
5. Tulija
6. Usumacinta
7. Chixoy
8. Pasion
9. San Pedro
10. Jatate
11. Lacanji
12. Lacantum
13. Candelaria
14. Champoton
15. Hondo
16. Azul
17. Xmoscha
18. Belize
19. Sibun
20. Sarstoon
21. Polochic
22. Dulce
23. Motagua

24. Chamelecon
25. Ulua
26. Jicatuyo
27. Otoro
28. Humuya
29. Aguan
30. Patuca
31. Guayape
32. Coco
33. Wawa
34. Cuçulaya
35. Prinzapolca
36. Grande
37. Escondido
38. Punta Gorda
39. San Juan (Desaguadero)
40. Tipitapa
41. San Carlos
42. Sarapiqui
43. Chirripo
44. Reventazon
45. Sixaola

PACIFIC WATERSHED

46. Lempa
47. Choluteca

48. Tempisque
49. Diquis
50. Chepo
51. Chucunaque
52. Tuira

LAKES

ATLANTIC WATERSHED

A. Bacalar
B. Yaxha
C. Peten-Itza
D. Tepancuapan
E. Izabal
F. Yojoa
G. Managua
H. Nicaragua
I. Arenal
J. Gatun

PACIFIC WATERSHED

K. Atitlan
L. Amatitlan
M. Guija
N. Coatepeque
O. Ilopango

Limited archaeology on the San Carlos Plain suggests there was a substantial population there by at least A.D. 300. Exploration also points to the area being regionally distinct. Current impressions are biased by pothunters' reports, but there appears to be a relatively high proportion of gold, jade, pyrite mirrors, and other trade goods—these probably reflect the multiple transportation routes offered by the extensive river systems. As Sheets noted during the seminar discussion, the problem of lowland tropical settlement relative to varying soil conditions has been greatly under-researched. In Mesoamerica the big lowland tropical rivers that drain from sedimentary areas with leached soils do not support dense populations on their floodplains and are not very fertile in terms of the nitrogen necessary for maize agriculture. On the other hand, rivers that drain from volcanic highlands periodically flood and renew soil fertility. In these settings civilizations like the Olmec, or very productive areas like the lower Motagua, emerged.

Artifacts from different time periods and in styles representative of Guanacaste have been found on the Solentenaime Islands at the southeastern corner of Lake Nicaragua. It is near this part of Lake Nicaragua that many tributaries drain into the San Juan, and where the San Juan begins its journey to the Caribbean. The Spanish made extensive use of the San Juan for transport in Colonial times (MacLeod 1973), and this practice was presumably modeled on existing indigenous trade routes.

The pattern of riverine systems is somewhat different along the southeastern cost of Costa Rica and along the coast of Panama. According to Tamayo,

South of the San Juan River the streams of the Caribbean drainage in Costa Rica and Panama are composed of short but voluminous rivers that drain the steep windward side of the central highlands. . . . The Reventazon River, 155 kilometers long, is the most important of the Caribbean streams in Costa Rica. (1964: 98)

Kennedy (1976) tested a number of sites along the middle and upper course of the Reventazon which, as Tamayo also notes (1964: 98), has long been used for communication between the Meseta Central and the Caribbean coast. Like Kennedy, Snarskis has focused more on the slopes and intermediate elevations than the coast; nothing is really known about the Atlantic coast of Costa Rica. Reports of site concentrations in the Sixaloa Valley, where the river has formed an extensive floodplain near the Panamanian border, have not been substantiated through scientific research. An Aztec trading post was reported in the area at Spanish contact (Lothrop 1942; Stone 1949; Laurencich de Minelli 1977).

The Panamanian coast of the Caribbean is "mountainous, broken only by the coalesced deltas of the Sixaloa and Changuinola rivers, the deeply indented Chiriqui Lagoon, and the small Chagres delta at the Canal Zone"

(West 1964a: 82). It is drained by 153 short streams, with the Chagres the most important river system (Tamayo 1964: 99). The area around the Chiriqui Lagoon, or Bocas del Toro, has been studied by Linares (1977b; Linares and Ranere 1980). East of the former Canal Zone, where the generally rocky shore is paralleled by coral reefs and innumerable small cays or islets, Drolet reported (1980) prehistoric settlement and subsistence patterns; in eastern Panama there is no real Atlantic-Pacific distinction, and basic ecological unity exists.

As classified by Vivo Escoto (1964: 210–12), the tropical Atlantic lowlands of lower Central America fall basically into two categories of the Koeppen system, *Afw'* and *Amw'* (fig. 3.4). "Both have rain in all months, but the latter receives the lesser amount (1500–2000 mm.) and is characterized by a short dry period of a few weeks during February or March [fig. 3.5] and concentration of rain in the months of September through November [fig. 3.6]. The *Afw'* climate usually receives over 2000 mm. of rain yearly, but with no dry period" (Vivo Escoto 1964: 213).

The Caribbean side of lower Central America is covered by tropical rain forest "extending continuously from the Gulf of Honduras to northern South America . . . reaching up to 800–1000 m. altitude, where the mean monthly temperature is well over 20 degrees C., and precipitation is as high as 4500 mm. annually" (Wagner 1964: 229).

While soil conditions are closely related to landforms and rainfall patterns (fig. 3.7 shows a general contrast between Atlantic coastal and Pacific coastal soil formation conditions in lower Central America), they have local variability and hence macro and micro significance for subsistence practices and settlement patterns. Selective occupation or avoidance of particular zones because of soil conditions probably affected regional development patterns. As Stevens (1964: 310) noted for general soil distributions along the Atlantic coast,

many soils of the interior plateaus and coastlands are too infertile for maize production. . . . Much of the quartz-sandy soil on the alluvial plains covered by pine savannas in Mosquito, eastern Honduras and northern Nicaragua, is definitely inadequate for maize. Bordering on, or interspersed with, these savannas are forested patches of broadleaf species which require a richer soil. These areas are planted to maize. . . .

These soil distributions are related to natural vegetation distribution (fig. 3.8) and suggest that soil survey data may be useful in locating areas with archaeological potential. It is perhaps no accident that extensive archaeological remains are often encountered in contemporary Atlantic lowland agricultural plantations, usually located in zones of higher soil fertility. While there has been substantial impact of volcanic deposition and destruc-

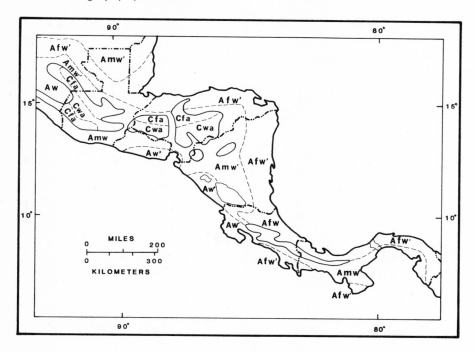

Figure 3.4.   Koeppen classification of lower Central American climatic types (Vivo Escoto 1964: 207).

tion or renewal of soils on the Pacific coast, there "has been little renewal of soil fertility on the Caribbean side. . . . the active volcanoes are very close to the Pacific shore, toward which the showers of ash and cinders are swept by the trade winds" (Stevens 1964: 310).

The most fertile soils along the Atlantic watershed are on the alluvial plains and levees of the major river systems, such as those drained by the Chamelecon and Ulua, which were "densely populated in pre-Spanish times" (Chapman 1957; West 1964a: 70). Tamayo (1964: 97) noted that, farther south,

in their lower and middle courses the rivers of the Mosquito coast have been of special significance for human settlement. Most of the forest Indians of northeastern Honduras and eastern Nicaragua . . . were riverine people living along the main streams and their tributaries. These people cultivated the fertile alluvium of natural levees and exploited the abundant riverine tropical fish resources. They were excellent canoemen, the rivers serving as highways for trade and migration.

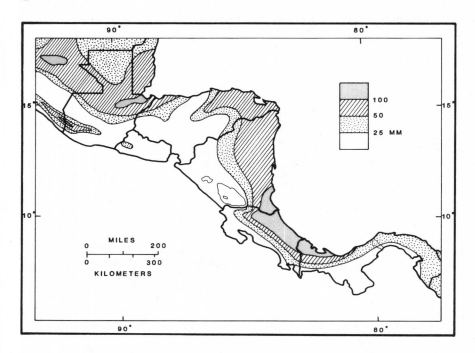

Figure 3.5.   Average March rainfall in lower Central America (Vivo Escoto 1964: 202).

This is very similar to patterns described by Lathrap (1970) for the Upper Amazon, suggested by M. Coe for the Olmec area (1979), and recently described in microcosm for the eastern Caribbean coast of Panama by Drolet (1980). In addition, the tropical rain forest provided an abundance of wild game, natural resources in wood and other vegetal products, and a wide variety of hallucinogenic and narcotic plants that were important in ritual and perhaps served as bases for regional and long-distance trade.

Palms of many kinds were important multipurpose plants of the area, and they might be considered a vegetal common denominator of the Atlantic-Caribbean coast which sweeps from South America to the Maya lowlands, where Puleston (1968) discussed in detail the importance of *Brosimum alicastrum* among the Maya. While the modern distribution of some palms reflects ancient patterns of forest cultivation, there are very few other firm indicators of subsistence behavior from the Atlantic coast.

Exceptions are most notably Magnus's detailed studies of adaptation in the Bluefields of Nicaragua and Healy's work along the northern coast of

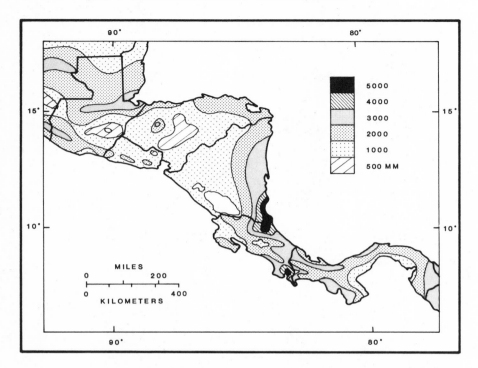

Figure 3.6. Mean annual rainfall in lower Central America (Vivo Escoto 1964: 200).

Honduras. Snarskis has some data from Costa Rica, and Drolet has detailed fishing and farming practices, using both archaeological evidence and eth-nographic analogy from Panama.

The Pacific Coast

The narrower Pacific coastal lowlands contrast with those of the Atlantic. West (1964a: 80) divided them into a northern plains sector, from the Isthmus of Tehuantepec to southern Nicaragua, and a more mountainous southern sector in Costa Rica and Panama (fig. 3.2). The two regions can also be contrasted in terms of the long, straight shore (with the exception of the Gulf of Fonseca) of the northern sector and the more irregular shoreline of the southern sector. Irregular shorelines create bays, form pen-insulas, and, in general, create much more favorable conditions for devel-opment of marine subsistence resources. The correlation between coastline form and availability of resources is seen in data obtained from the Bay of

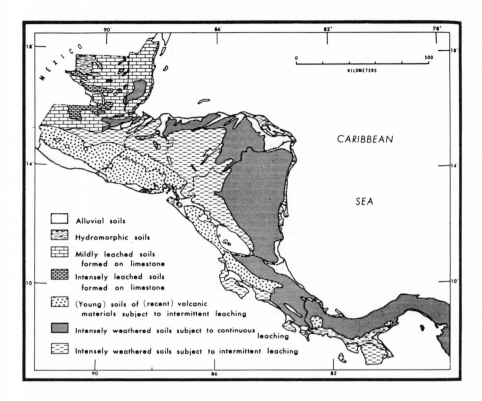

Figure 3.7.   Soils of lower Central America (reprinted with permission from Stevens 1964: 308).

Salinas, Santa Elena Peninsula, Bay of Culebra, and Tamarindo areas of Costa Rica. In those areas occupation was concentrated, and extensive shell middens provide ample evidence of marine exploitation. In contrast are the comparatively straight coasts of San Juan del Sur in Nicaragua and Nosara in Costa Rica where the evidence for human habitation is quite limited, with little, if any, evidence of the exploitation of marine resources.

In western and eastern Panama there is a large, lowland plain which extends from David to the Gulf of Panama. East of David the lowland is undulated, and there is a trough between the central mountain range and the mountainous Azuero Peninsula (West 1964a: 81). The Gulf of Chiriqui is almost unique along the Pacific coast, characterized by numerous small islands, some of which have been explored archaeologically (Linares de Sapir 1968b). While the Atlantic coast has been filling, extending, and

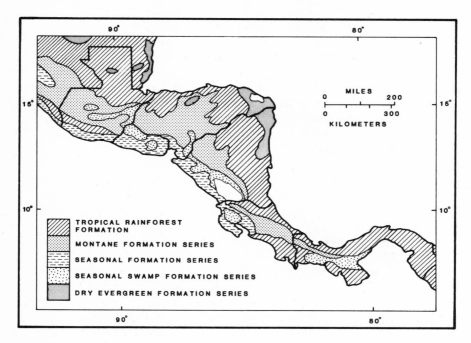

Figure 3.8.   Distribution of natural vegetation in lower Central America (Wagner 1964: 223).

depressing, plate action on the Pacific coast has probably contributed to significant coastal uplift during the time of human occupation. Early sites on the Pacific may be somewhat inland from modern shorelines, and one possible Dry Tropical Archaic site area was located near La Cruz along the Nicaraguan–Costa Rican border (Murray 1969 and Lange, this volume).

The Pacific coast receives much less rainfall than the Atlantic, and, being narrower, it is characterized by surface streams with relatively small discharges. Tamayo (1964: 101) described the setting in more detail:

In Central America the largest river draining to the Pacific is the Rio Lempa of El Salvador. . . . Moreover, a marked seasonal regime characterizes most of the permanent streams of the Pacific watershed, in accordance with the long winter dry season (five to seven months) and the summer rainy period. Many of the smaller rivers are intermittent. . . .

In Nicaragua hardly any major streams drain the Pacific coast. Their lack is emphasized by the concentration of prehistoric populations along the inland shore of Lake Nicaragua, and the principal stream is the Estero Real, which drains into the Gulf of Fonseca (Healy 1980a). The Tempisque River, surveyed and tested by Baudez (1967), the Rio Grande de Turrubares entering the Gulf of Nicoya at its mouth, the Rio Parrita farther south, and the Diquis area around the Rio Grande de Terraba, briefly tested by Lothrop (1963), are the principal rivers of Costa Rica's Pacific coast. According to Tamayo (1964: 109), more than 300 small streams "drain the Pacific slope of Panama, the largest rivers being the Chepo, the Chucunaque, and the Tuira in the eastern part of the country. . . ."

The Pacific coast of lower Central America was divided by Vivo Escoto (1964: 207) among four categories of the Koeppen system: Amw, Aw', Anw', and Afw' (fig. 3.4). He appears to have been in error in classifying parts of the area as Amw and Afw' since "both have rain in all months" (1964: 213). This clearly contradicts his rainfall data (1964: 202, fig. 11). The Aw' classification, indicating a definite and extended winter dry season from November to May, would seem to cover the entire area, since Am also implies at least some rainfall every month of the year (Vivo Escoto 1964: 212).

Prehistorically, these major fluctuations in seasonal rainfall affected Pacific coast settlement patterns, where year-round water was not available, and subsistence, where even single growing seasons are of marginal potential. Decreasing and increasing freshwater runoff into coastal areas also affected salinity, temperature, and other variables important to marine life.

Alterations in conditions for marine and human life on the Pacific coast are also related to changes in regional wind patterns and ocean currents (fig. 3.9). As Hubbs and Roden (1964: 161) pointed out, "Winds from the Atlantic are mostly felt during the dry season (November to April) . . . strong winds blow offshore in the gulfs of . . . Papagayo and Panama. . . ." These strong winds, or papagayos, make coastal sailing dangerous if not impossible and contribute to the natural aridity of the area by greatly accelerating the evapotranspiration rate. Finally, the winds create movement on the ocean's surface. These upwellings greatly enrich the lower end of the marine food chain and increase the productivity of marine resources.

In contrast to the Atlantic coast, the soils (fig. 3.7) of Pacific coastal regions are of recent volcanic derivation, and locally the soils have been affected by additional volcanic deposits during the past 10,000 years. As Stevens (1964: 268) pointed out, there is a general misconception that all volcanic soils are fertile. Such soils are in fact highly variable in quality; their fertility depends on both the original volcanic parent material and its susceptibility to the principal soil-forming processes of climate (temperature, moisture, and wind regimes), flora, fauna, relief and drainage, time, and human impact.

The soils of El Salvador are generally fertile (Stevens 1964: 308–9), having been subject to frequent renewal by volcanic activity. Soil porosity, a result

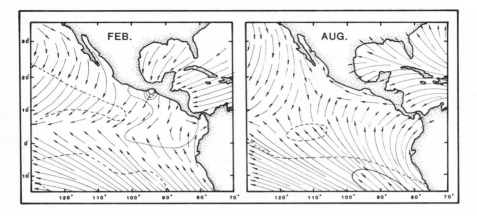

Figure 3.9. Predominant wind patterns in lower Central America (Hubbs and Roden 1964: 146).

of volcanic activity, permits cultivation on steep slopes. In Honduras the volcanic soils are somewhat older, weathered, and of reduced fertility; in some areas there is severe leaching, and the soils are very acidic. Nicaragua is similar to El Salvador in its volcanic soil quality along the Pacific coast. Some deep ashy soils tend to drain and dry rapidly, but the soils around the shores of Lakes Nicaragua and Managua, with higher clay contents, retain moisture better and hence have always been more favorable to human occupation. This cultural interpretation of the soils data is borne out by Willey, Norweb, and Healy's work on the Isthmus of Rivas. Abel-Vidor's assessment (1981a, 1981b) of the ethnohistoric data for the same area also indicates large populations in late prehistoric times. The Tempisque River drainge between the Nicoya Peninsula and mainland of Costa Rica is the only extended area of soil fertility in Pacific Costa Rica, and this is reflected in the density of pre-Columbian remains that seem to be concentrated there (Lines 1936a; Baudez 1967; Hoopes 1979).

This patchwork distribution of fertile soils on the Pacific coast had a definite effect on subsistence practices, most specifically on agricultural potential, not in placing absolute limits on agricultural practices, but in affecting the development of agricultural bases for permanent settlement. Sheets (1979) has confirmed agricultural practices in the volcanic soils of El Salvador by finding planted fields under volcanic deposits. The soil data and ethnographic information from the Isthmus of Rivas indicate a potential for extensive agricultural practices. The archaeological data contribute very little at present to an assessment of the overall role of agricultural products in the nutritional scheme. Problems of low soil fertility in northwestern Costa Rica seem to have caused a low emphasis on concentrated agricultural practices.

Chipped, "waisted" axes, which Snarskis described as being very common and indicative of agriculture on the Atlantic watershed (1978) and which he now feels are also indicative of warfare (Chap. 8, this volume), are almost totally absent from sites on the Pacific coast. In many parts of the New World, primitive populations are presumed to have spread along the coast and settled at the mouths of rivers. Eventually, according to the scenario, plants began to grow in the alluvial deposits as a result of "garbage plot" agriculture, and from there agriculture is supposed to have spread into adjacent areas. At least from coastal Costa Rica, the evidence suggests that the exploitation of marine resources was a post–A.D. 400–500 subsistence elaboration, and it, not agriculture, fed burgeoning populations. Where marine resources were not available, concentrations of coastal population did not develop.

Willey (1979: 850) observed that archaeologists working in Central America seem to have been concentrating on shell middens because, among other reasons, they are easily visible; other equally important sites may be further inland, but less noticeable and consequently less explored. It is true that research strategies on the Pacific coast have, in many cases, emphasized the immediate coastal zone; in these situations Willey's observation is quite apt. In other areas, concentrated efforts have been made to find sites away from the coast proper, and either a total lack of sites or a greatly diminished site density provides definite indications of settlement selection criteria and prehistoric population density.

The Lower Central American Highlands

Lower Central American highland basins are not as extensive as those in Mesoamerica, where the basins of Mexico, Oaxaca, and Guatemala became major focal points of population concentration and cultural development. In the Andean area as well, similar developments focused on areas with large amounts of contiguous cultivable land. Table 3.1 gives a comparison of Mesoamerican, lower Central American, and coastal Peruvian examples (all area calculations are approximate). Intensive occupation and complex cultural development seem to have occurred much less in the smaller basins in lower Central America than was the case elsewhere in Nuclear America. As West (1964a: 70) stated, "In central Honduras and northern Nicaragua flat-floored, grass-covered highland basins . . . probably never attracted Indians except for hunting." He continues (1964a: 77):

In both El Salvador and Nicaragua basins and valleys within the volcanic belt are low in elevation . . . located within a transisthmian depression. . . . this long

Table 3.1. Relative Areas of Contiguous Cultivable Land in Mesoamerica, Lower Central America, and the Andean Coastal Region.

Location	Approximate Area (km²)
Basin of Mexico	4,400
Teotihuacan	505
Oaxaca	730
Guatemala	1,200
Chalchuapa, El Salvador	400
San Andres (Zapotitan Valley, El Salvador)	250
Comayagua Valley, Honduras	240
Meseta Central, Costa Rica	250
Rio Chiriqui Viejo, Western Panama	31
Viru Valley, Peru	900
Moche Valley, Peru	1,500

narrow graben trends NW-SE from the Caribbean Sea to the Pacific Ocean. It forms the lowlands of Nicaragua, the central portion of which is occupied by the largest freshwater lakes of Middle America.

These lakes are surrounded by relatively fertile land and appear to have been centers of population for thousands of years. It may be partially a semantic difference with regard to "basins and highlands" but there is clearly a difference of opinion regarding prehistoric occupation of the central highlands of Honduras. Healy (this volume) feels that the valleys of Otoro, Sensenti, and Comayagua were densely populated.

West (1964a: 79) described the Meseta Central of Costa Rica as "the largest of the highland basins within the Central American volcanic hills that form a drainage divide. The smaller, higher basin of Cartago . . . drains to the Caribbean via the headwaters of the Reventazon; the larger, lower western basin of San Jose . . . drains to the Pacific through the Rio Grande." The Reventazon has long been a route of travel between the highlands and the Atlantic watershed, while the Gulf of Nicoya and lower Pacific coast are easily reached via the Rio Grande. The Central Plateau or large highland basin of Costa Rica not only provided a relatively large expanse for settlement, but also offered routes of travel connecting the Atlantic and Pacific coasts. The access to both coasts has been demonstrated in the variety of cultural materials recovered in the central highlands of Costa Rica. This central basin had long been considered to be relatively devoid of cultural remains, but recent work by Aguilar (1976), Snarskis and Blanco (1978), Guerrero (1981), and Vazquez (1981) has begun to confirm the presence of relatively extensive sites indicating large populations and long duration of occupation. However, there are no indications of anything like the concentrations of population in the highland basins of Mesoamerica.

Schuchert (1935) referred to Costa Rica and Panama as a "volcanic bridge" connecting Central America and South America, and West also described it (1964a: 79) in the following manner:

South of the Meseta Central the volcanic axis of Central America is interrupted by a hugh batholith, or granitic intrusion, which forms the Cordillera de Talamanca and extends southeastward to the Panamanian border. In western Panama vulcanism resumes with the large composite volcano of Chiriqui. . . . The Canal Zone . . . occupies a transisthmian fault rift [and] . . . the structure of the country east of the Canal Zone is related to a northwestern prong of the Andes. . . . Between these coastal ranges is a structural depression occupied by the Chucunaque and Bayano Rivers.

This "bridging" effect is also seen in the distribution of certain fauna and flora in the region. As West (1964b: 374–76) noted:

Although in general within the area of Neotropical fauna, the tropical highlands of Central America have been invaded by some Nearctic animals. Of these the white-tailed deer and a few species of rabbits and squirrels are the most important in terms of game. Associated with these as a predator is the North American cougar or puma (*Felis concolor*), who ranges into South America. True South American mammals of the lowland rain forests, such as tapirs, the spider monkey, the various tropical American cats (jaguar, margay, ocelot, etc.), anteaters, armadillo, and others, penetrate into the highland forests as far north as Guatemala and Chiapas. Among the birds, several trogons, including the beautiful quetzal, so important in ancient Mesoamerican trade and ceremony, are endemic to the Central American highlands. . . . Miranda (1959) has indicated that the plant assemblage in this area contains a large number of South American species, most of which find their northern limit on the eastern and southern slopes of the Sierra Maya in British Honduras.

The highland basins of lower Central America are all included within two classifications in the Koeppen system: *Cfa* and *Cwa* (fig. 3.4). As Vivo Escoto (1964: 210) noted,

The C climates are determined on the basis of the average temperature of the coldest (above 0° C.) and warmest (above 18° C.) months. . . . (*Cw*) is characterized by a distinct winter dry season and summer rains; the other (*Cf*), by rain in every month without a distinct dry period, but usually with most rain coming in the summer or autumn months. . . . (average temperature of warmest month *over* 22° C.) is indicated by adding the letter *a* to the climate designation. . . . Thus the climates *Cwa* and *Cfa* refer to temperate highland climates which occupy the lower mountain and plateau heights. . . .

Environmental Changes

While most studies of the prehistory of lower Central America implicitly assume that there has been a significant degree of continuity in the environment in the past 5,000 years, in reality few data are available either to support or to refute such assumptions. While the extent to which the environment has changed is uncertain, there is little doubt that it has not remained static during human occupation. It has changed significantly, perhaps more in the coastal zones, a factor noted previously by Lothrop (1961), and in areas of volcanic activity as discussed in this volume by Sheets (El Salvador), Lange (Costa Rica), and Cooke (Panama). On the Pacific coast, where there is a major volcanic axis, these examples of volcanic impact on human activity interact with both soil conditions and locations for human settlement.

Table 3.2 gives some idea of the level of volcanic activity. West (1964a: 76) stated there were more than 40 large symmetrical cones in the Central American axis and noted that Sapper (1913) had listed "101 first order volcanoes." Arenal Volcano in Costa Rica has been active almost continually since 1968.

The impact of volcanic eruptions on persons or populations in close proximity is immediate, but longer-term effects may be more subtle. Agricultural land may be rendered useless before fertility is gradually restored. Sheets (1979) has written in detail about the impact of the Ilopango eruption in El Salvador and the population movements it occasioned. Because of the proximity of the volcanic axis to the Pacific coast and the generally prevailing wind patterns, most of the ash and debris has been deposited along the Pacific coast. What has not been fully considered previously, however, is that a large percentage of this ash was deposited over water. In the open sea, this probably made little difference. However, in the coastal embayment and estuary systems, either as a result of direct deposit or as secondary accumulation of materials resulting from rain and runoff, the effect on marine life was probably substantial. This possibility was initially suggested by Moreau (1978) based on work in the Bay of Culebra region in Costa Rica, but so far we can say very little specifically about the probable dynamics of the introduction of volcanic materials into the coastal environment.

We need a better understanding of the relationship between volcanic deposition and our ability to locate archaeologic sites. By mapping the

Table 3.2. Volcanic Activity in Central America in Historic Times.

Volcano/ Synonym	Elevation of Peak Above Sea Level (m)	Relative Height, Base to Peak (m)	Dates of Major Eruptions in Historic Time	Character of Activity (1950–60)	Character of Activity (1961–72)	Relative Activity Since 1820[1]
Guatemala						
1. Tacana	4,030	2,200	None recorded	Dormant; fumarolic		2
2. Tajumulco	4,410	2,400	1863(?)	Dormant; slightly fumarolic		1
3. Santa Maria/ Santiaguito	3,768	2,200	1902, 1922–23, 1928–30, 1931–32, 1956(?)	Active; occasional emission of ash from adventive dome; strongly fumarolic	Very active; continuous growth of dome with periodic large pyroclastic explosions[2]	6
4. Cerro Quemado (Lava dome)	3,179	1,250	1785	Dormant; thermal springs		
5. Zuñil	3,533	1,600	None recorded	Dormant; solfataric; thermal springs		
6. San Pedro	3,024	1,500	None recorded	Extinct		
7. Atitlan	3,525	2,400	1827, 1853	Dormant; fumarolic(?)		3
8. Toliman	3,150	1,900	None recorded	Extinct(?)		
9. Acatenango	3,880	2,400	1924–27, Nov. 1972	Dormant; fumarolic	Minor ash and steam eruptions[3]	2
10. Fuego	3,835	2,700	1524(?), 1581–82, 1717, 1737, 1857, 1880, 1932, 1953, 1957, 1962–63, 1966–67, 1971	Active; occasional emission of ash and glowing avalanches; strongly fumarolic	Very active;[2] normal explosions and lava flows; ash clouds up to 12,000 m high; 1971 largest ash eruption in 70 years	8
11. Agua	3,752	2,600	None recorded	Extinct		
12. Pacaya	2,544	1,600	1565, 1651, 1664, 1775, 1854(?), 1961, 1965–72	Dormant; slightly fumarolic	Very active; large lava flow; eruptions[2]	2
El Salvador						
13. Santa Ana	2,381	1,800	1874, 1880	Dormant; slightly fumarolic		2

No. & Name	Elevation	Height	Historic eruptions	Condition	Remarks	
14. Izalco	1,965	800	1770 (birth), 1793, 1798, 1802–3, 1856, 1890, 1902, 1912, 1920, 1926, 1946, 1955–56, 1959, 1966	Active; occasional emission of ash, lava flows; strongly fumarolic; dormant since 1966	Very active;[2] lava flow from north flank	15
15. San Marcelino/Cerro Chino	1,324		1722(?)		Dormant	
16. Laguna Caldera	510	70	None historic; one small eruption A.D. 590±90		Dormant	
17. Playon	665	165	1658–59; lava flow and explosive eruption, pumice deposition; no activity since 1820		Dormant	
18. San Salvador/Boqueron/Quetzaltepeque	1,967	1,300	1659, 1671(?), 1917; one moderately large prehistoric eruption, ca. A.D. 1000	Dormant; slightly fumarolic		1
19. Isla Quemadas (Lake Ilopango)	450	sub-aquatic vent	1879–1880; one very large eruption ca. A.D. 260	Dormant		1
20. San Vicente/Chichontepeque	2,173	1,800	None recorded	Extinct		
21. Tecapa	1,603		None recorded	Dormant		
22. San Miguel/Chaparrastique	2,132	1,900	1699, 1787, 1819, 1844, 1867, 1924, 1964, 1966–67, 1970	Dormant; strongly fumarolic	Minor ash eruptions[3]	9
23. Usulutan	1,453	1,200	None recorded	Extinct		
24. Chinameca	1,402	800	None recorded	Dormant; fumarolic		
25. Conchagua	1,250	1,250	None recorded	Dormant; fumarolic		1
26. Conchaguita	550		1892	Dormant		1
Nicaragua						
27. Cosiguina	862	862	1835 super-explosion[4]	Dormant		1
28. El Viejo/San Cristobal/Chinandega	1,780	1,700	1684–85, 1971	Dormant; weakly fumarolic	Small ash eruption[3]	1

Table 3.2 (continued)

Volcano/ Synonym	Elevation of Peak Above Sea Level (m)	Relative Height, Base to Peak (m)	Dates of Major Eruptions in Historic Time	Character of Activity (1950–60)	Character of Activity (1961–72)	Relative Activity Since 1820[1]
29. Chichigalpa	1,592		16th century	Dormant; fumarolic		
30. Telica	1,038	900	1529, 1685, 1965–68, 1971	Dormant; strongly fumarolic	Minor ash eruptions[3]	1
31. Santa Clara/ San Jacinto	1,037		16th century	Dormant		
32. Cerro Negro	1,071	1,900	1850, 1867, 1914, 1923, 1947, 1950, 1952, 1954, 1968, 1971	Active; occasional emission of ash; strongly fumarolic	Very active; large ash eruptions and lava flow[2]	7
33. Las Pilas	1,072		1952–55	Fumarolic, solfataric; ash eruption	Dormant	1
34. Momotombo	1,258	1,200	1764, 1858–66, 1905	Dormant; fumarolic		5
35. Masaya (caldera)	650		1670, 1772, 1858–59, 1902–5, 1924, 1946, 1965, 1970–72	Dormant; strongly fumarolic	Very active; small lava flows[2]	5
36. Mombacho	1,363	1,350	1560	Extinct(?)		1
37. Concepcion/ Ometepe	1,557	1,557	1883–87, 1908–10, 1921, 1948–72	Active; occasional emission of ash; fumarolic	Less active; minor ash eruptions[3]	5
38. Madera	1,329	1,329	None recorded	Dormant(?)		

Costa Rica						
39. Orosi/Gongora	1,831	1,400	None recorded	Dormant; fumarolic(?)		
40. Rincon de la Vieja	1,643	1,200	1863, 1966–67, 1969	Dormant; fumarolic	Less active; several minor ash eruptions[3]	2
41. Arenal			1968–present		Very active; large directed blast[2]	1
42. Miravalles	1,980	1,500	None recorded	Dormant; fumarolic		
43. Tenorio	1,902	1,400	None recorded	Extinct(?)		
44. Poas	2,644	1,600	1910, 1953, 1961, 1963–64	Active; occasional emission of ash and scoria	Less active; minor steam and ash eruption[3]	5
45. Barba	2,898	1,800	1867	Dormant		
46. Irazu	3,414	2,600	1723, 1917–20, 1924, 1963–65	Dormant; slightly fumarolic	Very active; major ash eruption[2]	3
47. Turrialba	3,342	2,500	18th and 19th centuries; 1866	Dormant; slightly fumarolic		1
Panama						
48. Baru	3,474	2,000	None recorded; one small-moderate eruption ca. A.D. 500	Dormant		

1. Number of decades since 1820 in which eruptions were reported.
2. Very active 1961–72.
3. Less active 1961–72 than 1950–60.
4. "The explosions of 22 January 1835 were heard in Jamaica, Curacao, and Bogota, Colombia. Ash and pumice fell throughout Central America and southern Mexico, and over a radius of more than 150 km the sun was blotted out" (McBirney 1974: 110).

volcanic materials in El Salvador, Sheets demonstrated that the depth of deposits may be highly variable within a very small area. In northwestern Costa Rica, the presence of surface materials dating to about 300 B.C. in widely scattered locations seems to suggest there has been no volcanic deposition in some areas since that time. However, data obtained from the vicinity of Miravalles Volcano by the Costa Rican Electric Company (I.C.E.) demonstrated massive volcanic activity in some parts of the region about 10,000 B.C. Aguilar has found ca. 300 B.C. material at Arenal in the same area, and Sheets (personal communication) reported A.D. 300–500 ceramics in volcanic contexts during a May 1981 field trip to Arenal. Levels of volcanic ash occur at the Vidor Site on the Bay of Culebra between A.D. 800 and 1200. We cannot relate major cultural events or changes in Guanacaste to natural volcanic events, but we must be aware of the potential primary impact of major events on settlement patterns and subsistence practices in a given area as well as secondary impacts in surrounding areas.

Earthquakes related to major fault systems are also common to the Pacific coast of lower Central America, and they are interrelated with volcanism to the extent that some major volcanic events are considered consequences of subterranean structural shifts occasioned by earthquakes. The direct impact of earthquakes on the population was probably less than that of volcanic eruptions, since without monumental architecture, there was little danger of injury from collapsing buildings. Impacts were probably limited to occasional shifts in stream channels through blockage or course alterations and landslides.

Settlement Location and Trade in Natural Commodities

In Mesoamerica and other parts of the prehistoric world one of the main considerations in cultural geographical analysis is the identification of "central places," locations which for particular reasons were the focal points of settlement and cultural development. Usually the focal points were characterized by particular environmental factors such as a lake, fertile agricultural land, or marine resources; by locational access to trade routes; or by access to particular resources which became the foundation of local monopolies and profitable contacts with the external world.

Central America had no prehistoric population concentrations similar to those found at Teotihuacan, Oaxaca, or the valley of Guatemala. Smaller regional concentrations seem to have been found along the shores of freshwater inland lakes with fertile agricultural soils, along the fertile levees and middle-river-course soil formations of the Atlantic watershed, and around the subsistence-rich embayments and estuary systems of the Pacific coast. Marine produce was probably traded inland as well as consumed locally.

Limited areas of fertile soil along the Pacific coast also appear to have been favored for settlement.

No clearly identified formal trade centers have been scientifically investigated, and few exotic artifacts have been excavated. Obsidian sources are not known in either Costa Rica or Panama, and the nearest sources are unsampled outcroppings reported for northern Nicaragua along the Honduran border. The infrequent occurrence of obsidian in excavations in Rivas and in Guanacaste Province suggests it was not a greatly sought or easily obtainable commodity.[2]

While many serpentine and diopsite-like materials are found in northwestern Costa Rica, there is still no identified jadeite source in the region; recent geological and analytical studies suggest that there is probably none (Lange, Bishop, and von Zelst 1981). The presence of artifacts of actual jadeite in collections from the area, a very small percentage of all the reported Costa Rican jades, suggests social and perhaps economic significance of jadeite brought from the northern fringes of Central America, most likely from the Motagua Valley of Guatemala (R. Bishop, personal communication).

Gold occurs in small quantities from the cordillera of Guanacaste in Costa Rica and on the Santa Elena Peninsula, as does copper, but the major gold sources in the area appear to be on the Osa Peninsula of Costa Rica and in the Nueva Segovia region of Nicaragua. It is important to remember that while contact-period or modern geological identification of sources may establish their presence, simple presence does not automatically mean prehistoric utilization. In the case of gold, it is clear that sources in Osa and perhaps in Guanacaste were utilized, but the utilization of Nueva Segovia sources is less certain.

Many natural products are more perishable and less likely to survive archaeologically. Because of climatic considerations, the vast majority of woods, pelts, feathers, and other commodities probably came from the Atlantic coastal lowlands, but we are almost totally uninformed about the structure of the trade system. Some food products were probably traded, and based on parallels elsewhere, we must assume that trade in drug-type plants was also brisk. Purple dye, pearls, various mineral pigments, and salt were important products of the natural environments on the Pacific.

Sanders (1956) and Willey (1962) pointed out that "the variety of small environments within small areas and the subsequent interregional exchange of goods and ideas may have been an important key to the rise of high cultures" (West 1964b: 364). Similar conditions of environmental variability within a small area exist in lower Central America as well, and it is useful to look briefly at some of the reasons why, perhaps, the end result was not the same there prehistorically.

Principally, we should note that in Central America there were a limited number of commodities desirable for interregional trade. In addition, distances were so short that groups could obtain most items by direct access, rather than through regional trade networks. This capability of direct access probably impeded the local development of highly centralized or tightly controlled distribution systems, and thus placed one limit on development of complex social and economic organizations.

The Pacific-Atlantic contrast in lower Central America, recast in a wet-dry format, does not offer the potential for debating primacy or preeminence of cultural development that has evolved in Mesoamerica or South America, largely because in Central America neither area ever rose to state levels. Because of the relatively short distances involved, we must also assume, in the absence of strict boundary maintenance, that ongoing communication between the two zones existed from earliest time. Linares and Ranere (1980) definitely feel this was the case in western Panama. Nor was boundary maintenance highly elaborated in Costa Rica. This is demonstrated by the distinct parallels between the ceramic complexes of the Atlantic and Pacific coasts throughout the known period of culture history, even though the former was based largely on surface treatment by incision and appliqué, and the latter on polychrome painting.

The floral and faunal richness of the Atlantic watershed offers many more opportunities to peoples with limited technologies than does the Pacific, where organized efforts in hydrology and land management are needed to overcome environmental limitations. Such efforts apparently were not ever attempted during the pre-Columbian period along most of the Pacific coast, although Oviedo y Valdez did mention irrigation (extent unknown) by the Nicarao at Conquest.

Some of the probable reasons for lack of development of more complex societies are discussed in the Greater Nicoya chapter in this volume, but the main reasons, briefly, were lack of population; general lack of desired luxury resources; distance from major potential sources of external influence; absence of imitative models; and the already discussed ease of direct access to necessary resources.

Summary

The contrast between narrow, dry Pacific and broader, wetter Atlantic coasts and highlands in the area is apparent. Referring once again to the idea of a Central American cultural "bridge," West (1964b: 366) wrote:

The southern extent of high Mesoamerican culture in Central America appears to have been largely a result of diffusion into the semideciduous tropical woodlands and savannas of the Pacific coasts, whereas primitive forest cultures of South American affinity spread northward into the rain forests of the Caribbean coasts of Central America.

Lower Central America is a somewhat arbitrary unit blocked out of the Isthmian landform, with both the Atlantic and Pacific coasts being segments of ecological continuities extending to the north and south of the specific region under consideration.

Another interesting aspect of these two more or less parallel strips of ecologically contrasted tropical lowland is that the natural barriers between the two were relatively limited. In numerous locations throughout the Isthmus, the landform provides easy routes of communication between the Pacific and the Atlantic. This should have facilitated exchanges of ideas and material goods between the two major ecological zones, but to date research investigating the level of such contacts has been very limited. If evidence for structured and systemic relationships is found to be limited or lacking, we then need to pursue evidence that could lead to an explanation of boundary maintenance between the two ecological zones of a relatively small area.

We also need to determine whether we are dealing with influences from highland or lowland Mesoamerica or from both. Ecological patterns and cultural traits typical of the broader Atlantic coast of lower Central and South America did extend into the Maya lowlands and are also typical of the Veracruz coastal area. The narrow Pacific coast has ecological affinities with the more arid coastal and highland zones of Mesoamerica. The influences from the two different Mesoamerican zones are easily distinguished in lower Central America, and we need to consider the two zones separately in terms of access for contact, substantive bases for social or economic relationships, and ecological foundation. We also need seriously to reevaluate the relationship of the whole lowland Maya cultural zone to lower Central America, utilizing an ecological/geographical frame of reference.

Near-shore sailing conditions are relatively difficult along both coasts for significant portions of the year, and despite brief contact-period accounts of relatively large vessels, we are unable to assess the importance of open-water sailing within the lower Central American area. The ecological continuities do mean, however, that pre-Columbian peoples could traverse long distances, entering and leaving lower Central America, without changing ecological zones and without encountering persons whose settlement patterns, modes of subsistence, social organization, and life-styles were different from their own.

Lower Central America, although limited in land surface area, is highly varied in landform. Because of the contrast between the long dry Pacific coast and long wet Atlantic coast, separated by moderate highlands, lower Central America possesses a wide variety of ecological niches presenting variable potentials for human habitation and exploitation. Not only were the landforms and rain regimes important, but annual wind patterns, natural phenomena such as volcanic action and earthquakes, and offshore currents also were significant variables in the lives of the prehistoric inhabitants.

Note

1. This chapter has drawn on basic geographical and ecological data summarized in Volume 1 of the *Handbook of Middle American Indians*. Data relevant to lower Central America have been extracted and refined, corrected in a very few cases, and combined with an overview of ecologically oriented research results and problems in the region.

2. Survey by Lange and Sheets on the Pacific coast of Nicaragua in March 1983 found that obsidian use was basically a local practice and not strongly related to, or dependent upon, Mesoamerican stimulus or influence.

PART TWO

The Northern Frontier of Lower Central America

4
Lower Central America as Seen from Mesoamerica

ROBERT J. SHARER

University Museum, University of Pennsylvania

This paper seeks to define relationships between pre-Columbian cultures in Mesoamerica and lower Central America. The delineation of interaction between Mesoamerica and lower Central America requires a thorough understanding of cultural, historical, and evolutionary developmental aspects of prehistoric societies in both areas. Furthermore, an understanding of the nature and timing of such relationships is dependent upon the definition of the zone of interaction, the frontier or buffer between Mesoamerica and lower Central America (Lothrop 1939; Longyear 1947; Andrews V 1977; Lange 1979a; Fox 1981). While significant progress has been made, many basic questions remain concerning pre-Columbian cultural dynamics in both these areas and in the frontier between them. The frontier between Mesoamerica and lower Central America is gradually becoming better understood as a result of numerous research efforts. Space does not allow mention of all this research, but recent investigations at major sites within this frontier region include those at Quelepa (Andrews V 1976) and Chalchuapa (Sharer 1978a) in El Salvador, Los Naranjos (Baudez and Becquelin 1973), Naco (Henderson et al. 1979), and Copan (Baudez 1978–79) in Honduras, along with Quirigua (Sharer 1978b; Ashmore 1979) in Guatemala. Most of these projects have sought, either explicitly or implicitly, answers to questions bearing upon the nature of this pre-Columbian frontier.

These and similar studies provide the temporal and spatial definition of the frontier between Mesoamerican and lower Central American cultures and a starting point for delineating the kinds of relationships that existed between these areas in pre-Columbian times.

Themes and Processes of Interaction

A certain emphasis is inherent in any consideration of Mesoamerican–lower Central American interaction. This may be a result of the limitations of the data base (briefly outlined above) and of the author's inclinations. My own inclination, as can be seen in this paper, is to consider the principal factors involved in this interaction the economic ones, specifically, those subsumed under subsistence and exchange systems—access, transport, and allocation of certain scarce resources. By emphasizing these economic factors, I do not mean to diminish the importance of other aspects of culture, such as those defined in our own terms as social, political, or religious. But I am convinced that the dominant consequences of contact and interaction between Mesoamerica and lower Central America were mediated by economic connections.

Pre-Columbian exchange between these two culture areas served a variety of functions—most obviously trade of a variety of goods. This exchange also served as a primary mechanism for that most elusive of cultural processes—diffusion. Thus, economic systems developed, at least in part, as mechanisms to facilitate communication between cultural groups on both sides of the frontier. But pre-Columbian exchange systems also served socio-political and religious functions. This blurring of cultural boundaries between economic (in Western terms) and socio-political or religious institutions is best documented by ethnohistoric evidence from the Postclassic era (see, for instance, Scholes and Roys 1948). The most obvious example of relevance here are the pochteca of the Late Postclassic Mexica (Sahagun 1959). I do not intend to suggest that this specific Central Mexican institution should provide a model for the kinds of interaction existing at earlier points in time, but merely to point out that one may assume that socio-political and religious motives and consequences existed as part of economic interaction between Mesoamerica and lower Central America.

In the cultural areas of concern here we find the first signs of long-distance exchanges in Mesoamerica by the time sedentary societies emerged during Period III (ca. 4000–1000 B.C.). Among the earliest evidence is the widespread distribution of obsidian and jadeite artifacts outside their source areas in the Maya highlands (Hammond et al. 1977). Other products, including less durable goods such as feathers, pigments, and dyes, may have been exchanged over long distances from these early times. In the absence of evidence for either social or political elites, it is generally assumed that this early trade existed without centralized direction or control. Rather, it probably was accomplished by a series of local exchanges forming a "down-the-line" reciprocal system connecting distant sources to the ultimate consumer (Renfrew 1975: 41–42).

By the time the first complex societies (chiefdoms) emerged in Meso-america, long-distance trade appears to have come increasingly under the control of a theocratic elite class. In fact, long-distance exchange systems have been seen as a principal cause for the development of socio-political complexity in Mesoamerica (Rathje 1971), although long-distance trade has also been seen as a consequence of the same emerging socio-political complexity (Sabloff and Tourtellot 1969). Regardless of the cause and effect issue, elaborate long-distance exchange networks were established by the beginning of Period IV (ca. 1000 B.C.–A.D. 500). In Mesoamerica this development was associated with the Olmec and their contemporaries. By the time the Maya rose to prominence during the later part of Period IV, long-distance trade may have been controlled by elite merchants who carried out large-scale trading expeditions between Mesoamerica and lower Central America (similar to those known from Postclassic times) (Roys 1939: 61; Stone, this volume).

Trade Routes

Geography and the location of both natural routes and resources suggest that the Maya were the primary mediators in the relationships between Mesoamerica and lower Central America during much of the pre-Columbian era. Even as late as Period VI (ca. A.D. 1000–1550), ethnohistoric sources indicate that trade along the northern edge of Mesoamerica was controlled by the Mexica only as far as the boundaries of the Maya area, specifically Xicalango at the base of the Yucatan Peninsula on the Gulf of Mexico (Scholes and Roys 1948). While the pochteca seem to have traded via the Pacific coast of Mesoamerica at least as far as Costa Rica, Maya merchants were still active in the commerce passing along the south coast of their area (Feldman 1978). The reasons for this are obvious, as the Maya occupied (and still occupy) a geographically intermediate position between the peoples of Mexican Mesoamerica and the peoples of lower Central America. Maya merchants (Roys 1939: 61) were favorably situated to act as middlemen, or even dominate trade between these two areas, and appear to have done precisely that. In addition, the Maya area possessed rich resources that were in demand in both Mexico and lower Central America, including obsidian, jade, and a variety of other minerals (serpentine, slate, hematite, cinnabar, pyrite, talc), along with perishable commodities, such as animal pelts, quetzal feathers, bark paper, copal, and cacao.

Before turning to a chronological summation of these developments, we should briefly discuss the principal components of economic connections between Mesoamerica and lower Central America and the various forms such interaction may have taken at various times and places, and indicate some of the commodities involved.

Long-Distance Exchange

Since prehistoric exchange systems often leave tangible evidence in the form of durable trade goods, the distribution and patterning of these goods in time and space allow the reconstruction of ancient trading networks. Also, since these exchange systems require some sort of organization, their study often reveals information not only about economic systems, but about political and social structure as well. Thus, "the study of trade . . . offers a practical way of investigating the organization of society in social terms as well as economic ones" (Renfrew 1975: 4).

Long-distance exchange systems that reached beyond the confines of a single society also provided the basis for interaction between societies. As already mentioned, trade networks were not confined to the acquisition and distribution of material goods, but may also be seen as the mechanisms for information flow within and between prehistoric societies (Renfrew 1975: 21–25). In situations such as that considered here, long-distance trade was a primary means of communication across the Mesoamerican–lower Central American cultural frontier. In this way, long-distance trade contacts and the resulting information flow were stimulants for culture change in both areas.

There is the problem of the archaeological identification of a variety of different forms of exchange defined by Renfrew (1975). Transactions are often categorized according to the nature and scale of the economic system, as in differentiating between reciprocal, redistributive, and market exchanges (Polanyi 1971; Dalton 1975). Reciprocity refers to the exchange of commodities in noncentralized networks, while redistribution involves commodities collected by a central authority that are used to maintain an elite (ruling) class, its retainers, and to undertake public works. Markets are centralized and have specialized facilities for dispensing goods and services. Because of their common characteristic of centralization, it may be difficult or impossible to differentiate between redistribution and market exchange systems archaeologically, since both may leave similar spatial patterns of trade items (Renfrew 1975).

Both redistribution and market exchange operate under the aegis of an elite authority—whether political, religious, or economic in emphasis—while reciprocal exchange is generally not associated with a centralized authority. The question then emerges as to whether this distinction is significant in the specific case being investigated, and, if so, whether it can be recognized in the archaeological record. A complicating factor is that each of these basic types of exchange includes several variants which may coexist in differing degrees within any given society (Polanyi 1971).

Just as various trade modes may coexist at any given time, a chronological assessment of pre-Columbian trade in Mesoamerica and lower Central America reveals that both the relative importance of the various modes and the goods being exchanged changed appreciably over the thousands of years the economic systems functioned. Most emphasis was on local or regional distribution of goods, with long-distance trade becoming significant only with an expanding elite's increasing appetite for exotic commodities.

Most analysis of trade has been related to later periods and perhaps most heavily emphasized the contact period, when actual inventories were available. These analyses have emphasized precious materials usually consigned to elite utilization or benefit.

An earlier class of exotic materials, the basic "foodbasket" of agricultural and medicinal plants that were traded and exchanged throughout prehistoric America, were perhaps the first goods to move along pioneer exchange routes. Lathrap (1977) has strongly argued that not only were these used as foodstuffs, but that many of the plants were endowed with important cosmological properties as well.

It is currently not clear to what extent these earliest networks were truly exchange networks in which relatively balanced bilateral trade took place, or whether they were weighted in one direction or another. The fact that we are dealing largely with perishable remains makes such knowledge all the harder to come by.

Both redistribution and market exchange may be involved in long-distance trade of the kind that took place between lower Central America and Mesoamerica in the pre-Columbian era. The most useful model for the recognition of ancient exchange from the spatial distribution of archaeological remains is that outlined by Renfrew (1975). This model defines 10 different types or modes of trade. These types are illustrated in figure 4.1 and include several modes well suited to long-distance trade.

Prior to outlining the various modes of trade, it is worthwhile to summarize the major commodities that appear to have been traded back and forth across the frontier. Jade and related greenstones, obsidian, ceramics, gold, copper, marble vases, and pyrite mirrors seem to have been the most frequently traded items; only the first three were traded in even relatively significant quantities. Exchange of commodities such as cotton is suggested by the presence of spindle whorls, but quantification is impossible based on current data; neither can the volume of trade in such items as purple dye, feathers and skins, nor food, medicinal, or narcotic vegetal materials be calculated with any confidence. However, knowledge of some of the ma-

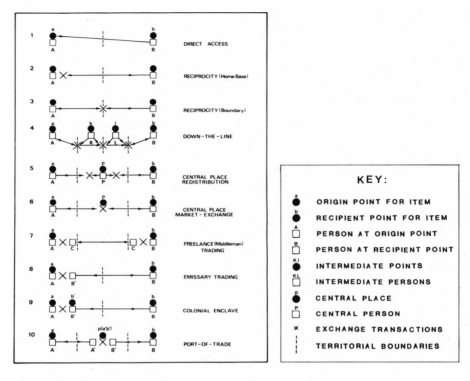

Figure 4.1.   The 10 modes of economic interaction (Renfrew 1975).

terials that were traded and of a range of possible trade modes that have facilitated exchange in other parts of the world will aid in the preliminary assessment of direction and mode of exchange for different goods.

This is clearly a trial formulation, restricted by available data. Nonetheless, as mentioned in the volume introduction, substantial amounts of new data have been acquired from controlled excavations and from physical analyses of chemical properties of natural materials. Such data do support such a preliminary formulation of Mesoamerican–lower Central American trade patterns. The application of Renfrew's model, however tentative, places these data in a framework suitable for further elaboration and promotes the discussion of exchange networks from the level of discrete, isolated artifact distributions that previously have been the basis for speculation and interpretation.

Economic Exchange Modes

Renfrew's modes 1 through 4 are most often associated with egalitarian societies, although they may coexist with more complex exchange networks in nonegalitarian societies. Mode 1 actually describes the lack of formal exchange, merely the direct acquisition of a resource by movement to the source. Modes 2 through 4 represent different kinds of reciprocity, that is, simple two-party reciprocal exchanges (mode 2 meeting at one group's home territory, or mode 3 meeting at the boundary between home territories) and a complex chain of reciprocal exchanges, as in mode 4, known as down-the-line trade. Modes 5 through 10 are normally associated with, or operate under the authority of, a ruling elite, and usually include a central place. Mode 5 corresponds to the classic definition of redistribution (see above), while mode 6 represents the usual kind of centralized market exchange.

Modes 7 through 10, along with mode 4, are most likely to be found in long-distance trade networks, with examples of each known or postulated from ethnohistoric and archaeological sources in the areas of concern here.

With this as background, we can now examine the extent to which these exchange modes can be recognized in the archaeological record of lower Central America and Mesoamerica. The remainder of the paper will outline the development of subsistence systems and exchange networks between Mesoamerica and lower Central America as presently understood from Period III through IV in the lower Central American chronological scheme developed in this volume (fig. 1.2).

Period III (ca. 4000–1000 B.C.)

Subsistence, Sedentism, and Long-Distance Exchange

The first indications of systematic interaction between the two areas appear with the origins of subsistence strategies that gave rise to permanent settled communities. One of these strategies, coastal gathering and root-crop agriculture (manioc and other species), appears earliest in lowland South America (Lathrap 1971, 1973a, 1973b). This subsistence strategy in Mesoamerica, although its origins are still imperfectly known, seems to derive from South America via lower Central America. A particular agricultural technology also found in Mesoamerica, and well adapted to poorly drained lowland soils and raised field systems, may also derive from South America (J. Parsons 1969; Parsons and Denevan 1967).

The other principal pre-Columbian subsistence strategy, based upon maize-bean-squash agriculture, developed independently in highland Mesoamerica (MacNeish 1964; Byers 1967). It soon appeared in South America, perhaps also imported via lower Central America, although separate South American origins for maize domestication have been proposed (Zevallos et al. 1977). The specific mechanisms for the spread of these subsistence strategies, and the permanently settled societies that they fostered, remain undocumented, although diffusion and migration are most often cited (Lathrap 1973b, 1977). The spread of various subsistence products and their recombination into dietary complexes was an important early stage in the development of long-range exchange systems. First, as noted earlier, long-distance exchange of plants may well have laid the foundation for subsequent more elaborate trading networks; second, improved agricultural practices were often pre-requisite to sedentism and permanent communities. The establishment of fixed populations and trading centers was obviously a basic need in per-manent trade relations.

Whether long-distance trade provided the avenue for the diffusion of these subsistence developments or whether in fact early subsistence ex-changes were the forerunners of more elaborate subsequent trade systems are significant problems for continuing research. No definite artifactual evidence reflecting the movement of exotic materials or finished craft prod-ucts yet exists for Period III. Trade modes 4 (down-the-line), 7 (free-lance), and 8 (emissary) are the most likely to have been employed.

Period IV (Early Phase: ca. 1000–400 B.C.)

During this interval, corresponding to the Middle Formative in Meso-america, the first clear signs of emerging social complexity appear in the archaeological record. At this time cultural differences can be defined both by differing levels of socio-political status and in the development of distinct monumental art styles. Of course the archetype of these attributes is Olmec civilization, still difficult to define precisely, yet nonetheless retaining an undeniably distinctive identity.

The available evidence indicates that by ca. 1200 B.C. the Olmec had developed a theocratic chiefdom, the first known in Mesoamerica (Sanders and Price 1968: 115–34). We can infer that the authority of the Olmec chiefdom derived from the manipulation of supernatural beliefs that reduced uncertainties for the populace and also reinforced the authority of the chief and his elite kinsmen. Economic power was based in the management of agricultural and other food-producing activities, along with the right to receive food tribute. In conjunction with, or perhaps as a causal factor in, these developments between Mesoamerica and lower Central America, eco-nomic power also derived from the control of the first long-distance trade networks that—and here there is direct archaeological evidence—provided a variety of exotic items, such as jade, serpentine, and magnetite, that were used as symbols of the elite's prestige and authority.

The Olmec trade network seems to have dominated the exchange of products throughout much of Mesoamerica and beyond into lower Central America. Olmec trading connections were established in the central Mexican highlands (Grove et al. 1976). The single most important route probably followed the Pacific coastal plain from the Isthmus of Tehuantepec into western El Salvador and farther south. This route can be traced by a series of centers with Olmec characteristics founded along its course, such as Abaj Takalik in southwestern Guatemala (J. Graham 1977) and Chalchuapa in western El Salvador (Sharer 1978a). Both these sites, as well as others along the Pacific coast, have furnished Middle Formative Olmec monumental sculptures and appear to have functioned to maintain trade between the Olmec heartland on the Gulf coast and resource areas located in the adjacent Maya highlands and in lower Central America to the southeast.

Obsidian from the Maya highlands and Central Mexico was imported and manufactured into cutting tools. More exotic items, many apparently reserved for elite use, included jadeite from the middle Motagua Valley in Guatemala and magnetite (used to fashion mirrors) perhaps from the Valley of Oaxaca or other areas in southern Mexico. Perishable commodities were undoubtedly traded also, but no direct evidence has survived. It is likely, however, that the Olmec imported cacao from the Pacific coast and quetzal feathers from the Maya highlands as well as textiles and other products from various sources.

The question of cacao cultivation is especially interesting. Ethnohistoric evidence indicates that its principal regions of cultivation were in the Maya area, including the Pacific coastal plain (Millon 1955), although its probable origins lie in northern South America (Stone 1979: 11, and this volume).

It is possible that cacao cultivation may have reached the Maya area as part of the spread of South American root-crop agriculture into lower Central America during the preceding period. Alternatively, it may have been introduced by the Olmec as a result of long-distance trading forays into lower Central America. In any case, Stone (1979) argues for a Pacific-coast introduction into the Maya area (perhaps by sea), which is consistent with the inferred location of the Olmec trade route to lower Central America.

The most obvious sign of trade with the newly emerging elite in several areas of lower Central America is the discoveries of Olmec-style artifacts, including the recent excavation of a jadeite shell effigy from Tibas, Costa Rica (Snarskis 1979a). Although a Costa Rican source for jadeite has long been postulated, recent mineralogical studies have been unable to document such a source (Lange, Bishop, and von Zelst 1981). It would appear, therefore, that much, if not all, the jadeite utilized by lower Central American peoples was imported from sources in Mesoamerica, such as those identified in the middle Motagua Valley of Guatemala (Foshag and Leslie 1955; Hammond et al. 1977). Present evidence indicates that the jade trade to lower

Central America was established during the early part of Period IV, probably under the aegis of the Olmec. Jade artifacts in lower Central America are found worked in both Mesoamerican (Olmec and Maya) and local styles, indicating that both worked and unworked jadeite was exchanged. The jade trade with lower Central America continued to flourish until just after the end of Period IV (see below), when metal artifacts appeared to supplant jadeite as the most esteemed elite-status commodity in the best-documented areas, such as Costa Rica.

The organization of Olmec trade remains unknown. Coe (1965a, 1965b) suggests a Formative pochteca, but other institutions are more probable, including an independent merchant class. Regardless, Olmec trade contacts seem to have had an important impact on non-Olmec peoples living in resource areas. It can be assumed that the Olmec used a variety of means to gain control over the distant resources they desired. Some areas, such as the middle Motagua Valley, were probably uninhabited or only sparsely settled. In such cases, the Olmec traders would have had little difficulty in securing jade or other products. In other cases, the Olmec may have bartered with local peoples to get what they wanted.

Resource exchange in the Olmec area proper was probably structured in a centralized fashion (modes 5 or 6) or subjected to direct control (mode 9). Long-distance exchange with lower Central America was most likely a result of mode 7 (free-lance) or mode 8 (emissary) contacts. Some evidence suggests mode 9 (colonial enclave), but only in the northern part of lower Central America.

Period IV (Late Phase: ca. 400 B.C.–A.D. 500)

It is now apparent that by the beginning of the Late Phase of Period IV, Olmec presence in both the Maya and lower Central American areas had disappeared. The impact of Olmec colonization and trade relationships, especially in the southern Maya area, where the best archaeological evidence exists, seems to have fostered further independent economic and political development during this era, corresponding to the Late Preclassic. Its impact on lower Central America has yet to be documented. However, Stone (1977) discusses the socio-political development of lower Central America as a series of local chiefdoms that emerge as early as the beginning of Period IV (see also Coe and Baudez 1961; Stone 1979). It can only be suggested that trade contacts with Mesoamerica during this era continued to contribute to this development by reinforcing the status and prestige of local ruling elites.

A series of Maya sites became more developed and prosperous than others in late Period IV. Significantly, these sites were either directly on, or had close access to, important land and sea trade routes. Such centers as Chiapa de Corzo, Izapa, El Baul, Kaminaljuyu, Chalchuapa, and, beyond the

Maya area, Quelepa probably emerged as independent mercantile powers during this interval. These centers were located on the Pacific coastal route, and each seems to have been the capital of a prosperous regional chiefdom and a focus for both ceremonial and economic activities. The economic sphere probably included the cultivation and distribution of cacao as well as commerce in highland minerals and commodities from lower Central America. It is reasonable to suggest that it was Maya elite merchants who controlled most of the movement of these goods, borne by human carriers up and down trails that followed natural overland routes of the area. A similar cultural development may be seen in centers located along the coastal and riverine routes of the Maya lowlands to the north, such as Cerros in Belize (Freidel 1979) and Tikal in the Peten (Jones 1979), respectively.

The Pacific coast route remained the most important for our purposes, running between lower Central America and the great centers in the Valleys of Oaxaca and Mexico via the string of former Olmec colonies. Thus, trade between Mexico and lower Central America, first consolidated by the Olmec, appears to have continued to prosper under the cooperative management of the ruling elite that controlled the regional chiefdoms along the Pacific coast and into Central America. Jade and related greenstone materials and finished objects continued to be important components of the trade inventory.

Southern Maya centers display the first evidences of florescent Maya civilization several centuries before the rise of the Classic-period sites in the lowlands to the north (Sharer 1975). Although no single center dominated the entire southern area, Kaminaljuyu, located in the largest basin of the southern Maya highlands, appears to have been the most powerful site in the southern region, if not the entire Maya area, during Period IV (Michels 1979). Kaminaljuyu directly controlled one of the most important obsidian quarries in the highlands, El Chayal, located several kilometers to the east. The power and wealth that accrued to the Late Formative chiefs of Kaminaljuyu is vividly demonstrated by the two spectacular tombs excavated by Shook and Kidder (1952) within Str. E-III-3, one of many large earthen mounds that probably served as platforms for ancestral shrines for the site's rulers. Obsidian first appears in lower Central America during the second half of this period, but its source is currently unknown.

The smaller site of Chalchuapa was probably allied with Kaminaljuyu during the Late Formative. In fact, Chalchuapa, which had seemingly been the southeasternmost direct Olmec trading colony during the early part of Period IV, may have served a similar function during the succeeding era (Sharer 1974). It may be suggested that, during the Late Formative at least, Chalchuapa served as an inland port of trade between the southern Maya and lower Central American areas. The most diagnostic Mesoamerican trade item found in lower Central America during this era is Usulutan pottery.

This distinctive ware (Demarest and Sharer 1982) was manufactured in the southeastern Maya area and traded widely. Its presence in lower Central America, especially in the Nicoya region of Costa Rica—although in limited quantities (Stone 1977)—testifies to the orientation of long-distance trade during the later part of Period IV. In fact, the Nicoya Peninsula may have served as a major focus for long-distance trade interaction by this period, a role it seems to have maintained for the remainder of the pre-Columbian era. Several factors undoubtedly contributed to the economic importance of the Nicoya area, including the availability of a valuable resource, murex dye, which had a ready market in Mesoamerica.

Finally, it is valuable to point out that the cult of human sacrifice and trophy head collecting appears in the southern Maya area during late Period IV. A particularly vivid example of these practices was excavated at Chalchuapa (Fowler 1979). Both these related cults may have originated in South America and lower Central America and could have been transmitted to Mesoamerica by trade contacts.

At the onset of the Mesoamerican Classic period, the southern Maya fell into a sudden decline. This setback is not confined to the Pacific coast and adjacent highlands. In the central Maya area, several lowland sites lost population, and a few were abandoned by the end of the Formative (Freidel 1979). But the effect of the decline appears to be most pronounced in the southern Maya area. Most, if not all, of the Formative centers lost population or were abandoned altogether (Shook and Proskouriakoff 1956; L. Parsons 1969: 27). The dynastic monument cult was extinguished only to be rekindled by the end of the third century A.D. in the central lowlands to the north.

The demise of the southern Maya corresponds in time and space to a major volcanic disaster, the eruption of Ilopango in central El Salvador during the third century A.D. It seems likely that this is more than mere coincidence. As has been suggested before (Sharer 1975), the eruption of Ilopango probably effectively severed the Pacific coast trade routes between Mesoamerica and lower Central America. Important research by Sheets (1976, 1979) has documented the date and cultural context of this eruption in western El Salvador. This work outlined Ilopango's severe consequences, one of which was to render uninhabitable a vast area within a 100-kilometer radius of Ilopango for at least several generations (and perhaps several centuries) because of heavy ashfalls. Within this region both subsistence and cash-crop agriculture, including cacao cultivation, were undoubtedly destroyed. While the Pacific coastal plain to the northwest probably escaped these drastic effects, ashfalls may have reduced soil fertility and production for a time. In addition, flooding from torrential rainfalls spawned by Ilopango's ash cloud could have affected a much wider area, and even light ashfalls could have reduced aquatic food resources harvested from rivers and coastal areas (Dahlin 1979). It has also been hypothesized that southern Maya refugees introduced cacao cultivation into the eastern Maya lowlands (Dahlin 1979).

The decline of the southern Maya certainly provided a vacuum for others to fill, including the lowland Maya. The weakening of the Pacific coast centers, and even, perhaps, Kaminaljuyu, was followed by an economic domination from Central Mexico. It would appear that the Pacific coast of the Maya area became a focus of Teotihuacan colonization in the Maya Early Classic era, probably so the Teotihuacans could control the production and distribution of cacao. This was followed by the eventual colonization of Kaminaljuyu, seemingly to exploit highland resources and trade, as well as to provide access to the lowlands to the north. Once the area devastated by Ilopango had recovered, Teotihuacan may also have expanded into the southern Maya area to control the traditional Pacific trade routes to lower Central America. Unfortunately, few of the archaeological remains from the colonization of the Pacific coastal plain have been adequately investigated or published. Instead, we can only rely upon descriptions of looted artifacts from private collections (Hellmuth 1978). Teotihuacan presence at Kaminaljuyu is better documented (Kidder, Jennings, and Shook 1946; Sanders and Michels 1977).

At about this same time the rapidly growing Maya sites in the central lowlands appear to have expanded to the southeast and spawned colonies along the frontier region with lower Central America. The major lowland power center behind this expansion was apparently Tikal (assuming a position apparently formerly held by El Mirador), which may have acted in concert with Teotihuacan allies from Kaminaljuyu (Coggins 1979). On the other hand, Tikal may have acted independently in its moves toward the southeastern frontier, in order to gain access to the resources and markets of lower Central America. In any case, lowland Maya colonies were established at Copan and Quirigua as early as the fourth and certainly by the fifth century A.D. (Sharer 1979). As a consequence, the long-distance trade network that formerly had connected Mesoamerica and lower Central America along the Pacific coast appears to have been realigned through the southeastern Maya lowlands. The resulting trading activity seems to have contributed to an era of unprecedented economic and political prosperity for the central Maya lowlands in general, and for Tikal in particular (Jones 1979).

The lowland Maya domination of trade between Mesoamerica and lower Central America during the later part of Period IV is reflected in the relative abundance of lowland artifacts from sites in lower Central America. These occur at sites on the Pacific coast in the Nicoya region (Stone 1979: 9), indicating at least some transport by oceangoing craft (Edwards 1969), although most relevant evidence derives from uncontrolled contents. Maya trade goods are also found at sites in the Caribbean watershed, such as Upala on the route to Lake Nicaragua, and at other sites including La Fortuna (Edwards 1969). Although exact chronological placement is often difficult, it is significant to note that trade in Maya lowland objects, such as jadeite artifacts, appears to peak during this era, corresponding to the later part of the Early Classic period (Edwards 1969: 13). This is the time of Tikal's apparent hegemony over the central Maya lowlands, its postulated dominance of trade with lower Central America, and the time of great prosperity that culminates in the reign of Stormy Sky (Coggins 1979).

In summarizing the forms of trade pertinent to this period, it is important to reiterate the apparent shifts from Mayan to Mexican control of the Pacific coast, and the enhancement of the trade routes in the Maya lowlands. Along the Pacific coast mode 8 (emissary trading) apparently continued as a major form, although nascent colonial enclaves (mode 9) or ports-of-trade (mode 10) may have been developing on the Gulf of Fonseca, in the Bay of Culebra, and in the Gulf of Nicoya. Some mode 4 (down-the-line) and mode 7 (free-lance) trading is also postulated, with the distance along the coast between points in the lineal succession extended by water-borne transport. On the Atlantic lowland Maya trade route, mode 8 appears again to have been the most likely form of trade, although a port-of-trade (mode 9) may have been established somewhere on the San Carlos Plain of Costa Rica.

Period V (A.D. 500–1000)

During the so-called hiatus in the middle of the Maya Classic period, the economic and political prosperity of the central lowland Maya seems to have been disrupted. The most plausible cause for this setback lies in the decline of Teotihuacan and a breakdown in the Mesoamerican long-distance exchange network (Willey 1974). Tikal, as Teotihuacan's principal lowland ally, seems to have suffered most, but other central Maya centers, including Tikal's former colonies and allies, appear to have gained new prosperity and power in the wake of this disruption. It might be expected that some reflection of this disruption, insofar as it affected trade relationships with societies to the southeast, would appear in the archaeological record of lower Central America.

There now seems to be good evidence that the trade in Mesoamerican jade in areas in lower Central America where it long enjoyed wide distribution in high-status contexts (such as elite burials) stopped by the end of Period IV or about A.D. 500 (Ryder 1980); but there are obvious problems in accurately dating the cessation of trade in a particular commodity. Local production of nonjadeite greenstone artifacts may have continued after the end of trade in Mesoamerican jadeite, thus further obscuring the issue. However, archaeological research in Costa Rica has provided excavations with good contextual and chronological controls that tend to support a cessation in jadeite trade by ca. A.D. 500.

At the site of La Fortuna, Costa Rica, burials containing jadeite pendants were excavated in association with Maya slate mirror backs, one notable example being inscribed with an Early Classic Maya hieroglyphic text (Stone and Balser 1965). These burials have been dated by their ceramic content to the period of A.D. 300–500 (Stone and Balser 1965; Baudez and Coe 1966). The more recent research by Snarskis (1978 and this volume) in the Atlantic zone of Costa Rica indicates that the latest occurrence of jadeite artifacts corresponds to the El Bosque phase (ca. 100 B.C.–A.D. 500), and two spectacular jade artifacts from the site of Tibas in the central highlands appear to have the same chronological placement (Snarskis 1979a and this volume). Finally, Ryder (1980) reports jadeite artifacts at the Grecia site also date to late Period IV, supported by a single radiocarbon result at ca. A.D. 425.

The dating of the present evidence suggests, therefore, that the end of the long-distance trade in Mesoamerican jade with lower Central America may be directly related to internal disruptions at the source (i.e., to the Middle Classic hiatus in the Maya lowlands). If the present chronological placement for the falloff in jade imports continues to be supported by future research in lower Central America, it may indicate that the negative impact on Maya commerce associated with the hiatus was not confined to the Maya lowlands but also affected the long-distance trade relationships far to the southeast in lower Central America.

By the beginning of Period V the Pacific coastal route to the lower Central American isthmus was undoubtedly reestablished. During this era a second wave of Central Mexican influence is detectable, probably the result of trade contacts that culminated in renewed colonization by Nahua-speaking ("Pipil") peoples by ca. A.D. 800–1000. From this time to the Spanish Conquest, Central Mexican powers seem to have dominated the economic and political interaction between Mesoamerica and lower Central America by using (and controlling?) the Pacific coastal routes (Lange, this volume).

Farther to the north, a new power emerged as the principal Maya trading center on the Mesoamerican frontier. Copan achieved its greatest period during the Maya Late Classic, and certainly its participation in trade with lower Central America contributed to its prosperity. Copan probably served as the principal inland port-of-trade for commerce between the Maya area (highlands and central lowlands) and lower Central America, thus, in effect, succeeding centers such as Chalchuapa that had performed this role in earlier times. But Copan's ascendance did not go unchallenged, for both archaeological and epigraphic evidence indicates that a rival, Quirigua, eventually defeated the ruler of Copan and thus secured control over at least a portion of this commerce (Sharer 1978b, 1980). After this, Copan appears to have expanded its economic activity into lower Central America, especially trade ties to the east and south (Willey et al. 1980), but declined rapidly before the close of Period V.

Given the increasing importance of the Pacific coastal route under Mexican control and the post-hiatus reestablishment of Maya commercial activity in lower Central America, it may be asked why there was apparently little recovery in the former trade in jadeite with lower Central America. The answer may be that by Period V metal artifacts were widely available throughout lower Central America, and these effectively replaced jadeite as the most highly prized symbols of status and power. There is a great increase in the quantity of archaeological data from lower Central America for this period. A much more concrete impression of the volume and distribution of trade materials has been gained as a result. In general, trade items that are clearly Mesoamerican in source were for elite consumption. This suggests continued prevalence of mode 8 (emissary trade), but some free-lance (mode 7) economic activity obviously also continued.

Period VI (A.D. 1000–1550)

The patterns of long-distance trade profoundly changed with the decline of the central lowland Maya and a renewed expansion of the Central Mexican states. The first of these events is reflected in the disappearance of most items of Classic Maya manufacture from the archaeological record of lower Central America. Similar shifts occur in localized artistic traditions influenced by contacts with the central Maya. For instance, Classic Maya styles are important in the local polychrome ceramic traditions of northeast Honduras throughout the Classic era; however, after the central Maya decline, there was a shift, and the local ceramic tradition reflects influences from lower Central America (Strong, Kidder, and Paul 1938; Healy, this volume). It seems likely that these shifts reflected changes in dominant trade relationships as well.

One important aspect of the shift in the patterns of long-distance trade begins before the end of Period V. By this time a group of sea-coast traders known as the Chontal or Putun Maya (Thompson 1970) seem to have perfected and monopolized commerce borne by large oceangoing canoes. Their base was the Acalan region of the Gulf of Mexico, where one of their principal ports, Xicalango, was located (Scholes and Roys 1948). There, as documented by Spanish Colonial sources, the land-based traders from Central Mexico exchanged a variety of products with Putun sea and riverine merchants who brought their goods from as far away as lower Central America (Scholes and Roys 1948).

The Putun merchants used sizable seagoing canoes capable of transporting larger loads with less manpower than land-based porters or even river canoes requiring portages. When the winds were correct, the oceangoing canoes may have had sails to supplement the paddlers (Edwards 1969; Stone, this volume). Of course this mode of transport was especially favorable for heavier and bulky products, such as salt, grinding stones, cacao, and other foodstuffs. The famous encounter between Columbus and a Maya trading canoe off the north coast of Honduras (Las Casas 1957) documents that these vessels carried crews of at least two dozen men, and cargos of cacao, copper bells and axes, pottery, crucibles, cotton textiles, and weapons (macanas).

Using these large craft the Putun Maya extended their trade routes around the Yucatan Peninsula, establishing their own colonies and ports at several strategic points. These included Cozumel Island, off the northeastern coast of Yucatan, perhaps the most important port-of-trade for the expanded sea-borne commerce between Mexico and lower Central America (Sabloff and Rathje 1975a). Other Putun colonies were established at Champoton on Yucatan's west coast, and at Nito near the mouth of the Rio Dulce, at the base of the east coast of Yucatan (Thompson 1970). Nito appears to have been the successor to Quirigua in the control of trade (in jadeite, obsidian, quetzal feathers, and other products) between the Maya highlands and the Caribbean, as well as a seaport for Putun canoe commerce (Sharer 1979). The role of the frontier inland port-of-trade for commerce between the Maya area and lower Central America seems to have been assumed by Naco. Naco, located nearer the Caribbean coast than its predecessor, Copan, was still in a good position to monitor and control overland trade between these two areas.

These trading centers maintained the dominance of Maya merchants in controlling both overland and the new seagoing commerce between Meso-america and lower Central America, at least along the Caribbean coast. However, as mentioned previously, on the Pacific coast Postclassic trade was seemingly dominated by Central Mexican powers—first the Toltec and later the Mexica, with their pochteca merchants. It was during this period that colonization and migration by Nahua-speaking peoples down the Pacific coast, in effect, expanded the Mesoamerican frontier as far as the Nicoya Peninsula (Lothrop 1926; Stone 1958b). The only examples of Mexica trade colonies on the Caribbean coast appear to have been a colony at the Desaguadero near the start of the San Juan River in Nicaragua and the Sigua colony in Panama (Peralta 1883: 117; Lothrop 1942). Postclassic Mesoamerican influences have been reported as far south as the Tairona of northeast Colombia, but may have been the result of sea contact (Reichel-Dolmatoff 1965b). This raises the possibility that Putun Maya trading voyages might have reached as far as northern South America.

Period VI provides the most plentiful archaeological evidence for trade contact between Mesoamerica and lower Central America. The earliest metal artifacts in the Maya area appear at the principal frontier sites toward the end of the Classic period (or late Period V), associated with burials or caches at Chalchuapa (Tazumal) (Boggs 1950: 270), Copan (Stromsvik 1941: 71), and Quirigua (Sharer et al. 1979: 59). By Period VI times, two widely traded pottery wares provide a good index of trade connections between Mesoamerica and lower Central America. Plumbate pottery, produced on the Pacific coast of the Maya area, was traded throughout Mesoamerica and well into lower Central America. For instance, small quantities of plumbate have been discovered in northwestern Costa Rica (Lange, personal communication, 1980). Polychrome pottery types from lower Central America (the Papagayo group in Nicaragua and Costa Rica, and the Las Vegas group in Honduras) have been found at numerous sites throughout the Maya area. In at least one case, related ceramics (probably Las Vegas Polychrome from Honduras) have been found as far north as Tula, Hidalgo (Diehl, Lomas, and Wynn 1974). Finally, as Coe and Baudez (1961) suggest, murex shell from the Nicoya region continued to be traded into Mesoamerica and contributed to the economic well-being of the peoples of the Nicoya Peninsula. Trade patterns during this period, again, reflect a division between highland Mesoamerica/Pacific lower Central America and lowland Mesoamerica/Atlantic and lower Central American contacts. The highland network seems to have been dependent on mode 9 and mode 10 networks, while the lowland Atlantic networks had a free-lance and emissary form of trading.

Conclusion

In conclusion, I wish to point out several issues raised by this all-too-brief summary of economic interaction in the hope that they will stimulate discussion and, perhaps, indicate directions for further archaeological and ethnohistorical research. While the available data are not adequate to identify explicitly the kinds of exchange that once existed between Mesoamerica and lower Central America, future archaeological research will undoubtedly include this area of investigation within its priorities. As a beginning step toward this goal, it may be useful to review and define the most likely types of exchange that characterized the development of interaction between Mesoamerica and lower Central America, using the model followed in this paper (Renfrew 1975: fig. 4.1).

Although Renfrew (1975) makes it clear that his trade-mode model is not an evolutionary scheme per se, he does note the obvious developmental implications within this typology. Thus, we might expect the distribution of archaeologically recovered items traded between lower Central America and Mesoamerica to reflect certain specific exchange modes and economic systems at different periods in the development of pre-Columbian society (table 4.1). During the first era discussed here (Period III), or even earlier (Periods I and II), there are few relevant data, but direct access and reciprocal

Table 4.1. Postulated Trade Modes (fig. 4.1) and Associated Economic Systems by Chronological Period for Long-Distance Exchange Between Lower Central America and Mesoamerica.

Chronological Period	Major Modes and Principal Agents of Long-Distance Exchange	Major Types of Associated Economic Systems	
		Mesoamerica	*Lower Central America*
VI (ca. A.D. 1000–1500)	9, 10 (Mexica) 7, 8 (?) (Putun Maya)	Redistributive Market	Redistributive Market
V (ca. A.D. 500–1000)	7, 8, 10 (?) (Maya)	Redistributive Market	Redistributive Market
Late IV (ca. 400 B.C.–A.D. 500)	4, 9, 10 (Teotihuacan) 7, 8, 9 (?) (Maya)	Redistributive Market	Redistributive Market
Early IV (ca. 1000–400 B.C.)	5, 6, 7, 8, 9 (?) (Olmec)	Redistributive Market	Reciprocal
III (ca. 4000–1000 B.C.)	1, 2, 3, 4, 7, 8 (?)	Reciprocal	Reciprocal
I and II (?–ca. 4000 B.C.)	(?)	(?)	(?)

trade modes (1 through 4) can be assumed. Because of its usual association with long-distance trade, down-the-line exchange (mode 4) may be the most likely form of trade to have existed between Mesoamerica and lower Central America during Period III, although modes 7 and 8 may also have been employed at times.

Beginning in Period IV, the emergence of the first chiefdoms and the development of elite-directed, long-distance trade have been noted in connection with the Olmec of Mesoamerica. With the establishment of long-distance trade in Mesoamerica, at least two relevant institutions can be considered in archaeological situations, based upon information from the later ethnohistoric record. These are the independent elite merchant or free-lance trader (mode 7), primarily associated with the Maya, and the state-controlled trade colony (mode 9), associated with the Mexica and, specifically, the pochteca, with or without ports-of-trade (mode 10; Chapman 1957). While the projection of these specific institutions back in time is a risky proposition, the archaeological evidence does seem to indicate that the Olmec established an early version of colonial enclave trade along the Pacific coastal plain of southern Mesoamerica. There is, however, no firm evidence that this form of exchange was extended into lower Central America during the first part of Period IV. Yet it is probable that the economic links between Mesoamerica and lower Central America included new exchange modes by this time, perhaps free-lance and emissary trade (modes 7 and 8). Earlier trade modes (1–4) probably continued as well.

By the time of the demise of Olmec power and the rise of the southern Maya during the later part of Period IV, there was a well-established and important network of exchange in exotic products between lower Central America and Mesoamerica along the Pacific coast. Modes 7 and 8, probably managed by elite Maya merchants, seem to be the most likely forms for this trade. These contacts continued under the auspices of the lowland Maya by the end of Period IV after new Maya centers were established in the southeastern lowlands (Copan and Quirigua), probably to secure the trade links with lower Central America. At the same time, after the collapse of the southern Maya, a new power, Teotihuacan, appears to have attempted to control trade across the southeastern frontier between Mesoamerica and lower Central America. Teotihuacan's presence in the Maya highlands almost certainly involved the establishment of a colonial enclave (mode 9) at Kaminaljuyu, and similar, albeit much smaller, enclaves and ports-of-trade (mode 10) may have been established in lower Central America, although none have been identified archaeologically. The Teotihuacan enclave at Kaminaljuyu, as well as postulated colonies in lower Central America, may have been associated with a pochteca-like institution, although this remains undocumented. Otherwise, less obvious trade contacts (modes 7 and 8) may have continued in lower Central America under the aegis of Teotihuacan and other Mexican states.

During Period V and the withdrawal of Teotihuacan, Mesoamerican–lower Central American trade seems to have declined, at least as far as can be determined from present evidence, although this apparent decline may be an artifact of archaeological sampling and preservation. Probably, however, it reflects changes in the economic systems that accompanied the development of increasing socio-political complexity in lower Central America, so that new products and trade modes may have characterized economic exchanges between Mesoamerica and lower Central America. Associated with these changes, we may expect an increased development of redistributive (and market?) economic systems in lower Central America (table 4.1), maintained, at least in part, by long-distance trade links with Mesoamerica. Trade modes 7 and 8, operating under the direction of Maya elite merchants, may have continued to dominate this interaction. Ports-of-trade (mode 10) may also have continued in existence. The principal routes seem to have continued through the southeastern lowlands, either by sea along the Caribbean coast or inland through Honduras. However, rivalries or conflicts between competing Maya centers may have affected the distribution of trade goods in lower Central America, such as the falloff in Maya jades observed in the Nicoya region of Costa Rica.

In Period VI we are no longer solely reliant upon the vagaries of archaeological evidence for trade contacts. For this era we possess documentary descriptions of Mesoamerican–lower Central American exchange involving colonial enclaves (mode 9), ports-of-trade (mode 10) associated with the Mexica Pochteca, and free-lance trading (mode 7) by Putun Maya merchants and their seaborne commerce. The problem remains to identify and systematically excavate examples of trade facilities described in the ethnohistoric literature in order to increase our understanding of exchange systems in archaeological contexts, although in at least one case where this was done, the task proved surprisingly difficult because of the paucity of remains directly associated with commercial activity (Sabloff and Rathje 1975b).

Future archaeological research may be directed toward the attempt to distinguish various kinds of economic contact between lower Central America and Mesoamerica to further our knowledge of the cultural development in both areas. At the most basic level, this would involve the recognition of evidence for direct access, reciprocal exchange, and centralized (elite-associated) exchange, or both redistributive and market systems. As has been suggested, the spatial modes defined by Renfrew (1975) may provide a useful way to distinguish specific exchange mechanisms as a significant step toward defining the developmental sequence and effects of long-distance trade in both Mesoamerica and lower Central America.

Assuming these steps can be taken, archaeologists would then be in a position to ask a variety of questions that bear upon the process of cultural development in these areas. For instance, provided that the trade interaction resulting from both the Maya (mode 7) and Mexican (mode 9) forms of economic institutions can be identified and distinguished, what were the developmental consequences for the lower Central American societies involved in these networks? Did sporadic interaction resulting from Maya freelance merchant contacts foster effects different from those produced by the more continuous interaction resulting from the establishment of Mexican trade colonies? Finally, recognizing that acculturation is always a reciprocal process, we need to consider the developmental consequences for both parties involved in the exchange process. Instead of emphasizing changes wrought in lower Central America, as is most often done, we need to examine as well the effects produced in Mesoamerica by trade contacts with lower Central America.

5
The Prehistory
of El Salvador:

An Interpretive Summary

PAYSON D. SHEETS

Department of Anthropology
University of Colorado, Boulder

This chapter reviews the prehistory of El Salvador, paying particular attention to external relationships, ecology and adaptation, volcanism, and regional economics. A problem in constructing such an overview is the geographic and chronologic inconsistency in research, with some areas and periods much more thoroughly known than others. Research designs and objectives of the numerous archaeologists who have excavated in El Salvador since the 1920s have also varied, and Salvadorean prehistory largely remains a thing of sherds and patches; an integrated understanding of internal dynamics and external relationships is at least a decade away.

One general trend from Preclassic to Postclassic is clear: there was an increasing intensity of external relationships. Ethnic and linguistic complexity during the Postclassic seems much greater than in the earlier periods. However, isolation from external contacts is a matter of degree, and complete economic or cultural isolation did not occur at any time. Ideally, the spectrum from autonomy through contact and integration should be studied culturally, politically, and economically—each initially examined separately—but in practice it is often difficult to separate the three. Research in the next decade or two may fill in some of the interstices and resolve some of the problems discussed in this chapter.

Periods I and II (?–ca. 4000 B.C.)

There are no known excavated sites in El Salvador dating to Periods I or II, equivalent to the Paleo-Indian and Archaic periods. El Salvador probably was occupied during these times, but evidence is still meager. A few fluted obsidian projectile point fragments stylistically most similar to Folsom points and some possible Archaic points are in private collections. A problem with early sites in El Salvador is exposure; deposition in many areas is rapid, with deep tephra, lava, and alluvial deposits having accumulated in the past few thousand years. However, that problem has potentially beneficial aspects. A Paleo-Indian or Archaic site buried by a sudden tephra fall would offer important archaeological data, since sudden tephra falls can preserve perishable artifacts as well as undisturbed activity areas. Given the duration of each period and the frequency of large explosive eruptions in the area, numerous Paleo-Indian and Archaic sites must exist under tephra deposits in El Salvador and elsewhere along the volcanic spine of lower Central America. For instance, a good place to look for such sites is along the contact between the Coatepeque tephra and the buried soil that is exposed along road and river cuts in western El Salvador. Coatepeque apparently erupted sometime between 40,000 and 10,000 years ago.

The outlines for Salvadorean prehistoric chronology after the Paleo-Indian and Archaic periods (i.e., for Neolithic horizons) were established as early as 1915 by Spinden. Although he misassigned a few individual artifacts, his categorization of Salvadorean artifacts into the following periods still is largely correct: Archaic (mid-Period IV, or the Late Preclassic or Late Formative), Maya (roughly Period V, or the Classic period), and Post-Maya and Aztec (Period VI, or the Early and Late Postclassic respectively).

At present only one site in the entire country, Chalchuapa (Sharer 1978a), has remains datable to the full span from Period III through Period VI. A few excavated sites, such as Quelepa, Santa Leticia, and Cambio, have briefer sequences of a few hundred years. Numerous sites, such as Cihuatan and Los Llanitos, have only a single component. Thus, this chapter uses the Chalchuapan culture-historical sequence as the chronological framework for all sites discussed (fig. 5.1).

Late Period III
(The Early Preclassic, 1200–1000 B.C.)

The earliest excavated evidence of sedentary human occupation in El Salvador is at Chalchuapa, dating perhaps as early as 1200 B.C. These early artifacts were found at two localities within the site and included extensive deposits of sherds, figurines, and lithics (chipped stone and ground stone, including manos and metates). The chipped stone industry was clearly a

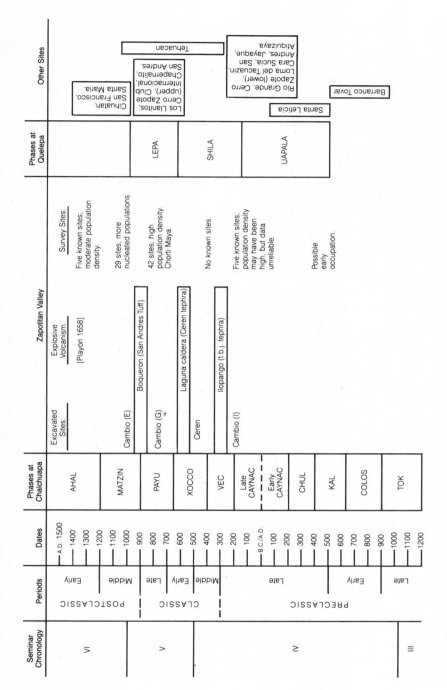

Figure 5.1. Cultural and volcanic chronology for El Salvador. Periods, dates, and Chalchuapa phases from Sharer (1978), Quelepa phases from Andrews V (1976), and Zapotitan Valley data from Sheets (n.d.a).

derivation from the northwest rather than the southeast. The sophisticated Mesoamerican core-blade technology was not yet as diversified as it would later become. Prismatic blades were carefully made, and although they are the most common implement, they account for only 7–9 percent of the artifacts (Sheets 1978). Ceramic and figurine analyses point more specifically to the Pacific coastal plain of Chiapas and Guatemala as the origin of these early colonists, and strong similarities are seen with the Cuadros phase in the Ocos area (Coe and Flannery 1967; Sharer 1978a).

The early Salvadorean colonists probably represent the expansion of predominantly seed-based agriculturalists, and they settled at Chalchuapa for at least three reasons. First, both early artifact concentrations at Chalchuapa are immediately adjacent to permanent sources of fresh water—the Trapiche Springs and Lago Cuzcachapa. Second, the site is in the center of a broad, fertile valley, where the moderate climate and almost 2,000 millimeters of mean annual rainfall make agroeconomic considerations for site location a strong probability. Third, Chalchuapa is precisely midway between the Pacific coast and the vast obsidian deposits at Ixtepeque (fig. 5.2). Considerable obsidian preforming and implement manufacture took place at Chalchuapa in Period III, as it did in all later periods up to the Conquest. Minimally, Chalchuapa seems to have served as a provisioning outpost for obsidian procurement parties as well as a location for workshops. Ixtepeque probably was not "owned" by any distinct ethnic or political group at this time, and it is not until the middle of Period IV that there is evidence for overt ownership and controlled access.

The archaeological Olmec of late Period III and early Period IV (the Early and Middle Preclassic periods) probably were Mixe-Zoque speakers (Kaufman 1976: 115), and it is possible that they extended across the Isthmus of Tehuantepec, along the Chiapas-Guatemala-Salvador coastal plain, and up into Chalchuapa. I agree with Fowler (personal communication) that the most likely linguistic affiliation of the early Chalchuapa residents was Mixe-Zoque, but there is, as yet, no reliable means of determining linguistic affiliations that far back in time. The contemporary Mixe and Zoque presently occupy a much restricted territory surrounding the Isthmus of Tehuantepec (Foster 1969).

Early Period IV
(The Middle Preclassic Period, 1000–500 B.C.)

It is unfortunate that Chalchuapa is the only excavated site in the country that has produced extensive information on this period. This would not be such a problem if Chalchuapa were representative of general Salvadorean developments, but it probably should only be considered representative of larger sites in the western part of the country. During this period it grew to

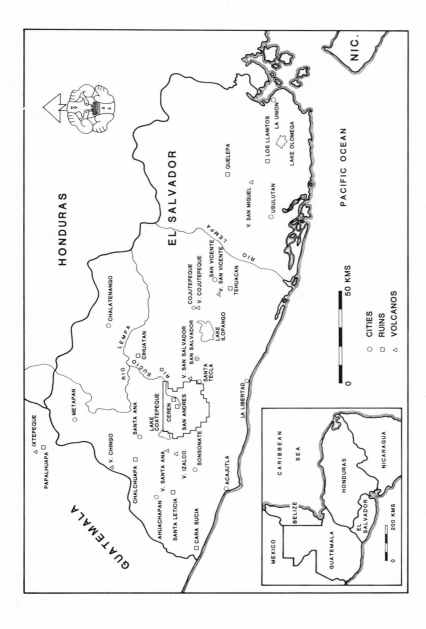

Figure 5.2. Map of El Salvador, showing major archaeological sites, volcanoes, and contemporary towns.

be a sizable community and crossed the threshold from an egalitarian farming community with occasional external trade contacts to a ranked society or chiefdom under sustained external cultural and economic influence by the Olmec.

The most striking physical addition to the expanding community is a 20-meter-high pyramid. The structure, E3–1, may have been conical in shape and may have been modeled after the pyramid at La Venta. It is one of the largest pyramids of its time anywhere in Mesoamerica and is indicative of controlled labor and centralized political authority well beyond the egalitarian farming community. The number and the geographical spread of Middle Preclassic artifacts in Chalchuapa has increased from the previous period, probably indicating population growth. Technological changes in lithic manufacture are quantitative rather than qualitative. Other artifact categories—particularly sculpture, ceramics, and figurines—show striking changes toward the Olmec model. These changes are both technological (e.g., firing atmosphere) and stylistic, and they may reflect an actual Olmec settlement at Chalchuapa. Such a strong Olmec presence 850 kilometers from the Olmec heartland (distance measured from La Venta) was probably to achieve more direct control over, or stable access to, Ixtepeque obsidian. Trace-element analyses of San Lorenzo obsidian indicate that the Olmec were using Ixtepeque obsidian by the Early Preclassic (Cobean et al. 1971), and the Ixtepeque obsidian that reached San Lorenzo probably traveled through Chalchuapa. In addition to being destined for the heartland, Ixtepeque obsidian was also almost certainly destined for use by numerous settlements along the Pacific coastal plain extending from Salvador through Chiapas. Other commodities, such as hematite, jadeite, amphibolite, cotton, and cacao, were probably also traded along this route, although we have yet to confirm that they were.

During the early part of Period IV, some of the ceramics of Chalchuapa are strikingly similar to Xe and Mamom ceramics of the Maya lowlands, and Sharer (1978a [3]: 209) suggests a migration from the southeast Maya area as an explanation.

Late Period IV
(Late Preclassic and Early Classic,
500 B.C.–A.D. 500)

A number of Late Period IV (Late Preclassic) sites are known from El Salvador (fig. 5.1). During this period Chalchuapa grew in size, complexity, and independence and emerged as its own complex polity, growing away from the earlier cultural and economic domination by the Olmec. The central ritual zone reached its greatest extent with the creation of a very large platform-plaza surrounded with large pyramids. A number of artifact categories including ceramics, lithics, sculpture, hieroglyphics, calendrics, and architecture point toward cultural contacts with the Guatemalan highlands. The southeast Maya area is one of the most culturally precocious of all Maya areas during this period, but not later.

It is during late Period IV that the sampling bias toward Chalchuapa decreases. In previous periods it almost appears that Chalchuapa was the sole occupied locale in all of El Salvador, but that is an artifact of research and publication. Numerous Late Preclassic sites, however, are known throughout the country. Longyear (1966) mentioned the following sites: Cerro Zapote, Barranco Tovar (but see below), Atiquizaya, Acajutla, El Trapiche, and perhaps Rio Gualacho. To these we can add Quelepa (Andrews V 1976), Santa Leticia (Demarest 1980), Loma del Tacuazin (Boggs 1966), numerous sites discovered during Cerron Grande research (Fowler 1976; Earnest 1976) and during recent fieldwork in the Zapotitan Valley (Sheets 1976, n.d.a), and Jayaque (L. Casasola, personal communication; fig. 5.3).

There are indications that Barranco Tovar was Middle Preclassic, not Late Preclassic. Robert Sharer (personal communication) believes that its ceramics typologically are Middle Preclassic, and the uncorrected C^{14} date (Porter 1955) ranges from 1400 to 680 B.C. A visually similar tephra layer buried charcoal in a soil at Santiago Texacuangos, some 11 kilometers southeast of Porter's site, and the charcoal was dated at 700–400 B.C. (Sheets 1976; uncorrected one-sigma range). Bill Hart (personal communication) found evidence of an Ilopango eruption earlier than the well-known "tbj" eruption of the third century A.D. Petrographic and stratigraphic data are not yet available to test the hypothesis that there was a Middle Preclassic eruption of Ilopango. If future research finds that it did occur, then the possibility of a volcanically induced migration explaining the Middle Preclassic Salvador-Belize similarities (Sharer and Gifford 1970) should be considered.

Space limitations do not allow for detailed descriptions of all sites, but some general conclusions can be drawn. The Late Preclassic (or late Period IV) was a time of high population density in "tierra caliente," the hot lowlands below 1,000 meters, and of expansion into "tierra templada," the areas above 1,000 meters and as high as Santa Leticia at 1,400 meters. Trade networks linked consuming populations with productive and extractive resources, and crafts show a high degree of similarity. Sites at the extreme western and eastern ends of the country have highly similar Usulutan ceramics, "Cara Sucia" mask sculptures, and lithic technology. The degree of relative cultural homogeneity and vitality achieved by Late Preclassic populations was never again achieved in Salvadorean prehistory. Agricultural technology was diversified, with intensive irrigation schemes in some river valleys and "high performance milpas" in others (Sheets n.d.b). Subsistence

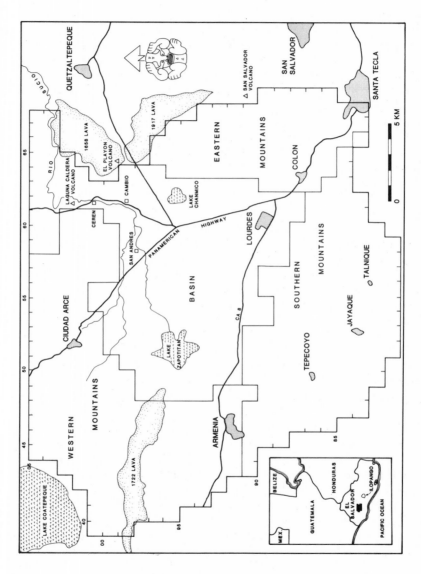

Figure 5.3. Map of the Zapotitan Valley, El Salvador. Research of the Protoclassic Project from 1978 through 1980 has taken place within the 550 square kilometers shown.

crops included maize, probably beans, and perhaps a variety of root and tree crops.

The highland site of Santa Leticia, located 18 kilometers southwest of Chalchuapa, has been investigated by Demarest (1980). It was occupied from about 400 B.C. to perhaps A.D. 200, with a brief reoccupation during the Late Classic. The site, only 15 hectares in area, is composed of earth-fill structures, a large artificial terrace, and several pot-bellied sculptures. These sculptures are almost certainly contemporaneous with those from Pacific and highland Guatemala, and Demarest is the first to provide reliable dating for that site. It has been speculated that the sculptures were as early as pre-Olmec times, but Demarest was able to date them to the Late Pre-classic. Cara Sucia–style carved stone masks were also associated with the site, and this find correlates with the Cara Sucia mask found in a Late Preclassic context sealed by Ilopango tephra at Chalchuapa (Sharer 1978a; Sheets 1979, fig. 17.3). Demarest was able to excavate numerous house platforms and associated bell-shaped pits. In the latter he found maize, sunflower seeds, and jocote (a tree fruit)—direct evidence of the Late Preclassic diet.

Quelepa, in eastern El Salvador, was founded during the middle of Period IV. Andrews V (1976) dates the earlier phase, the Uapala, from 500 or 400 B.C. to A.D. 150. He interprets the presence of comales, manos, and metates to imply maize agriculture and notes that the presence of dart points and deer bones indicates that hunting was practiced as well. The site contains evidence of Mesoamerican core-blade obsidian technology as early as 500 B.C., but the source for Quelepa obsidian is unknown. The only evidence of architecture was an oft-refurbished platform floor of unknown function. The imposing (ca. 3- × -3-meter) Jaguar Altar with a Cara Sucia–style jaguar mask sculpted in the center, flanked by serpents and stylized jaguars on both sides, is also of unknown function. The carving style and the motifs indicate inspiration deriving from the northwest; Andrews V (1976: 177) cites similarities to Kaminaljuyu, Izapa, and Abaj Takalik. He relates figurines to antecedents in western El Salvador and highland Guatemala. The ceramic trade wares, according to Andrews V, come from central and western El Salvador and points farther west, while the indigenous wares show strong similarities to ceramics from central-western El Salvador and the Maya highlands, indicating a Mesoamerican origin for the earliest Quelepa residents. However, Andrews V also notes some similarities to early ceramics at the following Honduran sites: Copan, Lo de Vaca, Yarumela, Los Naranjos, and Santa Rita. Usulutan-type ceramics are the most common.

Quelepa thus may represent the continued expansion of seed-based agriculturalists from the Pacific coastal plains of Chiapas and Guatemala. William Fowler (personal communication), however, feels that Quelepa was settled by Lenca speakers from Honduras, where population pressure may have necessitated their migrations. Andrews V supports his Meso-american identification of early Quelepa with a linguistic argument, holding that Lenca may be a Macro-Mayan language. Lenca often has been considered a northern Intermediate Area language with unclear or unknown affiliations (Linares 1979). If Andrews V is correct, then the ethnohistoric Lenca may be the direct descendants of the Preclassic peoples of the country, with the Chorti, Pipiles, and Pokomames being more recent immigrants. If some communities in eastern El Salvador were able to survive the Ilopango disaster (see below) that devastated communities in central and western El Salvador, then the ethnohistoric Lenca are the closest living relatives to Late Preclassic peoples of central and western El Salvador. The Ilopango eruptive plume was blown largely to the north and west, and according to Andrews V (1976: 182), Ilopango had little effect on Quelepa in the Early Classic. There was no detectable hiatus in occupation at Quelepa, and the transition from Preclassic to Classic was apparently a gradual one. There are still no confirmed deposits of Ilopango tephra (i.e., volcanic ash) in eastern El Salvador, although two sites have tephra deposits that could be from Ilopango. One is Los Llanitos, where Longyear (1944: 72) found a white volcanic ash layer under Late Classic construction. The other is a site reported by Lothrop (1927a: 177) near San Miguel.

Sharer and Gifford (1970) argue from ceramic evidence that direct contacts between western El Salvador and the Maya lowlands may have occurred twice in the Preclassic period. As mentioned above, the first occurred during the Middle Preclassic (ca. 900–500 B.C.) with Colos-Kal ceramics at Chalchuapa linked to Xe-Mamom ceramics of the Maya lowlands. The second connection is posited for the end of the Preclassic period, linking Caynac ceramics at Chalchuapa with Floral Park intrusive ceramics at Barton Ramie. Not only is the latter similarity extremely close, but an explanation for a migration from El Salvador to the lowlands exists in the form of the third-century eruption of Ilopango Volcano (Sheets 1976, 1979). The possibilities of similar site-unit intrusions, resulting from the volcanic disaster and resultant migrations, exist for other areas of Middle America.

Central and western El Salvador were severely affected by the third-century eruption of Ilopango (Sheets 1976, 1979). It erupted explosively, depositing more than 20 cubic kilometers of tephra across the countryside (the total volume may have been more than 40 cubic kilometers, according to William Rose, personal communication to V. Steen-McIntyre). Pyroclastic flows (density flows of volcanic gases and tephra) swept dozens of kilometers to the south, west, and north, killing flora and fauna in their paths. Tephra depths of more than 50 meters are known at locations close to the vent, and Chalchuapa, 77 kilometers distant, received over one-half meter. Much of central and western El Salvador evidently was abandoned for a few generations because of damage to agricultural land. As weathering and plant recolonization combined to form a soil on top of the Ilopango tephra, people began to recolonize the area.

The numerous cases of historical volcanic eruptions and their damage to agricultural land may be used as a guide to identify the areas of El Salvador severely affected by Ilopango. Of these, perhaps Paricutin in western Mexico is the best comparative case, as there is a high degree of climatic and adaptive similarity to El Salvador. Cornfields buried by more than 10 centimeters of Paricutin tephra could not be cultivated for a year, and more deeply buried fields required many years or decades for recovery sufficient to sustain maize agriculture. These data from Paricutin, relative to Ilopango, are conservative in that the Paricutin tephra was more mafic (i.e., contained more ferromagnesians, and it weathered faster with more plant nutriments) than the acid or sialic (greater silica content) Ilopango tephra; a given depth of Paricutin tephra, then, would be less damaging than the same depth of Ilopango tephra. Given the limited food-storage capacity of Late Preclassic Salvadorean society, migration must have been favored over a year or years with no food production. Geologists have estimated that two centuries of weathering and soil formation will be necessary for full recovery of the forest around Paricutin (summarized in Sheets 1976: 12–14).

Period V (Classic Period, A.D. 500–1000)

Following weathering, soil formation, and vegetation succession, human recovery of the devastated zones of central and western El Salvador was from the north. There is no evidence that Intermediate Area peoples from the east moved into the new territory. Chorti Maya expanded from the southern Peten-Belize area southward through the Copan and Quirigua areas in the late fifth and sixth centuries (Thompson 1970). Artifactual evidence from 1978 Protoclassic Project research indicates they reached the Zapotitan Valley by the sixth century (Sheets 1979). There they established an elaborate hierarchy of settlement types ranging from individual farmsteads to the large primary center of San Andres. Although soils were far from fully recovered following the Ilopango disaster, by the end of the sixth century, the Chorti Maya were able to sustain a moderately intensive form of maize agriculture. Soils derived from Ilopango tephra were comparatively rich in nitrogen and iron and neutral in pH, but they were very weak in phosphorus, magnesium, calcium, and manganese (G. Olson, personal communication 1978). The agriculture practiced at the sixth-century Ceren site (figs. 5.2 and 5.3) evidently was a short-fallow, dry-land (rainfall) system. The Ceren site, described in more detail below, was an agrarian village buried by a localized eruption of a nearby volcano at the beginning of Period V. The relatively low maize plant density, under 30,000 per hectare, is probably explained by the weak soil development and the fact that previous cultivation seasons had mismanaged the soils, leading to some erosion of the already weak topsoil (Sheets n.d.b).

Maize and bean agriculture has been confirmed for the Maya at Ceren, and future investigations may encounter tree crops and root crops, as well as possible swidden cultivation on the hillslopes. A swidden, or outfield, system is suspected, because each family at Ceren had an estimated one-third hectare of contiguous farmland around its house. They would have had to supplement infield production with some outfield cultivation.

Ironically, the natural event—the eruption of Laguna Caldera Volcano (fig. 5.4)—that destroyed the Ceren area so dramatically was the means for its extraordinary preservation. The eruption is radiocarbon dated to A.D. 590 ± 90 (MASCA-corrected composite of three dates). In contrast to Ilopango, it had negligible long-term cultural effects, in part because it affected such a small area. It deeply buried only 20 square kilometers, whereas Ilopango rendered about 10,000 square kilometers uninhabitable. The repercussions of Ilopango echo through centuries of southern Mesoamerican prehistory, whereas Laguna Caldera was only a brief perturbation in the flow of human events within part of the Zapotitan Valley of El Salvador.

The Protoclassic Project's regionally oriented research in the Zapotitan Valley has yielded information on settlement, subsistence, and economics from the Late Preclassic through the Postclassic periods. The most detailed information is about the Classic period, and therefore the results are discussed in this section on Period V.

The archaeological survey was under the field direction of Kevin Black (n.d.). Of the 546-square-kilometer research area, 82 square kilometers were surveyed in the form of square-kilometer quadrats chosen by a stratified random sampling strategy. The 54 sites discovered were classified into eight site types, ranging from the small, isolated residence to the primary regional center of San Andres (fig. 5.2). Only five sites were found that could be definitely dated to the Late Preclassic. Such a low figure could indicate an actual sparse occupation of the valley during the Preclassic, or it could be an underrepresentation; the latter is more likely. Because they are earlier, Preclassic sites tend to be buried by more tephra as well as obscured by Classic and Postclassic construction or refurbishing.

Not a single site datable to the Early Classic has been found in the valley, indicating the degree of environmental damage done by the Ilopango tephra. In marked contrast are the 42 Late Classic sites (about one per 2 sq km) scattered in the flat-lying basin lands and the rolling hilly lands to the west and north (fig. 5.3).

To continue the settlement figures (and temporarily violate the period framework used to organize this paper), the number of Early Postclassic, or early Period VI, sites diminished to 29. What at first glance might seem to be a considerable population decline is, in fact, only a very slight decline,

Figure 5.4.   Volcanic stratigraphy and Structure 1 at the Ceren site, Zapotitan Valley. The white volcanic ash from the third century Ilopango eruption (A) rests on the fertile Preclassic soil. The house was built upon the slightly weathered Ilopango tephra. The house was later buried by 4.6 meters of hot tephra from the Laguna Caldera eruption (B) at about A.D. 600. Boqueron, the main crater of Volcan San Salvador, erupted sometime around the tenth century, depositing the thin San Andres tuff (C). That was followed by the eruption of Volcan Playon, 1658, which deposited the uppermost tephra layer at the site (D). Only Ilopango was a large natural disaster; the three later eruptions affected residents only in the Zapotitan Valley. Photo by author.

as the mean site size increases in the Early Postclassic. The dramatic shift to defensible locations that characterizes the Guatemalan highland Early Postclassic is almost unknown in the Zapotitan Valley. Only five late Postclassic sites are known in the valley, and there are indications that this is an underrepresentation of the immediate preconquest population because many of the contemporary towns in the valley probably overlie Late Postclassic sites. Black (n.d.: 37) estimates minimal valley populations as follows: Late Classic 40,000, Early Postclassic 38,000, and Late Postclassic 27,000, which represent about 70, 70, and 50 people per square kilometer respectively. At all times the proximity of year-round fresh water and arable flat land outweighed defensibility as locational determinants.

Chipped-stone artifacts from the various types of valley sites have been analyzed to determine what was being transported and made, where it was made, who made it, and how it was used and discarded (Sheets n.d.a). Although the analysis is not yet complete, some general patterns of transport and manufacture can be summarized here. This aspect of lithic analysis is intended to indicate the economic interrelationships of the various types of sites in the past, particularly during the Late Classic. I have found it necessary to combine more traditional methods of lithic formal and technological analysis with a "hole in the donut" approach of also analyzing a site's lithics for what is not there. Missing implements, or debitage from a stage of manufacture, can be used to reconstruct what may have been made at a site and then traded, and that observation can be used as the beginnings of reconstructing regional intersite economic relationships. Before describing lithics within sites and the inferred relationships among sites, the variables and the indices used need to be explained in some detail.

Table 5.1 presents the results of sorting and analyzing obsidian artifacts by type of settlement. The settlement types, presented in ascending order of size and complexity in the table, are based on Black's categories (n.d.). The 11 types of lithics are the common, basic kinds of implements and debitage found across Mesoamerica from the Preclassic through the Postclassic, with the exception of the rare categories "shaped laja" and wedges. The six indices at the bottom of table 5.1 require explanation. Nonobsidian chipped-stone artifacts are tabulated to investigate the alternatives to obsidian manufacture. The use of alternatives, largely local basalt, was so rare as to be of little importance in comparing and contrasting settlement types. The percentage of hinge-fracture terminations in the debitage does vary with settlement type, apparently reflecting actual aboriginal patterning. Hinge fractures are interpreted as errors in manufacture and are employed here as a comparative device to explore occupational specialization. The assumption is that a greater degree of lithic specialization (i.e., a greater skill and success in manufacture) results in lower hinge-fracture frequencies. It would be better if this assumption had been tested on a variety of known lithic debitage

Table 5.1. Chipped Stone by Settlement Type, Valley Survey.

LITHIC TYPE	Isolated Residence (1)	Residence %'s	Hamlets (18)	Hamlets %'s	Small Villages (16)	Small Villages %'s	Large Villages (8)	Large Villages %'s	Isolated Ritual Precincts (4)	Isolated Ritual Precincts %'s	Large Villages with Ritual Construction (4)	Large Villages with Ritual Construction %'s	Secondary Regional Centers (2)	Secondary Regional Centers %'s	Primary Regional Centers (1)	Primary Regional Centers %'s	Totals—Valley Survey	%'s of Valley Survey
Bifacial Th. Fl.	0	0	20	4	5	1	1	-	0	-	2	1	0	-	0	0	28	1
General Debitage	4	40	224	43	377	78	257	59	31	94	25	15	374	62	4	20	1296	57
Macroblades	0	0	7	1	8	2	9	2	0	-	5	3	1	-	2	10	32	1
Prismatic Blades	5	50	254	49	89	19	155	36	2	6	118	69	219	37	13	65	855	38
Flake Cores	0	0	0	-	0	-	0	-	0	-	0	-	0	-	0	-	1	-
Polyhedral Cores	0	0	2	-	1	-	5	1	0	-	6	3	0	-	0	-	13	0.5
Pr. Blade Points	0	0	1	-	1	-	2	-	0	-	13	8	0	-	1	5	18	1
Scrapers	0	0	1	-	0	-	0	-	0	-	1	0.5	2	-	0	-	4	-
"Shaped Laja"	0	0	0	-	0	-	0	-	0	-	0	-	0	-	0	-	0	-
Bifaces	1	10	11	2	0	-	3	1	0	-	2	1	2	-	0	-	19	1
Wedges	0	0	0	-	0	-	0	-	0	-	0	-	1	-	0	-	2	-
TOTALS:	10	100	521	99	481	100	432	99	33	100	172	100.5	599	99	20	100	2268	99.5
Non-obsidian with % of total	0	0	5	1	1	-	2	0.5	0	-	0	0	9	1.5	0	0	17	1
# Hinge Fractures, with % of Debitage	1	25	8	3	39	10	19	7	0	0	1	4	7	2	0	0	75	6
# Ground Platforms on Prismatic Blades	0		23		3		7		0		2		0		0		34	
Mean wt/piece obsidian, in grams	1.4		1.9		2.1		2.8		2.0		2.3		2.0		3.8		2.1	
Cutting edge/mass, Pr. Blades, centimeter/gram	3.7		3.5		3.3		3.1		3.1		3.4		3.2		2.9		3.4	
# Cortex, with % of Total Obsidian	0	0	6	1	17	4	12	3	2	6	0	-	15	3	0	0	48	2

deposits (such as those generated by Crabtree's summer flintknapping schools), but it has not been.

The number of ground platforms on prismatic blades was tabulated, and although hamlets accounted for less than a tenth of valley populations, they turned out to have 68 percent of all survey specimens. The mean weight per piece of obsidian was recorded on an experimental basis to see if any patterns related to access were indicated. Larger sites tend to have larger mean weights, probably indicating that larger sites had closer connections with the obsidian supply system coming into the valley.

A more sensitive and well-tested index of obsidian access is the cutting edge per unit mass measurement (CE/M, in centimeters of acute cutting edge per gram of prismatic blade). Within the valley, people at sites farther down the supply and manufacturing chain would presumably have to pay more for their prismatic blades; a way to counteract the increased cost is to "stretch" the blades during manufacture by increasing the amount of cutting edge per unit mass. The hierarchical site-size pattern in the valley does correlate with the anticipated distribution system and with higher CE/M figures for sites farther down the access ladder.

The final index on the table is cortex frequency, an indicator of the manufacturing stage at which obsidian arrives at a locality. High cortex frequencies indicate a fairly close connection to the source, in that relatively little processing had taken place on the nodule prior to its arrival at a site. This index seems to be a reasonably reliable indicator of prior processing, and there are direct ways to check its validity in a collection. For instance, a high cortex frequency, indicating little prior processing, should be checked against expected high frequencies of core preforming debris and macroblades in the same collection.

The results summarized in table 5.1 show that large centers did not dominate the manufacture of obsidian implements in the valley. The primary and secondary regional centers did, not surprisingly, have more direct access to obsidian than smaller settlements. Both larger settlement types apparently served as redistributive centers for obsidian coming into the valley. Based on three indices (cutting edge per unit mass, mean weight per piece, and cortex frequency), it seems that the secondary regional centers were dependent on the primary regional center, San Andres, for their obisidan (see table 5.1). A high level of skill in core blade technology, based on occupational specialization, is evident for these two kinds of regional centers. This conclusion is based largely on the low error rate.

The next smaller settlement type is large villages with ritual construction. Evidently they were dependent upon the regional centers for macrocores but not for manufacture. Rather, they were making their own macroblades, prismatic blades, bifaces, scrapers, and blade points and doing so with only slightly less skill (i.e., with a slightly higher error rate) than were the major centers. Still unexplained is the emphasis on prismatic blade production; these settlements produced prismatic blades at about twice the frequency of the valley average (relative to the other artifacts they produced).

Large villages, the next smaller settlement taxon, are very similar to the overall valley mean in lithic manufacture. They are self-sufficient in lithic manufacture, but not in lithic access. The error rate in manufacture is markedly higher than in the larger settlements and is slightly larger than the valley mean, which I interpret as showing less lithic specialization and skill in large villages than in the larger settlement types. Although they were dependent upon the larger settlements for their obsidian, it was not a particularly scarce commodity for them, as indicated by the relatively large weight per piece figure. Large villages did not have to economize with their obsidian as much as did the three smallest kinds of settlements.

Small villages, the next smaller settlement unit, are extreme in a number of ways. They participated less in core-blade technology than did any other kind of settlement, larger or smaller. They used an alternative to core-blade technology, doing percussion manufacture of crude cutting flakes more often than any other type of settlement. The high error rate (the highest hinge-fracture rate of any settlement type with an adequate sample for comparison) indicates that this was an unspecialized cottage industry. These villages did have prismatic blades but in very low frequencies. The specialized core-blade secondarily retouched products such as scrapers and bifaces are notable for their absence. The absence of polyhedral cores probably is an indicator of manufacture elsewhere. The cortex percentage is the highest of all settlement types for which samples are adequate.

Hamlets, the smallest type of settlement with sufficient sample size, were surprisingly much more within the Mesoamerican lithic framework of core-blade technology than are the next larger settlements, small villages. An explanation of this anomaly could be that hamlets cooperated in employing itinerant lithic specialists.

The very small sample of isolated residences only allows for general comments. These households had trouble obtaining obsidian, as indicated by their high CE/M ratios. This high ratio also indicates maximization of cutting edge. The high hinge-fracture frequencies show that the workers were not experts or specialists but rather were part-time knappers.

One important implication of the above data, beyond reconstructing intrasite economic relationships, is the conclusion that *no single site is representative of the valley as a whole.* An excavated sample or a surface-collected sample from a single site, no matter how well controlled, is only a part of a complex system, and that system can be understood only by research that is regionally oriented and based on probability sampling. It is time to give up the search for typical sites and realize that the reality is in the diversity and the integration of sites. Attempts to understand how that integration was achieved and why it changed should be a principal research focus.

The recovery of the chipped-stone industry after the Ilopango natural disaster has a bearing on external relationships. Recovery of the industry can be studied in two ways. First, it can be viewed in terms of complexity, noting the point in time when the predisaster complexity in manufacture (the structure of the industry and the variety of implements produced) was achieved during recovery. Or, second, the volume of materials produced, the output, can be compared within the same geographic area. By the former measure, recovery can be said to have been achieved when the diversity of products produced after the disaster matches the predisaster production; by the latter, recovery may be considered achieved when as much material was processed postdisaster as predisaster.

Because of the above-mentioned Preclassic sampling limitations, an accurate assessment of only the former index of recovery, the structure of manufacture, is possible. The behavioral structures and the diversity of obsidian implement output for Preclassic times is known from survey and excavated samples. Macroblades and prismatic blades were made from cores. Macroblades were used as is, or were secondarily modified into scrapers. Thus, the Preclassic industry was basic core-blade technology with few frills.

During the Classic period the obsidian tool manufacturing industry recovered and surpassed the Preclassic in terms of variety of output. In addition to the prismatic blades, macroblades, and scrapers similar to those produced in Preclassic times, Classic knappers were producing prismatic blade points (probably for use as arrow points) and bifaces (knives and/or spearpoints). The best estimate of the time when the complexity of Classic manufacture would have equalled Preclassic manufacture is the sixth century A.D., indicating a recovery time of at least 200 years. Lithic recovery was relatively slow, because it was dependent upon the recovery of soils, vegetation, and human populations with their agroeconomic subsistence base.

It is frustrating not to be able to address satisfactorily the volume-of-production index of lithic recovery. If our Preclassic samples are representative of Preclassic habitation and lithic manufacture, Classic surpassed Preclassic production by 600 to 700 percent. However, we are fairly confident that the actual Preclassic settlement in the Zapotitan Valley is seriously underrepresented because of deeper burial by recent tephra. If Preclassic Chalchuapa is any guide, the volume of production at any time in the Classic or Postclassic did not equal Preclassic production. Given the information at hand, the latter interpretation probably is closer to the truth. If so, we have a case of the postdisaster obsidian industry being more diversified yet processing less raw material. Full recovery, in volume of materials possessed, may have been inhibited by sporadic explosive volcanism in the Zapotitan Valley during the past 1,500 years.

The source of technological expertise in recovery should be discussed.

There are three alternatives: (a) from the east (i.e., from eastern El Salvador, central or eastern Honduras, or even farther southeast in lower Central America), or (b) from the north (i.e., from western Honduras, eastern Guatemala, or Belize), or (c) from the west (i.e., from the Guatemalan highlands or Pacific coast (see fig. 5.2 inset). The hypothetical fourth alternative, from the south, involves floating Maya and is thus considered highly unlikely.

An eastern source can be discounted, for peoples living east of the area affected by Ilopango in the Protoclassic and Early Classic, as far as is known, did not possess sufficiently sophisticated core-blade technology. Likewise, a western source is also unlikely. During the Protoclassic and the beginnings of the Early Classic, there were numerous sites practicing core-blade technology, but none is known with the diversity of the Classic valley industry that could have served as the source. A technological source for lithic recovery from the west is possible, then, but not substantiated by data.

The best match of the known technology of recovery and potential sources is with the north, specifically, with sites such as Copan, Papalhuapa, and Quirigua. Thus, as judged by lithic analysis, the reoccupation of the Zapotitan Valley occurred most likely by a population movement from the north, probably via Copan and Quirigua. It is possible, but less likely, that groups in the Guatemalan highlands and Pacific coast participated. It is highly unlikely that people from central Honduras (Ulua drainage and eastward) or eastern El Salvador were involved.

In his overview of Salvadorean prehistory, Longyear (1966: 138–41) noted the ceramic types he felt indicated contacts outside the country. Copador polychrome commonly is found in central and western El Salvador and is part of a ceramic sphere which includes Copan. If Copador turns out to be earlier in El Salvador than Copan (M. Beaudry, personal communication), then the antecedents to Salvadorean Copador are unclear. Baudez (personal communication) believes Copador at Copan may be as early as A.D. 650. Ulua polychrome is found in most larger Salvadorean Late Classic sites, but it is much less frequent than Copador. Given the proximity of the Ulua and Comayagua valleys to El Salvador, Ulua polychrome is more notable for its relative absence than for its presence.

Quelepa witnessed large-scale ritual (fig. 5.5) construction faced by cut *talpetate* blocks during the Shila Phase (A.D. 150–625). These large structures were placed on top of long artificial terraces (Andrews V 1976). Although Andrews V sees continued artifactual similarities with western El Salvador and the Guatemalan highlands as well as with Los Naranjos and Copan, he notes the degree of similarity has lessened markedly. This may have been caused by the trade and interaction dislocations from the Ilopango disaster, isolating Quelepa from most acculturative influences deriving from the northwest.

Not surprisingly, Quelepa evidently increased social and economic in-

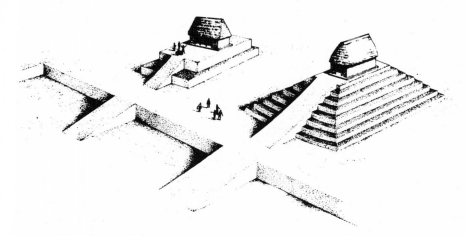

Figure 5.5. Isometric reconstruction of Structures 3 and 4 at Quelepa, eastern El Salvador. The pyramids were built on a large, artificially constructed platform. Structure 4, on the left, is Early Classic; the larger Structure 3 was built slightly later, probably during the sixth century A.D. This area of the site was largely abandoned when the Mexicans, perhaps from Veracruz, moved in and constructed the "West Group" as the center of their settlement. Drawing courtesy of E. Wyllys Andrews V.

teraction with the Intermediate Area. Andrews V (1976: 183) notes new "Central American" influences in the form of "small carved jadeite beads, carved legged metates, and pecked stone balls found in sets of three," positing Costa Rica as the likely source. The distance is not prohibitive, for it is less than 400 kilometers from Quelepa to northwestern Costa Rica.

The architecture and artifacts of the later phases at Quelepa are almost exactly duplicated at the large site of Tehuacan (W. Andrews V, personal communication), located on the eastern flanks of San Vicente Volcano (fig. 5.2). Andrews V would place Tehuacan contemporary with Quelepa's Shila and Lepa phases and perhaps extend it slightly later.

At Chalchuapa construction and ritual activity resumed in Period V in the central and southern parts of the site core (Sharer 1978a, [3]: 211), following the hiatus caused by Ilopango. El Trapiche, at the northern end of the site core, was largely abandoned. Lithic manufacture remains solidly within the Mesoamerican sphere, with a diversified core-blade strategy being employed. Sharer sees multiple external connections, including Copan, in the form of Copador pottery, the central Peten, and the Intermediate Area (based on Nicoya polychrome[1] and some of the earliest metallurgy of the Maya area). Compared with the Late Preclassic, Chalchuapa is much reduced in population, ritual construction, and general vitality.

Figure 5.6.   Oblique airphoto of Tazumal, at the southern end of the Chalchuapa site zone. The architecture visible is largely Late Classic and Early Postclassic in date. Photo by author.

Chalchuapa does contain some evidence of a connection with lower Central America in the form of three small gold or tumbaga castings found at Tazumal (fig. 5.6). Stone (1972: 150–51) gives a radiocarbon date of A.D. 751 (presumably uncorrected and lacking the standard deviation). Based on composition, she attributes them to Costa Rica but notes that one is stylistically closest to the Quimbaya style of Colombia. They could have arrived in Chalchuapa via Quelepa and Tehuacan along the trade route set up in the Shila phase and maintained in the Lepa phase by the Veracruz merchants.

Corresponding to the Late Classic and the beginnings of the Postclassic at Quelepa is the Lepa phase (A.D. 625–1000; Andrews V 1976: 183–86). It was a time of strong influences from the west, and the polychrome ceramics seem closely affiliated with Veracruz, Mexico. Because other Salvadorean sites seem to have received a similar infusion from Veracruz, this was probably associated with the general, widespread movements of Mexican-acculturated Maya from the southern Gulf area southeastward into the Maya highlands. This occurred during the Late Classic–Early Postclassic, and it probably was, at least in part, an attempt to take over the lucrative southern long-distance trade routes left in limbo by the collapse of Teotihuacan and the later decline and collapse of the Classic Maya in the lowlands.

In addition to ceramics, a number of cultural items found at Quelepa during the Lepa phase show a strong affiliation with Veracruz, and these include ball-game paraphernalia (yokes, palmas, and a hacha) and an I-shaped ball court, Quetzalcoatl Ehecatl, flutes with rolling pellets, and wheeled zoomorphic figurines. Andrews V (1976: 185) argues convincingly that more than just trade was involved, for in addition to portable items, the changes involve architecture and burial patterns. He argues that while many of the portable items were made locally at or near Quelepa, there was a takeover by a Veracruz foreign elite, perhaps with military backing, and possibly involving commoners from Veracruz and some direct imports.

It is significant that the artifact content of Quelepa is not representative of contemporary smaller sites in the area (analogous with Teotihuacan's presence at Kaminaljuyu, but on a smaller scale). The dominant polychrome pottery at Los Llanitos, only 20 kilometers south of Quelepa, is markedly different. Los Llanitos was a small ritual and residential site, with 10 small structures and a ball court arranged around two plazas in the center of the site (Longyear 1944, 1966). The construction method of facing earthen fill structures with cut talpetate masonry is similar to that used at Quelepa. Longyear found a layer of white volcanic ash underlying Late Classic construction in a few structures; it is unknown if this is from Ilopango or from a more local source. The distinctive Los Llanitos polychrome is most similar to Las Vegas Polychrome from the Comayagua Valley to the north, according to Longyear (1966: 147).

Period VI (Postclassic Period, A.D. 1000–1550)

During the Postclassic period, El Salvador was even less stable demographically and ethnically than during the Classic period, with numerous incursions by foreign groups. The Postclassic is also the least studied of the three Neolithic periods, and the literature is full of contradictions, confusing assertions, rampant speculations, and hazy sources. This overview does not presume to rectify these problems, but it is worthwhile to review what data are available and to present some tentative interpretations.

According to Sharer (1978a), the transition from Classic to Postclassic was a gradual one at Chalchuapa—not marked by the thorough demographic collapses of lowland Maya sites. This is not to say there were not significant changes, as numerous Pipil-associated characteristics begin to appear at Chalchuapa, including talud-tablero architecture, a round pyramid, a ball court, a life-size ceramic sculpture of Xipe Totec, chac mools, plumbate pottery, and other artifacts. These changes seem to represent more than acculturation from economic contacts; and probably they indicate that new people were moving into Chalchuapa.

The clear Maya-to-Pipil shift, as evidenced by architecture and artifacts at Chalchuapa, is almost entirely lacking in the Zapotitan Valley. A few plumbate sherds are known from the valley (cf. Longyear 1966; Black n.d.), but their paucity and the lack of other Pipil-associated characteristics argue against a rapid and large-scale population replacement. Yet by the Spanish Conquest the valley was supposedly densely populated by Pipiles (Daugherty 1969: 96ff.). If so, when and how did the Maya-to-Pipil shift take place in the valley? Our data are very weak, and it only can be suggested that the change may have been a long-term acculturative process owing to trade and social contacts with Pipiles to the east and west and perhaps occasional emigration of Maya families and immigration of Pipil families. Until Late Postclassic sites are excavated and ethnohistoric documents are consulted, this question will remain unanswered.

More significant demographic and cultural changes may have occurred at the beginning of the Late Postclassic (ca. A.D. 1200) than at the beginning of the Early Postclassic at Chalchuapa (Sharer 1978a[3]: 211). Ritual construction virtually ceased, and a diminished occupation shifted to the west, under the present town of Chalchuapa. Two ceramic types are diagnostic of the period at Chalchuapa: Marihua red-on-buff and Chinautla polychrome. These may be ethnically related to the Pipiles and Pokomames respectively. Neither is well understood in terms of trade, acculturation, and/or migration and conquest. In any event, in the sixteenth century the Spanish encountered a few enclaves of Pokomam speakers, such as Chalchuapa, within a supposed sea of Pipil speakers in western El Salvador (Miles 1957: 742).

Haberland (1964) suggested that Marihua red-on-buff may be a Postclassic horizon marker, based on its similarity in El Salvador to red-on-buff at the site of Tula, Hidalgo, Mexico. He suggested the similarity may be a result of a postplumbate Toltec southeastward migration at about A.D. 1200. There does seem to be evidence of such a ceramic sequence at the San Francisco site, as Marihua red-on-buff was stratigraphically superior to plumbate. However, at nearby Cihuatan, Marihua red-on-buff ceramics are found at the lowest levels of the Early Postclassic (Fowler 1977: 27). Marihua red-on-buff may not be an indicator of a single Mexican migration but may reflect a number of population movements throughout the Postclassic.[2] Not all movements should be expected to have been recorded in all archaeological sites; hence some apparent disparities are to be expected.

Fowler (personal communication) recently defined a new ceramic type, Tamoa red-on-buff, that is technologically and formally similar to Marihua but lacks the diversity of painted designs of Marihua. Fowler thinks the Tamoa ceramics from Cihuatan may be developmentally antecedent to

Marihua, and I suspect this might place them in the Late Classic period, prior to A.D. 900.

Fowler's (1977) summary of Postclassic El Salvador, focusing on the central portion of the country, is most useful. Only two sites have yielded appreciable Postclassic materials in the central part of the country—Cihuatan and Santa Maria. Cihuatan is a relatively large site, covering about 375 hectares (Fowler, personal communication). The residential pattern of settlement is dispersed, but the central area is dominated by a pyramid–plaza–ball court complex covering some 5 or 6 hectares. Bruhns's monograph (1980) summarizes the 1977–78 excavations at Cihuatan. One of her findings is that the habitation zone shows no overall planning. The center, composed of pyramids, plazas, and ball courts, apparently was well planned. She notes the strong Mexican character of Cihuatan artifacts, and she sees the Veracruz area as the most likely source. The strong artifactual similarities of Cihuatan to Quelepa and Tehuacan most likely indicate close economic and social relationships. This topic needs close examination; a controlled survey and testing program at the key site of Tehuacan is urgently needed.

Four uncorrected radiocarbon dates are available from Cihuatan. They are A.D. 795 ± 50, A.D. 922 ± 92, A.D. 940 ± 86, and A.D. 1010 ± 86 (Bruhns 1980: 121), with an uncorrected mean of A.D. 917 ± 79. The uncorrected date for Santa Maria, A.D. 1010 ± 76, is only slightly later. Although Cihuatan is typologically Early Postclassic, the conclusion should not be drawn that it must postdate the traditional A.D. 900 date. Cihuatan appears to have been founded by the ninth century, if not earlier, and therefore it could be viewed as an early example of Mexicanization, like Quelepa. If the early Pipiles had established a large commercial-residential-ritual (-militaristic?) settlement at Cihuatan by the ninth century, one wonders what their relationships were with the Maya settlements of San Andres and other sites in the Zapotitan Valley only 28 kilometers to the southwest.

Santa Maria is a moderate-sized ritual and residential site 16 kilometers east-northeast of Cihuatan, near the Lempa River (Fowler 1977). The site covers about 3.6 square kilometers. Housing was not nucleated. The planned central portion of the site is a smaller version of Cihuatan.

The major similarities between Cihuatan and Santa Maria (Fowler 1977), which also can be used to identify the central El Salvadorean Early Postclassic (and perhaps terminal Classic), include: pyramid–plaza–ball court complex, talud-tablero architecture, quarried talpetate slab construction, tubular ceramic drain pipes, circular rings on temple summits (probably column bases), plumbate pottery, Tlaloc braziers, thick-walled and spiked hourglass braziers, wheeled figures, ceramic Xipe Totecs, chac mools, Nicoya polychrome, Cajete polychrome (related to Mixteca-Puebla), Marihua red-on-buff, ladle censers, and molcajetes. Fowler concludes that Mexican populations had replaced Maya populations in central El Salvador.

Fox (1980) traced the Mexican characteristics that appear in the Motagua and Negro river valleys of Guatemala during the Epiclassic (A.D. 800–1000) to a Gulf Coast source area, specifically Veracruz-Campeche. As at Chichen Itza, these early migrations to the Maya highlands were precursors to major migrations, more thorough Mexican acculturative influences, and perhaps some overt conquests during the Early Postclassic. In some areas of the Maya highlands the hybrid chiefdoms or states, such as the Quiche, survived to the Spanish conquest and continued into historic times. In other areas the early hybrid communities, such as Quelepa, did not survive to the conquest. Quelepa evidently received a contingent of these aggressively expansionistic peoples, who then used the site as a way station along a southern long-distance trade route reaching into the Intermediate Area.

Fowler agrees (1977: 20) that the Pipil infusion into El Salvador was not a single event but rather a number of migrations at different times. According to documentary sources, Mexican groups moved southeastward from Xoconusco to El Salvador, and some as far as Nicaragua, to escape the onerous burdens of conquest and tribute placed upon them by the Olmeca-Xicalanca. The earliest Pipil migrations evidently followed the old, and temporarily abandoned, Preclassic trade route across the Isthmus of Tehuantepec and southeastward along the Pacific coastal plain. This Pipil expansion may also have been a competitive response to the somewhat earlier Chorti Maya southward migrations and economic expansions. It is possible that the Chorti expanded to achieve ownership of key resources for Maya consumption, whereas Pipil expansion was for the same resources, but with an eye to larger and ethnically more diverse consuming populations in south-central Mexico. The earliest Pipil expansions may have occurred as early as the seventh century, following the Chorti's southernmost expansion by about a century. A necessary but not sufficient condition for both expansions into El Salvador is ecologic recovery from the Ilopango disaster, and present data indicate that by the sixth century soil recovery was barely adequate to support moderately intensive agriculture in central El Salvador.

Both the Maya and the Mexican migrations into El Salvador may have been connected with Teotihuacan expansionism but in quite different ways. The Teotihuacan presence at Kaminaljuyu (ca. A.D. 400–600) must have been at least partially oriented toward influencing obsidian distribution (and probably that of jadeite, cacao, and other goods) in southern Mesoamerica. The Classic Maya may have regarded the presence of Teotihuacan as a clear threat to their access to obsidian; a prehistoric international obsidian cartel may have existed or at least been a threat. Chorti Maya colonization of the territory surrounding two obsidian sources (Ixtepeque and Media Cuesta) may have been a strategy to demonstrate ownership and thus ensure a steady supply and lower prices than from Teotihuacan-controlled sources.

But as Teotihuacan was pulling back from its far-flung control of trade routes sometime around A.D. 600, Gulf Coast groups may have seen the economic opportunities for taking over and expanding the declining Teotihuacan trade routes. Thus, the Pipiles may have been able to expand into El Salvador south and east of Chorti Maya–controlled areas. The extent of their penetration farther into lower Central America on this first migration is unclear. The northward movement of the Chorti Maya–Mexican frontier in Postclassic times is testimony to their success at expansion. Their northward growth left only a few Chorti communities in extreme northern El Salvador at the time of the Spanish Conquest.

In summary, the arrival of the Pipiles in El Salvador, the finding of Veracruz-style artifacts in Late Classic and Postclassic horizons at Salvadorean sites, and general Mixteca-Puebla or Tajin-associated expansionism may all be related. It is possible that a component of Mixteca-Puebla expansion was composed of Nahua speakers (H. Nicholson, personal communication), and these might have become known as the ethnohistoric Pipiles in sixteenth-century documents. The earliest indications of this Mexicanization occur at Quelepa, followed shortly by a number of other sites. Multiple migrations were likely; as the Maya hold over northern El Salvador waned, more Pipiles moved in to reap the benefits of trade route control and use of productive and extractive resources.

Comments

This paper concludes with a brief topical assessment of Salvadorean prehistory intended to cross-cut periods and geographic zones and points out certain strengths and weaknesses in prehistoric data and interpretation.

The recent publication of the Quelepa and Chalchuapa research programs (Andrews V 1976; Sharer 1978a) has added more substantive information on Salvadorean prehistory than all previously published research had contributed in total. These publications, used with previous research, do allow us to construct a preliminary regional prehistory, although a number of glaring geographic, chronologic, and topical lacunae remain.

One conclusion is clear: El Salvador, from the earliest sedentary societies through the Postclassic period, was much more closely affiliated with Mesoamerica than with the Intermediate Area; only a few sites show significant interaction with areas to the southeast. Quelepa is one such site; during the Shila phase, trade connections were opened with lower Central America, most likely with Costa Rica. Quelepa turned southeastward at this time probably because of its isolation caused by the Ilopango disaster. In contrast, Quelepa before and after the Shila phase evinces very close connections with western El Salvador and areas farther northwest in Mesoamerica.

Knowledge of pre-Columbian subsistence has advanced considerably during the past decade, with contributions falling into two general categories. First, specific cultigens have been identified in Preclassic, Classic, and

Postclassic sites; the maize complex is known from all three periods. Tree and root crops still largely remain unconfirmed possibilities. Second, agricultural land-use technologies have been discovered under, and preserved by, the tephra deposits from two explosive eruptions, Ilopango and Laguna Caldera. Both irrigated (Earnest 1976) and rainfall (dry-land) fields are known from the Late Preclassic. Detailed information from Middle Classic Ceren on maize cultivation, including plant density, soil management, and labor investment are also known (Sheets n.d.b).

Very few systematic data on population densities and distributions are available for El Salvador. To estimate regional populations, probability sampling on a regional basis is necessary, and Black's report (n.d.) is the first to meet statistical sampling demands. More surveys of other areas, based on similar research designs, are necessary before an understanding of even the outlines of Salvadorean prehistoric demography can be achieved.

Knowledge of extractive resource use is uneven, and obsidian procurement, distribution, implement production, use, and discard have been studied at only a few sites. Of all extractive resources, obsidian has received the most thorough treatment, but the weaknesses in obsidian data are indicated by the fact that, to date, only two sites in El Salvador have had trace-element analyses conducted for sourcing purposes.[3] Among the host of other resources that are still virtually unresearched with regard to sources and processing are jadeite, amphibolite and other greenstones, chert, various metamorphic and igneous rocks for grinding stones, hematite, and clay. The question of how such extractive resources were managed—by open (egalitarian) access or by various forms of restricted access and ownership—is all too rarely considered.

Judging external relationships from the data currently available is often a precarious activity. Both major published projects, Chalchuapa and Quelepa, have carefully assessed external relationships. Some of their conclusions—such as the Mexicanization of Lepa-phase Quelepa, or the Olmec, Chorti, and Pokomam infusions into Chalchuapa—are convincing, but other contacts remain unexplained. One difficulty in much of the Salvadorean literature is the chronic archaeological problem of attempting to determine linguistic affiliations from pottery (cf. Linares 1979). This is particularly hazardous, if not totally specious, when ethnicity, language, and pottery types are assumed to co-vary. To resolve problems in these areas a variety of analyses are needed, ranging from petrography—to identify imports from domestics—and chronometric dating to careful linguistic and archaeological studies of adaptation, continuity, and change.

Instead of blithely using the term *influence*, prehistorians in El Salvador are trying to differentiate between the acculturative effects of trade and the evidence left by migration. Although the current paradigm in archaeological theory gives preference to *in situ* cultural evolution and acculturation rather than to migration, a number of migrations into and out of El Salvador seem to have occurred. Strong candidates for migrations into El Salvador include the earliest settlers from Pacific coastal areas of Chiapas-Guatemala, the Chorti Maya in the Classic, the Mexicans from Veracruz at Quelepa and other sites, the Pipiles, and finally the Pokomames in central and western El Salvador during the closing centuries of prehistory. Two migrations from El Salvador to the Maya lowlands may have occurred—one possibly in the Middle Preclassic and one at the end of the Late Preclassic. Yet numerous other influences seem more likely to have derived from economic inter-actions and acculturative influences. The general similarities of Late Pre-classic settlements all over the country to their contemporaries in highland Guatemala is a case in point.

In summary, Salvadorean prehistory is becoming more clearly under-stood, but much remains to be done. The evolution of prehistoric societies in El Salvador can no longer be viewed in a uniformitarianist framework. Nor can autochthonous processes or migration be unicausal mechanisms for explaining external relationships. The improvement in Salvadorean pre-historic data, research strategies, and use of theory should continue in the decades ahead.

Acknowledgments

A number of scholars graciously consented to critique an earlier version of this chapter; they include Gordon Willey, Will Andrews V, Marilyn Beaudry, and William Loker. Fred Lange's experienced editorial hand has rectified some of my tortuous prose to make this almost readable. His efforts on both drafts are certainly appreciated. I wish to express my appreciation for their efforts, and I hope this revised version is seen by them as an improvement. Debbie Tyler's careful typing of the draft and the final version is greatly appreciated.

Notes

1. The problem of distribution of Nicoya Polychromes, especially Papagayo Polychrome, is presently under detailed study. Samples from Costa Rica, Nicaragua, and El Salvador have been submitted by various researchers to Dr. Ronald Bishop at the Brookhaven National Laboratory, and we are hopeful of having more precise information regarding the distribution of actual Papagayo specimens and Las Vegas Polychrome variants in the near future.

2. Smith and Heath-Smith (1980) and Abel-Vidor (1981) have also explored the nature of these migrations from the Costa Rican perspective and have come to the same conclusion that they were multiple in nature.

3. Recent trace element analyses have been performed on obsidian from two additional sites in El Salvador, to attribute artifacts to sources. Early Postclassic Cihuatan received obsidian from Ixtepeque, El Chayal, and Rio Pixcaya (San Martin Jilotepeque), according to William Fowler (personal communication 1983). Most of the obsidian at Late Preclassic Santa Leticia derived from Ixtepeque, with some from El Chayal (Arthur Demarest, personal communication 1981).

6
The Archaeology of Honduras

PAUL F. HEALY

Department of Anthropology, Trent University

Honduras is one of the largest Central American states, covering 112,087 square kilometers (fig. 6.1).[1] Archaeologically, geographically, and ethnographically, it is a microcosm of lower Central America. Archaeologically, our information is spotty, uneven, and in some places simply nonexistent, while available data show northern influences from Mesoamerica proper and southern influences perhaps from beyond Central America. Geographically, it is marked principally by a mountainous interior and lowland coastal plains. Ethnographically, it was fragmented into numerous tribes and different linguistic groups at the time of the Spanish *entradas*.

Because of this complexity, few archaeologists have attempted to synthesize the archaeology of Honduras. The most recent complete review was by Strong (1948), and in addition, there have been several major regional surveys (Strong, Kidder, and Paul 1938; Yde 1938; Stone 1941, 1957).[2] This paper reviews the pertinent information in a spatial/temporal format, summarizes some of the most recent data and interpretations, identifies the most glaring deficiencies, and suggests some possible future directions for Honduran archaeology.

Setting

The country lies totally within east-west-trending mountain ranges. Much of the land is rugged and difficult to traverse. The greatest elevations reach

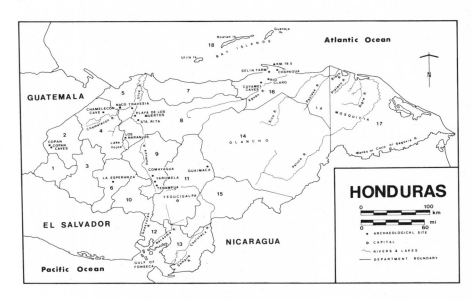

Figure 6.1.   Map of the Republic of Honduras detailing major archaeological sites, waterways, and political departments. Departments are numbered: 1, Ocotepeque; 2, Santa Rosa de Copan; 3, Lempira; 4, Santa Barbara; 5, Cortes; 6, Intibuca; 7, Atlantida; 8, Yoro; 9, Comayagua; 10, La Paz; 11, Francisco Morazan; 12, Valle; 13, Choluteca; 14, Olancho; 15, El Paraiso; 16, Colon; 17, Gracias a Dios; 18, Islas de la Bahia (Bay Islands). *Mapa General, Republica de Honduras*, 1970, Instituto Geografico Nacional, Tegucigalpa, D.C.)

2,700 meters near La Esperanza and Tegucigalpa. The volcanic axis of Central America cuts across only the southernmost strip of Honduras, leaving a few volcanoes as islets in the Gulf of Fonseca (West and Augelli 1976: 427). Consequently, Honduras lacks the rich volcanic ash that has created very fertile soils in most Pacific regions of Central America.

On the Pacific coast, the rainfall is somewhat higher than in the central highlands and supports a semideciduous tropical forest. Occasional patches of savanna give way to the narrow coastal plain and savanna lands of Choluteca and the mangrove-lined Gulf of Fonseca (West and Augelli 1976: 428). Except for some areas of the Caribbean lowlands, Honduran soils are generally infertile. Much of the interior mountain zone has shallow soils and is covered in pine and oak forest. At elevations above 2,100 meters, one enters *las montañas*, a much denser cloud-forest setting about which little is known archaeologically.

In terms of human settlement, the principal physiographic features of the interior highlands are numerous flat-floored valleys at 300–900-meter elevations. Several of these intermontane basins, such as the Valleys of Otoro, Sensenti, and, especially, Comayagua, have been very significant locales of settlement since prehistoric times.

The north coast or Caribbean lowlands, the next major distinctive physiographic unit, varies in width from almost nothing to a flatland 40 kilometers wide. *La costa* is marked by narrow river valleys and floodplains that often extend inland considerable distances, following the depressions of mountain ranges (West and Augelli 1976: 427–28). Instead of a single *cordillera* running parallel to the Pacific coast as in most of Central America, in Honduras the mountain zone forks into several separate, fingerlike ranges. The mountain ranges are oriented northeast to southwest with significant river valleys between them and run nearly parallel to both oceans. These valley floors and adjacent coastal plains have rich deposits of fertile alluvium and have been the focus of pre-Columbian activities and habitation. Two of the most significant and productive valleys were the Ulua in western Honduras and the Aguan in eastern Honduras. In the far northeast lies the most extensive Caribbean lowland, La Mosquitia, which continues into Nicaragua. This zone, which is largely pine-covered, sandy-soil savanna, is one of the least known areas of all Central America and is not included in this paper (J. Parsons 1955).

The Ethnographic and Linguistic Mosaic

Like the rest of Central America, sixteenth-century Honduras had an exceedingly complex ethnographic and linguistic composition. Our understanding of this diversity has been hindered by the scarcity of ethnographic studies and by the rapid rate of extinction of many aboriginal groups. The ethnohistoric record is also very uneven and generally inadequate. Stone (1941, 1948, 1957, 1966b), in several major surveys, has identified the important early chroniclers and discussed the types of ethnohistoric information which are available for Honduras and the balance of Central America. Over the years there have been some attempts at the correlation of ethnographic and archaeological data (see Stone 1941, 1942a, 1942b, 1969b). More research along this line needs to be conducted.

Based upon these works plus those of Johnson (1948a, 1962), Mason (1962), and recent linguistic reviews by Campbell (1976, 1979), we can identify seven major native groups which were present in Honduras at the time of the conquest and their approximate spatial distribution.

(1) *Maya*. Part of the Macro-Mayan linguistic family. The Maya were located primarily in far western Honduras. Some debate has taken place over which Maya dialect was originally spoken but Campbell (1976: 176)

argues that Copan was probably settled by Cholan-speakers (see Lothrop 1939; Longyear 1947; Thompson 1970: 84–102). Mesoamerican-affiliated group.

(2) *Jicaque*. The linguistic family probably is Hokan (Campbell 1976: 162). Distribution appears to cover much of northern Honduras, ranging from the Ulua-Sula zone eastward to Colon. Campbell (1976: 164) saw a coastal origin and spread but interior movement, to Yoro, after the Spanish conquest. Mesoamerican-affiliated group.

(3) *Lenca*. The linguistic family is Lencan (Campbell 1976: 164–66). Distribution is from eastern El Salvador and into southern central Honduras, such as the Departments of Lempira, Intibuca, La Paz, Comayagua, Francisco Morazan, and even Choluteca. Mesoamerican-affiliated group.

(4) *Pipil*. This Uto-Aztecan group of Nahua speakers was found in scattered pockets and larger regions throughout lower Central America, including Honduras (Stone 1969b; Reyes 1974; Campbell 1976: 172). At least two significant enclaves are known from contact-period descriptions in Honduras; the site of Naco in northwest Honduras and the sites of Papayeca and Chapagua in northeast Honduras (Stone 1941: 15–16; Healy 1976a; Henderson 1977b). The general belief is that these are late Central Mexican intrusions established principally for trading purposes. Mesoamerican-affiliated group.

(5) *Mangue*. Also called Chorotega-Mangue, this group belongs to the Oto-Manguean language family. It is found principally in south Pacific Honduras and the Gulf of Fonseca region (Chapman 1960; Healy 1976c; Martinez 1979). Some archaeological evidence of a fairly late (ca. 800 A.D.) movement into lower Central America (Healy 1980: 335–37). Mesoamerican-affiliated group.

(6) *Paya*. This group is part of the Chibchan family. Although traditionally linguists have expressed some uncertainty over the affinity of the Paya language, most recent studies show it to be Chibchan derived (Holt 1975; Campbell 1976: 157; Holt and Bright 1976). Precise distribution of this group remains unclear but apparently it was centered along the coast and in northeast Honduras, including the Departments of Colon, Gracias a Dios, and the Bay Islands of Honduras. South American–affiliated group.

(7) *Ulva*. Ulva is part of the Matagalpan linguistic family. Only limited information is available on this group, which is found in eastern El Salvador, northwest Nicaragua, and southern Honduras. The only information is linguistic (Lehmann 1920; Johnson 1948a: 59–61; Stone 1957: 77, 83–84). South American–affiliated group.

It is worth emphasizing that the native linguistic groups of Honduras manifest a distinct, marked division into Mesoamerican or South American origin (cf. Holt and Bright 1976: table 1). Judging from the linguistic evidence, the southern frontier of Mesoamerica cuts across Honduras, reaffirming the archaeological pattern for this area.

The Archaeological Regions

Honduras has six different regions defined primarily in terms of previous archaeological work, not of any particular linguistic or ethnographic boundaries. The divisions are the Far West region, the Ulua-Chamelecon-Sula region, the Lake Yojoa region, the Central region, the Southern Pacific region, and the Northeast region. Unfortunately, these units are not contiguous or of the same approximate size, nor are they evenly distributed. They do, as a rule, form unique and rather coherent geographic units. One unfortunate consequence of the process of selection for inclusion here is that vast areas of eastern, central, and northern Honduras must, by necessity, remain outside our review.[3]

Nevertheless, it is possible to extract a skeletonized time-space framework and, in a few instances, to go beyond and deal with many of the processual matters of these six better-studied regions. To do so, we look briefly at the physical settings, provide an abbreviated outline of research history in each region, and then highlight the archaeology, period by period, discussing significant research, sites, artifactual complexes, cultural changes, and problems.

Far West Region

This region falls squarely within the Mesoamerican culture area and the Maya lowlands subarea (Willey 1966: 88). Consequently, it is not within the direct scope of our review, and its inclusion is only indirectly germane to a discussion of lower Central America proper. However, because of the complete archaeological picture available on this western peripheral zone, it is extremely useful to refer to its culture history. Furthermore, because of the prehistoric cultural influences that this region apparently exerted on other parts of Honduras, it must be included for comparative purposes. More complete treatment of this region can be found in Longyear (1952) and Robicsek (1972).

The archaeology of the Far West region centers upon the Departments of Copan and Santa Barbara and, in particular, upon the impressive ruins of Copan.[4] This major Mayan ceremonial center, situated in the Copan River Valley among the mountains of the Sierra de Merendon, is located just east of the Guatemalan border. The Copan River is a branch of the larger Motagua in Guatemala, and Maya groups along both waterways were clearly in communication and interacted closely with one another (Sharer 1980). At 600 meters above sea level Copan is at a much higher elevation than that generally preferred by the Classic Maya. The valley floor is fairly flat, about 13 kilometers long and 2.5 kilometers wide. It is surrounded by steep, forested hills, a few of which contain caves of considerable archaeological significance. The flora and fauna are rich, a condition which probably existed throughout the pre-Columbian period. The soils and level terrain are quite good for cultivation.

Archaeology in this region has been extensive, dating well into the nineteenth century (Galindo 1836; Stephens 1841; Gordon 1896, 1898a, 1898b). Copan, as a premier Classic Maya center, has drawn archaeologists who have studied the site's hieroglyphics (Gordon 1902; Morley 1920), ceramics (Longyear 1952), sculpture and architecture (Rands 1969; Robicsek 1972), archaeoastronomy (Aveni and Hartung 1976) and, most recently, its settlement pattern (Willey, Leventhal, and Fash 1978; Willey and Leventhal 1979).

Lake Yojoa Region

Another very significant archaeological zone in western Honduras is the area about Lake Yojoa, situated between the Ulua-Chamelecon-Sula region and the Comayagua region. Lake Yojoa, the only sizable lake in Honduras, lies in a small mountain valley, 600 meters above sea level. It measures about 22 kilometers long and 14 kilometers wide. The lake water is clear and potable.

Northeast of the lake the land is marked by a pine forest and rolling hills. The remainder of the region is covered by a rain forest and high mountains with the exception of the southern end of the region, which is wetter and swampy in the rainy season. The flora and fauna are plentiful and diverse, not unlike those of the Copan Valley, but with the added advantage of the lacustrine resources.

This region was first surveyed by Squier (1858, 1870) and later by Stone (1934a, 1962b), Yde (1938: 27–40), and Strong, Kidder, and Paul (1938). This last publication, although designated a preliminary report, served as a benchmark for many years. The most recent work, carried out between 1967 and 1969, was done by Baudez and Becquelin (1969, 1973), particularly at the lakeshore site of Los Naranjos. It is one of the few detailed reports published for Honduras in recent years, and its direction, not surprisingly, is fundamentally chronological.

Ulua-Chamelecon-Sula Region

This is an extremely rich region of northwest Honduras also termed the "Ulua-Chamelecon drainage" (Strong, Kidder, and Paul 1938: 3). Indeed, the Ulua and Chamelecon river valleys, with their origins in the interior mountains of western and central Honduras respectively, join to become the massive, flat Sula Plain, 125 kilometers long by 45 kilometers wide, one of the richest agricultural zones of Central America. The two rivers meander across this broad coastal valley forming ox-bow lakes, natural levees, and marshes.

The soil in the plain is replenished nearly yearly with rich earth from the interior hills brought down by flooding rivers. This has not only made the Sula Plain an exceedingly fertile zone but has also buried prehistoric sites under meters of alluvium. The valley was originally covered by a rich tropical rain forest with mangrove zones near the coast, and Gordon (1898a: 5) described it as "deep bottomlands, very rich and covered in luxuriant vegetation." Rainfall, especially from the seasonal *nortes*, is plentiful and brings on the overflows and inundations. When the Spanish reached Sula in the sixteenth century, they found the lands heavily cultivated, with large, dense populations clustered in several major centers (Gordon 1898a: 34–35).

Archaeologically, the region has a long history of investigation dating again to Gordon's nineteenth-century efforts (Gordon 1898a). Blackiston (1910), Steinmayer (1932), and Popenoe (1934) also surveyed this region and published brief reports. The first major account was that of Strong, Kidder, and Paul (1938) and, for the northern zone, Stone (1941). The most recent work here has been by Henderson (1976, 1977a; Henderson et al. 1979) focusing upon the Naco Valley, an offshoot of the Chamelecon.

Central Honduras Region

The central highlands of Honduras are cut by a major fault zone running north to south (Canby 1949: 10). Within this zone lies the Comayagua Valley, a sizable highland depression that creates an important pass connecting the Ulua Valley to the north with the Gulf of Fonseca to the south (Stone 1957: 6).[5] The Comayagua forms a fourth major archaeological region and is made up of a series of environmental zones, including tropical forest in the lower portion of the plain and slopes of the surrounding hills, with oak and pine forests in the drier upland parts. The Humuya River, a branch of the Ulua, runs through the Comayagua Valley and serves as the main water supply. In some zones of the Comayagua depression, extensive savannas have evolved with near·xerophytic vegetation present (Yde 1938: 11–14). That such flat, level farm lands did not go unrecognized by the native populations of Honduras is evident from the many mounds and pyramid structures which cover the valley floor (Stone 1957: 9). At the time of the Spanish Conquest, the plain was touted as being the richest and best in all Honduras because of its abundance of flora, fauna, and pleasant upland climate (Stone 1957: 8). Although it is not clear what language was spoken in this region, Stone (1957: 9) believes that it probably was Lenca or a dialect of Lenca.

During the mid-nineteenth century, Squier (1853b, 1855, 1858) made some of the earliest published observations on this region. His excavations and survey work were limited, however, to the largest hilltop redoubts, such as Tenampua. In 1917, Lothrop mapped this same fortified site. The map was finally published by Stone (1957: fig. 3) with updated information. Tenampua was later examined and excavated by Popenoe in 1927. Yde described the Comayagua Valley in his report on northwestern Honduras, incorporating much of Squier's earlier archaeological information, including a detail furnished by Lothrop regarding a marble vessel from Yarumela (Yde 1938: 14–15). The first stratigraphic work in the valley was done by Canby (1949, 1951) at this site. In the 1950s, Stone published a major monograph, *The Archaeology of Central and Southern Honduras* (1957), which dealt with many of the previously described sites but in greater detail. She also discussed and illustrated, often for the first time, the artifacts characteristic of the region. The most recent work, still incompletely published, has been the 1964–65 survey and excavations by Baudez (1966) at the site of Lo de Vaca and various rock art analyses (Reyes 1976c, 1976d, 1977; Agurcia 1976).[6]

Southern Pacific Region

This region is located at the southernmost edge of Honduras, bordering the island-dotted Gulf of Fonseca, and includes the Departments of Nacaome and Choluteca (Stone 1957: 100–102; Baudez 1976a: 15). Several large and small rivers, such as the Goascoran, Nacaome, Choluteca, and Sampile, empty their waters into this gulf, but the coastal zones are swampy and mangrove-lined and are not particularly fertile. Baudez (1973, 1976a) noted a number of camp sites and some salt-making locales. Away from the coast are valley zones with richer soils and somewhat more abundant vegetation.

The Southern Pacific region is generally associated with two native groups: the Mangue and the Ulva, although there is some evidence of Lenca incursions by the time of the Spanish arrival (Stone 1957: 10). Aside from brief remarks on the archaeology by Lunardi (1945), Stone's survey (1957) has served as the principal source of information, including brief descriptions of ethnohistory, linguistics, and sites of this region. Archaeological work in 1964–65, again by Baudez (1966, 1976a), has provided the first chronological framework for the region. However, except for the pair of brief papers, no detailed report has appeared.

Northeast Region

This archaeological region includes the Departments of Colon and Islas de la Bahia.[7] Future investigation will probably reveal enough similarities to expand the region to include much of the interior Department of Olancho, the easternmost Department of Gracias a Dios, and perhaps the eastern edge of the Department of Atlantida. However, recent work has focused almost exclusively on the larger Bay Islands and the Aguan Valley of Colon.

The main portion of this region is composed of the Honduras north coast, its east-west mountain ranges close to the sea, and intervening river valleys.

The ranges catch moisture and support a heavy tropical vegetation, but otherwise the coast is largely covered by tropical forest, some savannas, and mangrove. Rich alluvial zones are present in the lowland river valleys, such as the Aguan, Sico, and Paulaya, the last two of which merge into the Black River. These valleys receive rich deposits from surrounding interior mountains and are superior areas for farming. Lopez Velasco, in an early account, described the Aguan Valley as a place where food supplies were abundant, with plentiful fruit, wildfowl, game, and fish (Lopez Velasco 1899, in Johannessen 1963). Prehistoric exploitation of the rich resources of the coastal lagoons is in evidence, as exemplified at the larger Guaimoretta Lagoon near Trujillo (Healy 1978b, 1983).

The Bay Islands lie just 21 kilometers off the north coast of mainland Honduras and are a significant part of this archaeological region. The chain of islets is made up of three large islands (Utila, Roatan, and Guanaja or Bonacca) and many smaller islands and cays. Although covering only 238 square kilometers, they are spread in an arc across 777 square kilometers of ocean (Davidson 1974: 5), and are low in elevation, not exceeding 425 meters above sea level. Mangrove and swampy zones are found on all the bigger islands, which are divided by deep sloping valleys with some small streams providing fresh water. Each island has a few flat, open areas. Coral reefs surround the islands and provide great quantities of seafood. Fish and molluscs were, not surprisingly, very significant paleonutritional factors. The climate and fauna are basically like those of the adjacent mainland, although some pine grows on higher parts of the islands, with rain-forest vegetation and savannas in lower zones.

Early investigations of the Honduran north coast, which included observations on the archaeology, were made by Spinden (1925) and Conzemius (1928). The area was explored by Bird, by Stone (1934b), and later by Strong (1934a, 1934b), who concentrated upon the Bay Islands (1935). Stone's (1941) descriptive monograph, *Archaeology of the North Coast of Honduras*, provided the first detailed overview of the region, as well as of some zones of the north coast, farther west. The first chronological sequence was established by Epstein (1957), using ceramics from both the mainland and the Bay Islands. In the 1970s work in the region was intensified, both on the mainland (cf. Healy 1973, 1974a, 1975, 1978a, 1978c; Veliz 1978b) and on the adjacent islands (Davidson 1975; Goodwin 1975; Veliz, Healy, and Willey, 1976; Hasemann 1977; Epstein and Veliz 1977).

Honduran Chronology

The archaeology and prehistory of Honduras can, for the sake of simplicity, be divided into the six broad chronological units established at the seminar (fig. 1.2), and labeled hereafter Periods I–VI. These unequal blocks of time have approximate but fixed dates, and they cross-cut the regional

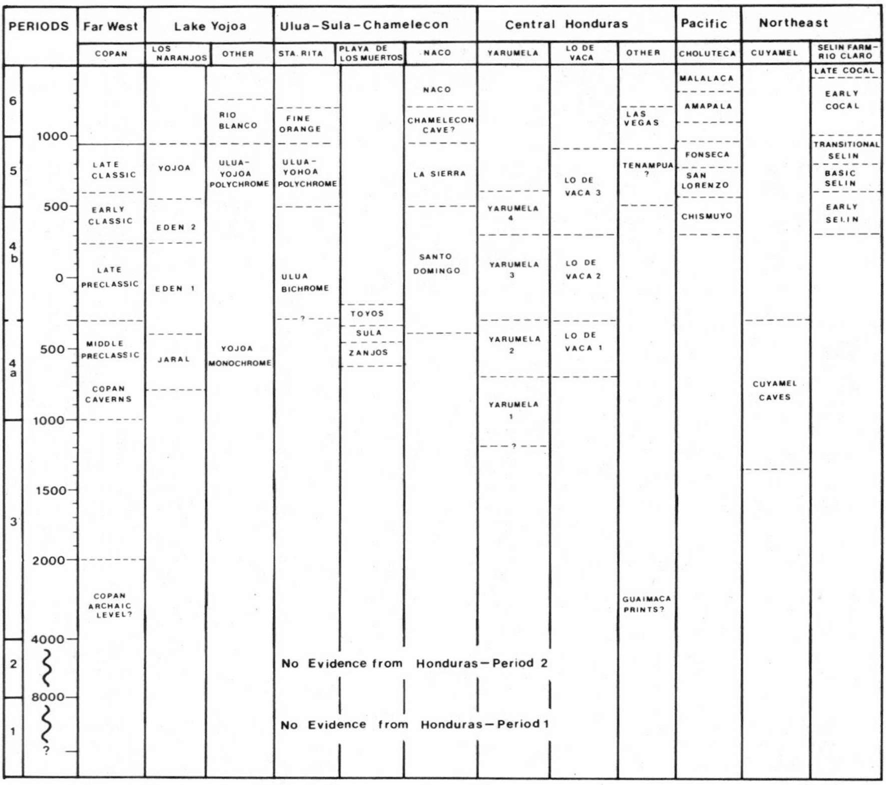

PERIODS	Far West	Lake Yojoa		Ulua–Sula–Chamelecon			Central Honduras			Pacific	Northeast	
	COPAN	LOS NARANJOS	OTHER	STA. RITA	PLAYA DE LOS MUERTOS	NACO	YARUMELA	LO DE VACA	OTHER	CHOLUTECA	CUYAMEL	SELIN FARM– RIO CLARO

Figure 6.2.   Chronological chart of Honduras periods and phases.

and local Honduras sequences established by various researchers (fig. 6.2).

Evidence from the three earliest periods ranges from skimpy to virtually nonexistent. By Period IV, however, our information begins to improve, though varying from region to region. About this same time, with the use of occasional radiocarbon determinations and, more frequently, the utilization of trade wares from better documented areas, it is possible to begin to see clear patterns of cultural evolution.

Period I (?–8000 B.C.) and
Period II (8000–4000 B.C.)

The entire question of the first arrival of man in the New World in general, and in lower Central America in particular, is widely debated

(MacNeish 1976; Bryan 1978). Although the highland zones of Guatemala (Coe 1960b; Gruhn and Bryan 1977) and neighboring countries to the south of Honduras, such as Costa Rica (Swauger and Mayer-Oakes 1952; Snarskis 1979b), Panama (Sander 1959; Bird and Cooke 1977, 1978b), and possibly Nicaragua (Espinoza 1976; Gruhn 1978), have now produced archaeological evidence of early man, no positive evidence of this early period has been found in Honduras. Similarly, there is no evidence of the early lithic development noted by Ranere (Ranere and Hansell 1978; Ranere 1980b, 1980c, 1980d, 1980e) from Panama between 5000 and 3000 B.C.

Period III (4000–1000 B.C.)

Almost equally lacking is evidence for Period III. This was primarily a late Archaic period, and three sites that have had some preliminary investigation may possibly be representative, although secure dating remains problematical. So little is known about this period that even equivocal evidence deserves comment.

The first locality, near La Esperanza in the Department of Intibuca, has 10 different small sites located at an elevation between 1,500 and 1,800 meters. These sites revealed strictly nonceramic artifactual remains. They are all located in a rough, mountainous region and were examined in 1962 by Bullen and Plowden (1963, 1964). These localities produced only lithic remains, including two points with fluted stems, a short, crude broad-stemmed point, and various small-to-medium-sized side-scrapers. Most of the lithics were of obsidian, and a possible obsidian source near La Esperanza has been mentioned (Lunardi 1948; Sidrys, Andressen, and Marcucci 1976). Bullen and Plowden (1964: 563–64) noted that the area has other sites with ceramics, but at least 10 sites they visited were unquestionably lithic only, hinting at a preceramic dating. The two fluted points suggest the possibility of a Paleo-Indian date, but the authors argued that the absence of a true Clovis point and the general form (large and stemmed) suggested an early Archaic date as more likely. The side-scrapers, they noted, could be either Archaic or Paleo-Indian.

The second possibility is the site of Guaimaca in the Department of Francisco Morazan about 60 kilometers north of Tegucigalpa. Here Veliz (1978a) has recorded the presence of a brief series of bare human footprints imbedded in stone. The site lacks any other cultural materials but is reminiscent of footprints found earlier in Nicaragua (Flint 1884; Richardson 1941; Williams 1952; Bryan 1973). Until the geology of Guaimaca is studied in more detail, or until some associated archaeological remains are unearthed, it is not possible to be sure if the Honduran footprints are of great antiquity. Similar prints are also known from El Salvador (Haberland and Grebe 1957).

Copan is the third site in Honduras that has produced probable Archaic remains. About half a meter below the lowest ceramic levels of the site, excavations produced a nearly horizontal layer of lithic artifacts, along with charcoal, charred nuts, and some broken and charred animal bones (Longyear 1948: 248–49). These are almost certainly Archaic, but the excavations, carried out in 1946, kept no charcoal for dating purposes. The lithic materials were only briefly reported and are mainly small-to-medium-sized chips and flakes of flint and obsidian that have some edge chipping. Although these excavations were very limited, they provide the most secure evidence of a Period III habitation within Honduras.

Period IV (1000 B.C.–A.D. 500)

Period IV in Honduras is divided into two parts: Period IVa runs from 1000 B.C. to 300 B.C., and Period IVb from 300 B.C. to A.D. 500. The first well-dated evidence of human occupation in Honduras falls in Period IVa. Sites dating to this period are found widely and are approximately coeval with the Mesoamerican Early and Middle Preclassic periods.

Some of the most complete archaeological evidence for Period IV comes from the Lake Yojoa region. Detailed excavations at the site of Los Naranjos on the north shore of this large lake have revealed signs of a fairly complex society functioning as early as the Jaral (800–400 B.C.) phase (Baudez and Becquelin 1973: 407–11). Los Naranjos at that time appears to have been marked by a sizable ditch, about 1,300 meters long, 15–20 meters wide, and 7 meters deep, which Baudez (1970: 37) interpreted as an early fortification. However, there is no clear indication of whom the early inhabitants of Los Naranjos feared, nor just why defenses were needed. There is also a rather impressive 6-meter-tall platform containing an elite burial with finely made jade ornaments and a few other interments, including a jade axe offering covered with cinnabar (Baudez and Becquelin 1973: 89, figs. 17b, 145a and b).

Baudez and Becquelin (1973: 89) have commented upon the Los Naranjos resemblances to approximately coeval burial practices at the Olmec site of La Venta on the Mexican Gulf coast. Similarly, some stone sculptures from Los Naranjos, which unfortunately lack secure stratigraphic provenience, have been dated on a stylistic basis to the Jaral phase (Baudez 1976b: 134) and labeled Olmecoid (Baudez 1971: 79; Stone 1972: 41, 53).

The ceramics of Jaral date are commonly jars with vertical necks and flat-bottomed bowls with wide-flaring sides and horizontally everted rims. Decoration is characterized mainly by deeply incised designs and by types of zoned decoration typical of many regions of Mesoamerica proper at this time. Baudez and Becquelin (1976: 7) see some Olmec design elements present in Jaral ceramics (Baudez and Becquelin 1976: 5). In general, the pottery is similar to Yojoa Monochrome (Strong, Kidder, and Paul 1938).

In the Ulua-Chamelecon-Sula region, the earliest remains are found at the famed site of Playa de los Muertos, first explored by Gordon (1898a) and later by Popenoe (1934) and by Strong, Kidder, and Paul (1938). This important site lies about 60 kilometers south of the north coast on the Ulua River, several kilometers downstream from the juncture of the Humaya and Ulua rivers (N. Kennedy 1978: 203). Because the Ulua meanders, substantial portions of the site have been washed away, and recent salvage excavations have been carried out by N. Kennedy (1980, 1981).

Earlier researchers divided the Playa de los Muertos ceramics into two separate periods or horizons (Strong 1948: 96; Stone 1972: 57). More recent investigations have shown clear evidence of three superimposed living floors and deposits, with cultural debris below the lowermost level suggesting at least four occupations (N. Kennedy 1978: 204–5). Today no mounds are visible at the site except for traces of wattle-and-daub briquets, and these house floors reveal that the Playa de los Muertos settlers lived in perishable pole-and-thatch-roofed structures. These settlers were almost certainly agriculturalists. Perhaps the most interesting aspect of the site is the burial of their dead in cemetery-like settings. Rich mortuary offerings again, as they do at Los Naranjos, suggest an advanced stratified society.

The Playa de los Muertos lithic artifacts are diverse. Jade was important, and carved jade axe gods are known from the site. Effigy vessels, spouted shoe-shaped vessels, and both solid and hollow pottery figurines were also found. Agurcia (1978) analyzed more than 100 Playa de los Muertos figurines and commented upon their remarkable range of variation, individuality, and high level of craft specialization (figs. 6.3, 6.4). The figurine decorative traits and the representations of jewelry and elaborate hairstyles all suggest marked social differentiation and provide some suggestions, at least, of the level of affluence in this ancient Honduran society.

N. Kennedy (1980: 2–8) has identified and tentatively dated three phases from Playa de los Muertos: Zanjos (650–450 B.C.), Sula (450–300 B.C.), and Toyos (350–200 B.C.). The earliest phase appears related to the Jaral Complex of Los Naranjos, and Kennedy sees the phase as belonging to a pre-Mayan tradition. Interestingly, some Olmec harpy-eagle designs occur in the Playa collections, as do double-line break motifs.

This important Ulua Valley site appears to have spanned a large portion of the Middle and Late Preclassic period. Agurcia (1978) considers the solid Playa de los Muertos figurines as basically Middle Preclassic, and Baudez and Becquelin (1973: 407–9) see Playa ceramics as Middle to Late Preclassic. It now seems probable that Playa de los Muertos had its beginnings in at least the Middle Preclassic and continued until a century or two before the time of Christ. The loss of so much of this important early site is one of the tragedies of Honduran archaeology.

Two sites in the Central region have early archaeological remains—

Figure 6.3. Hand-modeled figurine fragment from Playa de los Muertos, Honduras (Peabody Museum, Harvard University, photographed by Hillel Burger).

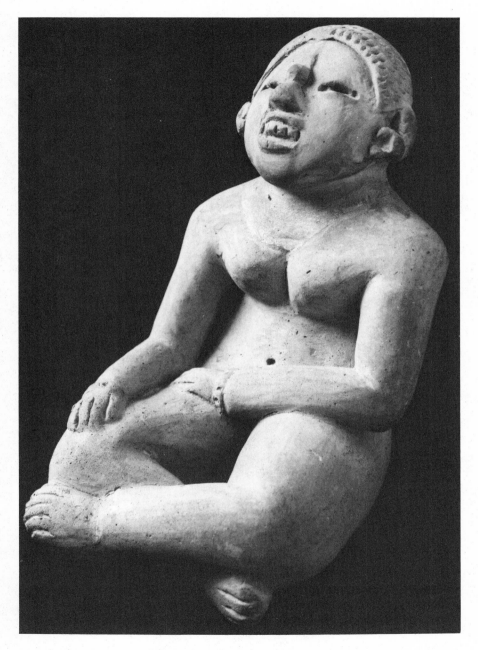

Figure 6.4. Hand-modeled figurine from Playa de los Muertos, Honduras (Peabody Museum, Harvard University, photographed by Hillel Burger).

Yarumela and Lo de Vaca. Both localities show that the Comayagua Valley has been a significant spot for settlement since Formative times and has probably always supported a substantial population. This early prominence may be a result of more than simply good farming lands, as the valley is located near the center of a transcontinental pass linking the Pacific coast with the Atlantic-Caribbean coast (Stone 1972: 38).

Yarumela, explored by Canby (1949), is located in the central part of the Comayagua Valley along the Humuya River, a tributary of the Ulua. It is marked by a series of rubble mounds, the largest of which measures about 20 meters tall. The site covers more than a square kilometer, and Canby (1951: 79) notes that it is visible from virtually any spot on the valley floor. He has delineated several periods that are clearly assignable to the Formative, with the Yarumela I and II periods falling primarily into Period IVa, and the Yarumela III (Archaic) period falling into Period IVb.

There are some decorative similarities between Yarumela I ceramics and the Tok Ceramic Complex of Chalchuapa—monochrome decoration, rim incising, and red-rim decoration—and between Yarumela II bichromes and Chalchuapa's succeeding Tok and Colos complexes. Stone (1972: 38) views Yarumela I as a contemporary of Ocos and Chiapa I–Cotorra (i.e., Early Preclassic).

Certainly these two very early ceramic units (monochrome and bichrome) at Yarumela can be clustered together by their lack of any ceramics with Usulatan decoration and by the absence of polychromes. The presence of Yarumela I bottle forms links the site to Cuyamel and the Copan Caverns (see below) and again places the first habitation as likely to have been in the Early Preclassic. The decorative techniques of pattern burnishing and reed impression link Yarumela II with the Yojoa Monochrome sites in the Lake Yojoa region, with early Playa de los Muertos levels, and with earliest components of nearby Lo de Vaca.

The most recent excavations in the Comayagua Valley have been carried out by Baudez in 1964–65 at Lo de Vaca, on the west bank of the Humuya and about 7 kilometers northwest of Yarumela (Baudez 1966). The site comprises two major groups of mounds, one to the northwest and one to the southeast, separated by about 100 meters, and each covering about 22,000 square meters.

The deepest excavation levels at Lo de Vaca revealed ceramics (Lo de Vaca I) that probably date to the later part of Period IVa. The pottery includes decorative techniques such as incised lines, pattern burnishing, impressions (shell impressed and rocker stamped), reed punctations, and bichrome pottery. Some specular hematite red slipping occurs, and white-slipped pottery not unike that of Yojoa Monochromes (Strong, Kidder, and Paul 1938: 113), Ulua Bichromes (Strong, Kidder, and Paul 1938: 62), and later Playa de los Muertos white-slipped wares (Strong, Kidder, and Paul 1938: 73) are also present.

The most recent, and some of the most tantalizing, information on the Honduran Formative comes from the Northeast region of Honduras. Here surveys have revealed a wide variety of Period IVa ceramics from cave sites in the Department of Colon. The limestone Cerro de Cuevas, located along the northern edge of the Aguan River Valley, is riddled with caverns and passageways. Three caves in particular, Matilde's Cave (H-CN-14), Cuyamel Cave (H-CN-15), and Cueva del Portillo (H-CN-16)—all grouped under the term Cuyamel Caves—were briefly surveyed by the author (Healy 1974a).

The cave entrances were all located near the summit of a 300-meter cliff face. All caves were multichambered, and, in some drier rooms, large quantities of human skeletons were scattered about. Associated with these ossuary-like burial remains were numerous whole vessels. These included flat-bottomed, flare-wall bowls; hour-glass, gourd-shaped jars; bird effigy forms; and a preponderance of monochrome spouted bottles (fig. 6.5). The rather striking similarities to ceramics from other Early Preclassic sites of southern Mesoamerica have been noted (Healy 1974a: 440).

There are further indications that the Cuyamel Caves continued to be utilized into the Middle Preclassic. Some Cuyamel-derived ceramics in the Instituto Hondureño de Antropologia e Historia collection in Tegucigalpa have bichrome and zoned bichrome decoration (Healy 1974a: fig. 4; Reyes and Veliz 1974: figs. 15–16). A pair of sphinx-like animal figures with humanoid faces (Healy 1974a: fig. 4), for instance, is very similar to the bulbous Playa de los Muertos hollow figurines of the Ulua Valley (Popenoe 1934: fig. 12; Porter 1953: plate 14). A marble-like bird effigy dish quite reminiscent of polished stone vessels from Kaminaljuyu and dating to the Miraflores phase (ca. 200 B.C.) was also recorded. The overall range of diversity in the Cuyamel materials and the fact that the caves are also known to have contained materials dating to the much later Selin and Cocal periods point to long-term usage beginning with the Early and Middle Preclassic.

The most interesting aspect of the Cuyamel pottery is the possible link to the Olmec culture of the Gulf Coast of Mexico. A finely made black polished and carved cylinder vessel from Cuyamel, with an Olmecoid design, has already been described (Healy 1974a: 440, fig. 4e, 1974c). In Trujillo in 1976, the author saw a private collection of pre-Columbian ceramics reported from the Cuyamel Caves. These included several more Early Preclassic bottle-shaped vessels and another black cylinder vessel which was heavily encrusted with calcium carbonate but with an Olmecoid motif still recognizable (fig. 6.6). Some of the bottle-shaped Cuyamel ceramics are very similar to Bajio-phase (ca. 1350 B.C.) pottery from the Olmec site of San Lorenzo in Mexico (Coe and Diehl 1980: vol. 1, 143–50).

No habitation sites of the Cuyamel period were identified in a 1973–76 site survey. All we can say at this time is that the caves appear to have been sacred areas for ritual disposal of the dead (both primary and secondary

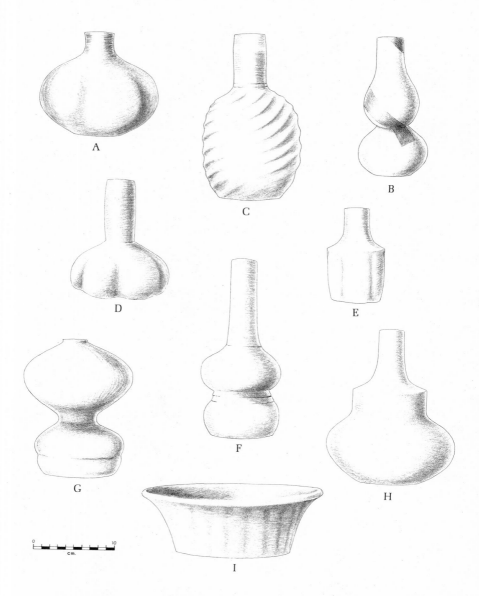

Figure 6.5. Preclassic vessels from the Cuyamel Caves, northeast Honduras (Healy 1974a: fig. 3).

Figure 6.6. Olmecoid vessels from the Cuyamel Caves, northeast Honduras (top, Instituto Hondureño de Antropologia e Historia collection in Tegucigalpa; bottom, private collection, Trujillo).

burials) and that during Period IVa northeast Honduras was in contact with southern Mesoamerican groups, including the Olmec. The similarity of ceramic forms and decorations suggests a significant connection at this stage.

Although the Far West region lies outside (*sensu strictu*) the primary area of concern for this chapter, it should be noted briefly that a group of only cursorily known ceramics from caverns above the Copan Valley also dates to this period (Gordon 1898b). In 1896 and 1897, five separate caves located in the Cerro Maria were visited by Gordon. The caves were about seven kilometers northwest of the main Maya ceremonial center of Copan, in a limestone ridge above the Sesemil Stream. The third cave described by Gordon (1898b: 5–7, plate 1) is particularly interesting in that it was composed of a series of very dry, naturally vaulted chambers which were littered with partly cremated human bones, mixed with ash and lime. Around the wall of this burial chamber Gordon found a series of small bottle vessels strikingly like those from the Cuyamel Caves of the Northeast region (Healy 1974a). Unfortunately, as in the case of Cuyamel, the location of and difficulty of access to these early caves at Copan has made systematic investigation virtually impossible. Longyear (1952) has reported on what are apparently Middle and Late Preclassic ceramics (what he termed Archaic) at the ceremonial center of Copan, beginning the lengthy sequence at that site which culminates in the tenth century A.D.

In sum, these early and usually modest-sized Honduras sites are marked by very similar ceramics, mostly plain, unslipped, and undecorated, but some with quite fancy zoned, incised, and plastic decoration. Generally speaking, the pottery across Honduras at this time conforms closely to the southern Mesoamerican ceramic tradition, and there is significant uniformity. Lithics were well developed, and people were utilizing imported, exotic minerals such as obsidian and jade.

The widespread presence of polished stone axes suggests clearing for agriculture. Although direct evidence for farming is scanty, the frequent location of Period IVa sites in rich river valleys well suited to agriculture and the substantial size of a few of these locales point strongly to a farming subsistence base. Thus, varying-sized sedentary farming villages existed by about 1000 B.C.

Burials at some Period IVa sites include the use of ritualized cave ossuaries, while at others there is evidence of cemeteries and special elite burials complete with jade jewelry and some Olmecoid funerary traits. Such grave offerings, along with individualized pottery figurines, indicate social stratification. Certainly the size of many earthen constructions shows the ability of the village elite to marshal the population for fairly large-scale public works. We may already be dealing with sites functioning as regional centers in a growing site and social hierarchy. Indeed, the suggestions of Olmec contact at this time—and there are several intriguing hints—may also imply something about socio-political development in Honduras. Some principal Period IVa sites must have had a significant minimal level of stratification to have appreciated contacts with such a complex, precocious Mesoamerican culture (Flannery 1968).

The question of the role of warfare as a triggering mechanism at this time needs further investigation. The data from the Lake Yojoa region suggest strongly that this early period may not have been uniformly tranquil and that disruption and conflict could have been responsible for the power concentrations recognized at several regional central places like Los Naranjos or Yarumela. We also know that long-distance trade was being managed and directed on a substantial scale by this era, and this could be another important factor in explaining the evolutionary course we recognize. Overall, Honduras is more cohesive as a singular subarea and more Mesoamerican in Period IVa than ever again in its evolution.

Period IVb (300 B.C.–A.D. 500) corresponds approximately to the Late Preclassic and Early Classic periods of Mesoamerica. It shows general continuity and evolution from Period IVa but with some evident changes in cultural complexity. Technological development is indicated along with population increase and site multiplication. One general unifying trait of Period IVb is the introduction and spread of the distinctive Usulutan decorated pottery over a wide area of western, central, and southern Honduras. The absence of Usulutan wares in northeast Honduras at this time probably signals this region's growing peripheral nature.

In the Lake Yojoa region, the Jaral phase is succeeded by the Eden (400 B.C.–A.D. 550) phase at Los Naranjos. It is a time marked by major building activity, and Baudez and Becquelin (1973: 417–19) have shown that some of the largest structures in the main group of seven pyramids date mainly to the Eden phase. Structure I, for instance, was then a stepped pyramid more than 18 meters tall, while Structure IV, a very large stepped pyramid topped by a rectangular plaza group, was built at this time and maintained (Baudez 1970: 65). The Eden-phase architecture at Los Naranjos is principally earthen in composition, except for the ramps, retaining walls of the steps, and structural exterior, which were made of undressed limestone blocks mortared with clay.

A second, larger ditch was also built during the Eden phase. This one was some 5 kilometers long, 4 meters deep, and 8–15 meters wide, with an earth embankment 2 meters tall along the southwestern edge. The new (defensive?) ditch now enclosed not only the main structures at Los Naranjos, but a great deal of surrounding fertile farmland as well (Baudez 1970: 65).

The artifacts of Eden times include metates, hinting at agricultural activities, while the ceramics show many forms continuing from the earlier Jaral phase. Some additions to the vessel form inventory include bowls with reinforced rims or with flaring sides, cylinder-like bowls, mammiform feet, and annular bases. Tripod *incensarios* appear and are similar to those known from Playa de los Muertos. Decorative techniques included the use of negative painting. Indeed, Baudez and Becquelin (1976: 7) saw Usulutan decoration as a major trait of the Eden phase at Los Naranjos.

The Eden phase has been divided into two facets—Eden I, which has some Jaral ceramic types continuing plus Usulutan decoration, and Eden II, marked by new ceramic types often with mammiform supports, horizontal grooves, Z-angle forms, rocker stamping, and bichrome and trichrome painting in zones. Eden I, then, is roughly comparable to the Late Preclassic, and Eden II is comparable to the Early Classic of Mesoamerica and the Far West region. Three C^{14} dates are available (appendix 2).

At the Ulua Valley site of Santa Rita in the Ulua-Chamelecon-Sula region, Strong, Kidder, and Paul (1938) identified a ceramic complex referred to as the Ulua Bichrome horizon. This collection of monochrome and bichrome pottery was found stratigraphically below polychrome-bearing levels, separated by a sterile sand layer (Strong, Kidder, and Paul 1938: fig. 6). The pottery is often flat-bottomed bowls with small, solid tripod and tetrapod feet. Strong (1948: 93) described one major Ulua Bichrome ceramic type as an orange-slipped Usulutan pottery. Baudez and Becquelin (1973: 408) see the Ulua Bichrome as probably chronologically between Eden I and II of Los Naranjos.

From Playa de los Muertos, N. Kennedy (1980: 2–8) has defined a Sula phase, with ceramics having marked similarities to Eden I–phase pottery of Los Naranjos, as well as Kal and Colos ceramics from Chalchuapa (Sharer 1978a). In this regard, N. Kennedy sees Playa de los Muertos being linked as much to the southeastern highlands as to the Isthmian zone of Mesoamerica. In the succeeding Toyos phase at Playa de los Muertos, the pottery recalls Middle and Late Preclassic ceramics of both the southeastern highlands and the Maya lowlands.

More recently, Henderson and colleagues (1979: 187) have reported ceramic complexes dating to Period IVb at Naco and at the site of Santo Domingo in the Naco Valley near the Chamelecon River. At Santo Domingo, there are more than three dozen structures ranging from small platforms less than a meter tall to structures six meters tall (fig. 6.7). The mounds and the site layout follow natural contours, and construction is entirely of river cobbles; no dressed stone architecture was noted. Bowls with thickened rims are common, as are vessels with Usulutan-style parallel-line decoration. The Period IVb materials from nearby Naco are similar and show that this site had a long history of occupation.

In the Central region, Period IVb is well represented by what Canby terms Yarumela III (Archaic). In fact, the majority of trenches at Yarumela revealed Usulutan ceramics, often with tetrapod feet, in the uppermost strata

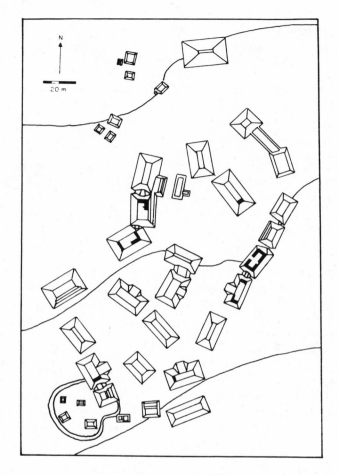

Figure 6.7. Map of Santo Domingo, a Period IVb site in northwest Honduras (Henderson et al. 1979: fig. 17).

(Canby 1949: 183). Canby (1951: 81–82) saw this Yarumela III as identical to the Ulua Bichrome phase at Santa Rita, farther down the Humuya River, in the Ulua Valley, and felt that it was equivalent to much of the Copan Archaic (Late Preclassic) and Kaminaljuyu's Miraflores phase (ca. 200 B.C.) on the basis of the presence of Usulutan ware with nipple feet. Most, and some of the largest, constructions at Yarumela (including mounds over 10 meters in height) appear to date from this period. These include large rectangular stepped platforms approached by stairs or ramps and aligned to cardinal points (Baudez 1970: 66). At nearby Lo de Vaca much the same pattern occurs.

The earliest evidence of any sort from the Southern Pacific region dates to terminal Period IVb. Baudez (1966, 1976a: 15) defined and dated a Chismuyo phase (A.D. 300–550) with one radiocarbon date (appendix 2). However, only three known sites belong to Chismuyo times. These are marked by oval-shaped earth mounds averaging about 20 meters across and 1 meter tall. The majority of these mounds cluster to form a rough circle.

As in other regions, ceramics of the Chismuyo phase include Usulutan decoration. Positive painted decoration is generally a bichrome with undulating lines applied with a multiple brush. Surface manipulation of pottery is quite variable (Baudez 1976a: 16).

In the Northeast region, there is a lengthy time gap between the earlier Cuyamel period (Period IVa) and the more firmly established Selin period (commencing ca. A.D. 300). We have no evidence of aboriginal habitation in this long intervening time span. The first part of the Selin period, called Early Selin (A.D. 300–600), falls within the last part of Period IVb and is marked by three C^{14} dates (appendix 2).

Early Selin remains are best known from site H-CN-5: Selin Farm, just north of Trujillo, Colon (Healy 1978a). The deepest deposits in several earthen and shell mounds revealed evidence of a farming and hunting-gathering culture. Mounds at the site include both residential house platforms and other mounds which probably were middens. Hardpacked house floors with burials beneath them have been identified.

Local pottery decoration includes zoning of different colored areas, and the painted area was sometimes zoned by incised lines or by simple painted borders. Spindle whorls suggest the use of cotton, and long, tubular jadeite beads are also characteristic.

A tripod slab-legged cylinder vessel from an Early Selin context resembles a form common in Mesoamerica during the Early–Middle Classic period and implies contact with external areas (Healy 1978a: 62). Curiously, no Usulutan pottery has been found in Northeast Honduras. Limited multiple brush painting does occur by the end of Early Selin times, but true negative painted ceramics have yet to be identified.

Manos and metates suggest corn-growing activities. Deep-sea fishing (jack, snook, snapper, and grouper), shellfish collecting, and the hunting of white-tail deer and manatee contributed to the diet of the Early Selin settlers at H-CN-5 (Healy 1978d, 1983). There are signs of expansion in later Selin times. Nevertheless, it appears that linkages between the artifactual complexes of the Northeast region and other parts of Honduras had lessened by Period IVb.

In the Northeast, almost from the beginning, there was less social stratification than elsewhere in Honduras. The mounds and structures known from most Selin-period sites were uniformly small and of roughly the same proportions. There was nothing developing here at this early date that can be compared to places like Los Naranjos or Yarumela. Obsidian, present and abundant nearly everywhere at this time, was rare in the Northeast. Additionally, there is a complete lack of a basic Period IVa time marker in the Northeast, as well as the absence of a significant Mesoamerican trade item, Usulutan pottery. Northeast Honduras by A.D. 300 appears to have developed along quite local, and not very Mesoamerican, lines. This trend of deviation from the Mesoamerican cultural pattern continues throughout the balance of the pre-Columbian era.

In sharp contrast to the Northeast region, the Far West region of Honduras shows signs of rapid population build-up in Period IVb. By A.D. 500, Copan is flourishing as a prominent Early Classic Maya center, a position which would be further enhanced in the succeeding period (Willey, Leventhal, and Fash 1978).

From about 300 B.C. to A.D. 500 we see a strong continuity in ceramics in most areas with the major change, and a useful archaeological marker, being the introduction of Usulutan ceramics. This also suggests increasing contacts between Honduras and El Salvador, where this technique appears first to have been developed (Demarest and Sharer 1980). There is a demonstrated increase in site density and, presumably, in the overall population, although we know virtually nothing about habitations in the Choluteca and the Northeast regions until after A.D. 300. Although there is no evidence of plastering or stucco work, some very large and elaborate mound constructions, with ramps and steps, were being erected in western and central Honduras. Indeed, at some sites, like Yarumela, the greatest amount of building occurred in Period IVb; more buildings were constructed, as well as the largest.

Period V (A.D. 500–1000)

In the Lake Yojoa region this was a time of expansion. Sites surrounding the lake were considerably larger now and marked by more mounds, and include La Ceiba and Los Naranjos (Strong, Kidder, and Paul 1938; Baudez and Becquelin 1973). At the latter site, Baudez and Becquelin (1976: 6) defined a Yojoa complex (A.D. 550–950) which closely corresponds to Period V. They also noted that at Los Naranjos the central group remained about the same, with only superficial changes, although the population reached its peak density. Much more building activity of better quality was carried out in the Yojoa phase, including the first use of stucco floors and stairs. Burials at this time were located in clear residential mounds and not within ceremonial structures.

The most distinctive artifactual changes of this period are again in the ceramics. A very large and varied class of polychrome pottery known as Ulua-Yojoa polychromes made its first appearance (Glass 1966: 164). This brilliantly decorated pottery group was concentrated in northwestern and central Honduras, with some traces also found in the Far West, Northeast, and Southern Pacific regions. In all instances it occurred on a basically Late Classic time horizon, although Baudez (1976b: 139) suggests that some elements of design and form were probably present as early as Tzakol II and III (Early Classic).

As Glass (1966: 164) has pointed out, despite the obvious significance of this ceramic group and the fact that Ulua-Yojoa polychromes have been identified and described in the literature for some time (Gordon 1898a; Yde 1938; Strong, Kidder, and Paul 1938; Stone 1941, 1957; Strong 1948), there is still no fully satisfactory typological classification of the group as a whole. Stone (1957, 1969a), Baudez and Becquelin (1973: 256–82, calling them Babilonia Polychromes), Viel (1978), and Wallace (1978) have all dealt with the polychromes recently; Glass's (1966: 164–74) survey in the *Handbook of Middle American Indians* is still one of the most significant reviews. Overall, the colors—black and red on orange—the decoration, and some of the basic forms of this ceramic complex—cylinders and hemispherical bowls—show clear connections with Classic Mayan polychromes (fig. 6.8).

In the 1950s, Longyear proved that the Ulua-Yojoa polychromes were Classic in date. A number of Ulua-Yojoa vessels were discovered in unquestionable Late (Full) Classic tombs at Copan and have been found in refuse deposits of the same date (Longyear 1952: 75). Glass (1966: 164) estimated that the Honduran polychromes are probably equivalent to Tepeu I and II. Indeed, distinctive Copador ware shows up in some Yojoa-phase deposits and is dated to Tepeu times at Copan. Epstein (1959) and Healy (1978a: fig. 5) have both reported Ulua-Yojoa sherds in the Northeast region, particularly from Basic Selin (A.D. 600–800) contexts. It is absent from Cocal (Postclassic) period deposits there. Other examples of this distinctive polychrome class have been identified from Guatemala (Kidder 1949: 16, fig. 6d), all over El Salvador (Boggs 1943b, 1945a, 1945b; Longyear 1944: 37), and as far south as El Cauce, near Managua, Nicaragua (Richardson and Ruppert 1942: 271). The Galo Polychrome pottery of the Greater Nicoya subarea is probably related.

Other than the introduction of Ulua-Yojoa Polychromes and the first appearance of mold-made figurines, the artifactual differences at Los Naranjos from the Eden phase are not remarkable (Baudez and Becquelin 1976: 6). There are two C^{14} dates (appendix 2).

As in the nearby Lake Yojoa region, the archaeology of the Ulua-Chamelecon-Sula region shows a major increase in population—more numerous sites with large numbers of mound concentrations. Some of the major

Figure 6.8. Ulua-Yojoa Polychromes, Period V (Glass 1966: fig. 5).

locales of Period V are Santa Rita, already mentioned, and Las Flores (Strong, Kidder, and Paul 1938), Santa Ana (Gordon 1898a), and Travesia (Stone 1941; Sheehy and Veliz 1977).

Pottery includes not only the Ulua-Yojoa polychromes, which some believe originate in this region (Baudez and Becquelin 1973: 282), but also a distinctive ceramic known as Bold Geometric (fig. 6.9). Unlike the Ulua-Yojoa polychrome, Bold Geometric is not found at Copan and is rare in El Salvador and at Lake Yojoa. It does, however, occur on the Bay Islands (Strong 1948: 80, fig. 4), in eastern Honduras at San Marcos (Strong 1934a: 47, fig. 54), and in the Northeast region at H-CN-5 (Healy 1978b). Glass (1966: 171–72) has summarized the range of design and form variation for Bold Geometric ceramics. The distribution of the type, and its differences from Ulua-Yojoa, are of interest.

Another fairly distinctive artifact class of the region during Period V is the so-called Ulua Marble vase carved with elaborate scroll and volute

Figure 6.9.   Bold Geometric vessel with bird-serpent motif, Sula Plain, Honduras, Period V (Peabody Museum, Harvard University, photographed by Hillel Burger).

designs. The common shape is cylindrical with protruding knobs (fig. 6.10). Again, despite the fact that these distinctive vessels have been frequently described in the literature, little is known about their function, origin, manufacture, and often their precise archaeological context (Gordon 1920; Stone 1938; Kidder 1947: 36–37).

Henderson et al. (1979: 174–87) have identified Period V occupations in the Naco Valley at El Regadillo, Naco itself, Monte Grande, Descalzada, and La Sierra. The latter locality is the largest and most thoroughly studied Period V site in this region. Henderson and colleagues (1979: 175) estimate that the total area of occupation exceeded a square kilometer (100 hectares), with more than 400 structures of various sizes, shapes, and arrangements (fig. 6.11). Formal plaza plans are rare and without consistent directional

Figure 6.10. Small marble vase, Sula Plain, Honduras, Period V (Peabody Museum, Harvard University, photographed by Hillel Burger).

orientation. The architecture includes a ball court, constructions reaching 5 meters in height, elaborate stairways and plastering, and structures built with cobbles set in clay with a pebble filler.

Among La Sierra ceramics were Ulua-Yojoa pottery, frying pan censers, *candeleros*, and various red and black on orange polychromes. Henderson et al. (1979: 190) see strong connections between this pottery and the Yojoa complex of Los Naranjos as well as with the ceramics of Travesia and Santa Ana (Strong, Kidder, and Paul 1938: 39–125; Stone 1941: 55–86). Some Copador pottery of Late Classic times from Copan was also found, which

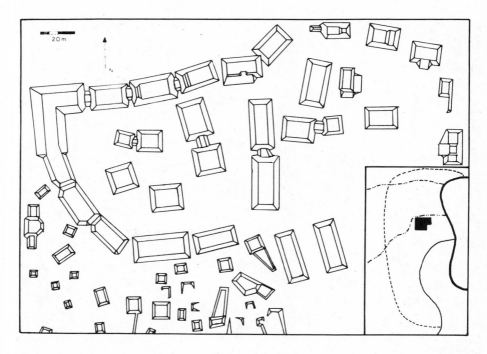

Figure 6.11.   Map of La Sierra, central section, a Period V site in northwest Honduras. Inset shows location of enlarged area within the site limits (Henderson et al. 1979: fig. 6).

reinforces the dating as well as suggesting contacts with the Far West region. Like so many sites elsewhere in western Honduras, La Sierra shows signs of abandonment at the end of Period V.

In the Comayagua Valley during this period, several locales are quite prominent. The sites of Las Vegas, Yarumela, Lo de Vaca, and possibly the fortress site of Tenampua have had some preliminary investigation (see also Agurcia 1980).

Las Vegas (or El Biscuital) is a large valley site located on the east bank of the Humuya River, between Yarumela and Comayagua, and is marked by a sizable concentration of mounds covering an area at least 7.8 square kilometers in circumference. The central zone consists of about 60 rectangular house mounds, with a smaller number of rectangular ceremonial mounds at the southern edge. These constructions range from 1 to 1.5 meters in height and average about 16 × 30 meters at the base. The two largest ceremonial mounds at Las Vegas are from 3 to 7 meters tall. Stone

(1957: 15–17) reported retaining walls of stone and living floors of adobe. Carved effigy stone metates, like those of the Northeast region and the Nicoya subarea of Nicaragua and Costa Rica, are reported from Las Vegas (Stone 1957: fig. 43a, b). The ceramics include examples typical of the Ulua-Yojoa polychrome complex (Glass 1966: 175) as well as some types which appear to be southern in origin. In particular, Las Vegas polychromes look quite like the Nicoya (Papagayo) polychromes of the Middle Polychrome period (A.D. 800–1200).

At Lo de Vaca, site utilization continues into the Lo de Vaca III phase (A.D. 300–900). It is characterized by large-scale construction, the appearance of Ulua-Yojoa polychromes, and Bold Geometric types (Baudez 1966: 312). At Yarumela, Canby (1951: 82) noted the same ceramics; he also found the Period V (Yarumela IV, A.D. 300–600) occupation to be primarily on the periphery of the site.

Throughout the Comayagua Valley are fortified locations such as Calamuya, Quelepa, and Tenampua. This last site has been described by Squier (1853b), Popenoe (1936), and Stone (1957: 50–53). It occupies the summit of a steep hill, with this natural defense complemented by site walls of undressed stone. The fortification has approximately 100 separate structures clustered in several different groups, including some very large mounds and a ball court (fig. 6.12). Baudez (1970: 101) suggested the possibility that Tenampua may have risen to prominence in the Comayagua Valley about the same time that Yarumela declined.

The presence of these hilltop, fortified sites might suggest a Period VI (Postclassic) date (Glass 1966: 175). Baudez (1970: 100–101) has argued, however, that Tenampua dates at least partly to Period V, and some of the polychrome ceramics of Tenampua certainly hint at such a placement. There are, for instance, some Ulua-Yojoa-like polychromes present (Stone 1957: figs. 55a, b, c, fig. 57a), although the site has some distinctive pottery elements of its own (Glass 1966: fig. 8). Until controlled excavations are carried out, the chronological position of Tenampua, the largest hilltop fort in the Valley, will remain uncertain. As in western Honduras, most Central region sites were apparently abandoned by the close of the period (ca. A.D. 1000).

Very little is known about Period V in the Southern Pacific region. There are two discernible phases: San Lorenzo (A.D. 550–750) and Fonseca (A.D. 750–950). In the first of these, we see a termination of many of the Chismuyo ceramics, the decline of Usulutan negative-painted decoration, and the appearance of the first Choluteca polychromes. Tripod cylinder bowls are a predominant vessel form. In the Fonseca phase, Ulua-Yojoa polychromes are quite prominent, including some like the Santa Rita Mayoid type.

Baudez (1976a) noted that the San Lorenzo phase is defined by some five sites known to cover an area that varies from four to nine hectares. The

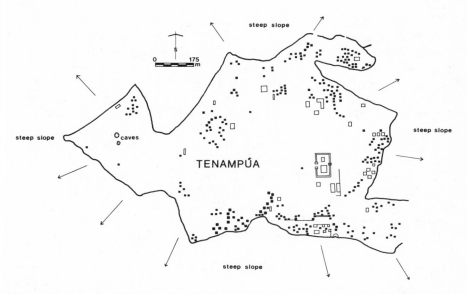

Figure 6.12.   Map of the fortified hilltop site of Tenampua, Period V–VI, Comaya-gua region, Honduras (Stone 1957: fig. 3).

mounds of this phase are of approximately the same proportions as those of the preceding Chismuyo phase and are now arranged in concentric rings with the apparently more important mound structures toward the center. The Fonseca phase is represented by only four sites and is even more sketchily defined. The one pure Fonseca site has been largely destroyed. Both Period V phases were only briefly defined by Baudez (1966: 319, 1976a: 15–17).

In northeast Honduras there was considerable continuity from the Early Selin (A.D. 300–600) to the Basic Selin (A.D. 600–800) phase in ceramics and other artifacts. During Basic Selin times—if we can utilize the number of sites known, quantities of mounds at these sites, and extent of refuse as indicators—the population may have reached its peak for the entire Selin period. H-CN-5: Selin Farm, at this time, covered 290 × 230 meters and was marked by 16 central mounds arranged in a roughly circular plan (fig. 6.13). Other Basic Selin sites, like H-CN-4: Williams' Ranch and H-CN-3: Km.29, were ringed by manmade ditches almost certainly constructed for defensive purposes (Healy 1973: 42, 1975: 65–66).

The Basic Selin ceramics include a number of types which continue from the preceding phase as well as new local ones (fig. 6.14). The presence of several Ulua Polychrome sherds shows at least limited contacts with western Honduras during this period (Healy 1978a: fig. 5).

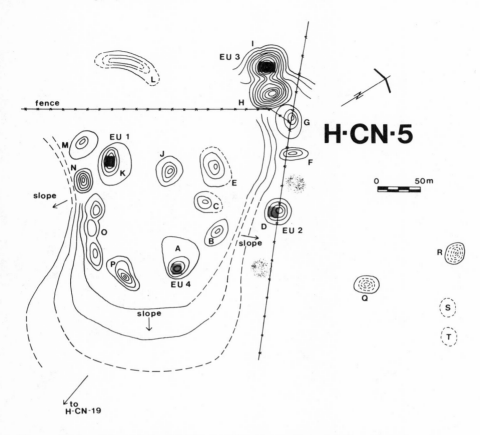

Figure 6.13. Map of site H-CN-5: Selin Farm, Period IVb–V, northeast Honduras. Contours approximately 30 centimeters (one foot); shaded zones show excavation areas (Healy 1978a: fig. 3).

Although burial information from the Northeast region is scanty, a few complete skeletons from primary extended burials have been recovered. A child's grave was found beneath a house floor and mound at H-CN-5 (Healy 1978a: fig. 13) and the skeleton of an adult at the bottom of the ditch encircling site H-CN-4 (Healy 1975: 65). In both cases grave goods were lacking, but the burials were clearly intentional. The remaining human osteological evidence comes from bones intermixed with the shells and other garbage in Mound I at H-CN-5. Examination and analysis revealed that these mixed bones were from different temporal units and different individuals (Healy 1978a: 64), raising the possibility of Selin-period cannibalism.

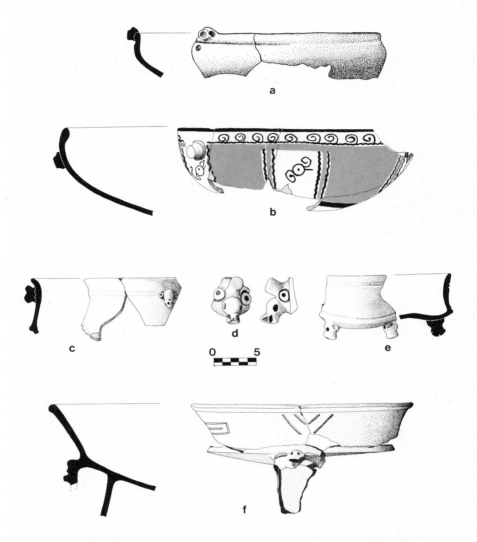

Figure 6.14. Basic Selin-period ceramics, Period IVb, northeast Honduras (Healy 1978a: fig. 7).

Our analysis of faunal remains from the Northeast region shows that, in addition to farming, Selin inhabitants were intensively exploiting virtually all their surrounding environments (Healy 1978d, 1983). By about A.D. 1000 and the end of the Selin period, the H-CN-5 settlers had apparently been increasing their reliance upon saltwater fish, although mammals like white-tail and brocket deer, armadillo, peccary, and manatee were still significant, as were iguanas, storks and herons, and a multitude of local shellfish.

Between A.D. 800 and 1000 it is possible to recognize some interesting alterations in the cultural assemblage which foreshadow more substantial changes in the subsequent Cocal period (i.e., post-A.D. 1000), although there are clear continuities from the Basic Selin phase. This 200-year span, labeled the Transitional Selin phase, sees painted ceramics starting to decline in popularity while a trend toward incised line and punctation decoration begins. Some new lithic types occur, especially the T-shaped axes and spherical jadeite beads. There are two radiocarbon dates for the Basic Selin phase, but none as yet for the Transitional Selin (appendix 2).

To the far west of Honduras, Late Classic Copan flourished and Maya culture reached its apogee. Classic Maya sites of the west, led by Copan, were marked by monumental building activity, spectacular carving of stelae, and an obvious population explosion until the collapse of this remarkable culture. At Copan, abandonment appears to have occurred around A.D. 800 or shortly thereafter (Willey and Leventhal 1979).

Period V, then, saw perhaps the greatest expansion of settlement and population. Everywhere there were signs of major building activity in the era roughly contemporaneous to the Mesoamerican Late Classic period. The first appearance of polychrome ceramics in Honduras occurred, many of which look Classic Maya in color, form, and general decorative style. Imitation of Classic Maya polychrome types, however, did not inhibit other, more regional styles from emerging at this time which are equally distinctive, among them Bold Geometric and Ulua Marble style. Analysis of the distribution of these types shows northeast Honduras having virtually no evidence of contact with the Maya and only traces of trade with Mayoid groups of the Ulua Valley. The foremost item in this category was the clay replica (or prototype?) of the Ulua Marble vase, which may have originated in the Northeast region (Strong 1934b: fig. 61; Stone 1938: 58–61; Healy 1978a: fig. 8a, b). The general impression of the period is of fairly pronounced Mesoamerican (Mayan) influence in western, central, and southern Honduras until about A.D. 900–1000.

The evidence of site size, artifact assemblages, burial elaboration, and settlement patterns in this period suggests a social order indirectly classifiable as a petty chiefdom. Long-distance trade from both the west and the south not only continued but increased. The lithics and ceramics were some of the finest examples of native workmanship ever produced in Honduras and suggest considerable technological skills and classes of professional artisans (lapidaries, potters, and so on). There was large-scale architecture, with Mesoamerican-style ball courts. Conflict and warfare, if not present before A.D. 500, certainly seem to have occurred in Period V; walled, fortified hilltop sites, like Tenampua, were being constructed by the end of the period. Another significant trend identifiable at this same time was the heightening of contacts between Honduras and lower Central America. In particular, coeval traits of the Greater Nicoya Subarea (polychrome ceramic styles, peg-based statuery, carved effigy metates) began showing up in greater number in Honduras.

In northeast Honduras, ceramics, settlement patterns, and burial customs were beginning to take on very non-Mesoamerican characteristics. By Period V (the Basic and Transitional Selin phases) burials still lacked grave offerings, though some residential mounds were now larger than others. However, sites were still nearly uniform in size and fairly small by contrast to contemporary developments in the west. Some sites were fortified. There is also evidence which suggests that by A.D. 800 the Northeast region was receiving substantially different cultural stimuli. Several of these trait changes are obvious forerunners of subsequent Cocal-period features. Unfortunately, our knowledge of the Transitional Selin phase at the end of Period V is based solely upon one site (H-CN-5) which, interestingly, was abandoned about A.D. 1000.

Period VI (A.D. 1000–1550)

The last major pre-Columbian era, Period VI, is approximately equivalent to the Postclassic period of Mesoamerica. It was a time characterized by a considerable population drop and widespread site abandonment in western and central Honduras during the first half of the period. The problems of the Maya subarea were unquestionably having an impact upon this portion of Honduras. At those sites still occupied after about A.D. 1000, there is evidence of Tohil Plumbate and Fine Orange pottery and some traces of metallurgy. Ceramics from the Greater Nicoya Subarea traded northward were still limited, but greater quantities entered central and western Honduras. In northeast Honduras, numerous changes also occurred, suggesting a major cultural realignment.

Baudez and Becquelin (1976: 6) reported that the main group of Los Naranjos, like Mayan centers farther west, was abandoned in Period VI. The only traces of settlement, belonging to the terminal Rio Blanco phase (A.D. 950–1250), are a few mound groups on the periphery of the Lake Yojoa zone. Several different polychromes were manufactured during the first half of Period VI before final and total site abandonment. Ceramics in general were quite inferior to earlier products. Some evidence of metallurgy also helps date the phase; presence of a Mixtec incensario and Tohil Plumbate sherds, like the metals, are indicative of an Early Postclassic chronological placement (Baudez 1970: 108; Baudez and Becquelin 1976: 7). The ware termed Las Vegas Polychrome is virtually identical to the Nicoya-Papagayo Polychromes of Rivas and Guanacaste to the south and corresponds well (e.g., Middle Polychrome period, ca. A.D. 800–1200) to dates from there. By A.D. 1200, however, habitation around Los Naranjos ceased completely.

As in the Lake Yojoa region, there are definite signs of a population decline at a number of sites in the Ulua-Chamelecon-Sula region. Glass (1966: 174) reported that his reexamination of the ceramics from Santa Rita, originally excavated by Strong, Kidder, and Paul (1938: fig. 6), revealed more than 50 sherds of Fine Orange Ware, a significant Mesoamerican time marker for the Early (A.D. 900–1200) Postclassic (Smith 1958). This pottery may also be present at Santa Ana (Gordon 1898a: plate 7j), and Sheehy (1978: 200) described a related fine orange pottery type of Travesia. It would seem, however, that although some sites continued into the beginning of Period VI, most declined before it was half over.

Closer to the coast, several sites in the vicinity of the Naco Valley have produced significant Period VI remains. The 1908 discovery of a cave near the headwaters of a stream that empties into the Chamelecon River about 40 kilometers from Naco produced a cache of artifacts unquestionably belonging in this time span. Blackiston (1910) described the cave as probably never used for habitation. Inside the cavern, however, were over 800 copper bells (fig. 6.15A–B) of various sizes, shapes, and forms of decoration (Blackiston 1910: plate 45). The Chamelecon Cave also produced a large, life-sized wooden mask covered with pieces of turquoise and other stones set with a natural pitch. This type of inlay mosaic work is almost certainly Postclassic in date, like the copper bells, and may be yet another indication of Mixtec contacts with western Honduras on this late time horizon.

One of the principal Period VI centers, and probably the best documented Late Postclassic site in northwest Honduras, is Naco in the Naco Valley along the middle of the Chamelecon. This late site is known to have participated in long-range Mesoamerican maritime trade stretching around Yucatan to at least the north coast of Honduras. Although Naco was still functioning when the Spanish first arrived in Honduras, the native trade networks were apparently quickly disrupted, and Naco was abandoned by the time Cortes arrived in 1525. Montejo (1539: 228) reported that Naco had a population of 10,000 persons, which is not out of agreement with Cortes's statement that there were more than 2,000 houses there, not including its neighboring hamlets (Pagden 1971: 407).

There is no direct evidence for the linguistic affiliation of Naco, though

Figure 6.15A. Copper bird effigy bells, Quimistan-Chamelecon Cave, Ulua-Chamelecon-Sula region, Period VI (Peabody Museum, Harvard University, photographed by Hillel Burger).

Henderson (1977a: 369) believed a Chontal-Maya enclave to be a reasonable possibility. Nahua-speaking Pipil are at least as likely and may have facilitated trade between the Pacific coast and the Gulf of Honduras (Stone 1941: 97; Baudez 1976b: 143; Henderson 1977a: 369–70).

Work at Naco has revealed that the site covers 90 hectares. First investigated by Strong, Kidder, and Paul (1938), the region has most recently been explored by a Cornell University project (Henderson 1977a, 1977b; Henderson et al. 1979). Because of heavy modern disturbance, the site boundaries are today blurred. Naco's main group, however, has been identified and includes small residential mounds and a cluster of larger elite residences and public structures, including a ball court (Henderson 1977a: 371). Period VI structures are located primarily on the north bank of the Rio Naco, but they extend to the other side as well. Ceramics are marked by the distinctive Naco Ware, which includes several types (Wonderley 1980, 1981).

Figure 6.15B.

In the Central region, there are no major ceremonial centers in Period VI in the Comayagua Valley comparable to earlier ones like Yarumela. Las Vegas consists of small, low house platforms about 10 meters across; some Tohil Plumbate pottery and Las Vegas (Papagayo) Polychrome are in evidence (Baudez 1976b: 141). The site of Tenampua and other hilltop fortifications above the Comayagua Valley may continue into Period VI, but the question is unanswerable based on present knowledge (Glass 1966: 177).

During the terminal period the Southern Pacific region of Honduras received considerable influence from the Greater Nicoya Subarea farther south (Healy 1974b, 1980). In the Amapala phase (A.D. 1100–1300), the first half of Period VI, Baudez (1966: 319) noted the appearance of Choluteca ceramics very similar to Middle and Late Polychrome (A.D. 800–1550) period types of Pacific Nicaragua and northwest Costa Rica (such as the Mombacho variety of Vallejo Polychrome and Papagayo Polychrome). Tohil Plumbate is also present and helps to identify a Choluteca equivalent to the Mesoamerican Early Postclassic. There is one C^{14} date for the Amapala phase (appendix 2).

For the last local phase, identified as the Malalaca phase (A.D. 1300–1500), Baudez (1976b: 143) noted some similarities between Malalaca ceramics and Naco pottery of the same date. Still other polychromes of the Choluteca region look reminiscent of the Vallejo Polychrome type of the Greater Nicoya Subarea, which dates there to the Late Polychrome (A.D. 1200–1550) period (Healy 1980: 242–46).

Concerning Period VI sites, Baudez (1976a: 16) defined the Amapala phase based upon evidence from three localities ranging in size from 12 to 42 hectares. Mound size and distribution at Amapala sites were variable, with some mounds clustered in groups and others more scattered. At site 14, the central zone is dominated by a platform 100×40 meters, standing 1.5 meters tall. Atop this base was a pair of mounds (about 30 meters in diameter and 3 meters tall). At site 13, there were pairs of elongated mounds, which were not ball courts, as well as platforms for large rectangular houses with traces of mud walls showing some signs of having once been painted. Interestingly, anthropomorphic stone (lava) statues with peg bases appeared in the Amapala phase and are almost certainly related to similar carved statuary of the lake zone of Rivas in Pacific Nicaragua. Tripod zoomorphic metates carved in low relief also occurred.

In the final phase of the Southern Pacific region, Malalaca, the only known site, is located within a mangrove zone. The topsoil is thin here, and recent cultivation activities have substantially destroyed the site's original features (Baudez 1976a: 16). The mounds were probably never very large.

In the Far West, remains of artifacts are scant but indicate what has been termed a "desultory occupation in the Postclassic" (Willey and Leventhal 1979: 78). Copan was abandoned, like so many other Classic Maya centers, with probable ramifications evident across Honduras, the principal exception being the Northeast.

In the Northeast region, Period VI is defined by the Early and Late Cocal phases (AD. 1000–1400 and A.D. 1400–1530 respectively). Of 23 prehistoric sites surveyed by Healy in the vicinity of Trujillo and the Aguan Valley, 12 sites were at least partly datable to this late period. Generally, Cocal sites were larger than Selin settlements, were more orderly in their layout, and were marked by larger constructions than ever before in the region (Healy 1973, 1976a). There are seven radiocarbon dates for the period (appendix 2).

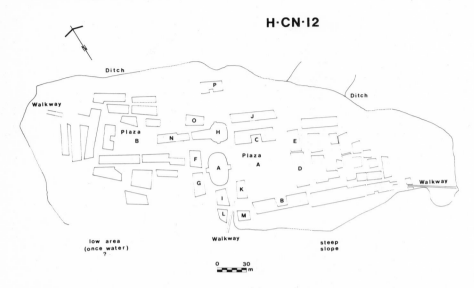

Figure 6.16. Map of site H-CN-12: Rio Claro, Period VI, northeast Honduras region (Healy 1978b: fig. 3).

Only one Cocal site, H-CN-12: Rio Claro, situated in a fortifiable location about 12 meters above the Aguan Valley floor, has been closely examined (Healy 1978b, 1978c) and belonged principally to Early Cocal. It is the largest prehistoric site known in the Northeast region, measuring 450 × 190 meters. More than 50 mounds were identified atop the natural platform. There were clay constructions, many faced with tons of stone boulders, and nearly all mounds had unmortared stone boulder ramps on one side (if residential) or both sides (if ceremonial) providing access to the summit. The whole site is dominated by one central construction which stands about 7 meters above the plaza area and is visible from almost anywhere in the immediate vicinity (fig. 6.16). Several other long, low, flat mounds are obviously residential "long house" dwellings arranged around plazas. Some of these houses measured over 50 meters long. The site itself had a man-made trench running around two-thirds of the locale and probably a body of water on the last third. Evidence of habitation beyond the site boundaries was virtually nonexistent.

Pottery of the Cocal period on both the mainland and Bay Islands is characterized by incised lines and punctations (fig. 6.17). It has been illustrated by Strong (1935: plate 5e–g, plate 18 #1d, plate 73), Stone (1941: fig. 36f–h), Veliz (1978b: figs. 5, 7, 11), and Healy (1978c: figs. 9–10). The

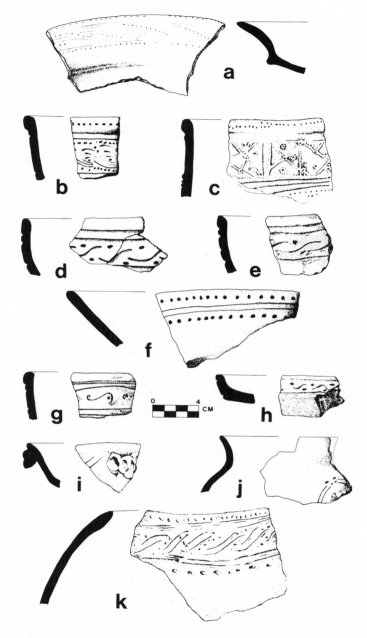

Figure 6.17. Incised-Punctate ceramics, Period VI, northeast Honduras region (Healy 1978b: fig. 10).

ceramic is quite unlike that of Period VI elsewhere in Honduras or Meso-america proper. Some general similarities to the pottery of eastern Nicaragua, Costa Rica, and Panama are discernible in design and mode of adornment.

Practically the only painted pottery attributable to the Early Cocal period is Bay Island Polychrome (Strong 1935). This is a well-made polychrome of red and black on orange. Geometric and anthropomorphic designs predominate; a plumed serpent motif is common. Bay Island Polychrome vessels are generally *jicara-*, egg-, or pear-shaped vessels with zoomorphic tripod legs (Strong 1935: plate 1, plate 6 #2, fig. 12, plates 21–22). In the Bay Islands, Strong noted the connection between this pottery (also called Polychrome 1) with Tohil Plumbate and copper bells (Strong 1935: 142–43, table 1 #12). Clearly, then, this polychrome falls into the first half of Period VI, and its contextual associations hint at a Mesoamerican derivation (fig. 6.18).

By Late Cocal times, incised line decoration became more haphazard and less complex. A Simple Incised-Punctate type is identifiable (fig. 6.19) and has been found with Naco Polychrome trade sherds at several sites.

Lithics of Cocal date show a marked increase in the appearance of obsidian. Crudely chipped, T-shaped axes are generally diagnostic of Cocal date (Healy 1978c: fig. 13). Stone manos and metates are present, and it appears fairly certain that the Cocal-period groups of the Northeast region produced the elaborate, and often giant-sized, grinding stones—some zoomorphic with feline traits—and carved stone bowls with bas-relief designs (Stone 1941: figs. 3, 27, 34).

Information on Cocal-period subsistence is limited, although grinding stones suggest that maize was significant. Some Cocal sites located near the coast have sizable shell middens, hinting that shellfish collecting was also important. Floral and faunal preservation, however, has been poor in contrast to Selin data (Healy 1978c: 26).

We also have very little information on Period VI burial customs for this region. No graves were uncovered in excavations at H-CN-12 or at H-CN-6: Gericki site. On the Bay Islands, at the 80 Acre site on Utila Island, Epstein (1957: 26–33) reports on three urn burials of probable Cocal date. At one Cocal period site, probably our H-CN-2: Km. 19.5 site, earlier excavations by Spinden (1925) in a low mound unearthed some eight skeletons that showed signs of dismemberment. The locality has recently been bulldozed for road fill (Healy 1978c: 26).

By and large, the Northeast region in Period VI shows significant changes from the preceding Selin times. As noted above, the pottery looks basically non-Mesoamerican. The Cocal period propensity for elaborate stone carving, especially legged metates and cruder sculptures, along with the overall ceramic pattern, points to more likely cultural affinities southward.

Figure 6.18. Bay Island Polychrome, Period VI, northeast Honduras region (Instituto Hondureño de Antropologia e Historia, photographed by author).

By contrast, some other traits of this date are more Mesoamerican; ladle censers, copper bells, ceramic cylinder stamps, obsidian, copper, and plumbate pottery are probably imported from Mesoamerica. It seems, then, that the Northeast region was becoming more receptive by Period VI to contacts and influences from both its southern and its northern neighbors. Indeed, in 1502, Columbus, on his last voyage sailing from the Bay Islands to the Honduran north coast, encountered a large, fully loaded native canoe. It was apparently bound with numerous trade goods (textiles, copper items, food supplies) for Yucatan. A quarter-century later, Cortes trekked to the Northeast region of Honduras and found Nahua speakers at several chiefdom sites (Papayeca and Chapagua) dominating the region. Although the basic regional culture in Period VI may have been non-Mesoamerican in foundation, it was obviously in contact with the north.

In sum, by the close of Period VI, as we get closer to the Historic period, our information becomes much better for ancient Honduras. There is evi-

Figure 6.19. Simple Incised-Punctate vessel, Period VI, northeast Honduras (private collection, photographed by author).

dence of continuing commerce, but we now know that at least some of this long-distance trade was via coastal sea routes in addition to the more traditional overland treks. Indications are that those remnant Period VI sites which survived the decline in the first half of the period were functioning as quite complex super chiefdoms of varying size and control. Some centers, like Naco in the Northwest or Chapagua and Papayeca in the Northeast, may have been outposts of colonizers of a state level of complexity.

In the Northeast, we see the appearance of pottery termed the North Coast Appliqué Style with incised and punctate decoration. This is totally unlike anything else in Mesoamerica proper. Disposal of the dead, judging from the Bay Islands data, is also distinctive. Unfortunately, a lack of data from the Atlantic side of Nicaragua makes it difficult to ascertain if the Period VI (Cocal) ceramics of the Northeast region are local in origin or, as several writers have suggested, "intrusive" from farther south. What is apparent from recent work in the Northeast is that the problems which severely affected the rest of Honduras in the first half of Period VI did not seem significant to the Northeast. Indeed, in some ways Early Cocal seems a time of marked regional prosperity, increased population, and expansion.

Problems and Questions for the Future

In 1948, when Strong's survey of Honduras archaeology appeared, he attempted to provide a rough chronological appraisal (Strong 1948: fig. 15). In the three decades since, archaeologists have established secure (if still broad) chronological sequences for those regions originally examined by Strong and for some others with which he was unable to deal. There are now 23 radiocarbon determinations for Honduras as a whole reinforcing the chronological framework. Strong, of course, had no real dates, only "guesstimates" based upon more firmly dated information from Meso-america, particularly the Maya lowlands.[8] Nevertheless, despite recent obvious progress on the temporal front, some regions of Honduras still lack any cultural sequences, relative dates, or time depth of any sort, let alone absolute dates. Until we have better control over the time variable, it will continue to be exceedingly difficult to discuss Honduras prehistory within an evolutionary framework or to make reliable cross-cultural comparisons with either Mesoamerica or the rest of lower Central America.

Similarly, as we noted in the introduction, vast areas of Honduras are still unknown archaeologically. Although the situation in the Far West, Lake Yojoa, and the Ulua-Chamelecon-Sula regions has improved as a result of recent attention, the Central, Northeast, and Southern Pacific regions are only beginning to be studied and are only superficially known. Furthermore, and perhaps most critical, huge expanses of eastern, central, and south-western Honduras are complete blanks in our archaeological picture. These zones are in desperate need of preliminary, basic investigation before large-scale agricultural activities and other modern developments obliterate all traces of the archaeological record there.

The problem of the first peopling of Honduras, the lack of positive information from the Paleo-Indian and Archaic stages, the questions of correlations of archaeological cultures with ethnographic groups, fundamental queries about regional settlement and subsistence patterns, technological development, determinations of the type of socio-political organization operating in different regions at different times—all are significant problems needing investigation.

The question of the Mesoamerican Frontier—what it was, if it can be recognized archaeologically, how the frontier groups may have operated and changed through time—needs attention as well (Baudez 1976b). It would seem, based upon ethnohistoric, linguistic, and our own archaeological work in the Northeast region, that at least part of the north coast of Honduras lay outside the Mesoamerican culture area during the prehistoric era. Unlike other parts of Honduras, this region never received Usulutan or true Classic Maya pottery, nor did it adopt stepped pyramids, ball courts, Mesoamerican deities, or other traditional hallmarks (Kirchhoff 1943). Unfortunately, the critical area between the Sula Plain of western Honduras and Trujillo in the northeast remains basically unexplored. Similarly unknown is the vast zone east of Colon and into Atlantic Nicaragua, an area which might help tie the Northeast region of Honduras to the southern zone of lower Central America (Baudez 1970).

The question of the significance and impact of Mesoamerican high cultures upon western, central, and southern Honduras needs analysis and fuller evaluation. The contacts are obvious, but just what role did the Olmec (in the Preclassic), the Maya (of the Classic), and the Pipil (of the Postclassic) play in the development of Honduras (Longyear 1969; Stone 1969b; Baudez and Becquelin 1973)? Traces of all three groups have been found, yet the patterns remain enigmatic. The impression one gets is that of fluctuating degrees of Mesoamericanization, but by what mechanisms (Willey 1969)?

Was this area being exploited by Mesoamerican groups for its natural resources? If so, what were these desired commodities, when did the extraction process begin, and why? Was exchange through itinerant trading groups, like the Aztec *pochteca*, the means by which Olmec pottery, obsidian, plumbate ware, and copper bells (to mention but a few items) came as far east as the Aguan Valley of Colon? If so, what routes (overland or by sea) were followed? What was being exchanged for these Mesoamerican-made products? Or, were the so-called Pipil enclaves known from Period VI less benign outposts of foreigners on Honduran soils? Were these garrisons of Nahua-speaking peoples part of the Postclassic Mexican expansion?

The interaction between Honduran groups and cultures of neighboring El Salvador, Pacific Nicaragua, and northwest Costa Rica needs new attention. Is the sudden and widespread distribution of Usulutan pottery, which marks our Period IVb, explainable from the archaeological record? On a somewhat later horizon, the rapid appearance of peg-based stone statuary, legged, tripod anthropomorphic metates, and Nicoya-Papagayo Polychrome pottery (Las Vegas Polychrome in Honduras) over much of Honduras about A.D. 1000 deserves investigation. In both eras Honduras appears to have been on the receiving end of large quantities of foreign-made goods. Here trace element analysis of so-called imported goods would be a most worthwhile endeavor.

The nearly simultaneous changes recorded in the Northeast region and the notable shift from Selin to Cocal cultural patterns may be related to the Maya collapse. Did the Classic Maya collapse of the Far West region in the tenth century A.D. so disrupt the balance of aboriginal life in the rest of Honduras that the remaining areas began to turn their focus southward to the Nicoya Subarea for most of Honduras and to Atlantic Central America and beyond for northeast Honduras?

The questions are almost endless, the data insufficient, and the many voids intolerable. To use the terms of a recent evaluation of the history of New World archaeology, we can only conclude that Honduras archaeology is operating in the Classificatory-Historical period of development, 20 or more years behind work being done elsewhere in the Americas (Willey and Sabloff 1980). We can take heart, perhaps, in seeing that the data base is steadily improving, and our areal coverage is expanding. This being the case, contemporary archaeology of Honduras is still in its formative stage with some of the most interesting problem-oriented research yet to unfold.

Notes

1. My research in Honduras has been supported by a number of individuals and institutions including the Peabody Museum of Archaeology (Harvard), National Geographic Society, Rutgers University, Trent University, and the Social Sciences and Humanities Research Council of Canada in the form of a leave fellowship. My investigations have benefited from a large number of scholars involved in lower Central American archaeology, several of whom were participants in the Santa Fe conference or whose works are cited herein. I am grateful to the Instituto Hondureño de Antropologia e Historia, particularly Lic. Vito Veliz R., and Dr. J. Adan Cueva, the former director. I am indebted to Dr. Gordon R. Willey for having first introduced me to Honduras and its archaeology. Figures 6.5 and 6.6 were republished with permission of *American Antiquity*, figures 6.7, 6.11, 6.16, and 6.17 with permission of J. S. Henderson and the *Journal of Field Archaeology*; figure 6.8 was republished with permission of J. Glass and the University of Texas Press; figure 12 is redrawn and reprinted with permission of D. Z. Stone from *The Archaeology of Central and Southern Honduras*, and figures 6.3, 6.4, 6.9, 6.10, and 6.15 from D. Z. Stone's *Pre-Columbian Man Finds Central America* (Peabody Museum Press). To all of the above, I am grateful for their assistance.

2. Two recent M.A. theses have been written by Honduran archaeologists reviewing the prehistory of their country (Reyes 1976a; Radillo 1978).

3. Stone (1957) discussed an Eastern Central Honduras region. Very little actual fieldwork has been carried out here, and we have not included such a region in our present discussion of the Central Honduras region.

4. In 1983, the Santa Barbara Archaeological Project was initiated with a focus on the important site of Gualjoquito, along the Ulua River, in the Department of Santa Barbara. Although research is currently in progress, the project has already produced datable evidence spanning from at least the Late Preclassic (ca. 400 B.C.) period to the Late Classic (ca. A.D. 900–1000) period. Given the intermediary geographic location of Gualjoquito, east of Copan and west of Lake Yojoa, it seems

likely to show evidence of influences from several archaeological regions during its lengthy history (Schortman, Urban, and Ashmore 1983).

5. This large rift through central Honduras creates a unique and natural passageway connecting the Caribbean and Pacific coasts. It would have served as the most efficient travel and communication route for pre-Columbian traders crossing the Central American landmass. Judging from the trade goods imported to Honduras from El Salvador (obsidian and Usulutan pottery) as early as Period IV, it may help to explain the precocious development of the Comayagua Valley sites in this great transcontinental pass.

6. Between 1980 and 1983, a large-scale rescue archaeological project has been conducted by the Instituto Hondureno de Antropologia e Historia in the region of the El Cajon Reservoir (Rio Sulaco and lower Rio Humuya) in the Central Honduras region. This ongoing research is sure to produce a substantial amount of new information on the region (Hirth, et al. 1981; Lara and Hasemann 1982).

7. Radillo (1978) divided mainland Colon and the Bay Islands into two separate regions. Our impression is that the archaeology of both localities is virtually identical (with a longer sequence on the mainland). Consequently, we have lumped them together for purposes of this paper.

8. A quick glance at Strong's (1948: fig. 15) time chart reveals his remarkable acuity on the overall cultural sequence. He tended to be a little on the conservative side, but basically he had the sequence correct.

PART THREE

The Lower Central American Core

7

The Greater Nicoya
Archaeological Subarea

FREDERICK W. LANGE

Department of Anthropology
University of Colorado, Boulder

This chapter examines similarities and differences among some sites and localities in the Greater Nicoya Archaeological Subarea (fig. 7.1) and broadly analyzes processes of ecological adaptation and cultural evolution as we presently understand them. Specifically, it assesses ecological influences on settlement pattern, the role of internal and external trade as cultural stimuli, and the overall limits placed on economic-political-social development. Common cultural characteristics present throughout the region continue to make "Greater Nicoya" as originally defined by Norweb (1961) a useful concept, but it is necessary to range north (Sheets, this volume; Healy, this volume), south, and southeast (Snarskis, this volume) to place Greater Nicoya patterns in a systemic areal context.

From north to south, reports on the following regions have been utilized: the interlakes area in Nicaragua (Wyckoff 1974); Ometepe Island (Haberland 1966b, 1978); the Isthmus of Rivas (Norweb 1961, 1964; Healy 1974b, 1980a); the Bay of Salinas and Rio Sapoa areas (Lange 1971b); the Santa Elena Peninsula (Coe 1962a; Sweeney 1975); the Bay of Culebra (Abel 1978; Lange 1978; Lange and Abel-Vidor 1980); the Rio Sabalo area (Murray and Jess 1976); the Tempisque River (Lines 1936a; Baudez 1963, 1967; Hoopes 1979; Day 1982); the Tamarindo area (Coe 1962a; Sweeney 1975); the Guanacaste–San Carlos corridor from the Tempisque Valley to the

Figure 7.1. The Greater Nicoya archaeological subarea and sites in its northern sector (Nicaragua).

Atlantic watershed (Finch 1977; Dawson 1979; Norr 1979a, 1979b; Creamer 1979; Ryder 1980); the Nosara Valley (Lange et al. 1974); the Gulf of Nicoya (Robison 1979; Creamer 1980, 1983); Barrahonda (Laurencich de Minelli 1975, 1979); and the Nicoya Peninsula (Herra n.d.). Some of the reports focus on isolated sites, while work in the Rio Sapoa, the Bay of Salinas, the Bay of Culebra, the Guanacaste–San Carlos corridor, the Gulf of Nicoya, and the Nosara Valley was based on controlled systematic surveys.[1]

The Vidor site on the Bay of Culebra has been extensively excavated; principal published references are: Abel 1978; Lange 1978; Accola 1978a, 1978b; Moreau 1979, 1980; Kerbis 1979, 1980; Bernstein 1980; Vazquez and Weaver 1980; and Abel-Vidor 1980a. To the south and east, reports by Snarskis (1978), Snarskis and Blanco (1978), and Finch and Honetschlager (n.d.) have been utilized to broaden the contextual setting. Many of the above authors attempted regional syntheses as part of their reports; the most complete overviews have been written by Ferrero (1977) in Spanish and by Stone (1977) in English. All segments of the relevant chronological sequence have been recently reviewed and revised (Accola 1978a, 1978b; Healy 1980a; Lange 1980a, 1980b); see Lange and Abel-Vidor (1980: fig. 3) for a summary.

Despite general areal unity, significant distribution differences in some ceramic types exist, as well as differing patterns of cultural development, subsistence orientation, and degrees of impact by external influences. Taking these differences into account, we distinguish a northern sector and a southern sector in the Greater Nicoya area. The former was focused on the inland Nicaraguan lakes (fig. 7.1) and the latter on the plains and coastal bays of northwestern Guanacaste Province, Costa Rica (fig. 7.2). Both archaeological and documentary data seem to support this distinction (Abel-Vidor 1981a; Healy 1980a). This division into northern and southern sectors illustrates the buffer-zone or frontier nature of the area (Lange 1979a). Abel-Vidor (1981) has suggested that the term *interaction sphere* (Caldwell 1964) may be more appropriate.

Greater Nicoya is south of the distribution of even minor public architectural remains, and there have been no demonstrated physical intrasite distinctions setting off ceremonial from other activity areas or separating an elite from more common people. The absence of architecture also makes it somewhat more difficult to establish site hierarchies. Settlement data suggest that areal hierarchies may be more appropriate. The absence of architectural remains also means that various researchers (including myself in the following synthesis) have focused on ceramics,[2] lithics, human skeletal remains, intersite spatial relationships, faunal and molluscan remains, and soil and morphological studies incorporating natural history data.

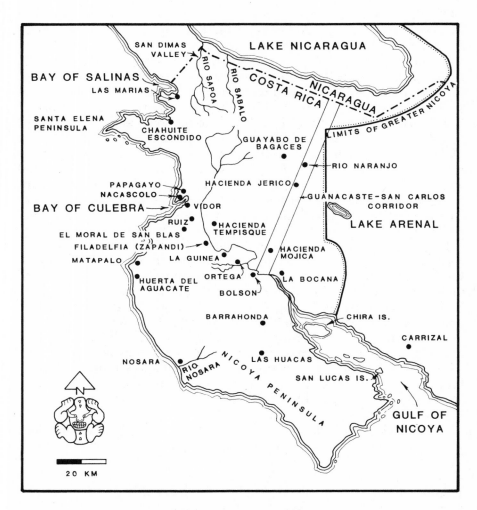

Figure 7.2. The Greater Nicoya archaeological subarea and sites in its southern sector (Costa Rica).

Period I: ?–8000 B.C.

The Paleo-Indian period was a major research focus in some earlier field investigations in northwestern Costa Rica (Lange 1969), but relevant data remain almost nonexistent. The so-called Hartman point, identified by Swauger and Mayer-Oakes (1952), is still a lonely example, and even its provenience is uncertain. The area may have been so dry that it was not suited to habitation by the fauna these hunters relied on. Espinoza's (1976) claim of a Paleo-Indian site in Pacific Nicaragua is of doubtful authenticity, while Snarskis's data from near Turrialba (1979b, this volume) suggest that such sites may more likely be found in lusher, non-Pacific coastal environments. However, the apparent geographical distribution may simply reflect the limitations of the data.

Period II (ca. 8000–4000 B.C.)

An area near the Bay of Salinas designated the Rio Antiguo (Murray 1969; Lange 1971b) had a number of sites with exclusively lithic artifact assemblages, although no temporally diagnostic artifacts were present. At the time of the research no comparable materials existed elsewhere in Central America, and the landowner's objections prevented any actual excavations. Morphologically, these lithic artifacts (fig. 7.3) have proven to be different from those found in association with ceramic-period materials and to be generally comparable to the lithic assemblages reported by Ranere (1976, 1980a, 1980b) from Panama. The placement of the Rio Antiguo materials is still somewhat tentative but more certain than it was a decade ago.

The impact of subsequent natural events on the archaeological record from this time period should also be considered. Radiocarbon-dated contexts bearing Zoned Bichrome–period ceramics (Aguilar, Abel-Vidor, personal communication; Sheets n.d.) have been found deeply buried under volcanic deposits in the Lake Arenal region of the cordillera section of Guanacaste. Also, as noted in chapter 3, in the Bagaces area of Guanacaste, in a higher, lusher habitat more suited to late Pleistocene fauna, the Costa Rican Electric Company (ICE) secured two radiocarbon dates slightly in excess of 10,000 B.P. from test drillings for geothermal exploration. Both dates came from beneath the same lava flow, some 12–15 kilometers apart, one more than 33 meters below surface and the other 15 meters or so below surface. The total flow is considerably wider than the distance between the two samples. No sites of earlier or contemporaneous date will readily be found under this or similar flows; while not totally explaining our paucity of early cultural data, this is one contributing factor. There are no known sites in Greater Nicoya dating from Period III (ca. 4000–1000 B.C.).

Figure 7.3.   Archaic lithic artifacts from near the Rio Antiguo locale, Guanacaste Province, Costa Rica.

Period IV (ca. 1000 B.C.–A.D. 500)

The Olmec are often thought to have been present during the Formative period in Greater Nicoya, but no supporting archaeological evidence exists. Various items of portable art bearing unmistakable Olmec motifs are attributed to the following sources: (a) post-Olmec prehistoric trade; (b) modern introduction into the Greater Nicoya area; or (c) pre-Columbian recycling of jade materials for reworking. Balser (1974, 1980) suggested that later people imported finished jade objects from Mesoamerica to replenish depleted local sources, or that the Olmec expansion into the Greater Nicoya area was oriented toward control of the Nicoya jade sources.

Current data suggest, although not conclusively, that there were no jade sources in Greater Nicoya; most so-called jade artifacts are made of non-jade material readily available and, hence, not a stimulus for long-distance trade (Lange, Bishop, and von Zelst 1981). The lack of jade sources would rule out one basis for Olmec desire to control the area, and Pohorilenko (1981) has summarized available data indicating that significant Olmec presence in Greater Nicoya is unlikely.

Coe and Baudez (1961) first described the Zoned Bichrome period for Guanacaste, defining it temporally from 300 B.C. to A.D. 300. Until very recently, this continued to be the earliest known ceramic period, despite subsequent research in many other Pacific coastal locations. Haberland (1966b, 1969: 232) felt that the Angeles phase on Ometepe Island and the presence of Schettel Incised in the San Dimas Valley (Lange 1971b: 131) represented earlier Zoned Bichrome phases. This evidence was generally considered inconclusive because of an absence of confirming comparative sequences, lack of relevant radiocarbon dates, or incompletely published data.

The physical composition of the majority of excavated coastal sites has also presented a problem in most research. Coastal sites in Guanacaste are characterized by large shell middens, and it is the intermixed mass of shell, potsherds, adobe, faunal material, and other cultural debris that is most impressive as excavation progresses downward. Prior to roughly A.D. 400–500, the shell does not occur, and without the protective context of the midden, faunal material (both marine/estuarine and terrestrial) ceases to be preserved. The cultural sequence, however, continues deeper, and it is from these levels at Vidor (up to 6.5 meters below surface) that the earlier data came.

Reexamination of excavation reports by Coe and Baudez (1961), Baudez (1967), and Sweeney (1975) suggests that failure to recover more than a trace of earlier data resulted from the time and labor limits imposed on deep testing the sites they reported. This was also true for my own work at Las Marias (1971b: 91).

Prior to 1975 most archaeological data from Greater Nicoya for the Zoned Bichrome period were from cemeteries, stratigraphic test contexts, and light surface scatters. The size of the cemeteries suggested large villages, but they were not readily apparent. At Vidor we encountered earlier levels underlying almost the entire site, demonstrating the existence of extensive habitation sites contemporaneous with the cemeteries.

Cultural contexts earlier than 300 B.C. have begun to appear in recent excavations. First, Snarskis reported one date as early as 1500 B.C. (with others clustering around 500 B.C. [appendix 6]) for the La Montaña complex on the Atlantic watershed of Costa Rica (1978: 105–6). More recently, a single date of 800 B.C. (appendix 3) was obtained at the Vidor site from a feature containing ceramics modally similar to those of La Montaña. A date (UCLA 2163) of 300 B.C. (appendix 3) was also obtained from the Rio Naranjo area along the Guanacaste–San Carlos continuum (Norr 1979b), again with modally similar ceramics. The Guanacaste ceramics show a general stylistic relationship to other Formative Zoned Bichrome ceramics present throughout Nuclear America.

Lange (1980a) has revised the Zoned Bichrome–period sequence based on excavations at the Vidor site and on reexamination of excavation data from other sites. The 800 B.C. date can also be considered only a current best effort, and earlier Formative ceramic complexes must eventually be found. Healy (1980a) has published the most recent cultural historical/ceramic sequence for the area, and should be referred to for detailed descriptions and illustrations of individual ceramic types.

The Zoned Bichrome period at the Vidor site was divided into three phases: the Loma B phase, roughly 800 B.C. to 300 B.C. and characterized by Bocana Incised Bichrome; the Orso phase, from roughly 300 B.C. to A.D. 300 and characterized by Rosales Zoned Incised, Ballena Incised, Tamino Incised, and Zelaya Painted (Bichrome variety) types; and the final Mata de Uva phase, from approximately A.D. 300 to A.D. 500 and characterized by Tola Trichrome, Guinea Incised, and Zelaya Painted (Trichrome variety). This new ordering fits well with previous sequences from the Greater Nicoya subarea. Not all significant cultural changes are paralleled by ceramic changes, and during this northwestern Costa Rican Formative period, important shifts in settlement and subsistence were occurring while the ceramics changes apparently evolved rather slowly.

Ceramics of the Loma B phase at Vidor have some modal similarities with the earliest so far identified in the intermontane Rio Naranjo area along the Guanacaste–San Carlos corridor and in certain examples of the La Montaña complex on the Atlantic watershed. They also were present in the Chombo phase on the Santa Elena Peninsula, in Minelli's work at Barrahonda, in the Aviles phase in Rivas, and in the Angeles phase on Ometepe Island—all demonstrating the broad distribution of a common cultural base. Bocana Incised Bichrome is pan-regional at this time, with the Toya variety most characteristic of the northern sector, and the Bocana variety most characteristic of the southern sector.

These people adapted to multiple ecological settings, but there is no evidence of utilization of marine mollusca. At Vidor and other sites, insufficient evidence exists to assess other subsistence practices. The horizontal extent of Loma B–phase materials at the Vidor site indicates a relatively large and settled population. Adobe-lined hearths and ovens are present. No mortuary data are available.

The succeeding Orso phase at Vidor is also well represented at other sites throughout the area (the San Jorge phase in Rivas and on Ometepe; the Chombo phase on the Santa Elena Peninsula/Bay of Salinas; the later Catalina phase on the Tempisque River; at Barrahonda and the Monte Fresco phase in the Matapalo area). Rosales Zoned Incised was a pan-regional type at this time, but it is not found frequently in the intermontane zone; Puerto Black/Red was characteristic of the northern sector, and Zelaya Painted (Bichrome variety) was characteristic of the southern sector. Close modal parallels are seen between El Bosque ceramics from the Atlantic coast and Zelaya Painted. Mortuary patterns from the phase reflect social stratification, with some graves containing finely made Rosales Zoned Incised ceramics, ornamental metate seats, and accompanying jades. The social stratification reflected in the mortuary patterns indicates that at least low-level chiefdoms had evolved by this time. Some of the population lived in permanent, year-round settlements, while others appear to have practiced a "restricted wandering" (Beardsley et al. 1955: 136) pattern. Artifacts indicative of subsistence practices continue to be rare, and inferences based on these limited data should be carefully considered.

The final Formative Mata de Uva phase at Vidor (A.D. 300 to A.D. 500) is also reflected throughout the region (the San Roque phase on the Isthmus of Rivas and on Ometepe Island; the Murcielagos phase on the Santa Elena Peninsula/Bay of Salinas; the Ciruelas phase in the Tempisque Valley; the Las Minas phase in the Tamarindo area), and at Hacienda Jerico, Rio Naranjo, and Hacienda Mojica along the Guanacaste–San Carlos corridor. At Vidor and other coastal sites in Costa Rica, we see not only a ceramic shift to nascent polychromes, but an adaptive change—the shift to exploitation of marine resources (Lange 1978: 109). This subsistence shift stimulated coastal settlement, population growth, and cultural elaboration. The preserving contexts of the shell middens also provide us with a fuller picture of pre-Columbian life from this time onward.

Las Marias on the Bay of Salinas, Chahuite Escondido on the Santa Elena Peninsula, many sites around the Bay of Culebra, and Huerta del Aguacate and Matapalo near Tamarindo all have shell middens arranged loosely around open plaza areas (fig. 7.4). Cemeteries are found consistently

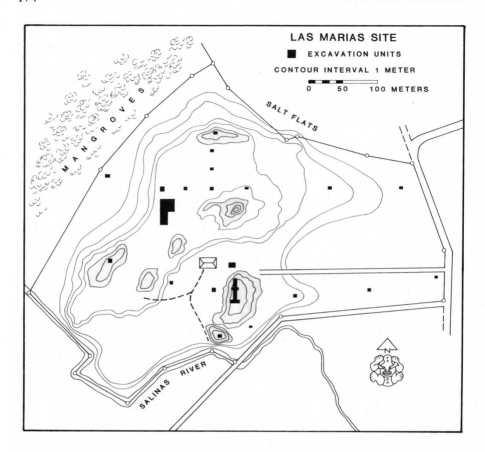

Figure 7.4. Las Marias site, Bay of Salinas. Typical configuration of coastal Guanacaste shell midden sites, with middens surrounding central plaza areas.

beneath these plazas, but no real architectural remains have been located. Some Middle and Late Polychrome mounds were superimposed on earlier burial locations, but the mounds were not used for burials.

Tola Trichrome and Charco Black/Red were pan-regional during this phase, Puerto Black-on-Red was characteristic of the northern sector, and Guinea Incised, Zelaya Painted, and Marbella Zoned Impressed were characteristic of the southern sector. Guinea Incised has strong Costa Rican Atlantic coastal analogs, as did Bocana Incised Bichrome and Zelaya Painted earlier in the period.

Mortuary customs from this time are known from limited examples. Inverted urn burials with infant and possibly fetal burials were found at

Vidor (fig. 7.5) and Chahuite Escondido. Excavations at Hacienda Mojica (Ryder 1980) near the Tempisque Valley produced an extensive cemetery almost exclusively from this period. No skeletal remains were preserved, but Tola Trichrome, Guinea Incised, Charco Black/Red, and Carrillo Polychrome vessels were prominent as grave offerings. No ornamental metates or jades were found. Ryder also noted a higher percentage of Atlantic ceramics at Mojica than had been found previously at any other site in Guanacaste.

At the Bolson site on the western side of the Tempisque, Baudez (1967: 304–5) excavated a cemetery from this period containing artifactual material similar to that from Mojica, but with skeletal material preserved. No analysis was made of the osseous remains. Day (1982) reported mortuary remains from this period from Hacienda Tempisque.

Burials at Hacienda Jerico, Guayabo de Bagaces, and Rio Naranjo along the Guanacaste–San Carlos corridor were in mounds filled with, and covered by, large river cobbles. These rock/rubble mounds are considered characteristic of Atlantic coastal rather than Pacific coastal mortuary patterns.

The only other extensive cemetery excavations from this period were those conducted by Hartman at Las Huacas early in the century (1907). Here, multiple tombs were found, the majority with more than one interment and most graves accompanied by metates, occasional mace heads, and jades. In contrast to Mojica, Las Huacas yielded only a few ceramic ocarinas and vessels, but no polychromes. On the basis of extensive pothunting, this same burial pattern is known from the Nosara Valley, but no controlled excavations have been carried out. The various elements in the burial complex, especially as they compare with broader distribution of particular artifacts, merit brief discussion, as they reflect patterns of social ranking.

The so-called metates are a misnamed component of the burial complex. Despite the thousands that have been recovered from mortuary contexts, very few have been found with manos. Other contextual and associated data have led Lothrop (1926), Lange (1971c), Baudez (1976b), and M. Graham (1979) to conclude that the metates found are ceremonial stools, thrones, seats, or "seats of power," rather than utilitarian items. Multiple functions must also be considered. Snarskis (this volume) has a somewhat different interpretation of this class of artifacts based on Atlantic coast data.

Mace heads have traditionally been referred to as war clubs. Until recently very little attention was paid to the contexts in which they were found, primarily because the vast majority were pothunted. Beginning with a reanalysis of Hartman's Las Huacas excavations (Lange 1971c), where the mace heads were found with the ceremonial seats, a number of mace heads were reported in mortuary contexts in the central highlands of Costa Rica (Snarskis 1979a). The discovery of a very similar mortuary complex at Grecia (also in the central highlands) and de la Cruz's analysis (1981) of mace

Figure 7.5.   Infant urn burial, Vidor site, Bay of Culebra, Costa Rica (photo by Ricardo Vazquez L.).

heads found on the Atlantic watershed, in the central highlands, and in Guanacaste make it conclusive that these mace heads were symbols of rank, of clans, or of status. Almost identical forms are repeated across the country and indicate social and hereditary ties among geographically dispersed upper classes.

Jadeite artifacts, or artifacts of jadeite-like stone, are frequently found in burial contexts, often lying on the ceremonial seats, and are also associated with mace heads. We now are almost certain that some of these artifacts were made from imported stone or were imported already made, while others are locally produced. We cannot say whether the difference between the foreign and locally obtained stones indicates differences between the buried individuals, but the foreign jadeite artifacts displaying clearly identifiable Mayan or Izapan motifs may, in fact, denote special relationships between the deceased and foreign political, economic, or social partners. Taken as a complex, the ceremonial stool/mace head/jade combination symbolizes persons of status within the society, and suggests that the status was at least partially derived from access to exotic goods or contacts with foreign persons and that persons of status in the southern sector of Greater Nicoya interacted with persons of similar status in other parts of Costa Rica.

Carrizal, an extensively looted mortuary/habitation site dating to this time period from the eastern lowlands of the Gulf of Nicoya, yielded no Guanacaste ceramic types, but it revealed many types previously undescribed for Costa Rica. Ceremonial seats were present, and pothunters reported finding jade. Modal similarities with Carrillo Polychrome, Zelaya Painted, and Guinea Incised ceramics were present.

External trade at this time is indicated by the jadeite utilized in the manufacture of offerings found with numerous burials. While serpentine and other diopsite-like raw materials were found in Costa Rica, no sources of jadeite have yet been identified. The closest indicated source is in Guatemala (Lange, Bishop, and von Zelst 1981), and a large number of specimens still cannot be related to any specific source.

In addition to the general Formative zoned bichrome techniques found in this period, a number of ceramic indicators suggest ties with other areas. These are almost entirely stylistic similarities rather than actual trade items. From the north, the influence of Usulutan Ware is seen in various combed types in the Greater Nicoya area, and Utatlan Ware seems to be quite similar to Rosales Zoned Incised; from the south, similarities are seen with Scarified Ware and Santa Maria Polychrome from Panama. A few trade pieces of Usulutan Ware are present in Costa Rica. By the end of the Zoned Bichrome period in northwestern Costa Rica, the bases for further developments were firmly laid.

Early Period V (A.D. 500–800)

On the Bay of Culebra, the Early Polychrome period is the later part of Accola's (1978a: 145) Culebra phase, distinguished ceramically by Carrillo Polychrome, Galo Polychrome, Chavez White-on-Red, and Potosi Appliqué. His sequence started with the Culebra phase, and the initial levels showed blurring from the preceding Mata de Uva phase. Regionally, this corresponds with the Palos Negros phase (Rivas and Ometepe), the Santa Elena phase, Santa Elena/Bay of Salinas, the San Bosco phase (Tempisque) and the Matapalo phase (Tamarindo).

In general, sites from this period are more oriented to the coast (ocean or lake), and we are beginning to see the influence of marine resources on site location. Kerbis (1979: 38) noted that during this period, "the first [intensive] exploitation of molluscan faunas as well as the subsequent trends toward marine vertebrate exploitation" occurred.

Polychrome ceramic decoration became prominent; Galo Polychrome and Chavez White-on-Red are pan-regional at this time; no predominant types are characteristic of the northern sectors, while Carrillo Polychrome continues to characterize the southern sector. Galo Polychrome vessels reflect the Ulua-Yojoa region of Honduras, but they are local imitations rather than imports. Careful comparative analysis of decorative motifs, as well as the paste itself, will be necessary to solve this problem. A few Ulua marble vases have also been found in Costa Rica, and these are definitely trade items. An occasional negative-resist vessel from Costa Rica's Central Valley is found at this time.

Two stuccoed polychrome vessels found by pothunters on the Bay of Culebra, one a cylindrical, slab-footed vessel with Tlaloc motifs and the other a double bird effigy false whistling jar, were definitely introduced from foreign sources, most probably the Guatemalan highlands. The Bay of Culebra in general and the site of Nacascolo in particular were established as a trade enclave by this time. Excavations during 1980 at Nacascolo found numerous adobe oven complexes from this period (Vazquez, personal communication).

A Maya jade was also found in the cemetery at Las Huacas. We see southern materials moving north, and Panamanian/Costa Rican gold work has been found in El Salvador (Bray 1977). However, as in the preceding period, the actual number of foreign source objects is quite limited. The presence of socially stratified mortuary remains and foreign trade objects indicates that the chiefdom structure noted in the preceding Formative period continued. There is no evidence for further evolution of the chiefdom level of organization; for example, on the basis of present settlement survey data, it is not possible to distinguish between any primary and secondary sites. As noted earlier, areas and regions seem to have been more important than individual sites.

Late Period V (A.D. 800–1000) and
Early Period VI (A.D. 1000–1200)

These periods are represented by two ceramic phases on the Bay of Culebra. Accola (1978b) took the initial step, dividing the period into an earlier Panama phase (A.D. 800 to A.D. 1000) and a later Monte del Barco phase (A.D. 1000 to A.D. 1200), with an approximately 30-centimeter-thick volcanic ash layer separating the two phases at the Vidor site. These correspond to the earlier Apompua and later La Virgen phases in the Isthmus of Rivas, to the single Doscientos phase on the Santa Elena Peninsula/Bay of Salinas and the single Palo Blanco phase in the Tempisque Valley. Accola feels that similar divisions can be made in the Tempisque and Santa Elena data. A brief reexamination of the Bay of Salinas data lends additional support to the division as do Healy's data from Rivas.

In the Middle Polychrome period, we see heavy dependence on marine resources and accumulation of large middens, some of which served as the bases for residences or other structures (as evidenced by daub fragments), while others were only garbage heaps. The refuse in these middens generally reflects mollusca gathering from the mud-flat and near-offshore areas with fish remains from the same niches. Kerbis (1979) does not feel that open water sailing or any particular technological expertise was necessary to obtain pelagic tuna. During this period we note an increase in significant differences between the northern and southern sectors of the Greater Nicoya archaeological subarea. The evidence is most obvious in ceramics and subsistence activities.

Ceramically, the Papagayo and closely related Pataky Polychrome ceramics have a northern sector concentration, and the Mora–Birmania–Santa Maria–Altiplano ceramics are typical of the southern sector. Papagayo Polychromes have strong similarities to Las Vegas Polychrome from the Lake Yojoa area of Honduras (Baudez and Becquelin 1973: 313) and are similar to trade ceramics found at Tula by Diehl et al. (1974). Persons familiar with both the Nicoya Polychromes and Las Vegas Polychrome agree with the opinion that the ceramics found at Tula are definitely not Nicoya in origin, and probably are Las Vegas (Baudez, personal communication; J. Day, personal communication). This does little to alter the significance of Diehl's trade network argument vis-a-vis Tula, but it does correct a factual error and redirect the pertinent trade vectors.

While Papagayo Polychrome does occur in Costa Rica and is quite prominent in northwestern Guanacaste, it has a limited extension to the south and east and decreases significantly as one descends the Tempisque River. Also, Papagayo is not found in Atlantic coast and central highland trade/mortuary contexts with anywhere near the frequency of the Mora-Birmania-Altiplano group. Papagayo styles in Nicaragua also demonstrate distinctive differences in polychrome treatment and a broader elaboration of decorative motifs than is seen in Costa Rica. Based on extensive study of the collection from Hacienda Tempisque and other collections and on compositional analyses done at Brookhaven National Laboratory, Day and Bishop can distinguish between Papagayo vessels made in Nicaragua and local imitations made in Costa Rica (Day 1982). On the other hand, representative specimens of the Mora-Birmania-Altiplano group are all but absent from collections from Nicaragua.

Both the Mora-Birmania-Altiplano group and Papagayo group occur infrequently in the Costa Rican Central Valley and on both Costa Rican and Nicaraguan Atlantic watershed sites, but there are practically no examples of Atlantic Coastal ceramics traded to the west. As Snarskis pointed out (this volume), the Costa Rica Central Valley is culturally considered part of the Atlantic watershed, even though hydrologically it is part of the Pacific. There is a continuous pattern of nonmutual ceramic exchange between the Atlantic and Pacific throughout the known chronological sequence and, during the Middle Polychrome period, even an absence of the modal decorative similarities between the two areas which were apparent in Bocana

Incised Bichrome, Guinea Incised, and Zelaya Painted in preceding periods. This may be a result of the overwhelming dominance of polychromes in the Greater Nicoya area during this time.

A major interpretive problem remains—the absence of polychromes from the Atlantic watershed. Some limitations were placed on Atlantic Poly- chrome production by the absence of suitable pigments, but it remains to be explained why trade across relatively short distances was either restricted or rejected. Where Mora Polychrome and Papagayo Polychrome are present in non-Guanacaste mortuary contexts (Snarskis and Blanco 1978), there are indications that their presence can be interpreted as offerings by social or political partners, or family members, from that area and not simply trade goods that were placed in the graves. This is similar to Adams's model (1971) for a major burial at Altar de Sacrificios, and I feel that it is applicable here as well (Lange 1980c).

Mortuary data from these periods are known from single and multiple primary burials at La Guinea excavated by Baudez (1967) and by Hoopes (1979). Some primary single burials were also recovered at Vidor (Vazquez and Weaver 1980). Semiarticulate multiple burials, usually containing one central figure and the associated elements of numerous other individuals (fig. 7.6), have been excavated from Middle Polychrome contexts at four different sites on the Bay of Culebra. Some individuals were accompanied by fine polychrome pottery and trade goods such as copper bells, while others have had multiple ceramic offerings of varying quality (Wallace and Accola 1980). One individual exhibited tooth filing, a trait, also noted by Stone (1977: 68), that apparently reflected Mexican influence. A semi- articulate burial from the same time period was reported by Baudez from the La Guinea cemetery (1967: 303). Stone (1977) reported a similar burial from El Moral de San Blas, and Lines also reported (1936a) a multiple burial from Zapandi on the Tempisque, but the human skeletal data are very sketchy in both cases.

While daub remnants from wattle and daub structures of the Middle Polychrome period have been recovered previously from many mound and midden contexts in the Greater Nicoya subarea and the midden profiles also revealed what have been considered living surfaces, the unstable nature of the midden context has prevented the careful excavation of a horizontal living floor. Hoopes (1979) has made a valuable contribution in his exca- vations at La Guinea; he not only increased our knowledge of mortuary behavior, but he discovered and reported on a habitation structure found with the cemetery. The house had a packed sand floor, indoor hearths, and was supported by poles covered with daub. He also described the recovery from inside the house of a bone implement referred to locally as a "cacho" and similar to what Flannery called a "piscador" in Oaxaca (1976: 37). Linares (1980: 139, citing personal communication from R. Cooke) notes

Figure 7.6. Multiple burial, Nacascolo, Bay of Culebra, Costa Rica (photo by Henry Wallace).

similar implements from central and western Panama. Hoopes (1979) also described the presence of a large shell, which, based on comparison with historical accounts, might possibly have been used as a hoe. If properly interpreted, the presence of both these implements in a domestic context would indicate the use of maize. Although Hoopes did not recover botanical evidence for corn, analyzed skeletal material from the Late Polychrome skeletal material from La Guinea (Norr 1980) indicates a 69 percent dietary dependence on maize.

Though difficult to determine from the published data, the emphasis on mollusca exploitation and fishing does not seem to have been nearly as intensive in Nicaragua as it was in Costa Rica. In Nicaragua documentary sources for the succeeding Late Polychrome period indicate an important emphasis on agriculture, but excavation data do not yet support this. The Guanacaste landscape presents different opportunities and challenges from those of the Isthmus of Rivas, and there are natural limitations on agriculture. The artifact evidence for agriculture is very limited. Whole manos and metates have not been found in domestic contexts anywhere in Greater Nicoya—except La Guinea—during these periods, and many fragments that are recovered have been reworked into nutting stones—pestles and mortars used to exploit locally available nuts, berries, and acorns. Even the presence of manos and metates is not conclusive evidence of agriculture, since many other uses for these implements are recorded in the Southwestern and Mesoamerican ethnographic literature. Conclusive evidence for agriculture is also absent from Nicaragua, and lithic evidence is surprisingly sparse, as Healy (1974b: 452) noted:

Chipped stone was rarer than ground stone in Rivas. In actuality, neither was especially plentiful in comparison to the quantities of stone artifacts from Meso-america proper. [With reference to Seibal] . . . the paucity of the Lower Central American materials was rather strikingly pointed out, considering we were dealing with seven sites in contrast to one Maya site. Not only were there four or five times as much Maya material in sheer bulk quantity, but the diversity and quality of tool types . . . was notable, especially in light of the natural stone resources of Rivas versus the Maya lowlands.

People were raising agricultural crops, regardless of the archaeological evidence, but either their relative importance in the diet or methods of preparation were such that the artifactual data are extremely sparse. Also, the primarily vertical excavations carried out to date do not yield household patterns in which such artifacts might be encountered. However, the total amount of excavation that has been done, vertical and horizontal, has yielded almost nothing but broken implements, and no blanks or other indications that manufacture and utilization of agriculturally related implements was taking place have been found.

Evidence of foreign trade during this period includes a limited number of Tohil Plumbate vessels and occasional copper artifacts such as the bell found with the Nacascolo multiple burial (Wallace and Accola 1980). Although none have been recovered from scientific excavations in the Greater Nicoya area, almost all known plumbate vessels (perhaps less than a dozen in total) are said to have come from the Bay of Culebra zone. One obsidian blade was recovered from Middle Polychrome contexts at the Vidor site, while other examples of obsidian blade fragments and flakes have been surface collected or recovered from looters' backdirt at this and other sites. Obsidian is found only in very limited quantities in the Greater Nicoya area, and trade in this commodity (whose nearest source is apparently in northern Nicaragua and may be as far away as Guatemala) probably began earlier. Mexican traders may well have been seeking cloth dyed with purple dye (Creamer 1983).

In the Bay of Culebra distinctions based on total site area and variations in the material culture recovered from excavations can be made for certain sites. There are differences between sites in terms of quantities and quality of polychrome ceramics recovered from mortuary contexts and the presence or absence of trade items such as plumbate, copper, and obsidian artifacts.

However, whether these differences resulted from the Bay's trade role or from further evolution of the chiefdom organizational structure, in which certain sites became more important than others, cannot presently be discerned. We can say that during the Middle Polychrome period, despite apparent increases in population size and the intersite differentiations noted above, there were no trends in the direction of permanent architecture or other archaeological indicators of collective activity that might indicate more distinct stratification of the social organization. Social evolution appears to have leveled off with chiefdoms at moderate stages of complexity. As Payson Sheets commented during seminar discussions, such leveling off need not indicate stagnation, but possibly a stable-state relationship between environment, population, and social organization.

Large portions of the Greater Nicoya area were apparently only sparsely occupied during this time, and there are no indications of competition or hostility between different groups. Day (1982) indicated that a significant percentage of the ceramics at Hacienda Tempisque pertained to this and the following period.

Late Period VI (A.D. 1200–A.D. 1550)

Sites with Late Polychrome components are generally concentrated on or near the many embayments of the northern coast of the Nicoya Peninsula but are absent from the straighter southern Pacific coast and inland areas. Related components are also found on islands in the Gulf of Nicoya and around the periphery of the gulf. Sites from this period are mostly concentrated along the shore of Lake Nicaragua and are relatively infrequent on the Atlantic coast of Costa Rica and Nicaragua (Snarskis, this volume).

This period is represented by the Ruiz phase on the Bay of Culebra, the La Cruz B phase on the Bay of Salinas/Santa Elena Peninsula, and the Alta Gracia phase on the Isthmus of Rivas. Sites from the period are apparently absent from other locations; Late Polychrome materials were quite limited in sites reported by Baudez for the Tempisque Valley (1967) and absent in inland work reported by Murray and Jess (1976) and Norr (1979a, 1979b). Salgado and Day (personal communication) have reported large Late Polychrome concentrations on the Tempisque River just east of the Bay of Culebra, but these are considered to be part of a general coastal system.

Polychrome ceramics reflect external cultural influences from various, and in some cases still unknown, sources. Vallejo Polychrome (fig. 7.7; Baudez 1967; Accola 1978a: 81) reflects Mexican influence and is representative of the northern sector, as is Madeira Polychrome. The exact nature of the cultural contact is still far from clear, but it is suspected that Vallejo Polychrome reflects the Mixteca-Puebla expansions; as Smith and Heath-Smith (1980) have pointed out, the Mixteca-Puebla expansion is a much

Figure 7.7.   Vallejo Polychrome (photo by Horace Day).

more complex phenomenon than previously detailed, and utilization as an explanatory device requires careful analysis of a number of different expansions which had different directions, strengths, and purposes.

The Greater Nicoya archaeological sequence provides no definite evidence of major Mexican population movements, such as the site-unit intrusion (Willey et al. 1955) at Kaminaljuyu. The lack of presence may be one reason for the leveling off of cultural evolution in the area. Abel-Vidor has observed (1980b, 1981) that in Greater Nicoya, Mexican trait-unit intrusions (Willey et al. 1955), seen in motifs on certain ceramics and in adaptation of Tlaloc vessels and motifs, have passed through the cultural filtering process that would have taken place during the course of a lengthy, overland dispersal of people from Mexico southward. Site-unit intrusions or more numerous specific trait-to-trait correlations would be expected had movement been via more rapid water routes. While we feel we have evidence that such water contacts did occur, we would currently infer that the primary dispersal of significant cultural traits took place overland.

Murrillo Appliqué (fig. 7.8; Baudez 1967; Accola 1978a: 75) is a ceramic type characteristic of the southern sector of the area, appearing as a well-defined type without apparent evolutionary roots in other ceramics. While

Figure 7.8. Murrillo Appliqué (photo by Horace Day).

the most likely source would appear to be the northern South American Caribbean area, given gross similarities between Murrillo and various appliqué-decorated types present in those areas (Lange 1971b), there has never been any firm evidence for external contacts on the basis of formal similarity. Ceramics illustrated by Linne (1929) do bear substantial resemblance and suggest one potential source area.

Surveys on Isla Caño (Finch and Honetschlager n.d.) on the south Pacific coast of Costa Rica, where Murrillo might be expected if it indeed had southern origins, revealed only a single sherd and a few additional examples of somewhat similar material. Creamer (1980, 1983) reported finding Murrillo on many of the islands she surveyed in the Gulf of Nicoya, as well as ceramics similar to those found on Caño. The island's ceramic assemblage is generally distinct from adjacent coastal assemblages. Creamer's excavations on islands in the gulf have indicated an interesting paucity of polychrome ceramics.

Bramadero Polychrome is also representative of the southern sector during this period. The fact that some types, such as Murrillo Appliqué and Bramadero Polychrome, extend just so far to the north, and other types, such as Jicote Polychrome and Vallejo Polychrome, extend just so far south, criss-crossing the area, again points out that this is indeed a cultural frontier or buffer zone (Lange 1979a), or, following Abel-Vidor's interpretation, reflects the limits of distribution of various elements in an interaction sphere.

Subsistence emphasis at this time in the Bay of Culebra area was on marine mollusca and estuarine fish, with minor emphasis on hunting (Kerbis 1979).Comparative data from Late Polychrome components of the Bay of Salinas and the Santa Elena Peninsula (Sweeney 1975: 456–57) also suggest that hunting was of minimal importance during this period. Agriculture was practiced, although, again, the amount of direct botanical or artifactual evidence is quite limited. The first non-legged, basin-shaped metate recovered from a controlled context in Guanacaste was found at the Ruiz site (Lange 1980b), and one similar specimen was reported from Rivas by Healy (1974b: 440). This form of metate is in a clear minority in contrast to the more elaborate three- and four-legged metates.

In addition to stone celts, lithic materials associated with the Late Polychrome components at the Ruiz site and Las Marias site included metate and mano fragments, many of which had been reworked into nutting stones (Lange 1971b: 53). Stone celts would appear to indicate land-clearing activities related to agriculture, although they may have been used for cutting wood for house construction, firewood, and possible watercraft. Bernstein's (1980) analyses of celts from numerous sites in coastal Guanacaste indicate a variety of uses.

Mortuary data are limited for this period. A multiple secondary burial at Las Marias on the Bay of Salinas, associated with a single Murrillo Appliqué bowl, a multiple burial associated with a zapatero form and other vessels at the Vidor site, and an interment with an undetermined number of individuals at El Moral de San Blas are typical. Filed dental mutilations were observed in this last burial (Stone 1977: 68). Creamer (1980: 5) reported a burial on San Lucas Island in the Gulf of Nicoya that contained "a child interred with three ceramic vessels, the annular base of a polychrome vessel, bone earspools and a necklace of shell beads, drilled human teeth, and a small eagle of gold/copper (*tumbaga*) alloy."

Healy summarized the major trends of the period in Pacific Nicaragua:

The archaeological remains suggest that there were fewer Late Polychrome sites . . . but that these, with numerous low mounds, were larger in overall dimensions than earlier times. . . . The last Rivas period was marked by more numerous and diversified stone tools . . . than previously. There was also a quantum jump in sheer quantity of ceramic remains. Altogether . . . there are strong impressions of a sizable Nicarao population living in nucleated villages. . . . Hunting, fishing, and farming were still important. (1974b: 525–26)

Wyckoff (1973: ms) suggested a major subsistence shift from heavy shell-fish reliance in Middle Polychrome times to more hunting in Late Polychrome times, based on data from the San Francisco site between Lake Managua and Lake Nicaragua, and from Healy's site J-RI-4: Santa Isabel "A" (excavated by A. H. Norweb) about four kilometers north of Puerto San Jorge on the shore of Lake Nicaragua. There is some doubt that faunal collection methods at either site were adequate to yield a picture of ecological trends. If this is so, it is a distinct and very interesting contrast to patterns observed on the Pacific coast of Costa Rica at the same time. Norr's (1980) analysis of C^{13} and C^{12} data from coastal Guanacaste human bone materials indicates a diet that included an 80–90 percent combination of marine fauna and C^4 plants, while only 10–20 percent of the diet came from C^3 plants and terrestrial fauna.

Direct indications of foreign objects are also limited for this period. Occasional copper artifacts are assumed to have a foreign origin, as are the very limited indications of gold metallurgy that have been identified. Metallurgy in northwestern Costa Rica during this period has been discussed by Lange and Accola (1979), but, in general, we suspected that the gold-working was being introduced from the south and copper techniques from the north. At about this same time, gold metallurgy was also introduced to the west coast of Mexico.

Obsidian has been found in Guanacaste and also on the Atlantic coast of Costa Rica from contexts of this period, indicating a further geographical extension of trade. The ceramic dissimilarity between Atlantic and Pacific Costa Rica, which was a strong feature of the preceding period, changes somewhat in the Late Polychrome period. Thin-walled, incised tripod vessels occur on both sides of the central range and share many form and decorative modes.

In Nicaragua, a very limited amount of Vallejo Polychrome has been found on the east side of Lake Nicaragua. The availability of gold in north-eastern Nicaragua also raises the possibility that some of the metal artifacts reported from the Chontales area may have been manufactured by local artisans, and goldworking in Greater Nicoya is described from the contact period (Fernandez Guardia 1889). These data directly contradict Helms's contention (1979: 3) that gold artifacts in the isthmian area were mostly introduced from external sources.

Beginning of the Historic Era

The prehistoric era in the Greater Nicoya Archaeological Subarea officially ended with the arrival of the Spanish in 1522. The use of 1550 as an end date for the Late Polychrome period indicates that the conclusion of relatively unaffected indigenous activity is purely arbitrary. The early Spanish *entradas* were casual, and Indian communities certainly continued beyond the 1520s. Abel-Vidor noted, "There is no doubt that Greater Nicoya was characterized by a plural society." Oviedo listed seven languages for the Nicaraguan colony: Chondales, Nicaragua, Chorotega, Oroçi, Orotiña, Guetares, and Maribios . . ." (Abel-Vidor 1981: 5). It is interesting that on the northern rim of the buffer zone in Honduras, Healy (this volume) also describes the pluralistic presence of seven languages at the time of contact. No contact-period sites have been definitely located or excavated, and this is one of the greatest shortcomings in our present knowledge of the area. Many researchers, most significantly Lothrop (1926) and Stone (1966b), have utilized some of the historical literature for the area, but a great wealth of documentary evidence remains unexamined. As long as sites facilitating the application of the Direct Historical Approach continue to be unexploited, the full advantages to be obtained from an interplay between the historical and archaeological data will not be realized.

Abel-Vidor (1980b, 1981) has recently studied many previously unutilized historic sources for Greater Nicoya and suggests that the northern sector had a considerably greater population density than the southern. She basically sees the Guanacaste coastal area as a hinterland to the Nicaraguan lakes region. The Nicaraguan part of Greater Nicoya has not seen active research in many years for various reasons, and it is essential that additional investigations be conducted there in the near future (see note 3). Such research will be necessary to try to resolve current discrepancies between documentary and archaeological data. An important example is in population estimates: Abel-Vidor (1981: 18) sees a population of about 500,000 in the lakes region of Nicaragua (although she has recently indicated [personal communication] that she views this number as being relative rather than absolute). Surveys in the area, although admittedly cursory, have not revealed settlement data that support such a high figure.

Discussion

The preceding period-by-period review of regional cultural development in the Greater Nicoya area summarizes current available data on prehistoric settlement patterns, ceramic distribution, subsistence practices, mortuary behavior, trade, and regional interaction. The same discussion reveals current weaknesses in the regional data base and pinpoints foci for future research. The following research themes are briefly summarized:

Chronological Framework

The areal chronology is still deficient in terms of total time depth relative to other known New World sequences and in the fineness of subdivisions within the known sequences at different locations. Some ceramic types do not always match the dated phases to which they normally correspond, but rather than assuming that the dates are in error or that the ceramics have a broader temporal range than we previously thought, we must consider that these data indicate something about the cultural development of the area. Within such a buffer/frontier zone, externally introduced motifs and techniques are going to reach different locations at different times and win varying degrees of local acceptance. Thus, I feel, we need to remain somewhat flexible in our use of correlations between particular dates, ceramic types, and cultural chronological devices such as horizon markers.

Settlement Pattern

Prior to 1978, most settlement data in the Greater Nicoya area were derived from the Lake Nicaragua shore in the northern sector of the area, the coastal Bay of Salinas and the Sapoa River Valley—an intermediate area which tends to have northern affiliations—and from coastal locations on the Santa Elena Peninsula, the Bay of Culebra, Tamarindo Bay, and the Nosara Valley in the southern sector. Only Baudez's Tempisque River survey was away from the coast, and even this area is tied ecologically and geographically to the Gulf of Nicoya area.

In 1978, research in the Bay of Culebra and other coastal areas was supplemented by an examination of Atlantic-Pacific coastal pre-Columbian contacts. Several surveys followed a transect from the Gulf of Nicoya inland through a natural corridor in the Guanacaste Cordillera to the southern shore of Lake Nicaragua. These Guanacaste–San Carlos surveys further emphasized the lack of sites dating post–A.D. 800 in the interior highland areas. This settlement distribution favors access to marine resources and growing dependence on these resources, and is of comparative value to a similar study in Panama (Linares and Ranere 1980).

Subsistence

Subsistence data are best documented for hunting, fishing, and marine mollusca exploitation. Artifact analysis also indicates utilization of nuts and berries and food processing carried out by mashing and pounding. Direct artifact evidence and botanical remains indicating agricultural practice are still so limited that we must reserve judgment regarding the significance of agricultural products, especially maize, for these people. Brewbaker (1979) has presented challenging botanical-pathological data on limits of maize utilization in the tropics. Given the lack of artifactual evidence, contact-period documentary data for agriculture must be carefully interpreted and, if accepted, utilized with caution as to temporal and geographical extrapolation. A mixed economy with local variation seems to be the best present interpretation. Changes in subsistence activity around A.D. 400–500 are seen as being significant in subsequent development of the area. These changes influenced settlement patterns and provided a basis for population growth and stable coastal settlements.

Mortuary Patterns

Data in this category are still very dispersed and sketchy. Practically the whole range of single, multiple, primary, secondary, and cremated burials representing both sexes and all ages, even fetal, have been found. Hilltops, riverbanks, middens, and central plazas between middens have all served as burial loci. From no single location, however, do we have a sufficient sample from a single time period to begin to characterize burial practices for specific age-sex-status groups during a particular time or to observe how these patterns compare throughout the subarea synchronically or change diachronically. We can say that different interment practices applied to various members of society and that some were interred with rather elaborate grave offerings, sometimes of foreign origin or locally available exotic materials.

Examination of the skeletal remains allows us to suggest that either fat/protein dietary deficiencies or chronic intestinal diseases afflicted a large percentage of the population (Vazquez and Weaver 1980). The bones occasionally show dental mutilation and are generally free of traumas suggesting either rugged activities or warfare.

The stable carbon isotopic analyses of bone collagen from Costa Rican skeletal materials have given us improved data regarding diet (Norr 1980). As Norr showed in her results, Late Polychrome–period skeletal remains from the La Guinea site (Hoopes 1979) suggest an estimated 69 percent of the diet can be attributed to C^4 plants (maize). La Guinea is sufficiently far from the Gulf of Nicoya or Pacific coast that we can assume that very few, if any, marine fauna entered the diet. The remainder of the diet at La Guinea was made up of C^3 plants (non-maize) and terrestrial fauna. From the Late Zoned Bichrome period (A.D. 300–500) she found no maize consumption indicated in samples run on bone collagen from the inland Mendez site. The total lack of maize in the diet would seem unusual, except that Linares (1980a: 246) also reported total lack of botanical or artifact evidence for maize at A.D. 600 in sites in the Bocas del Toro region of Panama.

From skeletal samples from three Middle and Late Polychrome–period coastal sites in the Greater Nicoya area, Norr reported estimates of 82–93 percent of the diet of these individuals consisted of some combination of C^4 plants (maize) and marine fauna. Given the greater archaeological evidence for marine exploitation at coastal sites than for maize agriculture, I am inclined to believe that the major portion of the represented dietary percentage was from marine resources. However, the inability to distinguish between C^4 plants and marine fauna is one of the current limitations of the stable carbon isotopic method of analysis of bone collagen. The analysis of bone collagen from these sample individuals for the stable nitrogen isotopic composition N^{15}/N^{14} is currently in progress for an estimate of the relative combination of terrestrial and marine organisms in the diet (Norr 1981), and this may help solve this particular problem.

External Contacts: The Frontier/Buffer Zone Interaction Sphere

Some ceramic parallels are seen with the Atlantic watershed of Costa Rica throughout the known prehistory of the two regions, but there are only limited indications of active trade between the two. The barrier maintenance factors between the two zones have yet to be defined. From farther afield, north or south, we find the evidence for external influence almost always appears as filtered ideas or representations, very seldom as actual trade items, and never as intrusive components indicative of actual foreign occupation.

Conclusion

The Greater Nicoya Archaeological Subarea, although exposed for two millennia to external cultural impulses from more developed societies, remained relatively isolated, and strong local traditions persisted. The extent to which these external forces actually influenced local developments has been variously appraised, but this area never underwent substantial development or change as a consequence. There is a particularly distinct lack of architectural features, generally assumed to reflect available and organized labor groups. Factors limiting growth in lower Central America and the Greater Nicoya Subarea relative to that achieved in El Salvador, Guatemala, western Honduras, and Mexico can be summarized as follows:

1. *Geographical distance from major centers of political and economic power in Mexico, Guatemala, and Peru was of primary importance.* Distances, given prehistoric transportation and communication, were simply too great to allow an external group effective control over the area. From what we know of the *pochteca*, elite group interaction, runner-messenger systems, and coastal travel, such communication might have been established given suitable economic or social incentives; however,

2. *there were insufficient concentrations of desirable/unique natural resources to justify such efforts.* Jade sources are no longer assumed to be within the area. Necessary raw materials were generally distributed and equally available. In terms of a simple economic model, other local raw, perishable, or exotic items simply did not have a high enough yield ratio to make the effort worthwhile; and

3. *human resources that could be harnessed for labor projects were lacking.* The population density in this area was low, with major concentrations

early in central areas and later principally along the coast. The Nicaraguan lakes appear to have attracted a steady and large population. There were no large geographical units within this area, such as the valleys of Teotihuacan, Oaxaca, or Guatemala (Lange, chap. 3, this volume), which in contrast to rugged or barren countryside surrounding a large oasis would attract population concentrations, particularly agriculturalists.

4. *Hydraulic controls have been another factor often noted as a possible explanation for the development of complex societies, but in Greater Nicoya* (a) there are no arid areas with major water sources where control of water would be important; (b) water courses tend either to be very small or to be raging tropical torrents uncontrollable by any means either prehistoric or modern; and (c) the population density was simply insufficient, relative to supplies, to bring about competition for and, hence, a desire for control of water with attendant social and economic mechanisms.

The current archaeological data base represents broad regional comparisons based on survey of selected zones, limited stratigraphic test excavations, and even more limited horizontal excavation. Such data do not yet permit the detailed comparison of multifaceted patterns. If we are to develop a useful understanding of this complex frontier/buffer zone, future research emphases must: (a) focus on excavations that will give us comparative data based on patterns, (b) gradually fill the many spatial lacunae that dot the research area, (c) renew work on the Isthmus of Rivas in Nicaragua, and (d) systematically utilize the ethnohistoric data for the region.

In addition to considering the foci of future research, we must also consider who the researchers will be. The vast majority of the research in the Greater Nicoya area has to date been done by foreigners, but the mention of Costa Rican students, even minimally, in the bibliography of persons who contributed to the preceding data is a significant step. For myriad reasons, students whose cultural roots are in the Greater Nicoya area should assume a greater responsibility for research.

The National Museum of Costa Rica has developed a core of well-trained students.[3] In terms of financial resources, international interest in the area will continue to be necessary and, indeed, appropriate to the extent that we consider its broad implications for New World culture history. Nonetheless, it is very clear we have entered a new era in which the spirit of true cooperation and mutual benefit must prevail.[4]

Notes

1. Research in Costa Rica from 1969 through 1979 was assisted by grants and support from the Organization for Tropical Studies, Inc., the National Geographic Society, the University of Wisconsin-Madison, Beloit College, and the Associated Colleges of the Midwest. From 1976 through mid-1979, financial support for field

research was provided primarily by the National Museum of Costa Rica. Numerous Costa Rican, North American, and European students participated in the fieldwork, and the efforts of many of them are reflected in the bibliographic citations for this chapter. Their work has been dedicated and their ideas stimulating. In addition, I would like to specifically acknowledge the assistance of Dr. Andrew Hunter Whiteford in getting the fieldwork started in 1969 and Dr. J. Robert Hunter of the Associated Colleges of the Midwest for keeping it going in the early stages. It is most appropriate that Bud Whiteford, in a letter I received on a rainy night and read by flashlight in a tent on the Bay of Culebra, first suggested I contact Doug Schwartz and the School of American Research with the idea for a seminar, and for which this paper was eventually prepared. Hector Gamboa P., head of the Department of Anthropology and History, and Luis Diego Gomez P., director of the National Museum of Costa Rica, both had tremendous influence on the course of the research. Daniel Oduber Q. made archaeological research an emphasis of his presidential administration from 1974 to 1978; he stimulated significant research and supported increased levels of training for Costa Rican students. Jan and Frederick Mayer of Denver, Colorado, have helped support various avenues of analysis and publication through the years.

2. In July 1982 the JFM Foundation of Denver, Colorado, sponsored a conference on Greater Nicoya ceramics. Participants included Suzanne Abel-Vidor, Claude Baudez, Ronald Bishop, Winifred Creamer, Jane Day, Paul Healy, Frederick Lange, Robert Stroessner, and Alice Tillett. Four days of discussions were devoted to clarifying terminology and classification of principal Greater Nicoya ceramic types, and the implications of the typological system. A follow-up conference on the same theme was also held in Costa Rica during the fall of 1982, again under the auspices of the JFM Foundation. Jan and Frederick Mayer are again recognized for their crucial support.

In 1982–83, the JFM Foundation supported the neutron activation analysis of 1,200 Greater Nicoya ceramic samples by the Brookhaven National Laboratory. The preliminary results indicated that Greater Nicoya ceramic production was initially relatively dispersed and became very centralized after ca. A.D. 800. In addition, in May 1983, the JFM Foundation supported a second conference in Denver. This meeting was attended by all the 1982 participants, as well as by Lorena San Roman de Gallageos (director of the National Museum of Costa Rica) and Silvia Salgado and Juan Vicente Guerrero (employees of the National Museum of Costa Rica and students at the University of Costa Rica). The assistance of the Costa Rican Tourist Institute in facilitating the participation of the two students is gratefully acknowledged. Discussions at this conference led to a further refinement of nomenclature and chronological periods, all of which will be reported in a forthcoming summary report.

3. Since the completion of the field research on which this chapter is largely based, investigations have continued in two different areas of Greater Nicoya. On the Bay of Culebra, Ricardo Vazquez and Silvia Salgado of the National Museum of Costa Rica have supervised excavations at Nacascolo and Playa Panama, respectively; both of these projects have added to our knowledge of site patterning on the Bay of Culebra, and at Nacascolo significant additional mortuary remains have also been recovered. A UCLA research team under the direction of Dr. Brian Dillon

has also been working at Nacascolo in cooperation with the National Museum of Costa Rica. Winifred Creamer of Tulane University has been finishing (1983) a three-year project in and around the Gulf of Nicoya that promises to greatly enhance our knowledge of the prehistoric role of that important region. Luis Ferrero, ethnohistorian with the National Museum of Costa Rica, is also continuing important research into attempts by the protohistoric Mexican groups to extend their domain south and east of Greater Nicoya and into the Central Valley of Costa Rica.

Lange (in November 1982) and Lange and Sheets (in March 1983) had the opportunity to visit the Republic of Nicaragua and conduct surface surveys on the Pacific coast and on the eastern side of Lake Nicaragua. Sheets concluded that the obsidian industry on the Pacific coast was basically a local entity and not subject to Mesoamerican influence or control. On the eastern side of the two lakes almost no obsidian was present and lithic technology was devoted almost entirely to locally available cherts; these data are very closely related to the point Sheets made during the seminar with regard to the use of lithic criteria to help determine the southern boundary of Mesoamerica. Lange found that the northern sector/southern sector distinctions that had been established were validated by the surface distribution data and that the northern frontier of Greater Nicoya can be drawn at approximately the location of Managua and slightly to the east of Lake Nicaragua and the southeastern corner of Lake Managua. Only in the Late Polychrome Period does there appear to have been a significant amount of trade between the Pacific coast and the area east of the lakes. Likewise, only Late Polychrome ceramics such as Vallejo Polychrome were found in small numbers near the Bay of Fonseca.

The assistance, interest, and cooperation of the Gobierno de Reconstruccion Nacional of Nicaragua and Olga Martha Montiel, Amelia Barahona, Leonor de Rocha, and Anibal Martinez of the Ministry of Culture is gratefully acknowledged. Dr. Jaime Incer B. and Roberto Parrales S. also helped to make both visits a complete success.

4. My wife, Holley, and daughters, Heather and Kathy, have been involved in almost all of the research I have done in Costa Rica. I have been grateful for their participation and support.

8
Central America:
The Lower Caribbean

M. J. SNARSKIS[1]

Museo Nacional de Costa Rica

This chapter emphasizes Atlantic Central America from Nicaragua to Panama, and especially eastern central Costa Rica, where I have done extensive fieldwork during the last five years (Snarskis 1976a, 1976b, 1978, 1979a, 1979b, 1981, 1982a, 1982b). Archaeological developments in northern South America and the Caribbean will be mentioned only as they appear to affect this subarea.

The natural environments of Central America have been described in chapter 3. Prehistoric man was a part of this biota, and it would not be unusual to find that his traditions of land use, resource procurement, craft technology, and even social organization exhibited a rather similar range of variation throughout the extent of this environmental zone. The definition of Central America as a distinct culture area must ultimately rest on bio-geographic foundations, and its frontiers are, first and most important, environmental ones. This is not environmental determinism à la Meggers (1954); the abundance, not the lack, of viable eco-zones played an important part in the arrested development of Central American cultures vis-à-vis those of the northern and southern ends of Nuclear America. In the following review of the archaeology of Atlantic lower Central America, emphasis has been given to the changing patterns of human adaptation to the natural medium and their expressions in the archaeological record.

Early Man Sites: Period I (?–8000 B.C.)

Solid evidence of human presence in eastern lower Central America is absent before 11,000–8000 B.C. Dated sites just to the north (Gruhn and Bryan 1977) and south (Rouse and Cruxent 1963: 34–35, 155; Haynes 1974; Lynch 1974) suggest that these must be present. Well-established dates for projectile point sites far to the south (Bird 1969; Schobinger 1973) seem to guarantee the existence of similar sites in Central America. For the period 11,000–6000 B.C. evidence does exist, even though it is only typological, without supporting radiocarbon dates. The regions specifically covered in this chapter, Madden Lake in Panama and Turrialba in Costa Rica, are examples of sites from this time period. Paleo-Indian points from the former site—a periodically exposed, lacustrine environment—have been noted in the archaeological literature for almost 20 years, and it has been the object of repeated surface collections by several investigators (Sander 1964; Bird and Cooke 1974).

The Turrialba site is an open site located on the eastern rain-forest slopes of the Costa Rica Cordillera Central at an elevation of 700 meters (fig. 8.1). It is on a multitiered bluff overlooking one of the largest rivers in Costa Rica, the Reventazon. The nearby Las Animas calcareous formation contains occasional large nodules of a chert- or jasper-like stone, many of which can still be found in a stream bed below the site. This resource proximity probably explains why Turrialba was a workshop site for several occupations spanning thousands of years. Although a multicomponent site bearing mixed materials, Turrialba (Snarskis 1979b) has yielded several kinds of Paleo-Indian chipped stone artifacts.

Turrialba was originally interpreted as a single, component El Bosque–phase ceramic site (Snarskis 1979b) with an atypical chert-jasper lithic assemblage. This interpretation was altered by the discovery of 18 whole and fragmentary fluted points and preforms, along with numerous snub-nosed, keeled end scrapers, end scrapers with lateral spurs, large blades, burins, and skillfully made side scrapers (fig. 8.2). Lynch (1967, 1970), confronted with a similarly poorly stratified site at Quishqui Puncu, Peru, was nevertheless able to distinguish probable preceramic lithics from ceramic-age lithics; this was also the case at Turrialba.

Although morphology alone allows for a Paleo-Indian placement of the points and preforms, the presence of an El Bosque ceramic component at Turrialba raises a question about the secure attribution of other lithics to Paleo-Indian times. Other preceramic components at the site which are not Paleo-Indian may possibly be represented by two scallop-based triangular points and crude bifacial wedges like those of the Talamanca (5000 B.C.–3000 B.C.) and Boquete (3000 B.C.–500 B.C.) phases of Chiriqui, Panama (Ranere 1976, 1980d; Richard Cooke, personal communication). Another

Figure 8.1. Map showing the locations of some sites discussed in chapter 8.

typically Archaic point is a more rounded triangular shape with a well-defined peduncle; Carlos Aguilar (personal communication) found a very similar point with Pavas-phase pottery near San Jose. It remains to be seen whether such points or still another variety of small triangular points—this one flat-based and serrated on all edges—are associated with El Bosque ceramics. For certain scraper types and other enigmatic tools, let alone unmodified cores and flakes, a secure temporal placement cannot be established. However, in addition to the evidence for less skillful stone knapping technology in ceramic times, the following data support the hypothesis that the majority of recognizable, frequently found chert tool types at Turrialba are assignable to the preceramic. First, of 12 El Bosque sites excavated or collected on the Atlantic watershed, only one (CATIE) has produced even a single chert tool (a heavily used keeled end scraper) like those found at Turrialba; it was also located on the highest Reventazon terrace just over a kilometer downstream. Even unretouched chert flakes were extremely rare in El Bosque sites, but artifacts of ground volcanic stone (manos, metates, and others) as well as chipped and ground slate or andesite tools were invariably present in considerable quantities. Second, except for two preform

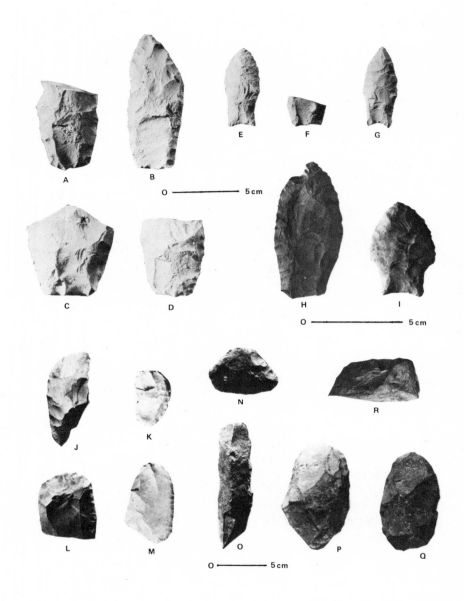

Figure 8.2. Chipped stone tools from the Turrialba site: *a–d*, preforms for fluted points; *e–h*, Clovis-like fluted points; *i*, fishtail or Magellan fluted point; *j–m*, unifacial side scrapers or knives; *n*, bifacial knife; *p–r*, large keeled scrapers or scraper planes (*r* is side view of *p*).

tips and the fishtail point, all Paleo-Indian points at Turrialba were found on the highest of the three large terraces. The western half of the lowest terrace shows a marked reduction in the quantity of chert fragments, while slate, andesite, and ceramics continue in lesser amounts. A fourth, very small terrace that did not exist in Paleo-Indian times and is only three to five meters above the present stream level, was also surface collected. El Bosque ceramics, andesite, and unmodified thick flakes and blocky fragments of chert were found, but no thin flakes, blades, or recognizable tool types appeared.

In terms of present evidence, all from surface-collected, nondated sites, lower Central America (Costa Rica and Panama) seems to be the borderline between the spatial distributions of two Paleo-Indian point types: the waisted and eared fluted point similar to some Clovis-derived waisted points of eastern North America, and the stemmed fishtail or Magellan point, sometimes fluted, known from several Paleo-Indian sites throughout South America. The converging or straight-sided classic Clovis points of western North America and Mexico are represented as far south as Costa Rica by at least two possible candidates, the Hartman point (Swauger and Mayer-Oakes 1952) and a basal fragment from Turrialba. Three waisted Clovis-like points and one resharpened fishtail were also found at Turrialba. The Madden Lake region in Panama, on the other hand, has produced only two waisted Clovis-like points, but six fishtails. At present, in other words, all Paleo-Indian fluted points known to the north of Costa Rica are either classic or waisted Clovis types, while all those south of Panama are fishtails.

Willey (1966: 68) noted the morphological evolution of the classic western Clovis point into waisted variations in the eastern United States as well as in lower Central America, where it may have further developed into the stemmed fishtail variety. An acceptable hypothesis for this evolution would be changing patterns of human ecological adaptations, in this case changes from resource procurement technology used in arid highlands and plains to that used in forested areas. The precise reasons why waisted and then stemmed projectile points should be more efficient in the forest are unclear. Rouse (1976 and personal communication) disagrees with the above hypothesis, and, citing early C^{14} dates for fishtail points to the south, he sees them diffusing northward later in time and finally degenerating into the waisted Clovis-like fluted points.

Lynch (1976, 1978) has presented the most recent summary of geologial and botanical evidence for climate changes in lower Central America at the end of the Pleistocene, all pointing to a cooler, drier climate facilitating man's passage of the Darien. If true, this would tend to deemphasize the importance of heavy forests (and the consequent shifts in human adaptive strategies) as a causative factor in the change of shapes observed in fluted points. However, repeated opening and closing of the Darien Gap would tend to promote more rapid speciation in the South American continent but still allow the periodic interchange of both fauna and flora. As the Darien remained passable for two or three thousand years or more, the Nearctic fauna coeval with fluted-point-bearing man could drift into South America, and Neotropic fauna could drift northward. Man could drift along with them, bearing his point of choice, and fishtails should be found some distance to the north of the Darien (as they have), while waisted Clovis varieties should be found somewhat to the south (they have not as yet). There was probably a period in which they were manufactured simultaneously.

The Tropical Archaic:
Periods II (8000–4000 B.C.)
and III (4000–1000 B.C.)

If we assume that the relatively large Paleo-Indian spear points reflect an emphasis on mega-faunal hunting complemented by the collecting of wild nuts, fruits, seeds, tubers, and possibly some riverine protein (Lynch 1978), then their disappearance or significant modification might reflect a concomitant shift in man's resource-procurement strategies. Several factors could have been involved: (a) change in the type, size, and quantity of animals most frequently hunted, (b) a cyclical, seasonal round for the efficient gathering of plant resources, which tended to limit spatially the scope of human groups, resulting eventually in (c), incipient agriculture, sedentism, and land or resource tenure, which in turn engendered increasingly different artifact complexes.

The Archaic stage of cultural development, linking the Paleo-Indian hunters to the Formative villagers, has been a neglected issue for most Central American archaeologists, probably because of the difficulty of locating and dating such sites. In the Caribbean, where true big game hunters were absent, this stage is perhaps the initial one and has been better studied. It was for some years called the Meso-Indian epoch (Rouse and Cruxent 1963), but now, on a purely technological basis, is known as the Archaic age (Rouse and Allaire 1979). Willey (1971) refers to this stage as Preceramic Periods IV and V.

Archaic sites are rare in lower Central America so far, and unreported above Panama with the possible exception of Magnus's unavailable results from Pearl Lagoon, Nicaragua. Ranere (1971, 1976, 1980b) has published extensively on the Talamanca and Boquete phases of northwest Panama, and Linares (1976a) has written an excellent review of this stage for the Intermediate Area as a whole. Linares agrees with Ranere's (1971) hypothesis of an "earlier generalized tropical hunting-gathering mainland adaptation" as the source for sites falling in Willey's northwest South American (we may add, Central American) littoral tradition. Both Ranere and Linares visualize a root- and tree-crop subsistence base for these supposedly earlier inland sites, based on stone tool replication experiments by Ranere. A few sites which probably date to this period have been surface collected in eastern and northwestern Costa Rica, but identifications are not definite as yet (Lange, this volume).

Recent surveys by Drolet (1980) in the Caribbean Costa Arriba, the coast east of the Canal region of Panama, did not encounter preceramic sites. A small rockshelter excavated by Bird and Cooke near Maje, the Cueva Bustamante, did seem to contain a preceramic lithic assemblage similar to that of the Pacific Chiriqui shelters in its lower levels (Cooke 1976a). Linares (1976a: 75) mentions an unconfirmed verbal account by J. E. Espinosa of a site in Caribbean Nicaragua (Angi, on Monkey Point) with deposits radiocarbon dated to 5000–3000 B.C.

Early Ceramics and Sedentism: Periods III (4000–1000 B.C.) and IV (1000 B.C.–A.D. 500)

4000–1000 B.C.

Investigators, among them Baudez, Coe, Magnus, Snarskis, and Drolet, have begun their projects in lower Central America expecting to find early Formative ceramics; none has done so. It seems advisable to stop looking for Puerto Hormiga clones and instead try to understand local cultural evolution in depth, perhaps using models very different from those of the northwest South American littoral.

1000–300 B.C.: The La Montaña and Chaparron Complexes

The earliest pottery presently known from Caribbean lower Central America is the La Montaña complex from the Turrialba Valley in Costa Rica, a site only five kilometers to the west of the Paleo-Indian workshop previously described. La Montaña pottery was found at a depth of 80–100 centimeters in a buried organic soil horizon visible as a darker 20-centimeter-wide band in a yellow sandy clay subsoil. This layer underlies a cemetery dating to approximately A.D. 300–700.

When compared to the later ceramics in the eastern Costa Rican sequence, the La Montaña complex is radically different (fig. 8.3). In a sample of some 7,000 sherds, 99 percent were a light orange-brown monochrome with plastic decoration predominating; only a very few sherds showed painted linear designs or a zoned wash in a fugitive red color. The most striking form is a flat, raised-rim griddle (fig. 8.3l, m) identical to the so-called *budares* which supposedly attest to bitter manioc use in many Brazilian,

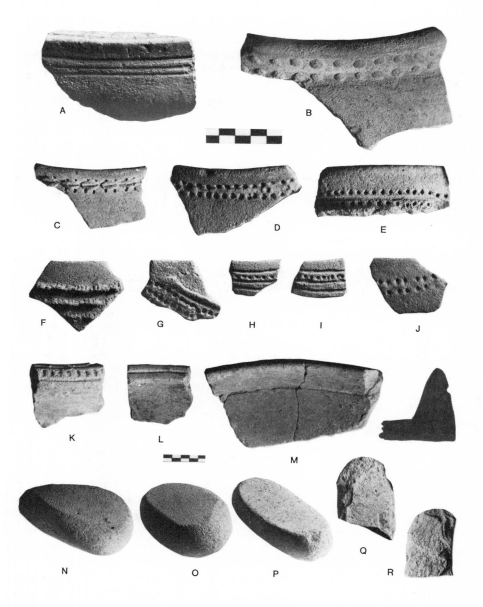

Figure 8.3. Ceramics and lithics of La Montaña complex (1000–500 B.C.): *a*, slightly incurving bowl with fugitive red paint on lip; *b–e, k*, collared ollas; *f–j*, slightly to strongly incurving rims (tecomates); *l, m*, flat, raised-rim griddles; *n–p*, manos with one or more surfaces beveled flat by use; *q, r*, cleavers made on andesite spalls.

Venezuelan, and Colombian sites (Reichel-Dolmatoff 1965a: 63–65; Lathrap 1970: 48–57). Some griddles have carbonized deposits.

If forms expanded at the exterior lip are included, tecomates or globular neckless jars make up over 40 percent of the rim forms recovered in the La Montaña sample. Another diagnostic form is a tall, cylindrical vessel with a flat, flaring base. Although only fragments were found at La Montaña, a nearly whole example, decorated in zoned dentate rocker stamping, was found at a construction site (ZIP) near San Jose, Costa Rica. This form, which may be a drum, is echoed in many similar vessels of the Concepcion or "Scarified Ware" and earlier complexes in Chiriqui, Panama.

Plastic decoration in the form of broad-line incising with round-tipped stylus, conical and rectangular punctation, and appliqué pellets and fillets predominates in the La Montaña complex. A very few sherds (always smudged grey-black or perhaps differently fired) have excised/incised areas filled with red ochre, an Early/Middle Formative technique discussed by Ford (1969: 131–33, 146). An unusual form of cord marking is also present and described by Coe (1961: 58–59) as rocker cord stamping. It was apparently achieved by binding a small tool with twine and rocking it lengthwise over the damp clay surface.

Like the ceramics, the lithic artifacts from La Montaña are strikingly different when compared to other lithic assemblages in the eastern Costa Rican archaeological sequence. The most frequent artifact is a cleaver, made from a spall which has been detached from a water-smoothed slate or volcanic cobble (fig. 8.3q, r). The cleaver is commonly oval in shape and ranges from 15×7 centimeters to 25×11 centimeters. Only 12 percent of these tools were recovered unbroken, and the lines of fracture on the rest are almost always perpendicular to the long axis, suggesting the tool was used to strike a cutting blow, perhaps in chopping tubers. The La Montaña cleavers do not show the narrower waist or signs of hafting that characterize the similarly made double-bitted axes of later periods, although their number (79) and relative ease of manufacture suggest a common, everyday use in food processing.

There are two kinds of manos among La Montaña lithics. One is a small ovoid cobble, unmodified except by slight-use polish and battering at the ends—it might better be called a pounder. The other is a longer cobble beveled (ground flat) on one or more sides, apparently as a result of use. This seems to imply a polishing, rubbing kind of manipulation, as opposed to the push-pull or rocking motion used with manos of later periods, which produced a characteristic bar-of-soap shape. The second kind of La Montaña mano, in contrast, has precise, sharply defined edges at the juncture between the working surface and the natural curvature of the cobble (fig. 8.3n, o, p). It is suggested that this form of mano is related to a food-processing activity, as yet unknown, which did not persist into later periods. Since manioc was still being cultivated when the Spanish arrived, it was not the use of manioc per se; it may represent, however, a distinctive mode of preparing manioc or perhaps other root and/or tree crops. No metates or fragments thereof were found.

Many small backed knives of chert were also recovered at La Montaña. Only two scrapers, both small and of chert, were found. Two trapezoidal basalt celts (which oxidize to a light green color) were excavated, one in association with a tiny volcanic stone bowl, in what was taken to be the only possible tomb or cache. None of the lithic tool types, ground or flaked, which characterize the Boquete phase in Chiriqui, Panama, was found.

Although an area of 13×22 meters was completely hand troweled, no definite features like hearths or post holes appeared; in some cases, clusters of artifacts lying flat in the same horizontal plane suggested former living floors. Fire-cracked rocks and flecks of charcoal were common. Among the charcoal samples were a few which could be tentatively identified. One was part of a large seed (minimum diameter 23 mm), apparently of the genus *Persea* (avocado); another was a porous, apparently dicotyledonous seed fragment; a third was a tiny, unidentifiable piece of animal bone (Richard Ford, personal communication). Five charcoal samples from the La Montaña component yielded dates ranging from 1515 B.C. to 280 B.C., clustering around 500 B.C. (appendix 6).

A final, speculative hypothesis is stimulated by the La Montaña artifact complexes. It is reasonable to conclude that the southern (northern South American) cast of most prehistoric cultures in eastern lower Central America is the natural result of a core of adaptive strategies and their associated artifacts related to human ecology in the tropical forest (Snarskis 1976b, 1978: 10–12). Traditionally, this interpretation has been extended to subsistence systems, postulating the priority of root and tree cropping in all pre-Columbian periods characterized by agriculture (Stone 1956b, 1958a: 25, 1961: 200, 1966a: 27). As will be seen, this was not the case in Atlantic watershed Costa Rica and similar regions after about the middle of Period IV. I postulate that the La Montaña–phase peoples were the last to depend primarily on root and tree crops. Although sympathetic to the arguments of DeBoer (1975) and Linares (1979), I suggest that the griddles (*budares*) and unusual manos of the La Montaña phase were associated with the preparation of root and tree crops in ways that did not persist. Sites of this phase were small and scarce because of the nature of swidden root cropping (Meggers 1971; Harris 1972; Linares 1977b).

Not long after the La Montaña site was excavated, a second early ceramic complex was discovered in the San Carlos region of the northern Atlantic watershed of Costa Rica near the town of Chaparron (fig. 8.4). Unlike La Montaña pottery, the Chaparron ceramic complex is almost totally bichrome with a hard, lustrous, dark red slip applied zonally to vessel lips and shoul-

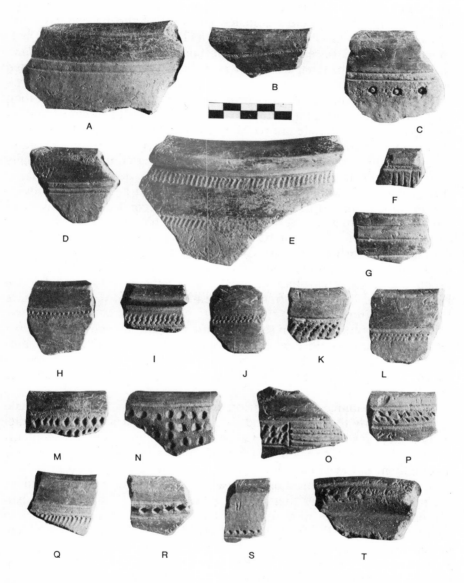

Figure 8.4. Ceramics of the Chaparron complex: *a–d, f–s,* tecomates with lips expanded on the interior; *e,* collared olla; *t,* bowl with lip expanded on the interior.

ders, almost always delimited by circumferential round-bottomed wide incised lines. Including expanded-lip varieties, more than 85 percent of the Chaparron rim forms were tecomate-like. Most of the La Montaña rim forms also appear in Chaparron pottery, including the distinctive flat-bottomed, cylindrical vessel. However, the raised-edge, flat griddle (*budare*) does not occur in the Chaparron pottery, although bowls with lips expanded on the interior do.

Although the sample of Chaparron complex sherds is small (less than 500), there is no mistaking the Mesoamerican cast of this pottery. Neither the expanded-lip tecomate nor red slip zoned by broad, incised lines occurs early in the Ecuadorian and Colombian sequences (Ford 1969: 92–95, 125–28). While the earliest Mesoamerican tecomates were thin walled, zonally slipped in specular red hematite, and occasionally decorated with crisscrossed grooves below the rim, later varieties (1100 B.C.–700 B.C.) were thicker walled, slipped in nonspecular red, and decorated in an unslipped band below the lip with precisely those plastic techniques observed in Chaparron pottery, plus brushing (Coe and Flannery 1967: 25–26; Ford 1969: 93). Among published materials, Chaparron pottery has its closest analogues in Dinarte-phase ceramics from Ometepe Island in Nicaragua (Haberland 1966b) and in Conchas-phase material from Pacific coast Guatemala (Coe 1961; Coe and Flannery 1967); certain early pottery from Chiapas (Lowe 1975) is also similar.

In a stratigraphic pit dug in search of pure Chaparron deposits, a flat river stone 90 centimeters in diameter was encountered; it displayed two pronounced concavities produced by grinding, the larger in the center. Chances are good that it belongs to Early-Middle Period IV. A radiocarbon date was not obtained.

After La Montaña and Chaparron provided in 1977 the first adequate samples of Early to Middle Period IV pottery in Costa Rica—the Schettel Incised sherd reported earlier by Lange (1971b) is almost certainly contemporary—sherds from this period began to be recognized at several other sites, among them in Guacimo, Linea Vieja, Guayabo de Turrialba (Oscar Fonseca, personal communication), Tatisco, near Cartago, Pavas, Barrial de Heredia, and four other sites within 30 kilometers of Chaparron in San Carlos. Small samples were recovered below Orso-phase materials at Sitio Vidor, Guanacaste (Lange 1980a), and near Rio Naranjo, in the Cordillera between Guanacaste and San Carlos (Norr 1979b; Lange 1980a). Carlos Aguilar excavated pottery like some of Norr's near Tilaran, Guanacaste, and dated it with one charcoal sample to A.D. 120 ± 80 (I–10,804).

As in Paleo-Indian times, the limited artifactual evidence from Early Period IV in lower Caribbean Central America suggests a fluctuating cultural frontier; red-on-buff Mesoamerican-like ceramics coexisted with monochrome pottery with forms and decoration much like those of earlier traditions in northern South America.

300 B.C.–A.D. 500: A Surge in Population

For many years, in much of lower Central America, sites dating to this time span were the earliest known, occasioning much discussion of the inhospitality or nonproductivity of the area as compared, say, to Meso-america. Now we know the earlier sites are there, but in numbers much fewer than those of the second half of Period IV. In the Atlantic watershed of Costa Rica, at least, this span was one of explosive population growth; this may have been related to a modified agricultural system and the avail-ability of more farmland. In Atlantic Panama, the geography is more re-strictive, with a larger percentage of coastline and steep slopes relative to recent alluvial plains, and its prehistory followed a rather different course. Furthermore, eastern Panama cannot really be divided into Atlantic and Pacific sectors, as is done in the rest of lower Central America; similar climatic patterns have resulted in a rather homogeneous cultural distribution in both watersheds.

Cooke (1973: 91–96) has discussed the ceramic styles of eastern Panama, the earliest of which is Zoned Linear–Incised (the last few centuries B.C.). It shows wide linear incisions often enclosing lines of punctations, shell and fingernail stamping, combing (brushing), and fillet appliqué. Sherds asso-ciated with a C^{14} date of 70 B.C. $\pm$ 155 were collected at the Isla Carranza site on the Rio Chagres (Cooke 1976a: 34, 1976b); they are very similar to pottery from contemporary sites on the Pacific like Guacamayo, Tonosi, and Isla Tobogilla (Stirling and Stirling 1964b). Interestingly, Cooke (1976a: 34) has noted that, after this time, the stylistic traditions of eastern and central Panama, as well as Chiriqui, begin to diverge markedly. The same can be said of pottery styles in northwest, southwest, and eastern Costa Rica.

From the first to the seventh centuries A.D., ceramics with plastic dec-oration unlike that of contemporary complexes in the central Pacific part of Panama appeared in sites to the east of the capital (Miranda 1974; Cooke 1976a: 34). This pottery, known as Incised-Relief Brown, sometimes occurs along with a black-on-red ware, often outlined by incision, called Zoned Bichrome (Drolet 1980: 224). In Playa Ventana and Panama Viejo many tombs similar to those of Sitio Conte have been found, but the Zoned Bichrome style apparently does not continue farther east in the Costa Arriba and Darien regions, suggesting its manufacture on the Pacific side (Drolet 1980: 225). Incised-Relief Brown was found in association with Conte Poly-chrome in the Playa Venado and Panama Viejo sites and in the fill of a later funerary context at the Miraflores site on the Rio Bayano (Cooke 1973, 1976a). Drolet (1980: 228) traces the appearance of Incised-Relief Brown through the Pearl Islands, Darien, and all the way to the site of Cupica in Pacific Colombia (Reichel-Dolmatoff and Reichel-Dolmatoff 1961). By far the most frequent pottery encountered by Drolet in the Costa Arriba region is a utilitarian ware he calls Santa Isabel Undecorated (1980: 195), tying it in to the monochrome pottery described by Linne (1929) and others throughout eastern Panama.

Drolet also describes a cobble-based lithic industry which produced tools for forest clearance, woodworking, fishing, hunting, and food processing. It appears that these tools were produced at specialized manufacturing centers and distributed to other sites in the region. Located on rather small inland riverine terraces, these sites lay between the heavily forested mountains, a band of estuaries, and periodically flooded swamp forest. No architecture was recorded, but apparently pole-and-thatch structures were constructed in small groups atop small natural mounds. Shell scatters occur at several sites.

Citing the frequent occurrence of manos and metates, Drolet (1980) sees a population of maize-based swidden agriculturists who primarily utilized floodplain plots but cleared forest as needed. The higher upriver forest was an important hunting ground and source of hardwoods for dugouts, while the predominantly palm swamp forest provided oil and vegetable protein (palm nuts), plus other hunting or collecting venues (molluscs, crabs, and other marine creatures). Reef collecting and marine fishing also figured importantly in Drolet's scenario. He describes in detail a very similar ecology for the Choco and black groups who occupy the region today. The first accounts of the region by Columbus and others also confirm this reconstruction and mention, in addition, an orchard complex of domesticated or semi-domesticated tree crops like cacao, papaya, mamey, and avocado (Drolet 1980: 323).

In Caribbean Nicaragua, Magnus (1975, 1976) has briefly described the results of survey and excavations from Pearl Lagoon to Bluefields Bay, almost to the Costa Rican border. Sites from this period (his Siteioid tradition) were coastal shell middens composed almost entirely of *Donax denticulatus* and *Neocyrena* cf. *nicaraguana*. Magnus notes with surprise the limited number of mollusc species and the apparent lack of fish and terrestrial mammal bones (1975: 688). In a later article (1978), he sees an important shift in settlement systems in eastern Nicaragua. Prehistoric data indicate sedentary inland villages based on maize agriculture, with seasonal fishing camps on the coast (perhaps explaining the selectivity of species in mollusc collection), while the modern, mostly black population sustains its villages near the coast and makes inland forays for hunting and other activities, much like the situation observed in Caribbean Panama by Drolet.

Magnus's Siteia ceramic complex is unusual for this period, defined around a locally made polychrome (black lines and dots, red zones, and lines on cream); he sees stylistic similarities with the early Caño del Oso polychrome from Venezuela (Zucchi 1972) and postulates an influx of South American people around the time of Christ (Magnus 1975: 570). Manos, metates, and celts were found with Siteia complex pottery, as were a few Costa Rican Zoned Bichrome trade sherds, and there are two C^{14} dates: 25 B.C. ± 85 (I–7100) and A.D. 80 ± 85 (I–7480).

The succeeding Smalla and Jarkin complexes did not contain local polychrome. They featured incising and punctation instead, sometimes in textile-like motifs. There is one C^{14} date of A.D. 490 ± 85 (I–7099) for the Jarkin complex.

In the central Atlantic watershed of Costa Rica, the El Bosque complex dominates the period of roughly 100 B.C.–A.D. 500. These sites, 12 of which have been excavated in part, are numerous and large. As yet, it is impossible to tell if the large amounts of pottery found represent contemporaneously occupied dispersed settlements or a series of sequentially occupied smaller sites; the latter is the favored hypothesis because of swidden agriculture's dynamics. All sites encountered were on fertile coastal plains or valley floors.

Ceramics of the El Bosque complex are most often red on buff, with polished dark red lips, interiors and bases, with a collar of naturally buff-colored clay smoothed but left exposed around the vessel shoulder and neck. This panel usually shows a variety of impressed or appliqué as well as maroon and red painted decorative modes (Snarskis 1976b). The zoned red-on-buff aspect of both Chaparron and El Bosque suggests a stylistic linkage more direct than that between monochrome La Montaña pottery and El Bosque.

The large quantity and ceremonial character of many El Bosque grave goods imply differential burial customs and consequently a ranked, hierarchical social structure. Decoratively (or better, symbolically) carved flat-topped metates and jade necklaces or pendants are key high-status markers, but it is important to note that small ceramic figurines, rattles, whistles, ocarinas, stamps, pipes, and nasal snuffers are found almost exclusively in higher-ranking burials, suggesting a ceremonial or shamanistic context for their use.

Chipped chert artifacts, except for a rare scraper or perforator, are absent in El Bosque contexts. Slate or hard stone celts, axes, and daggers were roughed out by percussion flaking and then often ground to their final form. Pecked and ground stone tools abound, mostly made of basalt or andesite, and they are presumably related to food processing and agriculture. Large petaloid celts show signs of hafting and were probably used for forest clearing. In two graves at the Severo Ledesma site (7.1–SL), what appear to be complete woodworker's kits were found. Each includes a large petaloid celt, one or more small sharp-edged trapezoidal celts, two chisel-drills (small cigar-shaped tools with a sharp edge at one end, hafted at the other, and with noticeable vertical and circumferential use striations), a small chert or quartz core, and worn sandstone celt sharpeners. Typical ground stone artifacts include bark beaters, pestles, edge-battered cobbles—sometimes modified with lateral depressions for easier grasping—stirrup-shaped mullers, crude andesite mace heads, loaf-shaped manos, and several kinds of mortars and metates.

Of this last artifact class, it has been said that the rimmed types were used for processing a softer vegetable substance with water, and the rim held the mixture on the plate (Stone 1961: 200–202, 1966a: 27), the idea being that Atlantic watershed cultures depended more on root crops than on maize as a staple. Controlled recovery of metates from funerary and domestic contexts in El Bosque sites has suggested that this interpretation is erroneous. The quotidian El Bosque metate type is most often a roughly oval stone slab, often with stubby cylindrical tripod feet, usually worn down to a deep, trough-like shape but without a purposefully carved raised rim around the perimeter. At Severo Ledesma both unfinished prototypes of these metates—pecked out on oval river cobbles—and used examples were found. Only used metates were found as grave goods, while both kinds were sometimes utilized to make up part of the tomb wall. These metates usually show heavy wear when found in finished form. The mano was apparently used in a push-pull motion and slightly rocked, its loaf shape corresponding well with this wear pattern.

The rimmed type of metate described by Stone and others may be either rectangular or round, but it is always tripod, with legs from 10 to 50 centimeters or more in length. A salient characteristic is a carefully carved raised edge around the entire perimeter. Occasionally, the flat plate or table itself is remarkably thin (2–3 cm), rendering the metates virtually useless for long-term daily food preparation. A different wear pattern also has been observed; in many cases a small section at the center of the table, not exceeding 20 centimeters in diameter, has been worn down as if hammer-like blows as well as rubbing strokes were employed. The raised edges are very seldom worn away. As it is this type of metate which is most often associated with jade artifacts, a ceremonial role is suggested, perhaps the preparation of special foodstuffs or drugs. Since the edges of these metates are almost always carved in the shape of small heads (or notched, a stylized representation), I believe the taking and shrinking of trophy heads by warriors in battle is somehow connected with the metates, perhaps because raids were carried out to obtain more farmland or because sacrificial victims were seen as necessary for the maintenance of adequate harvests. Such decorated special-purpose metates probably belonged to persons of politico-religious power or to warriors. Their hypothesized use as seats (Lange 1971b: 212–17) would fit this model also; some show virtually no wear and were either used exceedingly sparingly or made as tomb furniture.

Most manos are loaf- or bar-of-soap shaped. This is the classic maize-processing mano shape in Mesoamerica, and I believe it served the same function in Costa Rica. A slightly rolling, crushing motion is more apt for seeds than for bulky tubers. Contrary to the opinion of Stone and Balser

(1957: 167–68), this kind of mano was encountered most frequently, as was the trough-shaped rimless metate. Rimmed, flat-table metates and stirrup-shaped mullers were found less often in our excavations, as one would expect of higher status articles.

I believe that El Bosque subsistence centered around maize agriculture, with important adjuncts in the form of root and tree crops plus some game and riverine exploitation. In general, archaeologists have not challenged Stone's hypothesis (1956b, 1966a) of a purely root- and tree-crop subsistence for Atlantic and central Costa Rica, with maize, although known, being relegated to a minor, perhaps ceremonial role. Stone further stated in regard to the Talamanca region that "the introduction of the use of maize can be dated from the advent of the first Mexicans in this region" (1956b: 192); by Mexicans, she meant fifteenth-century migrants and warrior traders. A stratigraphically excavated maize cob from El Bosque deposits (Snarskis 1976b: 348) was thought to tend to disprove this hypothesis, suggesting that even early maize, like manioc and pejibaye, may have conformed to a tropical South American subsistence pattern. Dunn (1978), although misquoting the relevant parts of this article (actual "contact" between Period IV peoples of eastern Costa Rica and northern South America was not suggested), questioned the validity of attempting to prove a rather large point with one piece of botanical evidence, especially of the maize race Pollo, whose etiology and taxonomy are increasingly ambiguous (Galinat 1980). Improved maize races were appearing all around the Intermediate Area in the several centuries before and after Christ, and it is by no means certain that they derived from a single source. Still, Stone's early suggestion as to the time of the appearance of full-scale maize agriculture in central and eastern Costa Rica can now be discarded; more botanical evidence of maize and other cultigens has appeared in Late Period IV contexts, and even Stone seems to be shifting ground in her latest book (1977: 170).

Excavations of El Bosque middens at Severo Ledesma in 1978 yielded almost 100 fragments of carbonized palm nuts (inner kernels). These have been identified as *Elaeis oleifera* HBK, previously known as *Corozo oleifera*, an American oil palm related to the commercially important African oil palm (Robert McK. Bird, personal communication). Drolet (1980: 316–21) describes the harvesting and processing of *Elaeis* among black and Choco groups in eastern Panama today, where wooden mortars and pestles are used. He suggests that archaeological stone pestles may have served a similar purpose. Drolet has also emphasized that the oil obtained from the *Elaeis* palms, which are known in Panama as *corozo*, is much esteemed by modern consumers, who use it as a food additive or on their hair and body (personal communication). The only other carbonized floral samples associated with El Bosque materials have been identified as grass stems and a "dicotyle-donous charcoal, diffuse and porous, with many rays, possibly Legumi-

Figure 8.5. Two adjoining rectangular structures of the El Bosque phase at Severo Ledesma, perhaps with shared patio at center. Two-meter stadia rod lies along north-south axis at right center.

nosae" (C. Earle Smith, personal communication). No faunal remains of any kind have been found, but this is obviously a function of poor preservation.

The discovery of the first El Bosque structural remains in 1978 showed they were of a very different form than those of late sites like Las Mercedes and Guayabo (Snarskis 1978: 164). A large (25 × 15 m) rectangular complex of wall foundations, built of river cobbles, was excavated at Severo Ledesma (fig. 8.5). Chocked holes were observed where timbers had been along the perimeter and interior walls. There were three main rectangular sections, the center one containing many more cobbles. Palm nuts, mano and metate fragments, and charcoal were scattered within the structure, but no definite hearths could be discerned. Underneath the structure numerous caches and/or burials were discovered; some of the burials were defined by standing rows of cobbles, and one contained 27 pieces of grave furniture, including a jade necklace, the plate of a flying panel metate, fancy tripods, ocarinas, rattles, and celts. Two C[14] dates from the fill of this structure were 50 B.C. ± 90 (UCLA 2175–D) and A.D. 350 ± 60 (UCLA 2175–C).

More El Bosque–phase structures were sought at the same site in 1979—they were recognized by very slight mounds—and this time we uncovered

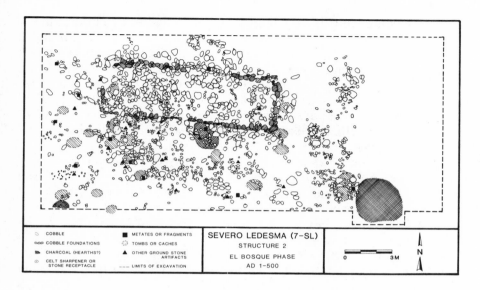

		SEVERO LEDESMA (7-SL)	
○ COBBLE	■ METATES OR FRAGMENTS	STRUCTURE 2	N
◎◎◎ COBBLE FOUNDATIONS	⬨ TOMBS OR CACHES		
▬ CHARCOAL (HEARTHS?)	▲ OTHER GROUND STONE ARTIFACTS	EL BOSQUE PHASE	0 3M
⊙ CELT SHARPENER OR STONE RECEPTACLE	--- LIMITS OF EXCAVATION	AD 1–500	

Figure 8.6.   Rectangular structure of the El Bosque phase at Severo Ledesma.

two smaller rectangular foundations of 3.5 × 12 meters (fig. 8.6). As their proportions were similar to the inner divisions of the larger 1978 structure, I now feel that it was in fact two houses, with a shared, perhaps open-air patio (the cobbled center section). Each of the 1979 El Bosque structures had two round or oval cobbles with cup-like depressions placed near the middle of one wall, reminiscent of offertory receptacles, like those at the entrance to the main mound at Guayabo de Turrialba (Fonseca 1979). Because the concavities varied in form, however, they could also be interpreted as celt sharpeners or mortars.

It might be said that most architecture in all prehistoric periods of eastern Costa Rica is found underground. Cemeteries are extensive, many covering 5 to 20 acres, the tombs themselves being fairly elaborate constructions of river cobbles. These cobbles, some of which weigh more than 100 kilograms, were carried from river beds anywhere from 50 meters to several kilometers distant. El Bosque–phase tombs may be 1 × 2-meter rectangles of cobbles, ellipses, long corridors up to 12 meters, or simply a scooped-out oval area in the subsoil, with no cobble edifice. Tombs in the large cemeteries always have delimiting walls of cobbles and are usually long rectangles, often ordered neatly in ranks and files, with a space between groups of 15 to 30. These tomb groups may correspond to clan, lineage, or other social units.

Lines of standing stones marked prestige burials in the large El Bosque house found in 1978, but the smaller structures located in 1979 were surrounded by simple, unmarked tombs cut into the subsoil. Since we have not found a single bone, or even a tooth, I cannot confidently say that all burials, no matter how humble, are accompanied by grave goods. However, this seems to be the case; ceramics are ubiquitous, usually arranged in the typical El Bosque fashion of one pot inverted over the mouth of another. Whole or fragmented stone artifacts like celts, pestles, manos, daggers, and metates are also found frequently.

A sophisticated lapidary industry also characterized El Bosque times, and some burials, probably of higher status, are accompanied by necklaces and pendants of jade or other hard stone. Most of the evidence suggests that these articles were worn by the deceased when buried. Stirling (1969) obtained a date of A.D. 144 associated with a string-sawed jade under what he called a low circular cobble house foundation of 15 meters in diameter at Mercocha, Linea Vieja. One wonders if this is another El Bosque house form or if Stirling simply found El Bosque and La Selva material under later architecture. In any case, the associated grave pottery is early and fits the date. Kennedy (1968, 1976) published a date of A.D. 420 ± 210 (5–5975A) for what are here called El Bosque ceramics at the El Cardel site near Turrialba. I have chosen not to follow Kennedy's periodization and ceramic typology for reasons explained elsewhere (Snarskis 1978: 48–62).

Carlos Aguilar (1973, 1975) has described the Pavas ceramic complex in the central highlands of Costa Rica as being similar to the El Bosque complex but with a greater emphasis on orange slip and channeled (gadrooned) decoration. Vessels are also larger as a rule. Ground stone implements are like those described for El Bosque. Although the central highlands are actually within the Pacific drainage, they have always been considered as part of the Atlantic watershed archaeologically, and rightly so, if we can judge by recovered artifacts.

In the type site of Pavas to the west of San Jose, Aguilar found what he called bottle-shaped tombs, containing large ollas and other ceramic offerings along with poorly preserved human skeletal material. At Barrial de Heredia, we recently excavated two of these bottle-shaped features which had been exposed in profile by a deep trench made for sewer pipes. They did not contain preserved human bone and yielded only fragmentary Pavas ceramics, chunks of fired clay, and pieces of manos and metates, but they were carpeted along the floor, which was two meters in diameter, with 10 to 20 centimeters of carbonized plant remains, the largest such sample encountered to date and one of the very few for the Pavas phase. Although botanical analysis is still in progress, it is known that the feature contained thousands of maize kernels, five maize cob fragments similar to Swasey 1 and 2 types from Cuello, Belize, several pieces of unidentified nuts or hard-shelled fruits, unidentified rhizomes, and several desiccated, cherry-like pitted fruits (Robert McK. Bird, personal communication). Also present in the feature were two varieties of *Phaseolus vulgaris* (common bean) that are "closer to Mesoamerican than Andean types" (Lawrence Kaplan, personal communication), and seeds of the Convolvulaceae Family, probably *Ipomoea nil* (L.) Roth (Daniel F. Austin, personal communication).

The majority of the maize kernels were found squeezed together in fist-sized bunches along with the cherry-like fruit and the *Ipomoea* seeds. During the excavation, some of these bunches were thought to be very large maize ears because many of the kernel rows had been shaved off the cob whole and were still lined up; a closer examination revealed that there were no cobs within.

We observed several other bottle-shaped features cut into a clay subsoil to a depth of 1.5 to 2.5 meters. Almost all carbonized floral remains were found in the bottom 40 centimeters, which suggests an alternative hypothesis as to their function: since the bottle-shaped features appear to be up to 50 to 100 meters apart, and since we know a fairly extensive Pavas-phase occupation exists at the site, they might instead be bell-shaped storage pits associated with the domestic activity zone surrounding a dwelling, much like the early Formative Mesoamerican pattern (the "household cluster" of Winter 1976: 25). Winter notes their occurrence in highland Mesoamerica from the Valley of Mexico to Guatemala City and emphasizes their almost universal use as maize storage pits which, upon eventual abandonment, were often "filled with household debris including burnt daub with pole impressions, ashes, carbonized corn cobs and fruit seeds, animal bones, cooking pots, and discarded manos and metates; some also had burials" (Winter 1976: 29, speaking of pits in Las Charcas, Guatemala). This description fits the Pavas-phase feature very well, especially as many fired adobe fragments were found scattered over part of the surface at Barrial in association with only Pavas sherds. Construction activities prevented us from searching for contiguous Pavas-phase houses.

In neither the Pavas nor the El Bosque phase do we see much evidence of intensive trade with other regions. An exception to this pattern was the small but important burial ground partially salvaged at Tibas, only 15 minutes from the National Museum of Costa Rica. Here, an array of prestige grave goods was found accompanying burials of the period A.D. 100–500. Although ceramics and metates typical of the Central and Atlantic regions were present, many jade-like mace heads, one large jade axe-god pendant, and a zoned engraved monkey effigy vessel with a spout and bridge design were probably products of middle to late Period IV (300 B.C.–A.D. 500) in northwest Costa Rica. In the most impressive tomb found, a body was laid on top of three Atlantic-style metates, two round and one rectangular, along with a broken Curridabat-phase tripod, the very large Guanacaste-style axe-god jade pendant mentioned above, two effigy mace heads, and an Olmec jade clamshell, 33 centimeters long, decorated on the interior with a low-relief carving of a human hand holding a composite feline-insect animal (Snarskis 1979a). The dental eruption pattern showed that the deceased was 18 to 25 years old (Ricardo Vazquez and David Weaver, personal communication). The Tibas burial and many other El Bosque–phase examples show that differential burial practices and strongly rank-ordered societies existed in eastern and central Costa Rica at least by the time of Christ.

In sum, then, Early Period IV in lower Caribbean Central America saw the establishment of scattered, sedentary, pottery-making, probably agricultural villages, the earliest of which may have appeared near the end of Period III. As yet, only one such site, La Montaña, has been systematically excavated in part and radiocarbon dated; settlement patterns, house forms, and socio-political organization are still unknown, as are burials reflecting a ranked society. A dramatic surge in population growth seems to have begun around 300–200 B.C., culminating in numerous but dispersed agricultural settlements in the first few centuries of the Christian era, especially in alluvial plains or fertile highland valleys. Architecture was rudimentary, but crafts like pottery, stone carving, and lapidary work with jade-like material were highly developed. A complex religious symbolism is evident, head hunting was probably practiced, and mortuary evidence indicates ranked societies, possibly at or near the chiefdom level.

The size and ubiquity of El Bosque– and Pavas-phase sites has only recently been appreciated, and an analysis of the cultural processes involved is yet to be done. In the interim, I would offer this hypothesis: the explosion of sites observed during the 100 B.C.–A.D. 300 lapse can be directly attributed to the adoption of full-scale maize agriculture, perhaps with improved varieties. The large number and dispersed nature of El Bosque and Pavas sites can be in turn attributed to the rapid colonization of fertile alluvial soils, stimulated by faster population growth and the budding-off of new communities. Other foods did not cease to be of importance (polycropping undoubtedly continued), but the sudden quantities of celts and grain-processing manos and metates argue persuasively for the priority of maize.

Where did the stimulus for increased and better maize agriculture come from? Drolet (1980: 340–45) favors the Colombian highlands, while Linares, in several recent articles (Linares, Sheets, and Rosenthal 1975; Linares 1976b, 1977b), has restricted her inferences to a generalized highland-to-lowland diffusion in western Panama. Revising my own earlier interpretations (Snarskis 1976b), I suggest that intensive maize agriculture, as well as a reverence for carved jade amulets, were integral components in a mythic complex or politico-religious world view that was propagated in the northern half of Costa Rica by an elite-oriented trade network that directly or indirectly included "classic" Gulf coast Olmec sites (600–400 B.C.) or the heirs of that cultural tradition. Two lines of thought led to this hypothesis.

First, Easby (1968: 81–97) thought that the presence in Costa Rica of Olmec and "Olmecoid" jades, coupled with the lavish quantities of local lapidary art and the similarity of the raw materials used in the two traditions, pointed toward an Olmec exploitation of Costa Rican jade sources. However, first results of trace-element analyses show that Costa Rican lapidaries used mostly serpentine, chalcedony, and other locally available jade-like stones, whereas Mesoamerican trade pieces found there are usually true jadeite (Lange, Bishop, and von Zelst 1981). These results suggest an opposing hypothesis, that the Olmecs brought or traded jade to Costa Rica, and acceptance of the associated mythological framework created an elite market for similar native stones. More physical analyses are needed to determine if these cultures distinguished consistently between, say, blue-green chalcedony and blue-green jadeite.

The second line of thought has to do with the predominance of celt and bird forms in the Costa Rican lapidary corpus. Can these be likened to Olmec iconography, and if so, why were they emphasized? "Several hundred celts" of serpentine and jade were found in 1942–44 excavations at La Venta, many of them in carefully placed caches which suggested that they were "endowed with some ceremonial importance" (Drucker 1952: 164). Significantly, two of the only four decorated celts from La Venta (Drucker 1952, fig. 47, b, c) were incised with the four dots and bar motif which Joralemon (1976: 47–52) indentifies as a stylization of the face of God I (the Olmec Dragon), and from which sprout maize symbols. Joralemon also notes that God I and God II, the Olmec Maize God, sometimes share facial features. Joralemon classifies his God III as the Olmec Bird Monster and, citing Drucker and Lathrap, tends to accept the harpy eagle (*Harpia harpyja*) as the model for the dominant avian component of this hybrid creature (1976: 52). The harpy eagle was found to be one of the two most frequently occurring and well-defined avian effigies (the other being the quetzal) portrayed on the axe-god pendants from Hartman's (1907) excavations of the Period IV Costa Rican cemetery Las Huacas (Fonseca and Scaglion 1978: 285). Identical effigies appear on many Atlantic watershed pendants, on the ceremonial mace heads often found with pendants, and on carved metates in both Atlantic and Pacific Costa Rica. Besides its primary celestial and solar associations, Joralemon links the Olmec Bird Monster to maize agricultural fertility and the trance produced by psychotropic substances, noting the concurrence of the respective symbolic motifs on many Olmec objects, especially the Arroyo Pesquero figure at Dumbarton Oaks (Joralemon 1976: 52–58). An avian effigy celt was part of the Cerro de las Mesas jade cache, which contained mostly later pieces, Drucker (1955: 58–60, 66, plate 36, f), noting the Bird Monster motif, considered the unusual piece "unquestionably Olmec . . . although probably a trade object, made to be used for ceremonial purposes."

Summing up, we see that, almost certainly, the Olmec jade carving industry preceded that of Costa Rica and probably stimulated its development through trade in ceremonial jade artifacts to Costa Rican elites. We know that celts were prominent in Olmec material culture, that representations of these agricultural tools were associated with maize, and that several principal Olmec deities, including the Bird Monster, had important links with maize agriculture. The ceremonial axe-god, while not common, was definitely part of the Olmec artifact inventory, and the Cerro de las Mesas example is strikingly similar to typical Costa Rican forms. The most common Costa Rican lapidary motifs, then, combine iconographic elements associated with maize in the Olmec cultural tradition. The demonstrable link between ceremonial metates and the best Costa Rican lapidary art further suggests a ritual complex having to do with agriculture and its products. Recovery of actual maize remains from Middle Period IV sites and a better understanding of Costa Rican mythological symbolism are still needed to confirm this hypothesis.

A key factor in the interpretation of the latter may be a Period IV petroglyph analyzed and described by the author and Clement W. Meighan near Liberia, Guanacaste, in 1979. It appears to be a mythic cosmography. Central and highest in the panel is a human head with a U-shaped headdress, accompanied by a bat with extended wings. Beneath the bat, an inverted human head releases long parallel lines (rain?) which fall to a horizontal plane with spiral plumes on one side and the trilobed maize symbol on the other. Along the same plane are several avian effigies in profile and a serpent, while beneath it are inverted avian forms and more spiral plumes. The bat is an important and undeciphered symbol in the Period IV mythology of northern Costa Rica, and it may not be coincidental that two Olmec jade figures reportedly found in Guanacaste are winged (Coe 1965b: 766–67, fig. 16). Finally, it is of interest that Linares in her most recent discussion of the cultural dynamics of maize agriculture in Middle Period IV western Panama (Linares and Ranere 1980: 241) now sees the rapid development of numerous and large sedentary agricultural villages with craft specialization and a socio-political order stressing rank and status as a result of the "expansion of seed-crop agriculture (and/or agriculturists) from the adjacent area of eastern Costa Rica. . . ."

We should not assume that a Mesoamerican-type mythology eradicated other belief systems in eastern Costa Rica during the second half of Period IV. Indeed, a patina of Mesoamerican symbolism appropriated by high-status groups, combined with preexisting tropical forest animist beliefs, may have produced the menagerie of zoomorphic *adornos* typical of Atlantic pottery. Again, it is significant that the food processing metate became a major plastic vehicle of this complex naturalistic-religious symbolism (Graham 1979, 1980, 1981). As social organization in most of the subarea at this time was already what Fried (1967: 115) calls rank society, I suggest that the rituals in which the decorated ceremonial metates played a part had to do with warlike behavior (land acquisition, the taking of captives for sacrifice), resource procurement, and redistribution. During rituals, the high-ranking owner of such a metate may have sat on it, but its principal function would have been the preparation of food and/or drugs for elites or perhaps for warriors prior to battle. (Remember the carved human heads on these metates.)

Although their scarcity precludes the inclusion of sites dating to 500 B.C. or earlier in a discussion of long-distance trade, it seems that some Olmec artifacts make their appearance in Costa Rican contexts several centuries later, suggesting that they were heirlooms, or reached Costa Rica very gradually in down-the-line trade. The operationality of the so-called Southern Maya route, basically the same overland Pacific trading route set up by the Olmec (Sharer, this volume), is slightly better founded owing to the presence of small amounts of Usulutan pottery in northern Costa Rican cemeteries dating to around the time of Christ or slightly after (F. W. Lange, Bernal Monge, personal communication). The variety of this Usulutan, which would allow a more exact temporal placement, has not been established.

To date, there are no firm archaeological indicators in eastern Costa Rica of the hypothesized rupture of the Southern Maya trade route by the Ilopango volcanic eruption around A.D. 200–300 (Sheets, this volume). However, the most notable trade objects found in Costa Rican contexts dating to A.D. 300–600, slate-backed pyrite mirrors occasionally inscribed with Maya glyphs (Stone and Balser 1965; Baudez and Coe 1966), definitely reflect a Central or lowland Maya hegemony over trade with Central America during the Early Classic. Finally, it is worthwhile to observe that, while some seagoing exchanges may have occurred since Olmec times, the evidence is strong for the arrival of northern goods through the Rivas corridor into northwest Costa Rica, whereafter their distribution is bifurcated by the Cordillera Central, with Mesoamerican articles appearing sporadically as far as the central Atlantic watershed on the east and the central Pacific region on the west. Thus, it might be that eastern Nicaragua, like northeastern Honduras (Healy, this volume) did not participate in these trade networks, interacting in unknown ways with the Caribbean, or with northern South America, as Magnus (1975) suggests. Only more work in eastern Nicaragua will clarify the picture.

Transition and Southern Influence:
Period V (A.D. 500–1000)

During the first two or three centuries after A.D. 500, drastic changes in material culture, from house forms to ceramics, occurred in those regions of lower Caribbean Central America that had until this time kept fingers on the Mesoamerican cultural pulse, however faint. Most evidence suggests that these changes were the result of undefined southern influence, especially from Colombia. As yet, our chronologies are not fine enough to detect with precision the beginning of this influence, if indeed the seeds had not already existed for a considerable time in the lower Central American regional cultures. For the present, we may hypothesize that the fall of Teotihuacan in the sixth century A.D., with the resulting disruption in central lowland Maya centers and the Pacific trade route to the south, was a factor. Whether this stimulated, or was merely contemporaneous with, important introductions from the south, especially metallurgy, remains to be seen.

In the Panamanian province of Bocas del Toro, teams led by Olga Linares have surveyed on the Aguacate Peninsula and excavated the Cerro Brujo site. By ceramic cross-dating, she placed the earliest occupation between A.D. 600 and 700, calling it the Aguacate phase. These first inhabitants were not traditional coast dwellers and did not have a shellfishing economy; their ceramics were closely related to late Bugaba-phase pottery (A.D. 400– 600) from the interior valleys and coastal plains of western Panama. A comparison of the Aguacate-phase faunal remains showed a greater percentage of forest-dwelling species than the later Bocas phase; five celts and a chisel were the only lithic tools recovered (Linares and Ranere 1980: 63– 64, 96–101, 123, 188). The Bocas-phase component of Cerro Brujo is discussed with Period VI.

Lack of data is also the fundamental problem in Nicaragua. Nothing certain is known about Period V, although Magnus believes his Jarkin ceramic complex (Smalloid tradition) carries well into the period with no marked changes (1976: 68).

In eastern central Costa Rica the La Selva phase corresponds roughly to Period V. Ceramics show linear designs painted in maroon on orange, red incised vessels (sometimes with resist decoration), brown slipped ollas, and some brown incised pottery, as well as delicate hollow-legged tripods; white paint applied with a multiple brush appears in this complex as well. There is no doubt that the El Bosque and La Selva complexes overlap in time, but La Selva seems eventually to dominate, as its decorative modes, not those of El Bosque, lead directly into later complexes. Most metate forms previously described for El Bosque persist, but some manos become more squared-off and flatter, while others take on a tapered cylindrical or bullet shape. Some changes occur in celt forms, and a greater variety of waisted, double-bitted axes appears. While lapidary work continues at least through La Selva A (A.D. 500–700), the quality of the greenstone employed seems to decline, suggesting a greater dependence on local sources.

Carbonized plant remains, including a maize cob, were found in a long-legged tripod vessel excavated in a Turrialba Valley cemetery. The presence of burnt maize in a mortuary offering may be a symbolic representation of the funeral maize chicha, the tripod vessel being the drinking container. In another part of the same cemetery, a mass of 15–20 of these tripods was found, smashed near the surface at one end of a corridor tomb, a possible prehistoric vestige of the lengthy funeral *chichadas* (rowdy, drunken feasts) described for historic times by Bozzoli de Wille (1975). Another possibility is that the tripods were incense or offertory burners, since many are smudged on the exterior.

The maize found in the La Selva–phase cemetery was identified by W. C. Galinat as a slender popcorn similar to the primitive popcorn races Confite Morocho and Confite Puntiagudo of Peru and Pira from Colombia. Galinat observes that the low condensation trait typical of such maize helps drying in humid climates; rather than being primitive, these popcorn races can justifiedly be viewed as a highly developed form. Slender popcorns were widely spread throughout the Americas well before Period V (Galinat 1978).

No house forms are definitely known as yet for the La Selva phase, although uncompleted excavations in the Turrialba Valley suggest long, rectangular shapes for La Selva A houses as well as tombs. The introduction of circular houses and stone cist tombs must have taken place around A.D. 500–800, a time span as yet poorly documented in the central Atlantic watershed. There are two C^{14} dates for La Selva A, both from the La Montaña cemetery: A.D. 220 ± 60 (UCLA 2113–C), too early, and A.D. 640 ± 60 (UCLA 2113–E). Two dates for La Selva B are A.D. 940 ± 90 (I–8913) and A.D. 1110 ± 195 (I–8914), both from stone cist tomb contexts at the Turrialba Valley site of La Isabel.

In the central highlands of Costa Rica, it is the Curridabat phase which spans most of Period V. Curridabat artifact complexes are very similar to those of the La Selva phase. Fortunately, more settlement data have been provided by two salvage excavations of Curridabat villages, La Fabrica de Grecia and Barrial de Heredia. At La Fabrica (Guerrero 1981), the earlier of the two sites according to ceramic evidence, 13 circular house foundations made of river cobbles were uncovered; they ranged from 9 to 15 meters in diameter. The largest house had two opposing rectangular entry ramps, and contained deer antlers and a copper bell.

In spite of its typically late architectural configuration (all circular structures, with at least one major *calzada*, or cobble-paved causeway), no stone cist tombs were found at La Fabrica. Instead, many burials were unmarked; some have only a few scattered cobbles or columnar stones above, some were beneath house floors, and others were placed within and beneath huge, unstructured masses of cobbles and field stone.

In a cemetery associated with the La Fabrica site, a notable find was a burial resting on three decorated metates (Lange 1979b). This burial included a banded jade-like tube identical to examples found in the Cenote of Sacrifice at Chichen Itza, which Proskouriakoff describes as coming into common use only in Late Classic times in the Maya area (Proskouriakoff 1974: 25). Carlos Aguilar (personal communication) has described a Curridabat A burial at the Cartago Valley site of Tatiscu which included red incised and alligator tripod ceramics, plus an identifiable fragment of a tumbaga piece in the Cocle or Sitio Conte style, datable to around A.D. 500. Through ceramic cross-dating, we can now place the grave goods described by Stone and Balser (1965) in Early Period V, the only time in which jade and gold artifacts coexisted in eastern Costa Rica.

The Barrial de Heredia site is multi-component, having been occupied in all phases from Barba B (500–200 B.C.) to Cartago A (A.D. 1000–1300). The occupation of most interest is associated with architectural remains and seems to have run from Curridabat B into Cartago A, perhaps from A.D. 800–1100. Whether for temporal or geographic reasons, house forms at Barrial did not conform to the circular pattern expected for that time period. Two shapes were found—quadrangular (square or slightly rectangular) and ellipsoidal—the latter sometimes showing straight sides and rounded ends. This shape difference seemed to correlate with a difference in function. Of the eight cobble foundations excavated, four were quadrangular with burials incorporating imported Nicoya polychrome pottery beneath their floors; these are considered to be primarily domiciles. The rounded structures, only one of which was excavated completely, contained much greater quantities of charcoal, used stone tools and flakes, sometimes large sunken ovens or hearths, and did not contain burials with polychrome ceramics.

Both stone cist tombs and a modified version of corridor tombs are present at Barrial; the latter showed just one line of standing cobbles and was found only beneath the principal quadrangular structures. Of seven vessels included as grave goods in the main burial within the largest square house excavated, five were Nicoya polychromes. The Nicoya polychromes found at Barrial were almost all from the period A.D. 900–1200. In all, 20 such vessels were recovered, representing 4.5 percent of the total number of vessels found in burials or caches. Polychrome sherds from surface collections and excavations totaled 356, 1.15 percent of all sherds collected. Within the largest quadrangular structure, five types of Nicoya polychrome were found: Mora, Birmania, Highland, Papagayo, and Chircot (Accola 1978a). It was interesting to note the high percentage of polychrome trade sherds at the site which showed evidence of cracklacing; obviously, the bright Nicoya-Guanacaste ceramics were highly valued, and their quantity suggests well-established trade channels with northwest Costa Rica (Snarskis and Blanco 1978).

Metates associated with the architectural component at Barrial were all of the crude, trough-shaped variety made on volcanic cobbles. The food-processing tool most often recovered was a hand-sized stone rhomboid with grinding wear on its flat facets and battering on its extremities. According to W. C. Galinat, the last prehistoric inhabitants of Barrial possessed two kinds of maize, Pollo and a slender popcorn previously described, suggesting that they were purposefully cultivated for their different traits. Two samples of *Phaseolus vulgaris* were also found, as well as many fragments from large, as-yet-unidentified seeds (Galinat 1978; Lawrence Kaplan, personal communication). The architectural component at Barrial has three C^{14} dates so far, one from just below a house floor (A.D. 950 ± 60; UCLA 2175–H), and the other two from charcoal within a rock-filled oven (A.D. 870 ± 80; UCLA 2175–F) and a hearth (A.D. 890 ± 40; Beta–2802).

It is unfortunate that relatively few Period V sites have been excavated in eastern lower Central America, for a finer chronology and more complete archaeological record are needed to understand this period of flux. In the Atlantic watershed of Costa Rica, there is a distinct sense of fewer sites at this time; no single-component Period V site has been found, although systematic surveys have not been carried out. Keeping in mind the substantive archaeology reviewed earlier, the following speculations on Period V cultural processes in lower Caribbean Central America can be offered, although the data permit many other hypotheses. Down-the-line trade from powerful, emergent chiefdoms in Colombia and Panama brings sophisticated products of metallurgy into Costa Rica for the first time, perhaps as early as A.D. 500. Their introduction and increasing acceptance by ranking elites is coeval with breakdowns in the Pacific trade route to Mesoamerica during the sixth to eighth centuries, caused by volcanic events and the fall of controlling centers like Teotihuacan and, later, Copan and Quirigua. Leaders dependent for their status upon products and liaisons of the Mesoamerican trade in lower Caribbean Central America were displaced by those with contacts to the south; lapidary work in jade-like stone wanes, and eventually, southern craft traditions and belief systems, as expressed by changes in pottery styles, house forms, and mortuary customs, prevail. The burgeoning of a southern-oriented Caribbean sector at this time is also apparent in northeast Honduras, where Selin-phase sites show a spurt in population growth, even as the Mesoamerican west declines (Healy, this volume).

While interpreting the components of cultural change in Period V as southern is supportable, with metallurgy replacing jade carving, incised and resist-decorated pottery supplanting red-on-buff, and circular houses replacing rectangular ones, it is quite another thing to be able to point to specific regions and periods in northern South America as sources (Bray, this volume). Quimbaya-style gold pieces have been found in eastern Costa Rica along with jade-like pendants from around A.D. 500 (Stone and Balser 1965). Circular mounds, resist-painted pottery, and stone cist tombs existed in the Colombian highlands around San Agustin and other zones during the first few centuries after Christ (Duque Gomez and Cubillos 1979), and many of these important ceremonial centers with their impressive stone sculpture were abandoned by Period V (Reichel-Dolmatoff 1972: 119–20). Bray (1978b: 113) illustrates three Musica pottery figurines that are identical to many excavated from the La Fabrica site and others found throughout central and eastern Costa Rica. Still, stylistic ties to the material culture of Colombia are not nearly as strong as those in southwest Costa Rica, which exhibits, after about A.D. 800, many shared motifs in gold, three-color resist-decorated pottery, and even coca-chewing paraphernalia. Obviously, the cultural processes behind the southern influence during Period V remain to be elucidated. Linares (1979: 35–36) has noted that much trade between South American tropical forest groups is subsistence related, and it is doubt-less correct that disproportionate attention has been given to status-linked artifacts like gold and jade.

Warfare and Balkanization:
Period VI (A.D. 1000–1550)

While the fertile plains and valleys of eastern central Costa Rica showed numerous agglomerated villages characterized by cobble architecture and definite site hierarchies, coastal settlements in Caribbean Panama and Nic-aragua were much more modest. This appears to have been the result of a less propitious natural environment, especially as concerns agriculture. Dro-let (1980: 340–45) did not locate sites specifically datable to the last several centuries before the Spanish arrival, but recognized in the Conquest de-scription of the Costa Arriba region of Panama an indigenous settlement pattern and human ecology which closely matches that suggested by the material culture of his archaeological sites, occupied over a thousand years earlier. He sees the entrance of maize farmers into eastern Panama from the moist floodplains of northern Colombia as early as 500 B.C., noting that the Costa Arriba region offers one of the few hospitable biotopes for maize farming between the Atrato river and eastern Costa Rica. He believes that the Cuevan polities originally derived from Colombia dominated the region at the Conquest and had a long history there. Drolet emphasizes that the Costa Arriba settlements were not just isolated farming communities, but were incorporated into the extensive commercial and political networks overseen by Cuevan chiefdoms based in the interior and Pacific regions. He posits the existence of similar networks while these sites were occupied, citing the presence of traded pottery and stone. A seasonal pattern of resource exploitation in several biotopes (forest, alluvial plains, rivers, swamp forest, reef, ocean) apparently persisted up into historic times and even to the present, a remarkably stable situation if confirmed by future archaeology.

The tenth-century-A.D. occupants of Cerro Brujo in the Bocas del Toro region of Panama apparently employed a series of adaptive strategies similar to those described for Costa Arriba sites, with a critical exception—they were not maize farmers (Linares and Ranere 1971: 354). Linares deduces the absence of seed agriculture from the lack of manos and metates (Linares and Ranere 1980: 124) and the results of nearby pollen cores, which show no record of forest disturbance over a long period of time (Linares 1976b: 337). Instead, a root- and tree-cropping system is proposed, augmented by the collection of shellfish with an intertidal shallow-water distribution, reef fishing, and the hunting of small game, primarily agouti, paca, and armadillo. By careful analysis of the Cerro Brujo faunal remains, Linares shows that these three animals are present in the archaeological middens far in excess of their normal percentage in the biomass, concluding that they were selected by the Cerro Brujo inhabitants for their habits of visiting or living near forest borders, recently cleared areas, or human settlements. She calls this "garden hunting" and shows how a comparison with the prey of other tropical forest groups suggests that trapping and spears were the probable implements used, with no effort made to capture hard-to-get species in the forest or the deeper ocean (Linares and Ranere 1980: 181–88).

Linares sees the origin of this adaptive strategy in the arrival in the Bocas del Toro region of farmers from the high, fertile valleys of Chiriqui sometime early in the first millennium A.D. (Linares, Sheets, and Rosenthal 1975). In another article, Linares (1977b) discusses the possible mechanisms that could have produced such a migration, favoring a developing scarcity of animal protein in the highlands plus a possible volcanic catastrophe (Linares 1977b: 313). Because of the lack of alluvial plains suitable for seed crop agriculture in the Bocas del Toro region, Linares's farmers shifted to the root-tree crop, collecting, garden-hunting adaptive pattern. This ecology resulted in notably smaller population concentrations in Bocas—villages of 25 to 30 people, a distribution of only about three people per square kilometer (Linares 1976b: 335)—when compared to those of Pacific Chiriqui lowlands, where, besides most of the biotopes mentioned for the Bocas region, fertile alluvial plains were to be found. Linares compares the small, transient archaeological occupations she perceives on the Caribbean side to the frequently shifting settlements of the historic and modern Guaymi in the region (1977b), much as Drolet likens his archaeological evidence to Conquest and modern data.

One of the conclusions to be drawn at this point is that an efficient and diversified coastal-estuary adaptation in lower Central America tends to be persistent and stable, while successful seed crop agriculture results in dynamic, perhaps even explosive, population growth, with its concomitant intensification of resource competition, societal complexities and ranking, warfare, and regional politico-commercial networks. This is, of course, an oversimplification and probably a truism in many parts of the world (Linares 1979: 34). Still, it seems to be supported by Magnus's data from eastern coastal Nicaragua, where his Cukra Point ceramic complex of this period closely resembles the earlier Smalla and Jarkin complexes in the same region. A date of A.D. 1185 ± 80 (I–7451) is supported by Costa Rican Middle Polychrome trade pottery. The presence of nonshell mounds in a nearby riverine context, as well as manos and metates, suggests that the shell heaps represent periodic, perhaps seasonal, collecting, and that the major sites were located inland and used a broader subsistence base which included agriculture (Magnus 1975, 1978).

This period in eastern Costa Rica saw developments quite different from those so far described for coastal Panama and Nicaragua, although the as-yet-poorly understood Nicaraguan inland plain may have witnessed a similar phenomenon (R. Magnus, personal communication). Settlements seem to have nucleated into small ceremonial centers (perhaps better characterized as city-states), almost invariably with rudimentary architectural features like earth-filled, cobble-faced mounds and cobble-paved causeways. Early investigators focused on this period (Hartman 1901; Stone 1958b) in the region, primarily, I think, because its remains are the easiest to recognize. Too often, facile conclusions are projected back into an only sketchily understood past, with no mention made of the long-term cultural processes that made the protohistoric period what it was; even Linares (1979: 36–37) is guilty of this, when she mistakenly places the Las Mercedes site (Hartman 1901) in the highlands and assumes that such sites date to the period around the time of Christ on speculative and scanty evidence (Kennedy 1975; Lange and Murray 1972).

The ceramics of this period (the La Cabaña complex), while capably executed, are inferior in technical quality to those of the earlier El Bosque complex. The zoning of orange and purple slips survives from La Selva times, as does a preoccupation with appliqué decoration. The feline motif becomes more popular, and bowls with hollow tripod supports in the form of stylized animal heads are diagnostic of pottery after A.D. 1000. Brown incised/excised pottery becomes common, and Nicoya polychromes are frequently seen as trade items, even inspiring an inferior local imitation of the brilliant red-on-white slip painting (Cartago Red Line). The number of clay figurines, rattles, ocarinas, and the like decreases noticeably.

Metates and manos actually sculpted for quotidian use declined sharply; instead, unmodified, large, flat river stones were used for grinding, and appropriate cobbles were used as manos. Mortars and pounding tools increased and celts were smaller in size and number. A large, triangular-stemmed projectile point of flaked chert was found in a stone cist tomb at Najera which can be dated by associated pottery to A.D. 1000–1300. An unworked block of chert accompanied this point, suggesting that it was not a chance find or heirloom. Decoratively carved ceremonial mortars, trays, and metates, especially the tetrapod jaguar effigy metate, are diagnostic of this period, as are circular Atlantean and anular-based forms. Beginning in the last half of Period V and continuing in Period VI, there is an increase in stone sculpture portraying human beings, from seated "sukia" (shaman) figures and what look like individual portrait (or trophy?) heads, to stylized poses of warriors holding an axe and a shrunken trophy head, and females holding up their breasts.

Only a handful of the nucleated villages made up of circular mounds and house foundations that characterize this period have been partially excavated. The first was Las Mercedes in the Atlantic lowlands, found when Minor Keith put the Old Line railroad through the middle of it. Carl Hartman excavated parts of it more than 80 years ago (Hartman 1901) and drew a map showing the main mound 20 meters in diameter at the top of its 6-meter height, faced with cobbles. On three sides were a series of ridges, also stone-faced. Judging by what is known of sites like Guayabo (Fonseca 1979), this was probably just a small part of Las Mercedes, but apparently it did include the principal mound; today Las Mercedes has been totally destroyed by looters and agriculture. Costa Rica Farm, less than 10 kilometers from Las Mercedes, has two large circular mounds with stairways adjoining a rectangular plaza delimited by stone-faced ridges; a cobble-paved causeway connects it and another similar feature some 300 meters away (Lothrop 1926: 462).

A team from the National Museum of Costa Rica recently excavated horizontally a similar, although smaller, site near Guacimo, called La Cabaña (fig. 8.7). It is located in between Las Mercedes and Costa Rica Farm (Snarskis and Herra 1980). Only a portion of the La Cabaña site containing the more prominent main mound, and the probable focus of the community, was exposed, as it was at Las Mercedes. Here, Mound 1 was also 20 meters across but only 2.5 meters high. Adjoining it was a lower circular mound with a projecting curved porch. Stairways from both mounds led into a square, empty plaza, outlined by cobble-faced ridges that, upon closer inspection, proved to be arms of a double-walled, earth-filled enclosure which contained tiny caches or burials with prestige grave goods. A cobble-paved causeway led into the plaza opposite the stairways of the two main mounds, after skirting a non-mound, circular house foundation of cobbles, some 12 meters in diameter. It is significant that the major sites mapped so far for Period VI in eastern Costa Rica—La Cabaña, Costa Rica Farm, Las Mercedes, and Guayabo (Oscar Fonseca has recently found and mapped several new features)—have a quadrangular plaza formed by raised ridges associated with the principal mounds. This suggests a ritual or civic use, perhaps as the locus of ceremonial encounters between the ruling group and the rest of the population or for the redistribution of goods.

Careful troweling of the house floors at La Cabaña revealed that, while all three circular structures uncovered had central hearths, only Mound 2

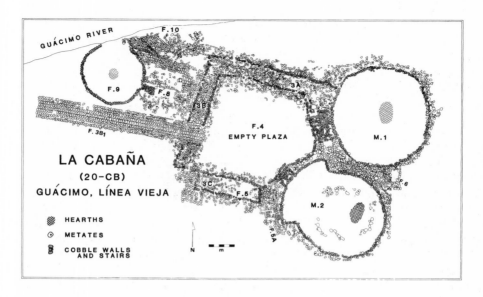

Figure 8.7.   La Cabaña, a partially excavated site of La Cabaña phase (A.D. 1000–1550).

(the large, eccentrically shaped structure next to Mound 1) had definite domestic activity foci, composed of large, flat river stones with marked grinding wear, some with other stones as seats and manos still associated. This evidence for functional difference between the two main structures suggests the inhabitants of Mound 2 had to do with the maintenance of the Mound 1 residents. This interpretation is strengthened by a document sent to the King by Fray Agustin de Cevallos in 1610 in which he describes several customs of the people then living in eastern Costa Rica: "They live in palenques, which are forts built in the native fashion . . . the chiefs have the women that they desire *all in the same house* and the common people generally have one" (Lothrop 1926: 446, emphasis added).

Tombs for this period in the eastern and central region of Costa Rica are usually of the well-known stone cist type, which can be circular, ellipsoidal, or rectangular. The excellent ethnographic work of Stone (1962a) and Bozzoli de Wille (1975) has allowed archaeologists to make feasible analogies between prehistoric material culture and historic data of many kinds but has been especially valuable for funerary contexts. Thus it is known that in this late period the stone floors and lids frequently encountered in stone cist tombs probably were the result of taboos against the deceased's body touching earth, even in the tomb; in historic times wooden, not stone, slabs served this purpose. Tombs are still found both under and around houses and in separate cemeteries. Spanish artifacts have been found in stone cist tombs by Hartman (1901) at Las Mercedes and Orosi, and by Stone (1977: 167) at Tuis, Chirripo.

In the Turrialba Valley many architectural sites of this period exist. Kennedy (1968, 1975) describes mounds, cobble pavements, and an unusual circular plaza (ridge-outlined) with several entrances at Najera. Originally worked by Carlos Aguilar (1972), the national park site of Guayabo de Turrialba has been reinvestigated in recent years by Oscar Fonseca and teams from the University of Costa Rica. Always impressive, Guayabo has now been shown to have a paved entrance causeway which first passes through a gate guarded by two square mounds half a kilometer from the center of the site. Additionally, a mound with nine stone sculptures around it was excavated, and Fonseca has devised an architectural classification of site sectors and features which seems to have a functional significance (Fonseca 1979). Guayabo covers up to one square kilometer, including over 50 mounds and circular house foundations, roadways, stairs, and even an underground water-control system.

The author has also mapped part of a large architectural complex, including a paved causeway nine meters wide, at the site of La Zoila (5–ZT) near Turrialba; this means that large centers like Guayabo, Najera, and La Zoila (and Las Mercedes, La Cabaña, and Costa Rica Farm in the lowland plain) all lie within a 10-kilometer circle. It remains to be seen if they were part of a contemporaneously occupied site network—they all have similar ceramics for this period—or were constructed sequentially in response to changing cultural frontiers. Similar sites have been reported from the Cartago Valley by Hartman (1901), Stone (1977), and Carlos Aguilar (personal communication), and the National Museum of Costa Rica has recently excavated sections of large stone cist cemeteries there, much like those described by Hartman at Chircot and Orosi (Vazquez 1981; Blanco 1981).

Findlow, Snarskis, and Martin (1979), using a modified version of Zarsky's (1976) method for site catchment analysis, have discerned an interesting trend in settlement patterns for eastern Costa Rica. Sites dating to 800–300 B.C. are still located near biotopes important for hunting or collecting, while sites through other periods up to A.D. 1000 show an increasing preference for alluvial farmland. In the last 500 to 600 years before the Conquest, however, the site location pattern becomes random, indicating to the author that factors other than agriculture were predominant; I think these factors were socio-political boundaries and defense.

Among cultures thought to be intrusive in eastern Central America during the late prehistoric periods, the Arawak is often cited (Stone 1972: 204–5). While Arawaks were apparently encountered in eastern Panama, no evidence of their influence is found in eastern Costa Rican archaeology, unless the ridged enclosures seen at some late sites are Caribbean-style ball courts! Certainly the circular stone foundations seen at so many sites are not ball courts or *areytos*, as Stone (1977: 169) suggests, but bases for perishable houses. Resemblances between sites like Guayabo and those of the Tairona culture in the Santa Marta region of Colombia are striking, and the temporal correlation is good (Fonseca 1979).

Floral remains, unfortunately, are very scarce for this period in eastern and central Costa Rica. A few maize kernels were found at the stone cist cemetery site of Hacienda Molino (27–HM) near Cartago, while the La Cabaña site yielded a sample of "diffuse, porous charcoal perhaps dicotyledonous," and "a wall fragment from a polished gourd container, probably *Curcubita pepa*" (R. I. Ford, personal communication). At this time there is no reason to propose subsistence systems for Period VI that are radically different from earlier ones; Spanish chroniclers repeatedly described the polycropping of maize and various root and tree crops. La Cabaña has two C^{14} dates, A.D. 1220 ± 60 (UCLA 2113–I) and A.D. 1360 ± 60 (UCLA 2113–G), and a charcoal sample from beneath a Period VI mound at La Zoila gave a date of A.D. 1270 ± 40 (I–8915). Both Stirling (1969) and Kennedy (1968, 1975, 1976) have at least two dates after A.D. 1000 for sites of this period.

Conclusions

In sum, the archaeological data for Caribbean lower Central America appear to indicate two general patterns of cultural ecology and evolution. In one, the use of coastal, riverine, and, to a lesser extent, forest biotopes for collection of floral and faunal resources on a seasonal basis was combined with small-scale root and tree cropping, producing small, anchoritic settlements with a tendency toward population equilibrium rather than rapid growth. This appears to have been the predominant pattern in Caribbean Panama in the Costa Arriba and Bocas del Toro regions (probably including much of the Costa Rican eastern watershed south of Puerto Limon) and in parts of coastal Nicaragua since Period IV times.

In the other pattern, recognized to date only in the central Atlantic watershed of Costa Rica but possibly applicable to parts of eastern Nicaragua and Caribbean Panama, the following trajectory is seen, starting at the beginning of Period IV: Small and few sedentary communities with pottery and perhaps a subsistence pattern similar to those of northern South America (i.e., mostly root cropping); toward the middle of Period IV a rapid increase in population and social complexity, perhaps stimulated by a tendency toward full-scale maize agriculture, complimented by polycropping in regions of fertile, alluvial soils and abundant rain, and by hunting; a culmination in the centuries around the time of Christ in a pattern of sedentary, fairly large nodes of population characterized by rank society with complex ritual paraphernalia, connections to Mesoamerican trade networks, and probably a redistributive hierarchy; a long period of intergroup resource competition and warfare, with headhunting and sacrifice of captives indicating population pressure, possible intromission of foreign groups (probably southern), restructuring of politico-religious hierarchies, changes in house and tomb forms, gradual degradation of ceramics, although not of other status-reinforcing prestige items; the balkanization of these regions during Period VI into relatively small, agglomerated, rudimentary architectural settlements, for reasons of political control (probably use of corvée labor) and defensive strategy, with occasional strong leaders able to organize several of these centers into a site hierarchy or alliance for brief periods.

It is probable that this summary view will be altered in the near future by more and better work in the subarea, but for now it represents interpretation of the substantive data. A final question remains. Why did the cultural evolutionary process in lower Caribbean Central America (and by extension the Intermediate Area in general), similar in its early stages to that observed in Mesoamerica and Peru, sputter and stall? Carneiro (1961) has stressed the difference between what he calls "circumscribed" and "open" environments. The Amazon basin is seen as an example of a large, relatively homogeneous area with plenty of room for population expansion. This would tend to lengthen the time required for population densities to reach a critical stage in which warfare was waged over habitable land. The Costa Rica Atlantic watershed, and indeed most of Central America, could be described as homogeneous, not, of course, referring to topography but to the land's potential for supporting human populations. The huge expanses of extremely arid land that characterize parts of Mesoamerica and the west coast of South America do not exist in Central America, and even the regions which are somewhat arid today were probably less so in the past before most of the forest cover was altered.

In a later article Carneiro (1970) explains why he favors "coercive" rather than "voluntaristic" theories about the origin of the political state. Carneiro believes that historical evidence shows that no autonomous socio-political unit, large or small, will voluntarily relinquish its sovereignty in the name of cooperation or the "greater social good." Only through forceful domination (war), he feels, are states and empires forged.

Meggers (1971: 159) feels that endemic warfare in an "open" environment like Amazonia, overtly waged for reasons like revenge, supernatural mandates, and the taking of exogamous marriage partners, is in reality a regulatory device for human population in an area with a precarious ecological balance. Warfare in eastern Costa Rica may have functioned similarly, and even have been more intense, given greater population densities. Why did this conflict not result in the amalgamation of larger, more complex socio-political structures, as it apparently did in parts of Mesoamerica and Peru? The answer is that oppressed populations could successfully flee the threatened domination, emigrating to other, similar localities which provided much the same kind of resources instead of being incorporated by force into the larger or more powerful conquering group (Carneiro 1970: 735). Sanders and Price (1968: 130) concur, noting that it is not so much the lack of productive potential in tropical forest areas like Amazonia that prevented the development of a complex society there (Meggers 1954), but rather that the presence of huge amounts of at least nominally agricultural land acted as an incentive to successful emigration. They emphasize that the juxtaposition of very different environments in Mesoamerica produced a cycle of competition and cooperation between "symbiotic regions," and produced growth and expansion trends in all participating "environmental niches," culminating in a socio-political whole bigger than the sum of its parts. They also note that while highly nucleated, urban population centers are dysfunctional in tropical forest areas where swidden agriculture is practiced, such centers are necessary to the survival of large populations in less hospitable environments, requiring as they do centralized political organization for successful agricultural exploitation. In those areas oppressed populations could not emigrate, facing instead the choice of submitting to the oppressor or being extinguished.

In this view of prehistoric eastern Central America, then, the living was easy—too easy to compete in the make-or-break, big-time cultural stakes to the north and south. Ironically, the abundance of viable eco-zones, not their lack, may have stifled the cultural evolutionary development of much of the area between Mesoamerica and the Andes.

Note

1. This article is a product of the cooperation, both in the field and in the laboratory, of all the members of the Departamento de Antropologia e Historia in the Museo Nacional de Costa Rica, especially Hector Gamboa P., Carlos Enrique Herra, Aida Blanco, Maritza Gutierrez, Juan Vicente Guerrero, Ricardo Vazquez, Silvia Salgado, and Carlos Valldeperas. Others who served as crew chiefs were John Hoopes, Ann Peters, Marcella Crump, and Robert Markens. Helpful comments on earlier drafts were provided by fellow archaeologists Carlos Aguilar P., Oscar Fonseca Z., Robert Drolet, Erika Wagner, and all the participants in the School of America Research seminar, especially F. W. Lange. The noted Costa Rican ethnohistorians Luis Ferrero and Maria Eugenia Bozzoli de Wille also contributed valuable facts. Drawings were done by Carlos Enrique Herra and photographs were taken by Maritza Gutierrez and the author.

9

The Archaeology of Greater Chiriqui

WOLFGANG HABERLAND

Hamburgisches Museum für Völkerkunde

Extension and Geographical Setting

Defining the geographical extension of Greater Chiriqui is by no means easy, since investigations, especially in the frontier areas, are either non-existent or only recently published. According to our present knowledge, Greater Chiriqui is thought to cover the territory between the Continental Divide—the crest of the Talamanca chain—in the northeast and the Pacific Ocean in the southwest (fig. 9.1). Whether parts or all of the Atlantic slope, especially in the Panamanian province of Bocas del Toro, are included in Greater Chiriqui is still an open question. The extension from northwest to southeast is even more difficult to determine. In the northwest the Rio Diquis drainage in Costa Rica is included, and on the coast the territory may extend as far as the present port of Dominical, Costa Rica, where the author encountered material related to Chiriquian types during a short survey in 1959. In the southeast the Estero de Horconcitos and the Panama river drainages emptying into it should pertain to Greater Chiriqui, but the exact boundaries on the east are unknown because of the lack of investigations in the eastern parts of Chiriqui Province.

The surface of Greater Chiriqui is very broken, and mountain chains and river drainage systems divide it into many different ecological units. One larger coastal plain is situated more or less between Puerto Armuelles and the Estero de Horconcitos, while all others are either small alluvial fans

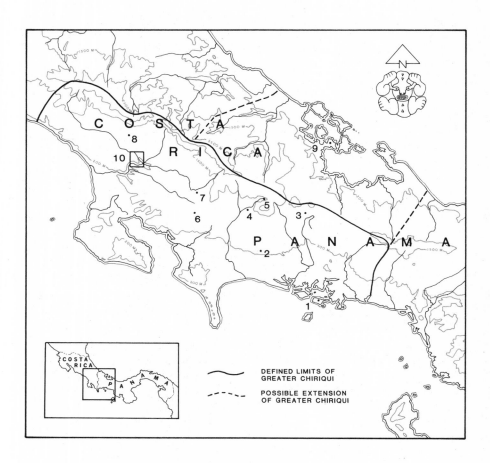

Figure 9.1. Area of Greater Chiriqui (dotted lines) and important sites.

at the mouths of the larger rivers, such as the Rio Diquis or the Rio Coto, or are remnants of older surfaces cut up by rivers running in deep ravines. Elevations in the region range from sea level at the Pacific and Atlantic coasts to the 3,823 meters of Cerro Chirripo Grande. Because of differences in altitude, rainfall, soil conditions, and vegetation, Greater Chiriqui contains a number of distinct ecological niches, which influenced the cultural development of this region.

State of Knowledge

The famous gold discovery at Bugavita in 1859 (Haberland 1959: 70–71) was followed by extensive looting. Despite the fact that by about 1900 every major museum owned a collection of Chiriquian antiquities, the pioneering publications of Holmes (1888) and MacCurdy (1911) were solely based on museum collections and hearsay. Scientific fieldwork in Greater Chiriqui began only in 1949, and then only a small number of investigators dedicated their work to the problems of Chiriquian archaeology (Laura and Luigi Minelli, Olga Linares, Anthony J. Ranere, Robert de la Guardia and his associates of the Museo Chiricano, Richard Cooke, and Haberland).

These studies have resulted in a somewhat better understanding of Chiriquian prehistory and in a certain outline of the development of the human occupation. Unfortunately, however, most fieldwork is only known through preliminary reports. That holds true for all investigators mentioned above, including the author. This is especially unfortunate for the work of Linares and associates, whose investigations are essential to our present knowledge of the archaeology of the Panamanian part of Greater Chiriqui. Many of their excavations could only tentatively be included here, and some, because of the lack of information, not at all.[1] For instance, the exclusion or inclusion of Bocas del Toro Province or, more specifically, of the Laguna de Chiriqui region in Greater Chiriqui depends much on the still-unpublished excavations of Linares at Cerro Brujo. What is known will be mentioned in this paper but is certainly subject to revision.

The situation for the C^{14} dates (appendix 7) gathered from several preliminary reports is somewhat similar. Most of them are only known by site name, without indications of their stratigraphic context, and often also lack an indication of which phase is actually dated.

Period II (8000–4000 B.C.)

The regional overview begins with Period II, since no archaeological finds that could be assigned to Period I are known from Greater Chiriqui. The oldest sign of human presence is a lithic assemblage from rockshelters along the Rio Chiriqui near the present eastern boundary of the area, at elevations between 645 meters and 900 meters above sea level (Ranere 1971; Linares and Ranere 1971; Ranere 1975b: 176). The older of the two preceramic phases, Talamanca, has been dated by Ranere (1975b: 177) to before 3000 B.C., while Cooke (1976a: 22) suggested a dating between 5000 and 3000 B.C. Taking the corrected C^{14} dates into account, 6000 to 3000 B.C. seems appropriate. Talamanca, therefore, belongs partly in Period III, although it lacks ceramics and has a very generalized tool kit; bifacially worked stone tools, including projectile points, polished stone celts, and most other ground stone tools are absent. This points to an economy based on general hunting and gathering (Cooke 1976a: 22), but the rockshelters may also have been specialized working stations for stone and woodworking. The implements for more specialized economic activities, including projectile points—which might have been made from bone and/or other perishable material—are missing here. Nothing definite is known about the origin of these people. They might have belonged to or split from the same generalized group of hunters and gatherers in central Panama, who possessed a comparable lithic tool kit. It is difficult, however, to reconstruct connections on the basis of a rather small and restricted tool kit, and definitive statements should wait until more is known about burial customs, group size, and living patterns, for which we have no data.

Period III (4000–1000 B.C.)

The rest of Period III, which in most other regions sees the advent of agriculture and pottery, is characterized in Greater Chiriqui by a second lithic (preceramic) assemblage, Boquete. It stratigraphically overlies the Talamanca phase at the Casita de Piedra and Trapiche rockshelters (Ranere 1975b: 176–77). The single C^{14} date, slightly later than 3000 B.C. when adjusted, came from the top of layer D at Casita de Piedra and either antedates the Boquete phase or reflects its very beginning (Linares and Ranere 1971: 350). The end should be around 1000 B.C., since SI–1844 is said to date the transition to the following ceramic phase at Casita de Piedra.

Boquete represents a gradual development out of the Talamanca phase. The lithic tools that were present before continue, but polished celts, grinding stones (manos), and pestles are added. Linares (1977b: 311) and Cooke (1976a: 22) postulate a shift in economy from a generalized hunting and gathering to specialized gathering and an incipient root- and tree-crop agriculture. Remnants of nance (Brysonima crassifolia (L.)DC), algarrobo (Prosopis spp.), and palm nuts have been found in Boquete layers, but whether there are any indications of their being cultivated is not known. Since edge-ground cobbles for grinding and/or mashing, mortars, stone bowls, and nutting stones as well as grinding-stone bases form part of the lithic assemblage of both phases (Ranere 1975b: 202–6) and obviously did not increase in their percentage, the shift does not seem to be as pronounced as suggested. In spite of the fact that elsewhere in Panama (Cooke, this volume) agriculture emerged during this period, Boquete might only indicate a shift to greater use of vegetable food, not necessarily a shift in the method of obtaining it. Linares (1977b: 311) and Cooke (personal communication) think that root crops might have been present, but firm proof is lacking.

Population increased from the Talamanca to the Boquete phase, at least in the Rio Chiriqui region. While Talamanca-phase material was only found in two rockshelters, Boquete-phase material was present at five sites. One of them was an open site, perhaps indicative of a shift in settlement patterns. All other data about living conditions during the Boquete phase are missing. The same is true for population distribution in Greater Chiriqui. One of the most important questions is whether there was some population on the coast, but to date, no sites of this time are known from the Pacific coast of Chiriqui, in spite of an intensive survey by McGimsey (1964). This might be a result of a shift in the coastline or a deep burying of sites by recent alluvial soils.

Period IV (1000 B.C.–A.D. 500)

This period sees the beginning of pottery and, presumably, settled agricultural village life in Greater Chiriqui. It is, therefore, consistent with the development on the Atlantic watershed of Costa Rica, where La Montaña and Chaparron appear about the same time (Snarskis, this volume).

Linares and Ranere reported that at the Trapiche and Horacio Gonzales rockshelters as well as at the open Schoolyard site, a ceramic phase overlies Boquete (Linares and Ranere 1971: 351, 354; Ranere 1975b: 177). Linares has termed these ceramics the "Scarified–Concepcion–Aguas Buenas tradition," giving the impression of a single ceramic complex overlying the preceramic Boquete material. However, slides of the ceramics show two different ceramic complexes on top of the preceramic, one of which appears older, and might, as Cooke believes (personal communication), be stratigraphically earlier, while the other undoubtedly belongs to the Aguas Buenas phase. The SI–1844 date, around 3000 B.C., might be applicable to the unnamed and presumably older complex. SI–1846 might apply to Aguas Buenas, thereby ending the discrepancy of more than 500 years between the two C[14] dates that are used to identify the transitional time between the preceramic and ceramic phases at Rio Chiriqui. Two completely different cultures, Concepcion and Aguas Buenas, seem to have been present in Greater Chiriqui, but since there has been contoversy about them, some remarks must be made concerning their differences.

Concepcion, as characterized by the Scarified pottery (fig. 9.2), actually the Solano Pottery Group (Haberland 1961c: 57–58), is well known through the studies of Holmes (1888: 87–90) and MacCurdy (1911: 96–100). Aguas

Figure 9.2. Solano Incised: Mata variety, Concepcion phase, from Chiriqui. Hamburgisches Museum für Völkerkunde.

Buenas (fig. 9.3) has been described intensively (Haberland 1959: 42–79, 1961b). As stated elsewhere (Haberland 1962: 386, 1969: 235), the ceramics of the Concepcion and the Aguas Buenas phases do not share a single mode, and any common origin or joint manufacture must be precluded until more information or sites belonging to these phases are available.

Assuming that Concepcion and Aguas Buenas are different cultural entities, the question arises whether they are contemporary or represent a time difference and/or sequence; if the latter is true, which is the older? Since most of the C[14] dates covering this time in Greater Chiriqui do not state explicitly which phase or ceramic complex is dated by them, only a few of them can be used for this purpose (appendix 7). These dates seem to indicate contemporaneity, but that has still to be verified in the field. Excluding the C[14] dates, arguments for both possibilities have been brought forth at various times (Haberland 1962, 1969: 235, 1976: 116, 1978: 414).

One of the arguments, and an important one, for contemporaneity is the occasional occurrence of Concepcion vessels and/or sherds in Aguas Buenas sites, which can easily be explained if the phases flourished at the same time. Otherwise, it is most difficult to understand, and the situation needs

Figure 9.3. Typical Aguas Buenas ceramics; foreground and right from type site El Tigre, Costa Rica. Hamburgisches Museum für Völkerkunde.

a very complicated explanation (Haberland 1969: 235). It should be added here that only one of the four Solano varieties of vessels, a chimney-like one with three solid columnar feet (Haberland 1962: fig. 3), has been found together with Aguas Buenas pottery types, and, therefore, probably was imported into Aguas Buenas settlements. It might have served a special purpose such as metal melting.

Contemporaneity is also indicated by some new C^{14} dates from San Vicente, which are said to date Concepcion material (Catherine Einhaus, personal communication). They fall right among the known or probable Aguas Buenas dates, strengthening, therefore, the argument for two different cultures during this time in Greater Chiriqui.

By the distribution of the pottery, still very inadequately known, we can conclude that the Concepcion people occupied the large coastal plain in the province of Chiriqui but did not venture into the highlands. They are obviously absent in the Costa Rican part of Greater Chiriqui. Their point of origin was probably the central provinces of Panama, since related ceramics have been found there (Haberland 1969: 236–39). The time of their arrival is difficult to ascertain, but appears to be no later than 500 B.C. Nothing can be said about their settlement patterns or settlement sizes, since only one pure Concepcion site, the cemetery of Solano near La Concepcion, is known, which, significantly, did not yield a single Aguas Buenas vessel.

The Concepcion people were maize agriculturalists, as shown by the numerous metates of a special shape, legless with high boards or rims on three of the four sides, which sometimes line the walls of their graves. Cylindrical and roller stamps were used (Sander 1960, personal communication), presumably for body ornamentation. Their art was, as far as we know, not well developed. This is demonstrated not only by the adornments of their pottery and the lack of any stone sculpture, but also by the handle of a pottery stamp shaped as a double figure, a nude pregnant female (Sander 1960: fig. 25a). Whether this figure also had religious significance is an open question. Finally, it should be mentioned that the large, partly stone-lined graves indicate primary burials, and the big, formal cemetery at Solano suggests rather large and probably well-organized villages or settlements.

While the Concepcion people came from the east, as mentioned above, the Aguas Buenas culture originated, in all probability, in the northwest (i.e., in central Costa Rica) and probably beyond. The links with the El Bosque complex of the Atlantic watershed of Costa Rica (Snarskis, this volume) in pottery and other features are striking. Whether both derived from a common source or whether Aguas Buenas developed from the unnamed pottery complex found in the Rio Chiriqui region and mentioned above is still unknown. In the latter case a derivation of that pottery, and presumably agriculture, from central Costa Rica should be considered. In all probability no ceramic traditions originated in Greater Chiriqui during this period. Ceramics and, by implication, agriculture were brought into this area from the outside, from central Panama as well as central Costa Rica or the Atlantic watershed region of that country. Greater Chiriqui, during Period IV, was obviously the meeting ground of different cultural trends as represented by the Concepcion and the Aguas Buenas complexes.

In spite of the fact that appendix 7 shows a considerable number of C^{14} dates for Aguas Buenas, the time depth of this culture is uncertain. One reason is that the Aguas Buenas affiliation of these dates can only be inferred. Nevertheless, with some caution it might be said that Aguas Buenas flourished in the mountainous regions of Greater Chiriqui not later than 500 B.C. One date, I–5871 from Sitio Piti, which ranges between 920 B.C. and 765 B.C. (one sigma range, new corrected date), falls outside, but whether it really is applicable to Aguas Buenas cannot be said at the moment. The end dates of this culture are difficult to ascertain, for as published, neither their position in the local stratigraphy nor, as a rule, the phase or culture which they actually dated is stated.

Sites of the Aguas Buenas cultural entity have been found in Costa Rica around Cañas Gordas on the frontier of Panama (type site Aguas Buenas, Haberland 1959: 42–79), around San Vito de Java (Laurencich de Minelli and Minelli 1973), and in the Diquis Delta on the coast (Lothrop 1963). In Chiriqui Province proper, numerous settlements are known from the highlands around the Volcan Baru (Haberland 1961e: 26–30, 1962: fig. 5; Linares, Sheets, and Rosenthal 1975), on the coast of Burica Peninsula (Ranere 1968: 112–13), near Puerto Armuelles (personal investigations), and in and around the Estero de Horconcitos (Linares 1977b; Jurado and Castro 1967) as well as on Rio Chiriqui (Linares and Ranere 1971: 351, 354; Ranere 1975b: 177). Finally Linares (1977b: 311) reports Aguas Buenas material or something very similar (no illustrations have been published to date for this excavation) from Cerro Brujo, a site on the Laguna de Chiriqui, in Bocas del Toro Province, on the Caribbean coast. Even excluding the last-mentioned site, Aguas Buenas culture obviously covered a large territory—at least 175 kilometers as the crow flies along the coast and 75 kilometers from the coast to the highlands. It also lasted about 1,000 years, if our present dating is correct. These facts should call for temporal as well as regional differences and make Aguas Buenas more a tradition, like later Classic Chiriqui, than a single culture. The differences are already apparent in local modes, such as shell stamping at Toreto on the coast (my own investigations, not yet published), as well as temporal differences as indicated by Linares, Sheets, and Rosenthal (1975: 141). I am certain that further investigations, as well as already excavated but not yet published material, will show more local and/or temporal diversity, establishing a number of subcultures or entities inside the Aguas Buenas phase or tradition.

Some time ago Linares (1977b) put forward a model of the spread of Aguas Buenas culture (she does not call it that), with which I agree. Linares (1977b) believes, and I agree, that the Aguas Buenas people migrated into Greater Chiriqui from central Costa Rica and/or its Atlantic watershed, wandering perhaps through the Valle de General (no Aguas Buenas ceramics have yet been found there, but no extensive survey has been conducted in or published about this area either). From here, all locations where Aguas Buenas material has been found could easily be reached following rivers and crossing over rather short stretches between them.

Linares also believes that the people from the Volcan area gradually moved down to both coasts, but we shall, for the time being, ignore the Caribbean side. People, in her opinion, "spent a long time moving down, assuming that the prevailing movement was from highland to coast" (Linares 1977b: 313). This idea of a slow movement or trickling down is substantiated by Aguas Buenas–like (she calls them "Volcan-like") sites found halfway between coast and highland and dated between 300 B.C. and A.D. 600. I am not familiar with these sites nor the dates which have not been mentioned elsewhere. Therefore, I cannot judge or verify this statement.

I offer another hypothesis for these settlement patterns: perhaps Aguas Buenas people did not settle the fertile coastal plains not because of ecological reasons, as indicated by Linares and others, but because this area was already occupied by another group, the Concepcion culture. Only after the Aguas Buenas people, or at least parts of them, were consolidated into small chiefdoms did they have the strength to dislodge or conquer this block and reach the coast. I should not wonder if one day we might find that it was the chief of Barriles who led the conquering army and added the new land to his realm, enhancing his prestige. Through this conquest he might have become the mightiest chief of this territory, expanding his capital into the largest and most important village or town of the Aguas Buenas culture. The statement by Linares, Sheets, and Rosenthal (1975: 142) that the so-called ceremonial complex is probably late in the history of Barriles would fit this idea well. That this model is not pure fantasy can be seen by comparing it with the known conquest of the coastal regions of Pacific Guatemala by the Quiche and Cakchiquel not long before the advent of the Europeans (Termer 1948: 24–25).

Barriles was probably the largest, most elaborate settlement of its time in Greater Chiriqui. In addition, a number of large sites may have been of regional importance. Linares, Sheets, and Rosenthal (1975: 140) propose this for Sitio Piti in the Cerro Punta area. Cooke (1976a: 32) interprets Linares and Ranere (1971) to mean that La Pitahaya on Isla Palenque in the Estero de Horconcitos was another one, but I think that the remarks of Linares and Ranere concern the Classic period and not the time in question. To this roster of major sites I add Piedra Pintada near San Vito de Java (Laurencich de Minelli and Minelli 1973: 222–23) and at least one other in the Diquis Delta area, either not yet discovered or completely destroyed by modern agricultural activities. The famous stone balls should have been associated with it (Stone 1954; Lothrop 1963).

Besides the larger capital settlements of regional or overall importance, people lived in small hamlets along the numerous rivers or on the shore. There seem to be differences in the pattern of village size and setting depending upon the geographical area. My own excavations indicate a preference for mountain spurs and high river terraces. Sometimes, however, hamlets were also situated at canyon bottoms or on low river terraces (Linares, Sheets, and Rosenthal 1975: 140–41). Dwellings were probably of the *rancho* type, and post holes of one of the dwellings have been excavated at Sitio Piti (Linares, Sheets, and Rosenthal 1975: 141). No plan of it has been published, but according to Sheets (personal communication) it looked like a figure eight, its sides being either oval or rectangular. Obviously settlement pattern and the size of the normal village or hamlet, as opposed to those cities presumed to have been capitals, were largely dependent upon natural formations and the availability of fertile soils necessary for agriculture, which was the basis of their economy.

Maize and beans were the main crops, attested to not only by the numerous metates but also by remains of these plants discovered by Linares, Sheets, and Rosenthal (1975: 142) at Sitio Piti. At the same site seeds of corozo palm and avocado have been unearthed. Linares (1977b) thinks that root crops were present also and at least moderately important. Since squash is normally associated with or part of the maize-bean complex, Linares (1977b: 314) and I think it was probably cultivated by the Aguas Buenas culture as well. Chili pepper was also grown.

Hunting and fishing did not play an important role in the interior. A very quick inspection of the Toreto site near Puerto Armuelles, however, yielded a small fishhook made of shell and a small shell ornament. Molluscs seem to be rarely present, even in coastal sites (Linares 1977b: 310), except perhaps for Toreto. There are indications of some craft specialization. Celts were manufactured centrally, perhaps because of the availability of the raw material (Sheets, personal communication). The large urns with zoned bichrome decoration found at Barriles and elsewhere were probably not fashioned by amateur potters. The same must be true for the carved statues and other elaborate stonework. Finally, some of the stone figures from Barriles show pendants that might have been made of gold (Torres 1972: 83–84, fig. 6, 88–90, fig. 2). If this is true, then gold-working was presumably another specialization. No gold, however, has been found in connection with Aguas Buenas material in scientifically controlled excavations. Gold might also have been imported from central Panama, but again this can only be proved through actual finds and detailed investigations. That there was a well-established trade network inside the Aguas Buenas territory is shown by the distribution of celts and/or their preforms from major sites down to the smallest hamlets (Sheets, personal communication). The already mentioned presence of Concepcion vessels and/or sherds in Aguas Buenas sites is another indication of exchange, this time with a near neighbor. Long-distance trade with central Panama might have been present, depending whether Linares's remarks on La Pitahaya (1977b: 310) refer to the earlier (Aguas Buenas) or later (Classic) occupation. Trade with central Costa Rica or regions farther north is indicated by a tubular jade bead from an Aguas Buenas grave near Boquete (Dan Sander, personal communication).

Different types of interment were obviously in use during Aguas Buenas times. Those at Boquete were roughly oval in shape and used either for primary or secondary burials (Dan Sander, personal communication). These burials were grouped together as a cemetery—the only one reported for this time period besides possibly the graves excavated by Stirling at Barriles (Stirling 1950: 243), although these were of a different nature, being shaft-and-chamber tombs. Their only contents were large metates, and these may be the last remainder of the "ceremonial stool–mace head–jade combination" of Greater Nicoya origin (Lange, this volume), which is also present in central Costa Rica (Snarskis, this volume), again strengthening the evidence for ties with Costa Rica.

Stirling also found another type of burial at Barriles, consisting of large urns with a bowl as a lid. No bones have been found inside these large vessels, perhaps owing to acidic soil conditions. The occurrence of at least one of the urns beneath a meter and a half of topsoil (Stirling 1950: 243) points to their use as burial vessels and argues against their being *chicha* jars, as has been put forward recently (Linares, Sheets, and Rosenthal 1975: 141). Normally, however, graves seem to be ill defined and scattered (i.e., not grouped together in a graveyard). They are often only indicated by a few pottery vessels lying together, generally at the bottom of an occupational layer (Haberland 1959: 44–56; Laurencich de Minelli and Minelli 1973: 219). I suppose, as did the Minellis, that the normal method, exemplified by this type of grave, was to inter the dead under the floor of the dwelling. The significance of the Boquete graveyard is unknown because of the rather meager information as to its layout, but the graves at Barriles, found by Stirling, should be interpreted as those of nobles and/or chiefs. Whether there are also regional and/or temporal factors involved we cannot say as yet because of lack of excavation reports.

Aguas Buenas was certainly a class society, containing at least a nobility and/or a chieftain class, commoners, and slaves. This is not only indicated by the graves and the stone statues, but also by the so-called metates, which sometimes are up to two meters long and elaborately carved, with human figures adorning the legs and with heads around the rim (Torres 1972: figs. 85, 90). They were probably seats of power like those of Greater Nicoya, as shown by Lange (1971c, this volume; Snarskis, this volume). Their burial (after the death of a chief?) reinforces this idea. The metates could also have been bifunctional, used for ceremonial making of chicha at the funeral. These thrones, as well as the statues, barrel-shaped objects, and stone spheres already mentioned, were probably the work of specialists living at the courts and forming another class of Aguas Buenas society. There are scarcely any indications about the religion, which might have centered on a cult of ancestors and, perhaps later, of deified chiefs, pictured in the famous stone statues (fig. 9.4). The same statues also indicate that trophy heads played a role. Whether the stone spheres and the barrel-shaped stone objects had any religious significance cannot be ascertained at this time.

Conditions were obviously different at the Laguna de Chiriqui (i.e., the Caribbean coast of Bocas del Toro Province). Linares (1977b: 311; Linares and Ranere 1971: 354) states that the oldest level of the Cerro Brujo site had Aguas Buenas ceramics. The economy was, in Linares's opinion, completely different from that on the Pacific side—the lack of metates is thought to indicate that maize was not present or played no important role. Linares, therefore, postulates root and tree crops as the agricultural basis. A rather large percentage of the food intake came from mollusc gathering, fishing, and hunting. The settlements, mostly on small hills, were tiny, consisting only of one or two houses (Linares and Ranere 1971: 353–55; Linares 1977b:

Figure 9.4. Stone figures from Barriles. Museo Nacional de Panama (photo by author).

314). This is a most interesting hypothesis, and it is certainly possible that the people on Laguna de Chiriqui changed food habits because of different ecological conditions, and, because they lived in the back wash, gradually became a marginal group. On the other hand, maize growing is possible in this area, and wooden mortars and pestles could have been used to crush maize. Perhaps more investigations have to be conducted before we can completely understand this area and link it with others, especially through sites higher up the Atlantic slope of the Chiriqui mountains.

Period V (A.D. 500–1000)

The end of Aguas Buenas came about A.D. 600. Linares and associates (Linares, Sheets, and Rosenthal 1975: 141, 144; Linares 1977b: 313) think that a larger than usual eruption of the Volcan Baru was the beginning of the end of this period since a massive layer of pumice capped the Aguas Buenas occupation at Sitio Piti and at Barriles. This might be possible, but the eruption is obviously not dated directly and might have occurred later, since Baru has been active into historical times (Sapper 1913: 124–27). On the other hand, there are chisel marks and other evidence of a violent destruction of the Barriles statues (Haberland 1968: 10). About this same time (A.D. 600–800) central Costa Rica and its Atlantic watershed see a sharp change in patterns, with an influx of foreign groups, which might come from the south (Snarskis, personal communication and this volume). There is a possibility that the end of the Aguas Buenas culture was caused by invasions, probably from or through central Panama and not, or not exclusively, by a natural disaster like the Baru eruption.

What follows Aguas Buenas is unclear, since no real stratigraphy has been established or found, especially in the interior. There seems to be a gap in the occupation of Barriles (Linares, Sheets, and Rosenthal 1975: 141; Linares 1977b: 310–11), perhaps a result of the pumice layer, which divided the earlier (Aguas Buenas) and later (Classic) occupation. Along the Pacific coast a special phase called Burica intervenes at La Pitahaya (formerly Isla Palenque), nearby Villalba, and sites on the eastern coast of Burica Peninsula (Linares 1968b: 68, 85–86; Ranere 1968: 115). Burica pottery as described from the sites mentioned seems vaguely related to Aguas Buenas, but it may be a late, somewhat impoverished, development. Maize agriculture was again the economic base, but not much else is known. Whether the large burial urns Linares illustrated from Las Tinajas and Eolega (Linares de Sapir 1968b: fig. 13; Miranda, Perez, and de la Guardia 1966; de la Guardia 1966) belong to the Burica phase does not seem to be certain, but it is possible, since secondary urn burial (a continuation of the Barriles urn burials?) was practiced during this time. Burica might only have covered 200 years, from A.D. 600 to 800, but may extend up to A.D. 1000, depending on the interpretation of its only C^{14} date (M–1470) and those of the following Chiriqui phase (I–5767 and I–5879).

In the Valle del General the gap may be filled by an up-to-date isolated site, Sabana de Caracol.[2] This site consists of a number of rectangular burial mounds with stone cist graves, none of which contained a single vessel. The few sherds from the mound fill are vaguely reminiscent of Burica material (Haberland 1961b: 32–33, 1976).

Period VI (A.D. 1000–1550)

The last archaeological entity of the sequence of Greater Chiriqui is the "classic" Chiriqui phase, known since the earliest publications (Bollaert 1863) and especially featured by Holmes (1888) and MacCurdy (1911). While the economic basis remained unchanged, many other material aspects represent an almost complete break with the earlier phases. The stone sculpture complex, so well represented in Aguas Buenas times, disappeared with the possible exception of a few remnants (Haberland 1973: 138–40). Among the ceramics there is a radical change in shapes and modes. Decorative techniques are now dominated by three-color polychromes, two- and three-color negatives, and a very thin, well-fired light-buff ceramic called Bisquit (either Tarrago Bisquit, Linares de Sapir 1968b: 38–41; or San Miguel Bisquit, Haberland 1961c: 58). The introduction of triangular projectile points, shaft-and-chamber graves and, possibly, gold techniques are other characteristics.

The date for the beginning of this phase is difficult to ascertain, because many C^{14} dates are missing, but most of this phase probably occurred some time between A.D. 800 and A.D. 1000, although it may have already begun in Period V. All indications, especially the painted pottery, point to the east, to the Panamanian central provinces and regions beyond, as the point of origin. It might represent the entrance of Chibcha-speaking peoples to Greater Chiriqui, but that is difficult to prove (see Haberland 1957a).

The "classic" Chiriqui cultures covered the whole region of Greater Chiriqui as described at the beginning of this chapter, excluding the Atlantic slope, at least for its lower (Caribbean) part. I use the plural, *cultures*, advisedly, since regional as well as possibly temporal differences exist among the archaeological entities known today as the Chiriqui phase.

The regional variations as far as known or published to date are (a) highland Chiriqui (i.e., the region around the Volcan Baru) (Haberland 1961c); (b) lowland Chiriqui, possibly limited to the slope itself and excluding the coastal plain (Haberland 1961e); (c) coastal Chiriqui (i.e., the coastal part of Chiriqui province in Panama) and especially around and in the Golfo de Chiriqui (Linares de Sapir 1968b); (d) the Boruca area in the Valle del General in Costa Rica (Haberland 1959, 1961b), possibly including the Diquis Delta (Lothrop 1963); (e) the Peninsula de Osa, also in Costa Rica (Haberland 1960c); and (f) possibly the region around San Vito de Java in Costa Rica near the Panamanian border (Laurencich de Minelli and Minelli 1966). Judging from the ceramics and some other modes, the first three areas are rather close together (Panama group), as are areas d and e (Costa Rica group). Area f might be included with the Panama group. Certainly, further investigation will reveal more subareas. An area that comes to mind from the evidence I have seen is the upper part of the Atlantic slope. The same is probably true for the Puerto Armuelles area and/or Burica Peninsula, regions that are scarcely known.

These small entities certainly demonstrate separate cultural subareas, joined together by a common bond but developing in different directions and creating different styles and/or modes. They might reflect archaeologically the small chiefdoms referred to by the early Spanish chroniclers (Linares de Sapir 1968b: 75–81). Regional differences were certainly encouraged by the diverse ecological conditions among the subareas.

The temporal differences during the Chiriqui phase are intimately connected with one pottery type, San Miguel (Tarrago) Bisquit, already mentioned earlier (fig. 9.5). At Buenos Aires, in the Valle del General, the graves in one burial mound sometimes contained this type of pottery, while in the graves of the other mound none has been found (Haberland 1961b: 37, 40). It is thought that the first-mentioned mound is younger than the other and that San Miguel Bisquit makes a rather late appearance, at least in the Valle del General. Proof from either stratigraphy or C^{14} dates does not yet exist, however. The idea of a later temporal unit or subphase characterized by the presence of Bisquit pottery is, on the other hand, strengthened through excavations by Linares at the Estero de Horconcitos. Her San Lorenzo phase, following Burica, shares a number of traits, especially in pottery, with the following Chiriqui phase but lacks Tarrago (San Miguel) Bisquit (Linares de Sapir 1968b: 66). Here the Bisquit pottery appears late in the sequence—the same phenomenon as at Buenos Aires. According to the dating obtained from the Estero de Horconcitos, Bisquit ceramics first appeared about A.D. 1200. They were obviously added to the inventory without any other important changes, at least as far as can be seen today.

San Miguel Bisquit is extremely well fired, often completely oxidized, and very thin, actually much better made technically than any other pottery of this time, not only in Greater Chiriqui but also in all of lower Central America. It comes in a large number of shapes, sometimes rather fancy ones. All this points to the fact that Bisquit is the work of specialists, probably made in one village or small group of adjoining villages. That it may come from only one source is also indicated by the fact that thin sections of Bisquit pottery are all identical, regardless of where the material was found. The most probable area of origin seems to be the lower slopes of the Pacific side of Chiriqui Province; here, as far as can be judged, the greatest variety of

Figure 9.5. San Miguel Bisquit from grave V, mound I, Buenos Aires, Costa Rica. Hamburgisches Museum für Völkerkunde.

shapes and also the largest percentage of Bisquit pottery have been found. Some of the shapes, but not all, were exported to the more remote subareas. For instance, four out of five Bisquit vessels at Buenos Aires were large tripod bowls, which are otherwise quite rare (Haberland 1959: plates VIIIi–1, IXa–b).

Bisquit pottery was not the only type produced commercially in Greater Chiriqui during the late period. Areas obviously specialized in certain types and traded them to other subareas. Osa, for instance, produced a heavily appliquéd tripod (Haberland 1960c: 83–84), which has also been found in the highland Chiriqui subarea (Haberland 1961c: plate VIj). Another group of tripods, Lerida Red-on-orange (Haberland 1961c: plate VIa), was obviously introduced into highland Chiriqui from the Atlantic slope, if not from the Caribbean coast itself, since Stirling, in his excavations at Darkland Cave (BOC–2), found not only several tripods of this type (Stirling 1964: 268–69, plates 30a–b), but also many other vessels with an exterior-roughed body, one of the characteristics of Lerida Red-on-orange (Stirling 1964: 267–75, plates 30c, 31b, 34a). Obviously only one shape, the most elaborate one, was exported; the simpler ones were used locally. Many of these tripods have been found in graves on the upper slopes of the Caribbean side (i.e., nearer their source of origin), strengthening the argument presented earlier.

Additional internal pottery trade might have involved Banco Red Line and Cangrejal Red Line from the coastal subarea (Linares de Sapir 1968b). These types were abundant there but rare in the interior (Haberland 1961c: plate XIIIh). Negative-painted pottery might have been another specialty of lowland Chiriqui.

Pottery was also imported from outside Greater Chiriqui. Polychrome ceramics from the Panamanian central provinces have been found repeatedly in Greater Chiriqui (Holmes 1888: figs. 207–15; Linares de Sapir 1968b: plates 14b–j), and White Line pottery from central Costa Rica appears in the Boruca subarea (Haberland 1959: plates VIm–q). Sherds from Nicoya are said to have been found at La Pitahaya (Linares and Ranere 1971: 352), and one Nicoya vessel is illustrated by Holmes (1888: fig. 216). As Cooke (1976a: 32) correctly pointed out, it is most interesting to note that pottery originating from Chiriqui has never been found outside the area. In view of the excellence of the Bisquit ceramics, this cannot be ascribed to inferior quality; there must have been other reasons.

Trade in durable goods was not restricted to pottery alone. This is shown by the presence of the jaguar metates, which were either seats of honor (Stone 1958a: fig. 4i) or altars. They were most probably carved in central Costa Rica and imported into Greater Chiriqui, where they are rarer than publications indicate. As Stone (1963: 341–42) demonstrated, molluscs from the Atlantic coast were imported into the Diquis Delta subarea, and manatee bones may also have been traded (Stone 1963: 343).

The spatial distinction between subareas does not rest solely on pottery types but can also be traced through grave construction. Graves differ from subarea to subarea, while following the basic pattern of a strongly modified shaft-and-chamber type with a stone cover. The burial type is difficult to verify since bones are almost completely gone, but the sizes of the graves and the distribution of the grave goods are such that in many cases, especially in the Boruca subarea, no primary burials seem to fit into them (Schmidt 1968: 27–30; Schmidt n.d.: parts G and H). The differences in grave construction are indicated by wall construction and the presence or absence of stones.

Graves of the Chiriqui phase always form cemeteries, showing another difference among the subareas. In the Boruca subarea circular mounds surrounded by a retaining wall constructed of water-worn stones and with a surface pavement (mostly gone today) are the rule. These mounds are sometimes marked by upright stone pillars or slabs (Haberland 1961c: 34–35). In highland Chiriqui such mounds do not exist, but stone slabs seem to have been present (Bateman 1861: 29–30). Most graves here and in the Valle del General were not oriented in a specific direction, with the possible exception of some parts of Mound I at Buenos Aires. The situation in lowland Chiriqui is not settled. Here, too, some parts of graveyards may contain parallel rows of graves, as have been encountered by the author at San Miguel del Juco. Graves in the cemeteries near San Vito de Java were roughly oriented in an east-west direction, but whether in rows is not mentioned by the excavators (Laurencich de Minelli and Minelli 1966: 421).

All Chiriqui-phase graveyards in Greater Chiriqui are similarly placed. Most often they are found on an elevated or commanding spot, like a mountain spur, an isolated hill, a slight elevation, or the rim of a river canyon. Since these locations were often also those preferred for settlements by the Aguas Buenas people, Chiriqui-phase graveyards sometimes cut into or through these older sites, and Aguas Buenas sherds might be found in the fill.

The positions of the cemeteries and of the settlements were obviously not identical. Settlements have been excavated only around the Estero de Horconcitos, but the special situation on the coast and the islands prevents a generalization. In the Valle del General there are indications that the villages or houses were placed on the lowest river terrace and, therefore, have been destroyed by the meandering of the river. The recent discovery of a settlement at Rey Curre, between Buenos Aires and Palmar Sur, seems to confirm this idea (Snarskis, personal communication). The settlement is situated on a low terrace near the river and has a possible plaza with a stone-covered mound.[2] Today a modern settlement is on top of it.

Graves and other indications, including the very meager notices of the Conquest time, show a class society, with chiefs and/or nobles and commoners. Slaves were probably also present. Among the commoners were some specialists, probably with an elevated status, like the potters manufacturing the Bisquit ceramics, gold workers (Stone 1977), some of whom were possibly itinerant, warriors, and shamans (Haberland 1961d).

As for religion, it centered probably around a number of gods, among which a fertility goddess was especially prominent or beloved. She can be seen in many polychrome figurines found in graves. Sitting spread-legged, she is sometimes shown with an infant on her back or nursing an infant or a puppy. Sometimes, but not very often, she is pregnant. Whether this goddess and her representation are intimately connected with similar figurines either to the northwest or in northeastern South America (Lothrop

1926:[2]: 260–61) is an interesting and puzzling problem, especially since
in Greater Nicoya and elsewhere these figurines are part of a rather old
tradition, while in Greater Chiriqui they have no known antecedents.

Another important god, this time with connections to the east, is the
alligator god, sometimes wrongly called the jaguar god. He is rather rare
among pottery figurines (MacCurdy 1911: fig. 244), but is often seen on
gold pendants (Holmes 1888: figs. 27, 30, 35; MacCurdy 1911: figs. 330,
361, 365–68, 374–77; Stone 1977: fig. 162). The alligator god also adorns
intricately carved antlers, part of a ceremonial outfit of either religious or
political significance, which were found at Jalaca in the Diquis Delta region
(Stone 1963: figs. 17, 18, 21, 25a, 26, 1977: fig. 161). As for a jaguar god,
he probably did not play a prominent part in Greater Chiriqui. He is more
characteristic of the northwestern part of lower Central America and was
replaced in Greater Chiriqui and farther to the east by the alligator god of
South American origin. The same origin might pertain to the raptorial bird
variously called eagle or vulture and depicted in ceramics (MacCurdy 1911:
figs. 248–49, plate XLVII; Stone 1963: fig. 3c) and gold (MacCurdy 1911:
figs. 353–58; Stone 1963: figs. 2a–c) if it also was a deity in animal disguise.
In that case its prototype may have been the condor deities of the central
Andes. There is also the tradition that "sibu" (i.e., god) took the form of a
buzzard (vulture) to teach the people how to dance (Stone 1962a: 64). Many
other aspects of daily life can be reconstructed, at least partially, from the
archaeological finds of Chiriqui—dress and ornament, musical instruments,
and so on. These subjects, however, go beyond the scope of this paper.

Graves with a strong affiliation to the Chiriqui phase have been found
in the Bocas del Toro Province on the Caribbean coast. For the Laguna de
Chiriqui, however, Linares stated that "the archaeological settlements of
Bocas Province appear to represent marginal populations organized on the
basis of small family (?) groups, without status differentiation or political
centralization of any recognizable kind" (Linares 1977b: 311). This is contrary to what Columbus found during his visit to this region in 1502. His
son Hernando mentions settlements, extensive agriculture, and the presence
of "principales," which I should translate as "noble vassals" (Lines 1952:
157–58; Sauer 1966: 131). It was also here that Columbus got the first gold
objects during his fourth voyage! On the whole, the cultural standard in
Bocas del Toro was probably not much lower than on the Pacific side, at
least not at the time of the Conquest.

Whether the Caribbean lowlands were, culturally speaking, part of Greater
Chiriqui is hard to decide since the finds of the recent excavations have not
been published yet. It is only said that "crude ceramics . . . and no trade
wares are characteristic" (Linares and Ranere 1971: 354–55). "Trade wares,"
I suppose, refers here to the painted ceramics of the Pacific side of Chiriqui.
Judging from the ceramics published by Stirling (1964) from the Bahia del
Almirante and referred to earlier, the connections with Greater Chiriqui

were only slight. Therefore, at this moment, Bocas del Toro, or at least its lowlands, is not included in Greater Chiriqui.

The Chiriqui phase or tradition was the last pre-Columbian cultural entity flourishing in Greater Chiriqui. It continued into early Colonial times, as is demonstrated, for instance, by the finds from Rio Changuina, a tributary of the Rio Diquis. Here a grave contained, besides typical Ceiba Red-brown tripods, rolled gold beads, iron implements, and millifiori glass beads (Stone 1958: 47–48).

The early Colonial accounts, especially those of Conquest times, are rather meager in their ethnographic content, giving only a very superficial picture. Those concerning the Panamanian portion of Greater Chiriqui were compiled and interpreted by Linares de Sapir (1968b: 75–81), while Stone (1977: 132–35) did the same for the Costa Rican part, where the conditions were only slightly better than in Panama.

Summary

The cultural history of Greater Chiriqui can be summarized as follows: The first settlements found up to now have been caves and date to Period II at 6000 B.C. Whether the inhabitants were the first human beings entering the region is more than doubtful, since people settling South America had to cross this territory. These early peoples probably wandered along the coast on paths now inundated. The first known settlers were hunters and gatherers whose remains have certain similarities to entities in the central provinces of Panama. This era is called the Talamanca phase. About 3000 B.C., during Period III (Boquete phase), a change occurred, probably involving a shift in subsistence pattern and perhaps the beginning of plant cultivation, with tree and possibly root crops becoming prominent. No major influx of people is thought to have triggered this change.

Period IV, beginning at about 1000 B.C., saw the first appearance of ceramics and, by inference, of maize and related crops. Since these ceramics have not yet been published, their origin is unknown. Equally unknown is whether this unnamed entity gave rise to one of the following traditions, which occupied Greater Chiriqui from about 800 to 500 B.C. One of them (Aguas Buenas) came from the northwest, where the El Bosque phase of the Costa Rican watershed shows many similarities, while the other (Concepcion) has connections with the east (i.e., the Panamanian central provinces). The two traditions settled in different environments. At first there were only small agricultural communities, but later, at least among the Aguas Buenas people, they agglutinated into political entities with a class society. They probably subjugated and/or drove out the Concepcion people, and Barriles might have been the capital of their united territory. This development ended about A.D. 600 either through a natural catastrophe or the invasion of new people, or both.

New groups came from the east at the beginning of Period V, bringing a more South American–based culture with them. This migration may represent the arrival of Chibcha-speaking peoples. Their culture, which appeared at least between A.D. 800 and A.D. 1000, is called the Chiriqui phase or tradition. It occupied all of Greater Chiriqui, including the higher slopes of the Atlantic side but probably not the Caribbean lowlands. Politically, Greater Chiriqui was, during this time, split into many small chiefdoms, contrary to what may have been the case during Aguas Buenas times. Trade was expanded during this era, with connections to the east (central provinces of Panama), northwest (central Costa Rica and Nicoya), and north (Atlantic lowlands), while during Period IV the main emphasis was on trade with the northwest. Curiously, only the imports but not the exports are known. The Spanish Conquest ended this indigenous development.

The cultural development in Greater Chiriqui is characterized by rather stable conditions. As far as it is known to date, only two sharp changes occurred—at the beginning of or during Period IV (Aguas Buenas and Concepcion invasion) and during Period V or the beginning of Period VI (Chiriqui invasion). While the first brought a basically Central American culture to Greater Chiriqui, the latter emphasized South American elements.

Editors' Notes

1. Haberland unfortunately did not have access to Linares and Ranere (1980) prior to revising his chapter. The book would certainly have provided Haberland with substantial quantities of data for reference in his chapter, but it would not have altered the general thrust of his chapter or the areas in which he agrees and disagrees with various interpretations.

2. Since the seminar, Robert Drolet (under the auspices of the National Museum of Costa Rica) has undertaken significant research in the southwestern part of Costa Rica. This area was totally unrepresented by recent research in the seminar presentations, and Drolet has kindly consented to prepare a summary of that work for inclusion here, with Haberland's agreement.

Proyecto Boruca 1980–81

Residence and Community Integration
During Aguas Buenas and Chiriqui Phases
in the Diquis Valley, Southeastern Costa Rica

ROBERT P. DROLET
Museo Nacional de Costa Rica
San Jose, Costa Rica

Newly acquired information regarding settlement during the Aguas Buenas (500 B.C.–A.D. 600) and Chiriqui (A.D. 800–1500) phases from the Gran Chiriqui region expands the data base presented by Haberland in the preceding chapter. Survey and mapping operations in the Diquis Valley have located and defined new habitational and cementery complexes. This evidence, when combined with the surface and lithic assemblages from 56 sites, makes it possible to link the Diquis Valley with early communities known over the Gran Chiriqui region.

One year of archaeological survey and selected site investigation has been completed on the project, encompassing an area of 400 square kilometers of valley land. Work was concentrated in the valley bottom and in upland areas along approximately a 20-square-kilometer stretch of the Terraba River (Drolet and Markens 1980a, 1980b, 1981a, 1981b). Of the 56 sites located, approximately half belonged to Aguas Buenas– and half to Chiriqui-phase occupations. Sites associated with each phase are found in distinct ecological zones of the valley, and each contains distinct cultural materials. The presence of these deposits in the Diquis Valley extends the known range of related early tropical farming populations to more than 100 kilometers, from the Diquis Valley on the west to the Chiriqui highlands on the east.

Aguas Buenas Settlement

A total of 25 Aguas Buenas habitation sites is clustered in four separate upland areas, located on flat ridge tops close to secondary and tertiary drainages. The four areas include Buenas Aires, Las Animas, Bolas, and Terraba, all at elevations between 300 and 600 meters (fig. 9.6). Sites are characteristically small (one hectare or less), dispersed, featureless, and contain sparse surface ceramic and lithic material. Badly distrubed stone cist tombs at a few sites indicate interment within the habitation complex, a pattern which probably influenced household abandonment and residential movement. This burial pattern appears to be an important feature of this early phase and is distinct from the later Chiriqui-phase burial pattern characterized by cemetery sites separated from habitation sites.

Site clustering in the four highland areas of the Diquis Valley suggests a settlement pattern organized into local community zones. In each area the habitational zone extends over an area of four to seven square kilometers, with 7 to 10 dispersed habitation deposits. The survey procedure was to systematically locate all deposits within a randomly chosen one-kilometer-square area (Findlow et al. 1980), then to survey the adjacent areas to determine the extent of the deposits.

The same pattern of clustered but dispersed Aguas Buenas habitation sites was documented for the Volcan Baru area of western Panama, located well to the east (Linares, Sheets, and Rosenthal 1975; Linares and Ranere 1980: 267–75). There, three major settlement areas each contained between 5 and 22 predominantly small-sized sites, suggesting a dispersed community pattern similar to that found in the Diquis Valley during the same Aguas Buenas phase. Reports of single Aguas Buenas– phase sites between the Diquis Valley and the Volcan Baru, in the area of San Vito de Java and Aguas Buenas (Haberland 1955, 1976; Laurencich de Minelli and Minelli 1973), most probably represent complexes that were part of larger community zones. Evidence from the Diquis Valley shows small-sized Aguas Buenas population clusters organized into separate highland communities and clearly indicates an orientation to upland forest and valley areas for resource exploitation.

Higher order Aguas Buenas sites have also been investigated within the Gran Chiriqui region (Linares, Sheets, and Rosenthal 1975; Linares and Ranere 1980: 280–92; Laurencich de Minelli and Minelli 1973). Survey conducted in the Bolas

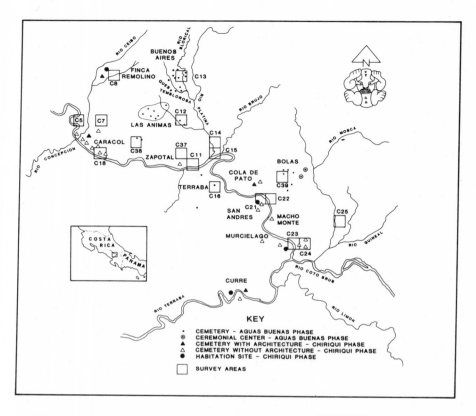

Figure 9.6. Distribution of sites located during the Boruca Valley survey.

area of the Diquis Valley located and mapped a similar site. This site contains numerous rectangular mounds with stone cist tombs, some with ramps and some with stone cobble facing. A restricted area of the site contains densely concentrated occupational debris and suggests special residence status. The site extends over an area of approximately five hectares and is surrounded by numerous smaller, featureless habitation sites along the flat ridge tops.

Besides the large mound construction, there are numerous stone balls, some measuring two meters in diameter. These massive granite stone carvings do not occur in other Aguas Buenas complexes to the east; in the Diquis Valley they indicate special manufacture and function associated with higher order habitation and cemetery sites. The Aguas Buenas settlement in the Diquis Valley clearly shows a demographic pattern of small, separated highland communities linked together by a large center, implying political integration. The site hierarchy and sociopolitical activities in the Diquis Valley during this phase closely resemble those associated with settlement complexes further east, implying a regional link between local occupations in Gran Chiriqui.

Ceramic affinities between Aguas Buenas sites in the Diquis Valley and those complexes located farther east are now quite clear. Linares's discussion (Linares and Ranere 1980) of ceramic material associated with the western Panama Late Formative phase now makes it possible to link the Bugaba-style ceramics of Chiriqui with the Aguas Buenas ceramic wares of southern Costa Rica, both representing a single ceramic tradition within the Gran Chiriqui region. The range of vessel forms associated with the Aguas Buenas–Bugaba style are typical of the Diquis Valley material, representing restricted-wall bowls, tecomates, slightly flaring-wall jars, other flat-rimmed jars, and plate forms. These sherds contain a similar range of incised, slipped, and modeled decoration, as well as legged and ring-based supports and circular handles typical of the Cerro Punta Orange and Valbuena ceramic types described for the Volcan Baru habitation sites (Linares and Ranere 1980: 85–96).

The ceramic inventory of the Diquis Valley Aguas Buenas–phase sites also represents the same industry as described for sites in the San Vito de Java and Aguas Buenas areas (Laurencich de Minelli and Minelli 1973; Haberland 1955, 1976). Bugaba-phase sites in western Panama are securely dated from A.D. 200 to A.D. 600 (Linares and Ranere 1980: 109); earlier Aguas Buenas settlement in the Diquis Valley appears likely, lending support to the idea shared by both Haberland and Linares of an early eastern spread of the Late Formative complex out of Costa Rica.

Only limited evidence has been collected from Aguas Buenas–phase sites in the Diquis Valley that would indicate what kinds of subsistence activities were practiced. Most sites contain only small, scattered concentrations of lithic debris from cores, flakes, double-faced axes, scrapers, hammerstones, and other groundstone tools. The exclusive orientation of all Aguas Buenas sites to the upland zone points to agricultural as well as hunting activities. As Haberland pointed out, the evidence for maize, fruit, bean cultivation, and arboriculture is well documented for the Volcan Baru area (Linares and Ranere 1980). There is no reason to suspect any different practices in the Diquis Valley.

Chiriqui-Phase Settlement

A totally different occupation phase is found in the lower valley bottom, where only Chiriqui-phase cemetery and habitation sites are located. Cemetery sites are present on 200–250-meter-high hilltops in front of the Terraba River and also are found on hilltops along its major tributaries. Habitation sites representing large nucleated villages are located along lower terraces close to flat, fertile alluvial fans. These two categories of sites have been found at San Andres, Murcielago, Curre, and Caracol, along a 17-kilometer stretch of the Terraba. Another area of Chiriqui-phase sites is near Finca Remolino on the Ceibo River, a major tributary of the Terraba. Occupation in this phase forms a lineal pattern of settlement along the major drainages with site complexes separated from one another by approximately 5 kilometers, a pattern which appears to be representative of the Chiriqui-phase occupation throughout the valley.

A complete survey of the valley bottom was not attempted, but rather, randomly chosen squares were established for survey work. A procedure identical to that used in the upland survey was followed in surveying the valley bottom. This procedure proved successful in determining the areal extent of the late-phase sites, as well as the relationship between the habitation and cemetery complexes.

Each of the large Chiriqui-phase habitation sites had similar distributions of refuse deposits. Lithic tools, waste flakes, and cores were recovered, as were similar types of monochrome and occasional polychrome ceramics. Heavy refuse concentrations were present at all sites, but at only one (Murcielago) were residential features also preserved. At the other sites these features had been largely destroyed by agricultural operations.

Intensive cleaning, collecting, and mapping were conducted at Murcielago. This site covers four square kilometers, with undisturbed areas (fig. 9.7). Six residential sectors have been identified at the site, each ranging from five to six hectares in size. Thus far, two of these have been mapped and reported on (Drolet 1980; Drolet and Markens 1980b, 1981b). Each residential sector contains circular cobble house foundations forming clusters of two to three units. These foundations measure 30–35 meters in diameter and are often connected by short causeways. Around the perimeters of the house structures are dense clusters of refuse pits and built-up daily work areas. In one sector (complex 4), foundations of what appear to be public structures have been found, with size and shape plans different from those of the adjacent round residential structures. A causeway links these structures to the house structures in the same sector.

A dense concentration of chipped river stone has been found within the refuse deposits and household activity areas associated with the residential sectors. Hundreds of manos and metates outnumber other artifacts around the house structures. Repair tools, used to peck off the smooth surface luster on the manos and metates, indicate constant maintenance of these utensils. Numerous unidirectional cores, waste flakes, and hammerstones make it possible to determine the process of tool manufacture and repair and the categories of material used. Scrapers, knives, polished stone axes, celts, and chisels manufactured from hard andesite and basalt cobbles are other categories of tools found around the house area. Large, boulder-shaped, metate-sized celt sharpeners present in these localities point to the repair of celts, axes, and chisels. Double-faced axes made from large granular flakes of igneous stone probably represent weeding and agricultural clearing tools. Small, stub-legged, plate-like grinding stones with slightly concave ground surfaces, along with circular-shaped milling stones with rounded grinding surfaces and nutting stones, exemplify the variety of utensils probably used for processing palm nuts and tubers.

All tools were found in densely concentrated and separated refuse areas located directly around the house perimeters. The tools associated with the assemblage point to a variety of activities associated with food processing, woodworking, and tool production and repair. The similar distribution of lithic debris and artifacts indicates similar daily activities within each barrio-like sector of the community. Judging from the large number of manos, metates, and edge-bearing tools, maize and wooden utensils appear to have been principal products of the community. These activities at Murcielago, however, represent only one component of a wider network of community interaction and resource exchange. Evidence from other Chiriqui-phase sites in the valley, especially cemeteries, indicates a wider range of lithic specialization than found on Murcielago. This suggests levels of economic and political community organization for manufacturing and distribution of resources established over territorial zones.

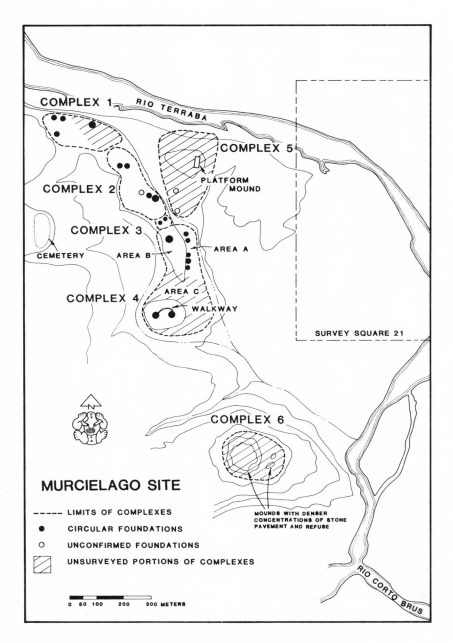

Figure 9.7. Details of site patterning at Murcielago.

A single residential sector at Murcielago contains up to 30,000 sherds on the surface of the numerous refuse deposits that ring the house structures. These sherds indicate the predominance of bowl, plate, and jar vessel forms, with few showing decorative treatment other than a simple red or brown slip. Conical hollow leg supports and ring bases were occasionally placed on these vessel forms. Jar forms sometimes were given simple circular handles, which were frequently decorated with incision and punctation. Modeled frog heads project from the upper portions of some vessels, apparently placed as functional stub handles. Few polychrome sherds were found, indicating a predominant use of monochrome vessels for domestic activities. Throughout all residential sectors investigated at Murcielago, the same homogeneous range of ceramic material occurs, pointing to similar vessel categories used for related household tasks. The relative absence of polychrome ware at the site suggests nondomestic use and may indicate that it was manufactured principally for interment in cemeteries where red, black, and white painted vessels have been frequently reported (Haberland 1961b; Stone 1963; Lothrop 1963: 78–86). Furthermore, special polychrome production seems to have been limited to a few sites; Murcielago does not show evidence of having been one of these manufacturing centers.

Not only are the details of settlement activities clearly visible on the site of Murcielago, but also the community arrangement of large-diameter house clusters in residential sectors offers the first evidence for identifying large-sized social units. These structures housed the most significant social units of the community, possibly representing lineage or other higher level groupings. The organizational design to this community implies social divisions for activities within the site as well as information and resource flow between Murcielago and similarly structured communities in the valley.

The other sites found in the valley consist of cemeteries which cover a large portion of the terraces that overlook the Terraba River and its major tributaries. Internal features were mapped and surface materials were collected at these sites. No excavations were conducted.

In one class of cemetery, located on lower-level terraces, tombs are arranged in lineal rows and covered by a circular cluster of cobbles. Survey conducted in the Caracol area of the Terraba River found seven cemeteries of this class, stretching over three kilometers in length, all situated on the narrow one-meter-wide northern bank. Tombs mapped in these cemeteries were easily located due to raised circular piles of cobble stones, occasionally sprinkled with light sherd remains and some double-faced axe artifacts. Some tombs were clustered tightly into restricted-sized cemeteries (one-half hectare or less) and others were spaced further apart in row-like arrangements within larger-sized cemeteries (four to seven hectares). The completed survey in this area found no refuse deposits associated with the cemetery complex, indicating the exclusive use of this entire area for funerary purposes. Typically, these cemeteries had no special features associated with them; however, one did have two petroglyphs and another had a large granite stone ball, suggesting variation in these burial lots possibly associated with social distinctions. The cemetery divisions at Caracol perhaps correspond to sector or household divisions within a nearby Chiriqui community, a hypothesis worthy of future investigation.

Other cemeteries of the same class occur along narrow channel banklands further downstream from Caracol, and around broader lowland areas even further downstream, near habitation sites in the areas of San Andres, Murcielago, and Curre. These cemeteries occur as dispersed, single sites, characteristic of one of the tomb cluster cemeteries described for Caracol. None were found with habitation refuse deposits, and all contained tomb features similar to that of Caracol, but without other constructions or specially made artifacts placed on the surface. Their placement near nucleated habitation sites suggests localized use, although this cannot be confirmed.

Another cemetery class was found associated with Chiriqui occupation in the valley bottomlands. This class of cemetery is usually more restricted in size but more elaborate in funerary design, with special architectural constructions, worked stone artifacts, and fancy polychrome pottery. These sites tend to be located on a second-level terrace, above the habitation sites and first class of cemeteries. One of these multifeature cemeteries is located above the Ceibo River, on top of a flat ridge, overlooking the deep canyon formed by the river. Thirteen rectangular and square mounds were mapped on this site, each containing badly disturbed stone cist tombs. The cemetery extends over a three-and-one-half-hectare area. Long basalt columns measuring between one and two and one-half meters were found on a number of mounds, apparently placed to mark special tombs. Systematic walking of the site showed no occupational refuse areas. The only surface sherd material recovered was from disturbed tomb fill.

Other cemeteries of this latter class were found in Curre, Caracol, Cola de Pato, Macho Monte, and San Andres. These sites contain large mound constructions with stone cist tombs. In every case the tombs were disturbed. Some of the mounds in Curre and Macho Monte were faced with river cobbles. Caracol, a site excavated by Haberland in 1958 (Haberland 1961b: 32–33, figs. 11–20), was constructed with a series of rectangular mounds faced with straight-sided retaining walls made from river cobbles. These special burial mounds housed hundreds of tombs. Basalt stone pillars found in this cemetery complex were similar to those mentioned from the Finca Remolino cemetery near the Ceibo River. A carved granite sphere was also found at the south side of the cemetery, below the terrace top containing the burial mounds. Other cemeteries of this class contained mound features associated with petroglyphs.

Sherds with polychrome designs were found on most of these latter class sites. These sherds were obtained not from refuse deposits, as mentioned, but along the sides of disturbed tomb fill, the only areas of these sites where collections could be found. The presence of this fancier pottery in cemeteries reinforces the idea that polychromes possibly represent funerary ware; their association with other well-crafted artifacts and well-constructed mounds implies an association of special funerary offering. The apparent difference found in ceramic association between habitational sites and cemetery sites in the Diquis Valley Chiriqui phase points to the necessity for defining patterns for ceramic production and distribution of diversified wares reported over both the valley network and the regional network.

Chiriqui-phase sites in the Diquis Valley indicate specific demographic and hierarchical patterns associated with settlement. The population was oriented exclusively to the rich valley bottom zone. Distribution of large nucleated sites in fertile alluvial zones along the Terraba River and its major tributaries indicates the use of the lowlands for maize farming, the rivers for travel, and the bank lands for obtaining cobble materials, timber, and probably hunting, fishing, and wild fruit collection. This network of communities probably left few available alluvial lands unoccupied, a condition which must have stimulated the growth of intervalley networks for resource exchange, social interaction, and political integration. Communities such as Murcielago indicate this network was well established in the valley well before the conquest. The residential organization of this site not only reflects a long period of valley adaptation, but also provides a clear design for social and economic organization associated with settlement. The house clusters and residential sectors on this site imply chiefdom domination of the valley. The distribution and hierarchical nature of cemetery sites appears to be directly related to social ordering in the valley and in communities like Murcielago, linking together the diversified sites associated with this phase.

The Diquis Valley represents only one geographical area in the Gran Chiriqui region colonized by Aguas Buenas– and Chiriqui-phase populations. The reported settlement of similar populations well to the east of the Diquis Valley in coastal and highland valley areas implies an integration of early complexes over a wide geographical region. Intensive work in the Diquis Valley is providing new evidence relating to this regional settlement. Considering the extent of deposits and the evidence for well-developed settlement in the Diquis Valley over a possible 2,000-year period, this part of the Gran Chiriqui may represent a center for regional networks in both the Aguas Buenas and Chiriqui phases.

10
Archaeological Research in Central and Eastern Panama:

A Review of Some Problems[1]

RICHARD COOKE

Smithsonian Tropical Research Institute

This paper discusses certain aspects of archaeological research in the Central and Eastern regions of Panama (fig. 10.1). After brief sections on the Paleo-Indian period and its sequel, it focuses on three problems only: (a) the Preceramic and Monagrillo (Willey and McGimsey 1954) occupation of Parita Bay, with special emphasis on new evidence for early maize cultivation, (b) the establishment of sedentary villages and social ranking, and (c) faunal analysis. I believe that it is more profitable in a review volume to concentrate on a few themes (see Linares 1979: 30–35) than to attempt an all-encompassing and superficial summary of two archaeological zones where serious investigations have been limited to a small proportion of the total area and span more than 50 years of rapidly changing research objectives (cf. Cooke and Camargo 1977).

Geographical Divisions and Culture Areas

Before embarking on the review per se, I should supply a brief comment about Isthmian culture areas, as the summaries published in the last two decades (Lothrop 1966; Willey 1971; de Brizuela 1972a; Haberland 1978) have employed a greater number of discrete cultural units.

The areal scheme I envisage for Panama (albeit provisionally) links the Atlantic and Pacific watersheds in three north-south zones which are con-

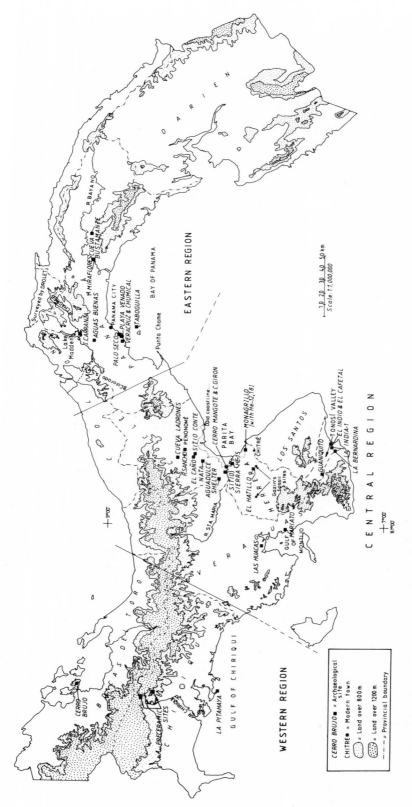

Figure 10.1. Map of Panama, showing the three major cultural divisions, provincial boundaries, modern place names, and archaeological sites mentioned in the text. (The cultural frontiers have not been proven empirically).

tiguous to each other (simply, the Western, Central, and Eastern regions) (Cooke 1976d: fig. 1). Notwithstanding criticisms (Roosevelt 1979) of my intentionally bland nomenclature (Cooke 1972: chaps. 1, 2), I remain adamant that this tripartite division of Panama coincides better with the archaeological, documentary, and ethnographic evidence for cultural and linguistic boundaries, territory formation, and exchange networks than do earlier attempts to subdivide the Isthmus strictly according to the modern political divisions of Cocle, Azuero, and Veraguas (Lothrop 1942: fig. 486; Ladd 1964).

In the Western region, Linares (1977b; Linares and Ranere 1980) has demonstrated that ceramic-using groups occupying ecologically dissimilar zones of the Atlantic and Pacific watersheds descended from a common cultural pattern and maintained contact because of, rather than in spite of, divergent adaptive strategies. Helms (1978: 124–28, 1979) has stressed that the distribution of certain chiefdoms in eastern Panama was related to the control of the Atlantic-Pacific trade routes, while her observation that some chiefly territories occupied environmentally diverse, north-south strips of land coincides with the ethnohistoric evidence for the Central region (Cooke 1979).

With regard to the contemporary peoples of Panama, the research of Young (1971, 1976, 1980) and Bort (1976, 1980) among the Ngawbere-speaking Guaymi of Chiriqui and Bocas del Toro, of students of Isthmian languages (cf. Young 1965; Gunn and Gunn 1974), and of the ethnographers of the Kuna (Stout 1947; Wassen 1949; Howe 1974, 1977; Stier 1979) has demonstrated clearly that populations living on the Caribbean and Pacific sides are, and have been, inextricably linked historically, linguistically, and culturally, and that establishing mutually exclusive social divisions along the axis of the Cordillera (cf. Johnson 1948b), makes little sense.

Differences in material culture, agricultural and hunting systems, and social organization obviously did exist between the Atlantic and Pacific watersheds in pre-Columbian times (Linares and Ranere 1980). Here I am simply endorsing Linares's approach to the archaeology of the Isthmus by reaffirming her belief that culture areas cannot be defined by reference to recent pottery types alone, and that the most positive research programs in the area are those that follow a regional and historical approach and pay close attention to tropical ecology and recent ethnography.

The Initial Occupation of the Isthmus

In earlier summaries of Isthmian archaeology (Cooke 1976a, 1976c), I favored the conservative view (cf. Haynes 1971; Martin 1973; Lynch 1974) that Panama was not occupied before a traditionally Paleo-Indian (i.e., fluted point) horizon that entered the Isthmus from the north. The dimensions and morphology of the Panamanian fishtail points are so close to those of South American examples (Bird 1969; Bird and Cooke 1977) that the similarities seemed best explained in terms of a very rapid migration from north to south (cf. Lynch 1976: 29). Besides, the indisputable rareness of fluted points in Panama appeared to give credence to this idea.

I now accept that more and more evidence to the north of the Isthmus and an increasing number of carefully investigated sites to the south (Bryan 1978), make a pre–12,000 B.P. occupation of Panama much more likely than it seemed five years ago. No sites, however, have yet provided acceptable stratigraphic or typological evidence for a pre-fluted-point occupation, be this hypothetical stage "pre-projectile point," "unifacial flake," or "willow-leaf point." Quarry detritus at the Aguas Buenas site in Panama Province, where Bryan and Cruxent had hopes of finding Pleistocene materials (Cooke 1977) and where there is no evidence of bifacial flaking, has been dated to 5785 ± 50 B.P. (3835 B.C.) (SI–3852), placing the deepest part of the refuse in the same general time period as the Talamanca-phase sites of Chiriqui (Linares and Ranere 1980), Cerro Mangote, the Aguadulce Shelter, and the Cueva de los Ladrones (this chapter). At the last three sites there is also no evidence for bifacial flaking, while in Chiriqui, the Talamanca-phase bifacial celt-like wedges seem to be a locally developed tool type adapted to forest conditions. For these reasons, it is not possible to argue that Aguas Buenas is somehow anomalous because it lack bifaces or that, in spite of a 4000 B.C. date, it can be accommodated into a much earlier, nonbifacial tool stage.

The only probable Paleo-Indian find that can be added to the eight reported fishtail- and Clovis-like fluted points from the Chagres Valley and Canal entrance (Snarskis, this volume; Bird and Cooke 1977, 1978b) is a fluted point that was recovered from the surface by Cruxent (personal communication 1980), near La Venta–1, a predominantly Colonial site on the northern bank of the River Chagres in the same general area as the earlier Lake Madden finds. This is similar to the largest fishtail points found at Lake Madden, but it has a large blade in proportion to the stem. There are fluting scars on both sides of the stem, and the blade has the typically lower Central American triangular thinning flakes that widen and deepen toward the center. The point seems to have been broken at the base while it was still fastened to the shaft, as were at least two of the earlier examples (Bird and Cooke 1978b: figs. 2c, d).

The Paleo-Indian Adaptation in Panama and Its Sequel

Views are divided over the nature of late Pleistocene adaptations and environments in Panama. Lynch (1974, 1976) proposes that the Pacific watershed would have been preferred by human populations as it would have included large tracts of open land perhaps maintained by man-induced fires. He feels that tropical forests, having a low biomass of large animals, would have been little suited to the communal hunting strategy he believes characterized the Paleo-Indian way of life in general.

Ranere (1972, 1976, 1981) has for long maintained a contrary opinion. He thinks that large expanses of savannas and/or grasslands did not exist anywhere in Panama until the advent of agriculture and intensive annual burning (between 7000 and 4000 B.P.). As the Paleo-Indians hunted large mammals which lived in many altitudinal zones, their obligatory occupation of tropical lowland biomes to the south of Nicaragua would have required little change in hunting strategies and instruments. Instead of balking at a barrier of impenetrable trees (MacNeish 1976; Cohen 1977) or migrating swiftly through a Pacific grassland corridor, the Paleo-Indians would simply have expanded to the limits of lowland tropical habitats on both slopes, before continuing southward into new areas. (This model, and the above, can be accommodated into any pre-Paleo-Indian stage.)

Obviously, these opposing views will only be clarified by more excavations and paleo-environmental studies (deep sediment and pollen analysis, for example). Nevertheless, the fact that the pollen diagram from Lake Gatun (Bartlett and Barghoorn 1973)—recovered from the same valley in which seven fluted points have been found—includes "predominantly rainforest tree genera" for the period 11,300–9600 B.P. (Bartlett and Barghoorn 1973: 235) indicates that the Paleo-Indian hunters in this region of Panama had to contend with a forest rather like that of Barro Colorado today. Snarskis's Turrialba site (this volume) was also, presumably, situated in a wet forest zone.

In regard to the Pacific watershed of Panama, if it really was drier in the terminal Pleistocene—the pollen data from neighboring areas are somewhat contradictory (c.f. van der Hammen 1961; Wijmstra and van der Hammen 1966; van der Hammen 1972; van der Hammen and Correal 1978; Carbone 1978)—would the forest have given way to grasslands, or would it simply have become more xerophytic? Rather than argue for forest barriers or for large expanses of open land, it seems more economical to predict, as Ranere (1980b: 35) has done, that the Pacific watershed would have included some open habitats in a generally wooded environment (seasonal swamp grasslands, for example). Such a situation could well have provided ideal conditions for the communal hunting of the different browsing, grazing, and swamp-dwelling organisms that have been recovered from late Pleistocene paleontological deposits in Herrera province (Gazin 1957).

All the artifacts that have been classified as Paleo-Indian in Panama have come from disturbed contexts. A terminal Pleistocene date has been attributed to them by reference to typologically similar tools from outside the

Isthmus (Bird and Cooke 1978b). Present evidence indicates that by 5000 B.C., pressure flaking and bifacial projectile points had dropped out of the Panamanian stone tool assemblages. It is possible, however, that these traits persisted into the early Holocene: a date of 6610 B.C. ± 160 has been recovered from the basal deposits of the Cueva de los Vampiros (AG–145), at the mouth of the Santa Maria River, in association with bifacially worked flakes, including a triángular thinning flake similar to those which were removed from the published fishtail- and Clovis-like points from Lake Madden (Cooke and Ranere in press).

This new information gives credence to the ideas that the transition from the Paleo-Indian Period I into the late Preceramic Period II B was gradual, and that the apparently drastic technological break between the Lake Madden materials and the post–5000 B.C. Chiriqui and Parita Bay assemblages is an artifact of the lacuna in the temporal record, and of an imperfect understanding of the nature of late Pleistocene and early Holocene stone tool kits. If the earliest occupants of the Isthmus (whatever the hierarchy of their subsistence base) had to adapt to a variety of tropical habitats, they must have developed a wide range of both percussion- and pressure-flaked tools for specifically tropical tasks (see the data from the Sabana de Bogotá [van der Hammen and Correal 1978]). It would seem, for example, that the morphological and probably functional similarities between the heavy, ovate scrapers from Turrialba and Ranere's Talamanca-phase scraperplanes are pointing toward a continuum in non-pressure-flaked tools between periods I and II B (compare Snarskis 1979b: fig. 6 with Ranere 1975b: plate 8, bottom, and fig. 11; Table 10.1 summarizes the regional chronology used in this paper).

Until very recently, it appeared that the lack of 8000–5000 B.C. sites in Panama and the extreme rarity of obviously Paleo-Indian materials substantiated Martin's (Martin 1973; Mosimann and Martin 1975) thesis of a rapid migration through the Isthmus and subsequent depopulation (Linares 1980e). Transect and purposive surveys undertaken by the Proyecto Santa Maria between 1981 and 1983 (Cooke and Ranere in press) indicate that the Panamanian preceramic settlement pattern has been poorly understood until now, and that Period II populations, though sparsely distributed, were well in excess of earlier estimates.[2]

The Advent of Agriculture:
New Data from Parita Bay

Of the countries under scrutiny in this seminar, Panama has the most complete record for the Preceramic. Eleven sites have been excavated— eight rockshelters, two open sites, and one shell mound (table 10.2)—and 27 radiocarbon dates are available for deposits that do not have ceramics

Table 10.1. A Summary of Aboriginal Cultural Development in the Central and Eastern Regions of Panama, with an Updating of the Chronological Sequence.

Period	Important Sites	Settlement and Subsistence	Diagnostic Artifacts	Approximate Dates
I (Paleo-Indian)	Lake Madden (Chagres Valley)	Hunting, probably concentrating on large terrestrial mammals. Possibly also plant gathering in forests and grassy areas.	Fluted points (Clovis-like and fishtail-like). Distinctive scrapers.	Terminal Pleistocene (There are no C[14] dates.)
IIA (Preceramic A)	La Cueva de los Vampiros	Hunting, fishing	Bifacially worked tools	ca. 8000–5000 B.C. (one C[14] date)
IIB (Preceramic B)	Aguadulce Shelter Cueva de los Ladrones Cerro Mangote	Settlements found to date are within 20 kilometers of the active coastline (shell mounds and rockshelters). (Many open sites have recently been recorded but not yet published). Box-type secondary burials at Cerro Mangote. Ritual cannibalism at the Aguadulce Shelter. Collection of aquatic resources; hunting iguanas, and terrestrial mammals; heavy reliance on shellfish and crabs. Wild plants gathered (with emphasis on palms). Some plants perhaps cultivated.	An entirely percussion-made chipped inventory (no pressure flaking, no bifacial tools), but some grinding stones and bases. (Many edge-ground cobbles at some sites.) A wide range of small scraping and boring tools, varying from site to site. Polished axes may have appeared by the end of the period.	5000–3000 B.C.
IIIA (Early Ceramic A)	Aguadulce Shelter Cueva de los Ladrones Monagrillo Zapotal (He–15) Cueva de los Vampiros	Apparently similar to Period IIB, though phytolith data suggest the use of maize by at least 1500 B.C. Palms still used intensively.	Stone tools similar to those of Period IIB, but need more detailed analysis. Grinding tools commoner—edge-ground cobbles, pestles, multi-faceted manos. Chipped stone adzes at the Monagrillo site may belong to this period. CERAMICS: Monagrillo-type ceramics had appeared by 2800 B.C., becoming slowly more complex in form and design.	3000–1200 B.C.
IIIB (Early Ceramic B)	El Limon (Cocle) Guacamayo Playa Venado (lower levels) Taboguilla-1 La Mula	Deep shaft-chamber tombs on mountain tops. Probably small but permanent maize-cultivating villages in the piedmont and on hill slopes. La Mula was a large, nucleated village.	CERAMICS: A poorly described group of plastically decorated wares, some of whose motifs survive into the early part of Period IV (i.e., Sarigua). Cylindrical vessels with flat bases. STONE TOOLS: Poorly known. Bread-board metates are found in tombs, and at La Mula, notched flakepoints.	1200–300 B.C.

Table 10.1 (continued)

Period	Important Sites	Settlement and Subsistence	Diagnostic Artifacts	Approximate Dates
IV (Aristide and Tonosi Pottery. Includes Ichon's Bucaro and El Indio phases)	Cerro Giron Ichon's Tonosi Valley sites Las Huacas Playa Venado (?) Sitio Conte (lowest refuse) Sitio Sierra	By at least 300 B.C. in Parita Bay (perhaps a little later elsewhere), permanent, large maize-cultivating villages. Flexed primary burials in group cemeteries. Continuing heavy reliance on aquatic resources. Intensive hunting of the white-tailed deer. Some ceremonial centers with stone columns perhaps functioning by the end of the period. Axe-maker and woodworker burials.	CERAMICS: Bichrome and three-color wares (Aristide and Tonosi). Also a wide variety of plastically decorated forms (cylindrical vessels, scarified jars, and so on). STONE TOOLS: Long, prismatic blades of silica and igneous rock appear. Legged metates, cylindrical manos, notched blade knives, elaborate stone jewelry, polished axes. GOLD: Hammered and lost-wax pieces are present by the final century of the period.	300 B.C.–A.D. 500
V (Conte Pottery, formerly Early Cocle).	El Caño La Cañaza and other Tonosi Valley sites Panama Viejo Playa Venado Sitio Conte Sitio Sierra	Large, nucleated, maize-cultivating villages. Ceremonial centers with lines of columns, many of which are sculpted. Burials generally primary and extended. Increasing social differentiation in cemeteries, with mass burials around central persons. Mutilations of (?) enemies. Caribbean slopes probably well populated.	CERAMICS: Four-color polychrome appears (with addition of purple and bluish paints). Zoomorphic designs added to geometric (these tend to be realistic). STONE TOOLS: Increasing sophistication in lapidary work. Tanged blade knives or points with triangular blades. The material culture of the Eastern and Central regions becomes more divergent. Eastern-region pottery consists mostly of modeled and incised forms. GOLD: Designs similar to those of Conte pottery.	A.D. 500–700 (There are no C14 dates.)

Period	Sites	Burial/Settlement	Artifacts	Date
VI (Macaracas Pottery, formerly Late Cocle)	Above sites Miraflores (CHO–3) El Hatillo and Nata become important	Above pattern continues. Urn burials and interments in artificial mounds become more common.	CERAMICS: *Central Region:* Increasing stylization of animal motifs, long, polychrome pedestals. Huge vessels (sometimes used for burials). *Eastern Region:* At CHO–3, very distinctive shapes, negative painting. Little polychrome, which is mostly imported from Central region. GOLD: Designs similar to those of Macaracas pottery.	A.D. 700–1100
VII (El Hatillo and Parita pottery)	Burial activities decline at Sitio Conte El Hatillo important Nata important El Caño active Guaniquito	Above pattern continues. Some evidence for a decline in the number, though not size, of sites, and for the artificial modification of hilltops. Urn and mound burials common.	CERAMICS: *Central Region:* Purple paint gradually drops out. Designs become stylized and rectilinear. Greater emphasis on modeled overpainted decoration. *Eastern Region:* Poorly documented. Modeled and incised bird effigies with white clay inlay. STONE TOOLS: Distinctive steeply chipped stemmed points with triangular cross sections. Probably an apogee of carved metates in western Veraguas. GOLD: Spread-eagled birds with decurved beaks (Veraguas eagles) (tentative).	A.D. 1100–Conquest

and are stratified beneath ceramic-bearing layers. At seven localities there is information on the *in situ* transition from the Preceramic into the Early Ceramic: at Cueva Bustamante in Panama (excavated by Bird and Cooke in 1973, unpublished), la Cueva de los Ladrones in Cocle (Bird and Cooke 1978a), the Aguadulce Shelter in Cocle (Ranere and Hansell 1978), three rockshelters in highland Chiriqui (Ranere 1980b, 1980e), and the Cueva de los Vampiros, in Cocle (Cooke and Ranere in press).

Over the past decade, archaeologists working on the Isthmus have questioned the once popular idea that pottery manufacture was related to a drastic change in prehistoric life-styles. When speculating about subsistence and settlement, they include the late Preceramic and Early Ceramic (IIIa and b) periods (5000–300 B.C.) under a single, transitional rubric: principally hunting and gathering in a seasonal round, but by at least the third millennium B.C., some kind of root- and/or tree-crop horticulture in which the proportions and species of cultigens employed slowly changed (Cooke 1976a, 1976c; Linares 1976a, 1976c; Ranere 1980a). To quote Linares (1976a: 66), "the addition of pottery made little difference either [to] the location of a site or [to] subsistence practices."

In spite of the uneven settlement data that are available for central and eastern Panama, it still seems as though there was no drastic change in the above pattern until the first millennium B.C., when populations rise, settlements nucleate, and sites cluster into obviously arable areas—apparently in response to the introduction of extensive seed-crop agriculture based on maize. Not until about 300 B.C. do we find incontrovertible evidence for maize-using villages in alluvial floodplains and fertile volcanic valleys in the highlands, whose establishment coincides with what looks like a rapid abandonment of the coastal shell mounds and rockshelters as regular, if impermanent, living sites (Linares, Sheets, and Rosenthal 1975; Cooke 1979; Linares and Sheets 1980). In fact, if the Monagrillo pottery was being made as far back as 3000 B.C. (which is reasonable in the light of recent evidence), fully sedentary villages employing the entire range of early sixteenth-century cultigens (Linares 1976a; Cooke 1979, 1981) might not have developed until as many as 3,000 years after clay utensils began to be used along the Parita Bay littoral. Certainly, it is difficult to argue for site hierarchies, political territories, craft specialization, and ceremonial centers until at least the beginning of the Christian era (Linares and Sheets 1980).

Although this scheme is difficult to refute, ongoing phytolith analysis of soils from Late Preceramic and Early Ceramic sites around Parita Bay and external evidence for maize movements and cultivation south of Mexico have affected its credibility, confirming the long-held suspicions of some archaeologists (Linares 1976c) and botanists (Galinat 1980) that maize was being cultivated in suitable areas of Panama long before the existing C[14] dates for charred macrofossils and instruments obviously used for maize preparation would indicate.

At the Aguadulce Shelter, Piperno has found that the proportions of large cross-shaped phytoliths with distinctive three-dimensional morphologies[3] demonstrate the presence of maize in the ceramic-bearing layers, while they are sufficiently underrepresented in the Preceramic levels beneath to show that, at this site, corn was not being used before the appearance of the Monagrillo ceramics. Ranere has put a date of 1680 ± 90 B.C. on the Preceramic layers at the Aguadulce Shelter that are immediately underneath the first ceramic-bearing layers. Hence Piperno concludes that maize was under cultivation in this area of Panama by 1500 B.C. (Piperno 1980b).

Before continuing with the specific problem of maize, however, I should discuss the radiocarbon chronology of the recently excavated Preceramic and Monagrillo sites, as there are a number of relevant discrepancies.

Excavations at the Cueva de los Ladrones (Bird and Cooke 1978a) and at the Aguadulce Shelter (Ranere and Hansell 1978) have confirmed that the pottery complex first described by Willey and McGimsey (1954) from the Monagrillo site (Herrera) is the earliest in the Central region. At both sites, sherds very similar to those from the type site occur stratified immediately above the Preceramic levels.

The date of 2140 B.C. ± 70 originally assigned to these ceramics at the Monagrillo shell mound (Deevey, Gralenski, and Hoffren 1959: 166–67) has been substantiated by Ranere's 1975 excavations (Ranere 1975a; Ranere and Hansell 1978; Ranere 1980a). Ten radiocarbon determinations have been added (table 10.2). These are, however, difficult to interpret. Ranere himself has pointed out (Ranere and Hansell 1978: 56) that the contradictions which characterize the dates in Block 1 could be explained by the very complex stratigraphy since "numerous pits dug by later Monagrillo phase inhabitants caused disturbance down to a level of 150 cms. in some parts" (Piperno 1979: 44).

In Block 2, the dates can be divided into two groups: the most recent three (1435 B.C., 1535 B.C., and 1665 B.C.) are stratigraphically consistent and were recovered from undisturbed cultural deposits. The three oldest dates, however, 3545 B.C., 3435 B.C., and 2400 B.C., came from deposits which Hansell and Adams (1980) have shown by reference to Rosin's Test to be the result of the natural water-sorting of materials, rather than cultural activity. The latest date, 2400 B.C., was taken on oyster (*Crassostrea*) shells, and corrected for C^{12}/C^{13} fractionation. As these shells were deposited naturally on the open beach that existed at this time, the much earlier charcoal dates should be intrusive, even though they may be culturally derived. Perhaps they were washed along the beach or down the Parita River.

Ranere now feels, in fact (on the basis of ongoing geomorphological studies), that ideal living conditions only existed at the Monagrillo shell mound between about 1700 and 1000 B.C. (see the section on faunal analysis), though it is possible that some form of occupation (and hence Monagrillo vessels) can be dated to the period 2400–1700 B.C. At the Cueva de

Table 10.2. All the C[14] Dates for the Five Central Region Sites Which Have Preceramic Deposits and Monagrillo-Type Ceramics.

Laboratory Number	Years B.P. (1-sigma)	Years (Gregorian)	Material	Archaeological Context
1. AGUADULCE SHELTER (AG-13)				
TEM-107	2570 ± 95	620 B.C.	*Crassostrea*	Layer B₁, Block 3, 5–10 cm below surface (see Ranere and Hansell 1978) Ceramics.
TEM-125	2540 ± 70	590 B.C.	*Crassostrea*	Layer B₂, Block 3, 10–15 cm below surface. Ceramics.
TEM-126	2960 ± 80	1010 B.C.	*Crassostrea*	Layer B₃, Block 3, 15–20 cm below surface. Ceramics.
TEM-108	3630 ± 95	1680 B.C.	*Crassostrea*	Layer C₁, Block 2, 20–25 cm below surface. No ceramics.
TEM-127	2790 ± 110	840 B.C.	*Crassostrea*	Layer C₃, Block 3, 25–30 cm below surface. No ceramics.
TEM-128	3700 ± 100	1750 B.C.	*Protothaca*	Layer C₃, Block 3, 25–30 cm below surface. No ceramics.
TEM-110	3540 ± 115	1590 B.C.	charcoal	Layers C₄ and D, Block 3, 35 cm below surface. No ceramics.
TEM-130	4210 ± 90	2260 B.C.	*Crassostrea*	Layer C₄, Block 3, 30–35 cm below surface. No ceramics.
TEM-131	6180 ± 120	4230 B.C.	*Anadara tuberculosa*	Layer C₄, Block 3, 30–35 cm below surface. No ceramics.
TEM-106	5840 ± 95	3890 B.C.	*Crassostrea*	Layer C₅, Block 5, 35 cm below surface. No ceramics.
2. CUEVA DE LOS LADRONES (LP-1)				
TEM-120	3770 ± 80	1820 B.C.	*Crassostrea*	Area 2A, layer 4 (see fig. 4). Associated with 2 Monagrillo-type sherds.
TEM-121	3860 ± 90	1910 B.C.	*Crassostrea*	Area 2A, layer 5. Associated with 1 Monagrillo-type sherd.
TEM-122	3880 ± 80	1930 B.C.	charcoal	Area 0, interface between layers 7 and 8. Possibly a small (intrusive) fire-pit (see fig. 4). 10 Monagrillo sherds.
TEM-124	4520 ± 100	2570 B.C.	charcoal	Area 1, at the base of a pile of shell and stones, perhaps a hearth, slightly underneath TEM-119 (see fig. 4).
TEM-119	4800 ± 100	2850 B.C.	*Crassostrea*	Area 1, within a pile of shell and stones, perhaps a hearth. Associated with 383 Monagrillo sherds.
TEM-123	6860 ± 90	4910 B.C.	charcoal	Area 2A, layer 6, stratified underneath the pile of shell and stones, directly on top of sterile clay. Base of cultural. No ceramics.
3. CUEVA DE LOS VAMPIROS (AG-145)				
Beta-5101	8560 ± 160	6610 B.C.	charcoal	Test pit 1 (April–May 1982). Beneath sterile hiatus. From levels 12/4–13/1 (2.90 to 3.60 meters below datum). Associated with bifacial thinning flakes.
Beta-5870	3800 ± 120	1850 B.C.	charcoal	Test pit 1. Bottom of ceramic occupation.

4. CERRO MANGOTE (AG-1)

Lab no.	Date		Material	Notes
Beta-1218	3555±100	1605 B.C.	charcoal	"Pothole 1," north wall (1979 excavations), 180–90 cm below datum.
TEM-207	5055±155	3105 B.C.	Crassostrea	"Pothole 1A," 145–55 cm below datum. Corrected for C^{12}/C^{13} fractionation. 4630±150 was reported.
TEM-175 and	5140±120	3190 B.C.	Crassostrea	Inside shell.
TEM-174	5990±180	4040 B.C.	Crassostrea	Outside shell. Same shell. "Pothole 1," north wall, 180–90 cm below datum.
TEM-176	5440±130	3490 B.C.	Crassostrea	Inside shell. "Pothole 1," red clay zone, 209–19 cm below datum.
Beta-1219	6670±215	4720 B.C.	charcoal	Combined sample from the red clay zone (base of deposit).
TEM-206	6710±175	4760 B.C.	Protothaca	"Pothole 1," north wall, 180–90 cm below datum.
Y-458d	6810±110	4860 B.C.	charcoal	Just above the red clay zone (McGimsey 1957).

5. MONAGRILLO (HE-5)

Block 2 dates (see Ranere and Hansell 1978 for drawings of the profiles)

Lab no.	Date		Material	Notes
SI-2838	3385± 75	1435 B.C.	charcoal	Block 2E, 20–30 cm below surface.
SI-2839	3485±100	1535 B.C.	charcoal	Block 2E, 50–60 cm below surface.
SI-2840	3615± 80	1665 B.C.	charcoal	Block 2E, 95–100 cm below surface.
TEM-208	4350±165	2400 B.C.	Crassostrea	Block 2E, 152–57 cm below surface. Corrected for C^{12}/C^{13} fractionation.
SI-2841	5385± 95	3435 B.C.	charcoal	Block 2E, 110–20 cm below surface. Possibly non-cultural.
TEM-109	5495±100	3545 B.C.	charcoal	Block 2E, 100–10 cm below surface. Possibly non-cultural.

Block 1 dates

Lab no.	Date		Material	Notes
SI-2843	3245±100	1295 B.C.	charcoal	Block 1E, 50–56 cm below surface.
I-9384	3325± 85	1375 B.C.	charcoal	Block 1E, 150–60 cm below surface.
SI-2844	4135± 80	2185 B.C.	charcoal	Block 1E, 97–100 cm below surface.
SI-2842	4405± 75	2455 B.C.	charcoal	Block 1E, 20–30 cm below surface.

Willey and McGimsey excavations

Lab no.	Date		Material	Notes
M-11	800±250	A.D. 1150	shell	Presumably related to "Alvina" pottery, i.e., post-Monagrillo period activities.
Y-585	4090± 70	2140 B.C.	charcoal	West trench, Section 6, 95 cm below surface, bottom of stratum 4 (Deevey, Gralenski, and Hoffren 1959).

A

B

Figure 10.2. *Opposite:* The northeastern profiles of areas 1A, 2A, 3, 01, and 0 at the Cueva de los Ladrones. *Above:* The depositional contexts of the six radio-carbon samples (for excavation plan, see Bird and Cooke 1978a: fig. 6).

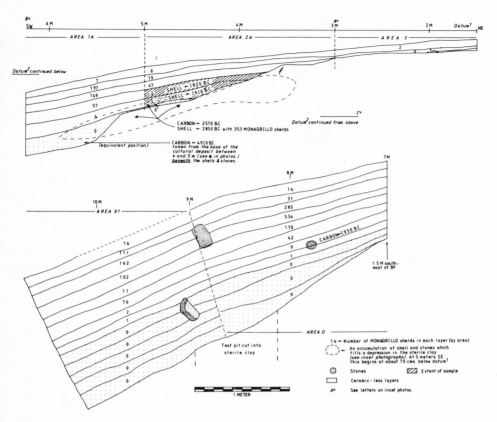

los Ladrones, however, the Monagrillo-type ceramics can be associated with a date of 2800 B.C.

Figure 10.2 shows the profile of the central trench at the site (Bird and Cooke 1978a: fig. 6) with the positions of the dated samples marked upon it. The earliest date, 4910 B.C. ±90, was run on charcoal and recovered beneath a pile of shells, hearth (?) stones, and potsherds found in a shallow depression near the dripline. Slightly downslope from this sample, but above it stratigraphically and clearly associated with 380 Monagrillo potsherds, a sample of *Crassostrea* shells yielded a date of 2850 B.C. ±100, while a charcoal sample from the same context gave 2570 B.C. ±100. Immediately above and to one side of these samples, a group of oyster shells was dated to 1910 B.C. ±90 and 1820 B.C. ±90. The artificially separated layers from which they were isolated contained three Monagrillo sherds. The sixth determination, 1930 B.C. ±80 (charcoal) came from further down the talus, in area 0, at the junction between the base of the ceramic deposit and the Preceramic layers.

Taken as a series, these dates are not incongruous. In areas 1 and 2 of the excavation, they are stratigraphically consistent when one considers the dipping of the sterile clay. The 4910 B.C. determination, taken from the base of the cultural deposit, coincides with the lowest dates at Cerro Mangote and should refer to the initial, Preceramic occupation of the shelter. The 2850 B.C. and 2570 B.C. samples recovered with the concentration of Monagrillo sherds came from a discrete kitchen area where shells, bones, and charred pots had been discarded. As shells are dating consistently younger in Parita Bay than charcoal (Ranere 1980a), 3000 B.C. would be a reasonable round figure for the beginnings of pottery manufacture at the site. This approximation coincides with the latest acceptable dates for the Preceramic occupation of Cerro Mangote.

At the Aguadulce Shelter, there are now eight radiocarbon dates that range from 3890 to 590 B.C. (Ranere, Cooke, and Hansell 1980). According to Ranere, the earliest reliable date for Monagrillo-type ceramics at the site is 1010 B.C. ± 80, while the top of the Preceramic deposits dates to 1680 B.C. ± 85. Hence Preceramic activities would seem to outlast the debut of ceramics at closeby sites by more than a thousand years. Though we are a long way from understanding these discrepancies, it is possible that at the Aguadulce Shelter (where, in some areas, less than 25 centimeters separated layers dated 3,300 years apart), the extremely compressed stratigraphy has mixed materials of slightly different ages, though the site was carefully excavated by reference to natural strata.

At Cerro Mangote, six dates have been added (Ranere, Cooke, and Hansell 1980; Ranere 1980a) to that collected by McGimsey (1957). The most recent of these (1605 B.C.) is very late. It is possible, however, that the primary flexed burials reported from the site (McGimsey 1956: fig. 3) postdate the intensive use of the outcrop as a living site and that this date is in some way related to these activities. At least one of the primary flexed interments encountered by McGimsey was accompanied by a "curly-tailed monkey" pendant (McGimsey, Collins, and McKern 1966: 9; cf. Lothrop 1937: fig. 171), an artifact type that has not yet been recovered from contexts earlier than about A.D. 200. Primary flexed burials have been reported from contexts dating to between 240 and 25 B.C. at the neighboring Sitio Sierra (next section), as well as at Cerro Giron, located at the base of Cerro Mangote (Ladd 1964; McGimsey quoted in Cooke 1972).

The 4720 B.C. result from the basal red zone and a C^{12}-C^{13}-corrected date of 4760 B.C. from immediately above it are a good corroboration for the 4860 B.C. determination acquired by McGimsey from a similar stratigraphic position, indicating that Cerro Mangote began to be used at the beginning of the fifth millennium B.C.. If the aforementioned late date is ignored, the latest result (3105 B.C.) coincides with the round figure I am putting on the beginning of ceramic manufacture in Parita Bay.

To summarize my own position on the dating of these four important sites, I would propose that the Ceramic-Preceramic boundary fell nearer 3000 B.C. than 2500 B.C., and that the best explanation for the late dates on the Preceramic deposits at the Aguadulce Shelter is the compressed stratigraphy at the site, and not the unlikely possibility that the locale was occupied by a different cultural group or used only for activities that did not require Monagrillo pottery until 500 B.C.

To return to the problem of the beginnings of maize cultivation and the Monagrillo ceramics, it is necessary to elaborate on the phytolith data Piperno has been gathering so carefully over the last few years.

Soil samples were recovered from Ranere's excavations at both Monagrillo and the Aguadulce Shelter. Unfortunately, soil from the former site had very few phytoliths (Piperno 1979). The opposite was true at the Aguadulce Shelter, where there were phytoliths in substantial quantities and of many different forms: the useful cross-shaped phytoliths that gave Pearsall (1977–78, 1978, 1979) her basis for separating maize from other grasses; other shapes from the epidermal cells of grasses; rod-shaped examples from monoctyledonous herbs; *Heliconia* and *Curatella americana*–type phytoliths; and spherical phytoliths which are probably from palms (Piperno 1980b, personal communication 1982).

Piperno's results from the analysis of the cross-shaped phytoliths from the ceramic and non-ceramic levels are given in table 10.3. They are compared with the phytolith count from two soil samples acquired at Sitio Sierra, a Period IV (300 B.C.–A.D. 500) maize-cultivating village only 12 kilometers from the Aguadulce Shelter (following section). The Sitio Sierra samples came from a refuse dump and a house floor in which carbonized maize was found. Conservative estimates for their ages would be A.D. 1–500. The comparative results can be summarized as follows:

From the Aguadulce ceramic levels, high percentages of cross-shaped phytoliths were isolated. In contrast, very few cross-shaped phytoliths were recovered from the preceramic deposits. The size distribution of the cross-shaped phytoliths from the ceramic levels falls much closer to the races of maize tested . . . than to any of the wild grasses, including those which produced some large-sized cross-shaped phytoliths. It is very similar to the distribution of maize from Sitio Sierra. Out of a total of 54 cross-shaped phytoliths, 14 (26 percent) fell into the large, and extra-large categories. No extra-large, cross-shaped phytoliths have been found in [any of the] wild grasses [tested]. The preceramic size distribution falls much closer to that of the wild grasses. (Piperno 1980b: 7)

When the chi-square statistical method was used on her data, the distribution of large, and extra-large, cross-shaped phytoliths in the ceramic levels was shown to be significantly different from the distribution that would be expected if wild grasses alone had accounted for the phytoliths present in

Table 10.3. Phytolith Distribution at the Aguadulce Shelter and Sitio Sierra (Piperno 1980b: table 2).

AGUADULCE SHELTER: PERCENTAGE OF CROSS-SHAPED PHYTOLITHS OF ALL SIZES

Layer	Percentage of Cross Shapes	Number of Phytoliths Counted
B	4.7	231
B	2.0	200
B	1.0	200
C	0	200
C	0.3	303
C	0	293
C	0	205
C	0	200

SIZE DISTRIBUTION OF CROSS-SHAPED PHYTOLITHS

	Small	Medium	Large	Extra Large
Aguadulce Shelter—Levels with Monagrillo-Type Ceramics				
Number	20	20	12	2
Percent of Total	37	37	22	4
Aguadulce Shelter—Preceramic Levels				
Number	17	11	2	0
Percent of Total	56	37	7	
Sitio Sierra—Period IV Domestic Contexts				
Number	14	13	11	0
Percent of Total	37	34	29	0

the deposit (p = between .001 and .01). Consequently, Piperno concludes that the Monagrillo-phase occupants of this site must have been cultivating maize.

Reconsidering the Early Ceramic (Monagrillo) Period in Parita Bay

Assuming that the earliest races of maize that arrived in South America between 6000 and 3000 B.C. (Lanning 1967; Pickersgill and Heiser 1977: 807; Zevallos et al. 1977; Pearsall 1979; Beadle 1980; Galinat 1980) did not do so by sea, it is reasonable to deduce that two aspects of data collection are preventing us from providing hard archaeological evidence from Panama for this cultigen's obligatory passage through the Isthmus—the nature of plant conservation in archaeological sites and the haphazard surveys that have been undertaken in key areas.

In the first place, Piperno is finding that phytolith preservation is dependent upon the amount of sand in the soils and upon the general soil pH (the more basic the soil, the fewer phytoliths). Both Cerro Mangote and Monagrillo are coastal shell mounds. Hence their deposits are inimical to phytolith preservation. Secondly, the conservation of charred maize material depends upon its ability to resist breaking up upon carbonization, the cooking methods used to prepare it, and its relative abundance in the overall plant supply. The more similar corn is to primitive popping varieties, the less likely it is to survive the carbonization process and subsequent trampling. Also, if the early race(s) of maize which passed through the Isthmus were not staples, but one of a large variety of equally important pot vegetables (Ranere 1980b: 41), their various parts—even if they were preserved—would not be found as frequently as they are at sites like Sitio Piti (Linares and Sheets 1980), or Sitio Sierra (next section), where cobs, kernels, and stalk fragments were recovered in large quantities, trampled into house floors, in pit fill, and around hearths.

It is likely, then, that phytolith and pollen studies will become more useful tools for testing for primitive maize in lower Central America than water-screening sediments for macrobotanical remains.

The second defective facet of research in Panama is site survey. In Parita Bay, where there are four known Preceramic sites (Cerro Mangote, Aguadulce Shelter, Cueva Ladrones, and Cueva de los Vampiros) and six with Monagrillo ceramics (Monagrillo, He–12, He–15, He–18, Aguadulce Shelter, and Ladrones), all the deposits that have been archaeologically tested are either coastal shell mounds or rockshelters. In Willey and McGimsey's words (1954: 101) the "site survey of the Parita Bay alvinas was not systematically pursued, but rather was carried out as an intermittent activity in conjunction with our excavations at the two principal sites, He–5 and He–

15." Since then, McGimsey and Cooke have surveyed adjacent areas of
Cocle (Cooke 1972), but the surveys cannot be called systematic. Cooke
was concerned with locating sites with painted ceramics and faunal remains
and not with searching for pre-1000 B.C. deposits. Ranere's reexcavations
of Monagrillo and Cerro Mangote, and the finding and excavation of the
Aguadulce Shelter, were part of a research program that did not include
survey as one of its very specific objectives. The Cueva de los Ladrones site
was located and excavated solely because it was believed that Paleo-Indian
material would be found here (Bird and Cooke 1978a).

The existing patchwork of information leaves a lot of room for doubt,
especially regarding Parita Bay, an area whose precipitation (1,000–1,400
mm annually), rainfall distribution, alluvial soils, and wide coastal plain
make it a perfect contender for the early cultivation of plants that require
dry periods. What if we have been missing Monagrillo, or even Preceramic
villages (the former already using maize, the latter relying on root and tree
crops), located some way inland from the coastal shell mounds and rockshelters, which were occupied only seasonally and/or for specific activities?

At all the Chiriqui and Parita Bay Preceramic and Monagrillo sites, plant-
preparing tools like edge-ground cobbles, grinding-stone bases, and multifaceted manos, mortars, and pestles are found. Whether these tools were
used for mashing root crops (Ranere 1980c) or for preparing the many palm
nuts and nances (*Byrsonima*) that occur in some of these sites (Ranere 1980c;
Ranere, Cooke, and Hansell 1980), or whether they were used for grinding
early forms of maize, cannot yet be determined with certainty from the
archaeological record. Smoothed and polished axes had appeared in the
highlands of Chiriqui by Ranere's (1980d: 350) Boquete phase (2300–500
B.C.), and at the Cueva de los Ladrones, chips from polished axes were
found well stratified below the Monagrillo layers (Bird and Cooke 1978a:
fig. 17).

With regard to the importance of coastal resources per se, there is no
doubt that Parita Bay, situated in a zone of heavy dry season upwelling,
and high fish and mollusc biomasses (Linares and Cooke 1975; Cooke 1979),
is a particularly productive area, noticeably more productive than the neighboring Gulf of Chiriqui, where there is no indication of human settlement
right on the coast until the beginning of the Christian era (Linares 1980c:
75). The size of the early settlements like Cerro Mangote and Monagrillo,
the fact that the former site seems to have been used as a special burial
area, and the production of ceramics perhaps 2,000 years before their appearance in Chiriqui (Linares 1980d: 109) are suggestive of a precocious
cultural development and a high human carrying capacity. What future
investigations must clarify is whether marine resources were the *sine qua
non* of early developments in Parita Bay or a vital adjunct to a primarily
agricultural, and even maize-using, settlement pattern centered on the pied-

mont and coastal plains, which is considerably older than what much of the existing field data suggest.

The publication of Linares and Ranere's (1980) monograph has made it clear that the seminal area for the cultural development of western Panama is the wide plain between the coast and the Volcan Baru (Linares 1980c: 75), where controlled archaeological surveys have only just begun (Einhaus 1980a). In Parita Bay, a team of geomorphologists employed by the Proyecto Santa Maria is gathering data on just how fast the coastline is prograding, how this progression can be correlated with existing graphs for sea-level changes, and how localized events have affected the subsistence potential of the excavated sites (Adams, Barber, and Dere 1980; Barber 1980; Ranere 1980a; Ranere, Cooke, and Hansell 1980). (I shall refer to this work in greater detail in the section on faunal analysis.) These studies are part of a major research project in the Santa Maria Valley that is attempting to clarify some of the problems mentioned in this section.

Real Village Life: A More Conservative View

Notwithstanding the as yet incompletely studied phytolith and geomorphological data, all the other lines of evidence suggest that it was not until the end of the first millennium B.C. that there was a rapid rise in population and a proliferation of permanent villages in central and eastern Panama. Monagrillo was abandoned as a regular dwelling site between 1200 and 950 B.C., the latest C^{14} date for the Aguadulce Shelter is 590 B.C. ± 70, and ceramic data indicate that the Cueva de los Ladrones was used little during the first millennium B.C. (Bird and Cooke 1978a). Conversely, the number of sites located in floodplain zones rises sharply during the Central region's Period IV (old Santa Maria phase), which begins about 300 B.C. (Cooke 1979: fig. 4).[4]

A similar development, beginning more or less simultaneously, has been documented in highland Chiriqui, where maize-cultivating villages proliferated during the last third of the first millennium B.C. (Linares, Sheets, and Rosenthal 1975; Linares and Sheets 1980). Even if we trace the origins of this development to a lower area to the southwest, it is not possible to put a relative date much older than 300 B.C. on the characteristic Concepcion pottery (Haberland 1962; Linares 1980d: 92). In the Eastern region, pollen cores taken from the Chagres Valley (now submerged under Gatun Lake) have indicated that deforestation and burning intensified from about 1200 B.C. to A.D. 150, and that maize, and possibly sweet potatoes, came under cultivation during this period (Bartlett, Barghoorn, and Berger 1969). Drolet (1980: 27) places the intensive occupation of the lowlands of Colon province at between A.D. 1 and 200, on the basis of ceramic cross-dating.

The agricultural village that provides the earliest concrete evidence (Cooke

1979) for a way of life drastically different from the known Preceramic and Monagrillo sites is Sitio Sierra (Cocle), where by at least 240–25 B.C. a number of features related to sedentary maize-farming communities have been identified.

At Sitio Sierra, at least three living floors were defined, one of which belonged to an oval or perhaps rectangular house measuring about 8×4 meters (Cooke 1979: fig. 6). Features on this last floor included at least one hearth, two hour-glass-shaped pits with sand linings and stones in their centers, and two or three elongated pits at the edges of the structure.

Wasp nests of the common tropical genus *Sceliphron*, found at the periphery of the house, bore the impressions of leaves from monocotyledonous plants, indicating that palms and grasses were used for roofing and walling. Very few fragments of *quincha*, or adobe, were recovered, and it is likely that the walls were made of vertically placed cane of palm slats.

Above this structure were the remains of at least one other, located slightly to one side. Two post holes and a channel probably caused by water dripping off the roof were identified. In another part of the site, the living floor of a smaller, more circular structure contained a central hearth and the same type of hour-glass-shaped pits that appeared in the completely excavated house.

On the floors of these structures were a number of items that indicate agricultural activities: (a) fragments of legged grinding tables (cf. Lothrop 1937: fig. 62a, b); (b) elongated, cylindrical manos (cf. Lothrop 1937: fig. 62d, e); (c) large quantities of carbonized maize (under analysis by Robert Bird); (d) rectangular blades of amorphous silicas (cf. Lothrop 1937: fig. 62h–k) and andesite; (e) polishing pebbles for axes (cf. Lothrop 1937: fig. 50a–e); and (f) the sharpening debris from the repair of polished axes. Though there are some discrepancies in the series of C^{14} dates from the site (Cooke 1979: fig. 5), the above-mentioned artifacts can be confidently associated with determinations of 65 B.C. ± 80, 25 B.C. ± 80, A.D. 115 ± 90, and A.D. 235 ± 90.

These essentially domestic remains at Sitio Sierra indicate that, at least between 65 B.C. and A.D. 235, the inhabitants were farmers who regularly cultivated maize and lived in oval, rectangular, and/or roundish cane- or palm-walled thatched houses. They may have stored vegetable materials in the elongated pits. They steamed, smoked, or roasted some foods in the hour-glass-shaped, sand-lined pits which occurred in each of the three excavated structures. They sharpened polished axes and chisels at the village and imported ready-made long, rectangular blades of silicas and andesite. The faunal sample, to which I refer in a later section, consists almost entirely of aquatic, ditch, and disturbed land forms, implying that by Period IV the land utilized by the village had been constantly cut over.

Beneath the roundish structure that dates between 65 and 25 B.C., we recovered a cemetery in which at least 25 individuals had been interred in flexed, primary positions (Cooke 1979). Carbon recovered beneath one of the earliest burials returned a date of 240 B.C. ± 80 (Cooke 1979). The following features are noteworthy: (a) the lowest interments had been pushed to one side, indicating that this was a community or family burial area which was used continually; (b) the pottery consists entirely of the Period IV Aristide bichrome group (Ladd 1964; Cooke 1972, 1976d) and plastically decorated vessels, such as little scarified jars (very similar to Lothrop 1942: fig. 346f); (c) two adult males had been buried with woodworking tools. An older man had a complete axe-making or axe-repairing kit (Cooke 1978a, 1979: figs. 6, 7); (d) one of the two males was associated with a lens of carbonized maize kernels which seem to have been an intentional offering (Cooke 1978a, 1979); (e) a number of individuals (mostly females) were buried with groups of long, rectangular blades which have pronounced silica gloss on their edges; (f) the only artifacts which could be described as luxury items were shell and iron pyrite (?) beads.

As these burial features duplicate the activities of a permanent maize-farming community that were represented on the slightly later house floors, it would seem that the cultural elements epitomized by the Central region's Period IV are so well established by the end of the first millennium B.C. at Sitio Sierra, and so markedly different from the cultural inventory of the preceramic and Monagrillo shell mounds and rockshelters, that we can make but a limited number of deductions to explain the polarity: (a) around 500/200 B.C. there was an influx of foreigners who introduced painted pottery and maize, or at least large-grained South American varieties (cf. Ichon 1980: 197–99, although he argues that such a migration would have occurred about A.D. 200); (b) all the changes in settlement types and artifact assemblages around Parita Bay occurred *in situ* between the end of the Monagrillo type site's occupation (ca. 1000 B.C.) and the founding of the Sitio Sierra village (by 240 B.C.); (c) the Preceramic- and Monagrillo-phase rockshelters and shell mounds reflect only certain aspects of the material culture and subsistence strategies of the 5000–500 B.C. period, and the true antecedents of the Period IV nucleated villages like Sitio Sierra and Sitio Conte must be sought away from the coast.

Deductions b and c seem more reasonable than a (though I must admit to a subjective aversion to boatlands of chuckling farmers from Ecuador). It is still a problem, however, to determine just how localized the Sitio Sierra cultural pattern might have been. It is possible that the precocious developments around Parita Bay caused demographic pressures much earlier than in adjacent areas and that there are more Early Period IV villages here than elsewhere in the Central region. In the Tonosi Valley, for example, where estuary systems are less extensive than around Parita Bay, where precipitation is higher (1750–3000 mm), and where the forest is less deciduous and less burnable (Ichon 1980: 7), evidence for human occupation before Ichon's Bucaro phase, C[14]-dated to A.D. 20 ± 110 at one site (Ichon 1980: 74), has not been found. Drolet (1980) has put a date of between A.D. 1 and 200 on what seems to have been a rapid initial colonization of the northeastern part of Colon Province. His assessments, however, are based on ceramic cross-dating—a difficult task in eastern Panama, where there is a dearth of well-stratified and well-excavated sites and a meager and inaccurate C[14] chronology (Cooke 1976b). Nevertheless, a date of 70 B.C. ± 155 on zoned shell-stamped and incised pottery (Cooke 1976d: figs. 3, 4) and cylindrical maize-grinding manos at Isla Carranza (Panama Province) appears to signal the beginning of the colonization of the middle Chagres River by farming groups. This date coincides with the pollen data from the Gatun basin to the northwest, where a noticeable increase in the frequencies of *Gramineae* and *Compositae* pollen and charcoal fragments has been detected in sediments that date from about 1150 B.C. to A.D. 150. *Zea mays* and *Manihot esculenta* pollen appear in the same context (Bartlett, Barghoorn, and Berger 1969).

Pottery like that of Isla Carranza and neighboring, unpublished sites on Butler Island has been found at the Taboguilla-I site, on a small island off Panama City (Stirling and Stirling 1964b: plates 59–69, 312–35). Similar ceramics are also appearing at the ongoing excavations conducted by the Patrimonio Historico near Palo Seco (Yangüez and Almanza, personal communication 1981) and have been reported from the poorly studied sites— Panama Viejo, Playa Venado, Veracruz, and Chumical—along the coast of Panama Province (personal observations on materials in the Smithsonian Institution, Washington, D.C., and in the Museo del Hombre Panameño).

I must repeat that without regionally based, historically oriented studies and excavations that concentrate on natural stratigraphy, it is difficult to assess this material. (Drolet's survey is a notable exception.) The data indicate, however, that there is a somewhat rapid expansion of maize-using groups with the same cultural antecedents in Panama and Colon provinces toward the end of the first millennium B.C., and that the islands in the Bay of Panama were colonized by this time, by the same people(s). At this stage, we have no idea where the center for this radiation might have been. By extrapolation from Linares and Ranere (1980), it would be logical to search for the nuclear area in the old savanna belt between Panama City and the Bayano Valley, where there are extensive fluvio-estuarine systems. When, and where, the cultural frontier between central and eastern Panama was established, and why certain coastal sites of Panama Province have early Central-region painted pottery types in appreciable quantities, remains to be determined.[5]

When Can We Identify Ranking in Panama?

The 240–25 B.C. flexed burial ground at Sitio Sierra would seem to be archetypally egalitarian. None of the 25 individuals was buried with noticeably more valuable goods than the others. In fact, the funerary objects are decidedly utilitarian: Aristide group (Ladd 1964; Cooke 1972) and allied plastically decorated vessels, polished axes and chisels with their sharpening accoutrements, blade knives, flake scrapers, drills, and a pounding stone. The only finds that could be considered exotic were a small set of stingray spines and the iron pyrite and shell beads. In sum, the burial goods seem to reflect sex and activity, rather than status.

The contrast between this cemetery and those of the Central region's Period V (Early Cocle: A.D. 500–700) is striking. At Sitio Conte, for example (Lothrop 1937, 1942; Mason 1940), the quantity and quality of funerary items in the oldest burials (e.g., 1, 31, and 32)—which must date from the very beginning of the period (Cooke 1972: 383–89)—indicate that status differences had already become accentuated in the Central region chiefdoms by at least A.D. 500. Both here and farther east at Venado Beach (Lothrop 1954, 1956)—another Early Period V or Late Period IV site—there are clear indications of ritual killings and mutilations which are probably related to the taking of elite prisoners in interchiefdom skirmishes (Espinosa 1913[1519]: 280).

Period V is heralded by the full development of the characteristic Central-region iconography on both gold and ceramics, replete with the aggressive, dangerous, and difficult-to-kill animals that Linares (1977b) interprets as metaphors of status rivalry. Luxury items, some of them imported from considerable distances, are encountered in a few burials in truly impressive numbers: metal objects, manatee bone, sperm whale ivory, peccary tusks, dog teeth, semiprecious stones, and lapidary work (Lothrop 1937; Ichon 1980). At El Caño (Cocle), some of the burials contain Conte (A.D. 500–700) polychromes (Verrill 1927; Cooke 1972), while other lines of evidence (Cooke 1976e) suggest that the Temple was operating during Period V, with raised roadways, lines of basalt columns, and elaborate carved altars.

It is reasonable to assume, then, that the antecedents of these developments should be sought during the Central region Period IV (300 B.C.–A.D. 500). In this section I shall refer to some data which suggest that the mechanisms by which the characteristic Panamanian ranked societies were formed were already in operation by the time of Christ. Rather than argue for "invasions" and "intrusions" (Ichon 1980), I shall stress continuity in material culture over the Central region, but not the structure and nature of chiefdoms, a topic which has recently received attention (Linares 1977b; Helms 1979).

In the Central region, Period IV is characterized by two classes of painted pottery: the Aristide group (Ladd 1964: 154–85; Cooke 1972: 128–62), and the Tonosi group (Ichon 1980: 79–204). The former is a carelessly made ware which uses a thin black paint on a meager red, cream, or whitish slip. The designs are always geometric and rather slapdash, and are arranged in discrete panels on the lips, on the interiors of bowls, or on the exteriors of collared jars, above the waist. The Tonosi pottery, on the other hand, is beautifully finished. It employs a thick, pinkish-white or red slip and uses white, red, and black paint for the designs. These are often completely geometric, like those of the Aristide group, but much more heterogeneous and complex. Several zoomorphic motifs which herald the later Conte (A.D. 500–700) pottery are used (curly-tailed monkeys, turtles, and amphibians), while a characteristic hummingbird figure (cf. Ichon 1980: plate XXIII) recalls the common bird forms of the gold pieces attributed to Veraguas (cf. Lothrop 1950: figs. 72–73). Human figures with their arms outstretched (Ichon 1980: figs. 36a, 39a, plate XXIa) seem to be antecedents of a common figure on the Conte polychrome pottery (cf. Lothrop 1942: fig. 91a). Other human forms are engaged in various activities—an idiosyncratic feature on Tonosi pottery.

The Tonosi group pottery was first isolated in the valley of the same name by Ichon (1980). He believed (1980: 197–99) that it had been introduced from outside Panama, replacing a cruder, native tradition of plastically decorated pottery and subsequently being manufactured only in southern Azuero and along the littoral of the Gulf of Montijo. I have contested these ideas (Cooke 1972, 1976a, 1976d), but more on intuitive, than empirical grounds. I believe that the Aristide and Tonosi pottery overlap in space and, at least partially, in time. The former, which probably represents the primeval tradition based on simple geometric motifs that evolved *in situ* out of incised patterns, was a poorly made utilitarian ware whose practical shapes reflect daily activities (drinking, cooking, and eating). The Tonosi pottery, on the other hand, was a luxury item that was produced not just in southern Los Santos and Veraguas, but at those important villages over the Central region which were in positions favorable for the import and exploitation of the raw materials necessary for its manufacture. The distribution of the Tonosi pottery should depend upon social context, rather than regional geography alone.

Some new data support this interpretation. First, Ichon is reluctant to begin his El Indio phase before A.D. 200 and places the apogee of the Tonosi pottery at about A.D. 400 (1980: 200). At Sitio Sierra, however, Tonosi sherds are present on the house floors and in the rubbish dumps of the structures that have been dated between 65 B.C. and A.D. 115. There is no doubt that the La Bernadina–type bowls (Ichon 1980) and the double vases were being manufactured by this time. Though Tonosi pottery is not common at Sitio Sierra (a low-rank village?), its temporal antecedence here over the same wares in the Tonosi Valley could be interpreted as showing that it was first produced in Cocle and then diffused to Azuero.

Second, ongoing studies by the Patrimonio Historico at the Cerro Juan Diaz site near Chitre (Herrera) have shown that the Tonosi pottery predominates in the Period IV deposits (Gonzalez 1980). The size and location of this site on a large hill overlooking the Parita River imply that it was a special community.

Leaving aside problems of provenience, the iconography of the Tonosi trichromes gives us some clues as to how society was organized in Period IV in the Central region. The scenes that depict human activities are particularly relevant. On a number of vessels, teams of men are seen lifting and carrying a long, apparently very heavy object with poles. Their legs are bent with the strain, they are being aided with ropes and/or poles, and little figures, often in red rather than black, seem to be giving them orders (Ichon 1980: fig. 41a, plates XXVIII, XXIX c; Miranda 1976: photos 1–4). In other scenes, an individual lifts up what looks like a clay vessel (as an offering?) (Ichon 1980: fig. 41a, d6). There are also some pin-like figures which wield two long sticks in both hands (Ichon 1980: fig. 41d, plate 21). At least one figure may be using a digging or planting stick (Ichon 1980: fig. 41, d7).

Ichon's interpretations of these scenes are quite reasonable; they represent domestic activities (preparing food), the erection of a public building, or, on a more ethereal plane, the creation of the world, or a ceremony involving fermented *chicha* (Ichon 1980: 140). Even though the men are obviously working as a group and there are fewer little red men than little black men, we cannot really force an argument for complex or stratified societies on the basis of these scenes. Nevertheless, the tree-trunk scenes could refer to the erection of a ceremonial precinct constructed with large basalt columns, such as El Caño, and the activity represented by the pin-men with sticks could be a communal game similar to the *balseria* of the Guaymi (Lothrop 1950: fig. 149; Young 1971), which was being played in the Cricamola River in 1620 (Resquexo Salcedo 1908: 86 ff.) and is, presumably, of pre-Columbian origin. In fact, it seems to me likely that the ceremonial areas at El Caño and Sitio Conte which are bounded by vertical stone columns could have been used for regular territorial *juntas* at which a perhaps more formalized version of the *balseria* was one of the ways by which a budding warrior gained prestige. A ball game similar to one played on Haiti was observed in the mountains of Veraguas by Espinosa in 1517 (1913: 176).

The burials that belong to Ichon's El Indio phase (A.D. 200–500) in the Tonosi Valley seem hardly more differentiated socially than those of Sitio Sierra, though the vessels they contain are mostly Tonosi trichromes. In none of the interments of this phase does a single individual have more than six funerary objects (Ichon 1980: 467–69), while in the succeeding Cañazas-phase cemeteries (A.D. 500–900), some persons are found with a far larger number of goods and a higher proportion of luxuries like metal objects and lapidary work (Ichon 1980: 469–74). Nonetheless, it is pertinent to the study of rank that some items which are found in the most splendid burials of later periods are already present in the Tonosi Valley between A.D. 200 and 500—bar pendants of polished agate and onyx (Ichon 1980: fig. 56e, f), mica, serpentine, agate, and animal bone beads, and some pieces of *tumbaga* whose technology includes *cire perdue* casting, filigree work, hammering, and *mise en couleur* (Ichon 1980: 285–87). Though it is difficult to date these pieces precisely (Ichon places them at the tail end of Period IV) and though they occur in small numbers, gold objects must have become sought-after luxury items in Pacific Panama some time between 300 B.C. and A.D. 500. At Rancho Sancho, Cocle, three copper-gold chisels were found in a deep, isolated tomb with Montevideo pottery (transitional between Tonosi/Aristide and Conte) (Dade 1960; Cooke 1972: 396–402; Ichon 1980: fig. 69h). Interestingly, eight maize kernels were found in the same tomb. At Venado Beach, where most of the unpublished pottery is Montevideo (Cooke 1976d: fig. 2; Ichon 1980), a number of exquisite cast pieces were recovered (Lothrop 1956). Their date should fall around A.D. 400–500 (Cooke 1976d).

Before closing this section, I refer once more to Sitio Sierra. At this site, as in the Tonosi Valley, Tonosi group pottery is found alongside a wide variety of plastically decorated vessels that include such generalized Formative techniques such as fingernail impression, stab-and-drag, zoned punctations, excisions filled with colored clay, zoned bichroming, cane punching, shell stamping, and the like (Ladd 1964: 179–81, plate 14; Cooke 1976d: fig. 3). Aristide, Tonosi, and the previously mentioned plastically decorated sherds are found trodden into the same house floors, the same pit fills, and the same rubbish dumps. Consequently, it is likely that they are contemporary. Many of the decorative modes and vessel shapes that are included in the Sarigua Complex by Willey and McGimsey (1954: 106) are common at Sitio Sierra. Hence they are well associated with maize and sedentary village life and do not represent sporadic boat trips from South America (cf. Willey 1971: 353). The technique known in Panama as scarification occurs in all Period IV contexts. Tall goblets, similar to Guacamayo ware (Harte 1966), are stratified in the refuse dumps of the lowest structures (65 B.C.–A.D. 235), while they are common in Ichon's El Indio phase (A.D. 200–500) in the Tonosi Valley (Ichon 1980: figs. 49, 51).

I firmly believe that the plastically decorated Period IV wares of Sitio Sierra, Cerro Giron (Ladd 1964) and Sitio Conte (Lothrop 1942: figs. 343–46, 349, 350), and the Tonosi Valley sites—all of which date between 300

B.C. and A.D. 500—represent the flowering of a ceramic tradition that, for all its obvious formativeness, is central Panamanian and endemic. In an earlier paper (Cooke 1976d) I tried to give an idea of how increasingly varied and complex this tradition became through time. The oldest incised pottery from Monagrillo and the Aguadulce Shelter, with its use of the volute, and the sherds that occur at the top of the Cueva de los Ladrones (Bird and Cooke 1978a: fig. 15), with their incised and brushed decorations arranged in zones, foreshadow the overriding concern of the Central-region potters with bilateral symmetry and the combination of simple curvilinear and rectilinear designs to form complex motifs. The Aristide and Tonosi pottery merely records in colors what the plastically treated ceramics depict with scratches, blobs, and pinches—taking advantage, of course, of the flexibility provided by different mineral hues.

Regarding the "Fordization" of Formative pottery in America, I take sides with Linares (1979: 35) and quote her in this context: "Peoples living in similar coastal environments would have at their disposal similar tools (reeds, shells, spines) to decorate their vessels, and would need the same simple vessel shapes to fulfil their daily needs." By saying this, I do not reject such interesting ideas as Stothert's (1977b) "Preceramic Interaction Sphere," which draws our attention to the similarities between Cerro Mangote and the Ecuadorean Vegas site, nor do I eschew the need thoroughly to investigate the problems of the origins and dispersal of the Macro-Chibchan-speaking peoples. I also find it likely that the introduction of large-kerneled South American flour corns, and not maize per se, is related to the population increase and proliferation of agricultural villages during the first millennium B.C. Nevertheless, I feel we must be cautious about attributing specific points of origin to plastically decorated pottery. It seems more pertinent, in an area where few excavations have been undertaken, to analyze intersite differences within a region (by means of trace-element analyses, thermoluminescence, and the study of discrete villages and structures) than to relate Panama prematurely to Ocos, Rancho Peludo, or Valdivia. Among the tons of potsherds that I have recovered from my own excavations around Parita Bay, I have yet to see a single sherd which I could classify as coming from Chiriqui (the only reference to Chiriquian pottery in Parita Bay is that in Ladd 1964: 179). This fact makes me believe that the intensive exchange of fine ceramics across culture areas in Panama was limited to frontier zones (Cooke 1980).

As far as gold is concerned, it is likely that the fully developed technology was introduced into Panama from Colombia. The Sinu and Quimbaya regions are the most likely contenders for stylistic influence (Bray, this volume). In my opinion, however, the iconography of the gold pieces found in the earliest datable contexts is recognizably Isthmian. For example, in the lowest graves at Sitio Conte (1, 31, 32), the designs on the hammered gold plaques (Lothrop 1937: fig. 84) are similar to the legged serpent forms on the Conte-group polychromes. This close stylistic relationship between ceramics and gold continues up to the Conquest. Macaracas-style standing, feathered saurians (cf. Lothrop 1942: plate 2a, b; Ladd 1964: plate 7a; Dade n.d.: plate following p. 83) occur on embossed plaques from the late grave, 26, at Sitio Conte (Lothrop 1937: figs. 85, 90).

I do not deny that some gold pieces were imported into the Isthmus from Colombia—their style is recognizably non-Panamanian. Nevertheless, the idea that all gold pieces other than simple, hammered forms were introduced into Panama custom-made, perhaps even being gilded there (Sauer 1966: 276; Helms 1979: 146–50), is simply not true. In the first place, there are obvious stylistic links between some lost wax gold pieces and designs on polychrome pottery like the Veraguan spread-eagled birds, which occur on Tonosi and Macaracas polychromes (Ichon 1980: plate XXIIIa). Secondly, there are at least two Veraguan lost-wax molds in the Museo del Hombre Panameño which exploded when the molten metal was poured in and have solidified, leaving the remains of the wax funnels at one end (Junius B. Bird, personal report to Marcela Camargo). In a country like Panama, where there have been some extremely productive gold mines like Concepcion/ Margaja, Remance, and Cana (cf. Castillero Calvo 1967), and where the Spaniards saw the Indians extracting alluvial gold from river banks (Oviedo 1944[8]: 9; Martyr 1912: 1, 404), one should ask what they did with all that ore—export it to Colombia?

The key to understanding the mechanisms of gold mining, distribution, and manufacture on the Isthmus of Panama is not only long-distance trade, or the desire for esoteric knowledge (cf. Helms 1979), but an archaeological study of the relationship between gold sources, trade routes, and population centers within the Isthmus, or within historically related chiefdoms. The Panamanian gold in the sacred cenote at Chichen-Itza (Lothrop 1952) is the end product of a local exchange system whose details have never been worked out.

Faunal Analysis in Panama: The State of the Art

During the 1970s, most archaeologists working on the Isthmus fell into line with current trends and began searching for tangible evidence for pre-historic subsistence. Most of the available techniques for the recovery and analysis of fauna and flora have been applied: sieving through meshes of graded sizes and with water (cf. Ranere and Hansell 1978); the conscientious identification of bone and shell, and their subsequent quantification by methods such as MNI (Grayson 1973; Linares 1976b; Cooke 1978b, 1979; Hansell 1979; Linares and White 1980; Wing 1980); precise estimates of meat weights (Linares and White 1980; Wing 1980); comparisons between natural and man-induced biomasses (Linares 1976b); pollen analysis (Clary 1980 and ongoing research); the identification of charred plant remains (Galinat 1980; Smith 1980); and phytolith studies (Piperno 1979, 1980). The detailed analysis of wear patterns on stone tools has also been employed to deduce methods of plant utilization (Ranere 1975b; Drolet 1980; Einhaus 1980b; Sheets, Rosenthal, and Ranere 1980).

Such a frontal attack has greatly improved our knowledge about the prehistoric subsistence of Panama. Gone (we congratulate ourselves) are the short sentences in the summary sections that refer to "agriculture along with some shell fishing . . . as the subsistence base" (Ladd 1964: 221). We should not, however, overestimate the available data. In Panama we are still hampered by such universal problems as differential conservation between and even within sites, lack of biological data about the utilized organisms, defective comparative collections for some taxa, and too few zooarchaeologists. In my own research zone, the best quality evidence is concentrated in a narrow strip along Parita Bay which has probably been dry and anomalous in regard to its soil chemistry for thousands of years. It would be most useful to compare the organic remains found at the Cocle preceramic sites with those of highland Chiriqui; but while in the former even the cartilaginous parts of anuran skeletons are well preserved, the latter have never provided the smallest sliver of bone.

In figure 10.1, I have identified the eight Panamanian sites from which archaeological bone samples have been recovered and, at least partially, analyzed. Animal bone has also been recovered at cemetery sites like Sitio Conte and El Hatillo (Lothrop 1937; Ladd 1964). Two sites (Cueva Ladrones and Nata) have provided very small samples which are difficult to quantify. Others (Cerro Mangote, Sitio Sierra) have large samples which are incompletely studied. The Aguadulce Shelter contains a lot of very triturated material. There and at Monagrillo, the shell has been thoroughly studied (Hansell 1979), but more work is needed on the bone. In fact, the only complete faunal analysis with its correct tabulation and quantification is from two Western region sites—Cerro Brujo and La Pitahaya (Linares and White 1980; Wing 1980).

It is not possible, then, to present a thorough cross-site and cross-regional analysis. Certain data and interpretive problems, however, should be of general interest. I shall concentrate on mammals, as they have been more completely studied than other groups. Wing (1980) has published a synthesis of the differences between fish samples at Cerro Brujo (Atlantic) and La Pitahaya (Pacific). The fish samples from the Parita Bay sites are too incompletely analyzed to be objectively interpreted.

When comparing the sites that have produced mammalian bone samples, we should carefully consider their specific locations. Only one site (Cerro Brujo) is situated on the Caribbean side of the Isthmus, in a very humid zone (Linares 1980b). The other seven sites are on the Pacific side, and all are within 18 kilometers of the present-day shoreline. Six are in the seasonally very dry Parita Bay zone where annual rainfall is between 1,000 and 1,400 millimeters. Of these the Cueva de los Ladrones is farthest from the coast and nearest the foothills. Today Monagrillo is nearest the sea, but geomorphological and zoological information suggests that Cerro Mangote was much closer to the coastline 7,000 years ago than it is today.

The mammalian sample from Cerro Brujo is dominated by three medium-sized species: the agouti (*Dasyprocta punctata*), the paca or tepescuintle (*Cuniculus paca*), and the nine-banded armadillo (*Dasypus novemcinctus*). These make up 78 percent of the skeletal remains (table 10.4) and 73 percent (table 10.5) of the MNI (Linares and White 1980: table 1).

Linares (1976b) has argued that these proportions are governed both by the nature of the habitats contiguous with the settlement and by factors of human selection. By comparing natural and archaeological biomasses, she shows how the two histricomorph rodents (paca and agouti) are commoner in environments which have been modified by man than in modern, forested habitats. She proposes that the establishment of cultivated fields and fallow plots in different successional stages near the human settlements was propitious not only to the pacas and agoutis, but also to the farmers, who could accommodate their trap- and blind-hunting activities into the annual agricultural cycle, without having to go on long trips into the rain forest. Her thesis is substantiated by the fact that three mature forest species which are very shy of man—the tapir (*Tapirus bairdii*), the brocket (*Mazama americana*), and the white-lipped peccary (*Tayassu pecari*)—are either absent or very rare at Cerro Brujo. This pattern is quite different from that of the Moskito of eastern Nicaragua, who take mostly white-lipped peccary on their long sorties into the primary forest (Nietschmann 1972).

Viewed as a spatial unit, the mammal samples from Parita Bay on the Pacific side, acquired at six sites whose dates range from 5000 B.C. to the Conquest (1521), are quantitatively different from that of Cerro Brujo, even though many of the same species were hunted. If the cricetine and heteromyid rodents are excluded, and the grey fox (*Urocyon cinereoargenteus*) is added to Bennett's (1968) list of mammals found in Panama between 80 and 81 degrees west, only 15 of the 43 species that could occur are actually present in the bone lots. Only eight species—the white-tailed deer, a raccoon, a paca, the agouti, the armadillo, a rabbit, the Virginia opossum, and the collared peccary—make up more than 2 percent of the total number of skeletal elements and/or MNI calculations at any of the studied sites (19 percent of Bennett's species list).

Three palatable species of the deep forest (the tapir, the brocket, and the white-lipped peccary) are absent. No primate, sloth, or squirrel bones have

Table 10.4. Relative Abundance of Mammals at Eight Panamanian Archaeological Sites (based on the percentage frequencies of skeletal elements in each sample).

Scientific Name	Common Name	Cerro Mangote 5000–3000 B.C. %	Aguadulce Shelter 4000–500 B.C. %	Cueva de los Ladrones 5000–500 B.C. %	Monagrillo 2400–1200 B.C. %	Sitio Sierra 300 B.C.–A.D. 500 %	Nata A.D. 1100–1520 %	La Pitahaya A.D. 800–1100 %	Cerro Brujo A.D. 600–900 %
Caluromys	Woolly Opossum	-	-	-	-	-	-	-	<1
Canidae cf. Urocyon	Grey Fox	-	-	-	-	<1	-	-	-
Cuniculus paca	Paca or Tepescuintle	<1	-	3	-	3	-	2	19
Dasypus novemcinctus	Nine-banded Armadillo	<1	7	3	17	8	7	-	21
Dasyprocta punctata	Agouti	-	*	5	5	-	-	<1	44
Didelphis marsupialis	Virginia Opossum	-	-	-	-	<1	29	<1	<1
Eira barbara	Tayra	-	-	-	-	<1	-	-	-
Felidae (medium-sized)	Medium-sized Cat	-	-	-	-	<1	-	-	-
Felis concolor	Puma	-	-	-	-	-	-	<1	-
Felis onca	Jaguar	-	-	-	-	-	7a	-	-
Felis cf. yagouaroundi	Jaguarundi	-	-	-	-	<1	-	-	-
Homo sapiens	Man	ni	ni	ni	2	ni	ni	ni	ni
Hoplomys	Armored Rat	-	-	-	-	-	-	-	<1
Mazama	Brocket Deer	-	-	-	-	-	-	-	<1
Mustela frenata	Least Weasel	-	-	-	-	<1	-	-	-
Odocoileus virginianus	White-tailed Deer	86	66	55	73	68	50	97	2
Oryzomys	Rice Rat	-	-	-	-	+	-	-	2
cf. Potos flavus	cf. Kinkajou	1	-	-	-	<1	-	-	-
Procyon	Raccoon	12	3	-	-	<1	-	-	-
Rodentia (small)	Small Rodents	-	17	-	-	16	7	-	-
Sigmodon	Cotton Rat	-	-	-	-	-	-	-	2
Sylvilagus	Rabbit	-	7	3	-	<1	-	<1	-
Tayassu cf. tajaçu/ and Tayassu tajaçu	Collared Peccary	<1	-	32	4	<1	-	<1	7
Tamandua tetradactyla	Anteater	<1	-	-	-	-	-	-	-
Trichechus manatus	Manatee	-	-	-	-	-	-	-	<1
Total Number of Skeletal Elements in Sample		1382	70	38	85	1495	14	263	920

Notes

  * agouti bones were included under small rodent
 ni not included as dietary bone, even though fragments were present in some sites
 + present in the small rodent sample (the other species are *Liomys adpersus* and *Zygodontomys brevicauda*)
 a an artifact (polished phalanx)
N.B. percentages have been calculated to nearest decimal place

Table 10.5. The Relative Abundance of Mammals at Four Panamanian Archaeological Sites (based on the percentage frequencies of MNI in each sample).

Scientific Name	Common Name	Cerro Mangote 5000–3000 B.C. %	Sitio Sierra 300 B.C.–A.D. 500 %	La Pitahaya A.D. 800–1100 %	Cerro Brujo A.D. 600–900 %
Caluromys	Woolly Opossum	-	-	-	<1
Canidae = Urocyon	Grey Fox	-	<1	-	-
Cuniculus paca	Paca or Tepescuintle	2	10	8	19
Dasypus novemcinctus	Nine-banded Armadillo	<1	20	-	16
Dasyprocta punctata	Agouti	<1	-	8	38
Didelphis marsupialis	Virginia Opossum	-	5	-	1
Eira barbara	Tayra	-	<1	-	-
Felidae (medium-sized)	Medium-sized Felid	-	<1	-	-
Felis concolor	Puma	-	-	8	-
Felis yagouaroundi	Jaguarundi	-	<1	-	-
Hoplomys	Armored Rat	-	-	-	3
Mazama	Brocket Deer	-	-	-	<1
Mustela frenata	Least Weasel	-	<1	-	-
Odocoileus virginianus	White-tailed Deer	38	53	58	6
Oryzomys	Rice Rat	-	ni	-	<1
cf. Potos flavus	Kinkajou	<1	1	-	-
Procyon	Raccoon	43	1	-	-
Sigmodon	Cotton Rat	-	-	-	2
Sylvilagus	Rabbit	-	8	8	-
Tamandua tetradactyla	Anteater	<1	-	-	-
Tayassu cf. tajaçu/ Tayassu tajaçu	Collared Peccary	<1	<1	8	10
Trichechus manatus	Manatee	-	-	-	3
Total MNI in Each Sample		108*	147	12	108

ni present in the sample but not included in the MNI count
 * the total MNI includes 12 individuals of medium-sized mammals which are not listed
N.B. figures are given to nearest decimal place

been found. Conversely, many of the species that were hunted are cursorial and prefer (though they are not necessarily limited to) open, shrubby areas: the white-tailed deer, the rabbit (*Sylvilagus* cf. *brasiliensis*), the grey fox, the tayra (*Eira barbara*), and the jaguarundi (*Felis yagouaroundi*). Others, like the opossum (*Didelphis marsupialis*), weasel (*Mustela frenata*), anteater (*Tamandua tetradactyla*), and armadillo (*Dasypus novemcinctus*) are catholic in their habitat preferences, but tolerate the presence of man. Raccoons are very common in Panama in mangrove swamps.

In direct contrast to Cerro Brujo, the agouti, paca, and collared peccary—the beneficiaries of Linares's garden hunting scheme—are much more sporadically distributed at the Pacific sites. Lack of suitable forested habitats would be the most logical explanation (Linares and White 1980: 190). At Sitio Sierra, where by the time of Christ, cultivated fields were probably quite extensive, the commonest rodent genera are *Zygodontomys* and *Oryzomys*, which are ditch and grassland forms (Cooke 1979, per Charles Handley). Two medium-sized rodents which are abundant in forest and are very palatable—the spiny rat (*Proechimys semispinosus*) and cotton rat (*Sigmodon hispidus*)—are not present in the Pacific samples. The latter occurs, however, at Cerro Brujo, where it represents 2 percent of the sample.

At all the Pacific coast sites the white-tailed deer (*Odocoileus virginianus*) prevails in the bone samples (ranging from 48 percent to 97 percent of the total number of mammalian elements). It was undoubtedly by far the most important game mammal, especially if MNI calculations are converted into meat weights (Linares and White 1980: table 7). Ethnohistoric data suggest that its hunting was governed by ritual and that its meat was consumed on occasions in extremely large quantities after being stored in special deposits (Cooke 1978a).

Another salient feature of the Parita Bay faunal samples is that at three sites, one species of mammal other than deer is much commoner than the remaining species; at Cerro Mangote, it is a raccoon (*Procyon*), at the Cueva de los Ladrones, the collared peccary (*Tayassu tajaçu*), and at Sitio Sierra, the nine-banded armadillo (*Dasypus novemcinctus*). At the first two sites, this pattern probably reflects localized vegetational conditions—Cerro Mangote was near mangroves, where raccoons fish and roost and can be caught easily, while the Cueva de los Ladrones, being nearer the mountains than the other sites, was relatively closer to the dense cover that peccaries require.

Only at Sitio Sierra were large bone samples of nonmammalian terrestrial forms recovered. These occupy habitats that are similar to those preferred by the mammals at the site. *Bufo marinus* (80 percent) and *Leptodactylus bolivianus* (ca. 18 percent) are the commonest anuran species, and both were apparently used regularly for food (Cooke, material in preparation). *Ameiva ameiva* and *Kinosternon scorpioides* prevail in the reptilian sample. The former is a heliophile species which is abundant around human dwellings and in cultivated fields. Conversely, related forms which prefer forested habitats, like *L. pentadactylus* and the *Rhinoclemmys* turtles, are absent.

The bird sample (Cooke 1979 per S. Olson) comprises almost exclusively marsh, river, and savanna species: herons, egrets, and ducks; the bobwhite quail (*Colinus cristatus*), which is the commonest individual *species* in the sample; the white-tailed nightjar (*Caprimulgus cayennensis*), an uncommon bird of short-grass areas; two species of ani (*Crotophaga*); various kinds of doves, including *Zenaida* and *Columbigallina minuta*; the aplomado falcon (*Falco* cf. *femoralis*), spottily distributed in grasslands throughout the Americas; the barn owl (*Tyto alba*), a commensal of man; and two open-country passerines—the great-tailed grackle (cf. *Cassidix mexicanus*) and fork-tailed flycatcher (cf. *Muscivora tyrannus*). Of the bones that could be identified to the species level by Olson, only the red-lored parrot (*Amazona autumnalis*) is out of context in a savanna biomes; it is found today only in the rain forest (Ridgely 1976: 131).

In sum, the archaeological bird sample from the Period IV deposits at Sitio Sierra mirrors very closely the avifauna of present-day southern Cocle—rice, cane fields, and all.

Faunal Analysis and Prehistoric Environments

The existing faunal evidence appears to favor the thesis that unforested, or at least highly disturbed, habitats, have prevailed around Parita Bay for 7,000 years (Cooke 1976a, 1977, 1978b, 1979). Nevertheless, it is obviously premature to use a limited number of bone samples acquired at four coastal sites to make statements about the terrestrial environment of the cultural region in general. Faunal samples are required from a greater variety of ecological zones, more pollen and phytolith data have to be collected, and the social parameters that are relevant to hunting territories and habitat destruction should be worked out.

Localized cultural phenomena that might have affected species composition need also to be identified. For example, archaeological evidence (Lothrop 1937; Cooke 1979; Ichon 1980) indicates that dogs were common in pre-Columbian Panama. If they were used for hunting, which seems likely (Gilmore 1950: 425; Rouse 1948: 542), they must have affected the local abundance of some species over others—pacas over agoutis, for example (Cooke 1979; Smythe 1978).

The fact that truly and facultatively arboreal mammals (monkeys, sloths, squirrels, and coatis) are absent from midden samples at all Panamanian sites could be the result of the lack of suitable weapons (blowguns and bows and arrows) as much as of dietary preferences and habitat destruction. Though blowguns are, and were, used by Talamancan peoples in Costa Rica (Stone 1962a: 31; Fernandez Guardia 1969: 17), sixteenth-century references to these weapons and to bows and arrows are rare in Panama (Oviedo 1944[7]: 300). The favorite Isthmian war and hunting instruments were spears propelled by spear-throwers and stones probably used with slings (cf. Espinosa 1913[1517]: 179, 1913[1519]: 284–85; Osorio, Salazar, and Diaz 1974: 131), while nets, firing the grasslands, and pitfalls were employed for catching peccaries and deer (Andagoya 1913: 197, 199; Martyr 1912: 1, 407).

With regard to the coastal sites, geomorphological evidence can be collated with faunal data to reconstruct the changing availability and proximity of collecting niches.

At both Cerro Mangote and Monagrillo, the timing and intensity of human occupation depended primarily upon their distance from the active coastline. The drilling program begun by Temple University under the direction of John Adams in 1979 has already provided data that indicate that the annual sedimentation rate of the Santa Maria River is about three millimeters in its central part (Barber 1980, 1981; Adams, Barber, and Dere 1980). When this figure is projected against the graph for sea-level changes calculated by Bartlett and Barghoorn (1973), a preliminary reconstruction of the coastal sequence can be established.

In the case of Cerro Mangote, the following events have recently been proposed by Barber (1980, 1981): (a) at about 8000 B.C., the coastline was about 15 kilometers from the site; (b) between 8000 and 6000 B.C., the sea approached rapidly, but its advance slowed down dramatically from about 6000 to 4500 B.C. (Cerro Mangote could have been occupied by coastal collecting groups as early as 6000 B.C.); (c) at about 4500 B.C. the sedimentation rate began to outstrip the rising sea level, and the coastline progressed rapidly between this date and 3000 B.C.; (d) between 3000 and 1000 B.C., the sea again rose faster than the delta could prograde, and transgressed over the estuarine sediments; (e) from 1000 B.C. to the present day, the coastline has continued advancing and is now about 8 kilometers away.

When Cerro Mangote was first occupied as a collecting station about 5000 B.C., the shore would have been only about two kilometers away, but by the time the site was abandoned (3000 B.C.), it had advanced a further three kilometers seaward. The vertebrate faunal sample reflects this change: in the lower levels, mud-flat- and mangrove-dwelling molluscs are commoner than crabs, but as the site got farther from the coast, it became more profitable to concentrate on the latter. Some of the more recent deposits are packed solid with the claws of *Cardisoma*, a seasonally active genus (Ranere 1980a; Ranere, Cooke, and Hansell 1980).

Preliminary information from the vertebrate sample also corroborates Barber's sequence. Of the four bird bones from McGimsey's sample, one is from a willet (*Catoptrophorus semipalmatus*) and another from a white ibis (*Eudocimus albus*) (Olson, personal information). These are species which rarely venture far from strictly coastline habitats. In McGimsey's unsieved mammal sample (summarized in tables 10.4 and 10.5), raccoons (*Procyon*) represent 12 percent of the skeletal elements and 43 percent of the MNI (Cooke 1978a). In the 1979 sample, which was sieved through one-eighth-inch mesh (Ranere 1980a), raccoons make up 12 percent of the mammal bone weight (Ranere, Cooke, and Hansell 1980).

Some inferences can already be drawn from the aquatic organisms. The freshwater species that are commonest upstream at Sitio Sierra (beyond the limits of salt water)—*Pimelodella* sp. and *Hoplias microlepsis*—are either absent or very rare in the 1979 (sieved) Cerro Mangote samples. The hicatee turtle (*Chrysemys scripta*) is represented by very few skeletal elements at Cerro Mangote, while it is abundant at both the Aguadulce Shelter and Sitio Sierra. These observations, in addition to the fact that Ariid (estuarine) catfish predominate in the fish samples, suggest that the inhabitants of Cerro Mangote fished little in fresh water.

The preliminary results of the drilling program at Monagrillo can also be used to make some deductions about niche use. Ranere and his associates now believe that while the site might have been occupied occasionally as early as 2400 B.C., ideal conditions for the intensive collections of *Tivela* clams, the economic mainstay of the site (Willey and McGimsey 1954), did not materialize until about 1700 B.C. when there was a high-energy sandy beach nearby (Ranere 1980a). By at least 950 B.C., a mangrove swamp had formed around the site, making clam collection less profitable. (This last date, TEM 149, was run on mangrove peat from the drilling cores and corresponds roughly to the 1200 B.C. terminal date for the in situ cultural materials.)

Hansell (1979) has worked with acetate peels from the Monagrillo shells and has indicated that many specimens are about a year old. As many species breed during the dry (windy) season, it is likely that the site was occupied seasonally at this time of year.

In closing, I make a plea for the collection of more data on the aquatic organisms that are being recovered from Isthmian sites. Specific areas of importance are: (a) ethnographic studies of local fishermen and shell collectors in order to determine what species they catch, when, and in what substrates, and how simple technologies (seines, weirs, fishing with hook and line from dugouts) are affected by local weather and tide conditions—very high winds in Parita Bay, for example; (b) the establishment of regularly manned collecting stations up and down rivers to monitor the seasonal availability and salt-water tolerance of some species; (c) a thorough synthesis of fishing journals which often have pertinent data on seasonality; (d) better coordination with government programs which provide useful data on shell-fish and fish catches up and down the coast.

Conclusions

The archaeological investigations of the 1970s in the Central and Eastern regions of Panama have achieved three major goals: (a) they have amplified our knowledge about the Late Preceramic and Early Ceramic (Monagrillo) periods, especially in regard to C^{14} chronologies; (b) they have provided primary subsistence data from particular sites of different ages and have offered a broad outline of how agricultural communities arose and developed; (c) they have pointed out that the archaeological sites of the area are sufficiently complete repositories of cultural information to warrant research strategies more broad-based than those that have been employed in the past.

We need, however, to employ new field approaches. It is all very well to theorize blandly about "chiefdoms incorporating different microenvironments," about "cross-mountain trade in luxury items," and about "intercommunity belligerence." Here and there we can dig out data to justify our points of view, but to do so we frequently have to resort to the archetypal cemetery sites like Sitio Conte, which have been ignored over the last decade as we have concentrated almost exclusively on subsistence materials. The next phase of research should be based on the valley-wide survey, well designed from the statistical point of view, well supported by environmental monitoring programs, and by identifying and sampling the whole range of available sites, not just shell mounds, shelters, and midden deposits with bones.

Notes

1. The writing of this summary would not have been possible without the collaboration of Anthony J. Ranere (Temple University), who has supplied me with a lot of unpublished data and permitted me to quote extensively from preliminary papers. He should be considered a coauthor. Dolores Piperno, John Adams, John Dere, Patricia Hansell, and John Barber—all from Temple University—have generously allowed me to refer to their preliminary data from Parita Bay. To Olga Linares and other staff members of the Smithsonian Tropical Research Institute, I owe my thanks for seven years of moral and intellectual support and facilities. Nicholas Smythe (STRI) provided me with useful ideas about animal behavior. Frederick Lange, Anthony Ranere, and Warwick Bray offered helpful comments on the preliminary drafts of the paper.

The Proyecto Santa Maria has been funded by National Science Foundation grant number BNS–8112475 awarded to Anthony J. Ranere and Richard G. Cooke.

This paper is dedicated to the memory of Junius B. Bird in sad gratitude for the many years of companionship and guidance he provided me in Panama.

2. Fully half of the over 350 sites recorded by the Proyecto Santa María lack ceramics, and many must be Preceramic. At least five sites, two on the coast (including AG-145) and three inland, have bifacially worked artifacts. A quarry

used for making bifacial tools, including long, extremely thin basally notched projectile points, has been located at La Mula–Sarigua.

3. Phytolith analysis of archaeological soils is still a controversial technique. Nevertheless, the reliance on a single criterion (size) for distinguishing between maize and non-maize cross-shaped phytoliths may soon become a problem of the past. Piperno has been finding that maize cross-shaped phytoliths possess a three-dimensional morphology that occurs but rarely in wild grasses. The large cross-shaped phytoliths attributed by her to corn at the Aguadulce Shelter have three-dimensional structures typical of *Zea mays* (Piperno in press).

4. Throughout the following sections "Period IV" and "Period V" refer to the local (Central region) sequence (fig. 10.1), and not to the areal sequence which was suggested for the Santa Fe symposium. Period IV, which in earlier works is referred to as the Santa Maria Phase, runs from 300 B.C. to A.D. 500. Period V (formerly Early Cocle) begins about A.D. 500 and ends around A.D. 700/800. The use of a numerical, seven-period system of chronological nomenclature in the Central region of Panama has been intentional on my part (for criticisms, see Roosevelt 1979). First, it eliminates the use of provincial names for periods (e.g., Cocle, Herrera), in a culture area which comprises five provinces, and, second, it permits the incorporation of localized variations of the same cultural patterns (e.g., Ichon's materials from southern Tonosi, which he classified into a local sequence).

5. Since this paper was written, the Proyecto Santa Maria has been working at the La Mula site (Willey and McGimsey 1954), located at the edge of the Parita Bay alvina. Covering at least 70 hectares, La Mula seems to have been a large village during the first millennium B.C. A sample of *Crassostrea* shells, corrected for C^{12}–C^{13} fractionation, has given a date of 870 B.C. ± 50 (Beta–6016); this was associated with zoned and incised pottery unlike the Monagrillo types and the Period IV plastically decorated wares. The size of La Mula and the presence of large quantities of agricultural implements suggest that population nucleation and village formation were well under way by the beginning of the first millennium B.C.

PART FOUR

The Southern Frontier of Lower Central America

11
Across the Darien Gap: A Colombian View of Isthmian Archaeology

WARWICK BRAY

London University, Institute of Archaeology

This chapter does not attempt to give a comprehensive review of Colombian archaeology. Rather, its objective is to examine those aspects of Colombian prehistory that have a bearing on developments in the Isthmus and to provide a model to describe the nature of the relationship between these two areas.

Interest is focused on the Caribbean lowlands from Uraba to Venezuela (fig. 11.1). My starting point is the situation described by the sixteenth-century Spanish cronistas, since I believe this kind of pattern is an old one and helps with the interpretation of purely archaeological data from earlier periods—if only by emphasizing the shortcomings and limitations of the evidence.

Caribbean Colombia in the Sixteenth Century

In 1502–4, the Gulf of Uraba was the hub of a trading network that linked the Isthmus with the Caribbean and the Cordilleran regions of Colombia. The upper reaches of the Tuira River system, in eastern Panama, provide convenient routes to Uraba and to the Rio Atrato which, in turn, gives access to interior Colombia. The Atrato tributaries, and also the Rio Leon, have always been the entry routes into Antioquia and the Cauca Valley—to the great gold-mining center of Buritica and the jewelry-man-

Figure 11.1. The Caribbean lowlands from Uraba to Venezuela.

ufacturing town of Dabeiba (Parsons 1967; Bray 1972) and, farther up the Cauca, to the Quimbaya zone, whose goldwork was a major influence on Isthmian styles before A.D. 1000. Eastward from Uraba, only low hills separate the Gulf from the drainage of the Rio Sinu, and there is no real obstacle to communication all along the Caribbean littoral.

Gold was a major article of commerce. In a letter written in 1513 to the Spanish king, Nuñez de Balboa commented: "From the house of the cacique Dabeiba comes all the gold that reaches this Gulf [Uraba] and all that the caciques of this region possess." Another chronicler, Cieza de Leon, noted that professional merchants from the Sinu traded to the interior and that there was a thriving business in slaves, fish, salt, cotton cloth, and live peccaries, as well as gold. Archaeological specimens show that Sinu goldwork was exported as far as Costa Rica. Esoteric knowledge may, as Helms (1979) suggests, have been another commodity exchanged between Colombia and Panama.

It is worth noting that most of the products on this list will leave no archaeological trace and that pottery does not figure at all. The only reference I have come across to trade in ceramics is a remark by Peter Martyr (Drolet 1980: 113) that the cacique of Comogra, in Atlantic Panama, obtained necklaces and pottery from his Carib neighbors to the east in return for foodstuffs and slaves.

A second crossroads region was the Mompos Depression, a vast basin consisting of floodplains, shallow lagoons, oxbows, and *caños* where the San Jorge, Cauca, and Cesar rivers converge on the Rio Magdalena. The combined river system unites much of the Caribbean lowlands. To the west, the headwaters of the San Jorge almost join the upper Sinu. To the east, the Rio Cesar is the traditional route of entry into Venezuela, passing south of the Sierra Nevada de Santa Marta to arrive at the Maracaibo basin. At the time of the Conquest, this route carried salt and fish from Maracaibo in exchange for gold objects from the Valledupar region (Sanoja 1966: 235–38).

The Magdalena, too, is the main route linking the Sierra Nevada and the Atlantic coast with the Muisca kingdoms of the high tableland in the Eastern Cordillera, a distance of more than 700 kilometers. Into this trading system the highland groups fed their emeralds, cotton cloth, and loaves of salt. In the other direction, salt from the coast of Santa Marta was traded more than 70 leagues upriver, and sea shells were traded as far inland as the Muisca towns. As Fray Pedro Simon reported, the Muiscas "procured these [shells] from the coast, from which they arrived, *passing from hand to hand*, at very high prices." The phrase in (my) italics gives some idea of the mechanism of contact between the different culture areas.

Like the Uraba connection, the Magdalena route was an old one. Muisca emeralds had already reached Sitio Conte (grave 26) by the Late Cocle period (Lothrop 1937: fig. 180), and the salt-boiling localities of Nemocon and Zipaquira have some of the earliest ceramic-period occupations in the Bogota basin (Cardale-Schrimpff 1976).

By putting together all this commercial information, we can define the limits of our study. The groups living north of a line from modern Bogota to Armenia were—however indirectly—in contact with the Isthmus. Those living south of this line were not. Applying the same principle to the northern frontier, we come up with an Isthmian Interaction Sphere which stretches from Yucatan to central Colombia (Bray 1977).

A Descriptive Model

In reviewing the archaeology of this Interaction Sphere I have been impressed by two things.

First, the frontiers between the discrete culture provinces remain constant for very long periods. A thousand years is not unusual. Thus, for example, Cooke (this volume) notes the ceramic continuity of the central provinces of Panama from the early centuries A.D. to the Conquest, and Drolet (1980) argues for a similar continuity in eastern Panama from A.D. 1 to the Cueva chiefdoms of the sixteenth century. I am not suggesting that there were never any boundary changes (there clearly were), but that stability, rather than continuous fluctuation, was the normal state of things. This same kind of stability can be demonstrated for Colombia.

Second, stability does not mean isolation. Each area traded with its neighbors and, by a sort of cultural osmosis, techniques and ideas were absorbed from one culture area into another. This kind of seepage operated in all directions. Although the spread of certain traits (metallurgy, for instance) was unidirectional, the overall pattern does not justify any simplistic division into donor and receiver cultures.

If this is so (and a large part of this paper is devoted to proving it), the Isthmus has a cultural individuality of its own and should not be regarded merely as a valve connecting the civilizations of Mesoamerica with those of South America. At all times, local adaptation, and adaptability, were the primary stimulus for development. This model does not require waves of invaders, but something much more like the "down-the-line" transmission described by Simon. I do not deny that there may have been long-range sea contacts with Ecuador or the central Andes (Paulsen 1977; Snarskis 1976a; Fonseca and Richardson 1978), but I do maintain that these contributed nothing of significance to Isthmian history.

For brevity's sake, I shall refer to my interpretation as a *chain model*. Each link, or culture province, has its own identity but, at the same time, interlocks with its neighbors to form a continuous and unbroken whole. Similarity falls off with distance; each area shares more traits with its immediate neighbors than with regions farther away. In these circumstances, where one draws the southern boundary of lower Central America becomes a matter of arbitrary choice. Depending on which traits one selects, the frontier can be placed anywhere between the Panama Canal and the foothills of the Colombian Andes.

A model of this kind fits the ethnohistorical evidence, and I believe that, in general terms, it can be projected back for several millennia.

The Paleo-Indian Occupation of Colombia

The archaeological evidence from Colombia sheds little light on the chronological problem of man's first entry into South America and his initial movement through Darien.

The earliest datable material in Colombia belongs to the terminal Pleistocene and falls into two quite distinct categories: sporadic, surface finds of projectile points in the Central and Western cordilleras, and a series of carefully excavated and meticulously analyzed sites in the Eastern Cordillera around the Sabana de Bogota. Since the relationship between these two groups of material is far from clear, they are best treated separately.

Projectile Points

Taking a general view of fluted points, I see no reason to change my opinion (Bray 1978a, 1980a) that we can recognize a northern subgroup, with Clovis and Folsom varieties, and a South American subgroup with stemmed points, whether fluted or not. In between, in the Isthmus, is a zone of transition or of overlap, in which are found both Clovis and stemmed forms, as well as varieties that may be intermediate between the two.

New discoveries in Belize (Hester, Shafer, and Kelly 1980; Hester, Kelly, and Ligabue 1981; MacNeish et al. 1980) and the reanalysis of the north Ecuadorean material (Mayer-Oakes 1981) reinforce this impression of a melting pot zone in Central America and also extend its boundaries. Clovis and Fell's Cave (fishtail) points are now known from Belize, while Correal (1983) reports a stemmed and fluted point of Madden Lake type from Bahia Gloria in the Colombian portion of the Gulf of Darien. With the recognition by Mayer-Oakes of the virtual identity between his El Inga broad-stemmed points and some of those from Panama, the melting-pot zone now embraces most of the Intermediate Area, extending northward to Chiapas, where Madden Lake points occur at the rockshelter of Los Grifos alongside a Clovis-related point in a stratum dated ca. 7300–6900 b.c. (Santamaria 1981).

In Colombia south of Darien, quite a few isolated finds of projectile points are recorded, many of which are not Paleo-Indian at all. We can now dismiss the tanged point published by Bruhns, Gomez, and Christiansen (1976), since this form has twice been found in tombs with pottery (Bray 1980b: fig. 22). Other possible Paleo-Indian specimens are illustrated by Reichel-Dolmatoff (1964a: 46–48). They include a point resembling an unfluted fishtail from near Manizales and a tanged and fluted point from Restrepo in the western cordillera. There is a second Restrepo point from Antioquia (Ardila 1982) and another from the preceramic levels in the Cueva de los Murcielagos in Darien (Correal 1983). The shape is matched at Lowe Ranch in Belize (Hester, Shafer, and Kelly 1980: fig. 1d). A broken lanceolate point from near Santa Marta (private collection) may also be of Paleo-Indian date.

The only item with a geological context is the tanged lanceolate point from El Espinal, in the middle Magdalena Valley, found beneath seven meters of sand and volcanic ash. Charcoal from the same deposit gave the figure 1830 b.c. ± 95 (GrN–5172), which is regarded as too recent (Vogel and Lerman 1969: 359).

These isolated finds are all we have at the moment to bridge the gap between Panama and El Inga in Ecuador (Bell 1965; Mayer-Oakes 1981). What may be significant is that they cluster in the Western and Central cordilleras, along the flanks of the Cauca and Magdalena valleys below 2,000 meters. In the high Eastern Cordillera, apart from the Tequendamian material discussed below, only a single point (undescribed, undated, and from a garden near Bogota) has been published (Hurt, van der Hammen, and Correal Urrego 1976: 16).

The Pleistocene Ecology of the Darien Region

Whether or not these projectile points, and their El Jobo counterparts from Venezuela, represent man's first thrust into South America, it is clear that the Darien Gap was not a total obstacle to human movement during the Pleistocene. Cooke (this volume) summarizes the Panamanian evidence and emphasizes the critical question, Did man have to adapt to forest conditions at some stage on his travels, or could he have threaded his way through Darien along corridors of open savanna, with no need to modify his technology or subsistence pattern? The other aspect of this problem, all too often overlooked, is, What did man find on the other side, after he had passed through the Darien bottleneck? Was it open grassland, with mammoth, horse, and magatherium, or a forested environment like the natural climax vegetation of this area today (Gordon 1957)?

Direct environmental evidence is lacking from the South American side of the Gap, but van der Hammen (1974) and Bradbury et al. (1981) have brought together the evidence from neighboring areas. An extremely dry period coincided with the time of maximum glaciation, ca. 19,000 to 12,000 b.c. During the epoch of extreme cold, the upper limit of the Andean forest was lowered to 2,000 meters (i.e., 1,200–1,500 m lower than today) with the result that, in the cordillera, isolated islands of open paramo grassland coalesced to form an almost continuous strip. At the same time, the dry, open vegetation of the Magdalena Valley extended farther upslope, connecting with the cold Andean paramo to create a broad corridor of open vegetation (the classic mastodon biotope) linking the Caribbean lowlands of Colombia with the Bogota Basin in the high Eastern Cordillera (van der Hammen 1981). In Venezuela, Guyana, and Surinam, pollen diagrams also show a correlation between glacial periods, dry climate, lowered sea levels, and extension of savanna vegetation.

Bearing in mind that the oldest radiocarbon date from El Abra is $10,510 \pm 160$ b.c. (GrN–5556) and that artifacts were found at some depth below this, it may not be coincidence that the oldest proven evidence for man in Panama and Colombia matches the earliest acceptable dates for Venezuela and Peru, and the date also falls just after the period when both lowland and highland grasslands were at their maximum extent. This leaves unanswered the question of whether the grassland was continuous (as Lynch, 1978, maintains) or interspersed with forest, as Cooke is inclined to believe (this volume).

The Abrian Industries of the Eastern Cordillera

The only detailed information on the Colombian Pleistocene comes from the Eastern Cordillera, where there are deep, stratified sites with good faunal preservation and multiple radiocarbon dates, all of this keyed to long pollen sequences. These sites are truly Andean, between 2,500 and 2,700 meters above sea level, close to the transition between forest and subparamo. Many of these localities cluster around the extinct lake that now forms the Sabana de Bogota.

The one open site from this period—Tibito 1, with a C^{14} date of 9790 ± 110 b.c.—is a typical kill site, with the smashed and burned bones of mastodon, horse, and deer, but no smaller animals (Correal 1980a, 1980c, 1981). The other sites (at Sueva, Tequendama, and El Abra) are rockshelters, whose faunal material gives a rather different picture (Correal 1979; Correal and van der Hammen 1977; IJzereef 1978). The dominant animal is deer (mainly *Odocoileus*, with some *Mazama* at Tequendama), followed in the list by guinea pig, agouti, armadillo, tayra, cotton rat, kinkajou, rabbit, birds, and land snails. Most of these animals abound in forest-limit and paramo conditions, and the predominance of deer skeletons leads the excavators to see the late Pleistocene inhabitants of the Bogota basin as specialized hunters.

The stonework from all these sites is of Abrian type. These tools are generally small, rarely more than five centimeters, and are made by the simplest possible technique of manufacture, with the working edges retouched by percussion flaking on one side only. Both cores and flakes served as tool blanks, though prepared striking platforms were uncommon. Artifacts tend to be of irregular shape. The most common implements are rectanguloid or oval chunks of chert with a single working edge trimmed to an obtuse angle to make a scraper. Most flakes are unretouched, though a few have their edges trimmed by percussion. The repertoire includes some triangular flakes, prismatic blades, choppers, and hammerstones. Projectile points and bifacial retouch are completely absent.

In functional terms, Correal and van der Hammen (1977) classify the late Pleistocene assemblage from the Tequendama rockshelter as more than 50 percent cutting implements, approximately 30 percent scrapers, and approximately 7 percent perforators. The missing projectile points were presumably made of hardwood, like those found in dry caves of the ceramic period in the cordillera.

Alongside these Abrian materials are a few artifacts of better quality, which have sometimes been separated out as a "Tequendamian" component of the assemblage. In contrast to Abrian tools, these are made with high technical skill and well-controlled pressure retouch. At Tequendama itself, the inventory included an ovoid, leaf-shaped biface, a broken projectile point, and an oval keeled scraper of Joboid type. Several of these tools are of alien raw material, probably from the Magdalena Valley (Correal and van der Hammen 1977). A Tequendamian scraper was found also at Tibito, and both Abrian and Tequendamian tools occur as surface finds in the Carare region of the middle Magdalena (Correal 1977).

The significance of these Tequendamian elements is hard to assess. Do these items represent technological anomalies in the Abrian assemblage, or do they indicate contacts with communities elsewhere in Colombia who habitually used projectile points and bifacial retouch? Or is it, as the excavators suggest, that the inhabitants of the high tableland lived there only seasonally, spending part of their year in the drier and semi-open lands toward the Rio Magdalena? Whatever the truth, attention is directed to the Magdalena Valley, which has been, at all times, the main corridor of communication between the Caribbean lowlands and the Eastern Cordillera. First, however, we must follow the cordilleran developments a little further.

The Preceramic Period in the Cordillera and the Lowlands

The cordilleran rockshelters provide one of the most complete preceramic sequences from northern South America and also a striking instance of stability and continuity lasting for thousands of years. El Abra, Tequendama, and Sueva continued in use, and there are other sites of this period at Nemocon (Correal 1979), Chia (Ardila 1980), and Gachala (Correal 1979: 13, 1980b: 18). This last site has dates of 7410 ± 45 b.c. and 7150 ± 160. The hiatus from 8000 to 5000 b.c. of which Cooke complains in Panama does not exist in this area of the Colombian Andes.

In the predominantly wooded environment of the early Holocene, changes took place in both technology and subsistence. The basic tool kit remained Abrian, though somewhat impoverished. Tequendamian elements disappeared; bone tools became more common; there was a rise in the percentage of hammers, mashing stones, and of cobbles with grinding and use-wear on their edges. Correal suggests that these changes are linked with an increased use of wild plant foods, and some support for this view comes from the human burials at Chia, where the teeth have the kind of dental caries associated with a diet high in carbohydrates.

In the faunal list the basic range of species stays the same, but there is a swing away from the specialized deerhunting of the glacial period to a more varied diet. At El Abra IV, in an admittedly small sample, deer and guinea pigs were present in roughly equal numbers before 5000 b.c., after which guinea pigs outnumber deer by about five to one (IJzereef 1978). A similar change of emphasis showed up at Tequendama (Correal and van der Hammen 1977). These guinea pigs may have been in a state of proto-domestication after about 5000 b.c. and were fully domesticated by 500 b.c. The presence at Nemocon, between 7000 and 6000 b.c., of nutria, jabali, and howler monkey shows contact with other environmental zones (Correal 1979), as does the continued import of foreign chert and Magdalena basalt.

At all these sites, the basic Abrian tool kit continued right through from the tenth millennium b.c. into the period of the first cordilleran maize-growing and pottery-using villagers of the final centuries b.c.

This technological continuity makes it hard to evaluate the mass of lithic tools found throughout the Caribbean lowlands of Colombia (Reichel-Dolmatoff 1965a: 48–50; Correal 1977, 1980b). Apart from the Medialuna rockshelter, most of this material comes from eroded, and sometimes mixed, surface sites without bone or plant remains. All the way from San Nicolas and Pomares in the west, to the Guajira in the east, are broadly similar assemblages lacking projectile points, ground stone, or pottery. These crude industries cannot be accurately dated, but (as in the highlands) Correal argues for continuity through the preceramic into the period of the oldest Caribbean pottery, dated ca. 3000 b.c., from Puerto Hormiga.

In the middle Magdalena Valley are numerous surface sites close to the lagoons of San Silvestre, Chuchuri, and Puerto Carare, with a well-defined chopper industry incorporating triangular flakes and prismatic blades of Abrian form and also keeled scrapers of Tequendamian type (Correal 1977; Hurt et al. 1976). Industries related in a general way to all the above occur along the Rio Magdalena almost to its headwaters (Correal 1974, 1977, 1980b).

In the Pacific Choco, similar percussion flaked tools, again without pottery, are recorded from the upper Baudo, the Juruvida, Catru, and Chori rivers, and from the Bahia de Utria (Angulo 1963: 56; Reichel-Dolmatoff

1965a: 49). The Catru artifacts are described as scrapers, blades with serrated edges, perforators, burins, and knives. If these assemblages are, in fact, of preceramic age, they demonstrate an early adaptation to rain-forest conditions, inland as well as coastal, and suggest that comparable material should be found in Darien. The lowest, nonceramic levels of Cueva Bustamante, with an estimated date older than 3000 b.c., may represent the first evidence for this (Cooke 1976c: 33), and I would be surprised if most of eastern Panama has not been continuously occupied since the late Pleistocene.

To sum up, we have in the Colombian lowlands and the adjacent Eastern Cordillera a series of simple industries that look like members of a single family and show a fundamental continuity from the Pleistocene to the ceramic period. Since these industries appear in many kinds of environment, this technology must be culturally conditioned rather than determined by ecology alone—though tools for working wood are a major constituent in all these groups. The evidence we have, from fauna in cordilleran shelters and from the preferred location of lowland sites, hints at unspecialized, broad-spectrum foraging and eating whatever the local environment offered.

Several authors have already postulated a "superfamily" of related, technologically simple industries all the way from Cerro Mangote in Panama to the southern end of what was, at this time, the mangrove coast in the Talara region of Peru (Stothert 1977a, 1977b; Richardson 1973). There has been a tendency to see these assemblages as a "littoral tradition" of Northwest South America, but I follow Hurt et al. (1976) in placing the Abrian industries firmly within this tradition and extending the distribution to the Colombian Andes. The southern frontier remains ill-defined, but it must fall somewhere to the north of the puna/camelid zone of the central Andes.

Within this vast area, each regional industry shares certain traits with the others, but each industry also has its own individual characteristics. There is no need to imagine long-distance voyages from end to end of this broad distribution, though short- and medium-range contacts are well attested— for example, the Peruvian Siches/Estero ground-stone axe from the Santa Elena peninsula of Ecuador, some 270 kilometers to the north (Stothert 1977b) or the links between the Magdalena Valley and the Bogota Basin in Colombia. The chain element in my introductory model seems to apply as early as the preceramic period.

So does its second element—great continuity through time. These unspecialized tool kits have a continuous distribution in space, seem to correlate with broad-range food gathering (usually in mixed environments), and persist for millennia. From Ecuador to Panama, the continuity extends into the ceramic period, and a common substratum—omnivorous feeding plus clumsy technology—seems to underlie the cultures of Monagrillo, Puerto Hormiga, Valdivia, and the (pre-Muisca) Herrera phase of the Colombian altiplano.

Manioc, Maize, and Early Agriculture in the Caribbean

This period (post-Pleistocene but preceramic) must be the time of the earliest experimental agriculture in the Caribbean lowlands, though the evidence is minimal. There has also been a tendency to assume a steady-state environment after the close of the Pleistocene, though this is manifestly untrue. Perturbation has been continuous, some of it natural or climatic (van der Hammen 1965; van Geel and van der Hammen 1973; Wijmstra 1967; van der Hammen and Correal 1978), and some of it human-induced, especially by deforestation, which has led to erosion and desiccation in the Guajira (Reichel-Dolmatoff and Reichel-Dolmatoff 1951) and to the creation of manmade savannas in the Sinu and San Jorge basins, with alluviation and silting up of lagoons and estuaries (Gordon 1975; Patiño 1964; Shlemon and Parsons 1977; Parsons 1978). It was, therefore, in an environment very different from today's that the first steps toward agriculture took place.

For the moment, it is easiest to work backward, from the known to the unknown, starting with the farming systems documented at the time of European contact. Patiño (1964) has brought together abundant sixteenth-century information showing that the Caribbean lowlands had, at contact, an efficient mixed economy that was based on maize, manioc, sweet potatoes and other root crops, palms, fruits, and economically useful plants such as cotton. The pollen evidence from Panamanian sites, Gatun Lake (Bartlett, Barghoorn, and Berger 1969) and Isla Palenque (Linares and Ranere 1980: 489), indicates that similar farming systems with both maize and root crops go back in some places at least to the early centuries A.D. The questions then arise, How, when, and where did this kind of economy develop? Any simple explanation is likely to be inadequate, but, as a first step, we can identify the two main components of Caribbean farming, one of them indigenous to the lowlands (the root-crop complex), the other (maize) intrusive from somewhere outside.

The Caribbean lowlands, and especially the drier, eastern portions, fit the ecologists' definition of the ideal zone for the beginnings of root and tuber cultivation (Harris 1969). This element of the economy, we may presume, developed in situ, though it is better to avoid the phrase "tropical forest agriculture" with all its diffusionist implications. In lowland tropical conditions, with much the same range of potential cultigens, similar agricultural systems will tend to develop all over the place, though they will be different in detail. We should, therefore, stop looking for a single center of origin "somewhere in northern South America."

In the case of manioc, the taxonomy is complex, the relationship between sweet and bitter strains is far from clear, and there are several possible centers of origin (Rogers 1965; Renvoize 1970, 1972). Since one center of varietal diversity is Mesoamerica, from Mexico to Nicaragua, it is dangerous to assume that manioc cultivation in the Isthmus necessarily implies an introduction from South America, though, on present evidence, the Mexican varieties of manioc do not seem to have given rise to the cultivated forms.

At the time of contact, Caribbean Colombia and Isthmian America constituted a single manioc province, utilizing only *yuca dulce*, in contrast to Venezuela, where *yuca brava* was important (Patiño 1964: 43–57). There is a solitary *Relacion* of 1579 which mentions bitter manioc (though not the characteristic processing equipment) on the Rio Magdalena near Tamalameque (Latorre 1919: 20), and a weedy, poisonous manioc is said to grow today near Mompos, farther downstream (Gordon 1957: 102, note 58). In addition, some bitter manioc was cultivated until recently in the Guajira (M. Schrimpff, personal communication), and the present-day Kogi of the Sierra Nevada plant a little bitter manioc for purely ceremonial purposes (Turbay, personal communication), but these are the only references I know of for Caribbean Colombia.

Maize, too, presents its problems. Leaving aside the question of where maize originated, and whether or not it derives from Mesoamerican teosintes (Beadle 1977; Smith and Lester 1980), we can at least say that it was not initially adapted to the conditions of the Caribbean lowlands, and it must, therefore, have been introduced into the local root- and tree-crop economies. But when? Looking around the periphery of our area, we find maize in highland Mexico by 5000 b.c., and races of maize adapted to humid tropical lowlands at Cuello (Belize) by 2000 b.c. (Miksicek et al. 1981). In Panama there is evidence for maize in the Gatun core by ca. 2750 b.c. (Piperno 1982). In addition, maize phytoliths occurred with Monagrillo pottery no later than 1500 b.c. (Piperno 1980b; Cooke, this volume), and in the fifth millennium b.c. in the preceramic deposits at Cueva de los Ladrones (Piperno and Clary n.d.). In Ecuador, maize has been found with Valdivia ceramics (Zevallos et al. 1977), and maize phytoliths have recently been identified in preceramic Vegas contexts around 6000 b.c. (Piperno 1981). Unless diffusion was entirely by sea, then the northern part of South America was in a position to have received maize at any time between 6000 and 2000 b.c. Where, then, is the evidence?

If pottery indicates that some sort of agriculture was practiced (and the consensus is that it does not), there may have been farming of a kind at Puerto Hormiga by 3000 b.c. In Colombia, this date coincides with a period of increased dryness. Most of the early ceramic sites are oriented to lagoons and estuaries and have nutting stones (for palm fruits) but no proof of agriculture. From the Monsu shell mound there are probable hoes of *Strombus* shell, which seem to indicate some turning of the soil in search of vegetable foods, but there is no maize in the pollen sample and no *budares* in Monsu pottery (Reichel-Dolmatoff 1978: 51–53).

After ca. 1000 b.c. there is a possible incursion, or diffusion, of bitter manioc from Venezuela to Malambo on the Rio Magdalena (Angulo 1962, 1981) to Momil on the Rio Sinu, and perhaps as far as La Montaña in the Turrialba region of Costa Rica (Snarksi, this volume). It is important to realize that, in every case, the evidence for bitter manioc is indirect and takes the form of *budares* (with some possible grater chips at Momil). As DeBoer (1975) has shown, these artifacts do not provide conclusive proof of manioc processing. Whatever this interest in *budares* may have meant, it was a temporary episode, and griddles eventually drop out of the record.

At Momil the excavators noticed a major break between Momil I (with rimmed *budares* and grater chips, but no milling stones) and Momil II (with manos and metates, but no griddle sherds or stone chips), and they suggested that this represented the replacement of a bitter manioc economy by one based on maize. Accepting the radiocarbon dates for Momil Ib at face value (see below, p. 323), this event took place after 200 b.c. (Reichel-Dolmatoff and Reichel-Dolmatoff 1974). However, I suggest that we should think not in terms of a total abandonment of manioc, but rather of the replacement of *yuca brava* (and its processing equipment) by *yuca dulce* once maize was available to provide an alternative storable surplus to take the place of manioc bread or farinha. The end product of this sequence of events would be precisely the kind of mixed economy recorded in the sixteenth century.

Nor should we generalize from the Momil case, for a comparative survey shows very diverse reactions to the arrival of maize. At the Estorbo shell mound on the eastern shore of the Gulf of Uraba, the story is rather similar to that of Momil (GIAP 1979, 1980). Phase I, bracketed by radiocarbon dates spanning 350 ± 95 b.c. to a.d. 420 ± 130, has griddle sherds, grinding and macerating stones, and pollen of manioc, palms, and tropical fruits. In Phase II (no dates), the griddles and manioc pollen disappear, while maize pollen and grinding stones enter the record. This fits the ethnohistorical evidence, which describes eastern Uraba in 1502–4 as a land of maize fields surrounded by thickets and woods (Sauer 1966: 163).

To the east, in Venezuela, the evidence for early cultivation of bitter manioc at Rancho Peludo turns out to be two unassociated griddle fragments (Roosevelt 1980: 9, note 2), and the occupation proves to belong in the period 400 b.c. to a.d. 1400, rather than the second or third millennium B.C. (Nuñez-Requeiro et al. 1983). This site must therefore be discounted. Still farther east, at Parmana in the Orinoco floodplain, maize enters the inventory at around 800 b.c. By a.d. 400 it was providing up to 80 percent of the total diet, and bitter manioc had lost its dominant position, though it was never completely displaced (Roosevelt 1980; van der Merwe et al. 1981). In the Venezuelan llanos this situation was reversed, and Zucchi (1973) argues that a maize economy, recognizable as early as 1000 b.c., was replaced by one based on manioc around a.d. 500. Instead of great sweeping migrations of maize farmers from Mesoamerica to South America, or of manioc cultivators from the Caribbean lowlands through the Isthmus, the totality of evidence seems to indicate a patchwork or mosaic pattern of local adaptations in which the same basic constituents are put together in different ways and with varying emphases.

Although maize was in theory available a long time earlier, there is no direct evidence in Colombia until the second millennium B.C., and this is in the Eastern Cordillera, with its Abrian-derived stonework. In rockshelter number 1 at Zipacon, with a radiocarbon date of ca. 1300 b.c., remains were found of maize, sweet potato, and avocado, together with the earliest types of pottery known from the Sabana de Bogota (Correal and Pinto 1982). The excavators believe that the crop plants and one of the pottery types may have been introduced from the Magdalena Valley. A thousand years later, these same pottery types, time-markers for the Herrera period, appear abundantly on sites of all kinds (rockshelters, open villages, and salt-boiling localities), with dates of 275 ± 35 b.c. (GrN-6536) from Tequendama (Correal and van der Hammen 1977: 61) and 260 ± 65 b.c. from the base of the Nemocon salt site (Cardale-Schrimpff 1976). At El Abra, maize pollen and pottery make a simultaneous appearance at the junction between Pollen Zones VII and VIII, which marks the start of a cooler and more humid period around 500 b.c. or somewhat earlier (Schreve-Brinkman 1978). At the same time, 600–300 b.c., maize pollen first occurs in sediments at the Laguna de los Bobos (van der Hammen 1962), coinciding with an episode of deforestation at Fuquene and throughout much of the cordillera (van Geel and van der Hammen 1973). Maize cobs return to the archaeological record, this time with Muisca pottery, in an offering or cache at Los Solares with a radiocarbon date of a.d. 310 ± 50 (GrN-4792).

These dates agree reasonably well with the bulk of the Panamanian evidence and with what Cooke (this volume) calls a "drastic settlement shift" associated with village life and maize agriculture. Nevertheless, in Colombia and Panama, there are still problems. If the teosinte school is correct in its botany, its argument requires a very early movement of maize from Mesoamerica to South America several thousand years before Christ. It is possible, and even likely, that the apparent time lag in Colombia is a result of poor preservation, and that the earliest maize in the lowlands has simply disappeared under tropical conditions. This could be directly tested by stable carbon isotope measurements (Burleigh and Brothwell 1978; van der Merwe et al. 1981).

Another line of approach is to study the distribution pattern of individual races of maize. The Panamanian maize from Sitio Sierra (Cooke 1979, this volume), dated 65 b.c.–a.d. 235, has cobs which include a Pollo-like form and another variety resembling Harinoso de Ocho. Maiz de Ocho is generally considered a South American race, and the modern distribution of Pollo is centered on northern Colombia and adjacent Venezuela. Other early finds of Pollo and Pollo-like forms are recorded at the following sites:

Parmana area, Venezuelan Orinoco, ca. 800 b.c. (Roosevelt 1980: 179); La Betania, Venezuelan llanos, a.d. 130±130 (Zucchi 1973: 188); Severo Ledesma, Costa Rica, in the El Bosque phase, dated a.d. 345±165 (I–7514) and possibly related to Momil II (Snarskis 1976a, this volume); and the Cerro Punta basin in Chiriqui, a.d. 200–400 (Galinat 1980). There are several later occurrences, after a.d. 1000, in the Venezuelan Andes (Mangelsdorf and Sanoja 1965; Wagner 1967, 1973).

Pollo and Pollo-like maizes have not been found archaeologically north of Costa Rica nor, so far, in southern Colombia. On distributional grounds, Pollo-like maize is therefore the Intermediate Area race par excellence. It occupied a coherent bloc of territory around the time of Christ, and its close relationship with Nal-tel (one of the first races to bridge the Darien Gap) is generally accepted (Pearsall 1977–78). I can see no archaeological objection to Galinat's belief that Pollo is an offshoot from Nal-tel, developing, perhaps as an evolutionary response to cold and wet conditions, somewhere (or possibly all over the place) within its archaeological distribution range from Costa Rica to Venezuela. It seems that there were indeed botanical contacts through Darien, but this is very different from saying that Pollo characteristics in Isthmian maizes necessarily prove South American influence.

Reconstructing the Colombian-Isthmian scenario so far, three stages emerge: (a) an early period with the emphasis on roots, tubers, and palm products, and no proof of maize; (b) a poorly documented episode during which bitter manioc and its processing technology may have spread westward from Venezuela or Amazonas; and (c) a later stage, recognizable by 300 b.c., when we have something like the crop mixture reported by the sixteenth-century Spaniards.

The fourth, and final, stage in this agricultural progression was the creation of an artificial, manmade landscape. As we have seen, this stage was reached with the forest clearances in the Eastern Cordillera around the time of Christ, or even before, and, in the lowlands, the San Jorge basin was converted from forest to farmland with raised fields, no later than the seventh century A.D. (San Jorge and Sinu section, this chapter). I doubt whether much of the natural landscape was left by the time of the first chiefdoms in Colombia and the Isthmus.

The Tecomate Tradition:
Early Ceramic Cultures 3000–1000 B.C.

Around 3000 b.c., two new phenomena—pottery and shell middens—make their first appearance in Caribbean Colombia. The late occurrence of shell mounds, by comparison with neighboring Panama and Venezuela, has never been adequately explained. If it is not just a sampling accident, it may have something to do with changing sea levels, or the fact that the date of 3000 b.c. also coincides with the onset of a period of increased dryness in Colombia, marking the start of Pollen Zone VII (van der Hammen 1965).

It is this series of shell mounds that provides most of the evidence for the next 2,000 years of Colombian prehistory. On the basis of radiocarbon dating, combined with the stratigraphies at the Monsu and Canapote mounds, a sequence of phases can be recognized around Cartagena that may be applicable to the whole area from the Gulf of Morrosquillo to the Rio Magdalena (Reichel-Dolmatoff 1955, 1965b, 1971, 1978; Bischof 1966, 1972).

The sequence begins ca. 3000 b.c. with the fiber-tempered and sand-tempered wares of Puerto Hormiga, followed successively by the Monsu, Canapote, Tesca, and Barlovento styles. The latest date for Barlovento is 1030 ± 120 b.c. (W–741).

It is not suggested that these materials form a single line of development. There are breaks in the continuity (e.g., between Puerto Hormiga and Monsu and between Monsu and Canapote) and signs that some phases may have been overlapping rather than strictly sequential, with possible site-unit intrusions (Bischof 1972). Illustrative of the problem is the difficulty of relating surface collections to the master sequence. There is no unanimity among the scholars who have studied these sherds, though most are agreed on a placement somewhere in the later half of the sequence for sites like Cienega de Totumo, Galera Zamba, Isla Baru, Tierra Bomba, Beruga, and Morrosquillo.

Nevertheless, there is unity behind this diversity, and we have here another of those cultural "superfamilies" that lasted some 2,000 years. This family relationship is demonstrated by a group of shared traits: (a) a liking for ring-shaped mounds (Puerto Hormiga, Monsu, Barlovento) which are different from the amorphous mounds of later periods (cf. Sutherland and Murdy 1979; though see Angulo 1978: 10), and presumably reflect shared ideas of social organization and settlement layout, (b) a lack of any definite evidence for agriculture, (c) a stone tool kit derived from the earlier pre-ceramic repertoire, (d) hoes made of *Strombus*, present in the Monsu, Canapote, and Barlovento occupations at the Monsu site, (e) almost total reliance on a few simple pottery shapes, in particular the hemispherical or subglobular bowl (tecomate), (f) a common stock of techniques for decorating pottery (broad and narrow incision, punctation, stamping, red fill, zones of red paint, modeling), though no single style employs all of these, nor uses the elements in precisely the same way as any other style.

Locations include coasts, offshore islands, river banks, and lagoons, often in places which seem designed to offer maximum ecological diversity. In these conditions one might expect a broad-range exploitation of several niches. Instead, the evidence, such as it is, indicates a deliberate specialization and restriction. Where possible, the protein supply came mainly from rivers, lagoons, estuaries, and the sea. Forest and savanna species are underrepresented, and small animals predominate over deer, though shell hoes may be linked with roots and tubers, while nutting stones, pestles, and grinders demonstrate an interest in seeds and palm fruits. The question of permanent versus seasonal occupation cannot yet be answered, but at Monsu, on the sand beach of a river, the post holes of a large oval structure hint at some permanency of settlement.

Aquatic resources were also the main food staple at the inland sites of the Magdalena drainage—at Isla de Indios on its island in the Cienega de Zapatosa (Reichel-Dolmatoff and Reichel-Dolmatoff 1953: 61) and at the Bucarelia/San Jacinto site, now buried deep under floodplain alluvium on the bank of the Rio Magdalena (Reichel-Dolmatoff 1965a: 59, 173, 1971; Bischof 1972). Bucarelia pottery has been compared both with Puerto Hormiga wares and with those of the Tesca/Barlovento group, but whatever the date, this site represents an early, inland adaptation to a floodplain, river, and lagoon setting different from that of the coast. The economic strategy was neither shellfish gathering nor small game hunting, but river fishing with bone harpoons, and reptile hunting in the oxbow lakes. This seems to have remained the general pattern in the area, for a *Relacion* of 1579 comments that the Tamalameque Indians had plenty of fish but rarely ate meat (Latorre 1919: 17).

These Colombian cultures constitute the central bloc within a single "supertradition" stretching from Venezuela to Panama. Its easternmost representative is the Kusu phase, a fishing station at La Pitia on the shore of the Venezuelan Guajira (Gallagher 1976). Its pottery includes ollas and the ubiquitous semiglobular tecomates. In Colombian terms, Kusu broad-line incision and punctate decoration are closest to those of Barlovento, though different in detail.

In Panama, Monagrillo appears to be a peripheral member of this family. Whatever its precise starting date (Cooke, this volume), Monagrillo aligns with the earlier part of the Colombian sequence on stylistic grounds. Shapes include tecomates, and certain of the Monagrillo decorative elements are shared with Puerto Hormiga, including incised lines ending in punctate dots, spiral ornament below horizontal rim bands, and the occasional use of excised areas where lines meet. On the other hand, Monagrillo lacks the exuberant modeled, stamped, punctate, and hatched designs of Puerto Hormiga, and Monagrillo painted decoration has no good parallel in Colombia (Myers 1978).

The differences among the constituent cultures of the Tecomate Tradition are as marked as the similarities, and each site shows an adaptation to purely local conditions. The overall impression is of a generalized family relationship, perhaps with sporadic contacts but with no systematic interaction or migration. The best case for long-range diffusion is, in fact, the possible introduction of fiber-tempered pottery and ring mounds from Colombia to the southeastern United States (Bullen and Stoltman 1972), but this—if it took place at all—bypassed the Isthmus entirely.

Colombian-Isthmian Contacts Around the Time of Christ: The Momil Site

A critical site for any discussion of Isthmian-Colombian relationships is Momil, a large village on the edge of an oxbow lake on the lower Rio Sinu (Reichel-Dolmatoff and Reichel-Dolmatoff 1956). In essence, the sequence seems to show the replacement of a local manioc-based culture (Momil I) by a maize-growing culture (Momil II) whose artifacts show strong Mesoamerican/Isthmian influence. Various cultures of Atlantic Costa Rica have been linked with Momil (Snarskis, this volume), and the site has come to occupy a pivotal role in nearly all studies of the Late Formative in Colombia.

Momil I was a sedentary village with a marked lagoon orientation. Its pottery marks a complete break with the old Tecomate Tradition. New forms are mainly composite shapes: carinated bowls and jars, flaring-rim jars, and ollas with overhanging collars. Many of the older decorative techniques of incision, stamping, punctation, and rouletting persist, though the designs are new. Into this basic incised and stamped tradition, innovations were introduced from time to time: red-on-white painting and simple negative painting in Phase 1b; then, in 1c, bichrome painting (black-on-white, black-on-red) and also polychrome (black- and red-on-white). Among the smaller artifacts are solid figurines, flat stamps, and the winged pendants discussed in the Early Painted Wares section.

Momil II is separated from the underlying material by a thin layer of sterile sand. There is no significant change in the fauna, but manioc-processing equipment disappears and is replaced by manos and metates. New pottery shapes also occur—tripods with solid or hollow feet, bowls with basal or medial flanges, zoomorphic adornos, mammiform supports, and bird-shaped whistles. All of these, and also the hollow figurines and roller stamps, have no obvious antecedents in Colombia but are present in various Isthmian and Mesoamerican cultures. In pottery decoration many of the old modes persist, though there are certain new ones. True rocker-stamping is confined to early Momil II; also exclusive to Phase II is zoned bichrome decoration, with zones of incision or dentate stamping outlined by incision.

Putting all this evidence together, the excavators argued that Momil II represents something new and exotic to the area. Reichel-Dolmatoff (1965a: 74) states that "it seems that maize was introduced at this time-level from Mesoamerica as a fully developed complex together with a number of new pottery shapes." If he is right, this is the only good instance of a Mesoamerican site intrusion in the entire history of Caribbean Colombia.

I have argued earlier that maize could have been adopted from almost anywhere at the time in question. Before considering the other claims, and seeing how Momil aligns with its possible Isthmian relatives, we must first solve the chronological problems.

Most of the evidence, unfortunately, is circumstantial. Bischof (1966: 484) reports Momil sherds from the surface of the Bocachica shell mound near Cartagena, presumably from a post-Barlovento occupation. This suggests that Momil began some time after 1000 b.c., perhaps considerably later, in which case the very early date proposed by Foster and Lathrap (1973) must be rejected. Two radiocarbon dates refer to Momil Ib, about halfway through the first period: 200 ± 60 b.c. (TK–131) and 175 ± 35 b.c. (GrN–6908) (Reichel-Dolmatoff and Reichel-Dolmatoff 1974). While the difficulties with shell dates must be acknowledged, these do seem about right. Typological parallels for Momil II suggest that the I/II boundary falls around the time of Christ, a figure that would be in keeping with the evidence from Estorbo in Uraba (Estorbo section of this chapter) and from Potrero Marusa in the San Jorge Basin (Cupica and the Pacific Connection section, this chapter).

It is gratifying to find that this internal Colombian dating fits with the quite independent radiocarbon chronology from Atlantic Costa Rica. The Montaña Complex, with its *budares* and its C^{14} dates ranging from 550 ± 60 to 280 ± 60 b.c., aligns, as it should, with the manioc horizon of Momil I, while El Bosque (with maize cultivation and good ceramic parallels with Momil II) is dated 100 B.C.–A.D. 500 (Snarskis, this volume). All this lends some plausibility to the belief in Colombian-Isthmian contacts along the Atlantic seaboard, though the stylistic parallels are general rather than specific.

Early Painted Wares, Venezuela to Panama

Along the middle reaches of the Rio Rancheria, almost on the Venezuelan frontier, the Reichel-Dolmatoffs (1951) discovered a number of substantial farming villages in what is today an arid region, useless for agriculture. The first two stages of the Rancheria sequence, the Loma and Horno periods, form a continuum, the so-called First Painted Horizon, characterized by bichrome and polychrome painting.

Designs are in red and/or black over a cream slip, and motifs are predominantly curvilinear: wavy lines, sigmoid patterns, comb-like devices, and bold, swirling scroll patterns composed of narrow parallel lines. Vessel shapes are more varied than during the Tecomate Period and now include composite forms (pedestal bases, bowls with nubbin feet) as well as shallow plates that may have been either manioc griddles or toasters for maize *arepa*. Figurines are hollow, with naturalistic faces and bulbous legs.

The precise chronology of the First Painted Horizon is difficult to establish. At the shell mound of La Pitia on the Gulf of Venezuela, the Hokomo

phase is clearly a lagoon and coastal manifestation of the First Painted
Horizon (Gallagher 1976). The excavator estimated that Hokomo may have
begun around 1000 B.C., which seems too early, given the radiocarbon date
of 70 ± 110 b.c. (Y–855) for a level about one-third of the way through the
Hokomo occupation. From Colombia there is a date of a.d. 585 ± 75 (Beta–
4842) for an early stage of the Horno period (Gerardo Ardila, personal
communication), and First Painted Horizon decoration appears on certain
vessels in the Nahuange tomb which Bischof (1969a, 1969b) places in the
sixth or seventh century A.D.

This chronology brings the First Painted Horizon roughly into line with
Momil and with the earliest painted wares of Panama. As Cooke (1976b:
96) notes, at Isla Carranza in Darien (with a date of 70 ± 155 b.c.) and at
La India 1, in Tonosi (a.d. 20 ± 100), painting appears rather tentatively in
the context of styles dominated by plastic decoration. The same is true at
Momil and perhaps at Taboguilla-1, in the Pearl Islands (Stirling and Stirling
1964).

Stylistically, the First Painted Horizon pottery belongs more with Venezuela than with Colombia, but it also has parallels with cultures to the
west. It has to be admitted that these similarities are general rather than
specific. They include bichrome and polychrome painting, vessels with
nubbin and tripod feet, hollow figurines, and, perhaps, knowledge of negative painting. There is also one artifact, the simplest form of winged pendant, which makes a more or less synchronous appearance throughout this
area. In Panama it is reported from the Rio Tabasera with a C^{14} date of
95 ± 45 b.c. and in the El Indio phase of Tonosi (Ichon 1980: fig. 56); at
Momil these items occur in levels 9, 10, and 12, roughly contemporary
with the radiocarbon dates of the second century b.c. (Reichel-Dolmatoff
and Reichel-Dolmatoff 1956); one pendant was excavated at El Horno in
the Rancheria (Reichel-Dolmatoff and Reichel-Dolmatoff 1951, plates 24,
6); in Venezuela the earliest record is from a burial at Las Locas (State of
Lara) with pottery of the Tocuyanoid series and an estimated date in the
second century A.D. (Perera 1979: 90–93).

For painted pottery, there is no unanimity about the nature and direction
of diffusion—if indeed there was diffusion at all. Coe (1962b) argued for a
gradual spread from Venezuela to Mesoamerica. Reichel-Dolmatoff (1965a:
120) suggested just the reverse:

The polychrome wares of La Loma and El Horno are probably in part derived from
Momil, but there are very strong resemblances with the polychrome pottery of
Panama, especially with the Cocle Complex. Although there is some evidence for
a west-to-east overland diffusion from Panama across northern Colombia to western
Venezuela, the possibility of diffusion by coastal navigation cannot be disregarded.

More than 15 years later, the controversy remains, though the balance
of the evidence favors Coe's view. With the discovery of the Caño del Oso

style in the llanos, the techniques of painting are present in Venezuela by ca. 1000 b.c. (Zucchi 1972). From the llanos, these techniques (though not the patterns) seem to have spread to northwest Venezuela, where Tocuyano has an unhelpful C^{14} date of 230 ± 300 b.c. (M–257). Gallagher (1976) makes out a good case for the spread of polychrome painting and of certain design motifs from this area, via La Pitia to the Rancheria.

West of the Rancheria, the case is less clear-cut, though the resemblances between wares of the Colombian First Painted Horizon and the earliest Panamanian bichromes and polychromes are close enough to demand attention. In black-and-white illustrations (which ignore vessel forms and color values), there is a marked family likeness between Rancheria painted sherds and those from Taboguilla-1 and also with those of the Aristide group of Period IV in the central provinces of Panama. These early wares have only geometric ornament, and the Conte iconography does not yet appear on the pottery. The common feel of these styles arises from a liking for rectilinear and swirling patterns made up from bands of parallel lines, the use of bundles of short, straight parallel lines, and a tendency to leave bubbles of open space within the overall design.

Two of the shared motifs are quite specific and carry the links through into Period V. The sigmoid zigzag (Reichel-Dolmatoff and Reichel-Dolmatoff 1951, plates 8, 146) occurs sporadically on Tonosi Polychromes of Period IV (Ichon 1980, plate 32) and on polychromes of Period V at Sitio Conte graves 4 and 13 (Lothrop 1942: figs. 110, 311h). The most interesting parallel of all—so exact that it can hardly be due to chance—is the Rancheria "volute sigmoid comb" pattern on an effigy jar from grave 32 at Sitio Conte (Lothrop 1942: fig. 122). This is one of the oldest tombs at Sitio Conte, and it can be dated ca. A.D. 450–500. The comb design is frequent at La Pitia and the Rancheria sites but is exotic at Sitio Conte. In this case, the direction of diffusion can only have been from Colombia to Panama.

In summary, a number of traits (winged pendants, pottery painting, certain design motifs, and metallurgical knowledge) appear to have been moving through Colombia and the Isthmus during the centuries immediately before and after A.D. 1. If pottery painting spread from Colombia to Panama (and I do not regard this as proved), the techniques were very quickly adapted to Panamanian decorative tastes. The view that Panama received more than it gave during these centuries is reinforced by the metallurgical evidence discussed in the next section.

Metallurgy

In the case of metalworking, archaeology demonstrates an unambiguous northward spread, starting in Peru during the second millennium B.C. and eventually reaching Mexico between A.D. 700 and 900. In Colombia the earliest datable metal (Bouchard 1979) is the hammered gold wire from

Inguapi, Tumaco, 325 ± 85 b.c. (Ny–642), and there is evidence (Duque
Gómez 1964: 409) for casting at San Agustin by about the time of Christ,
10 ± 50 b.c. (GrN–4205). Farther north, along the Caribbean littoral and
in Panama, the oldest metal objects belong to the early centuries A.D. Given
this south-north diffusion, there can be no doubt that metal technology was
introduced into the Isthmus from Colombia.

The first metal objects in Panama come from the central provinces, where
they may predate the Sitio Conte cemetery by a century or so. One of the
clearest associations is the fifth-century tomb at Rancho Sancho de la Isla,
with tumbaga chisels and Montevideo polychrome vessels (Dade 1960). The
ornaments from Las Huacas (Brizuela 1972a) also fall within the fifth century, as may those from Tonosi sites of the terminal El Indio Phase (Ichon
1980: fig. 56).

These early classes of ornament (double spiral pendants, multiple animals,
double-headed eagles) display none of the complex iconography of the later
Isthmian styles. In fact, they are pure Colombian in spirit and are numer-
ically much more common along the Caribbean mainland, though not
usually found in datable contexts. The double spirals are most frequent in
Tairona territory, though some have been found in the Sinu (Bray 1978b:
174; Falchetti, personal communication). From Panama, this form passed
to Costa Rica, where it occurs (wrongly identified as Ecuadorean) with a
Cocle bird at Guacimo (Stone and Balser 1965). The simple double eagles
have a similar distribution, with unassociated finds from Costa Rica, Panama, the Sinu (Falchetti 1976: fig. 70), and the Cauca Valley of Colombia
(Bray 1978b: 198). The same is true of the multiple animals.

Once the technical knowledge had been introduced into the Isthmus, a
whole series of local metallurgical styles emerged, incorporating regional
ideologies and sharing designs and iconography with the local pottery styles
(Cooke, this volume; Bray 1981).

From that time onward, Colombia and the Isthmus constitute a single
technological province, characterized by a preference for cast jewelry and
virtuoso work in false filigree. Copying was rife, and there was a thriving
trade in all directions. Sinu false-filigree ear ornaments and Tairona frogs
reached Costa Rica, Muisca *tunjos* were copied there, and Diquis-like
breastplates with conical bosses occur in a Sinu tumulus at Ayapel (Falchetti
1976: fig. 23). The so-called Darien pendants, whose greatest concentration
is in the Sinu, were imitated in Panama and Costa Rica, and these copies
were traded as far as Chichen Itza (Falchetti de Saenz 1979). The Isthmian
pendants in the shape of near-naked human figures, abundant throughout
Costa Rica and Panama, show clear influence from the Quimbaya style of
the Cauca Valley of Colombia (Bray 1981). In the other direction, Cocle
pieces reached the Sinu (Bruhns n.d.), and an Isthmian frog pendant traveled all the way to Armenia, in the Quindio (Museo del Oro no. 10.491).

At times, stylistic hybridization is so great that an object cannot be attributed to any particular manufacturing center. This is true of some categories whose distribution extends from Panama to Caribbean Colombia: curly-tailed animals, crocodilian forms, and human figures with recurved headdresses (Falchette 1976: figs. 19–21; Bray 1978b, nos. 227–29).

This flourishing exchange of small, portable, and valuable goods is reflected only palely in the ceramic evidence, and it is my conviction that *ceramic data grossly underrepresent the amount of interregional contact at all times.*

The "Darien Gap" is not so much the consequence of geography as of inadequate sampling. As we have seen already, sixteenth-century chronicles describe the Gulf of Uraba as a major center for the redistribution of raw gold and finished jewelry from all the surrounding areas. The evidence presented above shows that the identical pattern goes back about a thousand years.

Where, then, is the missing gold style from Darien, which should fill the void between Colombia and central Panama? There are the nose ornaments from CHO–3 (Cooke 1976a), a fine repoussé helmet in the Quimbaya-Sinu-Cocle fashion from the Rio Chucunaque (Lothrop 1937: 137), and the gold objects from Venado Beach—not much to set beside the documentary evidence.

It is Venado Beach which provides a possible clue. Situated on the frontier between eastern and central Panama, it has ceramics from both. The majority of the pottery falls around the fifth century, with some extension on either side. Of the 30 gold items reported from Venado Beach, only one has Cocle figurative ornament. The others include a Darien pendant, three sets of multiple animals, and nine objects (frogs, nose clips, a zoomorph, two tusk-shaped pieces) in an openwork, spiral, false-filigree style (Helms 1979: figs. 10, 12b). There are a few sporadic objects in this openwork style from points farther north, but no other site (including Sitio Conte) has anything like this proportion of openwork jewelry. If a separate Darien style of goldwork is eventually to be identified, this openwork group is the best candidate so far. For the latest stages, metal items in the terminal (i.e., post–Sitio Conte) style of the central provinces seem fairly abundant in private collections from Darien.

The Southern Fringe of Darien:
Estorbo and Cupica

The frontier between Panama and Colombia is an artificial creation that can be ignored for the prehistoric period. The Darien rain forest continues unbroken along the Pacific coast into the Colombian Choco and also along the Caribbean littoral well to the east of Uraba. In the sixteenth century, languages of the Chibchan family were spoken on both sides of the frontier, and Sauer (1966: 238) argues for the existence of a macro-Cuevan cultural and linguistic province extending from Panama, across the Atrato basin and into the Andes as far as Dabeiba. This southern frontier, in northwest Colombia, was a fluid and unstable boundary in the sixteenth century, and the precise relationship between its Cuna, Cueva, Choco, and Carib groups remains to be worked out (Isacsson 1980). For the moment, it is best not to tie ethnic labels to archaeological assemblages. One distinction that does seem to be valid is between the western and eastern (Carib?) shores of the Gulf of Uraba, where recent archaeological work corroborates the ethno-historical evidence.

Estorbo

Survey in eastern Uraba has concentrated on a series of shell mounds on the shore of the Gulf near Turbo and Neclocli (GIAP 1979, 1980) and along the main coast as far as Arboletes (Santos, Roman, and Otero de Santos 1980). In this area a single complex is identified, named Estorbo after a group of shell middens in the municipio of Turbo. The inland facies of this culture remains unknown, and we still have no archaeological material which matches the chronicle descriptions of the farming towns and the rich Uraba caciques of 1502–6, with their maize fields and their boxes full of golden axes, drums, and masks.

The key stratigraphy comes from the type site of Estorbo. At the base is a deeply buried shell midden with sherds and stone tools. This is capped by almost a meter of sterile yellow clay, representing a period of alluvial sedimentation that may have lasted a thousand years (GIAP 1979). Overlying this is a second shell midden (Estorbo Phase I) with four radiocarbon dates ranging from 350 ± 95 b.c. to a.d. 420 ± 130. The excavators believe that Estorbo I, with its manioc-based economy, ended somewhere around A.D. 750. Directly on top of this shell midden is a layer of dark organic soil (Estorbo Phase II) with no shells, though sherds, stone tools, and animal bones continue throughout. Maize pollen makes its appearance in this phase (Manioc, Maize, and Early Agriculture in the Caribbean section of this chapter), and the pottery derives from that of the previous period, though without manioc griddles. Although radiocarbon dates are lacking, Estorbo II is thought to carry the story, and the ceramic tradition, right up to the Conquest.

The ceramic inventory shows few similarities with Momil and leaves the two oldest Estorbo dates open to suspicion. None of the comparisons is earlier than Momil Ib, and the Mesoamerican traits, so marked in Momil II, are virtually absent from the corresponding wares in Uraba.

Instead, Estorbo I has very close links with the Tierra Alta phase of the Sinu, placed by seriation some time after the abandonment of the Momil site. The resemblances are general (urn burial, grater plates) and also quite specific: the hollow figurine type, plastic spiral ornament in combination with modeled faces, pedestal bases with cut-out panels, and several decorative motifs—concentric arcs bordered with dots, rows of excision or triangular stamping on rims, notched cordons at the neck/shoulder junction, and double-outline triangles filled with punctation.

In the context of Colombia as a whole, it turns out that the real international style is not Momil but Tierra Alta. In this connection, Bischof (1969b: 292) has already proposed that a single pottery series stretches all the way across the lowlands from the Magdalena to Panama. Its marker-traits are shallow platters, grater trays, ring bases, cut-out pedestal feet, urn burial (in the later stages), and also several decorative modes. Besides Estorbo, the component cultures of this series are late Malambo (Angulo 1962), the Crespo complex, from coastal villages and campsites everywhere from the Magdalena to Uraba (Dussan de Reichel 1954), the Tierra Alta and Cienega de Oro styles of the Sinu (Reichel-Dolmatoff and Reichel-Dolmatoff 1957), and a lot of the material collected by Linne (1929) in western Uraba and Pacific Darien. The presence of Uraba pottery at Crespo, which has a radiocarbon date of a.d. 1290 ± 80 (Y–1316), tends to confirm the long duration of Estorbo.

The logical extension of this route is northward along the Caribbean coast to Panama, where Drolet (1980) believes that maize farming arrived from Colombia around the time of Christ. The botanical evidence is dubious at best, as we have seen, nor does Drolet's pottery show anything like the complexity of the contemporary wares from Uraba. The only definite evidence for connections along the Caribbean coast is a report of Panamanian painted wares (type unspecified) from the Colombian littoral near Tolu (Reichel-Dolmatoff 1951: 20).

Cupica and the Pacific Connection

Although the ethnic composition of this area is unclear (Isacsson 1980) archaeologically, there is no doubt that Pacific Darien formed a single culture province from, at latest, the time of Christ right up to the Conquest. The northern frontier of this province coincides with the limit of Cueva speech near Chame, west of the Panama Canal, and the southern boundary falls near Bahia Solano, in the Colombian Choco.

One of the few stratigraphies in this entire province comes from near its southern edge, at the Bay of Cupica. Linne (1929) excavated 27 tombs in this locality, and then, in 1961, the Reichel-Dolmatoffs explored a funerary mound built of alternating strata of burials and fill, laid down over a considerable period (Reichel-Dolmatoff and Reichel-Dolmatoff 1961). The Cupica stratigraphy not only ties in sites and styles from the Caribbean coast, but also provides an independent check on the sequence proposed by Cooke (1976a) for Panamanian Darien.

The lowest burials (Cupica I) contain carinated bowls, pedestal cups, and everted-neck ollas decorated with incision, rows of punctation, and with shell dentate stamping. Although within the usual Darien repertoire, these designs can be compared in a general way with those of Momil and Cienega de Oro. In the same deposit are sherds of Incised Relief Brown Ware identical to those from Panama Viejo and Venado Beach, Utive, the Pearl Islands, CHO–3, and several other sites in the Pacific lowlands of eastern Panama. By contrast, this ware is recorded only once on the Atlantic slope, and here the sherds are thought to be imports from the Pacific side (Drolet 1980: 222–27). According to Reichel-Dolmatoff (1962), the fill sealing this lower burial stratum gave a C^{14} date of a.d. 1227 ± 100 (M–1313). Since this is out of line with the rest of the stratigraphic evidence, it should probably be dismissed as too recent.

The middle burials (Cupica III) have Zoned Bichrome vessels (Cupica Roja Fina) and also pots whose incised decoration has links with Tierra Alta of the Sinu. Zoned Bichrome is another of those wares distributed from one end of the Darien province to the other, though only on the Pacific side (Cooke 1976a; Drolet 1980: 221–22). The dotted triangle motif of the Zoned Bichrome recurs on the monochrome wares of the Estorbo complex and in the group of styles related to this. Sherds bearing a version of Incised Relief Brown decoration were still present in the fill overlying these middle burials (Reichel-Dolmatoff and Reichel-Dolmatoff 1961: plates X, 9–11).

The upper burials (Cupica IV) contain imported Macaracas Polychromes from Cocle, alongside local wares with deeply carved designs allied to those of Betanci, the most recent phase in the Sinu. Like the other marker wares, these Polychromes are scattered throughout the province and are reported from the Pearl Islands, CHO–3, and El Tigre. Most of the pottery found by Linne (1929: 176–90) in the rectangular pit graves at La Recasa is of local Cupica IV type, and similar material was discovered farther north at Garachine, Jaque, and Punta Patiño (McGimsey 1964). Sites are numerous wherever people have searched, and some of these settlements are large enough to be called towns (Sauer 1966: 174; Linne 1929: 157). The idea of a dense pre-Hispanic population in the Bayano and Chucunaque-Tuira drainages no longer seems far-fetched (Cooke 1976c: 33).

In Panamanian terms the Cupica pottery styles come out in their right relative order and also correlate quite correctly with the styles of Uraba and of Caribbean Colombia right across to Cartagena. All along the Pacific coast there was continuous and vigorous contact for some 900 years. The presence of just about every important trade ware in the Pearl Islands, together with Cocle goldwork, suggests that much of this traffic was by sea. Little of this internationalism can be recognized in Atlantic Darien, though there were clearly contacts across the divide. Ideas and products seem to have moved in all directions—Cocle animal art contributing to certain designs on Incised Relief Brown Ware, while Darien was probably the intermediary by which Colombian metallurgy reached central Panama. The region from Chame to Cupica is beginning to emerge as a significant culture area in its own right and should not be considered a mere buffer zone between the high chiefdoms of Cocle and Colombia.

The Chiefdoms of Caribbean Colombia, A.D. 500–1500

This section is less concerned with artifacts and pottery styles than with questions of organization. In particular, it sets out to establish three points: (a) that a similar level of organization, conventionally called a chiefdom, appears in the archaeological record at much the same time (before A.D. 500) in the Isthmus and in Colombia; (b) that the political, cultural, and commercial patterns described by Spanish *cronistas* can also be traced back to this period; (c) that the culture areas recognizable by A.D. 500 are still distinct entities at the Conquest. These culture areas are the individual links in my chain model.

Archaeologically, a chiefdom should possess several of the following characteristics: (a) a fairly large population, sustained by efficient agriculture, (b) a hierarchy of settlements, (c) organized political and ritual activities, which may be reflected in architecture and iconography, (d) social stratification, with the ruling elite appropriating for itself a large proportion of the luxury and high-status goods made by specialist craftsmen, (e) conspicuous consumption in life and, above all, in death, with rich burials of important personages.

Elements of this pattern are recognizable throughout the Isthmus and Caribbean Colombia by the early centuries A.D. In part, this progression to a new level of complexity seems linked to the expansion of maize production at the expense of root crops within the context of a mixed economy, though I am not suggesting that this was the sole cause of change. Economically, the existence of chiefdoms appears to require a food surplus in storable form, some of which is put back into the system by means of feasts and ceremonial drinking. In this connection, Linares, Sheets, and Rosenthal (1975) note the presence of large chicha jars in Panamanian Barriles tombs and conclude that "whatever its specific meaning and function, Barriles sculpture associates symbols of rank and warlike attributes with maize agriculture." For Colombia, the archaeological evidence for the replacement of manioc by maize has already been summarized. Here I will consider only the ecological and social consequences in the setting of northern Colombia.

Manioc is a perennial plant that is most productive of starch after a full year of growth. Although it can survive drought, acid soil, and a poor level of nutrients, its roots will not tolerate waterlogging, and two weeks of flooding can destroy the entire crop. Experiments have shown that growing manioc on richer soils does not enhance starch production in the tuber (Roosevelt 1980: 44, 112). On alluvial bottomland, flooded for several months of the year, manioc cannot therefore compete with seed crops in efficiency of exploitation.

By comparison with manioc, maize provides a diet much richer in vegetable protein (especially when combined with beans), but it makes high demands on soil nutrients. Maize is, however, the ideal crop for floodplain cultivation. Some varieties, such as the "two-month maize" of the Orinoco, have a growing season of no more than 60 days and are well adapted to land that is under water for much of the year. In addition, sediments derived from the Andes have the right chemical qualities for maize cultivation—a neutral pH, with adequate nitrogen, phosphorous, potassium, and trace elements (Roosevelt 1980: 115). These sediments are replenished annually and can sustain a high level of nutrient extraction.

All these arguments indicate that, once suitable races of maize and the appropriate cultivation techniques had been developed, some of the largest populations and most powerful chiefdoms should arise on the floodplains of the great rivers: the Magdalena and its tributaries, the Sinu and San Jorge basins, and the present-day banana belt south of Uraba.

For Colombia, this prediction seems to work. Ethnohistorical sources (e.g., Latorre 1919: 20–21) confirm that maize was, in fact, an important crop in the Mompos depression, though it did not displace manioc. Archaeologically, in the Caribbean lowlands east of Uraba, we can distinguish three major culture areas, each with its own long-lasting traditions in pottery, burial customs, and artifacts. These culture areas were not political entities. Like their counterparts in Panama (Helms 1979; Cooke, this volume), each was made up of several chiefdoms which, at the time of the Conquest, were competing actively among themselves.

San Jorge and the Sinu

This area comprises the three closely related provinces described in Spanish chronicles: Finecu (the Sinu basin), Pancenu (the San Jorge basin), and the gold-rich Senufana (the lower Rio Cauca and the Rio Nechi). By the sixteenth century all the classical features of chiefdom societies were present, and studies by Plazas and Falchetti have demonstrated both time depth and continuity for this pattern.

Since the 1960s, the San Jorge basin has been famous for its vast expanse of raised fields, covering some 200,000 hectares of seasonally flooded land (Parsons and Bowen 1966; Plazas and Falchetti 1981). Along the Caño

Carate, as many as four ancient soils have been observed, separated by bands of alluvium, indicating a long period of use with various episodes of land instability. More than two meters of river silt have been deposited on top of the original ridges, and it is suggested that increased sedimentation may have been one reason for abandonment (Shlemon and Parsons 1977; Parsons 1978). Radiocarbon dates from buried cultivation surfaces suggest that this abandonment had taken place before the twelfth century (Shlemon and Parsons 1977) and that the fields were in use during the early centuries A.D. (680 ± 120; Beta–2601).

Phosphate data from these layers confirm that they are anthrosols and indicate fairly intensive agricultural usage, with figures comparable to those from modern yuca plots (Plazas and Falchetti 1981; Eidt, personal communication). In addition, Parsons (personal communication) has tentatively identified a maize-like pollen from Caño Carate, which brings these San Jorge fields into line with their Belizian equivalents at Laguna de los Cocos (Puleston 1977) and Pulltrouser Swamp (Mikisicek and Wiseman in Turner et al. 1980).

The scale of these public works is an indicator of large and well-organized populations. The chiefdom model suggests that a hierarchy of settlements should be present, and this is corroborated by recent archaeological studies which have fitted the raised fields into their broader context (Plazas, Falchetti, and Saenz 1979a, 1979b, 1980; Plazas and Falchetti 1981). Interspersed among the fields are the house platforms, isolated or in small groups, but at Potrero Marusa there is a larger, more nucleated settlement (perhaps qualifying as a true town) with a formal layout of canals, and with nearly 100 house platforms arranged in rows (Plazas and Falchetti 1981). Some of these platforms have burial tumuli. The radiocarbon dates of a.d. 70 ± 90 (Beta–2596) and a.d. 150 ± 70 (Beta–2598) are the earliest so far recorded from the lower San Jorge, and the excavators comment on ceramic links with Malambo and with Momil II/Cienega de Oro, as well as with the wares of the Tradicion Modelada-Pintada.

It is this Tradicion Modelada-Pintada which dominates the subsequent history of the San Jorge basin and is clearly associated with the ridged fields, house platforms, and burial tumuli (Plazas, Falchetti, and Saenz 1979b, 1980). The characteristic wares are cream-colored, with appliqué and modeled decoration or with geometric designs in red paint. There is a clear separation between cooking-serving vessels and a range of forms exclusively for funerary use—these latter including anthropomorphic figures wearing jewelry in the Sinu style, defined by Falchetti (1976).

Burials are in tumuli, grouped into cemeteries. The size of the mound varies from small to very large, and, in general, the dimensions are proportional to the richness of the burial offerings. One mound at Ayapel, looted in 1919, contained 91 individual items of gold regalia in pure Sinu style (Farabee 1920), and similar high-status burials are reported from El

Japon, near Cuiva (Plazas and Falchetti 1979b). A few gold objects in this characteristic style were exported to Plato on the Rio Magdalena, to the Tairona region, and to the Isthmus (Falchetti 1976).

The Betanci complex of the Rio Sinu is closely related to these developments in the San Jorge Valley (Reichel-Dolmatoff and Reichel-Dolmatoff 1957). It shares the entire ritual of tumulus burial and the same style of goldwork. Moreover, the San Jorge wares of the Tradicion Modelada-Pintada have their counterparts in Betanci Modelada-Incisa and Betanci Bicromada. The other three Betanci wares do not occur in the San Jorge, and one of them (Betanci Incisa, with its deeply carved designs) seems rather to have affinities westward, with Uraba and Darien.

Along the lower San Jorge, the Tradicion Modelada-Pintada came to an end some time before a.d. 1300 (IAN–124), though probably no earlier than the tenth century. The old sites—and, presumably, the field systems also—were abandoned and the area occupied by new people coming from the Rio Magdalena, bringing with them a different pattern of settlement and pottery of the Tradicion Incisa-Alisada (next section). Further upstream, the old ways may have lingered on until the sixteenth century, for the Spaniards describe a flourishing chiefdom at Yapel (Ayapel) where there was a large town with satellite villages, burial tumuli, and extensive orchards and garden plots (Simon 1882–92[4]: 56; Castellanos 1955[3]: 76–77). There is no mention of raised fields, and, unfortunately for my argument, these authors insist that the Indians of Yapel grew only root crops and did not use maize. At Betanci, too, a version of this tumulus culture lasted until the Conquest, and its final stages can be equated with the chiefdoms described in Spanish chronicles (Simon 1882–92[4]: 25–51; Castellanos 1955[3]: 59–65; Gordon 1957). Finally, the Sinu style of goldwork seems to have continued in use, even in the Serrania de San Jacinto, where an impoverished version persisted in territory taken over by newcomers from the Magdalena (Plazas and Falchetti, personal communication).

The Chiefdoms of the Rio Magdalena

Spanish accounts of this region are summarized by Escalante (1955), who notes that in the sixteenth century, although there was no political unity, mutually intelligible dialects were spoken all over the Caribbean lowlands from Cartagena to the Magdalena, and upstream as far as the Laguna de Zapatosa. In this province, too, the Isthmian-Caribbean form of chiefdom is recognizable by A.D. 500.

The Zambrano area by this time had house platforms up to six meters thick, constructed of mixed earth and domestic rubbish. A few centuries later, compact villages with cemeteries of urn burials made their appearance (Reichel-Dolmatoff 1965a: 122–24, 1978). Some of these more recent sherd scatters are large, and may perhaps correspond with the Malibu towns mentioned in Spanish reports. Of these towns, Zambrano is listed as a commercial center; Mompox and Tamalameque had resident metalsmiths, as did Saloa, where metallurgical waste and goldsmiths' hammers have been collected (Reichel-Dolmatoff and Reichel-Dolmatoff 1953: 15, plate 12).

By now, the balance of power had shifted to the rich inland floodplains, and the coastal strip from Cartagena to the Magdalena begins to look decidedly peripheral, in spite of trade contacts with all the surrounding areas (Angulo 1951, 1978).

As in Panama, urn burial became general after ca. A.D. 900. Although there were regional differences, particularly in urn types, the whole of this Magdalena province (including the coastal strip from Tubara to the Cienega Grande) shared in a single pottery tradition, the Tradicion Incisa-Alisada (Plazas, Falchetti, and Saenz 1979b). This group of wares is characterized by well-made vessels, polished and sometimes red slipped, decorated with incised, crosshatched, and punctate motifs, all of them linear, rigid, and somewhat unimaginative by comparison with designs of the earlier periods.

The origins of this ceramic tradition appear to be in the lower Magdalena Valley, though the starting date remains uncertain. The early pottery from the Magdalena is still undescribed, and it is not yet clear what kind of material goes with the C^{14} date of a.d. 509 ± 120 (Y–730) from Las Mercedes at Zambrano (Stuiver 1969: 632). At the other end of the time range, persistence until the Conquest is confirmed by the radiocarbon dates from Las Palmas and Guaiquiri and by the presence of Spanish trade goods at Isla de Barrancon (Reichel-Dolmatoff and Reichel-Dolmatoff 1953: 58) and in the Serrania de San Jacinto (Plazas and Falchetti, personal communication).

The Tairona Chiefdoms

From Spanish chronicles it is evident that the sixteenth-century Tairona groups possessed one of the most sophisticated cultures in Caribbean America, with dense populations sustained by mixed-crop farming. Political organization was of chiefdom type. Smaller villages owed allegiance to the largest towns, which served as the capitals of mini-states, each one with its own cacique supported by a class of noblemen and specialist priests.

At Pueblito, excavations in ceremonial buildings, and also in ordinary family houses, gave evidence of a complex ritual life. Some elements of this persist among the present-day Kogi (Cogui) of the Sierra Nevada de Santa Marta, and many of these ritual practices may have Mesoamerican roots:

Among the Cogui Indians, an isolated and little-acculturated Chibcha-speaking tribe of the Sierra Nevada, which seems to have carried on the essential Tairona tradition, we find the greatest Mesoamerican element content registered so far. The most arresting parallels are: emphasis on "dawn" in creation myths; multiple creation of the universe and mankind; the concept of several stratified worlds difficult of access; association of colours, death and life forces, and theriomorphic beings with the four world quarters; special abode for those dying in childbirth or by drowning; reptilian origin of deities; duality (malevolent-benevolent) of deities; mono-poly-morphism and quadruplicity of deities; jaguar sun deity; masked dancers imper-sonating the deity; nine as a ritual number; illness attributed to sin; symbolism of "broom" and "sweeping" for forgiveness of sin; confession; divination by muscle twitching and fingernail tapping; a long training period for priests; a highly organized priesthood; a dog as guide to the Beyond; careful observation of solstices and equi-noxes, and astronomical markings. . . . It seems reasonable to assume that it was not a question of diffusion of isolated traits, but rather that these religious concepts and paraphernalia were transmitted as a complex. It would appear, therefore, that there existed a philosophic interrelation of religion, and that in the case of the Cogui we find the survival of an esentially Mesoamerican pattern in a still func-tioning culture of the Colombian mountain region. (Reichel-Dolmatoff 1965a: 157–58).

The archaeological Taironas are already well known from the publications of Mason (1931–39), G. Reichel-Dolmatoff (1954a, 1954b), Reichel-Dol-matoff and Reichel-Dolmatoff (1955), and Bischof (1971). In recent years the emphasis has moved toward settlement studies and ecological questions. Between 1973 and 1975, more than 200 sites were discovered, at all altitudes from sea level to 2,000 meters or higher (Cadavid and Turbay 1977), and new sites are still turning up. The presence of marine shells on high-altitude sites and historical accounts of trade in fish, salt, and gold hint at vertical control of the kind practiced by the Kogi and Ica today, in which each community maintains access to all the different ecological zones.

As predicted by the ethnohistorical data, settlements are ranked. Some of the new sites are small, with just a few houses, but others are large enough to have served as state capitals. Of these, Buritaca–200, with fourteenth-century radiocarbon dates, has some two square kilometers of stone-built house foundations, residential and agricultural terraces, tombs, staircases, roads, irrigation canals, and drains (Turbay 1980; Groot 1980).

Archaeology confirms, once again, that small and durable items travel farther than larger, breakable objects. Tairona pottery was traded to areas around the flanks of the Sierra Nevada (Angulo 1978; Reichel-Dolmatoff and Reichel-Dolmatoff 1959), but jewelry of stone, shell, or gold was ex-ported much farther—inland to the Muisca towns and to Sumapaz (Turbay, personal communication) and westward across the Caribbean lowlands to Tubara, Plato, the Sinu, and, eventually, to Panama and Costa Rica. Of the imports, the most extraordinary item is a Costa Rican stone sculpture found, without association, at Quebrada Valencia on the slopes of the Sierra (Dussan de Reichel 1967).

The great time depth of this Tairona tradition became apparent with the definition of the Nahuange phase, which is clearly proto-Tairona (Bischof

1969a, 1969b). Material of this phase was stratified below orthodox late Tairona in the fill of a terrace at Pueblito, and the funerary aspect is represented by the mound grave at Nahuange Site 1, with its wealth of offerings of pottery, shell, stone, resin, and metal (Mason 1931–39). The contents of the main grave simultaneously look back to the earlier cultures of the area and forward to the historical Taironas. The painted wares have decoration in the Horno style of the Rancheria and one form (the treasure jar) which persists into the full Tairona period. Other vessels suggest connections with Late Malambo and Mina de Oro, and a tumbaga figurine shows clear influence from the so-called Quimbaya style of the Cauca Valley, datable somewhere between A.D. 400 and 1000 (Bray 1978b: 51). With these early materials are stone and metal ornaments indistinguishable from mature Tairona forms.

Bischof favors a sixth- or seventh-century date for Nahuange. In support of this is the radiocarbon date of a.d. 580 ± 120 (Beta–3563) from Quebrada de las Animas, associated with Tairona Rojo Burdo sherds (Turbay, personal communcation).

An early start for the Tairona tradition, as well as long-distance trading connections, is further indicated by the clay spoons from La Fortuna and other sites in Atlantic Costa Rica. These items are almost certainly linked with snuff taking and drug use and are exact renderings in clay of a well-known category of Tairona stonework (compare Stone 1977: fig. 212b with Mason 1931–39[20], part 1, plate 101). Stone informs me that the Costa Rican specimens belong to her Early Period B, ca. A.D. 1–400.

At all events, the Nahuange burial, with its numerous ceremonial items and prestige goods, demonstrates that the Tairona chiefdoms, like their Sinu counterparts, were beginning to emerge as political and cultural entities during the early centuries after Christ. I suggest, too, that the emergence of chiefdoms at about the same time in the Isthmus and in Caribbean Colombia is part of a single phenomenon, and that neither area can be considered in isolation from the other.

Conclusions: The Role of Ideology

The Tairona case provides just one instance of the theme which is central to this paper: conservatism in the face of opportunity for change. The chain analogy describes this situation, but does not explain it. Contacts between the various regions of Colombia and the Isthmus were virtually continuous—why, then, did cultural frontiers maintain themselves for such long periods? Why, with all this to and fro, did neighboring cultures not become more like each other? And why is it always so easy to recognize, at first glance, a Magdalena pot, a Cocle zoomorph, or even a Colombian stone assemblage?

One answer is, perhaps, population stability. The evidence suggests that large-scale migrations and territorial encroachments were rare occurrences, and that a good deal of trade contact may have been of the indirect "down-the-line" type. Nevertheless, such contacts did take place, and geographical isolation cannot be the whole answer. The barriers must have been of a different kind, and I suggest that they were ideological, in the broadest sense of that word.

When borrowing does occur, what is usually taken over is the technology (metalworking, pottery painting, crop complexes), but this technology is used for purely local ends. There is surprisingly little direct copying. The more neutral the trait, the wider its distribution and the greater its chances of acceptance. As our comparisons have shown, geometrical designs travel faster and farther than figurative or symbolic themes, which are often strongly regional.

Since history shows that more people have died for their ideologies than for their art styles, we might begin by looking at the ideological content of pottery, metalwork, and the like. In the past, far too much attention has been paid to style, and far too little to subject matter, and the value of iconographic studies continues to go unrealized. One rare exception, which points the way to further development, is the essay by Linares (1976c) which demonstrates that the animal figures on the pottery and goldwork of Sitio Conte are charged with symbolic messages designed to reinforce the socio-political ideology of a particular society. We might then expect resistance to change. In this kind of context, borrowing a new motif from outside can be a major ideological event—as serious, in its way, as adding a hammer and sickle to the American flag or hanging an icon in a Baptist chapel.

Acknowledgments

For help with literature, unpublished information, or advice, I am indebted to Gerardo Ardila, Karen Bruhns, Richard Cooke, Gonzalo Correal U., Janice Darch, Robert Eidt, Ana Maria Falchetti, Norman Hammond, David Harris, Sven-Erik Isacsson, Fred Lange, William Mayer-Oakes, Charles McGimsey III, James J. Parsons, Barbara Pickersgill, Dolores Piperno, Clemencia Plazas, Marianne Schrimpff, Doris Stone, Luisa Turbay, Nikolaas van der Merwe, and Erika Wagner.

PART FIVE

Summary Statement

12

A Summary of the Archaeology
of Lower Central America

GORDON R. WILLEY

Harvard University

This summary is written to offer the reader a condensed version of the current knowledge and thinking on the pre-Columbian archaeology of what is hereinafter defined as lower Central America. It was prepared from the papers that compose this volume and from the week-long Santa Fe seminar discussions of these papers and of matters relating to them.

The summary, which in a general way follows the organization of the book and the seminar discussions, is divided into four parts. The first part, "Lower Central America: Archaeological and Natural Setting," pertains to the first two papers of the volume—those on a history of the archaeological research in the area and on the cultural-geographical setting. The second part, "Archaeological Cultures, Space, and Time," is a synopsis of the basic archaeological data as presented in the articles that compose the body of the book and as treated in the seminar discussions. A third, and briefer part, "A Chronological-Developmental Scheme for Lower Central America," follows. Although concerned with a time frame and with chronological relationships of the archaeological cultures, this chronological-developmental scheme is, by its very nature, interpretive to a degree. The scheme was devised by the conferees in a closing discussion, and it was designed to facilitate an archaeological overview of the area. When rewriting their papers for publication, the authors have referred to this general chronological scheme in a number of places; however, I do not refer to it in my regional synopses, preferring to present it after, rather than with, the basic data. The fourth and final division of the summary is devoted to "Interpretations"—to inferences, hypotheses, and models—which were advanced to deal with questions of ecological adaptation, subsistence, socio-political forms, trade and contacts, and overall cultural development. This closing portion of the summary is based in some degree upon the data papers, for even the leanest and most objective presentation of regional archaeological data must carry some interpretation within it; however, most of the interpretive treatment derives from the seminar discussions where such matters were explicitly addressed.[1]

Lower Central America: Archaeological and Natural Setting

Doris Stone opens her historical introduction to the development of lower Central American archaeological research with the reasonable question of just what is meant by "lower Central America." As Frederick Lange indicates in his cultural-geographical overview, our definition is provisional and to some degree arbitrary. For the purposes of the seminar, the definition, which is an archaeological one, includes most of El Salvador and Honduras and all of Nicaragua, Costa Rica, and Panama. We may also begin by saying that lower Central America is one of those archaeological areas that has long been considered as marginal to, or transitional between, better known areas. Thus, as Lange points out, it has been conceived as marginal to and derivative from Mesoamerica, which borders it on the north and west; and it has often been looked upon as a part of a transitional Intermediate Area between Mesoamerica and Peru, or a sort of conduit between these areas of New World high cultures. Fortunately, as both Stone and Lange relate, the amount and pace of archaeological research in lower Central America have increased greatly in recent decades, and with this has come a certain amount of what we can look upon as healthy archaeo-centrism. In other words, lower Central America, whatever its internal unity or disunity, is to be understood largely in terms of itself alone. Or, as Lange states, external Mesoamerican or South American "contacts were not the paramount cultural, or principal motivating, factors in development."

Lange's succinct natural environmental and ecological summary is difficult to reduce still further, but some salient points may be set out. Lower Central America is composed of three major physiographic zones: (a) a relatively broad Atlantic or Caribbean lowlands; (b) an interior spine of volcanic mountains, plateaus, and valleys; and (c) a relatively narrow Pacific coastal strip. The entire area lies in tropical latitudes, but a tropical climate and ambience varies according to moderating differences in elevation, winds, and ocean currents. The Atlantic lowlands are a tropical rain forest or savanna country and offer zones for human habitation not unlike those of the Maya or Veracruz lowlands of Mesoamerica on the one hand, and certain areas of South American tropical forest and savanna on the other. The interior highlands have a subtropical-to-temperate climate with some resemblances to the upland areas of southern Mesoamerica or Colombia, although the contiguous areas of prime agricultural land in Central America are generally much smaller. The Pacific side has less rainfall and vegetation than the Atlantic side and has a more seasonal precipitation pattern, resembling southern Pacific Mesoamerica.

The degree to which these broad environmental differences within lower Central America influenced cultural development and conditioned cultural diffusion from different parts of Mesoamerica and South America is a complex question, and it is one that engaged the attention of all of the seminar participants. The traditional archaeological (and anthropological) generalization about this has been that the Atlantic coastal lowlands saw a greater penetration of lowland South American tropical-forest-type cultural influences and peoples, while the Pacific strip was more closely allied with Mesoamerica. There is considerable evidence—including linguistic evidence—to support this generalization; yet, as Lange indicates, the situation is not altogether this simple. Southern Mesoamerica could be said to present two Mesoamericas, two basic cultural types, one highland and Pacific oriented, one lowland and Atlantic (the lowland Maya). How were these two types related to what went on in lower Central America? How and in what ways were South American cultures involved? And how and in what ways were local development and change generated in the natural environmental patchwork of lower Central America?

Lange emphasizes possible routes of communication between the two coasts of lower Central America, for the whole area is, in effect, a giant isthmus. As the substantive papers in the book amply demonstrate, there was a great diversity of regional-cultural differences, but at the same time there is abundant evidence of cultural contact among regions.

Lange summarizes the matter of volcanism in the area. As Lange, Payson Sheets, and others point out, volcanic activities occasionally had immediate negative effects upon human populations over the past several millennia; but they had positive effects upon social and cultural development as well: ash-enriched soils, fine clays, obsidian, and other valuable resources are all results of volcanic activity.

Lange tabulates and presents radiocarbon dates for the area, and he also sets out a lower Central American general developmental chronology—a chronology, referred to in the papers throughout the volume, which was a product of the seminar, and which I will discuss later. An area-wide chronological scheme such as this has been made possible as the result of regional chronological progress over the past few decades, as is both explicit and implicit in Stone's archaeological history.

From a review of this history we see that one of the first considerations in lower Central American archaeological research of a modern era was the definition of a Mesoamerican–lower Central American boundary. This has been in the process of formulation over the past 35 years and is intimately linked to the development of regional chronologies. Prior to that time, there was an implicit recognition that such major Maya sites as Quirigua and Copan, with their monuments and hieroglyphic texts, marked an eastern and southern edge or frontier of this civilization and Mesoamerican high cultures. Beyond this edge, to the east and south, extending for some uncertain distance into Honduras and El Salvador, was a discernible Mayoid periphery, so documented by pottery styles which, as one moved still farther eastward and southward, became less Mayan and more something else. When Mesoamerica began to take on a firmness of conceptual definition in the 1940s (Kirchhoff 1943), there was more concern about this archaeological border. Was the southern and eastern boundary a line running through western El Salvador and Honduras? Or should such a line be drawn to include all of El Salvador, a more appreciable slice of Honduras, and Pacific Nicaragua and northwestern Costa Rica? Or would we be better off if we conceived of a frontier zone of some geographical depth between Mesoamerica and the lands to the south and east? Such a zone might then be the territory between our two aforementioned lines. In any event, with the development of relative archaeological chronologies for these border regions, it began to be apparent that a lower Central American–Mesoamerican dividing line was something that had been quite fluid through time rather than a fixed demarcation. Thus, on a Formative or Preclassic time level Honduran and Salvadoran ceramics could be recognized as fully Mesoamerican in affiliation; then in the Classic period these regions began to show more stylistic independence from Mesoamerica; and finally, on the Postclassic horizon, strong Mesoamerican ties, as evidenced especially by trade wares, appeared as far south as northern Costa Rica. This is an overly simple statement about a complex set of situations; but the point to be made is that there were changing patterns of interaction between Mesoamerican cultures and those lying to the south and east.

Northeastern Honduras, most of Nicaragua and Costa Rica, and all of Panama lie outside of this zone of strong, if fluctuating, Mesoamerican influences. Stone recounts the archaeological explorations that have been carried out in these regions, some of them dating back more than a century. In general, archaeological information tended to be more readily available on the Pacific side of these regions—in historic times the more densely settled side; and it is probably fair to say, as Haberland did, that our interpretations are biased in this direction. Nevertheless, recent work in northeastern Honduras and in the intermontane basins and flatlands of Atlantic Costa Rica is beginning to redress the balance, as we have seen in this volume.

The question of a southern boundary for lower Central America has never received the same attention as that of the Mesoamerican frontier. The international line between Colombia and Panama is taken simply as an arbitrary cut-off point. For a long time there was very little archaeological information about either Panamanian Darien or northern Colombia, but there is more now, and the seminar, with Warwick Bray's help, made some attempt to review the state of knowledge at this southern end of the lower Central American area.

From Stone's paper and from these few remarks, it should be apparent that lower Central American archaeology is still largely in a stage of basic data definitions and space-time ordering. For a long time it had hardly reached this threshold, being concerned, for the most part, with grave excavations and descriptive presentations. Now, along with chronological control, other kinds of research are beginning to go forward. New questions are being asked. What were the ecological advantages and constraints influencing these Central American societies? How did these relate to trade and contacts within this area and outside of it? What was the nature of the socio-political structures in the area and how did these change or fail to change? There was some effort to address all of these and other questions in the seminar discussions, as I shall endeavor to summarize; but first let us review the basic data as they were presented.

Archaeological Cultures, Space, and Time

Lower Central America as Seen from Mesoamerica

In discussing lower Central American–Mesoamerican relationships, Robert J. Sharer was concerned to a very large extent with the processes of contacts and interrelationships between the two areas, especially those of economic systems and of trade. Sharer, however, lays down some groundwork basic to lower Central American prehistory. He recognizes the possibility of Early Preclassic connections between the two areas, especially between western El Salvador and western Honduras and Mesoamerica; and he suggested, in discussions, that we might view this even more broadly and ask if there might not have been such a continuity of Early Preclassic sharing from Mesoamerica to South America, with lower Central America being a vital link in the chain. Indeed, this seems quite likely—a community-to-community sharing of basic agricultural products and techniques and other traits. As yet, any indisputable pre-Olmec horizon complexes in western Salvador-Honduras have not been clearly defined, but Sharer, Sheets, and Haberland were all of the opinion that such probably exist. The first participation on the part of lower Central America in a more complex Mesoamerican world and system comes, however, with the Olmec horizon at ca. 1200 B.C. and persists to ca. 400 B.C. El Salvador and Honduras were most directly affected, although more remote influences are probably registered in jadework as far south as northern Costa Rica.

From about 400 B.C. to A.D. 250 (the Mesoamerican Late Preclassic and Protoclassic periods), or up until the time of the Ilopango eruption, El Salvador was firmly linked to a southern Maya world that extended from Chiapas, through Pacific and highland Guatemala, to Chalchuapa in western El Salvador. Beyond this, central and eastern El Salvador were undoubtedly linked to an economic system that had its principal node at Chalchuapa, whatever the linguistic affiliations of these regions. After A.D. 250 and the Ilopango eruption, the Chalchuapa part of the system broke down. Power in southern Mesoamerica continued at Kaminaljuyu, in the Guatemalan highlands, and began to be exercised from a new great base in the Maya lowlands, Tikal, in the Peten. Throughout the Classic period and into the Postclassic, there are indications that Maya lowland power, especially in the economic sphere, gradually shifted to the north. All of this was complicated by central Mexican influences into southern Mesoamerica—first, those radiating from Teotihuacan in the Early Classic and, later, those from Late Classic and Early Postclassic sources. These changes in Mesoamerica, involving shifts and balances in economic and political power, are reflected in trading influences seen in lower Central America. A specific case of such shifts and balances, relating very directly to lower Central America, would involve Copan's apparent isolation from the lowland Maya world, beginning in the eighth century A.D., and its response by turning increasingly toward lower Central America. This may have been the stimulus for the spread of both Copador and related (Ulua-Mayoid) pottery during this time (Sharer, personal communication).

El Salvador

Payson D. Sheets's coverage of the Salvadoran data conforms to the general structure laid down by Sharer. Sheets sees Chalchuapa as the easternmost full-scale "Mesoamerican establishment" in El Salvador. There are, however, other important Mesoamerican sites in the region such as the smaller one at Santa Leticia where Arthur Demarest has developed a related Preclassic sequence (personal communication 1979–81). This rooting in a Mesoamerican tradition can be traced back to about 900 B.C.; and from then until A.D. 250, Chalchuapa and western El Salvador might be considered a part of the same cultural subarea as Pacific and Highland Guatemala-Chiapas. This is expressed in ceramics, figurines, ground stone and obsidian technology, and even architecture. During the Late Preclassic the entire southern Mesoamerican-Salvadoran region enjoyed a florescence, as expressed in population growth, center construction, and ceramics (especially the Usulutan tradition).

Farther east in El Salvador, Sheets's surveys and excavations have provided a data base in the Zapotitan Valley with a sequence running from Late Preclassic into Postclassic times. During this time span, there is clear evidence for site nucleation; the Classic period site of San Andres is an urban zone of perhaps 10 square kilometers, and overall Zapotitan population figures are estimated at 50 to 70 persons per square kilometer. Still farther east, the long sequence at Quelepa runs from Late Preclassic through Classic. Ceramic ties in central and eastern El Salvador are predominantly, and easily recognizable as, Mesoamerican, and the same is true of obsidian technology. In this last connection, a special note should be made of Sheets's studies and emphases on obsidian manufacturing techniques and his definition of what might be called a "Mesoamerican tradition" in obsidian technology. In spite of this partial Mesoamericanization of central and eastern El Salvador, both Sheets and Sharer made clear in the discussions that such a diagnostic as architectural influence of a Mesoamerican type is weak or missing beyond the western confines of the country.

Sheets identifies three volcanic episodes in the Salvadoran cultural sequences. The first of these, the Ilopango eruption, occurred at ca. A.D. 250–300; and there cannot be much question but that it had a profound disruptive effect on the vigorous Late Preclassic culture with its major base at Chalchuapa. Indeed, this event seems to have ended the regional hegemony of this center for some centuries. Subsequent volcanic activities, which apparently had only very localized effects on human populations, include the Laguna Caldera eruption at ca. A.D. 600 and the Boqueron eruption ca. A.D. 900.

Honduras

Paul F. Healy's survey of Honduran archaeology also reveals strong Mesoamerican linkages, and, as in Salvador, the picture is one of the gradual thinning out of these influences as one moves from west to east. As a reading of his paper demonstrates, the ethnic-linguistic and archaeological mosaic is a complex one, and there are no easy one-to-one correspondences between language distributions and cultures. The definition of archaeological regions is also strongly conditioned by the amounts and nature of archaeological work which has been carried out. To date, this has been relatively limited and spotty; the western regions are better known, those to the east increasingly less so.

Healy's Far Western region is within Mesoamerica proper, being, in effect, the southeastern Maya zone with Copan as the most important center. It should be observed in passing, however, that this great Classic Maya site, while participating fully in the architectural, iconographic, calendric, and hieroglyphic systems of the lowland Maya, is, nevertheless, in its strong Usulutan and later polychrome traditions, essentially in a ceramic inter-action sphere that allies it closely with the Guatemalan highlands and Salvador.

Healy's Ulua-Chamelecon-Sula, Lake Yojoa, and Central regions are Mesoamerican outer peripheries, transitional into lower Central America. As in El Salvador, Early and Middle Preclassic ceramics ally closely to the west and north. This would include such pottery complexes as the Zanjos and Sula of the Playa de los Muertos site group, Jaral, and Yarumela I and II. Occupations are in rich agricultural valleys. In addition to pottery, the figurines, jades, and obsidians give a Mesoamerican cast to these complexes; and at both Jaral and Yarumela there is ceremonial center mound construc-tion. Just how far to the east and south these Mesoamerican networks of contact and exchange may have reached on these Preclassic levels remains to be determined; but it is of interest to note that the pottery of the Cuyamel Caves, in the distant and little known Northeast region, includes pieces that would be at home in Mesoamerica proper, especially a pair of vessels that are polished and carved in the Olmec style and that may have been man-ufactured in the west and transported to Honduras.

Between 300 B.C. and A.D. 500, corresponding to the Mesoamerican Late Preclassic and Early Classic periods, there was population growth in western and central Honduras, as borne out by increases in numbers and sizes of sites, including some large centers. Usulutan is the dominant pottery dec-orative technique of the time, and there are no polychromes comparable to those of the Guatemalan Maya Early Classic period. Instead, Usulutan tradition ceramics continue on until the Late Classic period.

In this 300 B.C.–A.D. 500 time period the Northeast region of Honduras is distinctly non-Mesoamerican. There is no Usulutan ware, no obsidian, and the largest constructions are house platforms of only modest size. The Southern Pacific region, centering on the Bay of Fonseca, may be a bit more within the Mesoamerican orbit at this time than the Northeast, al-though not much.

During the period A.D. 500–1000 the Ulua Mayoid polychrome cylinder jars, so obviously imitations of the Classic Maya polychrome genre of the Peten, were made. Ulua Mayoid is found in all of the Honduran regions we have just been considering except for the Northeast. Another polychrome style, sometimes referred to as Ulua Bold Geometric, is frequently found in association with Ulua Mayoid but tends to be more common as one moves toward the east. In the Southern Pacific region, both Ulua poly-chromes and a type known as Papagayo Polychrome, which is a part of the general Nicoya Polychrome tradition common to Pacific Nicaragua and Costa Rica, are found. This, and the presence of carved metates in this part of Honduras, indicate an increase in exchange with these regions outside of Honduras. In the Northeast Honduran region there is a local polychrome style, the Selin, which may be a stimulated response to a knowledge of the Ulua and Papagayo wares, although it is by no means a close imitation of them. Healy sees a continued population growth for all of the Honduran regions during this time. Big sites are constructed, including the fortified hilltop redoubt town of Tenampua in the Central region, and even in the far Northeast region there are sites with public buildings and fortifications.

Toward the end of the first millennium A.D. there are evidences of site abandonment in some places in Honduras—a curious parallel to what was going on in parts of the Maya lowlands; but there are still some important centers. Naco, in the Ulua-Chamelecon-Sula region, is one of these. Meso-american-derived styles, such as Fine Orange ware, are present there. The Northeast region still stands apart. It prospered in the A.D. 1000–1500 period when its largest sites were laid out and fortified. The ceramic tradition of this Northeast Postclassic Cocal phase is, however, quite distinct from that of the rest of Honduras and clearly relates southward to Caribbean lower Central America. This pottery is largely modeled and decorated with an appliqué technique, and this technique is generally known as the North Coast Appliqué tradition.

This brief history of Honduran archaeology might be further summarized by saying that, in chronological order, we see the following events and changes: (a) an early, Preclassic- or Formative-period Mesoamericanization that thins as one moves toward the east; (b) local styles and cultures that retain and develop, in their own ways, this Mesoamerican heritage; and (c) renewed Mesoamerican influences that are, however, countered by eastern and southern influences. This is a ceramic synopsis, of course, but it is probably paralleled by a trend in which a Mesoamerican hierarchically ordered settlement pattern extends into territories of simpler settlement systems and where the latter are then gradually transformed, presumably through combined processes of diffusion and internal growth.

Greater Nicoya

The name derives from the Costa Rican Nicoya Peninsula and the Gulf of Nicoya in the northwestern part of that country, but the cultural subarea also subsumes adjacent Pacific Nicaragua in the vicinities of the Nicaraguan lakes. Frederick W. Lange, who prepared this paper, was also at pains to indicate, in the discussions and in later comments, that there are some significant differences between the Nicaraguan and Costa Rican parts of the subarea. These are seen not only in the archaeological record but in the ethnohistorical sources as these have been researched recently by Suzanne Abel-Vidor. Both in prehistoric times and during the contact period, there were apparently greater concentrations of populations and wealth in Nicaragua than in the Costa Rican Nicoya region proper.

The earliest ceramic period for Greater Nicoya—preceramic evidences for the subarea are as yet only suggestive or inconclusive—is known as the Zoned Bichrome period (800 B.C.–A.D. 500), a name derived from the widespread use of incised-line-bordered color zones in pottery decoration. Technologically and aesthetically, the Greater Nicoya Zoned Bichrome wares are reminiscent of some Mesoamerican pottery types of the Early and Middle Preclassic periods, so that Mesoamerican ancestry may be involved in their origins; however, it should be made clear that the Greater Nicoya Zoned Bichrome types are not as indisputably Mesoamerican in appearance as are some of the Preclassic pottery styles of El Salvador or the Ulua-Chamelecon-Sula region of Honduras. They also show similarities to Formative-era styles elsewhere in the Intermediate Area and in Peru and, thus, might be said to have participated in a general sharing of technological-aesthetic properties common to much of Nuclear American pottery on a Formative time level. Direct evidence is lacking, but it seems likely that the Zoned Bichrome–period communities were supported by agriculture. The villages were found in inland valleys, and there was no recourse to nearby marine resources until near the end of the period. Lange subdivides the Zoned Bichrome period into three sequent phases which document a population growth as reflected in more and larger village sites. Zoned Bichrome–period burials are found in the villages and in separate cemeteries; those in the latter are often accompanied by such apparent symbols of social ranking as carved jades, elaborately carved metates (or stone seats?), and small stone statues. No good local jade source has ever been found in the Greater Nicoya subarea, and Lange is of the opinion that jade was imported from southern Mesoamerica and worked into pendants and ornamental axes or mace heads by the Zoned Bichrome societies. Such imports are definitely documented for the late phase by the appearances of associated jade ornaments of Mesoamerican manufacture, executed in Izapan or Mayan styles. On the other hand, obsidian, the other prime Mesoamerican commodity, is extremely rare in Greater Nicoya throughout the sequence.

In the Early Polychrome period (A.D. 500–800) there was a marked residential shift to coastal locations, and this can be correlated with some dependence on marine diet. Some of the middens of the period are of substantial size and indicate plaza arrangements of dwellings; however, there is nothing that would qualify as a public building. The coastal settlement orientation persists throughout the remainder of the Greater Nicoya sequence. A number of polychrome styles spring up during the Early and Middle Polychrome (A.D. 800–1200) periods. These are essentially local developments with some antecedents in the Zoned Bichrome period; however, they also reflect contacts and interchange with Honduran styles such as those of the Ulua Mayoid tradition. It will be recalled that Nicoya Polychrome styles were definitely present in Honduras in the Postclassic period, and possibly in the Classic. Exchange and influence must have moved in both directions. Lange also notes the widespread trade in Greater Nicoya polychrome styles well into Mesoamerica. The Greater Nicoya Late Polychrome period (A.D. 1200–1550) features a continuation of local painted styles, but there is now very definite Mexican influence in the form of designs of Mixteca-Puebla inspiration. Healy, who has worked with the Nicaraguan Isthmus of Rivas materials (Healy 1980), emphasizes this "Mexicanization" or "Mesoamericanization" of the Nicaraguan Middle and Late Polychrome pottery styles, and he speculates that they may have been introduced by the "displaced Mesoamerican groups" (personal communication 1981), such as the Chorotega (Middle Polychromes) and Nicarao (Late Polychromes). In his view, style motifs, as well as local legends, suggest such incursions; and he notes Mexican deities, such as Ehecatl, Quetzalcoatl, and Tlaltecutli, appearing on the principal pottery types.

How similar is the developmental profile of Greater Nicoya to that of Honduras? Early Mesoamerican influences seem more tenuous in Greater Nicoya than in western Honduras, although the jades and the Zoned Bichrome ceramics indicate some ties. Early and Middle Polychrome styles of Greater Nicoya show a strong localism, although this localism is more pronounced in Costa Rica than in Nicaragua. It is also expressed in the carved stonework of Costa Rica. Finally, in Late Polychrome times Greater Nicoya shows strong Mesoamerican influences, as does Honduras. These are more notable in Nicaragua than in Costa Rica and may involve not only trade but migrations into the former region. Nowhere in the Greater Nicoya subarea, however, does this late Mesoamericanization appear to be reflected in the kinds of archaeological evidence that would suggest major socio-political changes.

The Lower Caribbean

Michael J. Snarskis deals with the diverse cultures of the as-yet-little-known territories of Atlantic Nicaragua, Costa Rica, and Panama, and he also draws into this the Costa Rican Meseta Central. Previously, these regions have been the missing link between the better-known Mesoamerican outer periphery of El Salvador, Honduras, and Greater Nicoya, on the one hand, and Chiriquian–Central Panamanian regions to the south and east.

Snarskis devotes several introductory pages to Paleo-Indian- and Archaic-stage considerations. Fluted and fishtailed projectile points from Costa Rica and Panama are surely indicative of early hunting cultures in these regions, even though these are casual or surface finds. Although this question is covered in a general way, I think there can be little doubt but that lower

Central America was once a connecting pathway between North American
Clovis point hunters and the fluted point makers who lived down along the
Andes prior to 7000 B.C. Similarly, Archaic-like points and other implements
that have been recovered from various places in lower Central America
suggest environmental and cultural changes here in the millennia following
7000 B.C. that are comparable to those that took place elsewhere in the
Americas.

For the ceramic periods Snarskis presents his data from two principal
regions: the Atlantic watershed and the Meseta Central of Costa Rica. A
culture sequence in the Atlantic watershed begins with two early complexes,
both dated to about 1000–500 B.C. One of these is the La Montaña whose
pottery is described as being in a monochrome-plastic tradition that is reminiscent of the Barlovento of northern Colombia. The other cultural complex, located to the north of the La Montaña, is the Chaparron, whose
pottery features zoned bichrome decoration. Much of this Chaparron pottery
is in the form of tecomate bowls. The juxtaposition of the two cultures is
a fascinating one, suggesting a frontier between early South American–
derived societies and those that may be related to a far southeastern extension
of a Mesoamerican Formative orbit of influence. Both cultures are characterized by small, simple village settlements.

These two early phases of the Atlantic watershed are succeeded by the El
Bosque culture, with an estimated time range of 0–A.D. 500. "Succeeded"
may not be the right word here, as a chronological gap of 500 B.C.–0 is
suggested by the radiocarbon dates; however, Snarskis as yet has isolated no
intervening phase, and some cultural continuity is indicated. El Bosque
ceramics include zoned red-on-buff types, and this favors some continuity
from Chaparron into El Bosque. There is greater ceramic variety in El
Bosque than in either Chaparron or La Montaña. El Bosque has impressed,
appliqué, and bichrome painting and composite silhouette bowls and long-
legged tripods. Taken all in all, El Bosque sounds more Mesoamerican than
South American, although it is, of course, a very local culture complex.
El Bosque features symbols of rank as well, such as the ornamental stone
metates (or seats?) already mentioned for the contemporaneous Zoned Bichrome–period cultures of Greater Nicoya. Snarskis also refers to evidence
for chiefs' houses, and the chiefly graves (or some of them) are relatively
elaborate corridor tombs. Agriculture was firmly established by this time in
central and eastern Costa Rica, as indicated by the large numbers of metates
and other subsistence-related ground stone tools, as well as carbonized
samples of maize, beans, and palm nuts found in several sites.

The next Atlantic watershed sequence, the La Selva phase (A.D. 500–
800), includes such styles as the Curridabat ware, which emphasizes modeling and tripods. At this time jade, which was present in El Bosque, gives
way to gold as the most important status, ritual, or ornamental material,

signaling, perhaps, stronger connections with the east and south at the expense of those to the north and west. The later part of the La Selva phase (A.D. 700–1000) sees resist-painted decoration as an important mode in ceramics. Finally, the La Cabaña phase (A.D. 1000–1500) closes the Atlantic watershed region sequence. During this period ceramics present a variety of styles that may be derived from the earlier traditions: modeling, appliqué, tripods, and some painting, including the resist-decorated wares. La Cabaña has large ceremonial center sites with huge circular stone and earth platforms. The Las Mercedes site of the Atlantic drainage, well known in the earlier literature (Hartman 1901; Mason 1945) for its mounds, statuary and other stonecarving, and stone-cist graves, falls in the La Cabaña phase.

The Costa Rican Meseta Central sequence relates to that of the Atlantic slopes. The earliest phase, Pavas (200 B.C.–A.D. 400), has ceramics of the Zoned Bichrome tradition, linking it both to Greater Nicoya and to the Atlantic-drainage Chaparron phase. The next Meseta Central phase, Curridabat (A.D. 400–900), relates closely to La Selva, and the final Cartago phase (A.D. 900–1500) can be paired with La Cabaña in large-site construction.

Snarskis makes the generalization that the early pottery sites seem situated for a combination of hunting and farming; those of the intermediate periods for farming alone; and those of the late periods appear to be located with an eye to defense and frontier establishment.

Even in so brief a summary a word should be added about still a third Atlantic region. This is the territory of the southeastern Nicaraguan coast, and the information comes from recent surveys and excavations made by Richard Magnus and referred to in the seminar discussions. The earliest phase of this regional sequence, the Siteia, dating from about the time of Christ, is different from either La Montaña or Chaparron in its ceramics. These are red-and-black-on-white polychromes, which Magnus sees as reminiscent of an early northern Venezuelan Painted tradition. Siteia sites also have simple metates and manos and forest-clearing celts, with their implications of at least some farming activity. The succeeding Smalla (0–A.D. 400), Jarkin (A.D. 400–1200), and Cukra Point (A.D. 1200–1500) complexes are described as being in a plastic-decorated ceramic tradition suggestive of such sites as Momil in northern Colombia. In a general way, this would appear to link to the earlier La Montaña, Barlovento-like pottery, although these Nicaraguan coastal complexes are substantially later. In appraising all of this, Snarskis made the point in the seminar discussions that the Smalla–Jarkin–Cukra Point pottery groups could not be looked upon as similar to, or ancestral to, the modeled and appliqué pottery that begins to appear in El Bosque and then flourishes throughout the Atlantic watershed and Meseta Central sequences. This general line of pottery development, which climaxes in La Cabaña and Cartago, is almost certainly related to the North Coast Appliqué styles that are found in Northeast Honduras in the Late or

Cocal phases. Smalla–Jarkin–Cukra Point, at least to judge from current descriptions, may be a thing apart. I dwell on this to the length that I have to indicate that the concepts of Mesoamerican and South American inter-penetrations in the regions in question, while of some general validity, are very gross statements of what went on and that the schematics of the pre-history here are obviously complex.

Greater Chiriqui

The highlands and Pacific side of southern Costa Rica and western Panama include the Chiriqui region proper (situated along both sides of the international border) and the adjacent Costa Rican Boruca and Diquis regions (Willey 1971: 334–38). All of this is reasonably subsumed into a Greater Chiriqui archaeological subarea of lower Central America by Wolf-gang Haberland. Whether or not the Atlantic portions of these sections of Costa Rica and Panama should also be included in such a subarea is, in Haberland's opinion, still undetermined, although Richard Cooke, as we shall see further along, would be inclined to make such an inclusion.

The preceramic horizons of Talamanca (4800–2300 B.C., following Rich-ard Cooke's recent radiocarbon datings in this volume) and Boquete (2300–500 B.C., also following Cooke) are known from the work of Linares and Ranere in Panama. The Talamanca lithic assemblage has some distinctive stone tools—heavy bifacial splitting wedges or woodworking implements. There are no points in the complex, but small game hunting and plant collecting is the inferred economy. No Clovis-like or other lanceolate points have yet been found in the subarea, but as they have been reported from regions to both sides of it, there seems a reasonable possibility that more specialized early hunters may have once passed this way. Boquete introduces polished celts and grinding tools, and its discoverers have surmised that this phase saw a gradual shift to more specialized collecting and incipient cul-tivation. The chronological positions of the two phases are verified by stra-tigraphy and by some radiocarbon dates. Both phases are so far known only from upland terrain. Talamanca and Boquete sites are known from both shelters and open sites.

The long Aguas Buenas phase of the highlands, dating from 800 B.C. to A.D. 600, marks the inception of pottery for the subarea, at least by current evidence. The principal ceramic decorative technique is incised color zon-ing. This raises the obvious question as to what extent this may be a distant derivation from Mesoamerica, via Greater Nicoya and central Costa Rica. Such a question takes us into the larger question of Nuclear American Formative diffusions of technological and aesthetic properties in ceramics—and, in effect, leaves us there. Suffice it to say that the Aguas Buenas styles are local and distinctive and are not closely duplicated in any of the other zoned bichrome potteries that we have been mentioning. The most spectacular site of the Aguas Buenas culture is Barriles in Panama. Barriles was a major center, and it is clear that Aguas Buenas society had a hierarchically ranked settlement organization. There is large stone sculpture of human figures, and elaborate tables or thrones at Barriles; some of the tables have been found in graves. Just where in the long Aguas Buenas period the Barriles site—or at least the most elaborate aspects of that site—fits remains problematic; but it seems most likely that it (or these features of sculpture) falls in the later part.

The Concepcion phase of the western Panamanian Pacific lowlands is thought by Haberland to be the chronological equivalent of Aguas Buenas, for the most part, but to have been overrun by Aguas Buenas peoples in its later centuries. Snarskis and Cooke, in seminar discussions, were inclined to disagree with this and saw Concepcion as essentially earlier than Aguas Buenas. Concepcion features pottery of a Panamanian tradition known as scarified ware. Decorated in a combination painted and scratched or scoring technique, scarified ware has some resemblances to zoned bichrome wares.

Some authorities place a Burica phase (A.D. 600–800) after Aguas Buenas; Haberland, in contrast, sees Burica as merely an earlier part of the Chiriqui phase (A.D. 600/800–1500). Chiriqui pottery, well known from grave excavations of the past 70 years, divides into a number of styles: positive painted (Alligator Ware), resist or negative-painted, modeled, and a Bisquit Ware. Carved metates (seats?) are a part of the complex, although these are neither as large and elaborate as those of Barriles nor as elaborate as those of the Costa Rican Atlantic watershed and Meseta Central cultures. And gold ornaments are notably present. Chiriqui-phase settlement is not well known, a self-evident result of the past concentration on gravedigging alone. Cemeteries are known to be on high hills, and graves are most frequently stone lined. It is surmised that living sites were in valley bottoms; and, given the earlier Aguas Buenas tradition of site hierarchies, together with indications of rank in grave goods, it can be further surmised that settlement was divided into centers and lesser sites.

Central and Eastern Panama

Richard Cooke is of the opinion that cultural regions in Panama are more meaningfully conceived of as three north-south zones, extending in each case from the Atlantic to the Pacific, rather than in the more traditional fashion which separates Pacific regions from those of the Atlantic. Cooke's three zones would be, following this, Western, Central, and Eastern Panama. His Western Panama region would be the one treated mainly by Haberland, although dealt with to a limited extent by Snarskis on the Atlantic side. His Central region is the one known best from the several studies of the Cocle and Parita Bay sectors of the Pacific side; and his Eastern region is essentially Darien. This line of cultural-geographical argument still remains to be demonstrated; however, research to date does, indeed, indicate that there was substantial Atlantic-to-Pacific contact across the Isthmus.

Cooke makes clear at the outset that he will be dealing with three main themes: (a) the dating of Monagrillo pottery and culture and its agricultural status; (b) the threshold of sedentary village life; and (c) a special attention to faunal analyses. In addition, it is also fair to say that he devotes some attention to the problem of the rise of chiefdoms or nonegalitarian societies in Panama. In this summary I shall be concerned with the first, second, and fourth matters; the data on faunal analyses are summarized succinctly in Cooke's tables.

We should begin, however, with a summary word about Paleo-Indian and Early Archaic remains. Fluted and fishtailed points have been found in Panama, but these have all been surface finds. It is logical to assume that they do represent man's early movements through, and occupation of, the Isthmus, and Cooke considers this in the context of ecological speculations. He makes the observation that, assuming the early projectile point forms do date ca. 9000–8000 B.C., there is a notable hiatus in the Panamanian archaeological record from about 8000 to 5000 B.C. or during the early part of the post-Pleistocene. The lithic cultures which follow would be the Talamanca, already referred to by Haberland in his discussions of western Panama, and the Cerro Mangote of central Pacific Panama. The common Cerro Mangote artifact is a pounding-grinding stone, and the cultural adaptation seems to be primarily a coastal one, although some interior hunting sites are known.

The Monagrillo culture succeeds the Cerro Mangote in central Pacific Panama, and there is now substantial stratigraphic and radiocarbon-dating evidence on this transition and on the Monagrillo occupation. Sites include shell mounds, open sites some little distance in the interior, and rockshelters. At the Monagrillo site proper, the safe limits of pottery dating are between 2400 and 1000 B.C. for a shell mound on Parita Bay; however, a bottom date of 3000 B.C. seems probable. Taking a more inter-American perspective, I would agree that the appearance of the Monagrillo ware, with its simple vessel forms and incision-punctation decoration, supports such a round dating. The Monagrillo style is reminiscent, in a general way, of early northwestern South American ceramics, such as those of Puerto Hormiga in Colombia and the San Pablo and Valdivia types of coastal Ecuador, which also date to this approximate time. Cooke reports maize phytoliths with Monagrillo pottery at one inland Panamanian site. There is a complication here, however, in that the earliest radiocarbon date on the Monagrillo pottery at this site is only 1500 B.C. Nevertheless, in view of early direct-maize-find dates in Mesoamerica and Peru and of maize phytolith dates in

Ecuador, Cooke believes that maize quite probably dates to at least 3000 B.C. in Panama.

The maize-Monagrillo 3000 B.C. date is not, however, as advanced as the sedentary agricultural threshold. Cooke speculates that Monagrillo residence may have been seasonal with a shore-to-interior shifting. Unfortunately, the Panamanian record from 1000 to 300 B.C. is still skimpy; but, presumably, it was during these centuries that maize, beans, root crops, and tree crops were extended or exchanged over most of Panama. The large-grained South American maize, or Pollo-like maize, appears in Panama at this time as well. By 300 B.C. settled village farming life was fully established, and it is also at about this time that painted pottery styles first appear in Panama. In the chronological interval between the end of the Monagrillo pottery tradition and the appearance of the painted wares, it seems likely that plastic-decorated or scarified wares were the predominant styles, such as those identified by the names Sarigua and Guacamayo. Not much is known of these, but they relate to the scarified Concepcion pottery discussed by Haberland.

The period from 300 B.C. to A.D. 500 saw the rise of the Panamanian polychrome pottery styles and also the rise of chiefdoms. An early style in this tradition is the Tonosi Three-Color Ware, which features narrative decorative motifs of chiefs, traders, and group activities. These artistic representations of growing cultural complexity are supported by status burials and large central sites. The period from A.D. 500 to 1500 can be further subdivided into the Conte (A.D. 500–700), Macaracas (A.D. 700–1100), Parita (A.D. 1100–1300), and El Hatillo (A.D. 1300–1500) phases. These cultures have important central sites, such as the apparent politico-religious precincts at El Caño or Sitio Conte, and they were well known for their rich status burials of important chiefs. And it was with such chiefly cultures and societies that the Spaniards had their first contacts in central Pacific Panama.

Cooke referred to recent researches in eastern Panama, or Darien Province, especially those by Drolet. Pottery there is estimated to date at least as early as the beginning of the Christian era, and there are later ceramics and rock-cut tombs reminiscent of the later pre-Columbian chiefdoms of Colombia. Darien, however, remains as a "gap" in archaeological knowledge, and it is to this "gap" and lower Central American–northern Colombian relationships that Warwick Bray addressed his paper.

Lower Central America as Seen from Colombia

As was noted previously, a lower Central American–South American border or frontier is a shadowy construct. Bray's effort in this volume is perhaps the first to address this question systematically. His geographical focus is the north Colombian lowlands, from the Gulf of Uraba to western Venezuela.

There are some projectile point finds in northern Colombia which suggest a Paleo-Indian presence, but the basic early lithic tradition is the Abrian percussion industry, which lacks points. This Abrian tradition has early (ca. 11,000 B.C.) beginnings, but the technology seems to persist until much later; indeed, it provides the stone artifact component found with the earliest north Colombian ceramics at ca. 3000 B.C. The Abrian industry appears to be one of woodworking tools. Its northernmost expressions would seem to be the preceramic Cerro Mangote and Talamancan complexes of Panama, so that an ancient cultural base and union of Isthmian America and northwestern South America is suggested. I once posited a "Northwestern South American Littoral Tradition" as such an entity (Willey 1971: 262–63), but Bray makes clear that this would be too restricted an environmental or ecological limitation, for the Abrian cultures are present in the Colombian wooded uplands and may have their origins there.

The story of agricultural development in northern Colombia is much like that in Panama, including the ambiguities of dating and firm evidence. Bray, in summarizing, suggests four stages. Stage 1 was an initial stage of roots, tubers, and palm products, with manioc presumably a part of it. While he does not specify dates directly, his other statements make it appear that this stage antedates 3000 B.C. Stage 2 probably spans the period from 3000 B.C., and the inception of pottery, to the beginnings of more complex cultures at about 300 B.C. Manioc, of both the bitter and sweet varieties, was a part of this stage, and maize probably was as well. Given the presence of maize phytoliths in coastal Ecuador at 6000 B.C., and its antiquity in southern Mesoamerica, maize may very well have been present in some places in northern Colombia even in Bray's Stage 1; however, it is unlikely that it became economically important until Stage 3. Stage 3 saw the mixed manioc-maize economy which existed in both northern Colombia and Panama until historic times. A Stage 4 which overlaps with Stage 3 is suggested. It refers to landscape modifications resulting from intensive farming, such as large-scale clearings and artificially raised fields. This kind of activity probably began sometime after the beginning of the Christian era and was well established by A.D. 500, the time of the north Colombian chiefdoms.

The earliest ceramics of northern Colombia are subsumed by Bray under the designation of the "Tecomate Tradition." The period is 3000–1000 B.C., corresponding in large part to his agricultural Stage 2. Puerto Hormiga, Monsu, Canapote, Barlovento, and other incision-punctation-decorated ceramic complexes are included in the Tecomate Tradition. Vessels are uniformly simple, and a subglobular bowl or tecomate is a commonly shared form. Sites of this tradition also share, as mentioned, in the long-lived

Abrian stone tool tradition. The ecological settings are those of coastal, estuarine, and riverine shell mounds. There is no definite evidence for agriculture, although I would suspect it, at least as a subsistence adjunct. As observed earlier, the Colombian Tecomate Tradition is clearly related to Panamanian Monagrillo. There the type site does not offer direct evidence of farming, but, it will be recalled, maize phytoliths were found in an inland site of the culture.

After 1000 B.C. significant change occurs, undoubtedly as agriculture became more important, and this change is paralleled in ceramic innovations and changes. These developments must be followed in Bray's text; they are complex, and he has already provided an admirable synthesis. In attempting to synthesize even further, I would say that the half-millennium from 1000 to 500 B.C. is poorly known. After the latter date, we might factor out two long-lived ceramic traditions—a western one, which features or emphasizes the plastic decorative techniques of incision-punctation-modeling, and an eastern one where multicolor painting is dominant.

The Momil site is representative of the western ceramic tradition. Bray, incidentally, points to similarities between Momil and La Montaña and El Bosque cultures which Snarskis defined from Atlantic Costa Rica. In later times the western tradition may be represented by the Tierra Alta pottery styles, the Estorbo style, and the Cupica phases, the latter of north Pacific Colombia; and in later times the ceramics of the (historic) chiefdoms of the San Jorge region and the Sinu (Betanci).

The eastern or painted tradition may have its roots in the Llanos of Venezuela. There is a suggestion of it in the Rio Rancheria region of northeastern Colombia, whose distinctive polychrome wares date to the late centuries B.C. As Bray indicates, there are cross-ties in ceramic forms, painting, and design motifs which correlate this painted tradition with the styles of central Panama; and Snarskis has also noted possible connections as far north as the Siteia complex of Caribbean Nicaragua.

Metallurgy, in gold and gold-copper alloys, spread from South America into the Isthmus in the early centuries A.D. The earliest metal ornaments of Panama are quite Colombian in style; later, as in the well-known Cocle goldwork of central Panama, the styles are clearly local. Bray remarks upon the "Darien gap" in gold distributions, but he is of the opinion that this is more a factor of research and exploration than a reality. He points to the early Venado Beach (Canal Zone) gold finds as probable samples of an as-yet-unappreciated Darien goldwork style.

Bray devotes considerable space to the controversy of manioc versus maize. In their remote origins these important food plants were, almost certainly, of lowland South American and upland Mesoamerican derivations, respectively. But there is considerable evidence to indicate that both were spread and interchanged at very early dates. Both were important subsistence items in northern Colombia, Panama, and Costa Rica by the later part of the first millennium B.C. It is difficult to say just how and where maize did supplant manioc as the most important staple; however, it seems highly probable that maize farming was associated with the rise of the largest population concentrations and the greatest socio-political complexity in the later pre-Columbian periods. This is true both for lower Central America and for the pre-Columbian and historic chiefdoms of northern Colombia. South American maize as a vital factor in this improved and expanded agriculture has been covered in this volume as well as seminar discussions. Bray is hesitant to leave it like this. He emphasizes, instead, that a Pollo-type maize is the archetypal Intermediate Area maize, developed somewhere between Ecuador and lower Central America. In this sense it is South American, but it is too simple to look at the mounting cultural complexity that one sees in northern Colombia and lower Central America after ca. 300 B.C. as the result of a sudden, explosive maize-carrying migration or diffusion out of South America.

A Chronological-Developmental Scheme for Lower Central America

Chronological-developmental schemes for archaeological areas have both advantages and disadvantages. For both methodological and practical reasons most archaeological research is conducted on relatively small regional scales. Certainly most archaeological research in lower Central America in the past has been so conducted. But, as more is known, there comes a logical point at which coordination of information among regions becomes a necessity. Archaeological research in lower Central America has now reached that point, and a broad frame of chronological reference is necessary for comparative study. At the same time, it is known that the developmental aspect of such schemes carries certain problems. Cultural development over large geographical areas rarely marched along in synchronous uniformity in all of its parts; indeed, certain kinds of phenomena which occurred in some regions may never have occurred in other regions. These matters have been dealt with in some detail elsewhere in the archaeological literature (Rowe 1960; Price 1976) and need not concern us longer here. While realizing the theoretical value of keeping culture content and culture development as free as possible from chronological restrictions, the lower Central American seminar group was of the opinion that a general chronological frame was of importance as a heuristic device at the present stage of archaeological knowledge in the area.

Accordingly, a scheme of six numbered periods was agreed upon. These are, admittedly, very provisional constructs which will undoubtedly be revised or eliminated as research progresses. The dating of these periods is based largely upon radiocarbon determinations which, as Lange has shown in his introductory paper, are reasonably numerous, although still too few and rather spottily distributed over lower Central America. The dating of the periods is also aided to a degree by comparisons with adjacent Mesoamerican sequences and general Mesoamerican chronology. Unfortunately, lower Central American cultures do not display widespread and easily recognizable horizontal stylistic features—as is the case in both Mesoamerica and Peru—which assist the archaeologist in devising an area-wide chronological scheme. As a result, we are thrown back upon general cultural content, or developmental characteristics, for period criteria. Nevertheless, conscious of the need to make a beginning, the seminar essayed the following period chronology.

Period I (?–8000 B.C.)

This the the Early Lithic or Paleo-Indian period. By analogy with North American data it may be assumed to include a late Pleistocene big game hunting tradition, characterized by certain bifacially flaked projectile points; and, as we have seen, such points have turned up, in surface contexts, in lower Central America. The degree, however, to which such a Pleistocene hunting strategy characterized the human populations of this period remains a question. Other lifeways, signaled by other lithic industries, such as the Abrian of Colombia, may also have played a part in this period. The relationships of the one—the big game hunters and the projectile point tradition—to the other—the forest hunters-collectors of the percussion industries—are still to be determined.

Period II (8000 B.C.–4000 B.C.)

Again, reasoning by analogy with other parts of the Americas, we might anticipate an Archaic-type culture for this period. This evokes the developmental model of various specialized hunting-collecting strategies replacing a more general Pleistocene hunting existence. There is some evidence from some parts of lower Central America, as in Costa Rica and Honduras, to support this (e.g., stemmed dart points); elsewhere, as in Panama, there are suggestions that a percussion tool tradition, featuring woodworking implements, as well as various coastal adaptations, may characterize the period.

Period III (4000 B.C.–1000 B.C.)

This period marks the transition from foraging economies to dependence on plant cultivation; and, as such, it has some parallels to Late Archaic–type intervals in other parts of the Americas. There is good inferential evidence that both manioc and maize appear during this period, although the degrees to which they were important subsistence factors remain to be determined. At about 3000 B.C. ceramics appear in some places (Panama, northern Colombia); however, it is unlikely that this corresponds to any significant socio-economic change.

Period IV (1000 B.C.–A.D. 500)

This period marks the threshold of sedentary village life based on farming. As such, it is comparable, in a developmental sense, to the Mesoamerican Early Preclassic or Early Formative period, whose beginnings are usually placed at ca. 2000 B.C. This would imply that the beginnings of sedentary agriculture are a millennium earlier in southern Mesoamerica than in lower Central America. Such a conclusion, however, should be viewed with caution at our present state of knowledge. The consensus of our colleagues is that Monagrillo of Panama (ca. 3000 B.C. for its beginnings) may be incipient horticultural, but it is not truly a sedentary farming situation. The nature of the evidence, as we know it, now leaves some room to challenge this. Also, sedentary farming communities have been reported from the coast of Ecuador at about 3000 B.C. (Lathrap 1975). While this by no means indicates that similar economies and societies were established in lower Central America at such an early date, it is further reason to give pause in any interpretations which would see lower Central America as only a delayed marginal reflection of the developments of Mesoamerica.

Various authors of the present volume have indicated that the earlier part of this period, from 1000 B.C. to 500 B.C., is not well documented; indeed, the record in most places east and south of the Mesoamerican frontier zone does not offer much until about 300 B.C., after which time there is rapidly accumulating evidence for the rise of sedentary villages and, beyond this, large villages, hierarchial settlement patterns, and other evidences of complex society. Thus, our Period IV not only includes the sedentary farming threshold, but it goes on to the emergence of chiefdom-type societies in the early centuries A.D. Certainly by A.D. 500, or the close of the period, this type of society was characteristic of much of lower Central America. Again, with this threshold, there is an apparent developmental lag vis-à-vis Mesoamerica, where such societies were definitely present by the beginning of the Olmec horizon at ca. 1200 B.C.

Period V (A.D. 500–1000)

It was more difficult to characterize this and the succeeding period in terms of socio-economic and socio-political development than the preceding periods. It was a period of notable population growth. The seminar noted that it was a time of more rapid cultural change than what had gone before; however, it must be remembered that much of this change is measured in pottery and ritual artifacts, things which were nonexistent or in short supply prior to our Period IV. Changes in trade routes, both within and outside of lower Central America, were noted for the period. In connection with this, we should note that goldwork (essentially southern in its origins) now tends to replace jade (of Mesoamerican derivation) as the important precious commodity.

Period VI (A.D. 1000–1550)

Regionalism in ceramics and other manufactures, which had begun to be manifest in the previous period, is now more marked. It was suggested in the seminar that this may have been a result of conscious attempts on the part of population groups to identify themselves ethnically and politically in a time of growing intergroup competition. Such competition is further reflected in fortified centers or capital towns. Trade contacts with both Mesoamerica and South America continue during the period, although trade patterns show some change in comparison to earlier periods.

This chronological-developmental sequence, which has been referred to in most of the regional papers in this volume, will also be used to provide a general chronological structure for the following portion of this summary.

Interpretations

After a preliminary review of the several regional data papers, including a critical discussion of these, the members of the lower Central American seminar devoted a series of sessions to various themes or cultural subsystems. These included ecological adaptations and subsistence, socio-political inferences to be drawn from a range of archaeological data, questions of trade and other contacts, both within and beyond the formal limits of lower Central America, and related questions of cultural development. These interpretive examinations of the data were carried out with reference to both culture history and process. In pursuing such a thematic or subsystemic approach in the context of culture history, it is obvious that there will be considerable overlap. Ecology and subsistence relate to demography; this, in turn, ties to socio-political development; and the latter links to trade, group interaction, and militarism. Consequently, attempting to relate all of this in summary fashion means that there will be some repetition or, at least, some looking at the same sets of facts from different perspectives; but it seemed to us that such an analytic-synthetic procedure was a useful exercise at the present state of knowledge and data control in lower Central American archaeology, and I will attempt to identify the main lines of seminar thinking on these matters.

Ecological Adaptations and Subsistence

It became apparent, early in our conferences, that lower Central America presented a mosaic of relatively small ecological zones or niches. But it was also pointed out that these zones or niches, although numerous for lower Central America as a whole, were repetitive in type. That is, a coastal stretch would abut upon wooded foothills; small alluvial valleys would intersect there; the higher forested mountains of the cordillera would rise at no great distance away, and so on. All of this meant that settings for human habitation and subsistence could vary greatly over relatively small geographic spaces; but it also meant that such variation could have been exploited by single social and cultural groups, at least under certain cultural conditions. For Period I (prior to 8000 B.C.) our data were too few to offer much in the way of conclusions or even intelligent speculations on just how this ecological niche variability had been exploited. Scattered projectile point finds gave hints of a Paleo-Indian big game hunter presence but little more. However, from the Colombian end of our survey, there is evidence that the concept of a uniform big game hunter horizon for lower Central America and the larger Intermediate Area offers much too simple an understanding of what went on in late Pleistocene times. The Abrian percussion industry suggests another kind of adjustment; variation within this industry, or among Abrian-like industries, would appear to relate to highland, littoral, or riverine settings in its artifact inventory modifications.

For Period II (8000 B.C.–4000 B.C.) artifact and site variability is seen in Panama when comparing the upland Talamanca culture with that of the contemporaneous Cerro Mangote culture of the Pacific littoral. The artifact complexes of both of these cultures would appear to have derivations in the Abrian tradition, and there are some similarities between the two; however, Talamanca shows a forest collecting-and-hunting subsistence while Cerro Mangote combines hunting-collecting with an important dependence upon marine foods. Both complexes share scrapers and cutting tools; but Tala-manca features heavy woodworking implements while Cerro Mangote emphasizes pebble chopper-grinders that would have been serviceable in plant grinding.

In Period III (4000 B.C.–1000 B.C.) the Boquete culture, which succeeds the Talamanca at about 3000 B.C., has a number of new tools, including some polished stone chopping and, possibly, digging implements. These changes have been interpreted as marking a shift from plant collecting to cultivation. Tree crops were apparently important to these people, yielding foods such as palm nuts and algarroba pods; however, the degree to which such trees may have been tended or cultivated remains uncertain. Manioc may have been grown by the Boquete communities, although there is no direct evidence for this. On the Pacific coast the Monagrillo culture succeeds the Cerro Mangote, in what appears to be a gradual transition in this setting at about 3000 B.C. The most notable artifactual innovation in Monagrillo is pottery; however, some investigators are of the opinion that both manioc and maize cultivation may have appeared at this time. The economic importance of these plants may have been of a limited or incipient nature at first, but, subsequently, both could have spread into the interior to settings like that of the Boquete culture.

Monagrillo pottery, with its simple vessel forms and incised-punctated decoration, appears to relate to what Bray designated as the "Tecomate Pottery Tradition" in northern Colombia. The sites of this tradition are often shell mounds, and the locations are on the littoral or in estuarine or riverine settings. A hunting–fishing–plant-collecting economy, like that of Monagrillo, is implied. There is no direct evidence for agriculture; however, an incipient cultivation of manioc, and perhaps maize, must be recognized as a reasonable possibility.

The archaeological histories—to a large extent the inferred histories—of these two plants, manioc and maize, have been discussed in some of the data papers (Bray, Cooke, and Sharer), and the topic was dealt with at length in seminar discussions. I believe that the generalizations with which most American archaeologists are familiar still hold. Manioc is of northern South American lowland origin, and it spread from here northward into lower Central America and, eventually, into southern Mesoamerica. Its antiquity as a cultigen is probably considerable, although this is largely undemonstrated by hard evidence. Maize most probably had its origins in the highlands of southern Mesoamerica and from here spread southward into lower Central America and South America. Beyond this, and when we come to specifics, there is considerable room for argument. There is some evidence from the northern Colombian lowlands and from the Atlantic watershed in Costa Rica that manioc precedes maize as a staple, and future investigations may bear this out with reference to much of lower Central America; however, early maize finds in Peru and maize phytolith discoveries in Ecuador and Panama would indicate the spread of this plant well to the south in Period III times or even earlier. What we may eventually come to know is that these two plants were adapted to local settings, at various times and places, and that their archaeological history is one of great complexity that defies easy generalization.

However this question, or these questions, about the early appearances and successions of manioc and maize may eventually be resolved, what does seem clear for lower Central America and northern Colombia is that an economically successful and expanding agriculture did not come into being until Period IV (1000 B.C.–A.D. 500); and this is linked to maize. This success is reflected in settlement pattern changes, for example, in both Panama and Colombia, which occur in the late centuries B.C. At this time we have the first sedentary villages in interior valley tracts suitable for intensive farming. Cooke, Bray, and Snarskis, the latter with his view of his Costa Rican data, all agree that this success is to be correlated with a new and improved variety of maize which has been called a large-grained South

American maize. Bray, however, has cautioned that this term may be a misnomer, for this genetically improved maize may have developed *in situ* in lower Central America or, at least, within the Intermediate Area.

During our seminar discussions, some pertinent observations were made about the cultivation of manioc and maize and the potential of each for social and cultural growth and change. With manioc, more food, as measured in caloric value, can be grown on smaller plots of ground than is the case with maize. As a result, it does not set up the same kind of land pressures as maize farming. Manioc cultivation takes less work and less labor organization than maize cultivation; manioc does not require the same kind of scheduled harvesting as maize, nor does manioc require special storage facilities, for the plant can be kept in the earth until ready for use, even in a wet climate. All of these circumstances suggest that manioc would be more compatible with smaller, simpler societies than would maize growing. Maize, and especially the maize-beans combination, is nutritionally more complete and satisfactory than manioc. It, too, can be grown simply or minimally; but to make it a successful economic staple demands a degree of agricultural expansion—the clearing of extensive fields, scheduled planting and harvesting, and, to continue this expansion, labor-costly techniques of raised field or terrace constructions. All of these make maize the amenable concomitant of expansionistic societies, in contrast to manioc. Bray, Cooke, and Snarskis all made this point, either directly or indirectly, in describing the rise of chiefdoms during the later part of Period IV in northern Colombia and the eastern part of lower Central America.

The same point was also made by Sharer and Sheets at the northern and western end of lower Central America. In southern Mesoamerica the main subsistence reliance was on seed crops—maize and beans—from Early Pre-classic times (ca. 2000 B.C.–1000 B.C.) forward. They speculate that root and tree crops probably were present there from early times, perhaps even prior to maize or to the rise of maize as the prime staple, but after the threshold of settled farming life the subsistence story through the rise of the Olmec chiefdoms and beyond is largely that of maize.

In summary, by A.D. 500 lower Central American life was based upon settled farming, probably maize farming in most places. By this time, complex societies or chiefdoms had appeared in most regions. The chiefdom type of organization dominated the area in the succeeding Periods V (A.D. 500–1000) and VI (A.D. 1000–1550); and this leads us to our next interpretive theme.

Socio-Political Inferences

A theoretical question, of general interest to archaeologists as well as to the members of the lower Central American seminar, concerns the processes by which foreign or outside influences may bring about social and political change in the receiving society. Salvadoran and Honduran data were looked at in this regard vis-à-vis Mesoamerica. In El Salvador it was assumed that simple village society had preceded Mesoamerican Olmec influences and that Olmec stimuli were important in changing these societies. A notable settlement aspect of this change was the establishment of a major politico-religious and commercial center at Chalchuapa in the western part of that country. This began at about 1200 B.C., and while local demographic and economic growth were undoubtedly necessary for the rise of such centers, it was conceded that contacts with the Olmec chiefdom, or chiefdoms, and their redistributive networks, were also a crucial factor in this development. The old question as to the degree to which this involved direct invasion or political conquest was raised and debated. It seemed clear that Chalchuapa had provided a node for the extraction of various goods from El Salvador as well as serving as a redistributive point for Olmec system exchange. This must have involved profit for Mesoamerican Olmec centers. Some political coercion and taxation may also have been involved, and an Olmec presence at Chalchuapa is certainly suggested by the elite art and large architecture at that site. No resolution of the conquest question was made beyond this, but it was the seminar's consensus that the mechanisms of trade, with the Olmec in the position of the patron to the Salvadoran client, were important processes in this Mesoamericanization of a periphery. After about 400 B.C., with the waning of Olmec power and its commercial network, what appears to have been an indigenous Salvadoran chiefdom continued at Chalchuapa and was evolving toward a state-type political structure until the disaster of the Ilopango eruption at about A.D. 250. The eastward extent of Chalchuapa's influence remains speculative, although Sharer made the point that Quelepa, a large site in eastern El Salvador, probably lay beyond the hegemony of Chalchuapa.

After recovering from the Ilopango phenomenon, El Salvador about A.D. 500 probably was tributary, at least in its commercial status, to a Chorti kingdom with its capital at Copan. Such a Chorti kingdom and trade network had come into being following the weakening of a Teotihuacan-Kaminaljuyu alliance and network, and Copan appears to have monitored the obsidian trade, originating in the Guatemalan highland sources, through most of the Late Classic period. Sharer describes the settlement system of the Chorti state as multi-tiered, with four levels of sites. The Chorti state withered with the Classic Maya collapse. Later, in the Postclassic period, the Pokomam nation of the Guatemalan highlands pushed south and east into El Salvador, replicating, to a degree, the structure and territorial control of the Chorti.

The archaeology of the Honduran periphery provides evidence for similar inferences concerning chiefdom and state formations. In western Honduras the Jaral phase of the Los Naranjos site shows Olmec contacts and gives evidence of a ranked society by 800 B.C. Afterwards, throughout Late Preclassic and Classic times, central places, a tiered settlement system, signs of warfare, and trade competition all indicate an evolution comparable to that of El Salvador. In the Postclassic the western Honduran centers of power shift to the north, to the Caribbean, and towns such as Naco appear as outposts of water-oriented trading systems directed out of Mexico.

One aspect of these contacts between lower Central America and the trading states of Mesoamerica relates to a statement made earlier in this summary that lower Central American relationships with Mesoamerica are to be understood in the context of two Mesoamericas. The reference there was to the highland and lowland Maya spheres. Actually it was more complicated than that. Some of the contacts, especially the organized trading contacts of Postclassic times, were Mexican or Mexicanized Maya.

Socio-political development stimulated through commercial contacts is also well attested in that far periphery, northeastern Honduras. In our sequence review we have referred to Mesoamerican (including Olmec) ceramic evidences in this region in Preclassic or Formative times. The early archaeological record here, however, is obscure, and it is not until the A.D. 500–1000 period that Healy finds settlement evidences suggestive of chiefly-type societies. Subsequently, after A.D. 1000, the data of both archaeology and history reveal a system of chiefs and paramount chiefs in a complex political hierarchy. Papayeca was one such important capital, and it was tied in to a Mexican-originated trading network.

In reflecting upon these Salvadoran and Honduran data, and in the interchange of arguments, the seminar participants reached general agreement about a processual model that could be described as follows. Socio-political systems, in competition and cooperation with other systems, will often adapt to effect a better articulation with more successful systems. Thus, they may become more state-like in the handling of goods and information and in the exercise of authority than previously. In this way, a society like that of Papayeca in northeast Honduras develops toward the norms of statehood as a result of its Mexican ties. These ties, in the beginning, may have been altogether commercial, but it is likely that other types of exchange also come into being if the contact is maintained over any period of time. Actual Mexicans may have held some posts of authority within the Papayecan community; but this need not indicate that the town is either a colony or a conquered province ruled in all matters from distant centers in Mexico.

For Greater Nicoya, Lange and Haberland felt that there was little evidence for Mesoamerican-stimulated socio-political change. For the Costa Rican portions of the region, at least, there are no large centers, no special architecture, and no tiered settlement organization. A chiefly society is indicated only by burial wealth. Special grave goods include the carved stone metates (or seats?), jades, and carved mace heads.

In viewing Greater Nicoya from the standpoint of political development and Mesoamerican stimulus for change, Paul Healy took an opposing view to that of Lange and Haberland. Here, it may be significant that his perspective comes from the Rivas sector of Nicaragua rather than Nicoya proper. It is his opinion that the Rivas societies of the Middle and Late Polychrome periods (Periods V and VI) were "basically Mesoamerican-derived to begin with, and these groups brought with them lots of changes, including sociopolitical changes" (personal communication 1981).

These questions about the Greater Nicoya archaeological cultures—questions which could not be answered readily, at least to the satisfaction of all of the seminar participants—led to a more general theoretical consideration of the chiefdom definition. The consensus was that an essential set of chiefly criteria comprised the inheritance of status, wealth, and power. It was also generally conceded that organized trade, including long-distance trade, could be maintained at a simpler, egalitarian level of political organization; however, it was noted that trade management can lead to control, taxation, and profit-taking—all steps toward hereditary consolidation of wealth.

It was suggested that the accumulation and placement of burial wealth was one of the first signs of chiefdom organization, or at least a step in that direction. Was this something that had been allowed in an otherwise egalitarian society because it did not present dangers of wealth concentrations? On the contrary, it had the effect of dissipating such concentration. But the classic anthropological-archaeological question remained. How was grave wealth, as represented by the Nicoya carved stone paraphernalia, to be translated into socio-political inferences about the society in question?

Another classic question addressed concerned the mechanisms whereby lineage or kin ties were replaced by more centralized power. Public works, large-scale monuments, or constructions—giving evidence of centralized labor organization—were generally seen as the best clues to such a social and political change. There is nothing particularly new in these questions or in the answers tentatively given; but they indicate the kinds of problems the seminar confronted as it began to move from basic field data to higher levels of interpretation.

Moving farther south, Snarskis interprets the simple village sites of his La Montaña and Chaparron phases (both ca. 1000 B.C.–500 B.C.) as indicative of an egalitarian tribal society. El Bosque and Pavas, of the first half of the first millennium A.D., are, in his opinion, chiefly societies. The evidence seems about the same as that marshaled by Lange for his Greater Nicoya cultures. Anything in the way of large constructions or public works is generally lacking, but there is an abundance of grave materials—again, jades, carved seats, and the like. Warfare and human sacrifice are indicated by the presence of trophy heads on the seats or carved metates. After about A.D. 500–600 new pottery styles appear, and the carved stone objects disappear. And then in the late period after A.D. 900–1000 in the La Cabaña and Cartago cultures, we see more signs of the mature or advanced chiefdom—platform constructions, stone causeways, compact fortified sites, and hydraulic management. There are also regional settlement hierarchies of two or three tiers. In sum, the social evolution here seems somewhat more advanced—at least in terms of the tribal-chiefdom-state model—than that of Greater Nicoya even though the regions in question are geographically more remote from Mesoamerica.

For Greater Chiriqui, Haberland speculates that the earliest Aguas Buenas sites—his first pottery horizon—may have been egalitarian villages at ca. 800 B.C. These may have been succeeded by small chiefdoms; and, late in the Aguas Buenas period, these were followed by a system of chiefs and paramount chiefs. The big Barriles site, with its stone statuary indicative of rank and warfare and its elaborately carved table-like metates (altars?), would be the primary center of such a paramount chiefdom of the first half of the first millennium A.D. This kind of a social order persisted into the later Classic Chiriqui culture of the region.

Haberland, in his seminar presentations, questioned craftsman specialization and the degree of such specialization in these lower Central American chiefdoms. He made the suggestion that for Greater Chiriqui there may have been itinerant professional potters and metalworkers. The standardized quality of Chiriqui Bisquit ware, comparable in his opinion to the standardizations seen in Peruvian Chimu pottery or, perhaps, Mesoamerican Plumbate ware, was the basis for this suggestion. In this context Sheets made the observation that there might have been such professional obsidian workers in the Chorti kingdom of the Zapotitan Valley. In goldwork the complex techniques of lost-wax casting and *mise-en-couleur* surface treatments of gold-copper alloys, as well as the masterly conceptual and stylistic renderings of the ornaments, imply full-time specialization which might have been carried out by traveling smiths. It was suggested that the chiefs may have been smiths. Bray's extended discussions of north Colombian metallurgy and the widespread similarities of gold products, extending from Colombia well into lower Central America, gave still greater strength to the opinion that goldworkers, of whatever institutional status or social background, may have crossed the probable ethnic or political boundaries defined by ceramic styles. There was considerable seminar argument on this matter of specialized craftsmen. Our consensus was that while full-time specialization may have existed in some instances, as in the example of the goldworkers, lower Central America was, for the most part, characterized by part-time craftsmen, and that large-scale craft specialization as an institution is more compatible with the state level of organization than that of the chiefdoms.

For central Panama, Cooke considers the semi-sedentary early societies and those of the sedentary agricultural early levels as egalitarian. The first evidence for chiefdoms comes in the 300 B.C.–A.D. 500 period, or toward the latter part of our major Period IV, and such chiefdoms flourished and proliferated from then until the end of the pre-Columbian era. The Panamanian chiefdoms were characterized by endemic warfare, the taking of trophy heads, elaborate burial customs for the elite, and, later, by public works. Cooke relied heavily upon ethnohistoric accounts of sixteenth-century chiefdoms but cautioned that these may often have been idealized. The importance of the hereditary factor in chieftainship is somewhat ambiguous, and he suggests that a combination of military prowess and heredity was probably decisive in filling the post. References to slavery in the accounts raised questions about the conditions of such slaves. Were they only captives in war?

Bray's Colombian data, both archaeological and ethnohistorical, conform to Cooke's conclusions. It seems likely that some of the northern Colombian chiefdoms of late times were territorially more extensive than the Panamanian ones.

This scan of regional evidence and inference about socio-political development can be readily summarized into our chronological developmental framework. For Periods I (?–8000 B.C.) and II (8000 B.C.–4000 B.C.), society must have been organized on an autonomous-band basis, with the good possibility of seasonal variation of micro-band/macro-band groupings and a greater settling in into ecological niches in the later millennia. The sedentary small autonomous village was probably the prevailing mode of organization in Period III (4000 B.C.–1000 B.C.), although a more complex chiefdom-type organization may have been present in western El Salvador and Honduras by the beginning of the first millennium B.C. In Period IV (1000 B.C.–A.D. 500), chiefly societies came into being early in the period in most of El Salvador and western Honduras; later in the period it appears that a Mesoamerican state-type society arose around Chalchuapa. However, it is unlikely that this kind of socio-political organization ever spread to the east and south. In the later part of this period of socio-political change we find good inferential evidence for chiefdoms throughout most of eastern Honduras, Nicaragua, Costa Rica, and Panama. The data are variable, however, suggesting greater political centralization and more rigidly structured rank societies in some regions than in others. Subsequently, in Periods V (A.D. 500–1000) and VI (A.D. 1000–1550), there is evidence for a continued trend toward political centralization, competition, and warfare; however, there are no clear indications of the kinds or levels of complexity in lower Central America that characterize the developed states of either Mexico or Peru.

Trade

Trade is not the only process of contact among societies, but it is certainly one of the most tangible or evidential from an archaeological standpoint.

Furthermore, evidences of trade or exchange in material goods usually alert
the archaeologist to the possibility of other types of contact, such as information flow. We have referred to trade in all of the basic data papers, it
was dealt with at length in the seminar discussions, I have alluded to it
throughout the resume of the socio-political inferences we drew from our
archaeological data, and I continue the discussion here.

From his perspective of southern Mesoamerica, Robert Sharer examined
trading contacts between that area and regions to the south and east. His
use of Renfrew's model, or set of typological models, of trade emphasized
the close relationship between that institution and the growth of political
institutions. The simpler trade models probably characterized our earlier
Periods I through III, or up until about 1000 B.C., although it should be
pointed out that at some time prior to 1000 B.C. Mesoamerican trade was
moving onto more complex levels of organization. The Olmec horizon,
which can be dated to 1300 B.C., or perhaps even earlier, was characterized
by nonegalitarian societies and the maintenance of extractive and distributional centers which pertain to Renfrew's "central place redistribution"
model. Shortly after this, in our lower Central American Period IV (1000
B.C.–A.D. 500), the evidences of trading contacts radiating out of southern
Mesoamerica begin to appear in El Salvador and western Honduras; before
the close of this period, signs of Mesoamerican-directed trading activities
from bases such as Late Preclassic Izapa and Kaminaljuyu and, later, from
Classic Maya lowland centers are manifest in El Salvador, Honduras, Nicaragua, and Costa Rica. At the lower Central American end of such exchange, as we have seen, chiefdoms and chiefly trading centers were springing
up, and the causal force of trade as a mechanism in societal and cultural
growth has to be reckoned with. By the later periods, or from A.D. 500 until
the Spanish Conquest, it is likely that trade as an institution involved, to
some degree or another, all of Renfrew's more complex models—"central
place market-exchange," "freelance (middleman) trading," "emissary trading," and "colonial enclaves" and "ports-of-trade." Indeed, as Sharer argues,
some of these forms may have been present earlier.

But what of the substance of trade, and how can we summarize this for
lower Central America? Presumably this trade operated on two principal
levels: one of essentially utilitarian materials and products and another of
nonutilitarian items. In practical archaeological analysis this dichotomy is
often difficult to maintain, but the seminar made some attempt to sort things
out along these lines.

To begin with, it was the general seminar assumption that exchange of
foodstuffs or utility trade did not involve long-distance trade in any large
way. This is an assumption carried over, I think, from what we know or
hypothesize about Mesoamerica and other parts of pre-Columbian America.
It needs further examination in lower Central America as well as elsewhere,

but because of the limitations of archaeological recovery, especially in a tropical area, it is difficult to verify or disprove. I think we should keep an open mind on the subject, especially for lower Central America, where distances between rather diverse environments are not always great and where the transportation of such things as maize or root crops between regions may have been of economic importance. With regard to cacao, in a sense a foodstuff but of a very special sort, it was generally conceded that it may have been an important item of long-distance trade on the Meso-american model.

For obsidian, that prize material for archaeological trading studies, there is firmer ground for postulating and proving long-distance distributions. In lower Central America it is found in the northwestern and western portions of the area. These are, of course, the regions nearest the raw obsidian sources of Mesoamerica. Sheets stated that all of El Salvador and all of Honduras, except the northeastern region of the latter country, were also within a Mesoamerican core-and-blade technological tradition. Beyond this, to the south and east, one moves out of this technological tradition and pretty much out of the obsidian distribution range. Lange informed us that in Greater Nicoya and Atlantic Costa Rica what little obsidian is found indicates access only to finished products, and there is no obsidian debitage in the sites.

Jade, or jadeite, in lower Central America outruns the distribution of obsidian, extending beyond El Salvador and western Honduras into northern Costa Rica. The sources of this jade are in the Maya highlands of Guatemala. In Costa Rica it appears both as finished objects and as blanks which were reworked locally (into effigy-celt pendants and the like). This jade trade was active in Period IV, but it began to drop off in the Period IV–V transition, and, as has been noted elsewhere, the jade trade tended to be replaced by gold as the most valued elite material. Some of the early Costa Rican jade celt-pendants and other elite ornaments are reminiscent of Olmec carvings of Mesoamerica, and actual Classic Maya carved jades have been found in later Costa Rican graves. This suggests that, from early on, there may have been a certain amount of information flow accompanying the trade items.

Other Mesoamerican trade items found in Greater Nicoya contexts in-clude occasional Teotihuacan-style tripod vessels (possibly from Classic Pe-riod Kaminaljuyu sources), Ulua marble vases, and Plumbate ware. All of these occur only in limited quantity.

Lange suggested that, in exchange for Mesoamerican jade and other items, the Greater Nicoyans proffered cloth dyed with shells of the *Murex* sp. (available in the local Pacific waters), cacao, and medicinal or drug plants. In the Postclassic we know that Nicoya Polychrome pottery was traded widely into Mesoamerica.

In an attempt to provide a synthesis, or synthetic framework, of Meso-

american–lower Central American trade and other contacts, Lange set forth
what he designated as a buffer-zone model of interaction. Such a buffer
zone would be the geographical area of alternating Mesoamerican expansions and retractions into lower Central America. This has been alluded to
in my opening remarks with reference to a boundary or a frontier between
the two areas. The buffer zone would include central and eastern El Salvador
(western El Salvador being considered a part of Mesoamerica), most of
western and central Honduras, and the Greater Nicoya region of Pacific
Nicaragua–Costa Rica.[2] These regions were influenced, by trade and other
mechanisms, successively, from Mesoamerica in Olmec (900–400 B.C.),
Teotihuacan-Maya (A.D. 400–550), Classic Maya (A.D. 550–900), and Mexican expansionist (A.D. 750–1500) times. There was also some trade and
counter-influence from these regions back to Mesoamerica. This probably
began in Mesoamerican Preclassic times, although on this early level the
main south-to-north flow was probably in raw materials of which we have
little or no trace. Subsequently, after the Maya hiatus (A.D. 550–600), and
certainly with the beginning of the Maya collapse (ca. A.D. 800), lower
Central American influences into Mesoamerica (as seen in the Nicoya Polychromes) involved manufactured goods and probably some degree of information flow.

What of the lands to the south and east of the buffer zone? The Costa
Rican Meseta Central and Atlantic watershed have some Mesoamerican
jade; and it will be recalled that the Chaparron pottery style of Period IV
has a zoned bichrome decorative technique which is reminiscent of Zoned
Bichrome Horizon pottery of Greater Nicoya and, beyond this, of Mesoamerican Preclassic pottery styles. Thus, there is a case for these central
and eastern Costa Rican regions having been a part of a Mesoamerican
trading orbit. At the same time, it will also be recalled that the La Montaña
ceramic complex of Atlantic Costa Rica, which is approximately coeval with
that of Chaparron, is strikingly different and reminiscent of South America
rather than Mesoamerica; and the same applies to the Siteia pottery complex
of Atlantic Nicaragua. Do we have here, in the Meseta Central of Costa
Rica, in Atlantic Costa Rica–Nicaragua, and in northeastern Honduras, a
zone of interpenetration between Mesoamerican and South American influences? If so, does such a zone lie intermediate between the Mesoamerican–lower Central American buffer zone and a South American–lower
Central American buffer zone?

Presumably, such a South American buffer zone would be in Panama
and perhaps Greater Chiriqui. As Bray has indicated, Colombian goldwork
influences are found in these regions in considerable strength. Undoubtedly,
trade, diffusion, and the possible movement of goldsmiths from South America into the Isthmus explain these influences. There is, thus, a parallel of
sorts to the spread of the Mesoamerican obsidian and jade traditions into

the northern buffer. Similarly, the ceramic styles of Panama, Greater Chiriqui, and parts of Costa Rica and Nicaragua show relationships, although by no means identities or even close similarities, to those of northern Colombia and northwestern Venezuela. Beyond saying these things, we cannot pursue the question much further in light of available data.

Some Developmental Questions and Hypotheses

Why did lower Central American societies and cultures develop the way that they did? Or, to put it in another way, why did lower Central America not develop more along the lines of Mesoamerica and Peru? The seminar discussed this at some length. It was pointed out in these discussions that value judgments were implicit in these questions, as indeed they are. Cooke observed that socio-political evolution is, after all, a nineteenth-century European concept, imbued with the values of its time and place; and Sheets noted that the "step up" to a new organizational threshold in such things as production, trade, and government is, at best, a mixed blessing. Socio-cultural organisms resist change and tend to adapt in ways that appear, at least at the time, to disturb old habits the least.

But, leaving value judgments aside, we are, as archaeologists, interested in explaining change and variability in the record. Why did the developmental profile in lower Central America differ in its configurations from those of Mesoamerica and Peru? Why was the development of the state, if not stunted, at least rejected in lower Central America? Cooke's model of the socio-cultural organism resisting and adapting to change opened up a line of questions and hypotheses addressed to the larger question.

This line of inquiry began with ecological concerns, especially the nature and availability of natural resources and the relationships of these to population sizes. The obvious proposition was put forward: Was sheer land size the initial determinative factor in the course of lower Central American cultural development? Were lower Central American populations, because of this, always smaller than those of the mainlands to the north and the south? If so, were there demographic inequalities, disadvantageous to lower Central America, dating back to Paleo-Indian times? We do not know, but the answer is probably yes. Larger land areas allowed for more hunting and more hunters on a general north-to-south drift through the Americas. Would the same be true on the early post-Pleistocene level, our Period II (8000 B.C.–4000 B.C.)? Again, viewed in the large, the answer is probably yes. At this point, however, it is perhaps fair to say that hunting-collecting bands of lower Central America at this time were probably as large as those exploiting various but similar ecological niches in Mesoamerica or South America; but there were fewer such niches and fewer bands.

When we move to the changeover from hunting-collecting to farming, this factor of fewer niches and fewer bands may have begun to work against subsistence efficiency and population growth in lower Central America. In Mesoamerica the greater number of ecological niches probably speeded up the agricultural revolution by offering a greater potential in the number and variety of cultigens and in the genetic improvement of some of these through niche-to-niche interchange and hybridization; and, to move away from the strictly ecological, this Mesoamerican multiplicity of niches and population groups could also have offered greater opportunities for cultural hybridization and change in various spheres of activity.

Another hypothesis was returned to at this point in the seminar discussions. It had been suggested by Snarskis and others that lower Central America offered, from region to region, a kind of redundance in natural resources. Suitable farmlands, water, salt, and materials for tools were available almost everywhere in adequate supply, at least for relatively small populations. On the other hand, there were few concentrations of resources that would lead to control of the same, with resultant complex trading monopolies developing around these. This situation would act as a conservative barrier to centralization and governmental growth. Obsidian and jade were not really exceptions as these commodities, as we have seen, were derived from Mesoamerican traders.

This hypothesis about the ubiquity or redundance of natural resources acting as a brake to, or a barrier against, lower Central American sociopolitical development needs some further brief comment. It has often been argued that a multiplicity of ecological niches has just the opposite effect, and the growth of Mesoamerican and Peruvian civilizations has often been explained as resulting from the interchange and stimulation deriving from a symbiotic situation of many niches. I think there is much to be said in favor of this argument, and we have already referred to it with reference to the early rise of an economically viable agriculture in Mesoamerica and Peru; but the lower Central American situation does differ from this, and it differs, I think crucially, in just what has been pointed out in the redundancy argument. Redundancy of resources, from niche to niche, tends to stultify trade and trading control and, thereby, complex organizational development.

Another question relating to lower Central American development that was considered by the seminar was why Mesoamerica did not take over lower Central America. In a sense it did so, in part, or at least attempted to do so. As we have seen, the buffer zone with Mesoamerica was a kind of Mesoamerican colonial sphere, reflecting as it does successive Olmec, Teotihuacan-Maya, Chorti-Maya, and later Mexicanoid encroachments. We do not know all the processes of these encroachments, but certainly resource extraction and economic dominance were one syndrome. The nature of further political involvement remains speculative. The preponderance of seminar opinion was that Mesoamerican imperialism was never fully enough organized on any of these levels—Olmec, Teotihuacan, Maya, or Mexican—to extend a political and military empire into lower Central America or at least to do so in any long-term, incorporative way. Even within the bounds of Mesoamerica proper it is a moot question how extensive and fully political such horizons as the Olmec, Teotihuacan, and Toltec may have been; and the Aztec empire, for which we have ethnohistoric as well as archaeological information, seems rather a fragile fabric despite its warlike excesses and terroristic tactics. In sum, we would say that Mesoamerica did try to take over lower Central America, but for various reasons could not do so in any very complete or lasting way; and, through the centuries, the Mesoamerican expansions to the south and east alternated with retreats, perhaps as the result of political crises within Mesoamerica, pressures from lower Central America in the opposite direction, or combinations of both.

What forces or pressures came from the south into lower Central America? We have made reference throughout to the spread of ceramic traditions from South America into the area, some of these reaching as far as Atlantic Costa Rica and Nicaragua, perhaps even to northeast Honduras. It would appear that influence from this direction began back as early as our Period III (4000 b.c.–1000 b.c.) and continued thereafter. Except for goldwork for the later periods, however, we have little information that suggests the kinds of specific trading contacts and relationships seen at the Mesoamerican frontier. We should also note that the adjacent regions of northern Colombia and Venezuela did not generate the kinds of state societies that we have in Mesoamerica. There were, it is true, some advanced chiefdoms in these regions in late pre-Columbian times, such as the Sinu and the Tairona, summarized by Bray. Could these be equated at least with the Mesoamerican Olmec societies? And, if so, could they not have developed trading systems and exerted other pressures upon adjacent lower Central America? Future archaeological work may shed light on this problem.

Finally, in closing, can we conceive of lower Central America as a culture-area-with-time-depth? The seminar was of the general opinion that we could not, at least not in the sense that we can conceive of such an entity for Mesoamerica or Peru. For one thing, lower Central America lacks the broad horizontal phenomena that we see in the other two areas. For Mesoamerica, the Olmec, Teotihuacan, Toltec, and Aztec stylistic diffusions serve to interlink regions within the area in some kind of a bond; and for Peru, the Chavin, Huari-Tiahuanaco, and Inca present a counterpart of this. To be sure, we do not yet understand the meanings of these horizons nor the processes which they signify; however, they serve to forge what Bennett (1948) once referred to as a "co-traditional" unity for their respective areas.

Lower Central America does not present a similar phenomenon or set of phenomena. In this it is like Ecuador and Colombia, and for the time being at least, the archaeologist is forced to view the whole of Ecuador–Colombia– lower Central America as an Intermediate Area of considerable regional diversity and great cultural complexity.

Notes

1. This summary was written some months after the seminar and after the authors of the various papers had had the opportunity to revise their original presentations in the light of the Santa Fe discussions. A draft of the summary was sent to all of the participating authors except Warwick Bray, who had not participated in the seminar meeting and who had been asked to prepare his paper at a later date. As his manuscript was not seen by me until shortly before my completion of the final summary draft, it was then deemed too late for him to review the draft. Otherwise, I have benefited from the other authors' checking of facts and emphases and their additional suggestions. As is to be expected, there were and are some differences of opinion among the seminar participants, and this is especially so with regard to interpretive matters. It should be emphasized that the way I have put things together in this summary, and the things I have selected or left out, are my own responsibility. Finally, let me add that bibliographic references have been kept to a minimum in the summary; substantial source material is cited in the accompanying papers.

2. In a recent paper John W. Fox (1981) has advanced the idea of a "Meso-american Eastern Frontier" zone which has some relationships to Lange's concept. Fox relies essentially on ethnohistoric and Late Postclassic–period data, and his "Frontier Culture Area" lies largely in western El Salvador and along the Motagua and Polochic drainages. As such, it is mostly within what was considered by the seminar as Mesoamerica proper; however, the trait characteristics of Fox's frontier resemble some of those of the buffer zone, and some of the processes envisioned in its formation are comparable to those suggested by Lange.

Appendixes

APPENDIX 1. RADIOCARBON SAMPLES FROM EL SALVADOR.

Sample Number	Site	Mat.	Uncorr. Date	S.D.	Range S.D. × 1 (68%)	MASCA Range or Midpoint	Phase/Period	Comments
P-1551	Chalchuapa	C	840 B.C.	60	900–780	999±57 B.C.	Tok	TR-1-3-11A, Structure E 3-1, Terminal Early Preclassic; *Radiocarbon* 16:230.
P-1801	Chalchuapa	C	571 B.C.	60	631–511	611±60 B.C.	Colos	TR-10-15, Structure G 3-1-2nd fill; *Radiocarbon* 16:230.
P-1806	Chalchuapa	C	507 B.C.	63	570–444	549±63 B.C.	Colos	Fill, Structure E 3-1; *Radiocarbon* 16: 230.
P-1550	Chalchuapa	C	147 B.C.	44	191–103	99±44 B.C.	Caynac	TR-10-2-30A, charcoal inside vessel from Cache 10, Caynac ceramic complex; *Radiocarbon* 16:230.
FSU-338	Quelepa	C	105 B.C.	65	170–40	60 B.C.–A.D. 10	Uapala	Test pit 4, Lot 321. Cache 7, sealed beneath floor of structure. As in Cache 6, a large amount of charcoal lay between two Izalco Usulutan flaring-wall bowls (Andrews V 1976:42).
P-1805	Chalchuapa	C	74 B.C.	61	137–15	15±61 B.C.	Caynac, Early Facet	Fill, Structure E 3-1; *Radiocarbon* 16:230.
FSU-337	Quelepa	C	70 B.C.	55	125–15	A.D. 30–50	Uapala	Test pit 4, Lot 307, 140–163 cm. Cache 6, no architectural association. Between vessels 1 and 2, both Uapala ceramic complex Izalco Usulutan flaring-wall bowls (Andrews V 1976:42).
TX-2324	Cambio	C	20 B.C.	60	80 B.C.–A.D. 40	A.D. 70		Ilopango "tierra blanca joven" eruption (Sheets, pers. comm.).
TX-3114	Cambio	C	A.D. 10	50	40 B.C.–A.D. 60	A.D. 90		Ilopango "tierra blanca joven" eruption (Sheets, pers. comm.).
P-1547	Chalchuapa	C	A.D. 79	38	41–117	A.D. 145±38	Caynac, Late Facet	Charcoal inside intact ceramic cache vessel. Contemporary with use of Structure E 3-1. *Radiocarbon* 16:230.
P-1803	Chalchuapa	C	A.D. 181	62	119–243	A.D. 241±62	Vec	Test pit 2-8, Level 5; *Radiocarbon* 16:229.
GFIGNR-264			A.D. 260	85	175–345	A.D. 320–350		Ilopango "tierra blanca joven" eruption (Sheets, pers. comm.).
GFIGNR-2534			A.D. 290	95	195–385	A.D. 370–390		Ilopango "tierra blanca joven" eruption (Sheets, pers. comm.).
TX-3122	Cambio	C	A.D. 320	70	250–390	A.D. 400		Ilopango "tierra blanca joven" eruption (Sheets, pers. comm.).
GFIGNR-5002			A.D. 360	70	290–430	A.D. 440		Ilopango "tierra blanca joven" eruption (Sheets, pers. comm.).
TX-3119	Ceren	C	A.D. 380	110	270–490	A.D. 450		Ceren house, Laguna Caldera eruption. Run with small sample (Sheets, pers. comm.).
GFIGNR-2535			A.D. 425	70	355–495	A.D. 500–530		Ilopango "tierra blanca joven" eruption (Sheets, pers. comm.).
TX-3123	Cambio	C	A.D. 440	90	350–530	A.D. 540		F.5 of T.P. 16 at Cambio (Sheets, pers. comm.).
EI5-40	Ceren	C	A.D. 510	135	375–645	A.D. 590		Ceren house, Laguna Caldera eruption (Sheets, pers. comm.).
TX-3119a	Ceren	C	A.D. 530	50	480–580	A.D. 600		Ceren house, Laguna Caldera eruption, supersedes TX-3119, a smaller sample (Sheets, pers. comm.).
Composite	Ceren	C	A.D. 550	90	460–640	A.D. 620		Ceren house, Laguna Caldera eruption. Averaged from TX-3120, TX-3113a, and TX-3119a (Sheets, pers. comm.).
TX-3113a	Ceren	C	A.D. 620	90	530–710	A.D. 670		Ceren house, Laguna Caldera eruption. Supersedes TX-3113, a smaller sample (Sheets, pers. comm.).
TX-3121	Cambio	C	A.D. 630	100	530–730	A.D. 680		F.8 of T.P. 19 at Cambio, the lower classic deposit (Sheets, pers. comm.).
FSU-354	Quelepa	C	A.D. 665	140	525–805	A.D. 700–725		Dates abandonment of the East Group (Andrews V 1976:42).

APPENDIX 2. RADIOCARBON SAMPLES FROM HONDURAS.

Sample Number	Site	Mat.	Uncorr. Date	S.D.	Range S.D. × 1 (68%)	MASCA Range or Midpoint	Phase/Period	Comments
Gif-1475	Los Naranjos	C	750 B.C.	110	860–640	840–820 B.C.	Early Eden phase	Eden phase dates 400–100 B.C. Dated carbon thought to come from redeposited Jaral-phase materials (Baudez and Becquelin 1973:405).
Gif-1324	Los Naranjos	C	A.D. 100	100	1–200	A.D. 160	Late Eden phase	From excavation unit T.10-5. Late Eden dates 100 B.C.–A.D. 550 (Baudez and Becquelin 1973:405).
Gif-1473	Los Naranjos	C	A.D. 250	100	150–350	A.D. 290–320	Late Eden phase	From excavation unit T.36-12 (Baudez and Becquelin 1973:405).
SI-278	Monte Libano	C	A.D. 370	100	270–470	A.D. 440	Chismuyu	Healy (pers. comm.)
UGA-1455	H-CN-5: Selin Farm		A.D. 375	60	315–435	A.D. 445	Early Selin phase	Early Selin dates A.D. 300–600. Mound D, Pit 2 (300–325 cm). Healy (1978:60).
Gif-1472	Los Naranjos	C	A.D. 420	100	320–520	A.D. 490–530	Yojoa phase (A.D. 550–1000)	Cross references with Gif-1474; from two successive occupation levels in house platform behind Structure 26 of Group 1. Baudez and Becquelin (1973:405–6) thought both dates were somewhat early.
UGA-1457	H-CN-5: Selin Farm		A.D. 420	65	355–485	A.D. 490–530	Early Selin	Mound A, Pit 4, 100–125 cm. Healy (1978a:60).
Gif-1474	Los Naranjos	C	A.D. 450	100	350–550	A.D. 540	Yojoa phase	See comments with Gif-1472, above.
UGA-1459	H-CN-5: Selin Farm		A.D. 595	65	530–660	A.D. 655	Early to Basic Selin	Spans transition period (A.D. 550 to 650). Mound I, Pit 3, 325–350 cm (Healy 1978a:60).
UGA-1456	H-CN-5: Selin Farm		A.D. 600	60	540–660	A.D. 660	Early to Basic Selin	Spans transition from Early Selin (A.D. 300–600) to Basic Selin (A.D. 600–800).
Gif-1326	Los Naranjos	C	A.D. 690	90	600–780	A.D. 730–760	Yojoa phase	A.D. 550–1000 (Baudez and Becquelin 1973:406).
Not given	H-CN-4: Williams Ranch		A.D. 695	65	630–760	A.D. 730–760	Basic Selin	Healy (1980b:306).
UGA-1458	H-CN-5: Selin Farm		A.D. 745	60	685–805	A.D. 800–820	Basic Selin	Mound I, Pit 3, 50–75 cm, "slightly too early" (Healy 1978a:60).
Not given	H-CN-4: Williams Ranch		A.D. 755	60	695–815	A.D. 800–820	Basic Selin	Healy (1980b:306).
UGA-1574	H-CN-12: Rio Claro		A.D. 1045	65	980–1110	A.D. 1085	Early Cocal	A.D. 1000–1400 (Healy 1980b:306).
UGA-1571	H-CN-12: Rio Claro		A.D. 1050	120	930–1170	A.D. 1090	Early Cocal	Healy (1980b:306).
UGA-1284	H-CN-12: Rio Claro		A.D. 1105	55	1050–1160	A.D. 1150–1180	Early Cocal	Healy (1980b:306).
UGA-1570	H-CN-12: Rio Claro		A.D. 1255	60	1195–1315	A.D. 1260–1290	Early Cocal	Healy (1980b:306).
UGA-1572	H-CN-12: Rio Claro		A.D. 1350	60	1290–1410	A.D. 1350	Late Cocal	Healy (1980b:306).
UGA-1573	H-CN-12: Rio Claro		A.D. 1500	65	1435–1565	A.D. 1430	Late Cocal	Healy (1980b:306).

Sample Number	Site	Mat.	Uncorr. Date	S.D.	Range S.D. x 1 (68%)	MASCA Range or Midpoint	Phase/ Period	Comments
UCLA-2167A	Mendez	C	1560 B.C.	80	1640–1480	1770–1870 B.C.		From sterile subsoil immediately below initial cultural level. TR-4, N6W1, 200 cm b.d.
UCLA-2177A	Vidor	C	880 B.C.	80	960–800	940–990 B.C.	Zoned Bichrome	N45–47, W13-14, Feature 13, associated with Toya "Loma B" Zoned incised ceramics; RC #22.
UCLA-2163	Mendez	C	300 B.C.	60	360–240	270–390 B.C.	Zoned Bichrome	Lot 129.
UCLA-2177B	Vidor	C	250 B.C.	60	310–190	210–370 B.C.	Orso Zoned Bichrome	N 56.5-57.5, Level 3; RC #30.
GSY-100	Ortega	C	245 B.C.	130	375–115	210–365 B.C.	Catalina Zoned Bichrome	From two separate runs (Haberland 1978:40).
UCLA-2167E	Mojica		160 B.C.	80	240–80	70–120 B.C.	Zoned Bichrome	Square 12, may be somewhat early; RC #3–4.
Y-850	Ortega		A.D. 250	70	180–320	A.D. 320–390	Zoned Bichrome	Coe and Baudez (1961); Haberland (1978:405); Catalina phase.
Y-811	Matapalo	C	A.D. 555	90	465–645	A.D. 620–630	Zoned Bichrome	G11/1E, Cut 1, 60–75 cm (Sweeney 1976:42); Matapalo phase.
Y-1124	Ayala (Gr-5)		A.D. 560	100	460–660	A.D. 620–640	Early Polychrome	Cut 2, 285 cm (Haberland 1978:405).
Y-1122	Ayala (Gr-5)		A.D. 570	70	500–640	A.D. 620–640	Early Polychrome	Cut 2, 195 cm (Haberland 1978:405); beginning of San Roque phase.
P-2177	Matapalo	C	A.D. 620	50	570–670	A.D. 670	Early Polychrome	G11/2D and 2E (Sweeney 1976:42).
HAR-2513	Vidor	C	A.D. 640	40	600–680	A.D. 690	Early Polychrome	Cultural Feature #2; see Abel-Vidor (1980).
UCLA-2129	Vidor	C	A.D. 655	60	595–655	A.D. 695	Early Polychrome	Cultural Feature #2; see Abel-Vidor (1980).
UCLA-2164	Vidor	C	A.D. 665	60	605–725	A.D. 700–725	Early Polychrome	Feature 36, IV 23–24, W 0–1, 66 cm b.s.; Culebra phase.
M-1173	Matapalo	C	A.D. 680	75	605–755	A.D. 730	Early Polychrome	Cut 1, 60–75 cm (Sweeney 1976:42); Matapalo phase.
Y-1125	Cruz. Ri-7		A.D. 780	120	660–900	A.D. 830–850	Early Polychrome	Cut 2, 260 cm (Healy 1980a:T20).
P-2181	Huerta del Aguacate	C	A.D. 820	40	780–860	A.D. 890	Middle Polychrome	G2/2G (Sweeney 1976:42).

Sample Number	Site	Mat.	Uncorr. Date	S.D.	Range S.D. × 1 (68%)	MASCA Range or Midpoint	Phase/ Period	Comments
P-2284	Chahuite Escondido	C	A.D. 830	40	790–870	A.D. 890–910	Middle Polychrome	B1/1K (Sweeney 1976:42).
P-2174	Chahuite Escondido	C	A.D. 840	40	800–880	A.D. 910	Middle Polychrome	B1/1L (Sweeney 1976:42).
P-2283	Chahuite Escondido	C	A.D. 910	50	860–960	A.D. 970	Middle Polychrome	B1/1H (Sweeney 1976:42).
P-2176	Matapalo	C	A.D. 910	50	860–960	A.D. 970	Middle Polychrome	G11/1D (Sweeney 1976:42).
P-2282	Chahuite Escondido	C	A.D. 920	50	870–970	A.D. 980	Middle Polychrome	B1/1E (Sweeney 1976:42).
P-2170	Chahuite Escondido	C	A.D. 920	50	870–970	A.D. 980	Middle Polychrome	B1/1F (Sweeney 1976:42).
Y-815	Huerta del Aguacate	C	A.D. 960	70	890–1030	A.D. 1020	Middle Polychrome	G2/2E, Cut 2, 60–75 cm (Sweeney 1976:42).
HV-2688	Los Angeles		A.D. 980	60	920–1040	A.D. 1030	Middle Polychrome	Gato phase, F1 (Haberland 1978:405).
P-2172	Chahuite Escondido	C	A.D. 1000	40	960–1040	A.D. 1040	Middle Polychrome	B1/1T (Sweeney 1976:42).
P-2179	Huerta del Aguacate	C	A.D. 1020	40	980–1060	A.D. 1060	Middle Polychrome	G2/2D (Sweeney 1976:42).
P-2173	Chahuite Escondido	C	A.D. 1070	50	1020–1120	A.D. 1090–1020	Middle Polychrome	B1/1J (Sweeney 1976:42).
P-2178	Huerta del Aguacate	C	A.D. 1140	40	1100–1180	A.D. 1190	Middle Polychrome	G2/1C (Sweeney 1976:42).
P-2180	Huerta del Aguacate	C	A.D. 1190	50	1140–1240	A.D. 1230	Middle Polychrome	G2/2F (Sweeney 1976:42).
WS	San Francisco		A.D. 1203	135	1170–1250	A.D. 1230		
P-2175	Matapalo	C	A.D. 1210	40	1170–1250	A.D. 1240	Middle Polychrome	G11/1C (Sweeney 1970:42).
P-2171	Chahuite Escondido	C	A.D. 1230	50	1180–1280	A.D. 1250	Middle Polychrome	B1/1G (Sweeney 1970:42).
Hv-2690	La Paloma		A.D. 1275	50	1225–1325	A.D. 1270–1300	Middle Polychrome	4-F, 100–120 cm (Haberland 1978:405).
Hv-2691	La Paloma		A.D. 1290	50	1240–1340	A.D. 1310	Middle Polychrome	Haberland (1978:405).
Hv-2692	San Lazaro		A.D. 1445	30	1415–1475	A.D. 1410	End of San Lazaro phase	Late Polychrome (Haberland 1978:405).

384

APPENDIX 4. RADIOCARBON SAMPLES FROM ATLANTIC NICARAGUA.

Sample Number	Site	Mat.	Uncorr. Date	S.D.	Range S.D. x 1 (68%)	MASCA Range or Midpoint	Phase/ Period	Comments
I-7100	Bluefields Area		37 B.C.	85	122 B.C.–A.D. 48	A.D. 60		Siteia Complex (Magnus 1976:68).
I-7450	Bluefields Area		A.D. 80	85	5 B.C.–A.D. 165	A.D. 150		Siteia Complex (Magnus 1976:68).
I-7099	Bluefields Area		A.D. 490	85	405–575	A.D. 570–590		Jarkin Complex (Magnus 1976:68).
I-7451	Cukra Point		A.D. 1185	80	1105–1265	A.D. 1225		Cukra Point Complex (Magnus 1976:68).

APPENDIX 5. RADIOCARBON SAMPLES FROM CENTRAL PLATEAU AND VALLEY, COSTA RICA.

Sample Number	Site	Mat.	Uncorr. Date	S.D.	Range S.D. x 1 (68%)	MASCA Range or Midpoint	Phase/ Period	Comments
UCLA-2167F	Grecia, Fabrica de Licores	C	960 B.C.	100	1060–860	1030–1100 B.C.		
UCLA-2167B	Grecia, Fabrica de Licores	C	A.D. 425	80	345–505	A.D. 500–530		S 3-6/E 2.5-4, 117 cm b.d., SE corner (Lange).
I-8010			A.D. 625	80	545–705	A.D. 675		Supposedly Pavas (according to Aguilar), but has Curridabat association (Snarskis, pers. comm.).
UCLA-2175H	Heredia 26-CN	C	A.D. 950	60	890–1010	A.D. 1010	Cartago Phase	26-M.1, Level 2 (Snarskis and Blanco 1978:107).
None given	Retes		A.D. 990			A.D. 1030	Early Cartago	Wood artifacts (Stone 1958a).

385

Sample Number	Site	Mat.	Uncorr. Date	S.D.	Range S.D. x 1 (68%)	MASCA Range or Midpoint	Phase/ Period	Comments
UCLA-2113A	La Montaña 18-LM	C	1515 B.C.	160	1675–1355	1770–1740 B.C.	La Montaña	Layer "D." "Too early" (Snarskis). Snarskis (1978:105).
UCLA-2113N, D	La Montaña 18-LM	C	550 B.C.	60	610–490	510–660 B.C.	La Montaña	Two identical dates. Layer "D." Snarskis (1978:106).
UCLA-2113M	La Montaña 18-LM	C	280 B.C.	60	340–220	250–380 B.C.	La Montaña	Layer "D." Possibly contaminated from later La Selva–phase cemetery (Snarskis 1978:106).
UCLA-2175D	Severo Ledesma 7.1-SL	C	50 B.C.	90	140 B.C.–A.D. 40	A.D. 50	El Bosque	M-1, rectangular El Bosque house, sample from fill (Snarskis).
B1 (Haberland 1978:406)	Mercocha	C	A.D. 130	140	10 B.C.–A.D. 270	A.D. 180–200	El Bosque	Grave, with some El Bosque and early La Selva ceramics, jade, slate-back pyrite mirrors (Snarskis, pers. comm.; Stirling 1969).
UCLA-2113H	Guacimo 20-CB	C	A.D. 150	60	90–210	A.D. 210	El Bosque	Corridor tomb (Snarskis 1978:176).
B2 (Haberland 1978:406)	Porvenir	C	A.D. 265	120	145–385	A.D. 320–340	El Bosque	Grave, with some El Bosque and early La Selva ceramics, jade (Snarskis, pers. comm.; Stirling 1969).
UCLA-2175C	7.1-SL Severo Ledesma Guacimo	C	A.D. 350	60	290–410	A.D. 430	El Bosque	7.5, levels 5–8, stratigraphic pit (Snarskis, pers. comm.).
SI-147	Marin (W-2)	C	A.D. 590	90	500–680	A.D. 650	La Selva	Near Williamsburg. Linea Vieja (Stirling 1969). Grave 11. La Selva pottery (Snarskis, pers. comm.).
SI-146	Marin (W-1)	C	A.D. 620	120	500–740	A.D. 670	La Selva	Near Williamsburg. Linea Vieja (Stirling 1969). Grave 4. La Selva pottery (Snarskis, pers. comm.).
UCLA-2113E	La Montaña 18-LM	C	A.D. 640	60	580–700	A.D. 690	La Selva	18-7. Early La Selva cemetery (Snarskis 1978:240).
I-8913	La Isabel 4-IT	C	A.D. 940	90	850–1030	A.D. 1000	Late La Selva B	4.-Tomb 3b. (Snarskis 1978:240).
UCLA-2175I	Guacimo	C	A.D. 1030	80	950–1110	A.D. 1070	La Cabaña	7.-Tomb VIII. La Cabaña pottery, Luna vessel, possibly mixed with El Bosque. This is too early for Luna, but Snarskis feels the date is good (pers. comm.).
UCLA-2113I	La Cabaña 20-CB	C	A.D. 1220	60	1160–1280	A.D. 1240	La Cabaña	20.-1-Tomb 3. (Apparently mislabeled 2113-II in Snarskis 1978:289). See A.D. 150 date for the El Bosque phase, above. Stone cist tomb associated with La Cabaña site (Snarskis, pers. comm.).
I-8915	La Zoila 5.2T	C	A.D. 1270	140	1130–1410	A.D. 1260–1290	La Cabaña	From beneath La Cabaña–phase mound (Snarskis 1978:289).
UCLA-2113G	La Cabaña 20-CB	C	A.D. 1360	60	1300–1420	A.D. 1360	La Cabaña	20-3-Level 1, midden context (Snarskis 1978:290).
None given	La'Maquina	C	A.D. 1364			A.D. 1364	La Cabaña	Date supplied by Snarskis. La Cabaña ceramics, jaguar metate, gold (Stirling 1969).
SI-145	Williamsburg (W-6)	C	A.D. 1470	90	1380–1560	A.D. 1420	La Cabaña	Near Williamsburg. Linea Vieja-Grave 2 (Stirling 1969); La Cabaña ceramics.

APPENDIX 7. RADIOCARBON SAMPLES FROM THE CHIRIQUI AREA, PANAMA.

Sample Number	Site	Mat.	Uncorr. Date	S.D.	Range S.D. × 1 (68%)	MASCA Range or Midpoint	Phase/ Period	Comments
I-6278	Casitas de Piedras		4570 B.C.	120	4690–4450	5280 B.C.	1	Lowest stratum of human occupation (Haberland, pers. comm.).
C1 (Haberland 1978:406)	Trapiche		3900 B.C.	110	4010–3790	4540 B.C.	2	Stratum E.
I-5765	Casitas de Piedra		3845 B.C.	105	3950–3740	4490 B.C.	2	Second preceramic occupation (Haberland, pers. comm.).
I-5764	Casitas de Piedra		3730 B.C.	105	3835–3625	4420 B.C.	2	Second preceramic occupation (Haberland, pers. comm.).
C2 (Haberland 1978:406)	Casitas de Piedra		2125 B.C.	105	2230–2020	2565 B.C.	2–3	Stratum D.
SI-1833 and SE-1835	Piti (BU-17)		430 B.C.	60	490–370	430 B.C.		Dated by Teledyne Isotopes (I) and Smithsonian Institution Radiation Biology Laboratory (SI). There is a marked discrepancy between dates by the two labs for levels in the same excavation unit (compare SI-1833, SI-1834, and SI-1835 with I-7259 and I-7260). Probably due to presence of hearth and other disturbances (Linares, Sheets, and Rosenthal 1975:144).
SI-1834	Lower Barriles (BU-24)		115 B.C.	75	190–40	60 B.C.–A.D. 10		Compare with I-7259 and I-7260 (Linares, Sheets, and Rosenthal 1975:144).
SI-1831	Piti (BU-17)		A.D. 265	105	160–370	A.D. 320–355		Linares, Sheets, and Rosenthal (1975:144).
I-6536	Piti (BU-17)		A.D. 295	95	200–390	A.D. 390		Linares, Sheets, and Rosenthal (1975:144). Said to be Aguas Buenas (Haberland, pers. comm.).
I-6537	Piti (BU-17)		A.D. 295	90	205–385	A.D. 390		Linares, Sheets, and Rosenthal (1975:144). Said to be Aguas Buenas (Haberland, pers. comm.).
I-6523	Piti (BU-17)		A.D. 315	90	225–405	A.D. 395		Linares, Sheets, and Rosenthal (1975:144). Said to be Aguas Buenas (Haberland, pers. comm.).
I-6836	Lower Barriles (BU-24)		A.D. 435	90	345–525	A.D. 535		Linares, Sheets, and Rosenthal (1975:144).
I-7259	Piti (BU-17)		A.D. 455	85	370–540	A.D. 545		Compare to SI-1833, -34, -35, Linares, Sheets, and Rosenthal (1975:144).
I-7260	Piti (BU-17)		A.D. 600	85	515–685	A.D. 660		Linares, Sheets, and Rosenthal (1975:144).
I-6834	Lower Barriles (BU-24)		A.D. 730	85	645–815	A.D. 780–800		Linares, Sheets, and Rosenthal (1975:144).

APPENDIX 7 (continued)

Sample Number	Site	Mat.	Uncorr. Date	S.D.	Range S.D. ×1 (68%)	MASCA Range or Midpoint	Phase/ Period	Comments
M-1470	La Pitahaya (IS-3)		A.D. 760	100	660–860	A.D. 820		Most recent occupation (Linares 1977b:319).
I-6835	Lower Barriles (BU-24)		A.D. 820	85	735–905	A.D. 890		Linares, Sheets, and Rosenthal (1975:144).
I-5330	Cerro Brujo (CA-3)		A.D. 960	90	870–1050	A.D. 1020		Most recent occupation (Linares 1977b:319).
I-5329	Cerro Brujo (CA-3)		A.D. 960	90	870–1050	A.D. 1020		Most recent occupation (Linares 1977b:319).
I-5328	Cerro Brujo (CA-3)		A.D. 960	90	870–1050	A.D. 1020		Most recent occupation (Linares 1977b:319).
I-5326	Cerro Brujo (CA-3)		A.D. 980	90	890–1070	A.D. 1030		Most recent occupation (Linares 1977b:319).
I-5327	Cerro Brujo (CA-3)		A.D. 985	90	895–1075	A.D. 1030		Most recent occupation (Linares 1977b:319).
M-1308	El Cangrejal (SL-1)		A.D. 1020	100	920–1120	A.D. 1060		Pit 3, 60–70 cm (Haberland 1978:406).
I-5766	La Pitahaya (IS-3)		A.D. 1075	90	985–1165	A.D. 1100–1130		Most recent occupation (Linares 1977b:319).

APPENDIX 8. RADIOCARBON SAMPLES FROM CENTRAL PANAMA.

Sample Number	Site	Mat.	Uncorr. Date	S.D.	Range S.D. x 1 (68%)	MASCA Range or Midpoint	Phase/Period	Comments
TEM-123	Cueva de los Ladrones	C	4910 B.C.	90	5000–4820			Area 2A, Layer 6, stratified under pile of shell and stones. Probably dates to earliest site use. No ceramics directly associated (Cooke, pers. comm.).
Y-458-d	Cerro Mangote	C	4860 B.C.	110	4970–4750		Preceramic, Phase I	From McGimsey's (1957) Stratum C. Probably not the earliest occupation. Dates pending from Ranere's 1979 excavations. Cooke (1976d:137).
TEM-131	Aguadulce Shelter	S	4230 B.C.	120	4350–4110	4960–4940 B.C.		Block 3, Layer C₄, 30–35 cm b.s.; *Radiocarbon* 21:472–76.
TEM-106	Aguadulce Shelter	S	3890 B.C.	95	3985–3795	4530 B.C.	Preceramic	Block 5, Layer C₅, 35 cm b.s.; no ceramics (Cooke, pers. comm.).
TEM-109	Aguadulce Shelter	S	3545 B.C.	100	3645–3445	4265–4215 B.C.		Block 2E, 100–110 cm b.s.; possibly noncultural (Cooke, pers. comm.).
TEM-176	Cerro Mangote	S	3490 B.C.	130	3620–3360	4180–4100 B.C.		Inside shell, "Pothole 1," red clay zone (209–219 cm).
SI-2841	Monagrillo (HE-5)	C	3435 B.C.	95	3530–3340	4080–4040 B.C.		110–120 cm b.s.; possibly noncultural (Cooke, pers. comm.).
TEM-175	Cerro Mangote	S	3190 B.C.	120	3210–3070	3760 B.C.		Inside shell (see TEM-174).
TEM-119	Cueva de los Ladrones	S	2850 B.C.	100	2950–2750	3400–3470 B.C.		Area 1, within a pile of shells and stones, perhaps a hearth; associated with 383 Monagrillo sherds (Cooke, pers. comm.).
TEM-124	Cueva de los Ladrones	C	2570 B.C.	100	2670–2470	3160 B.C.		Area 1, at base of pile of shells and stones (see TEM-119); associated with Monagrillo-like ceramics (Cooke, pers. comm.).
SI-2842	Monagrillo (HE-5)	C	2455 B.C.	75	2530–2380	3000–2975 B.C.		Block 1E, 20–30 cm b.s.; ash lens (Cooke, pers. comm.).
TEM-130	Aguadulce Shelter	S	2260 B.C.	90	2350–2170	2830–2700 B.C.		Block 3, Layer C₄, 30–35 cm b.s.; *Radiocarbon* 21:472–76.
SI-2844	Monagrillo (HE-5)	C	2185 B.C.	80	2265–2105	2615 B.C.		Block 1E, 97–100 cm b.s.; ash lens (Cooke, pers. comm.).
Y-585	Monagrillo (HE-5)	C	2140 B.C.	70	2210–2070	2580 B.C.	Monagrillo Phase II–III	West trench, section 6, 95 cm b.s., bottom of stratum (Willey and McGimsey 1954). Plastic tradition (Cooke 1976d:137).
TEM-122	Cueva de los Ladrones	C	1930 B.C.	80	2010–1850	2180 B.C.		Down slope from cave floor; junction between ceramic and preceramic layers; possibly a small intrusive fire pit; 10 Monagrillo sherds (Cooke, pers. comm.).
TEM-120	Cueva de los Ladrones	S	1820 B.C.	80	1900–1740	2140 B.C.		Area 2A, Layer 4; 2 Monagrillo sherds; just above TEM-121 (Cooke, pers. comm.).
TEM-121	Cueva de los Ladrones	S	1910 B.C.	90	2000–1820	2180 B.C.		Area 2A, Layer 5; 1 Monagrillo sherd (Cooke, pers. comm.).

389

Sample Number	Site	Mat.	Uncorr. Date	S.D.	Range S.D.×1 (68%)	MASCA Range or Midpoint	Phase/Period	Comments
TEM-128	Aguadulce Shelter	S	1750 B.C.	100	1850–1650	2110 B.C.		Block 3, Layer C_3, 25–30 cm b.s.
SI-2840	Monagrillo (HE-5)	C	1665 B.C.	80	1745–1585	2040 B.C.		Block 2E, 95–100 cm b.s.; associated with fire-cracked rock (Cooke, pers. comm.).
TEM-108	Aguadulce Shelter	S	1680 B.C.	95	1775–1585	2050 B.C.		Block 2, Layer C_1, 20–25 cm b.s.; no ceramics; end of preceramic occupation (Cooke, pers. comm.).
Beta-1218	Cerro Mangote	C	1605 B.C.	100	1705–1505	1875 B.C.		"Pothole 1," north wall, 180–190 cm.
TEM-110	Aguadulce Shelter	C	1590 B.C.	115	1705–1475	1910–1780 B.C.		Block 3, Layers C_4 and D, 35 cm b.s.; no ceramics (Cooke, pers. comm).
SI-2839	Monagrillo (HE-5)	C	1535 B.C.	100	1635–1435	1755–1715 B.C.		Block 2E, 50–60 cm b.s. (Cooke, pers. comm.).
SI-2838	Monagrillo (HE-5)	C	1435 B.C.	75	1510–1360	1655 B.C.		Block 2E, 20–30 cm b.s. (Cooke, pers. comm.).
I-9384	Monagrillo (HE-5)	C	1375 B.C.	85	1460–1290	1600–1570 B.C.		Block 1E, living surface 150–60 cm b.s. (Cooke, pers. comm.).
SI-2843	Monagrillo (HE-5)	C	1295 B.C.	100	1395–1195	1505 B.C.		Block 1E, hearth, 50–56 cm b.s. (Cooke, pers. comm.).
TEM-126	Aguadulce Shelter	S	1010 B.C.	80	1090–930	1110 B.C.		Block 3, Layer B_3, 15–20 cm b.s.
TEM-127	Aguadulce Shelter	S	840 B.C.	110	950–730	910 B.C.		Block 3, Layer C_3, 25–30 cm b.s.
TEM-107	Aguadulce Shelter	S	620 B.C.	95	715–525	760 B.C.		Block 3, Layer B_1, 5–10 cm b.s. (Ranere and Hansell 1978).
TEM-125	Aguadulce Shelter	S	590 B.C.	70	660–520	730–710 B.C.		Block 3, Layer B_2, 10–15 cm b.s.
I-9704	Sitio Sierra		240 B.C.	80	320–160	210–360 B.C.		Associated with probably the earliest burial in a cemetery with Aristide bichrome pottery, blade tools, and offerings of large-grained maize (Cooke, pers. comm.).
I-9702	Sitio Sierra		65 B.C.	80	145 B.C.–A.D. 15	A.D. 50		Hearth of a circular structure above cemetery (Cooke, pers. comm.).
I-9703	Sitio Sierra		25 B.C.	80	105 B.C.–A.D. 55	65 A.D.		Rubbish tossed out of the circular structure (Cooke, pers. comm.).
Gif-1643	La India (TI-1)		A.D. 20	110	90 B.C.–A.D. 130	A.D. 100	Phases II–III	Associated with plastically decorated, ?prebichrome pottery. Cooke (1976d:137); Ichon (1980).
I-9701	Sitio Sierra		A.D. 115	90	25–205	A.D. 175		House floor with Aristide ceramics (Cooke, pers. comm.).
M-1474	Mariato (MO-1)		A.D. 190	130	60–320	A.D. 260		Mound 4, 215–225 cms, near bottom of site. Tonosi ceramics. Cooke (1976:137).
Y-125	Playa Venado		A.D. 200	60	140–260	A.D. 260	Aristide/Tonosi/Early Cocle	From an unpublished urn cache in the cemetery. Area A, Trench 8. Lothrop (1952); Cooke (1976:137).

Lab number	Site		A.D. date	±	Range	A.D. (calibrated)	Ceramic phase	Notes
I-8613	Sitio Sierra		A.D. 235	90	145–325	A.D. 290–300	Aristide/Tonosi Phase IV	House floor with maize-grinding stones, but stratified below I-9701. Cooke (1976d:137).
M-1472	Mariato		A.D. 250	120	130–370	A.D. 290–320	Aristide/Tonosi Phase IV	Mound 4, 355–370 cm. Tonosi ceramics. McGimsey (1961); Cooke (1976d:137).
Gif-2346	Sitio Sierra		A.D. 310	90	220–400	A.D. 390	Aristide/Tonosi Phase IV	Rubbish lense over houses, Aristide ceramics. Cooke (1976d:137).
Gif-1641	El Cafetal	S	A.D. 390	100	290–490	A.D. 460–480	Aristide/Tonosi Phase IV	Tonosi-style pottery. Cooke (1976d:137); Ichon (1980).
I-5983	Las Huacas		A.D. 405	100	305–505	A.D. 470–500	Aristide/Tonosi Phase IV	Dates a burial ground with Tonosi and Montevideo ceramics. I do not know with which kind of ceramic the date was recovered (Cooke 1976d:137; de Brizuela 1971).
Gif-1642	El Indio	S	A.D. 450	100	350–550	A.D. 540	Tonosi/Conte phases IV–V	Tonosi-style pottery. Cooke (1976d:137); Ichon (1972).
M-1471	Mariato		A.D. 470	120	350–590	A.D. 560	Aristide/Tonosi/Conte phases IV–V	Mound 2, 190–205 cm. McGimsey (1961); Cooke (1976d:137); Haberland (1978:400).
I-8556	Sitio Sierra		A.D. 475	110	365–585	A.D. 565	Aristide/Tonosi/Conte	Rubbish lense over houses, Aristide ceramics. Cooke (1976d:137).
M-1473	Mariato		A.D. 550	120	430–670	A.D. 620		Mound 4, 130–150 cm. Cooke (1976d:137); McGimsey (1961). Apparently mislabeled as "M-1475" in Haberland (1978:406–7).
I-7309	Miraflores		A.D. 765	80	685–845	A.D. 825–840	Macaracas Phase VI	Tomb 2 of a cemetery with deep, complex rock-cut tombs. Associated with gold-working and Macaracas polychromes. Cooke (1976d:137).
I-7310	Miraflores		A.D. 815	80	735–895	A.D. 870–885	Macaracas Phase VI	Tomb 1 of the same cemetery as I-7309. Cooke (1976d:137).
GrN-2200	Playa Venado		A.D. 825	65	760–890	A.D. 895–905	Macaracas/Early Cocle	No date—apparently from a "burial urn" (Cooke 1976d:137). "Probably too early" (Haberland 1978).
Gif-1520	La Bernadina (TI-1)		A.D. 850	95	755–945	A.D. 920	Macaracas Phase VI	Underneath a circular structure, with Bisquit-like modeled ceramics. Cooke (1976d:137); Ichon (1969).
GX-1545	Guaniquito (TI-28)		A.D. 995	120	875–1115	A.D. 1035	Macaracas Phase VI	Cooke (1976d:137); Ichon (1969).
I-8381	Sitio Sierra		A.D. 1030	80	950–1110	A.D. 1070	Macaracas, Phase VI	Underneath a geometric polychrome vessel alongside a burial. Cooke (1976d:137).
I-8382	Nata (NA-8)		A.D. 1075	80	995–1155	A.D. 1100–1120	Macaracas/Parita phases VI–VIIA	From a hearth, probably associated with geometric (Parita–El Hatillo) ceramics (Cooke 1976d:137).
I-317	El Hatillo (HE-4)		A.D. 1535	90	1445–1625	A.D. 1440	El Hatillo Phase VIIIB	Apparently from a tomb with El Hatillo polychromes; data unpublished. Cooke (1976d:137).

APPENDIX 9. RADIOCARBON SAMPLES FROM CENTRAL AMERICA, ELIMINATED FOR ANALYTICAL OR IN-TERPRETIVE REASONS.

Sample Number	Site	Mat.	Uncorr. Date	S.D.	Range S.D. ×1 (68%)	MASCA Range or Midpoint	Phase/Period	Comments
El Salvador								
FSU-248	Quelepa	C	1370 B.C.	390	1760–980			Excessive deviation; probable sample contamination (Andrews V 1976:42).
TX-2323	Cambio(?)	C	550 B.C.	150	700–400			Earlier; Ilopango eruption(?); excessive deviation.
FSU-366	Quelepa	C	150 B.C.	150	300–1 B.C.			Excessive deviation; also suspected analytical error (Andrews V 1976:42).
GFIGNR-5004		C	A.D. 25	215	190 B.C.–A.D. 240			Ilopango "tierra blanca joven" eruption; excessive deviation.
TX-3113	Ceren	C	A.D. 100	360	260 B.C.–A.D. 460			Ceren house, Laguna Caldera eruption; excessive deviation; small sample.
FSU-367	Quelepa	C	A.D. 410	120	290–530			Rejected due to analytical error (Andrews V 1976:44).
TX-3120	Ceren	C	A.D. 440	390	50–830			Ceren house, Laguna Caldera eruption; excessive deviation.
FSU-353	Quelepa	C	A.D. 490	180	310–670		Shila I	Excessive deviation; probably dedicatory str. 4; contained two Chaparrastique Red-on-orange sherds; small sample (Andrews V 1976:42).
GFIGNR-5001		C	A.D. 500	310	190–810			Ilopango "tierra blanca joven" eruption; excessive deviation.
TX-3116	Cambio	C	A.D. 1690	80	1610–1770			Historic canal.
Honduras								
Gif-1325	Los Naranjos	C	1730 B.C.	110	1840–1620		pre-Jaral	Non-human charcoal; some animal disturbance (Baudez and Becquelin 1973:405).
UGA-1285	Rio Claro		A.D. 680	155	525–835			Spurious date, given its context (Healy 1980:T2); excessive deviation.
SI-280	Choluteca, site 13	C	A.D. 680	240	440–920		Amapala	Too early: phase runs A.D. 950–1250, according to Baudez (Healy, pers. comm.).
Greater Nicoya								
Y-810	Matapalo	C	A.D. 80	200	120 B.C.–A.D. 280		Zoned Bichrome	G11/2J, Cut 2, Monte Fresco Phase (Sweeney 1976:42); excessive deviation.
Y-809	Matapalo	C	A.D. 420	280	140–700		Zoned Bichrome	G11/1K, Cut 1, Monte Fresco Phase (Sweeney 1976:42); spurious date (Healy 1980:T2); excessive deviation.
P-2168	Chahuite Escondido	C	A.D. 880	50	830–930			Spurious date, given its context (Healy 1980b:T.xx).
GSY-99	La Bocana		A.D. 945	90	855–1035			1/M3; contaminated sample (Haberland 1978:406).
I-9866	Vidor	C	A.D. 965	165	820–1150			Mound B; small sample, excessive deviation.

Lab No.	Site / Provenience		Date	±	Range	Phase	Notes
M-1172	Chahuite Escondido		A.D. 1030	75	955–1105		Contaminated through grave mixing (Haberland 1978:406).
P-2169	Chahuite Escondido		A.D. 1080	40	1040–1120		Spurious date, given context (Healy 1980b:T.xx).
Y-816	Chahuite Escondido		A.D. 1110	70	1040–1180		B1/1B; apparently spurious date (Healy 1980:T2).
UCLA-2151	Mojica		A.D. 1290	80	1210–1370		Spurious date, contaminated sample.
GSY-98	La Bocana		A.D. 1435	150	1285–1585		1/G1 (Haberland 1978:405); excessive deviation.
HV-2669	Ometepe Island	Late Polychrome	A.D. 1490	75	1415–1565		Contaminated sample (Haberland 1978:405).
UCLA-2167 C	Nacascolo		Modern Carbon				
Central Valley Costa Rica							
UCLA-2167 D	Grecia	C	A.D. 1590	80	1510–1670		S7.9, Artifact #233. Contaminated sample.
UCLA-2175 G	26-CN Barrial de Heredia	C	A.D. 425	90	335–515		26-M.2, Level 3: "too early" (Snarskis, pers. comm.); Late Curridabat-Phase ceramics possibly mixed with Pavas-Phase materials.
Atlantic Watershed Costa Rica							
UCLA-2113 B	18-LM La Montaña	C	325 B.C.	160	485–165	La Montaña	Layer D, possibly contaminated from later La Selva–Phase cemetery (Snarskis); also excessive deviation.
UCLA-2113 C	18-LM Turrialba	C	A.D. 220	60	160–280	La Selva	18-8, Early La Selva cemetery, possibly mixed with Layer D; too early (Snarskis).
I-7514	Severo Ledesma 7-SL	C	A.D. 345	165	180–510	El Bosque	Strat pit 5, levels 5–8 (Snarskis 1976a), excessive deviation.
Sh-5-5475A	El Cardel (C-1)		A.D. 420	210	210–630	El Bosque	Middle Period A, Haberland (1978:406); TPI 75 cm (Kennedy 1976:88); El Bosque ceramics (Snarskis, pers. comm.); excessive deviation.
I-7721	Finoa Patricia 41-FP	C	A.D. 425	185	240–610	El Bosque	41-1: Level 3, stratigraphic pit (Snarskis); excessive deviation.
UCLA-2113 F	La Cabaña 20-CB	C	A.D. 740	60	680–800	El Bosque	Corridor tomb, possibly disturbed, "too late" (Snarskis).
Sh-50-5592A	Platanillo (C-27)		A.D. 810	220	590–1030		TP7 (Kennedy 1976:88) possibly mixed El Bosque, La Selva, and La Cabaña ceramics (Snarskis); excessive deviation.
Sh-7-5475A	Aquiares (C-74)		A.D. 900	240	660–1140		TP1 (Kennedy 1976:88) possibly mixed La Selva and La Cabaña ceramics (Snarskis); excessive deviation.
Sh-29-5592A	Aquiares (C-24)		A.D. 920	290	630–1210		TP1 (Kennedy 1976:88) possibly mixed El Bosque, La Selva, and La Cabaña ceramics (Snarskis); excessive deviation.

APPENDIX 9 (continued)

Sample Number	Site	Mat.	Uncorr. Date	S.D.	Range S.D. × 1 (68%)	MASCA Range or Midpoint	Phase/ Period	Comments
Sh-45-5211A	Rosa Maria (C-29)		A.D. 970	170	800–1140			TP2 (Kennedy 1976:88) possibly mixed El Bosque, La Selva, and La Cabaña ceramics (Snarskis); excessive deviation.
Sh-6-5475A	Monte Cristo (C-87)		A.D. 990	430	560–1420			TP2 (Kennedy 1976:88); possibly mixed La Selva and La Cabaña ceramics (Snarskis); excessive deviation.
LSU-70-173	Guayabo		A.D. 997	241	756–1238			Mixed mound fill (Aguilar 1972); excessive deviation.
UCLA-2175I	Guacimo	C	A.D. 1030	80	950–1110		La Cabaña	7-Tomb VIII, possibly mixed with El Bosque ceramics; "too early" (Snarskis).
SI-144	Marin (W-4)	C	A.D. 1050				La Selva (too late)	
Sh-8-5475A	Descanso (C-39)		A.D. 1080	390	690–1470			TP2 (Kennedy 1976:88); La Selva, La Cabaña (Snarskis); excessive deviation.
I-8914	Turrialba 4-IT	C	A.D. 1110	195	915–1305		La Selva	4-Ib., Level 6, La Selva B ceramics; "too late" (Snarskis); excessive deviation.
Sh-28-5592A	Guayabo 4		A.D. 1220	210	1010–1430			TP7 (Kennedy 1976:88); mixed fill(?), La Cabaña (Snarskis); excessive deviation.
Panama, Chiriqui								
I-5871	Piti (BU-17)		735 B.C.	110	845–625			"Too early" (Linares, Sheets, and Rosenthal 1975).
GrN-1516	El Volcan		340 B.C.	45	385–295			Relation between carbon sample and ceramic data uncertain (Haberland 1978:414).
I-7262	Lower Barriles (BU-24)		160 B.C.	275	435 B.C.–A.D. 115			Excessive deviation.
I-7261	Lower Barriles (BU-24)		A.D. 415	210	205–626			Excessive deviation.

Sample	Site		Date	±	Range	Comments
I-5767	La Pitahaya (IS-3)		A.D. 830	150	680–980	Most recent occupation (Linares 1977b:319); excessive deviation.
I-5879	La Pitahaya (IS-3)		A.D. 830	170	660–1000	Most recent occupation (Linares 1977:319); excessive deviation.
I-7236	Lower Barriles (BU-24)		A.D. 1210	150	1060–1360	Excessive deviation.
M-1309	Las Secas Island (IS-17)		A.D. 1835	100	1735–1935	Historic date.

Panama, East of Chiriquí

Sample	Site		Date	±	Range	Comments
FSU-300	Alvina de Parita	C	9449 B.C.	330	9799–9119	Excessive deviation.
Beta-5101	Cueva de los Vampiros		6610 B.C.	160	6770–6450	Test pit 1; beneath sterile hiatus from levels 12/4–13/1 (2.9–3.6 m); associated with bifacial thinning flakes.
TEM-206	Cerro Mangote	S	4760 B.C.	175	4930–4585	"Pothole 1," north wall, 180–190 cm.
Beta-1219	Cerro Mangote	C	4720 B.C.	215	4935–4505	Combined sample from red clay zone.
TEM-208	Monagrillo	S	4350 B.C.	165	4515–4185	Block 2E, 152–157 cm b.s.; corrected for C^{12}/C^{13} fractionation.
I-12,018	Hornito 1		4320 B.C.	280	4600–4040	Cut L, 27–42 cm b.s.
I-12,017	Hornito 1		4230 B.C.	180	4410–4050	Cut L, 15–30 cm b.s.
TEM-174	Cerro Mangote	S	4040 B.C.	180	4040–3860	Outside same shell as TEM-175; "Pothole 1," north wall, 180–190 cm b.s.
I-12,019	Hornito 1		3930 B.C.	260	4190–3670	Cuts E and C(E).
TEM-207	Cerro Mangote	S	3105 B.C.	155	3260–2950	"Pothole 1A," 145–155 cm b.d.; corrected for C^{12}/C^{13} fractionation.
I-7729	Isla Carranza		70 B.C.	155	225 B.C.–A.D. 85	Shell-stamped pottery in abandoned shaft, associated with maize grinding implements; excessive deviation.
M-11	Monagrillo (HE-5)	S	A.D. 1150	250	900–1400	Presumably related to "Alvina" pottery (post-Monagrillo period) (Cooke, pers. comm.).

APPENDIX 10. RADIOCARBON SAMPLES FROM NORTHERN COLOMBIA.

Sample Number	Site	Mat.	Uncorr. Date	S.D.	Range S.D. x 1 (68%)	MASCA Range or Midpoint	Phase/Period	Comments
GrN-5556	El Abra 2	C	10,450 B.C.	160	10,610–10,290		Abrian	Unit C3, 150–175 cm.
GrN-9375	Tibito	Bone	9790 B.C.	110	9900–9680		Abrian/ Tequendamian	Kill site, Pleistocene megafauna.
GrN-6539	Tequendama 1	C	8970 B.C.	260	9230–8710		Abrian	Square L&M, c. 330–360 cm.
GrN-6270	Tequendama 1	C	8780 B.C.	105	8885–8675		Abrian	Square M(-L), c. 300–325 cm.
B-2134	El Abra 2	C	8770 B.C.	400	9170–8730		Abrian	185–190 cm, El Abra stadial, Unit C4.
GrN-6505	Tequendama 1	C	8640 B.C.	90	8730–8550		Abrian	Square M(-L), ca. 180/205–290/310 cm.
GrN-6731	Tequendama 1	C	8510 B.C.	130	8640–8380		Abrian	Square L, ca. 320–350 cm.
GrN-7114	Tequendama 1	C	8200 B.C.	150	8350–8050		Abrian	Square F1, 150–160 cm.
GrN-7113	Tequendama 1	C	8190 B.C.	100	8290–8090		Abrian	Square L, ca. 305–320 cm.
GrN-6732	Tequendama 1	C	8180 B.C.	150	8330–8030		Abrian	Square I & G II, 160–170 cm.
GrN-8111	Sueva 1	C	8140 B.C.	90	8230–8050		Abrian	Square H, Unit 3, some tools of good chert.
GrN-6210	Tequendama 1	C	8070 B.C.	95	8165–7975		Abrian	Square JI.
GrN-6730	Tequendama 1	C	8040 B.C.	100	8140–7940		Abrian	Square EIII.
GrN-7115	Tequendama 1	C	7790 B.C.	135	7925–7655		Abrian	Square M&L.
GrN-8448	Gachala	C, and humic soil	7410 B.C.	45	7455–7365		Abrian	150–160 cm, with hearths.
GrN-5561	El Abra 2	C	7390 B.C.	90	7480–7300		Abrian	Unit D1, Feature 8; 100–125 cm.
GrN-5746	El Abra 2	C	7375 B.C.	100	7475–7275		Abrian	Unit D1, Feature 8; 125–155 cm.
GrN-8117	Gachala	C	7150 B.C.	160	7310–6990		Abrian	Lowest habitation floor (180 cm), with hearths.
GrN-5710	El Abra 2	C	7075 B.C.	90	7165–6985		Abrian	Unit D1, 75–100 cm.
B-2135	El Abra 4	C	6300 B.C.	100	6400–6200		Abrian	Unit D3, Feature 16; fireplace with clay lining.
GrN-5711	Nemocon 4	C	5580 B.C.	100	5680–5480		Abrian preceramic	Square 4, Unit 5, 130–140 cm.

Lab No.	Site/Culture	Material	Date	±	Range	Alt. Date	Phase	Notes
GrN-7477	Tequendama 1	Bone	5285 B.C.	60	5345–5225		Abrian preceramic	Burial No. 12.
GrN-6729	Tequendama 1	C	5140 B.C.	75	5215–5065		Abrian preceramic	Hearths.
GrN-6728	Tequendama 1	C	5040 B.C.	110	5150–4930		Abrian preceramic	Hearths.
GrN-8456	Nemocon 4	C	4875 B.C.	40	4915–4835		Abrian preceramic	Square A, Unit 5, 120–130 cm.
GrN-6537	Tequendama 1	C	4445 B.C.	70	4515–4375	5110–5185 B.C.	Abrian preceramic	Square A2.
GrN-8112	Sueva 1	C	4400 B.C.	40	4440–4360	5110–5170 B.C.	Abrian preceramic	Square H, Unit 5.
GrN-7478	Tequendama 1	Bone	4070 B.C.	45	4115–4025	4670–4690 B.C.	Abrian preceramic	Burial No. 13.
GrN-7476	Tequendama 1	Bone	3850 B.C.	50	3900–3800	4495 B.C.	Abrian preceramic	Burial No. 7.
SI-153	Puerto Hormiga	Shell	3090 B.C.	70	3160–3020	3700 B.C.	Puerto Hormiga	Trench IV, 110 cm.
SI-152	Puerto Hormiga	Shell	3020 B.C.	70	3090–2950	3650 B.C.	Puerto Hormiga	Trench IV, 78 cm.
SI-151	Puerto Hormiga	C	2870 B.C.	100	2970–2770	3410–3520 B.C.	Puerto Hormiga	Trench IV, 80 cm.
Y-1317	Canapote	C	1940 B.C.	100	2040–1840	2190 B.C.	Late Canapote	Layer 10, Pit A.
Y-1760	Canapote	C	1780 B.C.	120	1900–1660	2110 B.C.	Tesca Phase	Pit D, layer 4.
Y-1318	Barlovento	C	1550 B.C.	110	1660–1440	1720–1870 B.C.	Late Barlovento	Trench II, 150 cm; stratigraphically between W-743 and W-741.
W-739	Barlovento	Shell	1520 B.C.	120	1640–1400	1710–1750 B.C.	Middle Barlovento	Trench II, 600 cm.
W-743	Barlovento	Shell	1190 B.C.	120	1310–1070	1370–1390 B.C.	Late Barlovento	Trench II, 300 cm; slight discrepancy with Y-1318.
M-1176	Malambo	C	1120 B.C.	100	1220–1020	1270–1300 B.C.	Malambo	Trench 3, 100–110 cm; considerably earlier than other dates in the series.
W-741	Barlovento	Shell	1030 B.C.	120	1150–910	1160–1180 B.C.	Late Barlovento	Trench II, 100 cm; slight discrepancy with Y-1318.
IAN-148	El Infiernito (Moniquira)	C	930 B.C.	95	1025–835	1020 B.C.	Muisca?	See also IAN-119.
IAN-135	Estorbo 1	C	350 B.C.	95	445–255	410 B.C.	Phase 1	Lower part of midden; 140–150 cm.
GrN-6536	Tequendama 1	C	275 B.C.	35	310–240	240–380 B.C.	Early ceramic	Mosquera crushed rock; Mosquera Red Incised.

APPENDIX 10 (continued)

Sample Number	Site	Mat.	Uncorr. Date	S.D.	Range S.D. ×1 (68%)	MASCA Range or Midpoint	Phase/Period	Comments
GrN-6544	Nemocon	C	260 B.C.	65	325–195	210–380 B.C.	Pre-Muisca	3.10 m; lowest stratum, household wares (Cardale-Schrimpff 1976).
IAN-128	El Infiernito (Moniquira)	?	230 B.C.	140	370–90	200–250 B.C.	Muisca?	See also IAN-119.
IAN-134	Estorbo 1	C	225 B.C.	110	335–115	185–200 B.C.	Phase 1	Lower part of midden; 140–150 cm.
Tk-131	Momil	Shell	200 B.C.	60	260–140	140–190 B.C.	Momil 1b	
GrN-6908	Momil	Shell	175 B.C.	35	210–140	125 B.C.	Momil 1b	
GrN-8452	Zipaquira V	C	150 B.C.	60	210–90	70–110 B.C.	Pre-Muisca boiling site	Stratum 1a, 1.5 m; Cardale-Schrimpff excavations.
BM-805	Cueva de la Antigua	C	38 B.C.	98	136 B.C.–A.D. 50	A.D. 60	Antigua Phase	Bray, unpublished excavations. Pottery has links with the Rio Cesar material of the Caribbean lowlands, and was stratified below Carrizal pottery associated with protohistoric Guane Indians.
GrN-6542	Nenocon	C	25 B.C.	70	95 B.C.–A.D. 45	A.D. 50	Pre-Muisca	Layer 18; house floor.
GrN-8453	Zipaquira V	C	5 B.C.	40	45 B.C.–A.D. 35	A.D. 70	Pre-Muisca salt-boiling site	Stratum 2i; 0.85 m.
GrN-8454	Zipaquira V	C	A.D. 30	35	5 B.C.–A.D. 65	A.D. 90–110	Pre-Muisca salt-boiling site	Stratum 5, 0.55 m.
GrN-9240	Zipaquira V	C	A.D. 60	50	10–110	A.D. 140	Pre-Muisca salt-boiling site	Stratum 2f, 0.95 m.
M-1175	Malambo	C	A.D. 60	100	40 B.C.–A.D. 160	A.D. 140	Plato-Zambrano?	Tr. 3, 60–70 cm (cf. M-1176).
Beta-2596	Potrero Marusa (Japon, Cuiva)	C	A.D. 70	90	20 B.C.–A.D. 160	A.D. 140	Modelada-Pintada tradition	Rubbish from a house platform in prehispanic town (Plazas and Falchetti 1981).
GrN-6543	Nemocon	C	A.D. 70	100	30 B.C.–A.D. 170	A.D. 140	Pre-Muisca	Layer 24; industrial salt-boiling debris.
Beta-2598	Potrero Marusa (Japon, Cuiva)	C	A.D. 150	70	80–220	A.D. 210	Modelada-Pintada tradition	Rubbish from a house platform in prehispanic town (Plazas and Falchetti 1981).

Lab no.	Site	Material	Date	±	Range	Calibrated	Culture	Notes
IAN-10	Simijaca	Cloth	A.D. 170	80	90–250	A.D. 220–250	Muisca?	Mummy wrap of fique cloth.
Beta-2602	San Cayentano, Caño Carate	C	A.D. 270	140	130–410	A.D. 320–360	Modelada-Pintada tradition	Rubbish from house platform (Plazas and Falchetti 1981).
BM-806	Cueva de la Antigua	C	A.D. 280	44	236–324	A.D. 360–380	Antigua Phase	See also BM-805.
IAN-116	Estorbo 1	C	A.D. 280	130	150–410	A.D. 360–380		
GrN-4729	Los Solares	Charred maize	A.D. 310	50	260–360	A.D. 390	Muisca?	Cache of maize cobs; same context had Muisca sherds and tumbaga items.
IAN-90	Los Jagüeyes	C	A.D. 335	100	235–435	A.D. 405		Angulo 1978.
IAN-115	Estorbo 1	C	A.D. 420	130	290–550	A.D. 490–530		Burial.
IAN-12	Guatavita	C	A.D. 450	90	360–540	A.D. 540	Muisca	Core material from metal item, Museo del Oro.
IAN-61	Cuiva area	C	A.D. 450	90	360–540	A.D. 540	Modelada-Pintada tradition	Treasure-hunter sample from a burial tumulus (Plazas, Falchetti, and Saenz 1979b).
M-1475	Mina de Oro	C	A.D. 460	100	360–560	A.D. 550		65 cm; humus overlying stratum B. Radiocarbon 7:144–45; Angulo 1978.
GrN-4902	La Lusitania (Municipio Chiscas)	Cloth	A.D. 480	50	430–530	A.D. 570	Lache	Mummy wrapping.
M-1302-1306	Palmira	C	A.D. 500	110	390–610	A.D. 570–590		Angulo 1978.
IAN-60	Padula II (Bolivar)	?	A.D. 500	130	370–630	A.D. 570–590	?	David Behar A. (unpublished excavations).
M-1178	Malambo	C	A.D. 565	75	490–640	A.D. 630	Malambo	Tr. 4, 90–100 cm; excavator suspects too recent.
Beta-3563	Quebrada de las Animas	C	A.D. 580	120	460–700	A.D. 640	Tairona?	With Tairona "Rojo Burdo" sherds (Turbay, unpublished excavations).
BM-804	Cueva de la Antigua	C	A.D. 582	103	479–685	A.D. 640	Antigua Phase	See also BM-805.
Y-730	Las Mercedes	C	A.D. 590	120	470–710	A.D. 650	no detail	3.4 m below surface of a deep deposit; Radiocarbon 1969:632.
GrN-4730	Los Solares	C	A.D. 600	50	550–650	A.D. 660	Muisca	Part of a wooden structure.
IAN-69	Zipaquira III	C	A.D. 610	100	510–710	A.D. 650–670	Muisca	Excavator believes too early.

APPENDIX 10 (continued)

Sample Number	Site	Mat.	Uncorr. Date	S.D.	Range S.D. ×1 (68%)	MASCA Range or Midpoint	Phase/ Period	Comments
BM-1382	Cueva de la Antigua	C	A.D. 615	60	555–675	A.D. 670	Antigua Phase	See also BM-805.
I-1963	Guatavita	C	A.D. 645	95	550–740	A.D. 690	Muisca	Core material from nose ornament, Museo del Oro.
M-1174	Malambo	C	A.D. 650	75	575–725	A.D. 690	Plato-Zambrano?	Tr. 3, 40–50 cm.
Beta-2601	Caño Carate	C	A.D. 680	120	560–800	A.D. 730	Modelada-Pintada tradition	Buried soil from raised field and canal system (Plazas and Falchetti 1981).
IAN-36	Fuquene	Wood	A.D. 750	100	650–850	A.D. 800–820	Muisca?	Anthropomorphic wooden figurine.
IAN-42	Guasca	C	A.D. 800	80	720–880	A.D. 860–880	Muisca	With a metal tunjo in a burial; excavations A. Botiva.
GrN-4004	Laguna de Chisaca	C	A.D. 840	60	780–900	A.D. 910	Muisca	Charcoal from core of a cast copper shell.
GrN-9242	La Mireya, El Anclar 1	C	A.D. 905	45	860–950	A.D. 965	Modelada-Pintada tradition	Tumulus burial with pottery (Plazas, Falchetti, and Saenz 1979b).
M-1477	Loma del Cuchal	C	A.D. 930	100	830–1030	A.D. 980–1000		80 cm, end of first occupation (Angulo 1978); *Radiocarbon* 7:144–45.
M-1308-1310	Tasajeras	C	A.D. 950	105	845–1055	A.D. 1010		Angulo 1978.
Y-732	Bucarelia	C	A.D. 960	80	880–1040	A.D. 1020		1 m below surface; *Radiocarbon* 1969:632.
I-2362	Santo Domingo	C	A.D. 960	90	870–1050	A.D. 1020	Muisca	Core material from metal nose ornament, Museo del Oro.
UGa-819	Cangaru	C	A.D. 965	120	845–1085	A.D. 1020		Just before transition from lower levels with "Magdalena" pottery to upper with Tairona imports (Sutherland and Murdy 1975).
IAN-11	Buenavista	C	A.D. 1000	120	880–1120	A.D. 1040	Muisca	Charcoal from core of metal nose ornament, Museo del Oro.
M-1312	Loma de Lopez	Shell	A.D. 1005	100	905–1105	A.D. 1045		Cut 2, 2.8–3.0 m (Angulo 1978); *Radiocarbon* 6:17–18.

Lab no.	Site	Material	Date	±	Range	A.D.	Affiliation	Notes
M-1311	Loma de Lopez	S	A.D. 1045	100	945–1145	A.D. 1085		Cut 2, 2.2–2.4 m (Angulo 1978); *Radiocarbon* 6:17–18.
IAN-31	Guasca site 35, Tomb 2	Bone	A.D. 1050	120	930–1170	A.D. 1090	Muisca	With gold sheet and stone beads; excavations by A. Botiva.
GaK-3322	Tebaida, Tomb T-LP-1	C	A.D. 1050	120	930–1170	A.D. 1090	Caldas complex	Charcoal scraped from pottery in same tomb as GaK-3320.
BM-807	Unknown	C	A.D. 1055	59	996–1114	A.D. 1095	Muisca	Charcoal from core of cast copper figure.
GaK-3323	Cordoba, Tomb C-LSi-1	C	A.D. 1100	80	1020–1180	A.D. 1150–1180	Transitional Middle Cauca-Caldas	Charcoal from Quimbaya-style tomb (Bruhns, *Cespedesia* 5:103).
GrN-4903	Los Solares	Wood	A.D. 1110	50	1060–1160	A.D. 1180	Muisca	Wood from column of Sogamoso Sun Temple(?).
GaK-3320	Tebaida, Tomb T-LP-1	C	A.D. 1120	90	1030–1210	A.D. 1180	Caldas complex	One of the so-called "Quimbaya" styles (Bruhns, *Cespedesia* 5:103).
M-1310	Loma de Lopez	Shell	A.D. 1125	100	1025–1225	A.D. 1185		Cut 2, 60–80 cm (Angulo 1978); *Radiocarbon* 6:17–18.
I-8957	Cano Carate	Organic carbon	A.D. 1175	80	1095–1255	A.D. 1210	Equate with Modelada-Pintada tradition	From a buried soil associated with ridged fields. Perhaps too young due to root/humic acid contamination. Terminus ante quem for abandonment of fields (Parsons 1978). Cf. Beta-2601.
IVIC-159	Cueva de los Indios	Cotton cloth	A.D. 1185	85	1100–1270	A.D. 1225	Probably Carrizal	Textile from mummy burial on Mesa de los Santos, in Guane territory. *Radiocarbon* 8:209.
M-1476	Loma del Cuchal	C	A.D. 1230	100	1130–1330	A.D. 1250		Reoccupation, 60 cm (Angulo 1978). *Radiocarbon* 7:144–45.
Beta-2850	Cueva del Caucho	Human bone	A.D. 1230	90			Carrizal	Guane burial with ornaments of Caribbean shell.
IAN-8	Silva	C maize	A.D. 1240	50	1190–1290	A.D. 1260	Muisca	With maize.
BM-803	Carrizal	C	A.D. 1268	66	1202–1334	A.D. 1260–1290	Mixed	60–70 cm; mixed Guane and pre-Guane sherds.
BM-802	Carrizal	C	A.D. 1347	63	1284–1410	A.D. 1350	Carrizal Phase	30–50 cm. Pottery linked with protohistoric Guane Indians. Closely related to Muisca.

APPENDIX 10 (continued)

Sample Number	Site	Mat.	Uncorr. Date	S.D.	Range S.D. × 1 (68%)	MASCA Range or Midpoint	Phase/Period	Comments
GrN-9247	Buritaca-200	C	A.D. 1385	50	1335–1435	A.D. 1380	Tairona	Tomb with Tairona goldwork (Groot 1980).
GaK-3324	Cordoba Tomb C-LSi-1	C	A.D. 1400	70	1330–1470	A.D. 1390	Transitional Middle Cauca-Caldas	Charcoal from a vessel in the same tomb as GaK-3323.
GrN-9243	Las Palmas	C	A.D. 1415	50	1365–1465	A.D. 1390	Tradicion Incisa-Alisada	Urn burial in house site (Plazas, Falchetti, and Saenz 1979b).
IVIC-158	Department of Boyaca	Wood	A.D. 1420	100	1320–1520	A.D. 1390	Muisca	Wooden statue from burial cave; *Radiocarbon* 8:209.
I-8956	Caño Carate	Organic carbon	A.D. 1445	70	1375–1515	A.D. 1410	Modelada-Pintada	Cf. Beta-2601; Parsons 1978.
I-6362	El Abra 3	C	A.D. 1445	104	1341–1549	A.D. 1410	Muisca	Unit E1, 45 cm, child burial no. 2.
GrN-8892	Zipaquira III	C	A.D. 1475	25	1450–1500	A.D. 1420	Muisca	Cardale-Schrimpff excavations.
GrN-8455	Zipaquira III	C	A.D. 1500	50	1450–1550	A.D. 1430	Muisca	Cardale-Schrimpff excavations.
Beta-2898	Guaiquiri	C	A.D. 1510	60	1450–1570	A.D. 1430	Plato-Zambrano	Unpublished excavations, L. Reines.
I-8958	Caño Carate	Organic carbon	A.D. 1515	70	1445–1585	A.D. 1430	Modelada-Pintada	Cf. Beta-2601; Parsons 1978.
Beta-3564	Sitio Estrella	C	A.D. 1550	90	1460–1640	A.D. 1450	Tairona	Tomb 2; Turbay, unpublished excavations.
IAN-118	Buritaca-200	C	A.D. 1550	150	1400–1700	A.D. 1450	Tairona	Groot de Mahecha, unpublished excavations.
BM-1384	Llano de los Gallos	C	A.D. 1569	78	1491–1647	A.D. 1460–1500	Carrizal Phase	Northern variant from Mesa de los Santos; associated with protohistoric Guane Indians.
GrN-9329	Zipaquira III	C	A.D. 1590	30	1560–1620	A.D. 1470–1500	Muisca	Cardale-Schrimpff excavations.
Beta-2896	Las Palmas	C	A.D. 1640	50	1590–1690	A.D. 1510–1600	Tradicion Incisa-Alisada	Funerary offering from burial in house site (Plazas and Falchetti 1981).
M-1314	Rio Anija (Bahia de Solano, Choco)	C	A.D. 1615	100	1515–1715	A.D. 1520	Protohistoric	Incised pottery. A mission was in existence 1632–46 among the Idabaez Indians; *Radiocarbon* 6:17.

Radiocarbon Samples from Northern Colombia, Eliminated for Analytical or Interpretive Reasons

Lab No.	Site	Material	Date	±	Tradition	Comments
GrN-6538	Tequendama 1	C	26,940 B.C.	840		Square III, ca. 175–195 cm; archaeologically sterile.
GrN-6579	Tequendama 1	C	20,300 B.C.	470		Square D, 215–250 cm; archaeologically sterile.
I-6363	El Abra 4	C	7100 B.C.	470	Abrian	Unit D2A, 94 cm, clay-lined fireplace; excessive deviation.
B-2133	El Abra 3	C	6850 B.C.	430	Abrian	190–191 cm; excessive deviation.
B-2137	El Abra 3	C	6810 B.C.	350	Abrian	Unit D2A, 100–118 cm, occupation surface with deer bone; excessive deviation.
GrN-8447	Gachala	C	5250 B.C.	90	Abrian	1.7 m with hearths; too recent; cf. GrN-8448 and GrN-8117.
IS-445	Puerto Hormiga	Shell	2925 B.C.	170	Puerto Hormiga	Trench I, 100 cm; excessive deviation.
IS-1123	Puerto Hormiga	C	2552 B.C.	250	Puerto Hormiga	Trench I, 70 cm; excessive deviation.
GrN-5172	Quebrada Catarniquera	C	1830 B.C.	95		Charcoal from varved clay 8 m below terrace surface. Same geological deposit as El Espinal Point. Date is unacceptably recent (Vogel and Lerman 1969).
Beta-3562	Quebrada de las Animas	C	1430 B.C.	140		Stratigraphically below Beta-3563. No archaeological materials. Turbay, unpublished excavations.
IAN-82	Zipaquira III	C	795 B.C.	195	Muisca	Cardale-Schrimpff excavations; unacceptably early.
IAN-93	Zipaquira III	C	580 B.C.	185	Muisca	Unacceptably early for Muisca.
IAN-119	El Infiernito (Moniquira)	C	540 B.C.	195	Muisca(?)	Site with stone columns; Silva Celis excavation; appears too ancient.
IAN-121	Zipaquira V	C	500 B.C.	200		Stratum 2a, 1.2 m; excessive deviation.
IAN-81	Zipaquira V	C	350 B.C.	275		Stratum 5, 0.55 m; excessive deviation.
BM-1381	Cueva de la Antigua	C	A.D. 406	201	Antiqua	See also BM-805; excessive deviation.
Beta-2595	Potrero Jolon (Japon, Cuiva)	C	A.D. 600	160	Modelada-Pintada tradition	Rubbish from house platform (Plazas and Falchetti 1981); excessive deviation.

APPENDIX 10 (continued)

Sample Number	Site	Mat.	Uncorr. Date	Range S.D. ×1 (68%)	S.D.	MASCA Range or Midpoint	Phase/Period	Comments
IAN-89	Cecilio	C	A.D. 990	375			Cienega de Pajaral complex	Angulo 1978; excessive deviation.
I-6684	Sutamarchan	C	A.D. 1005	260			Muisca	Pottery manufacturing site; Falchetti excavations; excessive deviation.
IAN-91	Santa Maria de la Antigua de Darien	C	A.D. 1190	240			Contact period Spanish towns	G. Arcila Velez, unpublished excavations; excessive deviation.
M-1313	Cupica	C	A.D. 1227	100			Cupica II fill	Probably a few centuries too recent.
IAN-124	Las Palmas 1	C	A.D. 1305	170			Tradicion Incisa-Alisada	Rubbish from habitation site (Plazas and Falchetti 1981); excessive deviation.
IAN-86	Buritaca-200	C	A.D. 1360	160			Tairona	Turbay (1980); excessive deviation.
IAN-84	Cuiva area	C	A.D. 1370	370			Modelada-Pintada tradition	Treasure hunter's sample from a burial tumulus.
IAN-44	Cuiva area	C	A.D. 1505	80			Modelada-Pintada tradition	Treasure hunter's sample from a tumulus grave; appears too recent (Falchetti 1976:227).
IAN-32	Boavita	Textile	A.D. 1580	200			Muisca	Mummy wrap; excessive deviation.
M-1177	Malambo	C	A.D. 1600	75				Tr. 4, 80–90 cm (cf. M-1178); clearly wrong.
B-2136	El Abra 3	C	A.D. 1610	260			Muisca/Colonial	Unit E2, 50 cm; excessive deviation.
IAN-117	Buritaca-200	C	A.D. 1635	170			Tairona	Groot de Mahecha, unpublished excavations; excessive deviation.
IAN-120	El Anclar	C	A.D. 1670	180				Excessive deviation.
Beta-2815	Aguadulce (Municipio Matanza)	Human bone	post-A.D. 1780					Burial with pottery of grooved/channeled style; too early.

References

References

ABEL, SUZANNE
1978   "An Interpretation of Two Burnt
        Clay Features in an Early Central
        American Village: Vidor Site, Bay
        of Culebra, Guanacaste, Costa
        Rica" (M.A. thesis, Brown Uni-
        versity).
ABEL-VIDOR, S.
1980a   "Dos hornos precolombinos en
        el Sitio Vidor," Vinculos 6(1–2):
        43–50 (National Museum of
        Costa Rica, San Jose).
1980b   "The Historical Sources for the
        Greater Nicoya Archaeological
        Subarea," Vinculos 6(1–2): 155–
        86 (National Museum of Costa
        Rica, San Jose).
1981   "Ethnohistorical Approaches to
        the Archaeology of Greater Ni-
        coya," in Between Continents/
        Between Seas: Precolumbian Art
        of Costa Rica, ed. E. Benson
        (New York: H. N. Abrams).

ACCOLA, RICHARD M.
1978a   "A Decorative Sequence of Pre-
        historic Ceramics from the Vidor
        Site, Guanacaste, Costa Rica"
        (M.A. thesis, University of Texas).
1978b   "Revision de los tipos de cer-
        amica del Periodo Policromo
        Medio en Guanacaste," Vinculos
        4: 80–105 (National Museum of
        Costa Rica, San Jose).
ADAMS, JOHN K., JOHN BARBER, AND
CHRISTOPHER DERE
1980   "Investigaciones geo-arqueologi-
        cas en el Panama central: reporte
        preliminar," paper presented at
        the Third National Congress of
        Anthropology, Archaeology, and
        Ethnohistory of Panama, Pan-
        ama.
ADAMS, R. E. W.
1971   The Ceramics of Altar de Sacri-
        ficios, Papers of the Peabody Mu-
        seum of Archaeology and

Ethnology, vol. 63, no. 1 (Cambridge, Mass.: Harvard University).

AGUILAR P., CARLOS H.

1953   *Retes, un deposito arqueologico en las faldas de Irazu* (San Jose, Costa Rica).

1972   *Guayabo de Turrialba* (San Jose: Editorial Costa Rica).

1973   "Contribucion al estudio de las sequencias culturales en el area central de Costa Rica," paper presented at the Ninth International Congress of Anthropological and Ethnological Sciences, Chicago.

1974   "Asentamientos indigenas en el area central de Costa Rica," *America Indigena* 34: 311–17.

1975   "El Molino: Un sitio de la fase Pavas en Cartago," *Vinculos* 1: 18–56 (Museo Nacional de Costa Rica, San Jose).

1976   "Relaciones de las culturas precolombinas en el intermoñtano central de Costa Rica," *Vinculos* 2: 75–86 (National Museum of Costa Rica, San Jose).

AGURCIA FASQUELLE, RICARDO

1976   "Los petroglifos de Valladolid, Comayagua," *Fourteenth Mesa Redonda, Sociedad Mexicana de Antropologia* 2:229–36.

1978   "Las figurillas de Playa de Los Muertos, Honduras," *Yaxkin* 2: 221–40.

1980   "Asentamientos del Clasico Tardio en el Valle de Comayagua," *Yaxkin* 3: 200–215.

ALFARO, A.

1893   "Arqueologia Costarricense," *El Centenario* 4: 241–46.

1896   *Antiguedades de Costa Rica* (San Jose, Costa Rica: Tipografia Nacional).

ANDAGOYA, PASCUAL DE

1913   "Relacion de los sucesos de Pedrarias Davila en las provincias de Tierra-Firme y de lo ocurrido en el descubrimiento del Mar del Sur y costas del Peru y Nicaragua, escrita por el adelantado Pascual de Andagoya" (fragment), in *El Descubrimiento del Oceano Pacifico: Vasco Nuñez de Balboa, Hernando de Magallanes y Sus Compañeros. Tomo II: Documentos Relativos a Nuñez de Balboa,* ed. J. T. Medina (Santiago de Chile: Imprenta Universitaria).

ANDREWS V, E. WYLLYS

1976   *The Archaeology of Quelepa, El Salvador,* Middle American Research Institute, Publication 42 (New Orleans: Tulane University).

1977   "The Southeastern Periphery of Mesoamerica: A View from Eastern Salvador," in *Social Process in Maya Prehistory,* ed. Norman Hammond (New York: Academic Press).

ANGULO VALDES, CARLOS

1951   "Arqueologia de Turbara," *Divulgaciones Etnologicas* 2(3): 7–72.

1962   "Evidencias de la serie Barrancoide en el norte de Colombia," *Revista Colombiana de Antropologia* 11: 73–88.

1963   "Cultural Development in Colombia," in *Aboriginal Cultural Development in Latin America: An Interpretative Review,* Smithsonian Miscellaneous Collections, vol. 146, no. 1, ed. B. J. Meggers and C. Evans (Washington, D.C.: Smithsonian Institution).

1978   *Arqueologia de la Cienega Grande de Santa Marta* (Bogota: Banco de la Republica, Fundacion de Investigaciones Arqueologicas Nacionales).

1981   *La tradicion Malambo* (Bogota: Banco de la Republica, Fundacion de Investigaciones Arqueologicas Nacionales).

ARDILA CALDERON, GERARDO I.
1980   "Investigaciones arqueologicas en la Mana y las Peñitas (Chia)," *Micronoticias Antropologicas* (septiembre–octubre): 11–13.
1982   "Analisis y perspectivas de los estudios sobre la etapa litica en Colombia," MS prepared for the Seminario Nacional de Arqueologia, Bogota, November.

ASHMORE, WENDY
1979   *Quirigua Reports, Vol. 1*, Mu-
(ed.)   seum Monograph 37, University Museum, University of Pennsylvania (Philadelphia).

AVENI, A., AND H. HARTUNG
1976   "Investigacion preliminar de las orientaciones astronomicas de Copan," *Yaxkin* 1(3): 8–13.

BALSER, CARLOS
1953   *El jade precolombino de Costa Rica* (San Jose: Museo Nacional).
1962   "Notes on Resin in Aboriginal Central America," *Proceedings of the Thirty-fourth International Congress of Americanists* 1: 374–80 (Vienna).
1974   *El jade de Costa Rica* (San Jose, Costa Rica: Libreria Lehmann).
1980   *Jade precolombino de Costa Rica*, Instituto Nacional de Seguros (San Jose, Costa Rica).

BARBER, JOHN
1980   "The Influence of Geological Parameters on Man's Early Adaptation to the Coastal Environment of Central Panama," paper presented at the Annual Meeting of the Geological Society of America, Atlanta.
1981   "Geomorphology, Stratigraphy and Sedimentology of the Santa Maria Drainage Basin, Central Panama" (M.A. thesis, Temple University).

BARTLETT, ALEXANDRA S., AND ELSO S. BARGHOORN
1973   "Phytogeographic History of the Isthmus of Panama during the Past 12,000 Years (A History of Vegetation, Climate, and Sea-Level Change)," in *Vegetation, and Vegetational History of Northern Latin America*, ed. A. Graham (New York: Elsevier Scientific Publishing Co.).

BARTLETT, ALEXANDRA S., ELSO S. BARGHOORN, AND RAINER BERGER
1969   "Fossil Maize from Panama," *Science* 165: 389–90.

BATEMAN, J. T.
1861   "Account of a Visit to the Huacas, or Ancient Graveyards of Chiriqui," *Bulletin of the American Ethnographical Society* 1: 28–33.

BAUDEZ, CLAUDE F.
1962   "Preliminary Report on Archeological Research Projects in the Valley of Tempisque, Guanacaste, Costa Rica," *Proceedings of the Thirty-fourth International Congress of Americanists* 1: 348–65 (Vienna).
1963   "Cultural Development in Lower Central America," in *Aboriginal Cultural Development in Latin America: An Interpretative Review*, Smithsonian Miscellaneous Collections, vol. 146, ed. B. J. Meggers and C. Evans (Washington, D.C.: Smithsonian Institution).
1966   "Niveaux ceramiques au Honduras: une reconsideration de l'evolution culturelle," *Journal de la Societe des Americanistes de Paris* 55: 299–341.
1967   *Recherches archeologiques dans la*

vallee du Tempisque, Guanacaste, Costa Rica, Travaux et Memoires de l'Institut des Hautes Etudes de l'Amerique Latine, no. 18 (Paris: Centre National de la Recherche Scientifique).

1970   *Central America*, trans. James Hogarth (Geneva: Nagel Publishers).

1971   "Commentary on: Inventory of Some Pre-Classic Traits in the Highlands and Pacific Guatemala and Adjacent Areas," in *Observations on the Emergence of Civilization in Mesoamerica*, University of California Archaeological Research Facility, Contribution 11, ed. R. F. Heizer and J. A. Graham (Berkeley).

1973   "Les camps de saliniers de la cote meridionale du Honduras: donnees archeologiques et documents historiques," in *L'Homme, hier et aujourd'hui* (Paris: Editorial Lujas).

1976a   "Llanura costera del Golfo de Fonseca, Honduras," *Vinculos* 2: 15–23 (National Museum of Costa Rica, San Jose).

1976b   "Arqueologia de la frontera sur de Mesoamerica," *Fourteenth Mesa Redonda, Sociedad Mexicana de Antropologia* 1: 133–48.

1978–79 "Informe sobre las actividades del proyecto," Proyecto Arqueologico Copan, nos. 1–5 (mimeographed).

BAUDEZ, CLAUDE F., AND
PIERRE BECQUELIN

1969   "La sequence ceramique de Los Naranjos, Honduras," *Proceedings of the Thirty-eighth International Congress of Americanists* 1: 221–28.

1973   *Archeologie de Los Naranjos, Honduras*, Collection Etudes Mesoamericaines 2 (Mexico:

Mission Archeologique et Ethnologique).

1976   "Los Naranjos, Lago de Yojoa, Honduras," *Vinculos* 2: 5–14 (National Museum of Costa Rica, San Jose).

BAUDEZ, CLAUDE F., AND
MICHAEL D. COE

1962   "Archaeological Sequences in Northwestern Costa Rica," *Proceedings of the Thirty-Fourth International Congress of Americanists* 1: 366–73 (Vienna).

1966   "Incised Slate Disks from the Atlantic Watershed of Costa Rica: A Commentary," *American Antiquity* 31: 441–43.

BEADLE, GEORGE W.

1977   "The Origin of *Zea mays*," in *Origins of Agriculture*, ed. C. A. Reed (The Hague: Mouton).

1980   "The Ancestry of Corn," *Scientific American* 242: 112–19.

BEARDSLEY, R., P. HOLDER,
A. KRIEGER, B. J. MEGGERS, J.
RINALDO, AND P. KUTSCHE

1955   "Functional and Evolutionary Implications of Community Patterning," in *Seminars in Archaeology*, ed. B. J. Meggers, Memoirs of the Society for American Archaeology, vol. 11 (Washington, D.C.).

BELL, ROBERT E.

1964   *Investigaciones arqueologicas en el sitio de El Inga, Ecuador* (Quito: Casa de la Cultura Equatoriana).

BELT, THOMAS

1874   *The Naturalist in Nicaragua* (London).

BENNETT, CHARLES F.

1968   *Human Influences on the Zoogeography of Panama*, Ibero-Americana, no. 51 (Berkeley: University of California).

BENNETT, W. C.

1948   "The Peruvian Co-Tradition," in

A *Reappraisal of Peruvian Archaeology*, ed. W. C. Bennett, Memoirs of the Society for American Archaeology, no. 11 (Menasha, Wisconsin).

BERNSTEIN, DAVID J.
1980 "Artefactos de piedra pulida de Guanacaste, Costa Rica: una perspectiva funcional," in *Investigaciones arqueologicas el la zona de Bahia Culebra, Costa Rica (1973–1979)*, Vinculos 6 (National Museum of Costa Rica, San Jose).

BIESE, LEO
1964 *The Prehistory of Panama Viejo*, Bureau of American Ethnology, Smithsonian Institution, Bulletin no. 191 (Washington, D.C.: U.S. Government Printing Office).

BIRD, JUNIUS
1969 "A Comparison of South Chilean and Ecuadorian 'Fishtail' Projectile Points," *The Kroeber Anthropological Society Papers* 40: 52–71.

BIRD, JUNIUS, AND RICHARD G. COOKE
1974 *Excavaciones en la Cueva de los Ladrones, distrito de La Pintada, Provincia de Cocle, Republic of Panama, informe preliminar* (Panama: Instituto Nacional de Cultura).
1977 "Los artefactos mas antiguos de Panama," *Revista Nacional de Cultura* 6(1,2,3): 19–33.
1978a "La Cueva de los Ladrones: datos preliminares sobre la Ocupacion Formativa," *Actas de V Simposium Nacional de Antropologia, Arqueologia y Etnohistoria* (Universidad de Panama, Instituto Nacional de Cultura).
1978b "The Occurrence in Panama of Two Types of Paleo-Indian Projectile Points," in *Early Man in America from a Circum-Pacific Perspective*, ed. Alan Lyle Bryan, University of Alberta, Department of Anthropology Occasional Papers, no. 1 (Edmonton: Archaeological Researches International).

BISCHOF, HENNING
1966 "Canapote—An Early Ceramic Site in Northern Colombia, Preliminary Report," *Thirty-sixth International Congress of Americanists, Proceedings and Transactions* 1: 482–92 (Seville: Spanish Catholic Publishing House).
1969a "Contribuciones a la cronologia de la Cultura Tairona (Sierra Nevada de Santa Marta, Colombia)," *Proceedings of the Thirty-eighth International Congress of Americanists* 1: 259–69.
1969b "La Cultura Tairona en el area intermedio," *Proceedings of the Thirty-eighth International Congress of Americanists* 1: 272–80.
1971 *Die Spanisch-Indianische Auseinandersetzung in der Nordlichen Sierra Nevada de Santa Marta* (1501–1600), Bonner Americanist Studies, no. 1.
1972 "The Origins of Pottery in South America: Recent Radiocarbon Dates from Southwest Ecuador," *Proceedings of the Fortieth International Congress of Americanists* 1: 269–81 (Genoa: Tilgher).

BLACK, KEVIN
n.d. "The Zapotitan Valley Survey," manuscript, Department of Anthropology, University of Colorado, Boulder.

BLACKISTON, A. HOOTON
1910 "Recent discoveries in Honduras," *American Anthropologist* 12: 536–41.

BLANCO, AIDA
1981 "El Cristo (39–EC): un informe

preliminar," manuscript, National Museum of Costa Rica, San Jose.

BOEKELMAN, HENRY J.
1935   "Clay Phalli from Honduras Shell-Heaps and Their Possible Use," *Maya Research* 2: 167–73.

BOGGS, STANLEY H.
1943a   "Notas sobre las excavaciones en la hacienda 'San Andres,' Departamento de La Libertad," *Tzunpame* 3: 104–26.

1943b   "Observaciones respeto a la importancia de 'Tazumal' en la prehistoria salvadoreña," *Tzunpame* 3: 127–33.

1944   "Appendix C: Excavations in Central and Western El Salvador," in *Archaeological Excavations in El Salvador,* by J. M. Longyear III, Memoirs of the Peabody Museum of Archaeology and Ethnology 9: 55–72 (Cambridge, Mass.: Harvard University).

1945a   *Archaeological Material from the Club Internacional, El Salvador,* Carnegie Institution of Washington, Middle American Archaeology and Ethnology Notes 60 (Washington, D.C.: Carnegie Institution).

1945b   "Informe sobre la tercera temporada de excavaciones en las ruinas de 'Tazumal,'" *Tzunpame* 5: 33–45.

1950   "Archaeological Excavations in El Salvador," in *For the Dean,* ed. E. K. Reed and D. S. King (Tucson and Santa Fe: Hohokam Museums Association and Southwestern Monuments Association).

1966   *Pottery Jars from the Loma del Tacuazin, El Salvador,* Middle American Research Institute, Publication 28 (New Orleans: Tulane University).

BOLETIN DEL MUSEO CHIRICANO
1966   Numbers 1–3 (David, Panama).

BOLLAERT, WILLIAM
1861   "Observations on the Peruvian Tomb Pottery and Some Gold Objects from South America in the Museum of Joseph Mayer," *Transactions of the Historic Society of Lancashire and Cheshire* (n.s.) 1: 311–22.

1863   "On the Ancient Indian Tombs of Chiriqui in Veragua (Southwest of Panama), on the Isthmus of Darien," *Transactions of the Ethnological Society of London* (n.s.) 2: 147–66.

BORT, JOHN ROGER
1976   "Guaymi Innovators: A Case Study of Entrepreneurs in a Small-Scale Society" (Ph.D. diss., University of Oregon).

1980   "Ecology and Subsistence on Opposite Sides of the Talamancan Range," in *Adaptive Radiations in Prehistoric Panama,* ed. Olga F. Linares and Anthony J. Ranere, Peabody Museum Monographs, no. 5 (Cambridge, Mass.: Harvard University).

BOUCHARD, JEAN FRANCOIS
1979   "Hilos de oro martillado en la costa pacifica del sur de Colombia," *Boletin del Museo del Oro* 2 (mayo–agosto): 21–24.

BOVALLIUS, CARL ERIK ALEXANDER
1886   *Nicaraguan Antiquities* (Stockholm: Swedish Society of Anthropology and Geography).

1887   *Resa i Central-Amerika 1881–1883,* 2 vols. (Upsala: Almqvist & Wiksells boktryckeri).

BOYLE, F.
1868   *A Ride Across a Continent,* 2 vols. (London).

BOZZOLI DE WILLE, MARIA EUGENIA
1962   "Contribucion al conocimiento arqueologico de Pueblo Nuevo de Perez Zeledon," *Informe Se-*

mestral, July–December: 73–101 (San Jose: Instituto Geografico de Costa Rica).

1966   "Observaciones arqueologicas en los valles del Parrita y del General," *Boletin de la Asociacion de Amigos del Museo*, no. 19.

1975   "Birth and Death in the Belief System of the Bribri Indians of Costa Rica" (Ph.D. diss., University of Georgia).

BRADBURY, J. PLATT, B. LEYDEN, M. SALGADO-LABOURIAU, W. M. LEWIS, JR., C. SCHUBERT, M. W. BINFORD, D. G. FREY, D. R. WHITEHEAD, AND F. H. WEIBEZAHN

1981   "Late Quaternary Environmental History of Lake Valencia, Venezuela," *Science* 214: 1299–1305.

BRANSFORD, J. F.

1881   *Archaeological Researches in Nicaragua*, Smithsonian Contributions to Knowledge, no. 25 (Washington, D.C.: Smithsonian Institution).

1884   "Report on Explorations in Central America in 1881," *Annual Report of the Board of Regents of the Smithsonian Institution for 1882*: 803–25 (Washington, D.C.).

BRAY, WARWICK

1972   "Ancient American Metal-Smiths," *Proceedings of the Royal Anthropological Institute for 1971*: 25–43.

1977   "Maya Metalwork and Its External Connections," in *Social Process in Maya Prehistory*, ed. Norman Hammond (London and New York: Academic Press).

1978a   "An Eighteenth-Century Reference to a Fluted Point from Guatemala," *American Antiquity* 43: 457–60.

1978b   *The Gold of El Dorado* (London: Time Books).

1980a   "Fluted Points in Mesoamerica and the Isthmus: A Reply to Rovner," *American Antiquity* 45: 168–70.

1980b   *Pro Calima: Archäologische-ethnologisches Projekt im westlichen Kolumbien/Sudamerika*, Nr. 1 (Bern: Vereinigung Pro Calima).

1981   "Goldwork," in *Between Continents/Between Seas: Art of Precolumbian Costa Rica*, ed. E. Benson (New York: H. N. Abrams).

BREWBAKER, J.

1979   "Diseases of Maize in the Wet Lowland Tropics and the Collapse of the Classic Maya Civilization," *Economic Botany* 33(2): 101–18.

BRIZUELA, GLADYS CASIMIR DE

1972a   *Sintesis de arqueologia de Panama* (Panama: Editorial Universitaria).

1972b   "Investigaciones arqueologicas en la Provincia de Veraguas," *Hombre y Cultura* 2(3): 119–37.

BROWN, KENNETH L.

1980   "A Brief Report on Paleoindian-Archaic Occupation in the Quiche Basin, Guatemala," *American Antiquity* 45: 313–24.

BRUHNS, KAREN O.

1974   "Punto Zapote and Punto de Las Figuras, Zapatera Island, Nicaragua," manuscript.

1976   "Ancient Pottery of the Middle Cauca Valley, Colombia," *Cespedesia* 5: 101–96.

1977   "Settlement Archaeology in Cihuatan: A Preliminary Report," manuscript.

1978   "Commercial Agriculture in the Postclassic: A View from El Salvador," paper presented at the Forty-third Annual Meeting of the Society for American Archaeology, Tucson.

1979   "Trade and Migration in Postclassic El Salvador," paper presented at the Forty-third International Congress of Americanists, Vancouver.

1980   *Cihuatan: An Early Postclassic Town of El Salvador,* Monographs in Anthropology, no. 5, Museum of Anthropology (Columbia: University of Missouri).

n.d.   "Sinu Metalwork in the Collection of the De Young Museum, San Francisco, California," manuscript, Department of Anthropology, San Francisco State University.

BRUHNS, KAREN OLSEN, OSCAR OSORIO GOMEZ, AND OLE CHRISTIANSEN
1976   "A Projectile Point from the Department of Quindio," *Nawpa Pacha* 14: 69–72.

BRYAN, ALAN LYLE
1973   "New Light on Ancient Nicaraguan Footprints," *Archaeology* 26: 146–47.

1978   *Early Man in America from a*
(ed.)   *Circum-Pacific Perspective,* University of Alberta, Department of Anthropology Occasional Papers, no. 1 (Edmonton: Archaeological Researches International).

BULLEN, RIPLEY P., AND WILLIAM W. PLOWDEN, JR.
1963   "Preceramic Archaic Sites in the Highlands of Honduras," *American Antiquity* 28: 382–85.

1964   "Preceramic Archaic Sites in the Central Highlands of Honduras," *Thirty-fifth International Congress of Americanists, Proceedings and Transactions* 1: 563–64 (Mexico).

BULLEN, RIPLEY P., AND JAMES B. STOLTMAN
1972   *Fibre-tempered Pottery in Southeastern United States and Northern Colombia: Its Origins, Context and Significance,* Florida Anthropological Society Publication no. 6, *The Florida Anthropologist* 25(2), part 2.

BURLEIGH, RICHARD, AND DON BROTHWELL
1978   "Studies on Amerindian Dogs 1: Carbon Isotopes in Relation to Maize in the Diet of Domestic Dogs from Early Peru and Ecuador," *Journal of Archaeological Science* 5: 355–62.

BYERS, DOUGLAS S.
1967   *The Prehistory of the Tehuacan*
(ed.)   *Valley, Vol. 1: Environment and Subsistence* (Austin: University of Texas Press).

CADAVID, GILBERTO, AND LUISA FERNANDA HERRERA DE TURBAY
1977   "Arqueologia de la Sierra Nevada de Santa Marta: investigaciones culturales en el area Tairona," manuscript, Bogota.

CALDWELL, JOSEPH R.
1964   "Interaction Spheres in Prehistory," *Hopewellian Studies* 12: 133–43.

CAMPBELL, LYLE R.
1976   "The Linguistic Prehistory of the Southern Mesoamerican Periphery," *Fourteenth Round Table, Mexican Society of Anthropology* 1: 157–83.

1979   "Middle American Languages," in *The Languages of Native America,* ed. L. R. Campbell and M. Mithun, 902–1000 (Austin: University of Texas Press).

CANBY, JOEL S.
1949   "Excavations at Yarumela, Spanish Honduras," (Ph.D. diss., Harvard University).

1951   "Possible Chronological Implications of the Long Ceramic Sequence Recovered at Yarumela, Spanish Honduras," *Proceedings of the Twenty-ninth International Congress of Americanists* 1: 79–85.

CARBONE, VICTOR A.
1978   "The Paleoecology of the Caribbean Area," paper presented at the Symposium on Problems of the Archaeology of the Antilles, Puerto Rico.

CARDALE-SCHRIMPFF, MARIANNE
1976   "Salt Production in the Eastern Cordillera of Colombia Before and After the Spanish Conquest—A Preliminary Survey," *Proceedings of the Forty-first International Congress of Americanists* 2: 419–28 (Mexico).

CARMICHAEL, ELIZABETH
1973   *The British and the Maya* (London: Trustees of the British Museum).

CARNEIRO, ROBERT L.
1961   "Slash and Burn Cultivation Among the Kuikuru and Its Implications for Cultural Development in the Amazon Basin," in *The Evolution of Horticultural Systems in Native South America: Causes and Consequences*, ed. J. Wilbert (Caracas: Editorial Sucre, La Salle).
1970   "A Theory of the Origin of the State," *Science* 169: 733–38.

CASASOLA GARCIA, L.
1977   "Jayaque, un sitio pre-clasico en El Salvador" (M.A. thesis, Universidad Nacional Autonoma de Mexico).

CASTELLANOS, JUAN DE
1955   *Elegis de varones ilustres de Indias*, 4 vols. (Bogota: Editorial A.B.C.).

CASTILLERO CALVO, ALFREDO
1967   *Estructuras sociales y economicas de Veragua desde sus origines historicos S. XVI y S. XVII* (Panama: Impresora Panama).

CHAPMAN, A.
1957   "Port of Trade Enclaves in Aztec and Maya Civilization," in *Trade and Market in the Early Empires*, ed. K. Polanyi, C. M. Arensberg, and H. W. Pearson (Glencoe, Ill.: Free Press).
1960   *Los Nicarao y los Chorotega segun los fuentes historicas*, Serie Historia y Geografia 4 (San Jose: Universidad de Costa Rica).

CLARY, KAREN H.
1980   "The Identification of Selected Pollen Grains from a Core at Isla Palenque," in *Adaptive Radiations in Prehistoric Panama*, ed. Olga F. Linares and Anthony J. Ranere, Peabody Museum Monographs, no. 5 (Cambridge, Mass.: Harvard University).

COBEAN, ROBERT H., MICHAEL D. COE, EDWARD A. PERRY, KARL I. TUREKIAN, AND DINKAR P. KHARKAR
1971   "Obisidan Trade at San Lorenzo Tenochtitlan, Mexico," *Science* 174: 666–71.

COE, MICHAEL D.
1960a   "Archaeological Linkages with North and South America at La Victoria, Guatemala," *American Anthropologist* 62: 363–93.
1960b   "A Fluted Point from Highland Guatemala," *American Antiquity* 25: 412–13.
1961   *La Victoria, an Early Site on the Pacific Coast of Guatemala*, Papers of the Peabody Museum of Archaeology and Ethnology, vol. 53 (Cambridge, Mass.: Harvard University).
1962a   "Preliminary Report on Archaeological Investigations in Central Guanacaste, Costa Rica," *Proceedings of the Thirty-fourth International Congress of Americanists*, pp. 358–65.
1962b   "Costa Rican Archaeology and Mesoamerica," *Southwestern Journal of Anthropology* 18: 170–83.
1963   "Cultural Development in Southeastern Mesoamerica," in

Aboriginal Cultural Development in Latin America: An Interpretative Review, Smithsonian Miscellaneous Collections, vol. 146, ed. B. J. Meggers and C. Evans (Washington, D.C.: Smithsonian Institution).

1965a   *The Jaguar's Children: Preclassic Central Mexico* (New York: Museum of Primitive Art).

1965b   "The Olmec Style and Its Distribution," in *Handbook of Middle American Indians,* vol. 3, ed. R. Wauchope (Austin: University of Texas Press).

COE, MICHAEL D., AND
CLAUDE F. BAUDEZ
1961   "The Zoned Bichrome Period in Northwestern Costa Rica," *American Antiquity* 26: 505–15.

COE, MICHAEL D., AND
RICHARD A. DIEHL
1980   *In the Land of the Olmec,* 2 vols. (Austin: University of Texas Press).

COE, MICHAEL D., AND
K. V. FLANNERY
1967   "Early Cultures and Human Ecology in South Coastal Guatemala," *Smithsonian Contributions to Anthropology,* vol. 3 (Washington, D.C.: Smithsonian Institution).

COGGINS, CLEMENCY
1979   "Teotihuacan at Tikal in the Early Classic Period," *Proceedings of the Forty-second International Congress of Americanists* 8: 251–69 (Paris: Musee de l'Homme).

COHEN, MARK NATHAN
1977   *The Food Crisis in Prehistory: Overpopulation and the Origins of Agriculture* (New Haven: Yale University Press).

CONZEMIUS, EDUARD
1928   "On the Aborigines of the Bay Islands (Honduras)," *Proceedings of the Twenty-second International Congress of Americanists* 2: 57–68 (Rome).

COOKE, RICHARD G.
1972   "The Archaeology of the Western Cocle Province of Panama" (Ph.D. diss., University of London).

1973   "Informe sobre excavaciones arqueologicas en el sitio CHO–3 (Miraflores) Rio Bayano, Panama," paper submitted to Patrimonio Historico, Instituto Nacional de Cultura, Panama.

1975   "Excavaciones arqueologicas en el sitio AG–3 (Sitio Sierra), Distrito de Aguadulce, Cocle, Panama," preliminary report on the 1975 excavations on file at the Direccion de Patrimonio Historico, Panama.

1976a   "El hombre y la tierra en el Panama prehistorico," *Revista Nacional de Cultura* 2: 17–38.

1976b   "Informe sobre las excavaciones en el sitio CHO–3 (Miraflores), Bayano, febrero de 1973," *Actas del IV Simposium Nacional de Antropologia, Arqueologia y Etnohistoria de Panama,* Instituto Nacional de Cultura y Universidad de Panama, pp. 369–426.

1976c   "Nuevo analisis de Carbono-14 para Panama al este de Chiriqui," *La Antigua* 6: 88–114.

1976d   "Panama: Region central," *Vinculos* 2: 122–40 (National Museum of Costa Rica, San Jose).

1976e   "Rescate arqueologico en El Caño (NA–20), Cocle, Panama," *Actas del IV Simposium Nacional de Antropologia, Arqueologia y Etnohistoria de Panama,* Instituto Nacional de Cultura y Universidad de Panama, pp. 447–82.

1977   "Non-Aquatic Animal Resources in Central Panama: Unforested Environments, Habitat Destruction, or Selective Hunting?" paper presented at the Forty-second Annual Meeting of the Society for American Archaeology, New Orleans.

1978a "El hachero y el carpintero: dos artesanos del Panama precolombino," *Revista Panameña de Antropologia* 2.

1978b "Maximizing a Valuable Resource: The White-tailed Deer in Prehistoric Central Panama," paper presented at the Forty-third Annual Meeting of the Society for American Archaeology, Tucson.

1979 "Los impactos de las comunidades agricolas sobre los ambientes del tropico estacional: datos del Panama prehistorico," *Actas del IV Simposium Internacional de Ecologia Tropical* 3: 917–73.

1980 "Polychrome Pottery from the Central Region of Panama at La Pitahaya (IS–3)," in *Adaptive Radiations in Prehistoric Panama*, ed. Olga F. Linares and Anthony J. Ranere, Peabody Museum Monographs, no. 5 (Cambridge, Mass.: Harvard University).

COOKE, RICHARD G., AND MARCELA CAMARGO

1977 "Cocle y su arqueologia: una breve historia critica," *La Antigua*, Año 6º(9): 115–72.

COOKE, RICHARD G., AND ANTHONY J. RANERE

in press "The Proyecto Santa Maria: A Multidisciplinary Analysis of Prehistoric Human Adaptations to a Tropical Watershed in Panama," *Proceedings of the Forty-fourth International Congress of Americanists* (Manchester).

CORREAL URREGO, GONZALO

1974 "Artefactos liticos en la Hacienda Boulder, Municipio de Palmero, Departamento de Huila," *Revista Colombiana de Antropologia* 16: 195–222.

1977 "Exploraciones arqueologicas en la Costa Atlantica y Valle del Magdalena," *Caldasia* 11(55): 33–128.

1979 *Investigaciones arqueologicas en Abrigos Recosos de Nemocon y Sueva* (Bogota: Banco de la Republica, Fundacion de Investigaciones Arqueologicas Nacionales).

1980a "El sitio arqueologico Tibito 1," *Micronoticias Antropologicas* (marzo–abril): 7–8 (Sociedad Antropologicas de Colombia).

1980b "Estado actual de las investigaciones sobre la etapa litica en Colombia," *Antropologicas* 2: 11–30.

1980c "Evidencias culturales asociadas a megafauna durante el Pleistoceno tardio en Colombia," *Geologia Norandina* 1: 29–34.

1981 *Evidencias culturales megafauna Pleistocenica en Colombia* (Bogota: Banco de la Republica, Fundacion de Investigaciones Arqueologicas Nacionales).

1983 "Evidencia de cazadores especializados en el sitio de La Gloria, Golfo de Uraba," *Revista de la Academia de Ciencias Exactas, Fisicas y Naturales* 15(58): 77–82.

CORREAL URREGO, GONZALO, AND MARIA PINTO NOLLA

1982 "Investigaciones Arqueologicas en el Municipio de Zipacon Cundinamarca," *Boletin del Museo del Oro* 5 (enero–abril): 24–34.

CORREAL URREGO, GONZALO, AND
THOMAS VAN DER HAMMEN
1977   *Investigaciones arqueologicas en los Abrigos Rocosos del Tequendama. 11,000 años de prehistoria en la Sabana de Bogota* (Bogota: Banco Popular).

CREAMER, WINIFRED
1979   "Preliminary Survey near Upala (Alajuela), Costa Rica," paper presented at the Forty-fourth Annual Meeting of the Society for American Archaeology, Vancouver.

1980   "Evidence for Prehispanic Exchange Systems in the Gulf of Nicoya, Costa Rica," paper presented at the Forty-fifth Annual Meeting of the Society for American Archaeology, Philadelphia.

1983   "Production and Exchange on Two Islands in the Gulf of Nicoya, Costa Rica, A.D. 1200–1550" (Ph.D. diss., Tulane University).

DADE, PHILIP L.
1960   "Rancho Sancho de la Isla, A Site in Cocle Province, Panama: A Preliminary Report," *Panama Archaeologist* 3: 66–87.

n.d.   *Arte Precolombino de Panama* (Panama: Edilito).

DAHLIN, BRUCE H.
1979   "Cropping Cash in the Protoclassic: A Cultural Impact Statement," in *Maya Archaeology and Ethnohistory*, ed. Norman Hammond and Gordon R. Willey (Austin: University of Texas Press).

DALTON, GEORGE
1975   "Karl Polanyi's Analysis of Long-Distance Trade and His Wider Paradigm," in *Ancient Civilization and Trade*, ed. J. A. Sabloff and C. C. Lamberg-Karlovsky (Albuquerque: University of New Mexico Press, School of American Research Advanced Seminar Series).

DAUGHERTY, H.
1969   "Man-Induced Ecologic Change in El Salvador" (Ph.D. diss., University of California, Los Angeles).

DAWSON, SUSAN
1979   "Archaeological Survey in the San Carlos Plains: Upala, Costa Rica" (B.A. thesis, Lawrence University).

DAY, J.
1982   "New Approaches in Stylistic Analysis," paper presented at the Forty-fourth International Congress of Americanists (Manchester).

DAY, JANE S., AND
SUZANNE ABEL-VIDOR
1980   "The Late Polychrome Period: Guanacaste, Costa Rica," paper presented at Seventy-ninth Annual Meeting of the American Anthropological Association, Washington.

DEBOER, WARREN R.
1975   "The Archaeological Evidence for Manioc Cultivation: A Cautionary Note," *American Antiquity* 40: 419–33.

DEEVEY, EDWARD S., L. J. GRALENSKI,
AND VAINO HOFFREN
1959   "Yale Natural Radio-Carbon Measurements, IV," *Radio-Carbon Supplement*, no. 1.

DE LA CRUZ, E.
1981   "Costa Rican Mace Heads: Their Symbolic Significance in Information Exchange" (M.A. thesis, Southern Illinois University, Carbondale).

DE LA GUARDIA, ROBERTO
1966   "El sitio Tinajas," *Boletin del Museo Chiricano* 3: 7–13.

DEMAREST, ARTHUR
1980   "Santa Leticia and the Prehistory

of Western El Salvador," manuscript, Anthropology Department, Harvard University.

DEMAREST, ARTHUR A., AND
ROBERT J. SHARER
1982   "The Origins and Evolution of the Usulutan Ceramic Style," *American Antiquity* 47: 810–22.

DIEHL, RICHARD A., ROGER LOMAS,
AND JACK T. WYNN
1974   "Toltec Trade with Central America: New Light and Evidence," *Archaeology* 27: 182–87.

DROLET, ROBERT P.
1980   "Cultural Settlement Along the Moist Caribbean Slopes of Eastern Panama" (Ph.D. diss., University of Illinois).

DROLET, ROBERT P., AND
ROBERT MARKENS
1980a   "Informe mensual: investigaciones arqueologicas en el Valle de El General, Puntarenas, Costa Rica, P. H. Boruca," manuscript, Museo Nacional de Costa Rica, San Jose.

1980b   "Investigaciones arqueologicas en el sitio P-107-Mc y el Valle Intermedio del Rio Terraba, Region Diquis, Costa Rica, P. H. Boruca (ICE), Buenas Aires, Puntarenas," manuscript, Museo Nacional de Costa Rica, San Jose.

1981a   "Investigaciones arqueologicas en Murcielago, sitio P-107-Mc, Rio Terraba, Puntarenas: informe de labores, rescate arqueologico, P. H. Boruca," manuscript, Museo Nacional de Costa Rica, San Jose.

1981b   "Informe final, rescate arqueologico, Proyecto Boruca," manuscript, Museo Nacional de Costa Rica y el Instituto Costarricense de Electricidad, San Jose, Costa Rica.

DRUCKER, PHILLIP
1952   *La Venta, Tabasco: A Study of Olmec Ceramics and Art*, Bureau of American Ethnology, Smithsonian Institution, Bulletin no. 153 (Washington, D.C.: U.S. Government Printing Office).

1955   *The Cerro de las Mesas Offering of Jade and Other Materials*, Bureau of American Ethnology, Smithsonian Institution, Bulletin no. 157: 44 (Washington, D.C.: U.S. Government Printing Office).

DUNN, MARY EUBANKS
1978   "Suggestions for Evaluating Archaeological Maize," *American Antiquity* 43: 97–99.

DUQUE GOMEZ, LUIS
1964   *Exploraciones arqueologicas en San Agustin*, Revista Colombiana de Anthropologia Supplemento no. 1 (Bogota: Imprenta Nacional).

DUQUE GOMEZ, LUIS, AND
JULIO CESAR CUBILLOS
1979   *Arqueologia de San Agustin: Alto de los Idolos, Monticulos y Tumbas* (Bogota: Fundacion de Investigaciones Arqueologicas Nacionales, Banco de la Republica).

DUSSAN DE REICHEL, ALICIA
1954   "Crespo: un nuevo complejo arqueologico del norte de Colombia," *Revista Colombiana de Antropologia* 3: 171–88.

1967   "Una escultura litica de tipologia costarrincense de la Sierra Nevada de Santa Marta," *Razon y Fabula* 2: 39–42.

EARNEST, H. H., JR.
1976   "Investigaciones efectuadas por el proyecto no. 1: programa de rescate arqueologico Cerron Grande, en la Hacienda Santa Barbara, Departamento de Cha-

latenango," Segundo Informe Preliminar, *Revista Anales no. 49 del Museo Nacional "David J. Guzman*," November 30: 57– 67.

EASBY, E. K.
1968   *Pre-Columbian Jade from Costa Rica* (New York: Andre Emmerich).

EDWARDS, CLINTON R.
1969   "New World Perspectives on Pre-European Voyaging in the Pacific," Latin American Center Reprints, no. 6, from the proceedings of a symposium, *Early Chinese Art and Its Possible Influence in the Pacific Basin* (Milwaukee: University of Wisconsin).

EINHAUS, CATHERINE SHELTON
1980   "Stone Tools from La Pitahaya (IS–3)," in *Adaptive Radiations in Prehistoric Panama*, ed. Olga F. Linares and Anthony J. Ranere, Peabody Museum Monographs, no. 5 (Cambridge, Mass.: Harvard University).

EPSTEIN, JEREMIAH F.
1957   "Late Ceramic Horizons in Northeastern Honduras" (Ph.D. diss., University of Pennsylvania).
1959   "Dating the Ulua Polychrome Complex," *American Antiquity* 25: 125–29.
1978   "Problemas en el estudio de la prehistoria de las islas de la Bahia," *Yaxkin* 2: 149–59.

EPSTEIN, JEREMIAH F., AND VITO VELIZ
1977   "Reconocimiento arqueologico de la Isla de Roatan, Honduras," *Yaxkin* 2: 28–39.

ESCALANTE, AGUILES
1955   *Los Mocana: prehistoria y conquista del Departamento del Atlantico, Colombia*, Divulgaciones Etnologicas 4(6).

ESPINOSA, GASPAR DE
1873   "Relacion a proceso quel Licen-
ciado Gaspar Despinosa, alcalde mayor, hizo en el viaje . . . desde esta Cibdad de Panama a las provincias de Paris e Nata, e a las otras provincias comarcanas," *Documentos Ineditos de Indias*, 20.
1913   "Relacion hecha por Gaspar de
(1517)   Espinosa, alcalde mayor de Castilla de Oro, dada a Pedrarias Davila, lugarteniente de aquellas provincias, de todo lo que sucedio en la entrada que hizo en ellas, de orden de Pedrarias," in *El Descubrimiento del Oceano Pacifico: Vasco Nuñez de Balboa, Hernando de Magallanes y sus Compañeros, Tomo II: Documentos Relativos a Nuñez de Balboa*, ed. J. T. Medina (Santiago de Chile: Imprenta Universitaria).
1913   "Relacion e Proceso quel Licen-
(1519)   ciado Gaspar de Espinosa, alcalde mayor, hizo en el viaje que por mandado del muy magnifico señor Pedrarias Davila, teniente general de estos reinos de Castilla de Oro por Sus Altezas, fue desde esta cibdad de Panama a las provincias de Nata e Paris e a las otras provincias comarcanas," in *El Descubrimiento del Oceano Pacifico: Vasco Nuñez de Balboa, Hernando de Magallanes y sus Compañeros, Tomo II: Documentos Relativos a Nuñez de Balboa*, ed. J. T. Medina (Santiago de Chile: Imprenta Universitaria).

ESPINOSA E., JORGE
1976   "Excavaciones arqueologicas en 'El Bosque,'" *Informe 1* (Managua: Departamento de Antropologia e Historia, Instituto Geografico Nacional, Ministerio de Obras Publicas).

FALCHETTI DE SAENZ, ANA MARIA
1976   "The Goldwork of the Sinu Region, Northern Colombia"

(M.Ph. diss., Institute of Archaeology, University of London).

1979 "Colgantes Darien: relaciones entre areas orfebres del occidente Colombiano y Centroamerica," *Boletin del Museo del Oro* 2 (January–April): 1–55.

FARABEE, W. M. CURTIS
1920 "Ancient American Gold," *The Museum Journal* 11: 93–129.

FELDMAN, LAWRENCE
1978 "Moving Merchandise in Protohistoric Central Ququhtemallan," in *Mesoamerican Communication Routes and Cultural Contacts*, ed. Thomas A. Lee and Carlos Navarrete (Provo: New World Archaeological Foundation).

FERNANDEZ GUARDIA, LEON
1889 *Historia de Costa Rica durante la dominacion Española, 1502–1821* (Madrid: Tipografia de Manuel Gines Hernandez).

FERRERO ACOSTA, LUIS
1977 *Costa Rica Precolombina*, 2d ed. (San Jose: Editorial Costa Rica).

FINCH, WILL O.
1977 "Preliminary Survey of the Hacienda Jerico, Guanacaste, Costa Rica," manuscript, National Museum of Costa Rica.

FINCH, WILLIAM, AND
KIM HONETSCHLAGER
n.d. "An Archaeological Survey of Isla del Caño, Costa Rica," manuscript, National Museum of Costa Rica.

FINDLOW, FRANK J., MICHAEL J.
SNARSKIS, AND PHYLLIS MARTIN
1979 "Un analisis de zonas de explotacion relacionadas con algunos sitios prehistoricos de la Vertiente Atlantica de Costa Rica," *Vinculos* 5: 53–71 (Museo Nacional de Costa Rica, San Jose).

FINDLOW, FRANK, MICHAEL SNARSKIS,
PHYLLIS MARTIN, AND
ROBERT MARKENS
1980 "A Survey Design for the Boruca Archaeological Project," manuscript, Museo Nacional de Costa Rica, San Jose.

FLANNERY, KENT V.
1968 "The Olmec and the Valley of Oaxaca: A Model for Inter-Regional Interaction in Formative Times," in *Dumbarton Oaks Conference on the Olmec*, ed. E. P. Benson (Washington, D.C.: Dumbarton Oaks).

1976 *The Early Mesoamerican Village* (New York: Academic Press).

FLINT, E.
1882 Letters to George Putnam, beginning in 1882 and continuing for the years 1884–85 and 1889, in Peabody Museum Archives, Harvard University.

1884 "Human Footprints in Nicaragua," *American Antiquarian and Oriental Journal* 6: 112–14.

FONSECA ZAMORA, OSCAR
1979 "Informe de la primera temporada de reexcavacion de Guayabo de Turrialba," *Vinculos* 5: 35–52 (National Museum of Costa Rica, San Jose).

FONSECA ZAMORA, OSCAR, AND
JAMES B. RICHARDSON III
1978 "South America and Maya Cultural Contacts at the Las Huacas Site, Costa Rica," *Annals of Carnegie Museum*, vol. 47, art. 131 (Pittsburgh: Carnegie Museum of Natural History).

FONSECA ZAMORA, OSCAR M., AND
RICHARD SCAGLION
1978 "Stylistic Analysis of Stone Pendants from Las Huacas Burial Ground, Northwestern Costa Rica," *Annals of Carnegie Museum*, vol. 47, art. 12 (Pittsburgh:

Carnegie Museum of Natural History).

FORD, J. A.
1969   A *Comparison of Formative Cultures in the Americas*, Smithsonian Contributions to Knowledge, no. 11 (Washington, D.C.: Smithsonian Institution).

FOSHAG, W. F., AND R. LESLIE
1955   "Jade from Manzanal, Guatemala," *American Antiquity* 2: 81–82.

FOSTER, DONALD W., AND DONALD W. LATHRAP
1973   "Further Evidence for a Well-Developed Tropical Forest Culture on the North Coast of Colombia During the First and Second Millennium B.C.," *Journal of the Steward Anthropological Society* 4: 160–99.

FOSTER, GEORGE
1969   "The Mixe, Zoque, Popoluca," in *Handbook of Middle American Indians*, vol. 7, ed. R. Wauchope (Austin: University of Texas Press).

FOWLER, WILLIAM, JR.
1976   "Programa de rescate arqueologico Cerron Grande," *Anales del Museo Nacional, San Salvador* 49: 13–50.

1977   "Problems of the Postclassic Period of Central El Salvador," paper presented at the Forty-second Annual Meeting of the Society for American Archaeology, New Orleans.

1979   "Evidence of Preclassic Period Human Sacrifice at Chalchuapa, El Salvador," paper presented at the Forty-fourth Annual Meeting of the Society for American Archaeology, Vancouver.

FOWLER, WILLIAM, JR., AND E. M. SOLIS ANGULO
1977   "El mapa de Santa Maria: un si-

tio postclasico de la region Cerron Grande," *Anales del Museo Nacional "David J. Guzman"* 50: 13–30.

FOX, JOHN W.
1980   "Lowland to Highland Mexicanization Processes in Southern Mesoamerica," *American Antiquity* 45: 43–54.

1981   "Mesoamerica," *Acta Americana* 1: 92–107 (Mexico).

FREIDEL, DAVID A.
1979   "Towards a Late Preclassic Maya Horizon Style: Symbolism, Mediums, and Implications for the Evolution of Maya Civilization," paper presented at the Forty-third International Congress of Americanists, Vancouver.

FRIED, MORTON H.
1967   *The Evolution of Political Society* (New York: Random House).

GALINAT, WALTON C.
1978   "Additional Archaeological Maize from Costa Rica," manuscript, National Museum of Costa Rica, San Jose.

1980   "The Archaeological Maize Remains from Volcan Panama—A Comparative Perspective," in *Adaptive Radiations in Prehistoric Panama*, ed. Olga F. Linares and Anthony J. Ranere, Peabody Museum Monographs, no. 5 (Cambridge, Mass.: Harvard University).

GALINDO, JUAN
1936   "A Description of the Ruins of Copan in Central America," *Archaeologica Americana* 2: 543–50.

GALLAGHER, PATRICK
1976   *La Pitia: An Archaeological Series in Northwestern Venezuela*, Yale University Publications in Anthropology, no. 76 (New Haven).

GAZIN, LEWIS
1957   "Exploration for the Remains of Giant Ground-Sloths in Panama," *Annual Report of the Board of Regents of the Smithsonian Institution*, Publication 4979, 341–54.

GIAP (GRUPO DE INVESTIGACION DE ARQUEOLOGIA Y PREHISTORIA)
1979   *Boletin No. 4* (Medellin: Universidad de Antioquia).
1980   *Investigacion arqueologica y prehistorica de un yacimiento conchal en la costa Atlantica Colombiana, Turbo-Antioquia* (Medellin: Universidad de Antioquia).

GILMORE, RAYMOND M.
1950   "Fauna and Ethnozoology of South America," *Handbook of South American Indians*, vol. 6, ed. Julian H. Steward (U.S. Government Printing Office).

GLASS, JOHN B.
1966   "Archaeological Survey of Western Honduras," in *Handbook of Middle American Indians*, vol. 4, ed. Gordon F. Ekholm and Gordon R. Willey (Austin: University of Texas Press).

GOODWIN, R. CHRISTOPHER
1975   "Archaeological Sampling on Utila Island, Bay Islands, Spanish Honduras," manuscript, Trent University.

GORDON, B. LE ROY
1957   *Human Geography and Ecology in the Sinu Country of Colombia*, Ibero-Americana 39 (Berkeley: University of California).

GORDON, GEORGE BYRON
1896   *Prehistoric Ruins of Copan, Honduras: A Preliminary Report of the Exploration by the Museum, 1891–1895*, Memoirs of the Peabody Museum of Archaeology and Ethnology, no. 1 (Cambridge, Mass.: Harvard University).
1898a   *Researches in the Ulua Valley, Honduras*, Memoirs of the Peabody Museum of Archaeology and Ethnology, no. 1 (Cambridge, Mass.: Harvard University).
1898b   *Caverns of Copan, Honduras*, Memoirs of the Peabody Museum of Archaeology and Ethnology, vol. 1, no. 5 (Cambridge, Mass.: Harvard University).
1902   *The Hieroglyphic Stairway, Ruins of Copan: Report on the Explorations of the Museum*, Memoirs of the Peabody Museum of Archaeology and Ethnology, vol. 1 (Cambridge, Mass.: Harvard University).
1920   "A Marble Vase from the Ulua River Valley, Honduras," *Art and Archaeology* 9: 141–45.

GRAHAM, JOHN A.
1977   "Discoveries at Abaj Takalik, Guatemala," *Archaeology* 30: 196–97.

GRAHAM, MARK
1979   "A New Look at Mesoamerican Influence on Costa Rican Art," paper presented at the Forty-fourth Annual Meeting of the Society for American Archaeology, Vancouver.
1980   "Symbolic Agriculture: Utilitarian Sources of Elite Art in Guanacaste Province, Costa Rica," paper presented at Seventy-ninth American Anthropological Association, Washington, D.C.
1981   "Traditions of Stone Sculpture in Costa Rica," in *Between Continents, Between Seas: Precolumbian Art of Costa Rica*, ed. E. Benson (New York: H. N. Abrams).

GRAYSON, DONALD K.
1973   "On the Methodology of Faunal

Analysis," *American Antiquity* 38: 432–39.

GROOT DE MAHECHA, ANA MARIA
1980   "Buritaca–200: una fecha de radiocarbono asociada con objectos de orfebreria Tairona," *Boletin del Museo del Oro* 3 (mayo–agosto): 21–34.

GROVE, D., K. HIRTH, D. BUGE, AND A. CYPHERS
1976   "Settlement and Cultural Development at Chalcatzingo," *Science* 192: 1203–10.

GRUHN, RUTH
1978   "A Note on Excavations at El Bosque, Nicaragua, in 1975," in *Early Man in America from a Circum-Pacific Perspective*, ed. Alan Lyle Bryan, University of Alberta, Department of Anthropology Occasional Papers, no. 1 (Edmonton: Archaeological Researches International).

GRUHN, RUTH, AND ALAN L. BRYAN
1977   "Los Tapiales: a Paleo-Indian Campsite in the Guatemalan Highlands," *Proceedings of the American Philosophical Society* 121: 235–73 (Philadelphia).

GUERRERO, JUAN VICENTE
1981   "Informe preliminar sobre el proyecto de rescate arqueologico en el sitio La Fabrica, Grecia," manuscript, National Museum of Costa Rica, San Jose.

GUNN, ROBERT D., AND MARY R. GUNN
1974   "Fonologia Bocota," in *Lenguas de Panama, tomo 1: sistemas fonologicos* (Instituto de Cultura e Instituto Linguistico de Verano).

HABEL, S.
1878   *The Sculpture of Santa Lucia Cosumalwapa*, Smithsonian Contributions to Knowledge, no. 22 (Washington, D.C.: Smithsonian Institution).

HABERLAND, WOLFGANG
1955   "Preliminary Report on the Aguas Buenas Complex, Costa Rica," *Ethnos* 4: 224–30 (Stockholm).
1957a   "Black-on-Red Painted Ware and Associated Features in Intermediate Area," *Ethnos* 22: 148–61 (Stockholm).
1957b   "Excavations in Costa Rica and Panama," *Archaeology* 10: 258–63.
1958   "A Pre-Classic Complex of Western El Salvador, C.A.," *Proceedings of the Thirty-second International Congress of Americanists* 1: 485–90 (Copenhagen: Munksgaard).
1959   *Archäologische Untersuchungen in Sudost Costa Rica*, Series Geographica et Ethnographica, Nr. 1 (Wiesbaden: Franz Steiner Verlag).
1960a   "Ceramic Sequences in El Salvador," *American Antiquity* 26: 21–29.
1960b   "Beiträge zur Stratigraphie und zur Paläopedologie des mittleren El Salvadors," *Neues Jahrbuch für Geologie und Paläontologie*, Monatshefte 3: 111–32.
1960c   "Peninsula de Osa. Anotaciones Geograficas y Arqueologicas," *Instituto Geografico de Costa Rica, Informe Semestral* (enero–junio): 75–86.
1961a   "Affen auf Tongefafsen des präkolumbischen El Salvador," *Natur und Volk* 91: 433–41.
1961b   "Arqueologia del valle del Rio Ceiba, Buenos Aires," *Instituto Geografico de Costa Rica, Informe Semestral* (enero–junio): 31–62.
1961c   "New Names for Chiriquian Pottery Types," *Panama Archaeologist* 4: 56–60.
1961d   "Two Shaman Graves in Central

America," *Archaeology* 14: 154–60.

1961e   *Archäologische Untersuchungen in der Provinz Chiriqui, Panama*, Acta Humboldtiana, Series Geographica et Ethnographica Nr. 3 (Wiesbaden: Franz Steiner Verlag).

1962   "The Scarified Ware and the Early Cultures of Chiriqui (Panama)," *Proceedings of the Thirty-fourth International Congress of Americanists* 1: 381–89 (Vienna).

1964   "Marihua Red-on-buff and the Pipil Question," *Ethos* 1–2: 73–86.

1966a   "El Sur de Centroamerica," *Proceedings of the Thirty-eighth International Congress of Americanists* 1: 193–200.

1966b   "Early Phases on Ometepe Island, Nicaragua," *Proceedings and Transactions of the Thirty-sixth International Congress of Americanists* 1: 399–403 (Seville: Editorial Catolica Española).

1968   "Las Figuras liticas de Barriles, en Panama," *Boletin del Museo Chiricano* 6: 8–14.

1969   "Early Phases and Their Relationship in Southern Central America," *Proceedings of the Thirty-eighth International Congress of Americanists* 1: 229–42.

1973   "Stone Sculpture from Southern Central America," in *The Iconography of Middle American Sculpture*, ed. Dudley T. Easby (New York: Metropolitan Museum of Art).

1976   "Gran Chiriqui," *Vinculos* 2: 115–21 (National Museum of Costa Rica, San Jose).

1978   "Lower Central America," in *Chronologies in New World Archaeology*, ed. R. E. Taylor and C. W. Meighan (New York: Academic Press).

HABERLAND, W., AND W. H. GREBE

1957   "Prehistoric Footprints from El Salvador," *American Antiquity* 22: 282–85.

HAMMOND, NORMAN, ARNOLD ASPINALL, STUART FEATHER, JOHN HAZELDEN, TREVOR GAZARD, AND STUART AGRELL

1977   "Maya Jade: Source Location and Analysis," in *Exchange Systems in Prehistory*, ed. Timothy K. Earle and Jonathon E. Ericson (New York: Academic Press).

HANSELL, PATRICIA

1979   "Shell Analysis: A Case Study from Panama" (M.A. thesis, Temple University).

HANSELL, PATRICIA, AND JOHN K. ADAMS

1980   "The Application of Textural Analysis to the Interpretation of Cultural Deposits," paper presented at the Forty-fifth Annual Meeting of the Society for American Archaeology, Philadelphia.

HARRIS, DAVID R.

1969   "Agricultural Systems, Ecosystems and the Origins of Agriculture," in *The Domestication and Exploitation of Plants and Animals*, ed. P. J. Ucko and G. W. Dimbleby (London: Gerald Duckworth & Co.).

1972   "Swidden Systems and Settlement," in *Man, Settlement and Urbanism*, ed. P. J. Ucko, R. Tringham, and G. W. Dimbleby (London: Gerald Duckworth & Co.).

HARTE, NEVILLE A.

1966   "El Sitio Guacamayo," *Boletin del Museo Chiricano* 3: 3–7.

HARTMAN, CARL V.

1901   *Archaeological Researches in Costa*

Rica (Stockholm: Royal Ethnographical Museum).

1907   *Archaeological Researches on the Pacific Coast of Costa Rica*, Memoirs of the Carnegie Museum, no. 3 (Pittsburgh).

HASEMANN, GEORGE E.

1977   "Reconocimiento arqueologico de Utila," *Yaxkin* 2: 40–76.

HASEMANN, G., V. VELIZ, AND L. VAN GERPEN

1978   *Informe preliminar, Curruste: Fase 1*, Patronato Pro-Corruste (San Pedro Sula: I.H.A.H.).

HAYNES, C. V., JR.

1971   "Time, Environment and Early Man," *Arctic Anthropology* 8: 3–14.

1974   "Paleoenvironments and Cultural Diversity in Late Pleistocene South America: A Reply to A. L. Bryan," *Quaternary Research* 4: 379–82.

HEALY, PAUL F.

1973   "Archaeological Reconnaissance in the Department of Colon, Northeast Honduras," manuscript, Peabody Museum, Harvard University.

1974a   "The Cuyamel Caves: Preclassic Sites in Northeast Honduras," *American Antiquity* 39: 433–37.

1974b   "Archaeological Survey of the Rivas Region, Nicaragua" (Ph.D. diss., Harvard University).

1974c   "An Olmec Vessel from Northeast Honduras," *Katunob* 8: 73–79.

1975   "H-CN-4 (Williams Ranch Site): Preliminary Report on a Selin Period Site in the Department of Colon, Northeast Honduras," *Vinculos* 1: 61–71 (National Museum of Costa Rica, San Jose).

1976a   "Informe preliminar sobre la arqueologia del Periodo Cocal en noreste Honduras," in *Las Fron-*

teras de Mesoamerica, XIV Mesa Redonda, Sociedad Mexicana de Antropologia 2: 237–44 (Mexico City).

1976b   "La ceramica de la region Rivas suroeste de Nicaragua," *Vinculos* 2: 24–36 (National Museum of Costa Rica, San Jose).

1976c   "Los Chorotega y Nicarao: evidencia arqueologica de Rivas, Nicaragua," in *Las Fronteras de Mesoamerica, XIV Mesa Redonda, Sociedad Mexicana de Antropologia* 2: 256–65 (Mexico City).

1977   "The Archaeology of Northeast Honduras: Preliminary Report on the 1975 and 1976 Research," paper presented at the Forty-second Annual Meeting of the Society for American Archaeology, New Orleans.

1978a   "Excavations at Selin Farm (H-CN-5), Colon, Northeast Honduras," *Vinculos* 4: 57–79 (National Museum of Costa Rica, San Jose).

1978b   "La arqueologia del noreste de Honduras: informe preliminar de la investigacion de 1975 y 1976," *Yaxkin* 2: 159–73.

1978c   "Excavations at Rio Claro, Northeast Honduras: Preliminary Report," *Journal of Field Archaeology* 5(1): 15–28.

1978d   "Preliminary Report on the Paleoecology of the Selin Farm Site (H-CN-5), Department of Colon, Honduras," paper presented at the Forty-third Annual Meeting of the Society for American Archaeology, Tucson.

1980a   "The Prehistory of Northeast Honduras: Cultural Change on a Precolumbian Fronter," National Geographic Research Reports, 1975 (in press).

1980b   *Archaeology of the Rivas Region, Nicaragua* (Waterloo, Ontario: Wilfrid Laurier University Press).

1983   "The Paleoecology of the Selin Farm Site (H-CN-5), Department of Colon, Honduras," in *Civilization in the Americas: Essays in Honor of Gordon R. Willey*, ed. R. M. Leventhal and A. L. Kolata (Albuquerque: University of New Mexico Press).

HELLMUTH, NICHOLAS

1978   "Teotihuacan Art in the Escuintla, Guatemala Region," in *Middle Classic Mesoamerica: A.D. 400–799*, ed. E. Pasztory (New York: Columbia University Press).

HELMS, MARY W.

1978   "Coastal Adaptations as Contact Phenomena Among the Miskito and Cuna Indians of Lower Central America," in *Prehistoric Coastal Adaptations: The Economy and Ecology of the Maritime Middle America*, ed. Barbara L. Stark and Barbara Voorhies (New York: Academic Press).

1979   *Ancient Panama: Chiefs in Search of Power* (Austin: University of Texas Press).

HENDERSON, JOHN S.

1976   "Precolumbian Trade Networks in Northwestern Honduras," *Journal of Field Archaeology* 3: 342–46.

1977a   "The Valley de Naco: Ethnohistory and Archaeology in Northwestern Honduras," *Ethnohistory* 24: 363–76.

1977b   "Northwestern Honduras and the Eastern Maya Frontier," paper presented at the Forty-second Annual Meeting of the Society for American Archaeology, New Orleans.

1978   "El noroeste de Honduras y la frontera oriental Maya," *Yaxkin* 2: 241–53.

HENDERSON, JOHN S., ILENE STERNS, ANTHONY WONDERLEY, AND PATRICIA URBAN

1979   "Archaeological Investigations in the Valle de Naco, Northwestern Honduras," *Journal of Field Archaeology* 6: 169–92.

HERRA, C.

n.d.   "Informe sobre el sitio Nosarita (en Nicoya) y propuesta de excavacion," typescript, Museo Nacional de Costa Rica.

HESTER, THOMAS R., THOMAS C. KELLY, AND GIANCARLO LIGABUE

1981   A *Fluted Paleo-Indian Projectile Point from Belize, Central America*, Working Paper no. 1, Colha Project, Center for Archaeological Research, University of Texas at San Antonio and Centro Studi e Ricerche Ligabue, Venice.

HESTER, THOMAS R., HARRY J. SHAFER, AND THOMAS C. KELLY

1980   "A Preliminary Note on Artifacts from Lowe Ranch: A Preceramic Site in Belize," in *The Colha Project, Second Season, 1980, Interim Report*, ed. T. R. Hester, J. D. Eaton, and H. J. Shafer (San Antonio: Center for Archaeological Research, University of Texas).

HIRTH, K. G., P. A. URBAN, G. HASEMANN, AND V. VELIZ R.

1981   "Patrones Regionales de Asentamiento en la Region de El Cajon, Departamento de Comayagua, Honduras," *Yaxkin* 4: 33–55.

HOLMES, W. H.

1888   *Ancient Art of the Province of Chiriqui*, Bureau of American Ethnology, Smithsonian Institution, Fifth Annual Report

(Washington, D.C.: U.S. Government Printing Office).

HOLT, DENNIS
1975 "Paya as a Chibchan Language," manuscript, University of California, Los Angeles.

HOLT, DENNIS, AND W. BRIGHT
1976 "La lengua Paya y las fronteras linguisticas de Mesoamerica," *Las Fronteras de Mesoamerica, XIV Mesa Redonda, Sociedad Mexicana de Antropologia* 1: 149–56 (Mexico City).

HOOPES, JOHN
1979 "Recent Archaeological Investigations at the Site of La Guinea, Tempisque River Valley, Guanacaste, Costa Rica" (B.A. thesis, Yale University).

HOWE, JAMES
1974 "Village Political Organization Among the San Blas Cuna" (Ph.D. diss., University of Pennsylvania).
1977 "Carrying the Village: Cuna Political Metaphors," in *The Social Use of Metaphor*, ed. C. Crocker and J. D. Sapir (Philadelphia: University of Pennsylvania Press).

HUBBS, CARL L., AND
GUNNAR T. RODEN
1967 "Oceanography and Marine Life Along the Pacific Coast," *Handbook of Middle American Indians* I, ed. Robert C. West (Austin: University of Texas Press).

HURT, WESLEY, R., THOMAS VAN DER HAMMEN, AND GONZALO CORREAL URREGO
1976 *The El Abra Rockshelters, Sabana de Bogota, Colombia, South America*, Occasional Papers and Monographs, no. 2, Indiana University Museum (Bloomington).

ICHON, ALAIN
1968 "La mission archeologique française au Panama," *Journal de la Societe des Americanistes de Paris* 57: 139–43.
1980 *Archeologie du Sud de la Peninsule d'Azuero, Panama*, Etudes Mesoamericaines Serie 2, no. 3 (Mexico City: Mission Archaeologique et Ethnologique Française au Mexique).

IJZEREEF, G. R.
1978 "Faunal Remains from the El Abra Rockshelters, Colombia," *Palaeogeography, Palaeoclimatology, Palaeoecology* 25: 153–77.

ISACSSON, SVEN-ERIK
1980 "Gentilicios y desplazamientos de la poblacion aborigen en el noroeste colombiano (1500–1700)," *Indiana* 6: 209–24.

JOHANNESSEN, CARL L.
1963 *Savannas of Interior Honduras*, Ibero-Americana 46 (Berkeley: University of California).

JOHNSON, FREDERICK
1948a "Central American Cultures: An Introduction," in *Handbook of South American Indians*, vol. 4, ed. Julian H. Steward, Bureau of American Ethnology, Smithsonian Institution, Bulletin no. 143 (Washington, D.C.: U.S. Government Printing Office).
1948b "The Caribbean Lowland Tribes: The Talamanca Division," in *Handbook of South American Indians*, vol. 4, ed. Julian H. Steward, Bureau of American Ethnology, Smithsonian Institution, Bulletin no. 143 (Washington, D.C.: U.S. Government Printing Office).
1962 "The Linguistic Map of Mexico and Central America," in *The Maya and Their Neighbors*, ed. C. L. Hays et al. (Provo: University of Utah Press; reprint ed. of a volume published in 1940).

JONES, CHRISTOPHER
1979   "Tikal as a Trading Center," pa-
        per presented at the Forty-third
        International Congress of Amer-
        icanists, Vancouver.

JORALEMON, PETER DAVID
1976   "The Olmec Dragon: A Study in
        Pre-Columbian Iconography," in
        *Origins of Religious Art and Icon-
        ography in Preclassic Mesoamer-
        ica*, ed. H. B. Nicholson (Los
        Angeles: University of California
        at Los Angeles, Latin American
        Studies).

JOYCE, THOMAS A.
1916   *Central American and West In-
        dian Archaeology, Being an In-
        troduction to the Archaeology of
        the States of Nicaragua, Costa
        Rica, Panama, and the West In-
        dies* (New York: Putnam).

JURADO, OVIDIO, AND
ABELARDO CASTRO
1967   "La fase Aguas Buenas en Hor-
        concitos," *Boletin del Museo
        Chiricano* 51: 27–29.

KAUFMAN, T.
1976   "Archaeological and Linguistic
        Correlations in Maya Land and
        Associated Areas of Meso-Amer-
        ica," *World Archaeology* 8: 101–
        18.

KELLEY, J. H.
1980   "The 1979 Season at Cihuatan,
        Central El Salvador," paper pre-
        sented at the Forty-fifth Annual
        Meeting of the Society for Amer-
        ican Archaeology, Philadelphia.

KENNEDY, NEDENIA C.
1978   "Acerca de la frontera en Playa
        de los Muertos, Honduras,"
        Yaxkin 2: 203–15.

1980   "The Formative Ceramic Chro-
        nology from Playa de los Muer-
        tos, Honduras," paper presented
        at the Forty-fifth Annual Meeting

        of the Society for American Ar-
        chaeology, Philadelphia.

1981   "The Formative Period Ceramic
        Sequence from Playa de los
        Muertos, Honduras" (Ph.D. diss.,
        University of Illinois at Urbana-
        Champaign).

KENNEDY, WILLIAM J.
1968   "Archaeological Investigations in
        the Reventazon River Drainage
        Area, Costa Rica" (Ph.D. diss.,
        Tulane University).

1969   "Current Research, Costa Rica,"
        American Antiquity 34: 358.

1975   "The Appearance of the Chief-
        dom and Its Environmental Set-
        ting in the Reventazon River Area,
        Costa Rica," *Proceedings of the
        Forty-first International Con-
        gress of Americanists* 1: 560–67
        (Mexico City).

1976   "Prehistory of the Reventazon
        River Drainage Area, Costa Rica,"
        Vinculos 2: 87–100 (National
        Museum of Costa Rica, San Jose).

KERBIS, JULIAN
1979   "An Analysis of the Vertebrate
        Fauna from a Costa Rican Shell
        Midden" (M.A. thesis, Univer-
        sity of Chicago).

1980   "The Analysis of Faunal Re-
        mains from the Vidor Site," in
        *Investigaciones arqueologicas en
        la zona de Bahia Culebra, Costa
        Rica (1973–1979)*, *Vinculos* 6
        (National Museum of Costa Rica,
        San Jose).

KIDDER, A. V.
1947   *The Artifacts of Uaxactun, Gua-
        temala*, Carnegie Institution of
        Washington, Publication 576
        (Washington, D.C.: Carnegie
        Institution).

1949   "Certain Archaeological Speci-
        mens from Guatemala," in *Notes
        on Middle American Archaeology*

and Ethnology, 92 (Washington, D.C.: Carnegie Institution).

KIDDER, A., J. JENNINGS, AND E. SHOOK

1946   Excavations at Kaminaljuyu, Guatemala, Carnegie Institution of Washington, Publication 561 (Washington, D.C.: Carnegie Institution).

KIRCHHOFF, P.

1943   "Mesoamerica: sus limites geograficas, composicion etnica y caracteres culturales," Acta Americana 1: 92–107.

LADD, JOHN

1964   Archaeological Investigations in the Parita and Santa Maria Zones of Panama, Bureau of American Ethnology, Smithsonian Institution, Bulletin 193 (Washington, D.C.: U.S. Government Printing Office).

LANGE, FREDERICK W.

1969   An Archaeological Survey of the Rio Sapoa Valley: Report on a Preliminary Season of Archaeological Research in Northwestern Guanacaste Province, the Republic of Costa Rica (mimeographed, Chicago: Associated Colleges of the Midwest).

1971a   "The Late Polychrome Period in Northwestern Costa Rica," paper presented at the Thirty-sixth Annual Meeting of the Society for American Archaeology, Norman, Oklahoma.

1971b   Cultural History of the Sapoa River Valley, Costa Rica, Logan Museum of Anthropology, Occasional Paper no. 4 (Beloit: Beloit College).

1971c   "Northwestern Costa Rica: Pre-Columbian Circum-Caribbean Affiliations," Folk 13: 43–64.

1972   "Historia cultural en el Valle del Rio Sapoa, Costa Rica," Informe Semestral, Instituto Geografico de Costa Rica, pp. 61–76.

1976   "Bahias y valles de la costa de Guanacaste," Vinculos 2: 45–66 (National Museum of Costa Rica, San Jose).

1978   "Coastal Settlement in Northwestern Costa Rica," in Prehistoric Coastal Adaptations: The Economy of Maritime Middle America, ed. Barbara L. Stark and Barbara Voorhies (New York: Academic Press).

1979a   "Theoretical and Descriptive Aspects of Frontier Studies," Latin American Research Review 14: 221–27.

1979b   "Shells, Spoons, Maces, and Stools: A Look at Social Organization in Pre-Columbian Costa Rica," paper presented at the Seventy-eighth Annual Meeting of the American Anthropological Association, Cincinnati.

1980   "La presencia de metales precolombinos en Guanacaste," in Memoria del Congreso Sobre el Mundo Centroamericano de su Tiempo, V Centenario de Gonzalo Fernandez de Oviedo (San Jose, Costa Rica: Editorial Texto).

LANGE, FREDERICK W., AND SUZANNE ABEL-VIDOR

1980a   "The Formative Zoned Bichrome Period in Northeastern Costa Rica (800 B.C. to A.D. 500)," in Investigaciones arqueologicas en la zona de Bahia Culebra, Costa Rica (1973–1979), Vinculos 6 (National Museum of Costa Rica, San Jose).

1980b   "Una ocupacion del Policromo Tardio en sitio Ruiz, cerca de Bahia Culebra," in Investigaciones arqueologicas en la zona de Bahia Culebra, Costa Rica (1973–

1979), *Vinculos* 6 (National Museum of Costa Rica, San Jose).

LANGE, FREDERICK W., AND
RICHARD M. ACCOLA
1979   "Metallurgy in Costa Rica," *Archaeology* 32(5): 26–33.

LANGE, FREDERICK W., DAVID J.
BERNSTEIN, MARTI SIEGEL, AND
DONALD TASE
1974   "Preliminary Archaeological Research in the Nosara Valley," *Folk* 18: 47–60.

LANGE, FREDERICK W., RONALD
BISHOP, AND LAMBERTUS VON ZELST
1981   "Perspectives on Costa Rican Jade: Compositional Analyses and Cultural Implications," in *Between Continents/Between Seas: Precolumbian Art of Costa Rica*, ed. E. Benson (New York: H. N. Abrams).

LANGE, FREDERICK W., AND
THOMAS MURRAY
1972   "The Archaeology of the San Dimas Valley, Costa Rica," *Katunob* 7(4).

LANNING, EDWARD P.
1967   *Peru Before the Incas* (Englewood Cliffs, N.J.: Prentice-Hall).

LARA, G., AND G. HASEMANN
1982   "El Salvamento Arqueologico en la Region de El Cajon, Honduras," *Mexicon* 4: 42–45.

LARDE, J.
1926a   "Cronologia arqueologica de El Salvador," *Revista de Etnologia, Arqueologia y Lingüistica* 1: 153–62 (San Salvador).
1926b   "Arqueologia cuzcatleca: vestigios de una publacion pre-mayica en el valle de San Salvador, C.A., sepultados bajo una potente capa de productos volcanicos," *Revista de Etnologia, Arqueologia y Lingüistica* 1: 3–4 (San Salvador).

LAS CASAS, FRAY BARTOLOME DE
1957   *Historia de las Indias* (Madrid: Ediciones Atlas).

LATHRAP, DONALD W.
1970   *The Upper Amazon* (New York: Praeger).
1971   "Complex Iconographic Features Shared by Olmec and Chavin and Some Speculations on Their Possible Significance," paper presented at the First Symposium on Anthropological Correlations in Andean Mesoamerica, Salinas, Ecuador.
1973a   "Gifts of the Cayman: Some Thoughts on the Subsistence Basis of Chavin," in *Variations in Anthropology*, ed. D. Lathrap and J. Douglas (Urbana: Illinois Archaeological Survey).
1973b   "The Antiquity and Importance of Long Distance Trade Relationships in the Moist Tropics of Pre-Columbian South America," *World Archaeology* 5(2): 170–86.
1975   *Ancient Ecuador: Culture, Clay and Creativity* 3000–300 B.C. (Chicago: Field Museum of Natural History).
1977   "Our Father the Cayman, Our Mother the Gourd: Spinden Revisited or a Unitary Model for the Emergence of Agriculture in the New World," in *Origins of Agriculture*, ed. C. A. Reed (The Hague: Mouton).

LATORRE, GERMAN
1919   *Relaciones geograficas de Indias (contenidas en el Archivo General de Indias de Sevilla)* (Seville: Zarauela).

LAURENCICH DE MINELLI, LAURA
1979   "Informe preliminar sobre investigaciones arqueologicas en Barra Honda (Costa Rica)," *Indiana* 5: 177–91 (Berlin).

LAURENCICH DE MINELLI, LAURA, AND
LUIGE MINELLI
1966   "Informe preliminar sobre exca-
          vaciones alrededor de San Vito
          de Java," XXXVI Congreso In-
          ternacional de Americanistas,
          Actas y Memorias 1: 482–91
          (Seville: Editorial Catolica Es-
          pañola).
1973   "La fase 'Aguas Buenas' en la re-
          gion de San Vito de Java Costa
          Rica—informe preliminar," Atti
          del XL Congresso Internazionale
          degli Americanisti 1: 219–24
          (Genoa: Tilgher).
LEHMANN, W.
1910   "Ergebnisse einer Froschunge-
          reise in Mittelamerika und Mex-
          iko, 1907–09," Zeitung fur
          Ethnologie, 42: 687–749.
1920   Zentral-Amerika, 2 vols. (Berlin:
          Reimer).
LINARES DE SAPIR, OLGA
1968a   "Ceramic Phases for Chiriqui,
          Panama, and Their Relationship
          to Neighboring Sequences,"
          American Antiquity 33: 216–25.
1968b   Cultural Chronology in the Gulf
          of Chiriqui, Panama, Smithson-
          ian Contributions to Anthropol-
          ogy, no. 8 (Washington, D.C.:
          Smithsonian Institution).
1976a   "From the Late Preceramic to the
          Early Formative in the Interme-
          diate Area: Some Issues and
          Methodologies," Proceedings of
          the First Puerto Rican Sympo-
          sium on Archaeology, report no.
          1, ed. Linda Sickler Robinson,
          Agamemnon Gus Pantel, and
          Gary S. Vescelius (San Juan:
          Fundacion Arqueologicas, An-
          tropologica e Historica de Puerto
          Rico).
1976b   "'Garden Hunting' in the Amer-
          ican Tropics," Human Ecology
          4(4): 331–49.

1976c   "Plantas y animales domestica-
          dos en la America precolom-
          bina," Revista Panameña de
          Antropologia 1: 8–28.
1976d   "Animals That Were Bad to Eat
          Were Good to Compete With: An
          Analysis of the Conte Style from
          Ancient Panama," in Ritual and
          Symbol in Native South America,
          University of Oregon Anthropo-
          logical Papers no. 9, ed. P. Young
          and J. Howe (Eugene).
1977a   "Ecology and the Arts in Central
          Panama: On the Development of
          Social Rank and Symbolism in
          the Central Provinces," Studies
          in Pre-Columbian Art and Ar-
          chaeology, no. 17 (Washington,
          D.C.: Dumbarton Oaks).
1977b   "Adaptive Strategies in Western
          Panama," World Archaeology 8(3):
          304–19.
1979   "What Is Lower Central Ameri-
          can Archaeology?" Annual Re-
          view of Anthropology 8, ed. B. J.
          Siegel (Palo Alto: Annual Re-
          views).
1980a   "Conclusions," in Adaptive Ra-
          diations in Prehistoric Panama,
          ed. Olga F. Linares and Anthony
          J. Ranere, Peabody Museum
          Monographs, no. 5 (Cambridge,
          Mass.: Harvard University).
1980b   "Ecology and Prehistory of the
          Aguacate Peninsula in Bocas del
          Toro," in Adaptive Radiations in
          Prehistoric Panama, ed. Olga F.
          Linares and Anthony J. Ranere,
          Peabody Museum Monographs,
          no. 5 (Cambridge, Mass.: Har-
          vard University).
1980c   "Ecology and Prehistory of the
          Chiriqui Gulf Sites," in Adaptive
          Radiations in Prehistoric Pan-
          ama, ed. Olga F. Linares and
          Anthony J. Ranere, Peabody
          Museum Monographs, no. 5

(Cambridge, Mass.: Harvard University).

1980d   "The Ceramic Record: Time and Place," in *Adaptive Radiations in Prehistoric Panama*, ed. Olga F. Linares and Anthony J. Ranere, Peabody Museum Monographs, no. 5 (Cambridge, Mass.: Harvard University).

LINARES, OLGA, AND RICHARD G. COOKE

1975   "Differential Exploitation of Lagoon-Estuary Systems in Panama," paper presented at the Fortieth Annual Meeting of the Society for American Archaeology, Dallas.

LINARES DE SAPIR, OLGA, AND ANTHONY J. RANERE

1971   "Human Adaptation to the Tropical Forests of Western Panama," *Archaeology* 24: 346–55.

1980   *Adaptive Radiations in Prehistoric Panama*, Peabody Museum Monographs, no. 5 (Cambridge, Mass.: Harvard University).
(eds.)

LINARES, OLGA F., AND PAYSON D. SHEETS

1980   "Highland Agricultural Villages in the Volcan Baru Region," in *Adaptive Radiations in Prehistoric Panama*, ed. Olga F. Linares and Anthony J. Ranere, Peabody Museum Monographs, no. 5 (Cambridge, Mass.: Harvard University).

LINARES, OLGA F., PAYSON D. SHEETS, AND E. JANE ROSENTHAL

1975   "Prehistoric Agriculture in Tropical Highlands," *Science* 187: 137–45.

LINARES, OLGA F., AND RICHARD S. WHITE

1980   "Terrestrial Fauna from Cerro Brujo (CA–3) in Bocas del Toro and La Pitahaya (IS–3) in Chiriqui," in *Adaptive Radiations in*

Prehistoric Panama, ed. Olga F. Linares and Anthony J. Ranere, Peabody Museum Monographs, no. 5 (Cambridge, Mass.: Harvard University).

LINES, JORGE A.

1935   *Los Altares de Toyopan: estudio hecho con motivo de la Exposicion de Arqueologia de octubre 1934* (San Jose).

1936a   *Una Huaca en Zapandi: notas preliminares tomadas a proposito de las excavaciones arqueologicas hechas a raiz de la inundacion del Rio Tempisque en 1933, Filadelfia, Provincia de Guanacaste, Peninsula de Nicoya, Costa Rica* (San Jose).

1936b   *Notes on the Archaeology of Costa Rica* (San Jose: National Tourist Board of Costa Rica).

1942   "Dos nuevas gemas en la arqueologia de Costa Rica," *Proceedings of the Eighth American Scientific Congress* 2: 117–22 (Washington, D.C.).

1952   *Coleccion de documentos para la historia de Costa Rica relativos al cuarto y ultimo viaje de Cristobal Colon* (San Jose: Academia de Geografia e Historia de Costa Rica).

LINNE, S.

1929   *Darien in the Past: The Archaeology of Eastern Panama and North-Western Colombia*, Göteborgs Kungl. Vetenskaps- och Vitterhets-Samhälles Handlingar, Femte Följden, Ser. A, 1, 3, Bd 1, nr 3 (Gothenberg: Elanders boktryckeri aktiebolag).

1936   "Archaeological Field Work in Chiriqui, Panama," *Ethnos* 1: 95–102 (Stockholm).

LONGYEAR, J. M., III

1944   *Archaeological Investigations in El Salvador*, Memoirs of the Peabody Museum of Archaeology and Ethnology, vol. 9, no. 2 (Cambridge, Mass.: Harvard University).

1947   *Cultures and Peoples of the Southeastern Maya Frontier,* Carnegie Institution of Washington, Theoretical Approaches to Problems, no. 3 (Washington, D.C.: Carnegie Institution).

1948   "A Sub-Pottery Deposit at Copan, Honduras," *American Antiquity* 13: 248–49.

1952   *Copan Ceramics: A Study of Southeastern Maya Pottery,* Carnegie Institution of Washington, Publication 597 (Washington, D.C.: Carnegie Institution).

1966   "Archaeological Survey of El Salvador," in *Handbook of Middle American Indians,* vol. 4, ed. R. Wauchope (Austin: University of Texas Press).

1969   "The Problem of Olmec Influences in the Pottery of Western Honduras," *Proceedings of the Thirty-eighth International Congress of Americanists* 1: 491–97.

LOTHROP, SAMUEL K.

1926   *Pottery of Costa Rica and Nicaragua,* Contributions from the Museum of the American Indian, no. 8, 2 vols. (New York: Heye Foundation).

1927a   *Pottery Types and Their Sequence in El Salvador,* Museum of the American Indian, Heye Foundation, Indian Notes, vol. 1, no. 4 (New York: Museum of the American Indian).

1927b   "The Museum Central American Expedition, 1925–1926," Museum of the American Indian, Heye Foundation, *Indian Notes* 4: 12–33.

1933   *Atitlan: An Archaeological Study of Ancient Remains on the Borders of Lake Atitlan, Guatemala,* Carnegie Institution of Washington, Publication 444 (Washington, D.C.: Carnegie Institution).

1937–42 *Cocle: An Archaeological Study of Central Panama,* Memoirs of the Peabody Museum of Archaeology and Ethnology, vols. 7, 8 (Cambridge, Mass.: Harvard University).

1939   "The Southeastern Frontier of the Maya," *American Anthropologist* 41: 42–54.

1942   "The Sigua: Southernmost Aztec Outpost," *Proceedings of the Eighth American Scientific Congress* 2: 109–16.

1950   *Archaeology of Southern Veraguas, Panama,* Memoirs of the Peabody Museum of Archaeology and Ethnology, vol. 9, no. 3 (Cambridge, Mass.: Harvard University).

1952   *Metals from the Cenote of Sacrifice, Chichen Itza, Yucatan,* Memoirs of the Peabody Museum of Archaeology and Ethnology, vol. 10, no. 2 (Cambridge, Mass.: Harvard University).

1954   "Suicide, Sacrifice and Mutilations in Burials at Venado Beach, Panama," *American Antiquity* 21: 226–34.

1956   "Jewelry from the Canal Zone," *Archaeology* 9: 34–40.

1960   "C-14 Dates for Venado Beach, Canal Zone, Panama," *Archaeologist* 3: 96.

1961   "Early Migrations to Central and South America: An Anthropological Problem in the Light of Other Sciences," *Journal of the Royal Anthropological Institute of Great Britain and Ireland* 91: 97–123.

1963   *Archaeology of the Diquis Delta, Costa Rica,* Papers of the Peabody Museum of Archaeology and Ethnology, vol. 51 (Cambridge, Mass.: Harvard University).

1966 "Archaeology of Lower Central America," in *Handbook of Middle American Indians*, vol. 4, ed. R. Wauchope (Austin: University of Texas Press).

LOWE, GARETH W.

1975 *The Early Preclassic Barra Phase of Altamira, Chiapas: A Review with New Data*, Papers of the New World Archaeological Foundation, no. 38 (Provo: Brigham Young University Press).

LUNARDI, FEDERICO

1945 *Choluteca: Ensayo historico etnografico* (Tegucigalpa: Talleres Tipograficos Nacionales).

1948 *Honduras Maya: Etnologia y arqueologia de Honduras* (Tegucigalpa: Imprenta Calderon).

LYNCH, THOMAS F.

1967 "Quishqui Puncu: A Preceramic Site in Highland Peru," *Science* 158: 780–83.

1970 *Excavation at Quishqui Puncu in the Callejon de Huaylas, Peru*, Occasional Papers of the Idaho State University Museum, no. 26 (Pocatello, Idaho).

1974 "The Antiquity of Man in South America," *Quaternary Research* 4: 356–77.

1976 "The Entry and Postglacial Adaptation of Man in Andean South America," in *Colloque XVII, Ninth Congress of the International Union of Prehistoric and Protohistoric Sciences* 1: 69–100 (Nice).

1978 "The South American Paleo-Indians," in *Ancient Native-Americans*, ed. J. D. Jennings (San Francisco: W. H. Freeman & Co.).

MCBIRNEY, A.

1974 "Active Volcanoes of Nicaragua and Costa Rica," *Bulletin Volcanologique* 37(3): 109–46 (Naples).

MACCURDY, GEORGE G.

1911 *A Study of Chiriquian Antiquities*, Memoirs of the Connecticut Academy of Arts and Sciences, vol. 3.

MCGIMSEY, CHARLES R., III

1956 "Cerro Mangote: A Preceramic Site in Panama," *American Antiquity* 22: 151–61.

1957 "Further Data and a Date from Cerro Mangote, Panama," *American Antiquity* 23: 434–35.

1964 "Investigaciones arqueologicas en Panama: informe preliminar sobre la Temporada de 1961–62," *Hombre y Cultura* 1(3): 139–55.

MCGIMSEY, CHARLES R., III, MICHAEL B. COLLINS, AND THOMAS W. MCKERN

1966 "Cerro Mangote and Its Population," paper presented at the Thirty-seventh International Congress of Americanists, Mar del Plata, Argentina.

MCCLEOD, MURDO J.

1973 *Spanish Central America: A Socioeconomic History, 1520–1720* (Berkeley: University of California Press).

MACNEISH, RICHARD S.

1964 "Ancient Mesoamerican Civilization," *Science* 143: 531–37.

1976 "Early Man in the New World," *American Scientist* 64(3): 316–27.

MACNEISH, RICHARD STOCKTON, S. JEFFREY K. WILKERSON, AND ANTOINETTE NELKEN-TERNER

1980 *First Annual Report of the Belize Archaic Archaeological Reconnaissance* (Andover: Robert E. Peabody Foundation for Archaeology, Phillips Academy).

MAGNUS, RICHARD W.
1975   "La secuencia de la costa Atlan-
        tica y zona central de Nicara-
        gua," Boletin Nicaraguense de
        Biblioigrafica y Documentacion 4
        (Managua).
1976   "La costa Atlantica de Nicara-
        gua," Vinculos 2: 67–74 (Na-
        tional Museum of Costa Rica, San
        Jose).
1978   "The Prehistoric and Modern
        Subsistence Patterns of the At-
        lantic Coast of Nicaragua: A
        Comparison," in Prehistoric
        Coastal Adaptations: The Econ-
        omy and Ecology of Maritime
        Middle America, ed. Barbara L.
        Stark and Barbara Voorhies (New
        York: Academic Press).
MANGELSDORF, PAUL C., AND
MARIO SANOJA O.
1965   "Early Archaeological Maize from
        Venezuela," Botanical Museum
        Leaflets, Harvard University,
        21(4): 105–11.
MARTIN, PAUL S.
1973   "The Discovery of America,"
        Science 179: 969–74.
MARTINEZ GIRON, ERIC JORGE
1979   "Los Chorotegas de Mesoamer-
        ica meridional," Yaxkin 3: 1–25.
MARTYR, PETER
1912   "De Orbe Novo," trans. Francis
        MacNutt (New York).
MASON, J. ALDEN
1931–39 Archaeology of Santa Marta,
        Colombia: The Tairona Culture,
        Field Museum of Natural His-
        tory Anthropological Series, vol.
        20, parts 1, 2, 3 (Chicago).
1940   "Ivory and Resin Figurines from
        Cocle," University Museum Bul-
        letin 8(4): 13–21.
1941   "Gold from the Grave," Scien-
        tific American 165: 261–63.
1942   "New Excavations at the Sitio
        Conte, Cocle, Panama," Acts of

the Eighth American Scientific
        Congress 2: 103–7 (Washington,
        D.C.).
1945   Costa Rican Stonework, Anthro-
        pological Papers, American Mu-
        seum of Natural History, vol. 39,
        pt. 3 (New York).
1962   "The Native Languages of Mid-
        dle America," in The Maya and
        Their Neighbors, ed. C. L. Hay
        et al. (Provo: University of Utah
        Press; reprint ed. of a volume first
        published in 1940).
MATILLO VILA, J. (HNO. HILDEBERTO
MARIA F.S.C.)
1968   Estas piedras hablan. Managua:
        Editorial Hospicio.
MAYER-OAKES, WILLIAM
1981   Early Man Projectile Points and
        Lithic Technology in the Ecu-
        adorian Sierra, manuscript pre-
        pared for the R. E. Bell Festschrift.
MEGGERS, BETTY J.
1954   "Environmental Limitations on
        the Development of Culture,"
        American Anthropologist 56: 801–
        24.
1971   Amazonia: Man and Culture in
        a Counterfeit Paradise (Chicago:
        Aldine).
MERRITT, J. K.
1860   Report on the Huacals, or An-
        cient Graveyards of Chiriqui (New
        York: American Ethnological So-
        ciety).
MICHELS, JOSEPH W.
1979   The Kaminaljuyu Chiefdom,
        Monograph Series on Kaminal-
        juyu (University Park: Pennsyl-
        vania State University Press).
MIKSICEK, CHARLES H., ROBERT McK.
BIRD, BARBARA PICKERSGILL, SARA
DONAGHEY, JULIETTE CARTWRIGHT,
AND NORMAN HAMMOND
1981   "Preclassic Lowland Maize from
        Cuello, Belize," Nature 289
        (5793): 56–59.

MILES, S. W.
1957 "The Sixteenth-Century Pokom-Maya," *Transactions of the American Philosophical Society* 47(4): 735–81.

MILLON, RENE
1955 "When Money Grew on Trees" (Ph.D. diss., Columbia University).

MIRANDA, F.
1959 "Estudios acerca de la vegetacion," in *Estudios particulares*, vol. 2, ed. E. Beltran (Instituto Mex. Recursos Naturales Renovables).

MIRANDA, LUIS MAXIMO
1974 "Un aporte preliminar a la arqueologia del oriente de Panama" (Tesis de Licenciado, Universidad de Panama).
1976 "Interpretacion de las escenas que aparacen en algunas de las vasijas dobles de la fase El Indio," in *Actas del IV Simposium Nacional de Antropologia, Arqueologia y Etnohistoria de Panama* (Panama: Universidad de Panama e Instituto Nacional de Cultura).

MIRANDA, MAXIMO, LUAN B. PEREZ, AND ROBERTO DE LA GUARDIA
1966 "El Sitio Dolega," *Boletin del Museo Chiricano* 2: 7–12.

MONTEJO, FRANCISCO DE
1539 "Carta del adelantado D. Francisco de Montejo al Emperàdor, sobre varios asuntos relativos a la gobernacion de Honduras," in *Coleccion de documentos ineditos relativos al descubrimiento, conquista y organizacion de las antiguas posesiones españolas de America y Oceania* 2: 212–44 (Madrid).

MONTESSUS DE BALLORE, F. DE
1892 "Etudes archeologiques sur le Salvador precolombien," *Acta,* *Eighth International Congress of Americanists*, pp. 525–32 (Paris).

MOREAU, JEAN-FRANÇOIS
1978 "Some Paleoecological Consequences of Two Volcanic Eruptions as Evidenced by the Shells of a Costa Rican Shell Mi" paper presented at the Forty-third Annual Meeting of the Society for American Archaeology, Tucson.
1979 "The Inland Occupation on the Pacific Coast of Prehistoric Northwestern Costa Rica," paper presented at the Forty-fourth Annual Meeting of the Society for American Archaeology, Vancouver.
1980 "A Report on the Hunter-Robinson and Sardinal Sites," in *Investigaciones arqueologicas en la zona de Bahia Culebra, Costa Rica (1973–1979)*, *Vinculos* 6 (National Museum of Costa Rica, San Jose).

MORLEY, SYLVANUS G.
1920 *The Inscriptions of Copan*, Carnegie Institution of Washington, Publication 219 (Washington, D.C.: Carnegie Institution).

MOSIMANN, J. E., AND PAUL S. MARTIN
1975 "Simulating Overkill by Paleo-Indians," *American Scientist* 63: 304–13.

MURRAY, T. A.
1969 "Report on the Rio Antiguo Locality of the Rio Sapoa Valley," in *1969 Rio Sapoa Valley Field Report* (Chicago: Associated Colleges of the Midwest).

MURRAY, THOMAS, AND EDWARD W. JESS
1976 "Preliminary Report of the Rio Sabalo Valley Survey," manuscript, National Museum of Costa Rica.

MYERS, THOMAS P.
1978 "Formative-Period Interaction

Spheres in the Intermediate Area: Archaeology of Central America and Adjacent South America," in *Advances in Andean Archaeology*, ed. D. L. Browman (The Hague: Mouton).

NIETSCHMANN, BERNARD
1972   "Hunting and Fishing Focus among the Miskito Indians, Eastern Nicaragua," *Human Ecology* 1: 41–67.

1973   *Between Land and Water: The Subsistence Ecology of the Miskito Indians, Eastern Nicaragua* (New York: Seminar Press).

NORR, LYNETTE
1978   "Excavations of a Stone Burial Mound, Costa Rica," paper presented at First Annual Meeting, Midwestern Mesoamericanists, University of Illinois-Urbana.

1979a   "Summer Research Report on Fieldwork in Northwestern Costa Rica," manuscript, Department of Anthropology, University of Illinois at Urbana-Champaign.

1979b   "Stone Burial Mounds and Petroglyphs of the Zoned Bichrome Period," paper presented at the Forty-fourth Annual Meeting of the Society for American Archaeology, Vancouver.

1980   "Prehistoric Diet and Bone Chemistry: Initial Results from Costa Rica," paper presented at the Forty-fifth Annual Meeting of the Society for American Archaeology, Philadelphia.

1981   "Prehistoric Human Diet in Lower Central America: The Maize vs. Marine Fauna Problem," paper presented at the Third Annual Meeting of the Society for Archaeological Sciences, San Diego.

NORWEB, ALBERT H.
1961   "The Archaeology of the Greater

Nicoya Subarea," manuscript, Peabody Museum of Archaeology and Ethnology, Harvard University.

1964   "Ceramic Stratigraphy in Southwestern Nicaragua," *Proceedings and Transactions of the Thirty-fifth International Congress of Americanists* 1: 551–61 (Mexico City).

NUÑEZ-REGUEIRO, VICTOR A., JULIO CESAR VALDEZ, AND MARTA R. A. TARTUSI
1983   *Efectos de la contaminacion por carbon inerte en los fechados de C14 de Sitio Z-102, Rancho Pelado, Edo. Zulia, Venezuela (informe preliminar)*, Pub. no. 5 (Maracaibo: Programa Arqueologia de Rescate Corpozulia-Luz).

OSGOOD, CORNELIUS
1935   "The Archaeological Problem in Chiriqui," *American Anthropologist* 37: 234–43.

OTIS, F. M.
1895   "The New Gold Discoveries on the Isthmus of Panama," *Harper's Weekly*, August 6.

OVIEDO Y VALDES, GONZALO FERNANDEZ DE
1944   *Historia general y natural de las Indias*, ed. J. Natalico (Asuncion, Paraguay).

PAGDEN, A. R.
1971   *Hernan Cortes: Letters from*
(trans.,   *Mexico* (New York: Orion Press).
ed.)

PANAMA ARCHAEOLOGIST
1958–65 (Balboa, Canal Zone).

PARSONS, JAMES J.
1955   "The Moskito Pine Savanna of Nicaragua and Honduras," *Annals of Association of American Geographers* 45: 36–63.

1967   *Antioquia's Corridor to the Sea: An Historical Geography of the Settlement of Uraba*, Ibero-

Americana 49 (Berkeley: University of California).

1969   "Ridged Fields of the Rio Guayas Valley, Ecuador," *American Antiquity* 34: 76–80.

1978   "More on Pre-Columbian Raised Fields (Camellones) in the Bajo San Jorge and Bajo Cauca, Colombia," in *The Role of Geographical Research in Latin America*, Conference of Latin American Geographers Publication no. 7, ed. W. M. Denevan (Muncie).

PARSONS, JAMES J., AND WILLIAM A. BOWEN

1966   "Ancient Ridged Fields of the San Jorge River Floodplain, Colombia," *Geographical Review* 56: 317–43.

PARSONS, JAMES J., AND W. DENEVAN

1967   "Precolombian Ridged Fields," *Scientific American* 217(1): 92–100.

PARSONS, LEE

1969   *Bilbao, Guatemala*, vol. 2, Milwaukee Public Museum Publications in Anthropology 12 (Milwaukee: Milwaukee Public Museum).

PATIÑO, VICTOR MANUEL

1964   *Plantas cultivadas y animales domesticos en America equinoccial, tomo II, Plantas alimenticias* (Cali: Imprenta Departamental).

PAULSEN, ALLISON C.

1977   "Patterns of Maritime Trade Between South Coastal Ecuador and Western Mesoamerica 1500 B.C.–A.D. 600," in *The Sea in the Pre-Columbian World*, ed. Elizabeth P. Benson .(Washington, D.C.: Dumbarton Oaks).

PEARSALL, DEBORAH M.

1977–78 "Early Movement of Maize between Mesoamerica and South America," *Journal of the Steward*

Anthropological Society 9: 41–75.

1978   "Phytolith Analysis of Archaeological Soil: Evidence for Maize Cultivation in Formative Ecuador," *Science* 199: 177–78.

1979   "The Application of Ethnobotanical Techniques to the Problem of Subsistence in the Ecuadorian Formative" (Ph.D. diss., University of Illinois at Urbana-Champaign).

PECCORINI, A.

1913   "Algunos datos sobre arqueologia de la Republica del Salvador," *Journal de la Societe des Americanistes de Paris* 10: 173–80.

1926   "Ruinas de Quelepa," *Revista de Etnologia, Arqueologia y Lingüistica* 1: 249–50.

PECTOR, DESIRE

1892   "Notice sur l'archeologie du Salvador precolumbien," Internationales Archiv fur Ethnographie (Leiden).

PERALTA, MANUEL MARIA DE

1883   *Costa Rica, Nicaragua y Panama en el siglo XVI* . . . (Madrid: Libreria de M. Murillo).

PERERA, MIGUEL ANGEL

1979   *Arqueologia y arqueometria de las placas liticas aladas del occidente de Venezuela* (Caracas: Universidad Central de Venezuela).

PEREZ ZELEDON, P.

1907–8 *Las llanuras de Pirris valle del Rio General o Grande de Terraba*, informes presentados a la Secretaria de Fomento (San Jose).

PICKERSGILL, BARBARA, AND C. B. HEISER, JR.

1977   "Origins and Distributions of Plants Domesticated in the New World Tropics," in *Origins of Agriculture*, ed. C. A. Reed (The Hague: Mouton).

PIPERNO, DOLORES R.

1979   "Phytolith Analysis of Archaeological Soils from Central Panama" (M.A. thesis, Temple University).

1980a   "First Report on the Phytolith Analysis of the Vegas Site OGSE–80, Ecuador," manuscript, Temple University.

1980b   "Phytolith Evidence for Maize Cultivation in Central Panama During the Early Ceramic (Monagrillo) Period," paper presented at the Forty-fifth Annual Meeting of the Society for American Archaeology, Philadelphia.

1981   "Phytolith Analysis of Preceramic Soils from Southwest Ecuador: Evidence for Maize Cultivation by 6000 B.C.," paper presented at the Forty-sixth Annual Meeting of the Society for American Archaeology, San Diego.

1982   "The Application of Phytolith Analysis to Paleo-Environmental Reconstruction in the Tropics: Comparison with a Pollen Sequence from the Gatun Basin, Panama," paper presented at the Eighty-first Annual Meeting of the America Anthropological Association, Washington, D.C.

in   "A Comparison and Differentia-
press   tion of Phytoliths from Maize (*Zea mays* L.) and Wild Grasses: Use of Morphological Criteria," *American Antiquity* (1984).

PIPERNO, DOLORES, AND
KAREN HUSUM CLARY
n.d.   "Early Plant Use and Cultivation in the Santa Maria Basin, Panama," in *Recent Advances in Isthmian Archaeology*, ed. F. Lange (Oxford: British Archaeological Reports), in press.

PLAZAS, CLEMENCIA, AND ANA MARIA
FALCHETTE DE SAENZ
1981   *Asentamientos prehispanicos en el Bajo Rio San Jorge* (Bogota: Banco de la Republica, Fundacion de Investigaciones Arqueologicas Nacionales).

PLAZAS, CLEMENCIA, ANA MARIA
FALCHETTI DE SAENZ, AND
JUANA SAENZ O.
1979a   "Investigaciones arqueologicas en Montelibano (Cordoba): informe parcial," unpublished report, Museo del Oro, Bogota.

1979b   "Investigaciones arqueologicas en el Rio San Jorge," *Boletin del Museo del Oro* 2 (septiembre–octubre): 1–18.

1980   "Investigaciones arqueologicas en el Rio San Jorge," unpublished report, Museo del Oro, Bogota.

POHORILENKO, ANATOLE
1981   "The Olmec Style and Costa Rican Archaeology," in *The Olmec and Their Neighbors*, ed. E. Benson (Washington, D.C.: Dumbarton Oaks Research Library and Collections).

POLANYI, KARL
1971   *Primitive, Archaic, and Modern Economies: Essays of Karl Polanyi* (Boston: Beacon Press).

POPENOE, DOROTHY H.
1928   *Las ruinas de Tenampua* (Tegucigalpa: Tipografia Nacional).

1934   "Some Excavations at Playa de los Muertos, Ulua River, Honduras," *Maya Research* 1: 61–85.

1936   "The Ruins of Tenampua, Honduras," in *Annual Report of the Smithsonian Institution, 1935* (Washington, D.C.).

PORTER, MURIEL N.
1953   *Tlatilco and the Pre-Classic Cultures of the New World*, Viking Fund Publications in Anthropology 19 (New York: Viking Fund).

1955   "Material preclasico de San Salvador," *Comunicaciones* 4: 105–12.

PRICE, BARBARA J.
1976   "A Chronological Framework for Cultural Development in Mesoamerica," in *The Valley of Mexico: Studies in Pre-Hispanic Ecology and Society*, ed. E. R. Wolf (Albuquerque: University of New Mexico Press, School of American Research Advanced Seminar Series).

PROSKOURIAKOFF, TATIANA
1974   *Jades from the Cenote of Sacrifice, Chichen Itza, Yucatan* (Cambridge, Mass.: Peabody Museum of Archaeology and Ethnology, Harvard University).

PULESTON, DENNIS E.
1968   *"Brosimum alicastrum* as a Subsistence Alternative for the Classic Maya of the Central Southern Lowlands" (M.A. thesis, University of Pennsylvania).

1977   "The Art and Archaeology of Hydraulic Agriculture in the Maya Lowlands," in *Social Process in Maya Prehistory*, ed. Norman Hammond (London: Academic Press).

RADILLO, RUDY
1978   "Cultural Sequences in Honduras in Space and Time" (M.A. thesis, California State University, Los Angeles).

RANDS, ROBERT
1969   "Relationship of Monumental Stone Sculpture of Copan with the Maya Lowlands," *Proceedings of the Thirty-eighth International Congress of Americanists* 1: 518–29.

RANERE, ANTHONY J.
1968   "Analysis of Pottery Surface Collections from the Pacific Districts of Punta Burica, San Felix, and Remedios in Chiriqui, Panama," in *Cultural Chronology of the Gulf of Chiriqui, Panama*, ed. Olga Linares de Sapir (Washington, D.C.: Smithsonian Institution).

1971   "Ocupacion pre-ceramica en las tierras altas de Chiriqui," *Actas del II Simposio Nacional de Antropologia, Arqueologia y Etnohistoria de Panama*, 197–207.

1972   "Early Human Adaptations to New-World Tropical Forests: The View from Panama" (Ph.D. diss., University of California, Davis).

1975a   "Report on the 1975 Archaeological Investigations at Monagrillo and the Aguadulce Shelter, Central Panama" (mimeographed, Temple University).

1975b   "Toolmaking and Tool Use Among Preceramic Peoples of Panama," in *Lithic Technology: Making and Using Stone Tools*, ed. E. Swanson (The Hague: Mouton).

1976   "The Preceramic of Panama: The View from the Interior," *Proceedings of the First Puerto Rican Symposium on Archaeology*, Informe no. 1, ed. Linda S. Robinson (Fundacion Arqueologica, Antropologica e Historia de Puerto Rico).

1980a   "Nueva excavacion y re-interpretacion del sitio de Cerro Mangote, un conchero preceramico en la region central de Panama," paper presented at the III Congreso Nacional de Antropologia, Arqueologia y Etnohistoria de Panama, Panama City.

1980b   "Preceramic Shelters in the Talamancan Range," in *Adaptive Radiations in Prehistoric Panama*, ed. Olga F. Linares and Anthony J. Ranere, Peabody Museum Monographs, no. 5 (Cambridge, Mass.: Harvard University).

1980c   "Stone Tools and Their Interpretation," in *Adaptive Radiations in Prehistoric Panama*, ed. Olga F. Linares and Anthony J. Ranere, Peabody Museum Monographs, no. 5 (Cambridge, Mass.: Harvard University).

1980d   "Stone Tools from the Rio Chiriqui Shelters," in *Adaptive Radiations in Prehistoric Panama*, ed. Olga F. Linares and Anthony J. Ranere, Peabody Museum Monographs, no. 5 (Cambridge, Mass.: Harvard University).

1980e   "The Rio Chiriqui Shelters: Excavation and Interpretation of the Deposits," in *Adaptive Radiations in Prehistoric Panama*, ed. Olga F. Linares and Anthony J. Ranere, Peabody Museum Monographs, no. 5 (Cambridge, Mass.: Harvard University).

1981   "Human Movement into Tropical America at the End of the Pleistocene," in *Anthropological Papers in Honor of Earl H. Swanson, Jr.*, ed. C. N. Warren, D. R. Touhy, and L. B. Harten (Pocatello: Idaho State University Press), in press.

RANERE, ANTHONY J., RICHARD G. COOKE, AND PATRICIA HANSELL

1980   "Food Procurement in the Parita Bay Region of Panama: 5000 B.C.–A.D. 500," paper presented at the Forty-fifth Annual Meeting of the Society for American Archaeology, Philadelphia.

RANERE, ANTHONY J., AND PAT HANSELL

1978   "Early Subsistence Patterns along the Pacific Coast of Central Panama," in *Prehistoric Coastal Adaptations: The Economy and Ecology of Maritime Middle America*, ed. Barbara J. Stark and Barbara Voorhies (New York: Academic Press).

RATHJE, WILLIAM L.

1971   "The Origin and Development of Lowland Classic Maya Civilization," *American Antiquity* 36: 275–85.

REICHEL-DOLMATOFF, GERARDO

1951   *Notes on the Present State of Anthropological Research in Northern Colombia* (Bogota: Editorial Iqueima).

1954a   "Investigaciones arqueologicas en la Sierra Nevada de Santa Marta, partes I y II," *Revista Colombiana de Antropologia* 2: 145–206.

1954b   "Investigaciones arqueologicas en la Sierra Nevada de Santa Marta, parte 3," *Revista Colombiana de Antropologia* 3: 139–70.

1955   "Excavaciones en los conchales de la costa de Barlovento," *Revista Colombiana de Antropologia* 4: 249–72.

1962   "Una nueva fecha de carbono-14 de Colombia," *Revista Colombiana de Antropologia* 11: 331–32.

1965a   *Colombia* (New York: Praeger).

1965b   *Excavaciones arqueologicas en Puerto Hormiga, Departamento de Boliver*, Publicaciones de la Universidad de Los Andes, Antropologia 2 (Bogota).

1971   "Early Pottery from Colombia," *Archaeology* 24: 338–45.

1972   *San Agustin: A Culture of Colombia* (New York: Praeger).

1978   "Colombia indigena: periodo prehispanico," in *Manual de historia de Colombia, tomo I*, ed. J. C. Cobo and S. Mutis (Bogota: Instituto Colombiano de Cultura, Editorial Andes).

REICHEL-DOLMATOFF, GERARDO, AND ALICIA D. DE REICHEL-DOLMATOFF

1951   "Investigaciones en el Departamento del Magdalena, Colombia, 1946–1950," *Boletin de Arqueologia* 3(1–6).

1953 "Investigaciones en el Departamento del Magdalena, Colombia, 1946–1950, parte 3," *Divulgaciones Etnologicas* 3(4).

1955 "Investigaciones arqueologicas en la Sierra Nevada de Santa Marta, parte 4," *Revista Colombiana de Antropologia* 4: 189–245.

1956 "Momil: excavaciones en el Sinu," *Revista Colombiana de Antropologia* 5: 109–333.

1957 "Reconocimiento arqueologico de la hoya del Rio Sinu," *Revista Colombiana de Antropologia* 6: 29–157.

1959 "La Mesa. Un complejo arqueologico de la Sierra Nevada de Santa Marta," *Revista Colombiana de Antropologia* 8: 159–213.

1961 "Investigaciones arqueologicas en la Costa Pacifica de Colombia I: el sitio de Cupica," *Revista Colombiana de Antropologia* 10: 237–330.

1974 "Momil: dos fechas de radiocarbono," *Revista Colombiana de Antropologia* 17: 185–87.

RENFREW, COLIN
1975 "Trade as Action at a Distance: Questions of Integration and Communication," in *Ancient Civilization and Trade*, ed. J. A. Sabloff and C. C. Lamberg-Karlovsky (Albuquerque: University of New Mexico Press, School of American Research Advanced Seminar Series).

RENVOIZE, BARBARA S.
1970 "Manioc (*Manihot esculenta Crantz*) and Its Role in the Amerindian Agriculture of Tropical America," (M.Ph. thesis, University College, London).

1972 "The Area of Origin of *Manihot esculenta* as a Crop Plant: A Review of the Evidence," *Economic Botany* 26(4): 352–60.

REYES MAZZONI, ROBERTO R.
1974 "El nombre de Olancho y los grupos de habla Nahuat en Honduras," *Instituto de Investigaciones Antropologicas, Notas Antropologicas* 1(5): 31–39.

1976a "Sintesis de la arqueologia de Honduras" (M.A. thesis, National University of Mexico).

1976b *Introduccion a la arqueologia de Honduras*, 2 vols. (Tegucigalpa).

1976c "Influencias mayas y mexicanas en los petroglifos de la Quebrada de Santa Rosa Tenampus, Honduras," *Katunob* 9(3): 38–56.

1976d "Observaciones adicionales sobre los petroglifos de la Quebrada de Santa Rosa," *Boletin, Museo de Hombre Dominicano* 4: 47–61.

1977 "Posibles influencias epi-teotihuacanas en petroglifos de Honduras," *Vinculos* 3: 47–65. (National Museum of Costa Rica, San Jose).

REYES MAZZONI, ROBERTO R., AND VITO VELIZ R.
1974 "La Ceramica de Cuyamel," *Revista de la Universidad* (de Honduras) 8(5): 3–26.

REYNOLDS, L.A.
n.d. "A Ceramic Collection from Zapatera Island, Lake Nicaragua," manuscript, Department of Anthropology, San Francisco State University.

RICHARDSON, FRANCIS B.
1940 "Non-Maya Monumental Sculpture of Central America," in *The Maya and Their Neighbors*, ed. Clarence L. Hay et al. (New York: Appleton-Century).

1941 "Nicaragua," in *Carnegie Institution of Washington, Yearbook* 40: 300–302 (Washington, D.C.).

1954 "Las huellas de Cahualinca," *Cuaderno del Taller San Lucas* 4: 24–30.

RICHARDSON, FRANCIS B., AND
K. RUPPERT
1942   "Nicaragua," in *Carnegie Institution of Washington, Yearbook* 41: 269–71 (Washington, D.C.).

RICHARDSON, JAMES B., III
1973   "The Preceramic Sequence and the Pleistocene and Post-Pleistocene Climate of Northwest Peru," in *Variations in Anthropology*, ed. D. W. Lathrap and J. Douglas (Urbana: Illinois Archaeological Survey).

RIDGELY, ROBERT
1976   *The Birds of Panama* (Princeton, N.J.: Princeton University Press).

ROBICSEK, FRANCIS
1972   *Copan: Home of the Mayan Gods* (New York: Museum of the America Indian, Heye Foundation).

ROBINSON, EUGENIE
1978   "Mayan Design Features of Mayoid Vessels of the Ulua-Yojoa Polychrome" (M.S. thesis, Tulane University).

ROBISON, CATHY
1979   "Preliminary Archaeological Survey on Chira Island, Costa Rica," manuscript, San Jose, Associated Colleges of the Midwest.

ROGERS, DAVID M.
1965   "Some Botanical and Ethnological Considerations of *Manihot esculenta*," *Economic Botany* 19: 369–77.

ROOSEVELT, ANNA CURTENIUS
1979   "The Goldsmith: The Cocle Style of Ancient Panama," in *The Ancestors: Native Artisans of the Americas*, ed. Anna C. Roosevelt and James G. E. Smith (New York: Museum of the American Indian).
1980   *Parmana: Prehistoric Maize and Manioc Subsistence Along the Amazon and Orinoco* (New York: Academic Press).

ROUSE, IRVING
1948   "The Arawak," in the *Handbook of South American Indians*, vol. 4, ed. Julian H. Steward (Washington, D.C.: U.S. Government Printing Office).
1976   "Peopling of the Americas," *Quaternary Research* 6: 597–612.

ROUSE, IRVING, AND LOUIS ALLAIRE
1979   "Cronologia del Caribe," *Boletin del Museo del Hombre Dominicano* 8(12): 59–117.

ROUSE, IRVING, AND JOSE CRUXENT
1963   *Venezuelan Archaeology*, Yale University Caribbean Series 6 (New Haven: Yale University).

ROWE, JOHN H.
1959   "Carl Hartman and His Place in the History of Archaeology," *Proceedings of the Thirty-third International Congress of Americanists* 2: 268–79 (San Jose, Costa Rica: Lehmann).
1960   "Cultural Unity and Diversification in Peruvian Archaeology," in *Men and Cultures, Selected Papers, Fifth International Congress of Anthropological and Ethnological Sciences*, ed. A. F. C. Wallace (Philadelphia: University of Pennsylvania).

ROYS, RALPH L.
1939   *The Titles of Ebtun*, Carnegie Institution of Washington, Publication 505 (Washington, D.C.: Carnegie Institution).

RYDER, PETER R.
1978   "CODESA: La fabrica de cemento en Colorado de Abangares, Guanacaste, una prospeccion de sitios precolombinos," manuscript, National Museum of Costa Rica.
1980   "Costa Rica and the Maya, ca. A.D. 500–800," manuscript, Department of Anthropology, University of Pennsyylvania.

SABLOFF, JEREMY A., AND
WILLIAM L. RATHJE
1975a   A *Study of Changing Pre-Colum-*
         bian Commercial Systems,
         Monographs of the Peabody Mu-
         seum of Archaeology and Eth-
         nology, no. 3 (Cambridge, Mass.:
         Harvard University).
1975b   "The Rise of a Maya Merchant
         Class," *Scientific American* 233(4):
         72–82.

SABLOFF, JEREMY A., AND
GAIR TOURTELLOT
1969   "Systems of Exchange Among the
         Ancient Maya," paper presented
         at the Sixty-eighth Annual Meet-
         ing of the American Anthropo-
         logical Association, New Orleans.

SAHAGUN, BERNARDINO DE
1959   *Florentine Codex: General His-*
         tory of the Things of New Spain,
         Book 9, The Merchants, trans.
         A. J. O. Anderson and C. Dibble
         (Santa Fe: University of Utah and
         School of American Research).

SANDER, DAN
1959   "Fluted Points from Madden
         Lake," *Panama Archaeologist* 2(1):
         39–51.
1960   "Pottery Stamps from the Prov-
         ince of Chiriqui, Panama," *Pan-*
         ama Archaeologist 3: 99–104.
1964   "Lithic Material from Panama:
         Fluted Points from Madden
         Lake," *Proceedings and Trans-*
         actions of the Thirty-fifth Inter-
         national Congress of Americanists
         1: 183–92 (Mexico).

SANDERS, WILLIAM T.
1956   "The Central American Sym-
         biotic Region: A Study in Pre-
         historic Settlement Patterns," in
         Prehistoric Settlement Patterns in
         the New World, Viking Fund
         Publication in Anthropology, no.
         23, ed. Gordon R. Willey (New
         York).

SANDERS, WILLIAM T., AND
JOSEPH MICHELS
1977   *Teotihuacan and Kaminaljuyu:*
(eds.)   A *Study in Prehistoric Culture*
         Contact, Pennsylvania State
         University Press Monograph Se-
         ries on Kaminaljuyu (University
         Park: Pennsylvania State Univer-
         sity Press).

SANDERS, WILLIAM T., AND
BARBARA J. PRICE
1968   *Mesoamerica: The Evolution of a*
         Civilization (New York: Random
         House).

SANOJA, MARIO
1966   "Datos etnohistoricos del Lago
         de Maracaibo," *Economia y*
         Ciencias Sociales 8: 221–51.

SANTAMARIA, DIANA
1981   "Preceramic Occupations at Los
         Grifos Rock Shelter, Ocozocoau-
         tla, Chiapas, Mexico," in *Tenth*
         Congress, International Union of
         Prehistoric and Protohistoric Sci-
         ences, Miscellaneous Volume, pp.
         63–83.

SANTOS, GUSTAVO, GUSTAVO ROMAN,
AND HELDA OTERO DE SANTOS
1980   "Asentamientos prehispanicos en
         la region de Golfo de Uraba,"
         manuscript, Departamento de
         Antropologia, Universidad de
         Antioquia, Medellin.

SAPPER, KARL T.
1896   "Alterhümer aus der Republik San
         Salvador," *Internationales Archiv*
         für Ethnographie 9: 1–6 (Lei-
         den).
1902   *Mittelamerikanische Reisen und*
         Studien aus den Jahren 1888 bis
         1900 (Braunschweig).
1913   *Die mittelamerikanischen Vul-*
         kane, Petermanns Geogra-
         phische Mitteilungen, Ergan-
         zungsheft Nr. 178 (Gotha: Justus
         Perthes).

SAUER, CARL ORTWIN
1966   *The Early Spanish Main* (Berke-

ley and Los Angeles: University of California Press).

SCHMIDT, PETER J.
1968   "Die Bestattungsformen der Indianer des sudlichen Mittelamerika" (Ph.D. diss., University of Hamburg).
n.d.   "Indianische Bestattungsformen im sudlichen Mittelamerika," manuscript.

SCHOBINGER, JUAN
1973   "Nuevos hallazgos de puntas 'colas de pescado' y consideraciones en torno al origen y dispersion de la cultura de Cazadores Superiores Todense (Fell) en Sudamerica," *Atti del XL Congresso Internazionale degli Americanisti* 1: 33–50 (Genoa: Tilgher).

SCHOLES, FRANCE V., AND
RALPH L. ROYS
1948   *The Maya Chontal Indians of Acalan-Tixchel*, Carnegie Institution of Washington, Publication 560 (Washington, D.C.: Carnegie Institution).

SCHORTMAN, E. M., P. A. URBAN, AND W. ASHMORE
1983   "Santa Barbara Archaeological Project: 1983 Season," report presented to the Instituto Hondureno de Antropologia e Historia, Tegucigalpa (Honduras).

SCHREVE-BRINKMAN, ELISABETH J.
1978   "A Palynological Study of the Upper Quaternary Sequence in the El Abra Corridor and Rock Shelters," *Palaeogeography, Palaeoclimatology, Palaeoecology* 25: 1–109.

SCHUCHERT, CHARLES
1935   *Historical Geology of the Antillean-Caribbean Region* (New York: John Wiley and Sons).

SHARER, ROBERT J.
1974   "The Prehistory of the Southeastern Maya Periphery," *Current Anthropology* 15: 165–87.

1975   "The Southeast Periphery of the Maya Area: A Prehistoric Perspective," paper presented at the Seventy-fourth Annual Meeting of the American Anthropological Association, San Francisco.
1978a   *The Prehistory of Chalchuapa, El Salvador*, 3 vols. (Philadelphia: University of Pennsylvania Press).
(ed.)
1978b   "Archaeology and History at Quirigua, Guatemala," *Journal of Field Archaeology* 5: 51–70.
1979   "Classic Maya Elite Occupation in the Lower Motagua Valley, Guatemala: A Preliminary Formulation," paper presented at the Ethnohistory Workshop, University of Pennsylvania.
1980   *Quirigua Reports, Vol. 1*, Museum Monograph, University Museum (Philadelphia: University of Pennsylvania Press).
(ed.)

SHARER, ROBERT J., AND
JAMES C. GIFFORD
1970   "Preclassic Ceramics from Chalchuapa, El Salvador, and Their Relationships with the Maya Lowlands," *American Antiquity* 35: 441–62.

SHARER, ROBERT J., C. JONES,
W. ASHMORE, AND E. M. SCHORTMAN
1979   "The Quirigua Project: 1976 Season," in *Quirigua Papers;, Vol. 1*, ed. W. Ashmore (Philadelphia: University of Pennsylvania).

SHEEHY, JAMES J.
1978   "Informe preliminar sobre las excavaciones en Travesia en 1976," *Yaxkin* 2: 175–201.

SHEEHY, JAMES J., AND VITO VELIZ
1977   "Excavaciones recientes en Travesia, Valle de Sula," *Yaxkin* 2: 121–24.

SHEETS, PAYSON D.
1975   "Behavioral Analysis and the Structure of a Prehistoric Indus-

try," *Current Anthropology* 16(3): 369–91.

1976 *Ilopango Volcano and the Maya Protoclassic*, University Museum Studies no. 9 (Carbondale: Southern Illinois University).

1978 "Artifacts," in *The Prehistory of Chalchuapa, El Salvador*, ed. R. J. Sharer, vol. 2, pp. 1–140 (Philadelphia: University of Pennsylvania Press).

1979 "Environmental and Cultural Effects of the Ilopango Eruption in Central America," in *Volcanic Activity and Human Ecology*, ed. P. Sheets and D. Grayson (New York: Academic Press).

n.d.a "Research of the Protoclassic Project in the Zapotitan Basin, El Salvador," manuscript, Department of Anthropology, University of Colorado, Boulder. In translation, *Anales*, Museo Nacional D. Guzman, San Salvador.

n.d.b "Prehistoric Agricultural Systems in El Salvador," in *Maya Subsistence*, ed. K. Flannery (New York: Academic Press).

SHEETS, PAYSON D., E. JANE ROSENTHAL, AND ANTHONY J. RANERE
1980 "Stone Tools from Volcan Baru," in *Adaptive Radiations in Prehistoric Panama*, ed. Olga F. Linares and Anthony J. Ranere, Peabody Museum Monographs, no. 5 (Cambridge, Mass.: Harvard University).

SHLEMON, ROY J., AND JAMES J. PARSONS
1977 "Late Quaternary Cyclic Sedimentation, San Jorge River Floodplain, Colombia," *Abstracts, Tenth International Quaternary Association (INQUA) Congress*, Birmingham, England.

SHOOK, E. M., AND A. KIDDER
1952 *Mound E-III-3, Kaminaljuyu, Guatemala*, Carnegie Institution of Washington, Publication 596 (Washington, D.C.: Carnegie Institution).

SHOOK, E. M., AND T. PROSKOURIAKOFF
1956 "Settlement Patterns in Mesoamerica and Their Sequence in the Guatemalan Highlands," in *Prehistoric Settlement Patterns in the New World*, ed. Gordon R. Willey (New York: Viking Fund).

SIDRYS, RAYMOND, JOHN ANDRESEN, AND DEREK MARCUCCI
1976 "Obsidian Sources in the Maya Area," *Journal of New World Archaeology* 1: 1–13.

SMITH, C. EARLE
1980 "Plant Remains from the Chiriqui Sites and Ancient Vegetational Patterns," in *Adaptive Radiations in Prehistoric Panama*, ed. Olga F. Linares and Anthony J. Ranere, Peabody Museum Monographs, no. 5 (Cambridge, Mass.: Harvard University).

SMITH, J. STEPHEN C., AND RICHARD N. LESTER
1980 "Biochemical Systematics and the Evolution of *Zea, Tripsacum* and Related Genera," *Economic Botany* 34(3): 201–18.

SMITH, MICHAEL E., AND CYNTHIA HEATH-SMITH
1980 "Waves of Influence in Postclassic Mesoamerica? A Critique of the Mixteca-Puebla Concept," *Anthropology* 4(2): 15–50.

SMITH, ROBERT E.
1958 "The Place of Fine Orange Pottery in Mesoamerican Archaeology," *American Antiquity* 24: 151–60.

SMYTHE, NICHOLAS
1978 *The Natural History of the Cen-*

tral American Agouti (Dasyprocta punctata). Smithsonian Contributions to Zoology, no. 257 (Washington, D.C.: Smithsonian Institution Press).

SNARSKIS, MICHAEL J.

1975   "Excavaciones estratigraficas en la vertiente atlantica de Costa Rica," *Vinculos* 1: 2–17 (National Museum of Costa Rica, San Jose).

1976a   "Stratigraphic Excavations in the Eastern Lowlands of Costa Rica," *American Antiquity* 41: 342–53.

1976b   "La Vertiente atlantica de Costa Rica," *Vinculos* 2: 101–14 (National Museum of Costa Rica, San Jose).

1978   "The Archaeology of the Central Atlantic Watershed of Costa Rica" (Ph.D. diss., Columbia University).

1979a   "El jade de Talamanca de Tibas," *Vinculos* 5: 89–106 (National Museum of Costa Rica, San Jose).

1979b   "Turrialba: A Paleo-Indian Quarry and Workshop Site in Eastern Costa Rica," *American Antiquity* 44: 125–38.

1981   "The Archaeology of Costa Rica," in *Between Continents/Between Seas: Precolumbian Art of Costa Rica*, ed. E. Benson (New York: H. N. Abrams).

1982a   "The Precolumbian Art of Costa Rica," *Archaeology* 35: 54–58.

1982b   *La ceramica precolombina en Costa Rica/Precolumbian Ceramics in Costa Rica*, bilingual edition (San Jose, Costa Rica: Instituto Nacional de Seguros).

SNARSKIS, MICHAEL J., AND
AIDA BLANCO

1978   "Dato sobre ceramica policromada guanacasteca excavada en la Meseta Central," *Vinculos* 4:

106–14 (National Museum of Costa Rica, San Jose).

SNARSKIS, MICHAEL J., AND
CARLOS ENRIQUE HERRA

1980   "La Cabaña: arquitectura mesoamericana en el Bosque Tropical," *Memoria del Congreso sobre el Mundo Centroamericano de su tiempo: V Centenario de Gonzalo Fernandez de Oviedo* (Nicoya, Costa Rica).

SOL, ANTONIO E.

1929a   "Informe del director al departamento de historia sobre las ruinas de Quelepa," *Revista Departamento de Historia, Ministerio de Instruccion Publica* 1: 37–39 (San Salvador).

1929b   "Informe sobre las ruinas de Cihuatan," *Revista Departamento de Historia, Ministerio de Instruccion Publica* 1: 19–23 (San Salvador).

1939   "Informe de la inspeccion practicada en el estero de Jaltepeque y apreciaciones sobre la antigua ciudad de Tehuacan," *Revista Departamento de Historia, Ministerio de Instruccion Publica* 1: 51–56 (San Salvador).

SPINDEN, HERBERT J.

1915   "Notes on the Archaeology of Salvador," *American Anthropologist* 17: 446–87.

1917   *Ancient Civilizations of Mexico and Central America*, American Museum of Natural History, Handbook Series no. 3 (New York).

1925   "The Chorotegan Culture Area," *Compte-Rendu de la XXI Congres International des Americanistes* 2: 529–45 (Gothenberg).

SQUIER, EPHRAIM GEORGE

1850   *Decouverte d'anciens monuments sur les Iles du Lac de Nicaragua,*

Societe de Geographie de Paris, Bulletin 13–14.

1852   *Nicaragua: Its People, Scenery, Monuments and the Proposed Interoceanic Canal*, 2 vols. (New York).

1853a   "Observations on the Archaeology and Ethnology of Nicaragua," *Transactions of the American Ethnological Society* 3: 83–158.

1853b   "Ruins of Tenampua," *Proceedings of the Historical Society of New York*, pp. 1–8.

1855   *Notes on Central America, Particularly the States of Honduras and El Salvador* (New York: Harper and Bros.).

1858   *The States of Central America: Their Geography, Topography, Climate, Population, Resources, Productions, Commerce, Political Organization, Aborigines . . .* (New York and London: Harper and Bros.).

1859   "More About the Gold Discoveries of the Isthmus," *Harper's Weekly*, Aug. 20, p. 532.

1860   "Some Account of the Lake of Yojoa or Taulebe, in Honduras, Central America," *Journal of the Royal Geographical Society* 30: 58–63.

1869   "Tongues from Tombs," *Frank Leslie's Illustrated Newspaper*, March 20, July 24.

1870   *Honduras: Descriptive, Historical and Statistical* (London: Trubner and Co.).

STEINMAYER, R. A.

1932   *A Reconnaissance of Certain Mounds and Relics of Spanish Honduras*, Middle American Research Institute, Publication 4 (New Orleans: Tulane University).

STEPHENS, JOHN L.

1841   *Incidents of Travel in Central America, Chiapas, and Yucatan* (New York: Harper and Bros.).

STEVENS, RAYFRED L.

1964   "The Soils of Middle America and Their Relation to Indian Peoples and Cultures," in *Handbook of Middle American Indians*, vol. 1, ed. Robert C. West (Austin: University of Texas Press).

STIER, FRANCES RHODA

1979   "History, Demography, and Agriculture in San Blas" (Ph.D. diss., University of Arizona).

STIRLING, MATTHEW W.

1950   "Exploring Ancient Panama by Helicopter," *National Geographic Magazine* 97: 227–46.

1964   *Archaeological Notes on Almirante Bay, Bocas del Toro, Panama*, Bureau of American Ethnology, Smithsonian Institution, Bulletin 191 (Washington, D.C.: U.S. Government Printing Office).

1969   "Archaeological Investigations in Costa Rica," *National Geographic Society Research Reports, 1964 Projects*, 239–47.

STIRLING, MATTHEW W., AND MARION STIRLING

1964a   *El Limon, an Early Tomb Site in Cocle Province, Panama*, Bureau of American Ethnology, Smithsonian Institution, Bulletin 191 (Washington, D.C.: U.S. Government Printing Office).

1964b   *The Archaeology of Taboga, Uraba and Taboguilla Islands, Panama*, Bureau of American Ethnology, Smithsonian Institution, Bulletin 191 (Washington, D.C.: U.S. Government Printing Office).

STONE, DORIS

1934a   "A New Southernmost Maya City (Los Naranjos on Lake Yojoa,

Honduras)," *Maya Research* 1: 125–28.

1934b "A Mound and a House-Site on Jerico Farm, near Trujillo, Honduras," *Maya Research* 1: 129–32.

1938 *Masters in Marble*, Research Series, Middle American Research Institute, Publication 8 (New Orleans: Tulane University).

1941 *Archaeology of the North Coast of Honduras*, Memoirs of the Peabody Museum of Archaeology and Ethnology, vol. 9, no. 1 (Cambridge, Mass.: Harvard University).

1942a "A Delimitation of the Area and Some of the Archaeology of the Sula-Jicaque Indians of Honduras," *American Antiquity* 7: 376–88.

1942b "A Delimitation of the Paya Area in Honduras and Certain Stylistic Resemblances Found in Costa Rica and Honduras," *Proceedings of the First Session of the Twenty-seventh International Congress of Americanists* 1: 226–30 (Mexico).

1943 "A Preliminary Investigation of the Flood Plain of the Rio Grande de Terraba, Costa Rica," *American Antiquity* 9: 74–88.

1948 "The Basic Cultures of Central America," in *Handbook of South American Indians*, vol. 4, ed. Julian H. Steward, Bureau of American Ethnology, Smithsonian Institution, Bulletin no. 143 (Washington, D.C.: U.S. Government Printing Office).

1949 "Los Grupos Mexicanos en la America Central y su Importancia," *Antropologia e Historia de Guatemala* 1: 43–47.

1954 "Apuntes sobre las esferas grandes de piedra, halladas en el Rio Di-

quis o Grande de Terraba, Costa Rica," *Boletin Informativo del Museo Nacional de Costa Rica* 1(6): 6–10.

1956a *Don Anastacio Alfaro Gonzalez: su vida* (San Jose, Costa Rica).

1956b "Data of Maize in Talamanca, Costa Rica; An Hypothesis," *Journal de la Societe des Americanistes de Paris* 45: 189–94.

1957 *The Archaeology of Central and Southern Honduras*, Papers of the Peabody Museum of Archaeology and Ethnology, vol. 49, no. 3 (Cambridge, Mass.: Harvard University).

1958a *Introduction to the Archaeology of Costa Rica* (San Jose: National Museum of Costa Rica).

1958b "A Living Pattern of Non-Maya–Non-Mexican Central American Aborigines," in *Miscelanea, Paul Rivet, Octogenario Dicata*, vol. 1 (Mexico: Universidad Nacional Autonoma).

1959 "The Eastern Frontier of Mesoamerica," *Americanist Miscellany*, pp. 118–21 (Hamburg).

1961 "The Stone Sculpture of Costa Rica," in *Essays in Precolumbian Art and Archaeology*, ed. S. K. Lothrop et al. (Cambridge, Mass.: Harvard University).

1962a *The Talamancan Tribes of Costa Rica*, Papers of the Peabody Museum of Archaeology and Ethnology, vol. 43, no. 2 (Cambridge, Mass.: Harvard University).

1962b "The Ulua Valley and Lake Yojoa," in *The Maya and Their Neighbors*, ed. C. L. Hay et al. (Provo: University of Utah Press; reprint ed. of a volume published in 1940).

1963 "Cult Traits in Southeastern Costa Rica and Their Significance,"

American Antiquity 28: 339–59.

1966a *Introduction to the Archaeology of Costa Rica* (revised edition) (San Jose: National Museum of Costa Rica).

1966b "Synthesis of Lower Central American Ethnohistory," in *Handbook of Middle American Indians*, vol. 4, ed. Gordon F. Ekholm and Gordon R. Willey (Austin: University of Texas Press).

1967 "The Significance of Certain Styles of Ulua Polychrome Ware from Honduras," *Folk* 8–9: 335–42 (Copenhagen).

1969a "An Interpretation of Ulua Polychrome Ware," *Proceedings of the Thirty-eighth International Congress of Americanists* 1: 229–42 (Stuttgart-Munich).

1969b "Nahuat Traits in the Sula Plain, Northwestern Honduras," *Proceedings of the Thirty-eighth International Congress of Americanists* 1: 527–36.

1972 *Pre-Columbian Man Finds Central America* (Cambridge, Mass.: Peabody Museum Press).

1977 *Pre-Columbian Man in Costa Rica* (Cambridge, Mass.: Peabody Museum Press).

1979 "The Peripheral Importance of Lower Central America in Precolumbian Trade," paper presented at the Forty-third International Congress of Americanists, Vancouver.

1982 "Cultural Radiations from the Central and Southern Highlands of Mexico into Costa Rica," *Aspects of the Mixteca-Puebla Style and Mixtec and Central Mexican Culture in Southern Mesoamerica*, Middle American Research Institute, Occasional Paper 4: 60–70 (New Orleans: Tulane University).

STONE, DORIS, AND CARLOS BALSER

1957 "Grinding Stones and Mullers of Costa Rica," *Journal de la Societe des Americanistes de Paris* 46: 165–79.

1958 *The Aboriginal Metalwork in the Isthmian Region of America* (San Jose: National Museum of Costa Rica).

1965 "Incised Slate Discs from the Atlantic Watershed of Costa Rica," *American Antiquity* 30: 310–29.

STONE, DORIS, AND CONCHITA TURNBULL

1941 "A Sula-Ulua Pottery Kiln," *American Antiquity* 7: 39–47.

STOTHERT, KAREN E.

1977a *Proyecto Paleoindio: informe preliminar* (Guayaquil: Museo Antropologico del Banco Central).

1977b "Preceramic Adaptation and Trade in the Intermediate Area," paper presented at the Seventy-sixth Annual Meeting of the American Anthropological Association, Houston.

STOUT, DAVID B.

1947 *San Blas Cuna Acculturation: An Introduction*, Viking Fund Publications in Anthropology, no. 9 (New York).

STROMSVIK, GUSTAV

1941 "Substela Caches and Stela Foundations at Copan and Quirigua," *Contributions to American Anthropology and History*, Publication 528, no. 37 (Washington, D.C.: Carnegie Institution).

STRONG, WILLIAM D.

1934a "Hunting Ancient Ruins in Northeastern Honduras," *Smithsonian Institution Explorations and Field-work, 1933–1934* (Washington, D.C.).

1934b "An Archaeological Cruise Among the Bay Islands of Honduras,"

Smithsonian Institution Explorations and Field-work, 1933–1934 (Washington, D.C.).

1935   *Archaeological Investigations in the Bay Islands*, Smithsonian Miscellaneous Collections, no. 92 (Washington, D.C.: Smithsonian Institution).

1948   "The Archaeology of Honduras," in *Handbook of South American Indians*, vol. 4, ed. Julian H. Steward, Bureau of American Ethnology, Smithsonian Institution Bulletin 143 (Washington, D.C.: U.S. Government Printing Office).

STRONG, WILLIAM D., A. V. KIDDER II, AND A. J. D. PAUL, JR.

1938   *Preliminary Report on the Smithsonian Institution–Harvard University Archaeological Expedition to Northwestern Honduras, 1936*, Smithsonian Miscellaneous Collections, no. 97 (Washington, D.C.: Smithsonian Institution).

STUIVER, MINZE

1969   "Yale Natural Radiocarbon Measurements IX," *Radiocarbon* 11(2): 545–658.

SUTHERLAND, DONALD R., AND CARSON N. MURDY

1979   "Adaptaciones prehistoricas al ambiente litoral en la Isla de Salamanca, costa norte de Colombia," *Universitas Humanisticas* 10: 51–72 (Bogota: Universidad Javeriana).

SWAUGER, JAMES L., AND WILLIAM J. MAYER-OAKES

1952   "A Fluted Point from Costa Rica," *American Antiquity* 17: 264–65.

SWEENEY, JEANNE W.

1975   "Guanacaste, Costa Rica: An Analysis of Precolumbian Ceramics from the Northwest Coast" (Ph.D. diss., University of Pennsylvania).

1976   "Ceramic Analysis from Three Sites in Northwest Coastal Guanacaste," *Vinculos* 2: 37–44 (National Museum of Costa Rica, San Jose).

TAMAYO, J.

1964   "The Hydrography of Middle America," in *Handbook of Middle American Indians*, vol. 1, ed. Robert C. West (Austin: University of Texas Press).

TERMER, FRANZ

1948   *Quauhtemallan und Cuzcatlan*, Hamberger Romanistische Studien, B. Ibero-Amerikanische Reihe, Band 18 (Hamburg: Hansischer Gildenverlag).

THOMPSON, J. ERIC S.

1970   *Maya History and Religion* (Norman: University of Oklahoma Press).

TORRES DE ARAUZ, REINA

1966   *Arte precolombino de Panama* (Panama: Instituto Nacional de Cultura y Deportes).

1972   *Arte precolombino de Panama* (Panama: Instituto Nacional de Cultura y Deportes).

TSCHOPIK, HARRY

1937   "Textile Motifs from Ulua Valley Pottery," manuscript, Peabody Museum, Harvard University.

TURBAY, LUISA FERNANDA HERRERA DE

1980   "Buritaca–200: estudio del polen arqueologico," *Boletin del Museo del Oro* 3 (mayo–agosto): 1–20.

TURNER, B. L., II, P. D. HARRISON, R. E. FRY, N. ETTLINGER, J. P. DARCH, W. C. JOHNSON, H. J. SHAFER, A. COVICH, F. M. WISEMAN, AND C. MIKSICEK

1980   *Maya Raised Field Agriculture and Settlement at Pulltrouser Swamp*, report of the 1970–80 University of Oklahoma—National Science Foundation Pulltrouser Swamp Project.

VAILLANT, GEORGE C.
1927 "The Chronological Significance of Maya Ceramics" (Ph.D. diss., Harvard University).
1934 "The Archaeological Setting of the Playa de los Muertos Culture," *Maya Research* 1: 87–100.

VAN DER HAMMEN, THOMAS
1961 "The Quaternary Climatic Changes of Northern South America," *Annals of the New York Academy of Sciences* 95(1): 676–83.
1962 "Palinologia de la region de Laguna de los Bobos," *Revista de la Academia Colombiana de Ciencias Exactas, Fisicas y Naturales* 11(44): 359–61.
1965 "A Pollen Diagram from Laguna de la Herrera (Sabana de Bogota)," *Leidse Geologische Mededelingen* 32: 183–91.
1972 "Changes in Vegetation and Climate in the Amazon Basin and Surrounding Areas During the Pleistocene," *Geologie en Mijnbouw* 51(6): 641–43.
1974 "The Pleistocene Changes of Vegetation and Climate in Tropical South America," *Journal of Biogeography* 1: 3–26.

VAN DER HAMMEN, THOMAS, AND GONZALO CORREAL URREGO
1978 "Prehistoric Man on the Sabana de Bogota: Data for an Ecological Prehistory," *Palaeogeography, Palaeoclimatology, Palaeoecology* 25: 179–90.

VAN DER MERWE, NIKOLAAS J., ANNA CURTENIUS ROOSEVELT, AND J. C. VOGEL
1981 "From Manioc to Maize on the Middle Orinoco: Isotopic Evidence for Prehistoric Subsistence Change at Panama," *Nature* (in press).

VAN GEEL, G., AND THOMAS VAN DER HAMMEN
1973 "Upper Quaternary Vegetation and Climatic Sequence in the Fuquene Area (Eastern Cordillera, Colombia)," *Palaeogeography, Palaeoclimatology, Palaeoecology* 14: 9–92.

VAZQUEZ LEIVA, RICARDO
1981 "27–HM: un sitio en Cartago con tumbas de cajon" (Thesis, University of Costa Rica, San Pedro).

VAZQUEZ LEIVA, RICARDO, AND DAVID S. WEAVER
1980 "Un analisis osteologico para el reconocimiento de las condiciones de vida en sitio Vidor," in *Investigaciones arqueologicas en la zona de Bahia Culebra, Costa Rica (1973–1979), Vinculos* 6 (National Museum of Costa Rica, San Jose).

VELIZ R., VITO
1978a "Huellas humanas en Guaimaca, Honduras," *Yaxkin* 2: 263–69.
1978b *Analisis arqueologico de la ceramica de Piedra Blanca*, Estudios Antropologicos y Historicos 1 (Tegucigalpa: Instituto Hondureño de Antropologia e Historia).

VELIZ R., VITO, PAUL F. HEALY, AND GORDON R. WILLEY
1976 "Una preliminaria descriptiva clasificacion de la ceramica de la Isla de Roatan, Honduras," *Revista de la Universidad* (de Honduras) 11: 19–29.

VERRILL, A. HYATT
1927 "Excavations in Cocle Province, Panama," Museum of the American Indian, Heye Foundation, *Indian Notes* 4: 47–61.

VIEL, RENE
1978 "Etude de la Ceramique Ulua-Yojoa polychrome (Nord-ouest du Honduras): Essai d'analyse styl-

istiquie du Babilonia (Ph.D. diss., Rene Descartes University, Paris).

VIVO ESCOTO, JORGE A.
1964   "Weather and Climate of Mexico and Central America," in *Handbook of Middle American Indians*, vol. 1, ed. Robert C. West (Austin: University of Texas Press).

VOGEL, J. C., AND J. C. LERMAN
1969   "Groningen Radiocarbon Dates VIII," *Radiocarbon* 11(2): 351–90.

VOORHIES, BARBARA
1978   "Previous Research on Near-shore Coastal Adaptations in Middle America," in *Prehistoric Coastal Adaptations: The Economy and Ecology of Maritime Middle America*, ed. Barbara L. Stark and Barbara Voorhies (New York: Academic Press).

WAGNER, ERIKA
1967   *The Prehistory and Ethnohistory of the Carache Area in Western Venezuela*, Yale University Publications in Anthropology no. 71 (New Haven).
1973   "The Mucuchies Phase: An Extension of the Andean Cultural Pattern in Western Venezuela," *American Anthropologist* 75(1): 195–213.

WAGNER, PHILLIP L.
1964   "Natural Vegetation of Middle America," in *Handbook of Middle American Indians*, vol. 1, ed. Robert C. West (Austin: University of Texas Press).

WALLACE, HENRY, AND RICHARD M. ACCOLA
1980   "Investigaciones arqueologicas preliminares de Nacascolo, Bahia Culebra, Costa Rica," in *Investigaciones arqueologicas en la zona de Bahia Culebra, Costa Rica (1973–1979)*, *Vinculos* 6 (National Museum of Costa Rica, San Jose).

WALLACE, IRENE STERNS
1978   "Ceramica policroma en el Valle de Naco y sus relaciones externas," *Yaxkin* 2: 255–62.

WASSEN, HENRY S.
1949   "Contributions to Cuna Ethnography," *Ethnological Studies* 16: 7–139.

WAUCHOPE, ROBERT
1954   "Implications of Radiocarbon Dates from Middle and South America," *Tulane University Middle American Research Records* 1: 211–50.

WEST, ROBERT C.
1964a   "Surface Configuration and Associated Geology of Middle America," in *Handbook of Middle American Indians*, vol. 1, ed. Robert C. West (Austin: University of Texas Press).
1964b   "The Natural Regions of Middle America," in *Handbook of Middle American Indians*, vol. 1, ed. Robert C. West (Austin: University of Texas Press).

WEST, ROBERT C., AND JOHN P. AUGELLI
1976   *Middle America: Its Lands and Peoples*, 2d ed. (Englewood Cliffs, N.J.: Prentice-Hall).

WIJMSTRA, T. A.
1967   "A Pollen Diagram from the Upper Holocene of the Lower Magdalena Valley," *Leidse Geologische Mededelingen* 39: 261–67.

WIJMSTRA, T. A., AND T. VAN DER HAMMEN
1966   "Palynological Data on the History of Tropical Savannas in Northern South America," *Leidse Geologische Mededelingen* 38: 71–90.

WILLEY, GORDON R.
1962   "Mesoamerica," in *Courses Toward Urban Life*, ed. R. Braidwood and G. Willey, Viking Fund Publications in Anthropology, no.

32 (New York: Wenner-Gren Foundation for Anthropological Research).

1966 An Introduction to American Archaeology, Volume 1: North and Middle America (Englewood Cliffs, N.J.: Prentice-Hall).

1969 "The Mesoamericanization of the Honduras-Salvadoran Periphery," Proceedings of the Thirty-eighth International Congress of Americanists 1: 537–42.

1971 An Introduction to American Archaeology, Volume 2: South America (Englewood Cliffs, N.J.: Prentice-Hall).

1974 "The Classic Maya Hiatus: A Rehearsal for the Collapse?" in Mesoamerican Archaeology: New Approaches, ed. Norman Hammond (Austin: University of Texas Press).

1979 "Review of Prehistoric Coastal Adaptations: The Economy and Ecology of Maritime Middle America, ed. Barbara L. Stark and Barbara Voorhies," American Antiquity 44: 850–51.

WILLEY, GORDON R., T. PATRICK CULBERT, AND RICHARD E. W. ADAMS

1967 "Maya Lowland Ceramics: A Report from the 1965 Guatemala City Conference," American Antiquity 32: 289–315.
(eds.)

WILLEY, GORDON R., C. C. DIPESO, W. A. RITCHIE, I. ROUSE, J. H. ROWE, AND D. W. LATHRAP

1955 "An Archaeological Classification of Culture Contact Situations," in Seminars in Archaeology, Memoir 11 of the Society for American Archaeology.

WILLEY, GORDON R., AND RICHARD M. LEVENTHAL

1979 "Prehistoric Settlement at Copan," in Maya Archaeology and Ethnohistory, ed. Norman Hammond and Gordon R. Willey (Austin: University of Texas Press).

WILLEY, GORDON R., RICHARD M. LEVENTHAL, AND WILLIAM L. FASH, JR.

1978 "Maya Settlement in the Copan Valley," Archaeology 31(4): 32–43.

WILLEY, GORDON R., AND CHARLES R. McGIMSEY III

1954 The Monagrillo Culture of Panama, Papers of the Peabody Museum of Archaeology and Ethnology, vol. 49, no. 2 (Cambridge, Mass.: Harvard University).

WILLEY, GORDON R., AND JEREMY A. SABLOFF

1980 A History of American Archaeology, 2d ed. (San Francisco: W. H. Freeman and Co.).

WILLEY, GORDON R., R. SHARER, R. VIEL, A. DEMAREST, R. LEVENTHAL, AND E. SCHORTMAN

1980 "A Study of Ceramic Interaction in the Southeastern Maya Periphery," paper presented at the Forty-fifth Annual Meeting of the Society for American Archaeology, Philadelphia.

WILLIAMS, H.

1952 Geologic Observations on the Ancient Footprints Near Managua, Nicaragua, Carnegie Institution of Washington, Publication 596 (Washington, D.C.: Carnegie Institution).

WING, ELIZABETH S.

1980 "Aquatic Fauna and Reptiles from the Atlantic and Pacific Sites," in Adaptive Radiations in Prehistoric Panama, ed. Olga F. Linares and Anthony J. Ranere, Peabody Museum Monographs, no. 5 (Cambridge, Mass.: Harvard University).

WINTER, MARCUS

1976 "The Archaeological Household Cluster in the Valley of Oaxaca," in *The Early Mesoamerican Village*, ed. Kent V. Flannery (New York: Academic Press).

WONDERLEY, ANTHONY
1980   "Postclassic Naco, Honduras," paper presented at the Forty-fifth Annual Meeting of the Society for American Archaeology, Philadelphia.
1981   *Late Postclassic Excavations at Naco, Honduras*, Dissertation Series no. 86, Latin American Studies Program (Ithaca, N.Y.: Cornell University).

WYCKOFF, LYDIA L.
1973   "An Examination of Nicaraguan Late and Middle Polychrome Assemblages," manuscript, location unknown, cited in Healy (1974).
1974   "The Nicaraguan Archaeological Survey: A Preliminary Report," Museum of the American Indian, Heye Foundation, *Indian Notes* 10: 99–107.

YDE, JENS
1938   *An Archaeological Reconnaissance of Northwestern Honduras*, Middle American Research Institute, Publication 8 (New Orleans: Tulane University).

YOUNG, PHILIP D.
1965   "Nota sobre afinidades linguisticas entre Bogota y Guaymi sabanero," *Hombre y Cultura* 1(4): 20–25.
1971   *Ngawbe: Tradition and Change Among the Western Guaymi of Panama*, Illinois Studies in Anthropology, no. 7 (Urbana).

1980   "Notes on Guaymi Traditional Culture," in *Adaptive Radiations in Prehistoric Panama*, ed. Olga F. Linares and Anthony J. Ranere, Peabody Museum Monographs, no. 5 (Cambridge, Mass.: Harvard University).

YOUNG, PHILIP D., AND JAMES HOWE
1976   *Ritual and Symbol in Native*
(eds.) *South America*, University of Oregon Anthropological Papers, no. 9 (Eugene).

ZARKY, ALAN
1976   "Statistical Analysis of Catchments at Ocos, Guatemala," in *The Early Mesoamerican Village*, ed. Kent V. Flannery (New York: Academic Press).

ZELTNER, A. DE
1865   "Sepulturas indias del departamento de Chiriqui en el estado de Panama," *El Felix*, August 15.

ZEVALLOS, C., W. GALINAT, D. LATHRAP, E. LENG, J. MARCOS, AND K. KLUMPP
1977   "The San Pablo Corn Kernel and Its Friends," *Science* 196: 385–89.

ZUCCHI, ALBERTA
1972   "New Data on the Antiquity of Polychrome Painting from Venezuela," *American Antiquity* 37: 439–46.
1973   "Prehistoric Human Occupations of the Western Venezuelan Llanos," *American Antiquity* 38(2): 182–90.

Index

Index